THE BEAUTY OF BATH

A PHOTOGRAPHIC CELEBRATION & VISITOR GUIDE

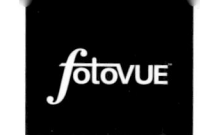

CASPER FARRELL

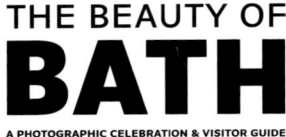

THE BEAUTY OF
BATH
A PHOTOGRAPHIC CELEBRATION & VISITOR GUIDE

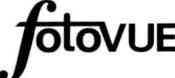

Copyright © fotoVUE Limited 2025.
Text and Photography: Copyright © Casper Farrell 2025.

Casper Farrell has asserted his right under the Copyright, Designs and Patents Act 1988
to be identified as the author of this work.

All rights reserved. No part of this book may be reproduced or transmitted in any form or by any means, electronic or mechanical, including photocopying, recording, or by any information storage and retrieval system without the written permission of the publisher, except for the use of brief quotations in a book review.

TRADEMARKS: fotoVUE, the fotoVUE wordmark, Explore & Discover and The Beauty Of, are the registered trademarks of fotoVUE Ltd.

Publisher: Mick Ryan – fotoVUE Ltd.
Edited by Mick Ryan
® Design by Ryder Design – www.ryderdesign.studio
Layout by Vicky Barlow – www.victoriabarlow.co.uk

All maps within this publication were produced by Don Williams of Bute Cartographics.
Map location overlay and graphics by Mick Ryan.
Map contains data from OpenStreetMap (openstreetmap.org/copyright).
© OpenStreetMap 2025 and Ordnance Survey data © Crown copyright and database right 2010–2025.

A CIP catalogue record for this book is available from the British Library.

ISBN 978-1-7395083-5-7
10 9 8 7 6 5 4 3 2 1

The author, publisher and others involved in the design and publication of this guide book accept no responsibility for any loss or damage users may suffer as a result of using this book. Users of this book are responsible for their own safety and use the information herein at their own risk. Users should always be aware of weather forecasts, conditions, time of day and their own ability before venturing out.

Front cover: The Circus (page 77)
Rear left: The Royal Crescent (page 43)
Rear middle: Bath Abbey (page 149)
Rear right: Pulteney Bridge (page 97)
Cover flap: Green Street and St Michael's Church (page 173)
Overleaf: an aerial image of Bath taken from above Somerset Place in the north behind the Royal Crescent,
and on the right a close up of Pulteney Bridge and the river Avon.

Printed and bound in China by Latitude Press Ltd.

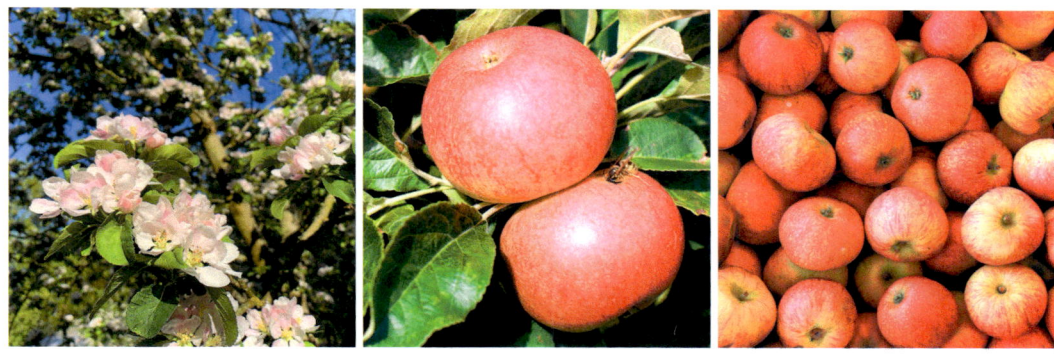

BEAUTY OF BATH

Dessert apple

The Beauty of Bath apple variety originated at Bailbrook, Bath, Somerset and was propagated by George Cooling of Bath in about 1864. Cooling received a First Class Certificate from the Royal Horticultural Society in 1887 for his work. This variety was once the most important early (July/August) commercial apple in the U.K. Fruits are soft, juicy, sweet and a little acid, with a distinctive flavour.
from the National Fruit Collection archives

As well as being the photographer and author of this book, Casper Farrell has an orchard that includes Beauty of Bath apples from which he makes proper west country cider.

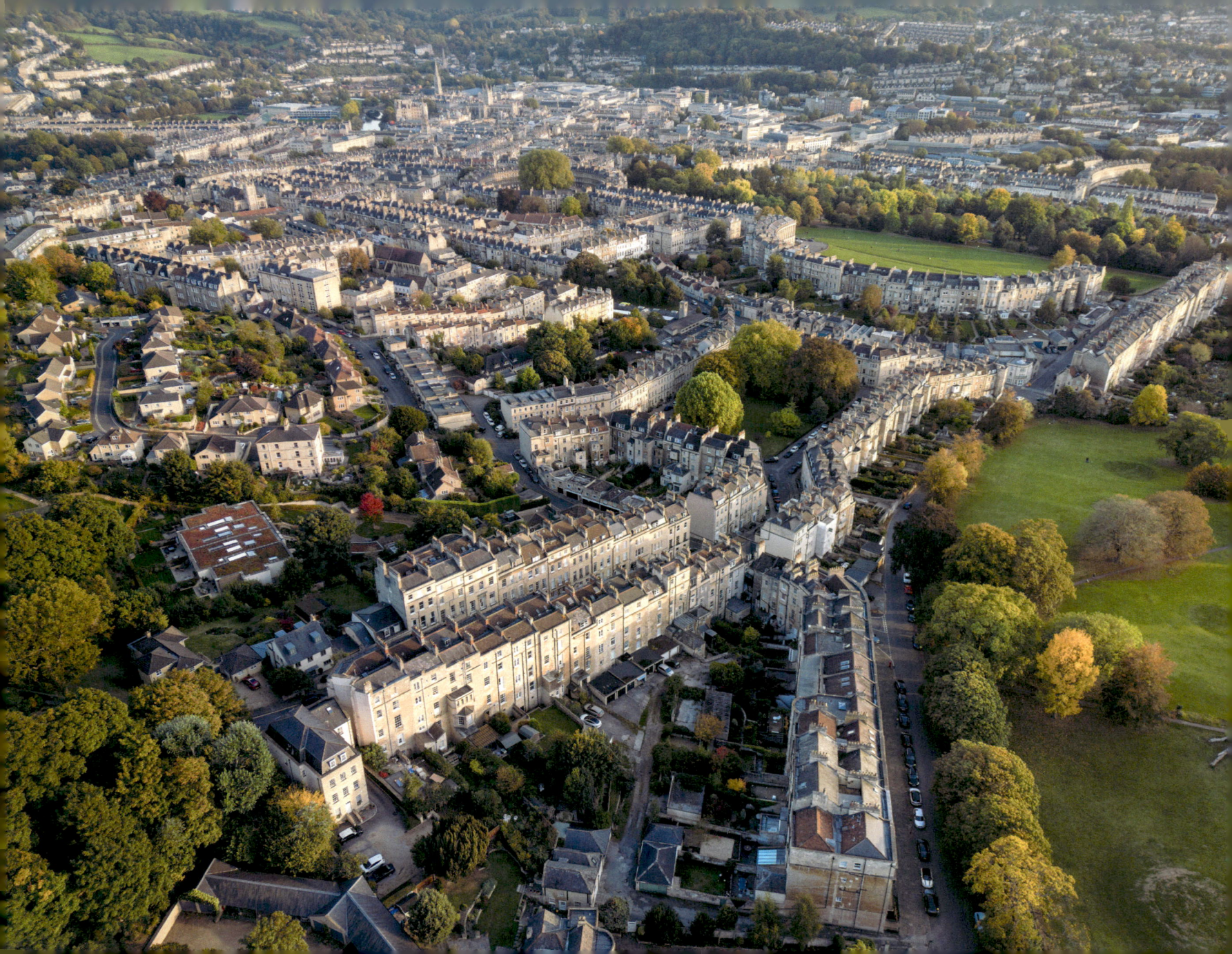

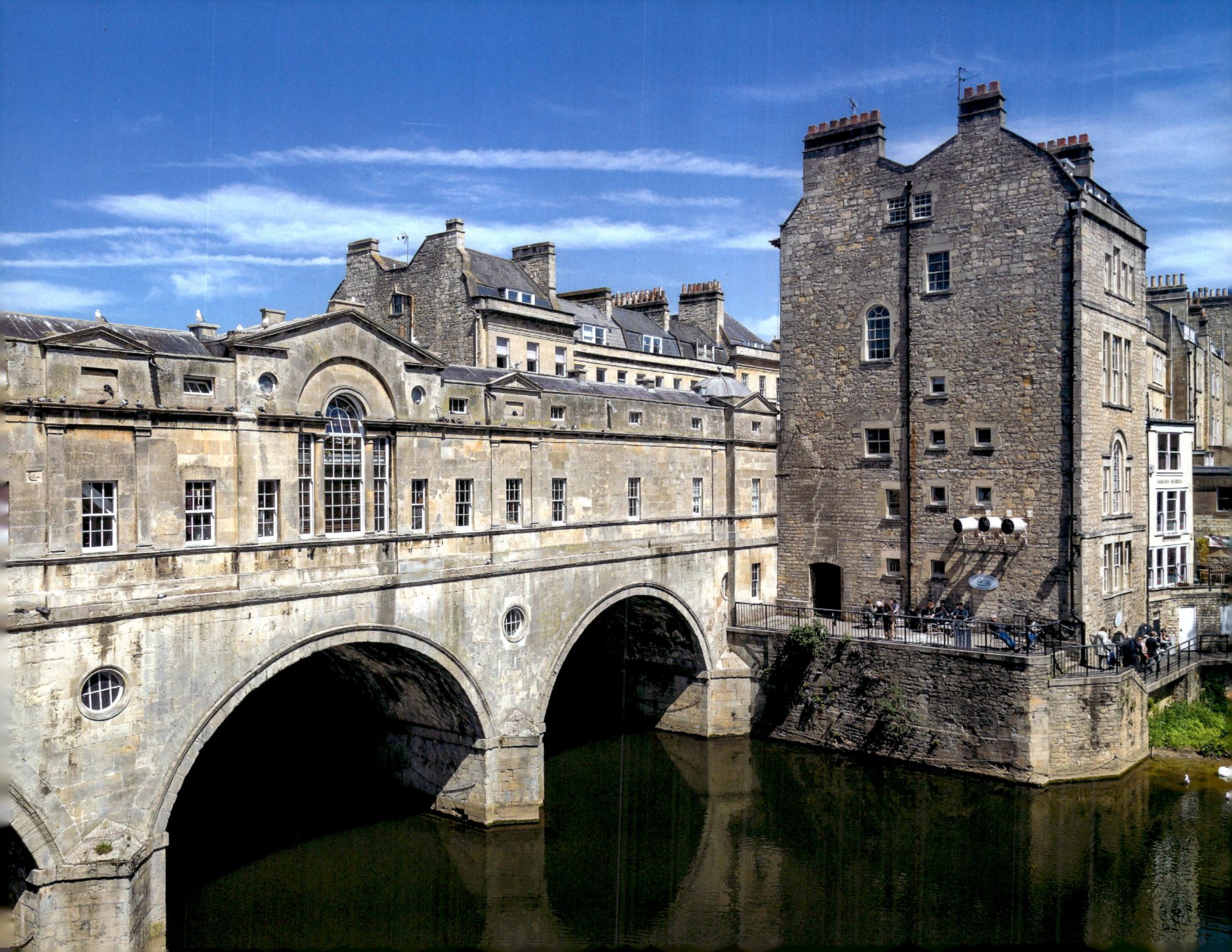

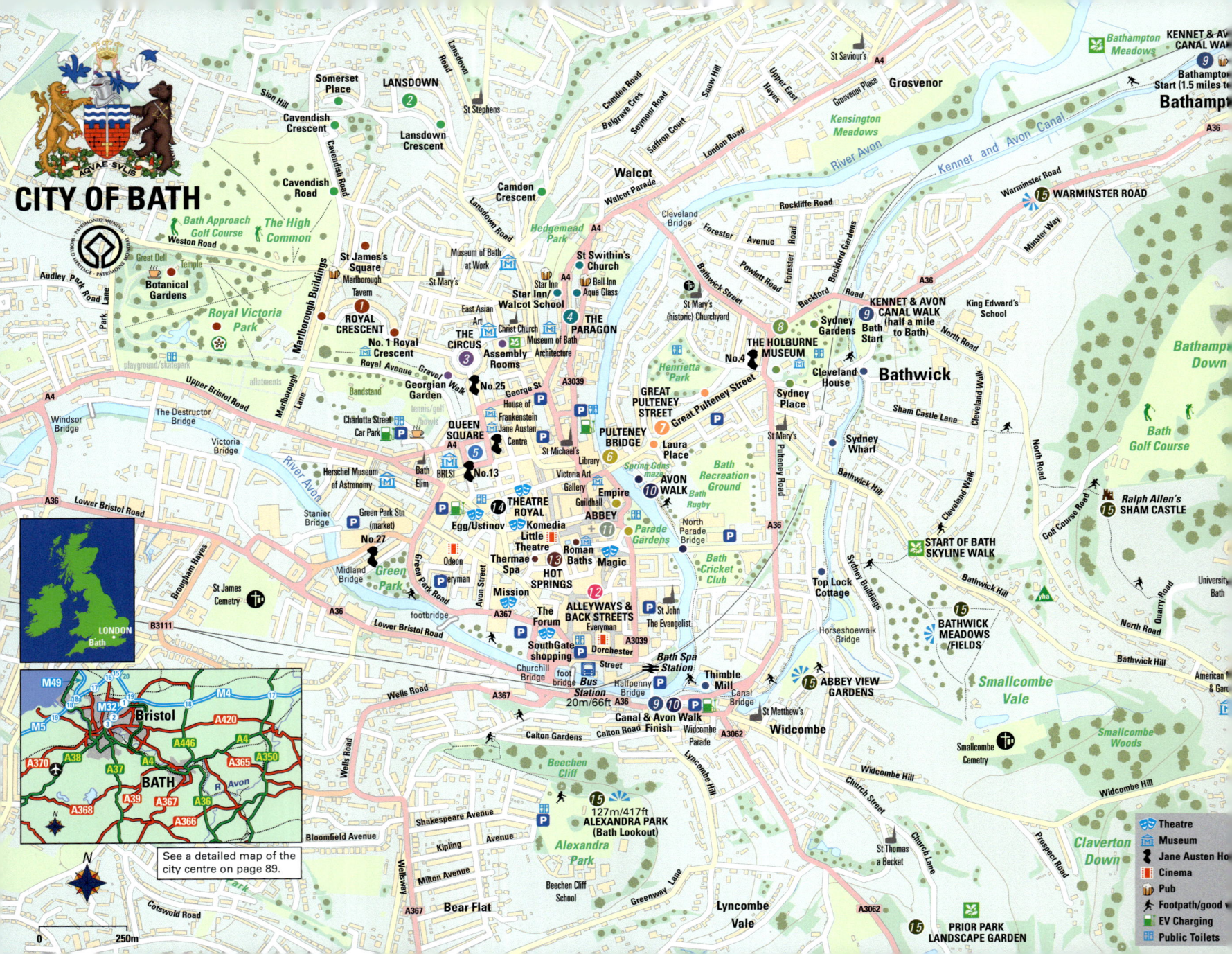

CONTENTS

Introduction	11
Acknowledgements	13
How to use this book	15
Timeline of Bath's history	18
A UNESCO World Heritage Site	21
Some facts about Bath	22
Inventions and Bath	24
The architecture of Bath in the Georgian Period	28
Georgian Balls and Beau Nash	30
Jane Austen and Bath	32
Mary Shelley, Frankenstein and Bath	34
The use of Bath for TV and Films – Bridgerton	38

❶ The Royal Crescent 43
- The Royal Crescent 45
- No.1 Royal Crescent 53
- Marlborough Buildings 54
- Royal Victoria Park 56
- The Botanical Gardens 58
- St James's Square 60

❷ Lansdown 63
- Lansdown Crescent 65
- Somerset Place 66
- Cavendish Road & Crescent 69
- Camden Crescent 72

❸ The Circus 75
- The Circus 77
- The Georgian Garden 78
- The Assembly Rooms 79

❹ The Paragon 81
- The Paragon 83
- The Star Inn & Walcot School 85
- St Swithin's Church 87

THE HEART OF BATH MAP 89

❺ Queen Square 91

❻ Pulteney Bridge 97
- The Empire 102
- Parade Gardens 106

❼ Great Pulteney Street 111
- Laura Place 117

❽ The Holburne Museum 121
- Sydney Gardens 126
- Sydney Place 132

❾ Kennet & Avon Canal 135
- Kennet & Avon Canal – Bathampton 137
- Kennet & Avon Canal – Bath Section 138

❿ River Avon 143

⓫ Bath Abbey 149

⓬ Bath's Alleyways & Back Streets 163
- Abbey Green 165
- North Parade Alleys 168
- Old Orchard Street 172
- Green Street 173
- Hay Hill 174
- The Corridor 176
- Northumberland Place 177
- New Bond Street Place 177

⓭ The Thermal City – Historic & Modern Hot Springs 179
- The Roman Baths 180
- The Pump Rooms 187
- Bath Street 189
- The Cross Bath & Hot Bath Street 191
- Thermae Bath Spa 192

⓮ The Theatre Royal 195

⓯ Bath Skyline & Viewpoints 199
- Alexandra Park 202
- Bathwick Meadows 206
- Sham Castle 210
- Prior Park Landscape Garden 212
- Abbey View Gardens 216
- Warminster Road 222

VISITOR INFORMATION 225
- Getting to and around Bath 226
- Bath climate, weather & seasonal highlights 228
- Where to stay, eat, drink and shop 232
- Bath's museums, and art galleries 236
- Bath's cinemas, theatres and live music 238
- Bath's parks and gardens 240
- Spas and wellbeing 242
- Family friendly activities and sports 244
- Bath guided tours 246
- Bath events 247
- Bath top ten: in a day 250
- Day trips from Bath 254
- Bath itinerary 260
- Bath pubs 261
- Further reading 264
- Visitor information websites 265

About fotovue 268
Index 270

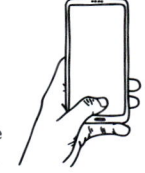

Take a photo of the map for reference.

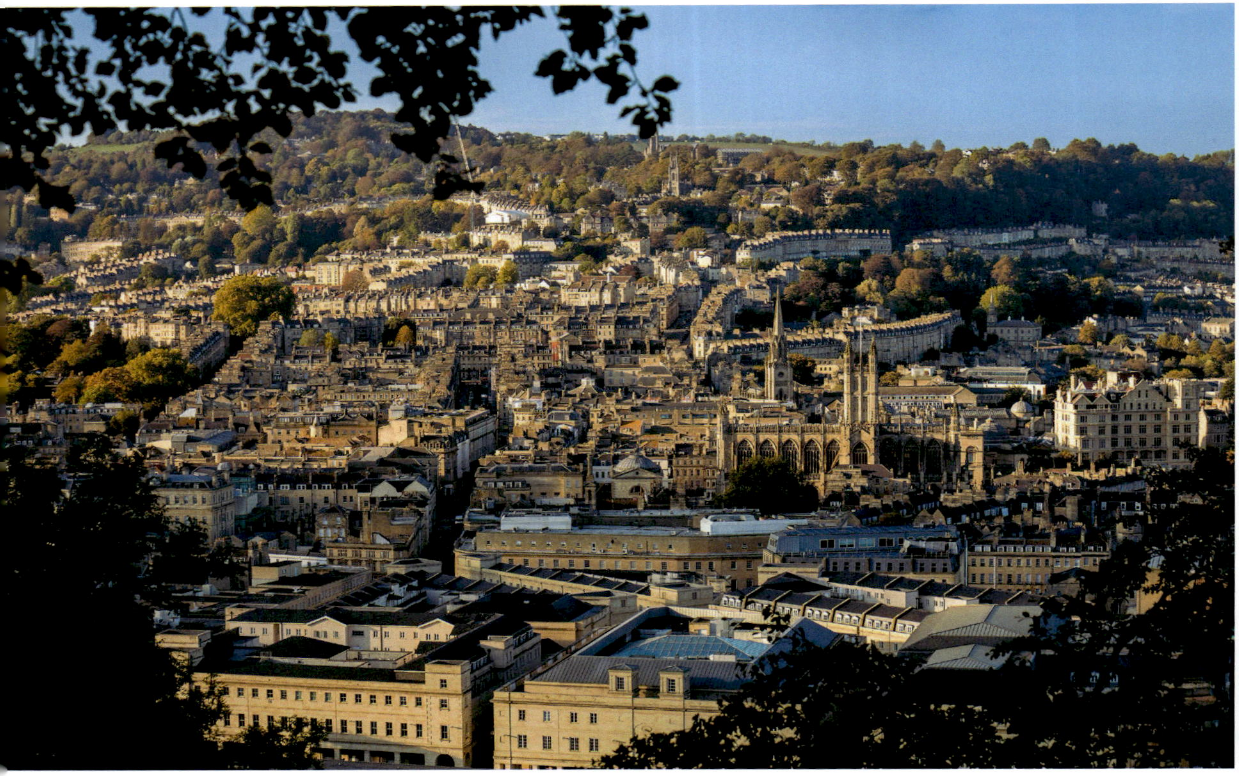

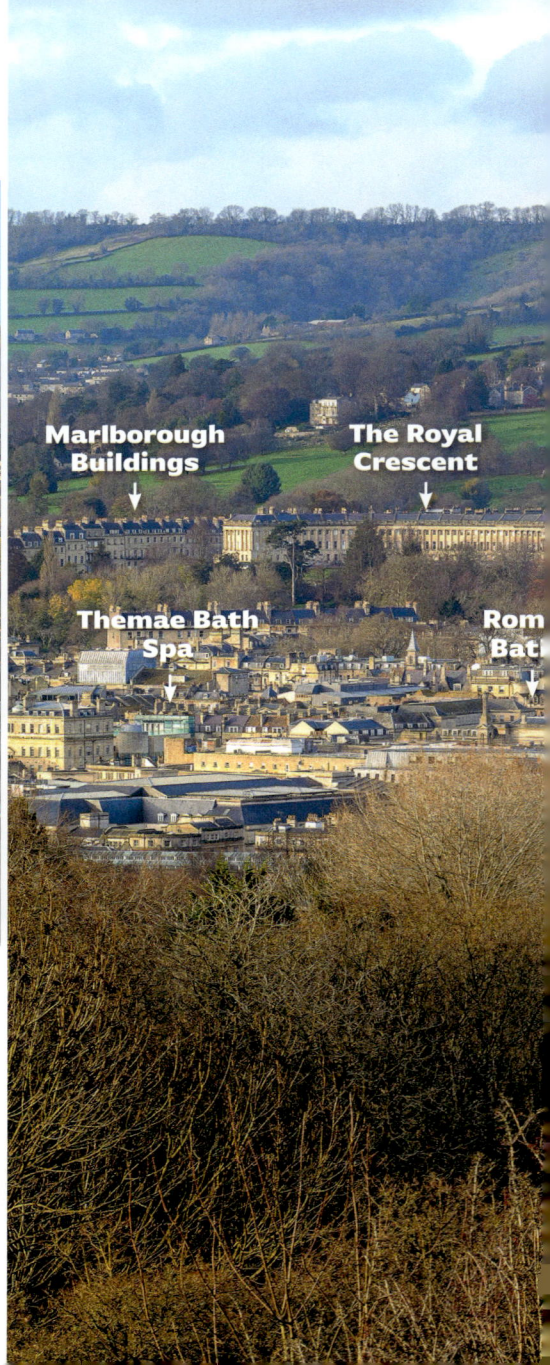

ABOVE: close to Bath is a fantastic viewpoint of the city from Beechen Cliff at Alexandra Park (see page 212). It's a short but steep 1 km (0.6 mile) walk from Bath Spa Station that takes about 20 minutes (you can also drive there). This peaceful spot is the perfect escape for breathtaking views and a quiet moment above the city. It is spectacular at any time of day, but especially so in the golden hour just after sunrise or before sunset.

RIGHT: a stunning panoramic view of the historic city of Bath from Prior Park Landscape Garden (see page 212). From this elevated spot, you can see Bath Abbey's Gothic spires rising above the honey-colored Georgian buildings, the winding river Avon, and the iconic Royal Crescent in the distance.

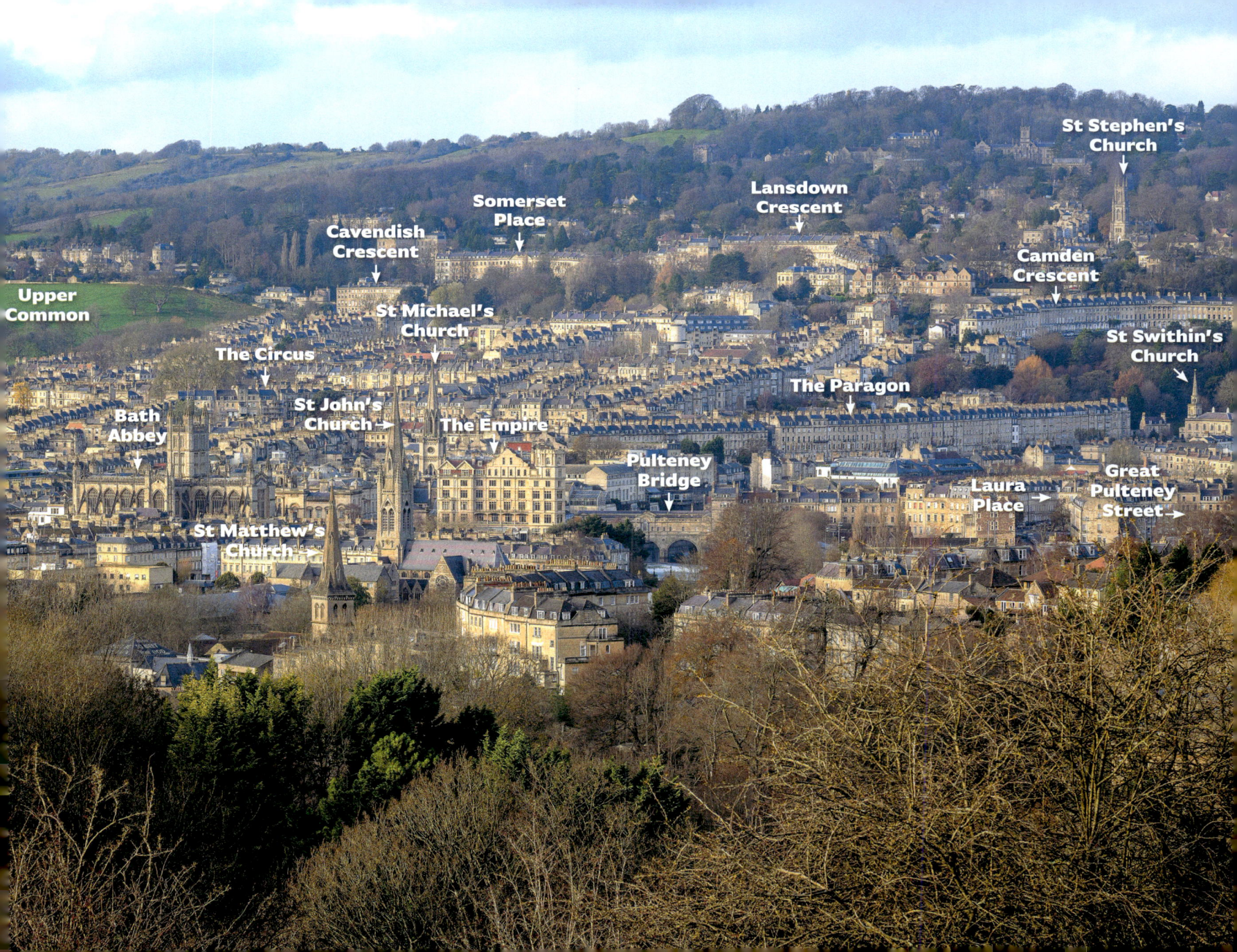

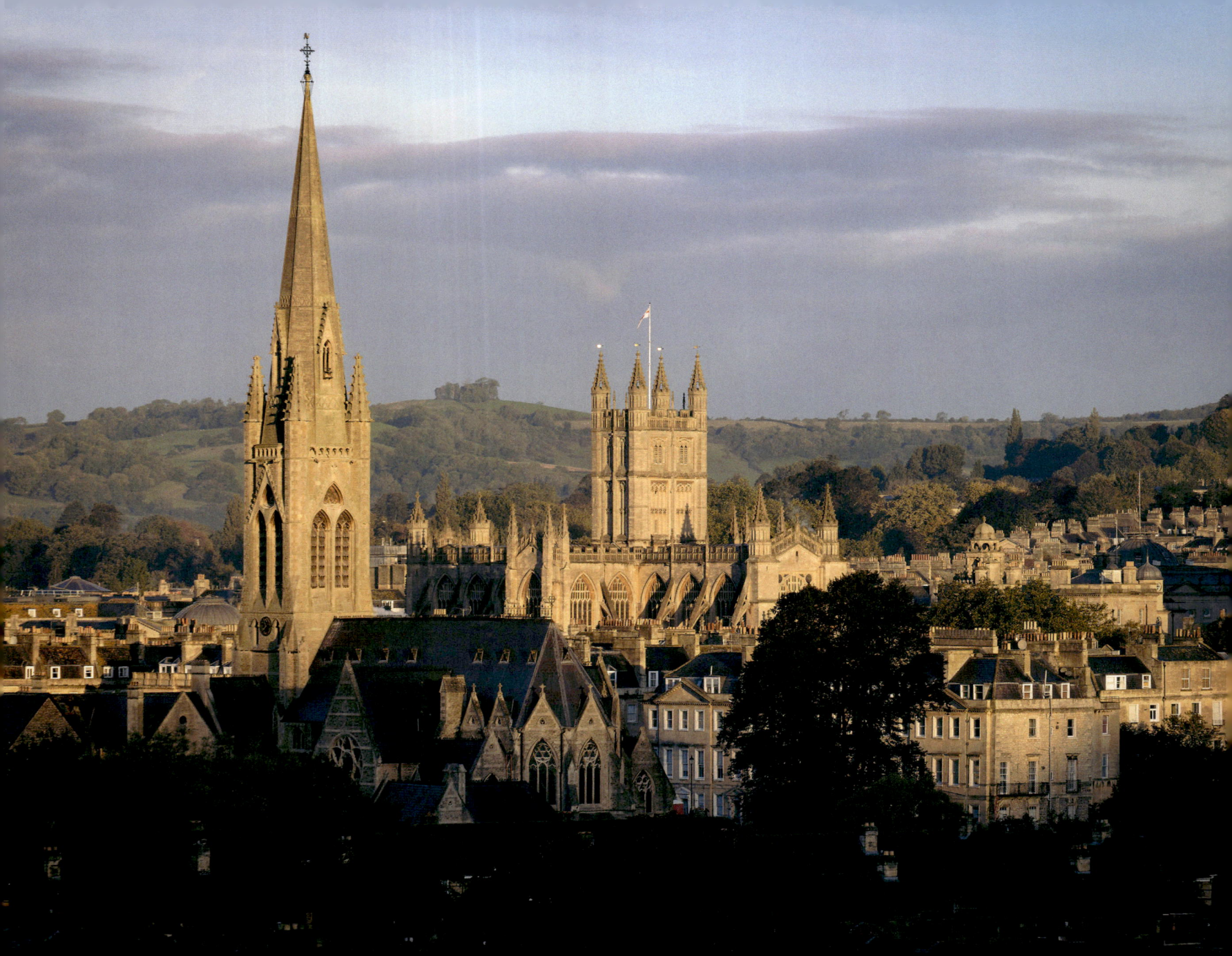

INTRODUCTION

Bath has never been just another city on the map, it is a place of wonder. From my earliest visits to its grand terraces, cobbled streets and sweeping crescents, the city captured my imagination, leaving an imprint that has shaped both my life and my work. As a local, Bath is woven into my own story; a place of endless inspiration, discovery and quiet familiarity, sparking a love of Georgian architecture and a fascination with the stories woven into the fabric of the city.

Photography has been my way of honouring that connection, a means of capturing not just the beauty of Bath's architecture, but also its atmosphere, the changing light and its timeless spirit. My work has allowed me the privilege of exploring Bath from many different angles from its iconic landmarks to the quieter, lesser-known corners that reveal the city's deeper layers. Through the years my camera has led me down hidden alleyways, beneath mighty columns and colonnades, to misty mornings by the river and into conversations with history itself, whispered from weathered stone and echoing in the shadows of incredible buildings.

Photographing Bath for this book has been both a personal and creative journey. Each image is in a sense, a love letter to the city. From the grandeur of the Royal Crescent to the delicate details that often go unseen. I wanted to create something that would resonate not only with those who are discovering Bath for the first time but also with those who know and love it as deeply as I do.

This book is a celebration of Bath: its rich history, its extraordinary architecture and its quiet enduring magic. Across fifteen carefully curated chapters, I invite you to walk with me through the city's most beautiful places, to uncover its stories and to lose yourself in its charms. In this book's introduction you can learn about the history of Bath, in the final section, you will find practical guidance to help shape your own journey here to ensure that your time in Bath is as rewarding and memorable as the city deserves.

Bath is a place to linger, to wander, and to return to. My hope is that, through these pages, you'll be drawn into its golden spell – if you haven't been already – and inspired to begin your own lasting connection with this remarkable city.

Casper Farrell
Bath, August 2025

LEFT: St Johns Church and Bath Abbey – the tallest landmarks in the city.

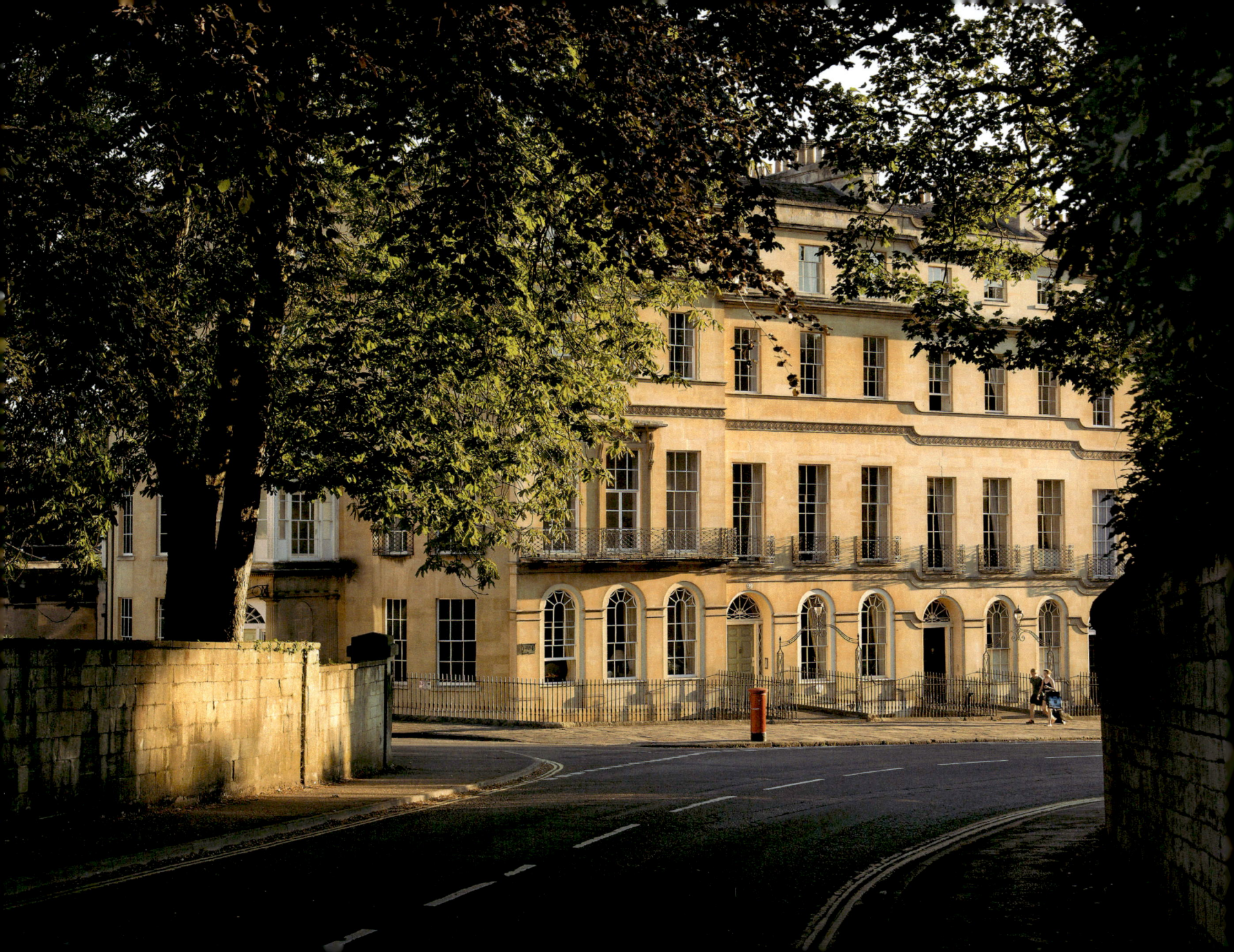

ACKNOWLEDGEMENTS

Writing The Beauty of Bath has been an incredible journey and I am deeply grateful to everyone who has supported, guided and encouraged me along the way.

First and foremost, my heartfelt thanks go to Mick Ryan of fotoVUE, whose belief in my work and love for this city made this book possible. Mick saw something in my photography and offered me the opportunity of a lifetime; to create a book that celebrates the city through my lens. It was an offer no photographer could possibly refuse and I'm so thankful he reached out.

A huge thank you also to Vicky Barlow, whose expert eye and tireless attention to detail shaped the layout of this book. Don Williams, for creating beautifully detailed maps of the city – he probably knows it better than I do now!

I owe deep gratitude to everyone in Bath who granted access to some of the city's most iconic landmarks, hidden gems and beloved visitor attractions. Your generosity has enriched this project in ways that words and pictures alone cannot fully express.

I'm also immensely thankful to the individuals and organisations who have championed my work over the years, including Visit Bath, the Bath Preservation Trust and Bath Life magazine. Your encouragement and support have played a vital role in helping my work reach a wider audience.

To my followers on Instagram and those who visit my website, thank you for your ongoing enthusiasm, your kind messages and unwavering support. It's a joy to share my work with a community that values heritage, beauty and photography as much as I do.

And finally, to my family – Mum, Dad and brothers. Thank you for keeping me on the tracks and for tolerating no end of "book talk" over the last few years. We finally finished it!

Casper Farrell
Bath, August 2025

LEFT: an example of Bath's fine architectural detailing at Sydney Place.

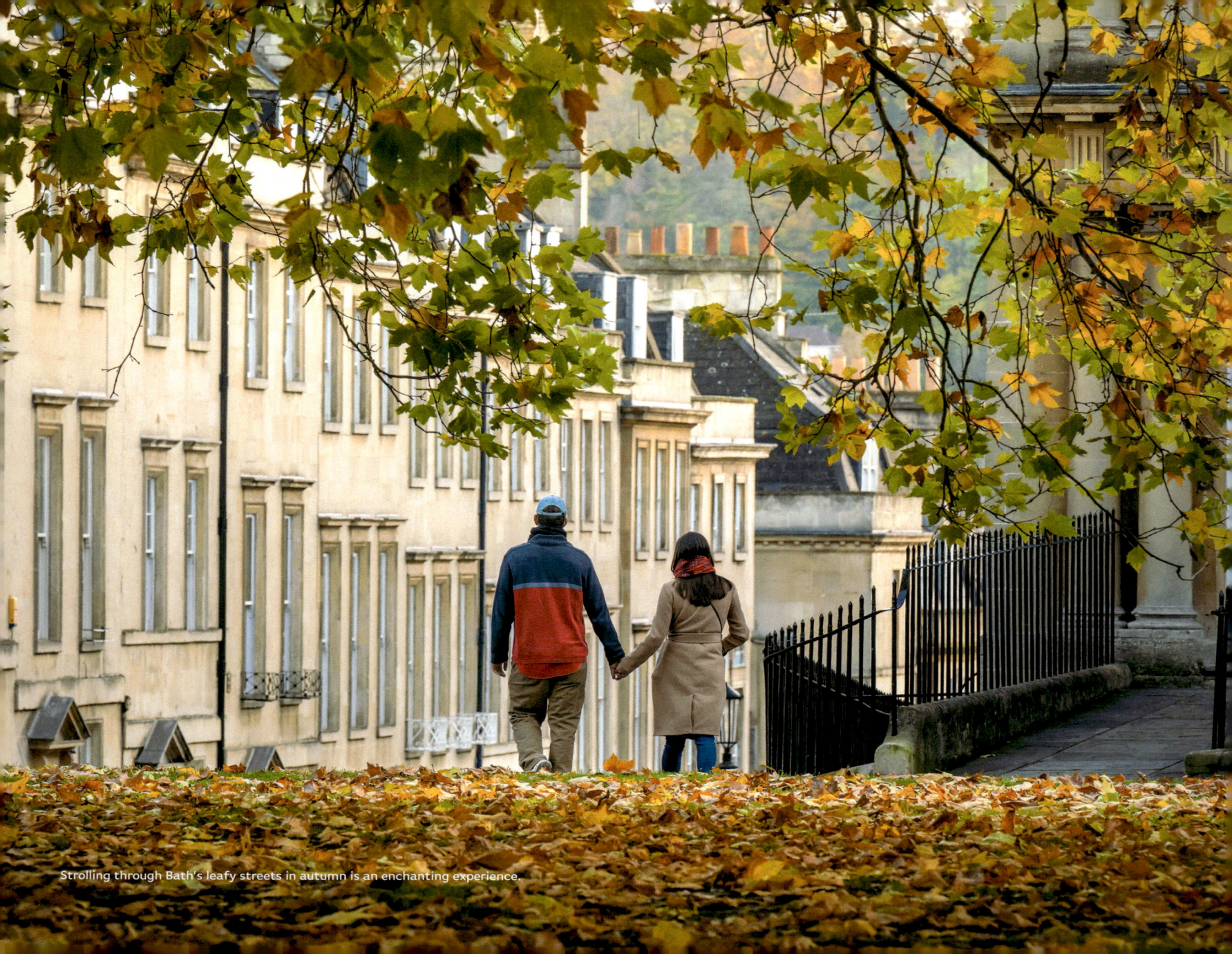
Strolling through Bath's leafy streets in autumn is an enchanting experience.

HOW TO USE THIS BOOK

fotoVUE's **Beauty of** series are hybrid books, a visitor guidebook with all the information you need for an enjoyable trip, and also a coffee table-type book with a rich array of beautiful images that you can enjoy at home, as a souvenir or memento of your trip, or even as gift for someone to show the beauty of the area.

We have divided Bath into fifteen areas to visit, each area has a chapter with an introduction, and alongside beautiful photography short essays describing the most beautiful and important places to visit. In the book's introduction are chapters about the history of Bath.

GETTING TO A LOCATION
Bath is small and compact. Bath city centre covers approximately 1.5 square miles (about 4 square kilometers). This includes the area with the main attractions, historic sites, and the city's central shopping and dining areas. Most of the locations are within walking distance of each other. See page **226** for more information about getting around Bath, including car parks, toilets and bus routes.

To help you get around there are maps on pages **7** and **89**. In each of the Bath city centre location chapters are co-ordinates to help you on your way. If a location is outside of Bath city centre we also include written directions.

THE ROYAL CRESCENT

Postcode: BA1 2LS
what3words: count.trade.slate

POSTCODE
Type the postcode of the location into the map app on your phone and you will get directions (by foot, car or public transport) from where you are to your chosen location.

///WHAT3WORDS
What3words, assigns each 3m square in the world a unique three-word address that will never change.

Download the free what3words app then either say, type or scan in the what3words of a location, click on navigate, open a map app and you will get directions to the location.

THE QR-CODE (LOCATION DIRECTIONS)
Using your smart phone camera point the lens at the QR-code and your camera will scan the code that contains the location information as a lat-long co-ordinate. Once read, your browser will open in Google maps and you can get directions (by foot, car or public transport) from where you are to your chosen location.

THE QR-CODE (MORE INFORMATION)
Some of the QR-codes once scanned by your smart phone camera are linked to specific websites providing more information about a location or attraction.

MORE INFORMATION

museumofbatharchitecture.org.uk
Visit the Museum of Bath Architecture website for opening times, admission and directions.

BATH VISITOR INFORMATION
At the rear of this book is a smorgasbord of information to help make your trip to Bath great. This includes how to get to Bath and the best times to visit, best places to stay and eat, best places to shop, spas, festivals and events, filming locations, live music and theatre venues. If you are short on time there are itineraries for Bath in a day, suggestions for weekend visits and suggested day trips outside of Bath.

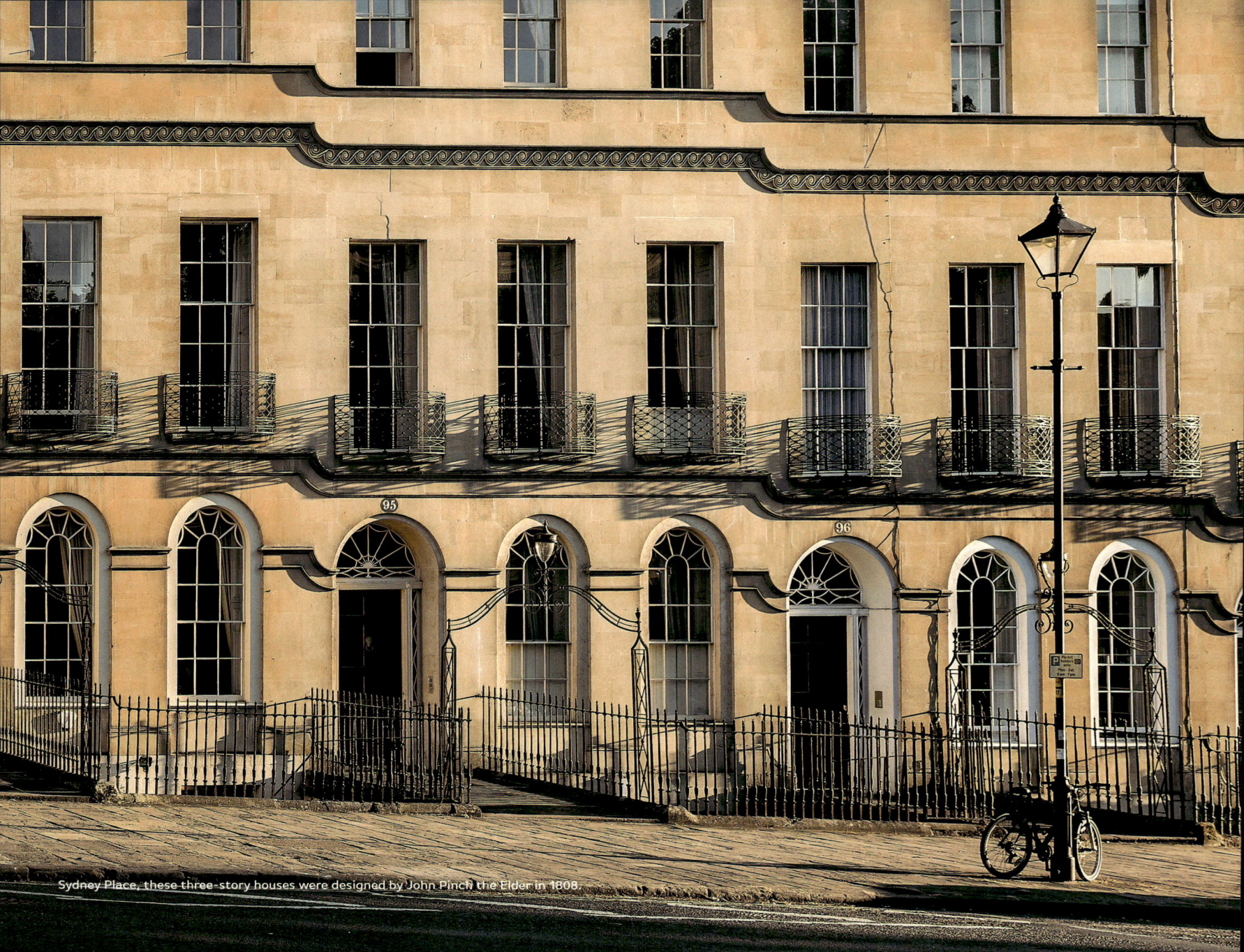
Sydney Place, these three-story houses were designed by John Pinch the Elder in 1808.

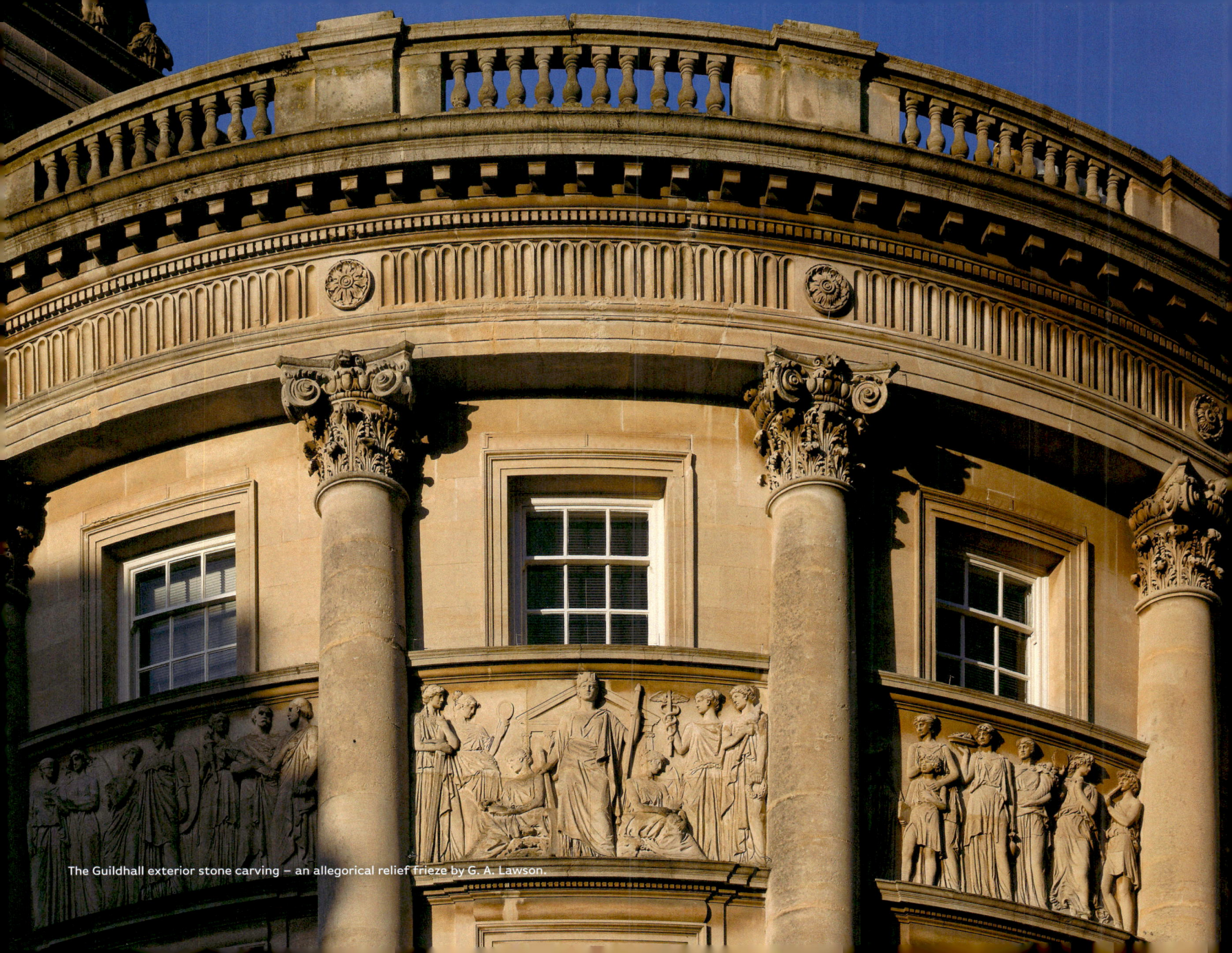

The Guildhall exterior stone carving – an allegorical relief frieze by G. A. Lawson.

TIMELINE OF BATH'S HISTORY

Before the Romans, Bath was home to the Dobunni, a Celtic tribe. They lived in small villages and hillforts, such as Solsbury Hill, located just outside modern Bath. The Dobunni were a relatively peaceful and agrarian people, known for their farming, metalwork, and trade. Long before the Romans, the area around Bath was known for its hot springs, which the Celts revered as sacred. They dedicated the hot springs to Sulis, a local goddess associated with healing and water. When the Romans invaded Britain in 43 AD, they encountered the Dobunni, who largely submitted without major resistance. The Romans recognised the religious significance of the hot springs and merged the local beliefs with their own, identifying Sulis with their goddess Minerva. This led to the development of Aquae Sulis, the grand Roman spa city that would eventually become modern Bath.

1st Century AD – Roman Bath (Aquae Sulis)
c. 60–70 AD – Romans build a bathing complex around the natural hot springs.
c. 75–80 AD – Temple of Sulis Minerva constructed, making Bath a major religious site.
3rd–4th Century AD – Bath thrives as a Roman spa town with public baths, temples, and townhouses.
5th Century AD – Romans withdraw from Britain, leading to the decline of Aquae Sulis.

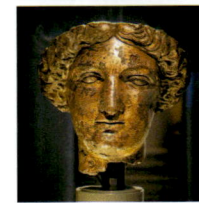

TOP: a Catti Stater of the Dobunni tribe c. 40 B.C. A type of Celtic gold coin, struck by the Dobunni tribe and bearing the name 'Catti'. The name "Catti" is believed to be that of a Dobunni chieftain.

6th–10th Century – Saxon & Early Medieval Period
7th Century – Bath falls under Anglo-Saxon control. The monastery of St. Peter (early Bath Abbey) is founded.
973 AD – King Edgar, the first King of England, is crowned at Bath Abbey in a grand ceremony that inspires future coronations.
Late 10th Century – Bath becomes an important religious and trading centre under the Benedictine monks

11th–16th Century – Norman & Medieval Bath
1088 – The Normans rebuild Bath Abbey, making it a grand Romanesque cathedral.
12th–14th Century – The wool trade brings prosperity to Bath. Merchants and monasteries thrive.
1499 – Bath Abbey is rebuilt in the striking Perpendicular Gothic style under Bishop Oliver King.
1539 – Dissolution of the Monasteries under Henry VIII leads to the decline of Bath Abbey's influence.

17th–18th Century – The Georgian Golden Age
1668 – Queen Catherine of Braganza (wife of Charles II) visits Bath for its healing waters, boosting its reputation as a spa town.
1704–1718 – Architect John Wood the Elder develops plans for grand streets and squares.
1728 – Ralph Allen improves Bath stone quarries, providing the city with its signature honey-colored limestone.
1767–1774 – The Royal Crescent is built by John Wood the Younger, becoming one of the most iconic pieces of Georgian architecture.

LEFT: the gilt bronze head of the goddess Sulis Minerva, discovered in 1727 while workmen were digging below Stall Street in Bath. Sulis Minerva was a syncretic deity worshipped in Roman Britain, specifically at the site of the hot springs of Bath (Aquae Sulis), representing the fusion of the Celtic goddess Sulis with the Roman goddess Minerva.

1771 – Pulteney Bridge is completed, inspired by Italian design, making it one of only four bridges in the world lined with shops.
1795 – Jane Austen visits Bath and later moves here (1801-1806), writing about its high society in Northanger Abbey and Persuasion.

19th Century – Victorian Expansion & Change
1841 – The Great Western Railway, designed by Isambard Kingdom Brunel, connects Bath to London, bringing more visitors.
1860s – The Roman Baths are rediscovered, leading to restoration efforts.
1897 – The Grand Pump Room is rebuilt, solidifying Bath's identity as a fashionable spa town.

20th Century – War & Reconstruction
1934 – Bath Preservation Trust was formed to safeguard the city's historic buildings.
1942 – Bath suffers heavy bombing during the Baedeker Raids in World War II, damaging historical buildings.
1960's & 70's – Large scale restoration threatens Bath's historic character, leading to a campaign to halt destructive developments.
1987 – Bath is designated a UNESCO World Heritage Site due to its Roman and Georgian heritage.

21st Century – UNESCO & Modern Bath
2006 – Thermae Bath Spa opens, reviving Bath's ancient spa culture with a modern thermal bath.
2021 – Bath gains dual UNESCO status, recognized as one of the "Great Spa Towns of Europe."
Today – Bath continues to attract visitors yearly, preserving its historical charm while embracing modern culture.

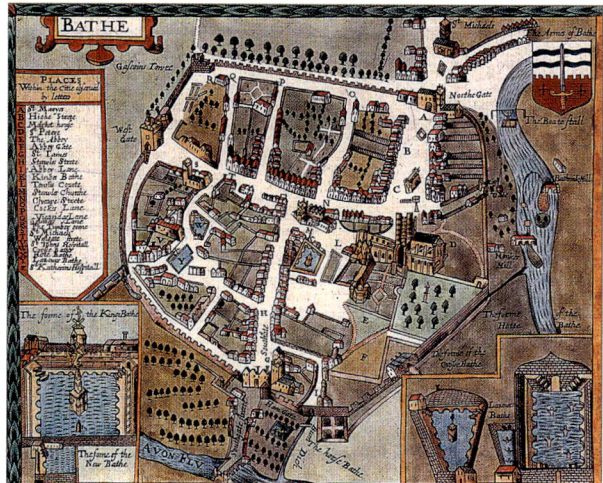

1610: Bathe map. Circa 1610 by John Speed. From an inset from his Somerset map which was included in his book the "Theatre of the Empire of Great Britaine", 1611.

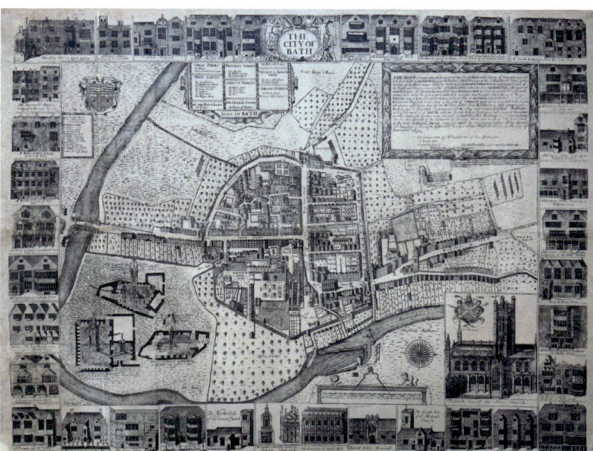

1694: a map of pre-Georgian Bath (1694) by Joseph Gilmore bordered by images of Bath's Lodging Houses, in the style of a modern day tourist map, it provides a revealing insight into Medieval Bath.

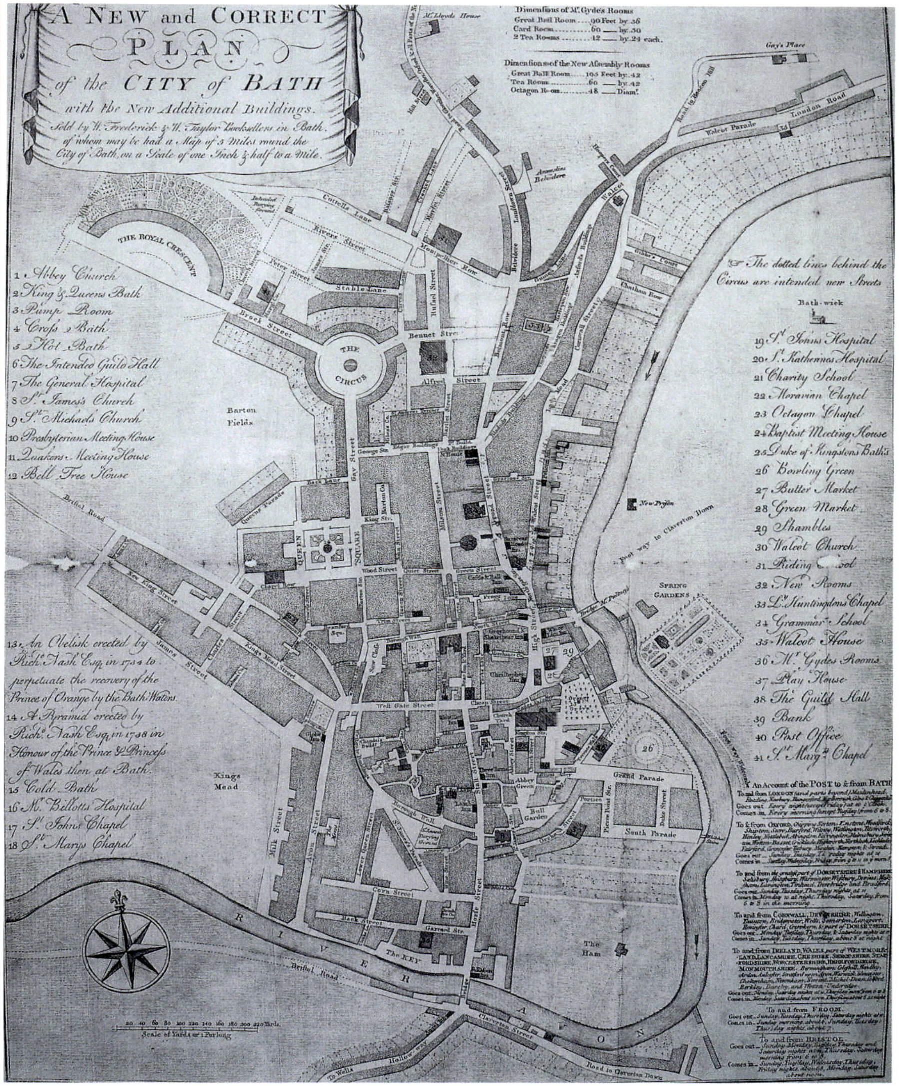

1780: A NEW and CORRECT PLAN of the CITY of BATH, 1780 by William Frederick and William Hibbert. Sold by W. Frederick & W. Taylor, booksellers in Bath.

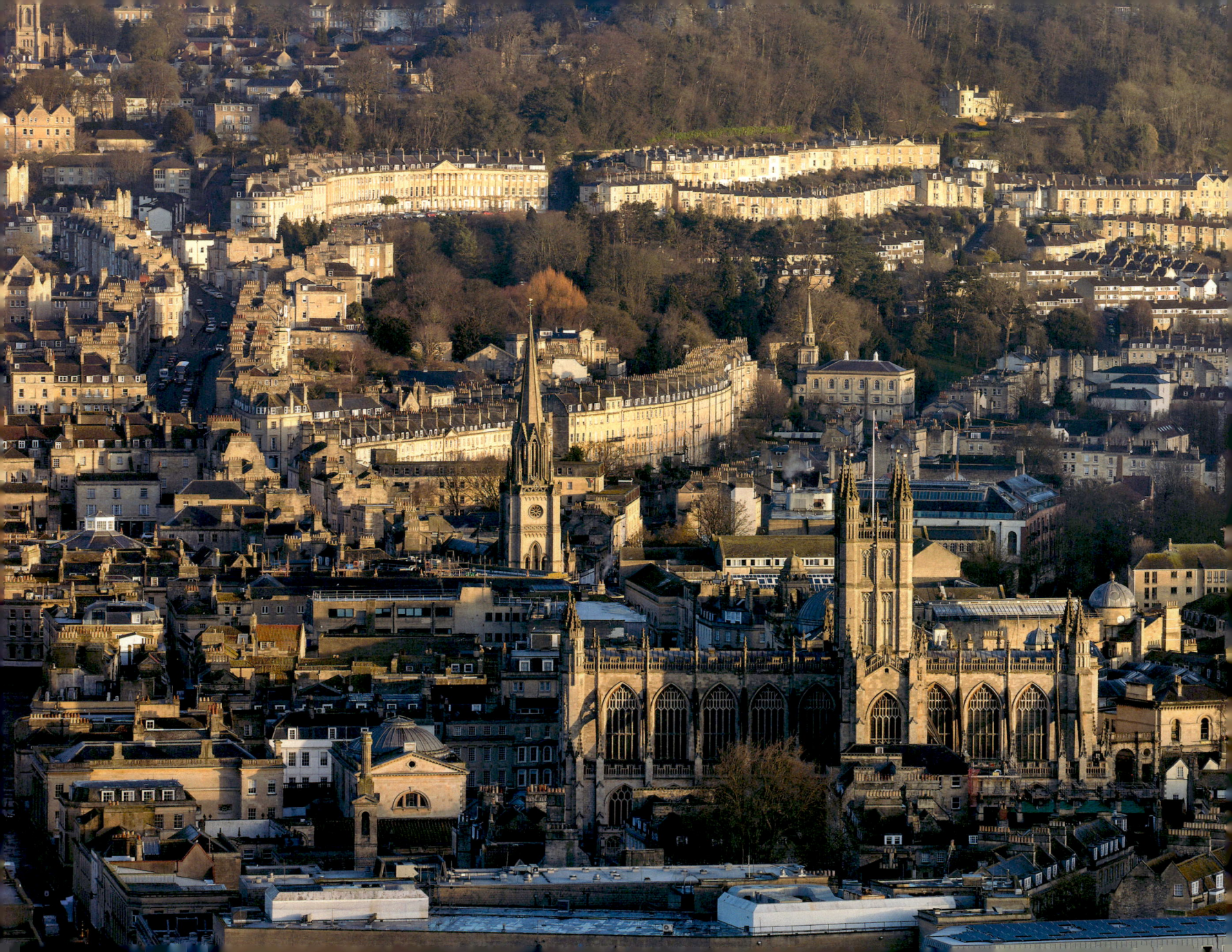

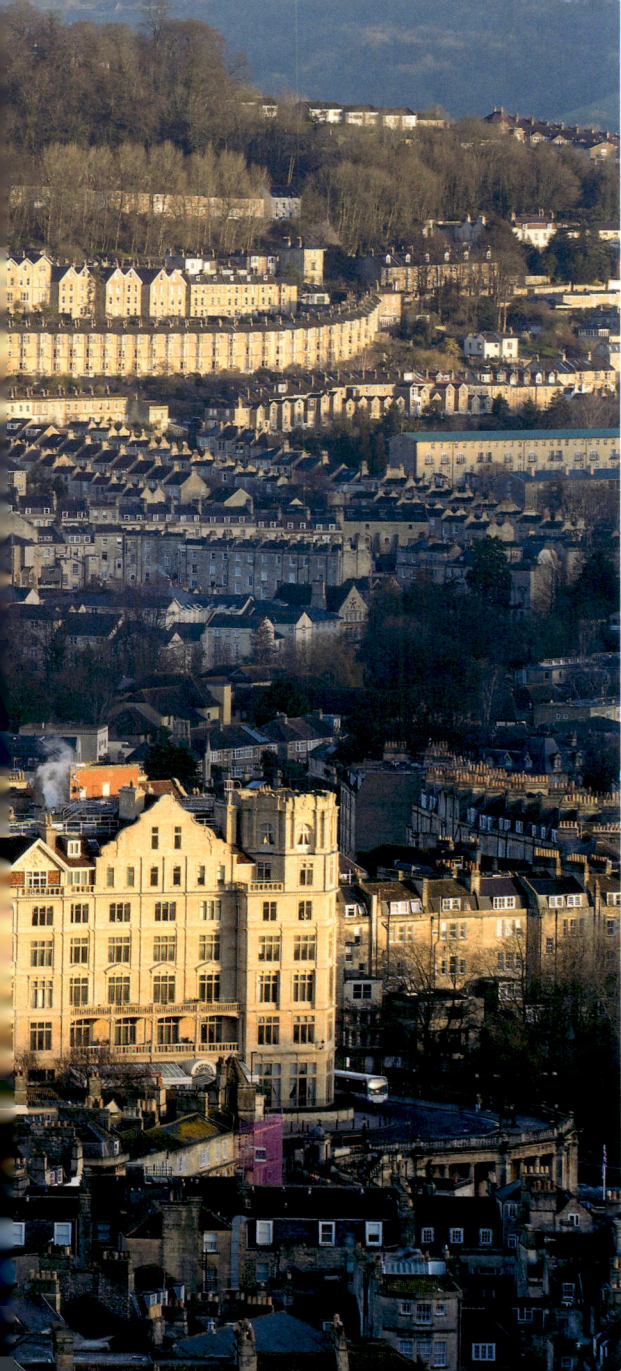

A UNESCO WORLD HERITAGE SITE

The city of Bath holds a double UNESCO World Heritage Site status due to its unique historical and cultural significance. The two designations are:

1987: UNESCO World Heritage City
Bath was inscribed as a World Heritage Site due to its Roman remains, 18th-century Georgian architecture, and natural hot springs. It is recognized for its harmonious urban design, influenced by classical ideals, and its role as a fashionable spa town in the 18th century.

2021: Part of the "Great Spa Towns of Europe" World Heritage Site
Bath was included in this transnational designation, which recognizes 11 historic spa towns across seven European countries. These towns were chosen for their role in the development of European spa culture, where mineral waters were used for health and leisure from the early modern period onward.

WHY BATH IS SPECIAL?
- **Roman Heritage**: The city is home to the famous Roman Baths, which date back to around 60 AD, built around natural thermal springs.
- **Georgian Architecture**: Bath is renowned for its Palladian-style buildings, such as the Royal Crescent, The Circus, and Pulteney Bridge.
- **Natural Hot Springs**: It is the only place in the UK with natural hot springs still in use today.
- **Cultural Influence**: Bath was a major centre of social life in the 18th and 19th centuries, attracting figures like Jane Austen.

This double UNESCO status highlights Bath's unique blend of Roman engineering, Georgian elegance, and spa-town heritage, making it one of the most historically significant cities in the world.

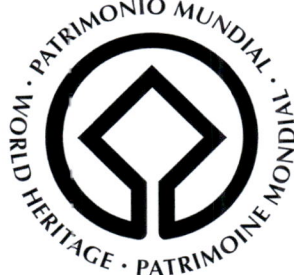

OPPOSITE: the view of Bath from Alexandra Park (page 202).

SOME FACTS ABOUT BATH

Bath is nestled in the valley of the River Avon in the South West England, surrounded by the rolling hills of the Cotswolds and Mendip Hills (both Areas of Outstanding Natural Beauty).

Elevation: Varies, but around 20-238 metres (60-780ft) above sea level.

The city of Bath is located at approximately:
Latitude: 51.3751° N Longitude: -2.3617° W

Bath shares its latitude with parts of:
- Southern Canada: Vancouver Island and Calgary
- United States: Seattle and Portland, Maine
- Southern UK cities: Reading, Oxford and Windsor
- Northern France: Rouen and Le Mans

Bath is historically part of the county of Somerset, but administratively, it is now governed as part of a unitary authority called: Bath and North East Somerset (B&NES)

Bath is 115mi/185km (2.5 hrs drive) from London, 170 mi/274km from Manchester (3.5h hrs drive) and 370mi/ 595km (7.5 hrs drive) from Edinburgh. Bath is accessible via the A4 and M4 Motorway. Bath Spa Station connects to Bristol (15 mins) and London Paddington (approx. 90 mins). The nearest airport is Bristol airport.

City Population: Around 94,000 (as of the latest estimates, 2023) Bath has two universities, the University of Bath and Bath Spa University, with a student population of around 25,000.

Notable schools include King Edward's School, Prior Park College and the Ralph Allen School

The Member of Parliament (MP) for Bath is Wera Hobhouse of the Liberal Democrats who was elected in 2017 General Election. Wera Hobhouse is known for her work on environmental issues, women's rights, and housing. She's held the seat since winning it from the Conservatives in 2017 and has been re-elected since.

Bath has a mayor, *The Right Worshipful The Mayor of Bath*, which is a ceremonial role, not an executive or political one. The mayor is elected by the Charter Trustees (made up of Bath's ward councillors) with a term of one year. The role includes: attending civic events, representing the city at official functions upholding traditions dating back to 1590 (when Bath was granted city status by Queen Elizabeth I).

Bath is governed by Bath and North East Somerset Council (B&NES) and its Council Leader.

The local newspaper is the *Bath Chronicle* which is published weekly on a Thursday. For online Bath news visit *somersetlive.co.uk*. Local radio stations include *BBC Radio Bristol*, *Heart West* and *Bath Radio* and for TV watch, *BBC Points West* and *ITV News West Country*.

The main sources of employment in Bath are: Tourism & Hospitality, Education, Health & Social Care, Public Administration and Professional Services & Creative Industries.

The tourism sector supports around 9,000–10,000 jobs directly and indirectly. Key employers include hotels, restaurants, attractions (Roman Baths, Thermae Spa), museums, and tour operators. Bath attracts over 6 million visitors per year; 1.3 million overnight visitor and 4.8 million day-trippers.

ARMS OF THE CITY OF BATH

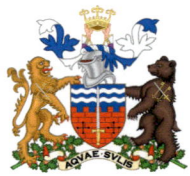

ARMS
The shield is that which was in use in the 16th century, depicts the Borough wall and the mineral springs and River Avon, and the sword of St. Paul, one of the patron saints of the Abbey.

CREST
The crest itself commemorates the Coronation of King Edgar in 973 and his crown, held aloft by the sleeved hands of St. Dunstan in the Edgar.

SUPPORTERS
The lion and bear. Their historical significance is

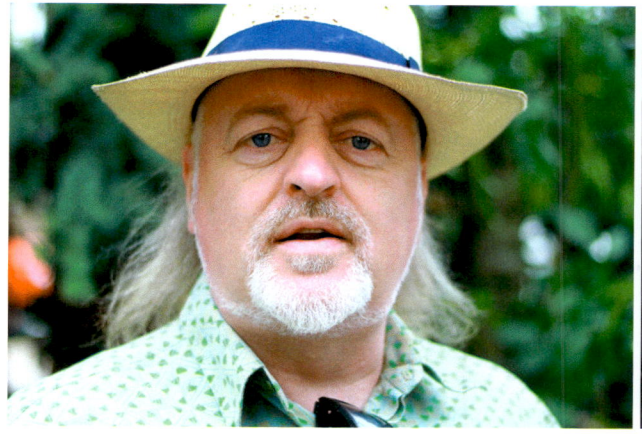 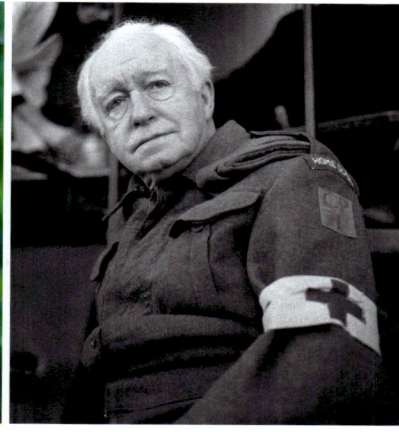 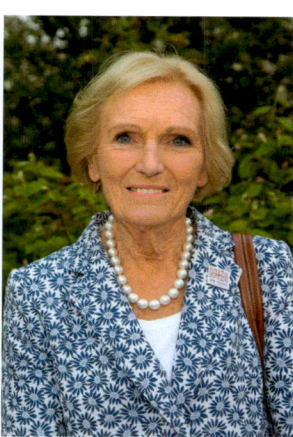

not clear, but they were certainly familiar to the citizens of Bath in Elizabethan times. The supporters stand on branches of oak with leaves and acorns refer to the legend of King Bladud, said to have discovered the medicinal springs while, as a swineherd he was feeding acorns to his pigs. The acorn is also a prominent architectural feature of Georgian Bath.

BADGE

A roundel of the arms within a civic crown proper, ensigned by a length of wall with four crenels gules masoned sable.

MOTTO

Aquae Sulis, the name for Bath from two thousand years ago, which epitomises the Romano-British associations with Sul-Minerva and the waters which made the City famous.

FAMOUS BATHONIANS

A selection of famous people born, educated or prominent in Bath:

Dame Mary Berry (born 1935) – chef, food writer and TV presenter (The Great British Bake Off)
Jennifer Biddall (born 1980) – an English actress who played Jessica Harris in Hollyoaks
Anthony Head (born 1954) – an English actor, singer and performer in musical theatre.
Indira Varma (born 1973) – a British actress
Bill Bailey (born 1965) – comedian, musician, actor, TV and radio presenter and author
Dame Jacqueline Wilson (born 1945) – children's author (The Story of Tracy Beaker) born in Bath
Russell Howard (born 1980) – comedian, TV presenter and actor
Charlotte McDonnell (born 1990) – YouTuber, filmmaker and screenwriter
Curt Smith (born 1961) co-founder of Tears for Fears – a musical group
Midge Ure (born 1953) – musician
Peter Gabriel (born 1950) – musician
Thomas Gainsborough (1727–1788) – painter
Caroline Herschel (1750–1848) – astronomer who discovered several comets.
William Herschel (1738–1822) – astronomer, discoverer of Uranus and musician
William Lonsdale (1794–1871) – English geologist and palaeontologist
Claire Calvert (born 1988) – ballet dancer, a first soloist at the Royal Ballet.
Amy Williams MBE (born 1982) – former skeleton racer and Olympic gold medalist
Sir Roger Bannister (1929–2018) – runner who ran the first sub-4-minute mile, doctor
Sir Arnold Ridley (1896–1984) – actor (Private Godfrey in Dad's Army), playwright
Chris Anderson (born 1957) – journalist, publisher, entrepreneur, the owner of TED and the curator of TED Talks.
Princess Claire of Belgium (born 1974) – born in Bath
Samantha Harvey – (born 1975) is an English novelist. She won the 2024 Booker Prize for her novel Orbital and she is a Reader on the MA in creative writing at Bath Spa University

TOP LEFT: Bill Bailey. **MIDDLE**: Sir Arnold Ridley. **RIGHT**: Dame Mary Berry.

INVENTIONS AND BATH

Bath has a rich history of innovation and creativity – especially during the Georgian and Victorian eras – here's a list of notable inventions, discoveries, and pioneering achievements associated with people who lived in the city of Bath:

SCIENCE & MEDICINE
Discovery of Palladium (1803)
By William Hyde Wollaston, who lived and worked in Bath. He isolated palladium before later discovering rhodium.

Early use of electrical therapy (18th century)
Dr. James Graham ran a "Temple of Health" in Bath, promoting electrotherapy long before it became mainstream in medicine.

Discovery of Uranus (1781)
William Herschel discovered Uranus while living at 19 New King Street in Bath. He was originally a musician and telescope maker before becoming a pioneering astronomer. There's a Herschel Museum of Astronomy in Bath, located in his former home.

ENGINEERING & INFRASTRUCTURE
Hydraulic Systems for Baths
The Romans pioneered underground plumbing and heating systems (hypocausts) in the Roman Baths – cutting-edge engineering for the time.

Crescent-shaped Urban Design
The Royal Crescent, designed by John Wood the Younger, was revolutionary in 18th-century urban architecture and influenced Georgian design across Britain.

First Flushing Toilet (1596)
Sir John Harington lived in Kelston, near Bath. He built the first documented flushing water closet, which he named Ajax, for Queen Elizabeth I (and one for himself). The term "the John" for a toilet traces back to him!

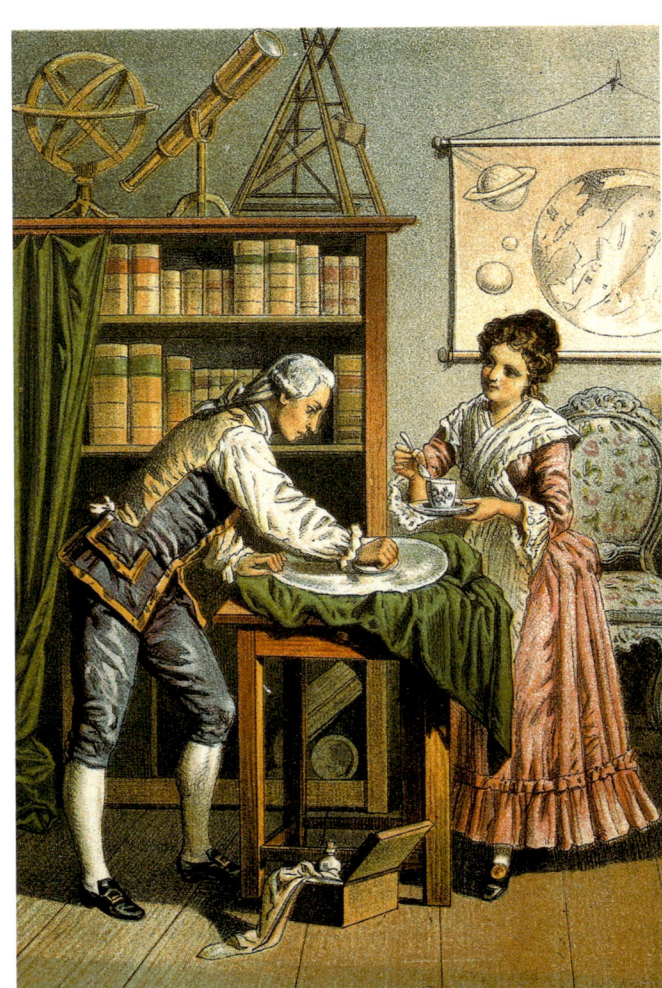

Sir William Herschel, polishing a telescope mirror and Caroline Herschel. Colour lithograph by A. Diethe, ca. 1896.
© Wellcome Library.

LITERATURE & CULTURE
Innovative use of free indirect speech
Jane Austen, who lived in Bath from 1801 to 1806, helped popularise this literary technique that blends a character's thoughts with the narrator's voice.

Sociological Observations in Bath Guide (1766)
Christopher Anstey's satirical poem The New Bath Guide was one of the first pieces of literature to poke fun at social behavior in spa towns – an early example of observational humor.

World's First Postage Stamp – The Penny Black (1840)
Sir Rowland Hill created the Penny Black which was issued in Bath in 1840. In addition, Ralph Allen, Postmaster of Bath (early 1700s), laid crucial groundwork for a national postal system decades earlier.

INNOVATION IN THE ARTS
Introduction of 'modern' stage lighting
The Theatre Royal, Bath, was one of the first to experiment with gas lighting in the early 1800s, preceding its broader adoption.

Plasticine (1897)
William Harbutt, an art teacher in Bathampton, invented Plasticine, a non-drying modeling clay used in art and education. Still used in schools, animation (e.g. Wallace & Gromit), and art therapy today.

ODD INVENTIONS
The "Bath Chair" (early 18th century)
Invented by John Dawson of Bath, this was an early wheelchair used by the frail to move about the city – especially common among spa visitors.

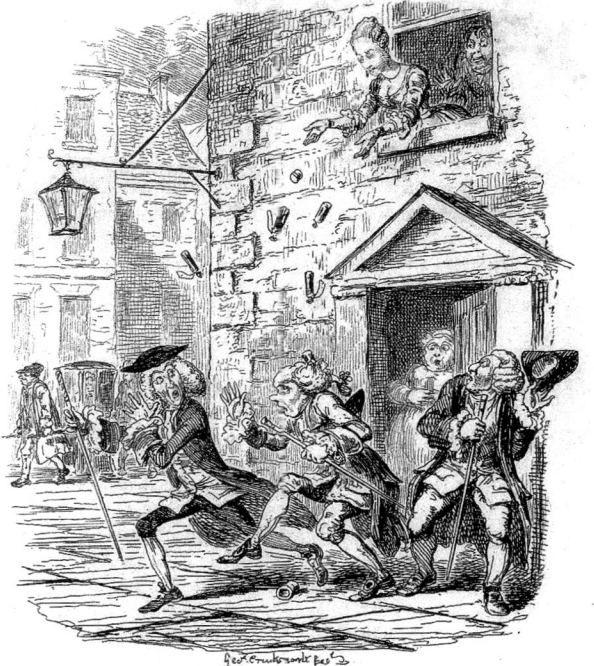

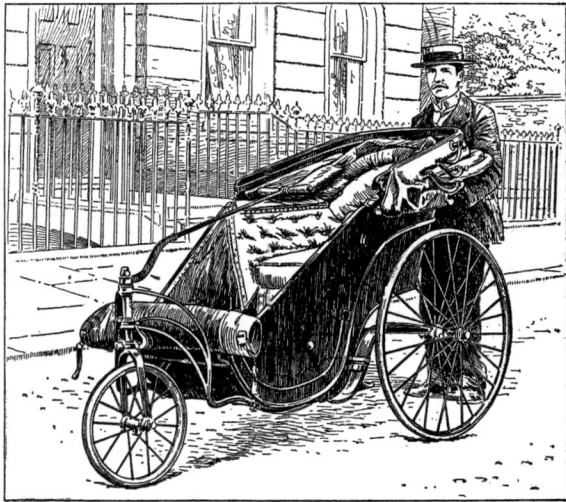

TOP RIGHT: one of George Cruikshank illustrations for Christopher Anstey's satirical poem The New Bath Guide, 1766.
RIGHT: Bath-chair, wheeled vehicle invented by James Heath of Bath.

INVENTIONS AND BATH

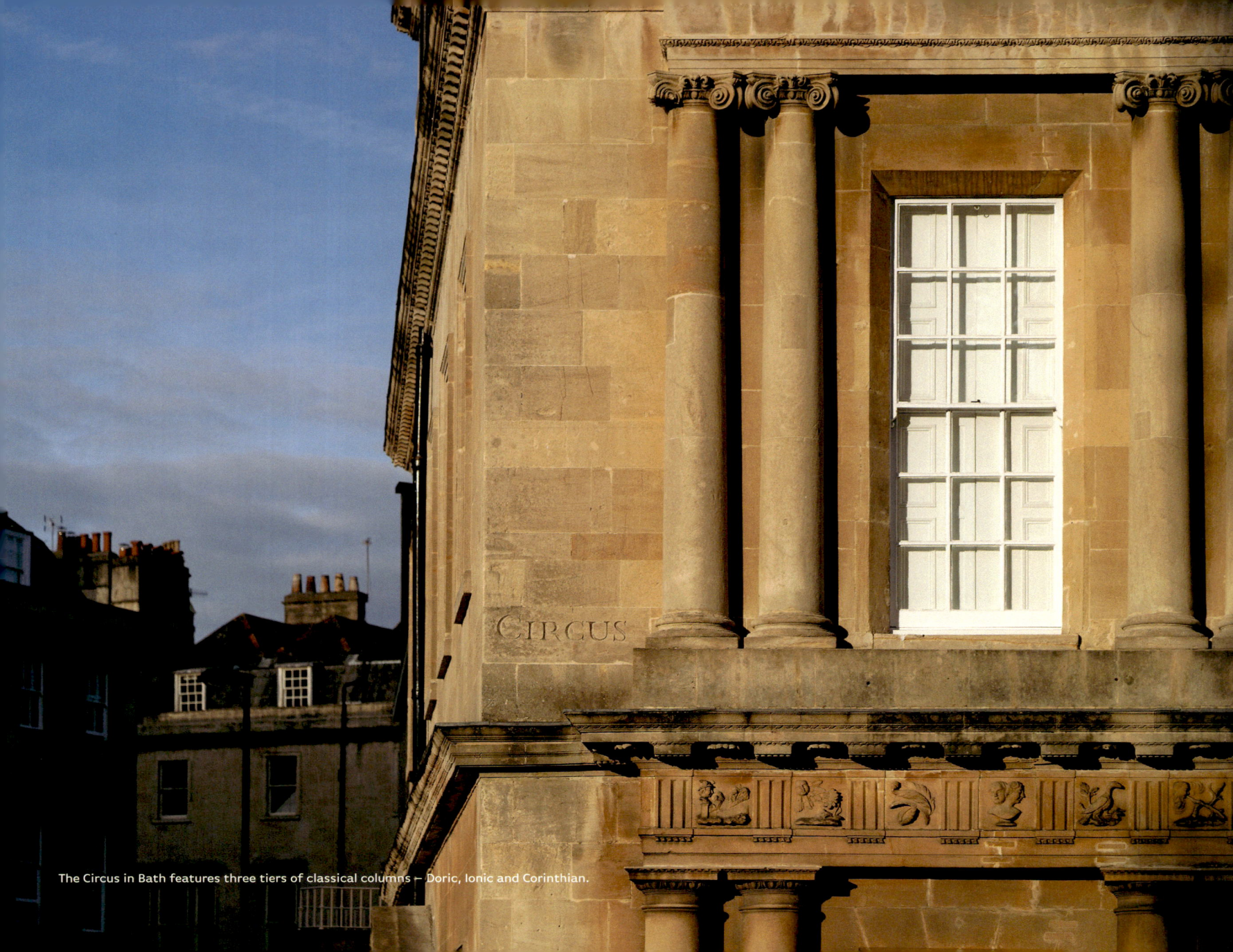
The Circus in Bath features three tiers of classical columns – Doric, Ionic and Corinthian.

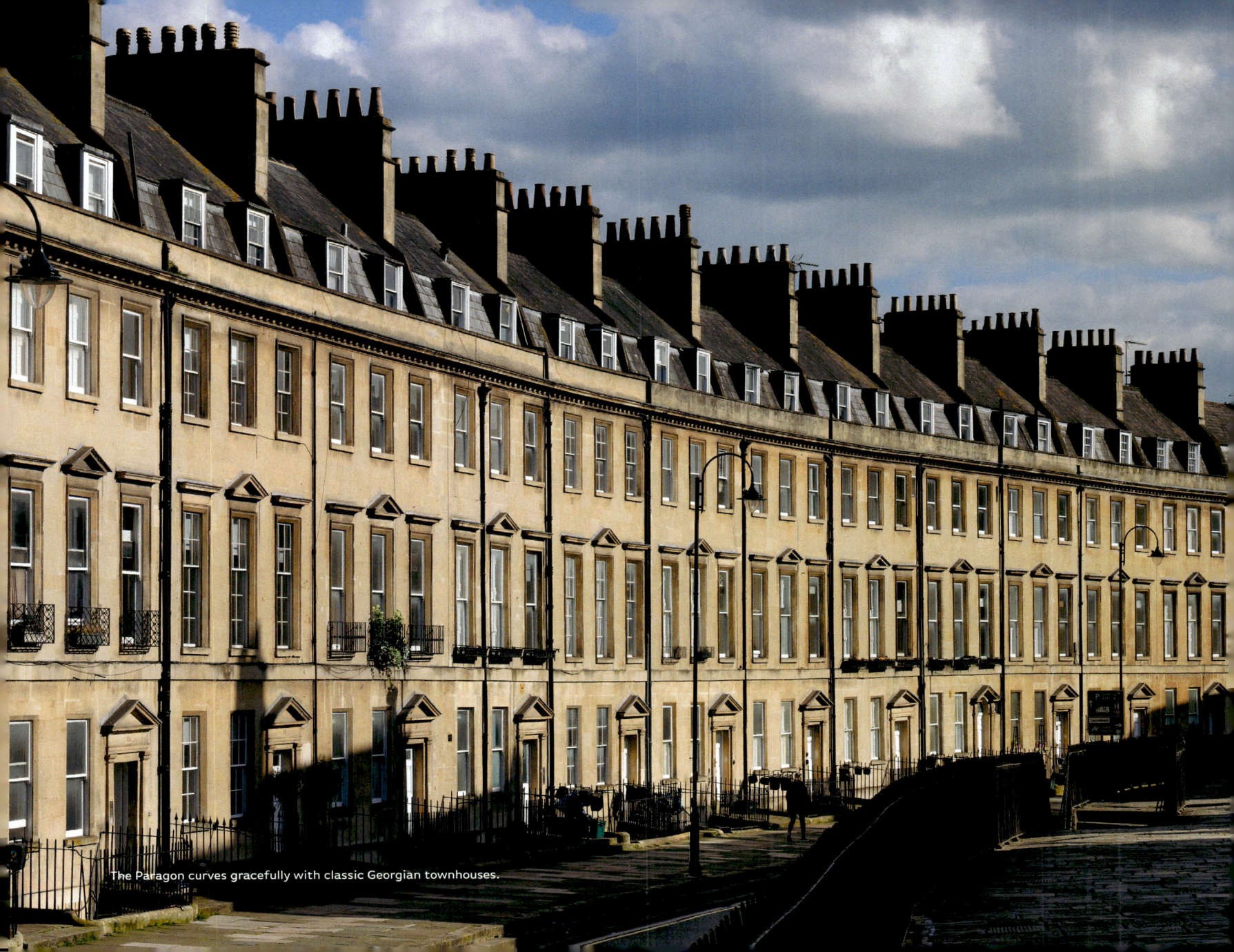
The Paragon curves gracefully with classic Georgian townhouses.

THE ARCHITECTURE OF BATH IN THE GEORGIAN PERIOD

Bath reached the pinnacle of its urban development during the Georgian period (1714–1830). It became a fashionable spa town, attracting aristocrats and gentry who sought both the reputed healing properties of its waters and the refined social scene. As a result, the city underwent significant architectural transformation.

BATH STONE: THE BUILDING MATERIAL OF A CITY

A defining characteristic of Bath's Georgian architecture (and earlier Roman architecture) is the use of Bath stone, a creamy limestone quarried from the surrounding region, particularly from Combe Down and Bathampton Down. This oolitic limestone, formed from sedimentary deposits in the Jurassic period, was prized for its warm hue, ease of carving, and durability. The availability of this high-quality material contributed significantly to the cohesive aesthetic of the city, allowing for uniformity in its grand terraces and civic buildings.

KEY ARCHITECTS AND THEIR CONTRIBUTIONS

Several notable architects played a crucial role in designing Bath's Georgian landscape, each leaving a lasting legacy:

John Wood the Elder (1704–1754)

John Wood the Elder was instrumental in laying the foundations for Bath's neoclassical style. Influenced by Palladian principles, he envisioned Bath as a grand classical city, inspired by ancient Rome. His major works include:

Queen Square (1728–1736): One of the first examples of unified Georgian architecture in Bath, it set the tone for future developments.

The Circus (1754): Inspired by the Colosseum in Rome, this circular arrangement of townhouses remains one of Bath's most iconic architectural achievements.

John Wood the Younger (1728–1782)

Following his father's death, John Wood the Younger continued his vision for Bath, executing some of its most famous developments:

The Royal Crescent (1767–1775): Perhaps the most celebrated architectural ensemble in Bath, this sweeping crescent of 30 terraced houses exemplifies Palladian elegance and symmetry.

Assembly Rooms (1769–1771): A social hub for Bath's elite, these rooms hosted balls and gatherings that defined high society in Georgian England.

Robert Adam (1728–1792)

Although primarily associated with the neoclassical movement in London, Robert Adam contributed to Bath's architectural heritage. He designed **Pulteney Bridge** (1769–1774), a unique structure spanning the River Avon, modeled after the bridges of Florence and Venice.

Thomas Baldwin (c. 1750–1820)

As Bath's official city architect in the late 18th century, Baldwin played a crucial role in expanding the city's urban plan. His notable works include:

The Guildhall (1775–1778): A grand civic building that remains a focal point in the city.

Great Pulteney Street (1789): A broad avenue lined with symmetrical Georgian houses leading to Sydney Gardens.

OPPOSITE BOTTOM RIGHT: The Four Bath Worthies on display at the Building of Bath Collection. Oil on Canvas, Anonymous. c.1735. This portrait features four of the key figures in the story of how Georgian Bath was built. On the right is John Wood the Elder in surveyor's clothes with an architectural drawing tucked under his arm, and next to him sits Robert Gay, one of Bath's major landowners. To the left of Gay, also seated, is Ralph Allen, the owner of the Combe Down stone quarries and Wood's patron-client. Allen was responsible for developing the stone mines in Combe Down and reducing the cost of Bath stone, making a fortune in the process. On the left is Richard Jones, the Clerk of Works who eventually replaced Wood as the builder-surveyor of Allen's mansion house, Prior Park. © Bath Preservation Trust.

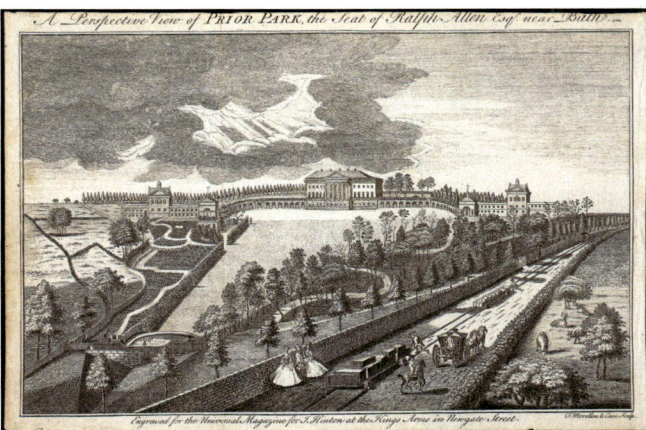

RIGHT: Prior Park, the Seat of Ralph Allen Esqr. near Bath. This celebrated image is believed to be the first depiction of a railway in Great Britain (1750) by Anthony Walker. © Bath & North East Somerset Council. Ralph Allen (1693–1764) was an influential businessman who helped reform the postal service and successfully managed the quarrying and promotion of Bath stone. Allen invested his wealth in Bath stone – the distinctive honey-coloured stone for which Bath is famous. He acquired quarries at Hampton Down and Combe Down and ran a very profitable business, employing many local people and providing the architect, John Wood the Elder, with the building blocks with which to build Georgian Bath.

TOP RIGHT: Robert Adam. Oil on canvas by George Willison. c.1770. Adams was a Scottish neoclassical architect and the designer of Pulteney Bridge. Utilising Palladian style, it is highly unusual in that it has shops built across its full span on both sides. The bridge is named after Frances Pulteney, wife of William Johnstone. Frances was the third daughter of MP and government official Daniel Pulteney (1684–1731) and first cousin once removed of William Pulteney, 1st Earl of Bath. © National Portrait Gallery, London.

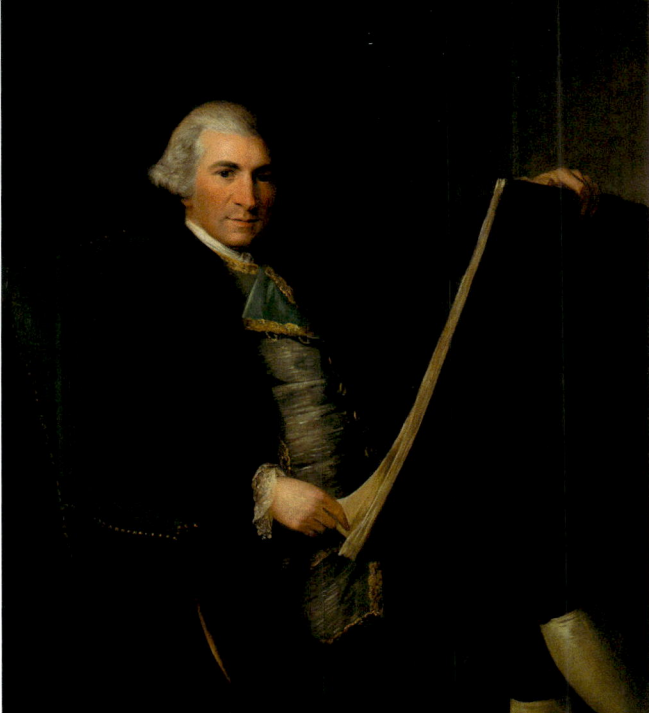

John Palmer (1738–1817)

Palmer succeeded Baldwin as city architect and continued the development of Georgian Bath, completing the **Bath Theatre Royal** (1805) and contributing to the expansion of the city's residential areas.

By the end of the Georgian period, Bath had become a masterpiece of urban planning, with its streets, squares, and crescents forming a remarkably consistent architectural ensemble. The city's reputation as a spa resort, combined with its magnificent buildings, led to its designation as a UNESCO World Heritage Site in 1987. Today, Bath remains one of the finest examples of Georgian architecture in Britain, a testament to the vision of its architects and the enduring beauty of Bath stone.

PALLADIAN PRINCIPLES

Palladian principles are architectural guidelines based on the works of the Italian Renaissance architect Andrea Palladio (1508–1580). His designs emphasised symmetry, proportion, and classical elements inspired by ancient Roman architecture which include the incorporation of columns (Doric, Ionic, Corinthian), an emphasis on geometric proportion, central halls or porticos with columns and pediments, and the use of temples fronts in residential architecture, all seen in Bath.

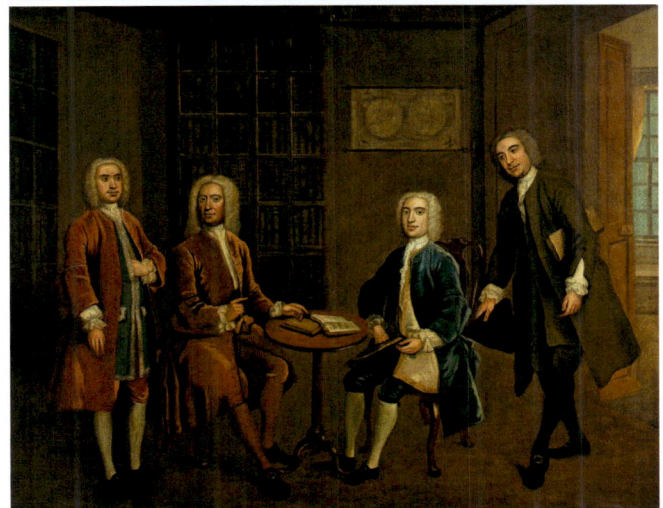

GEORGIAN BALLS AND BEAU NASH

The Georgian balls in Bath were glamorous affairs full of powdered wigs, elegant gowns, classical music, and a bit of social scheming. And right at the heart of it all? Richard "Beau" Nash.

Bath was a major social hub during the 1700s, drawing in aristocrats, wealthy merchants, and hopeful social climbers. The city was famous for its spa waters, but the real draw was the social scene – especially the evening balls held in grand venues like the **Assembly Rooms**.

But it wasn't just about dancing. Balls were a strategic game of matchmaking and status-building. It was where reputations could be made or broken.

RICHARD "BEAU" NASH

Beau Nash (1674–1761) was Bath's legendary **Master of Ceremonies** and the ultimate social influencer of his day. He wasn't born into nobility – he was actually the son of a glassmaker – but his charm, style, and ambition helped him climb the ranks.

Nash laid down the rules of polite society in Bath. He created a code of conduct for the balls, making sure the balls started on time, that dancing rotated fairly among guests, and that gambling didn't overshadow the more "refined" elements of society. Nash was so influential that even dukes and duchesses would defer to him when it came to proper conduct in Bath. He essentially *curated* the social scene and made Bath fashionable.

But … Nash was no stranger to drama, scandal, and a fair bit of hypocrisy. Nash was a notorious gambler, despite trying to keep Bath's vices in check. He started his career as a dandy and a professional gambler in London, and though he preached moderation and elegance in Bath, he was often neck-deep in gaming tables himself. He lost fortunes – both his own and others. Nash never married, but he had his share of complicated romances, and one in particular turned heads: Juliana Popjoy. She was his long-time mistress – about 30 years younger than him – and completely devoted, but he refused to marry her.

Beau Nash styled himself as a moral guardian of society – he banned swords at events and discouraged duels. But he was a womaniser, a bit of a party animal and a gambler. When Nash died in 1761, he was broke, despite having presided over one of the wealthiest, most fashionable cities in England for decades. He had no real fortune, no children, and very few remaining allies. He was given a lavish funeral at Bath Abbey, complete with a public procession, paid for by the city.

There's even a statue of him in the Pump Room today. So, the man who lived for public drama got one last moment in the spotlight.

OPPOSITE RIGHT: an 1823 engraving of a Regency ball dress, with a diaphanous overskirt that can be lifted for certain dance moves, such as the pas d'été'. **FAR RIGHT:** portrait of Richard ('Beau') Nash (1674–1762) by William Hoare © National Portrait Gallery.

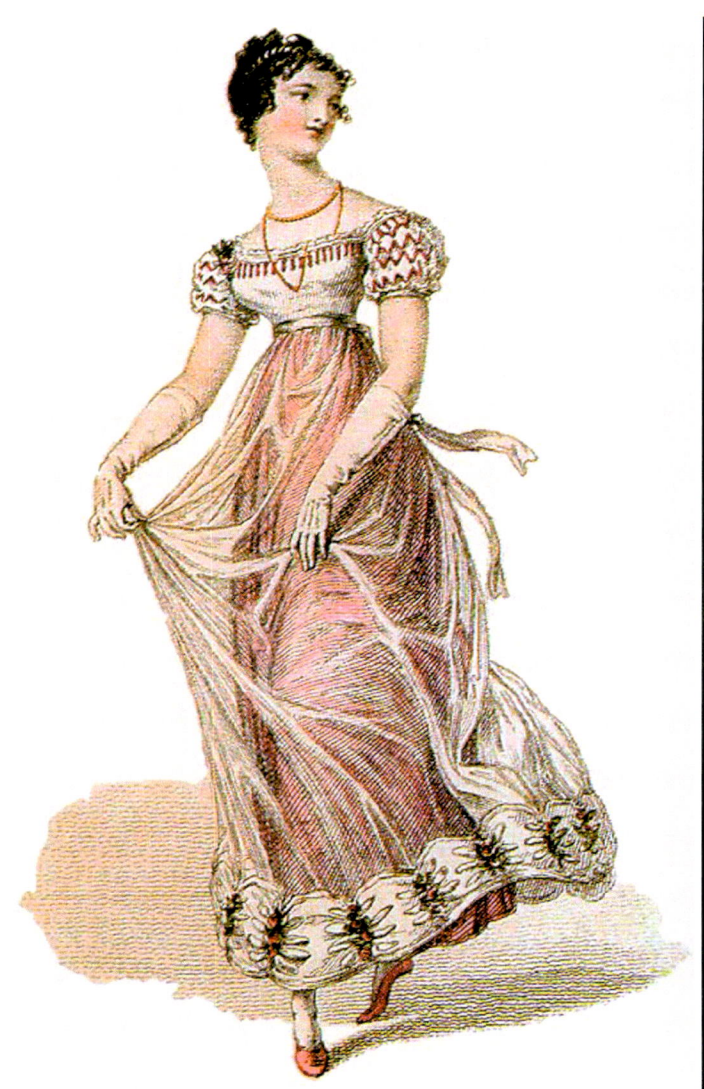

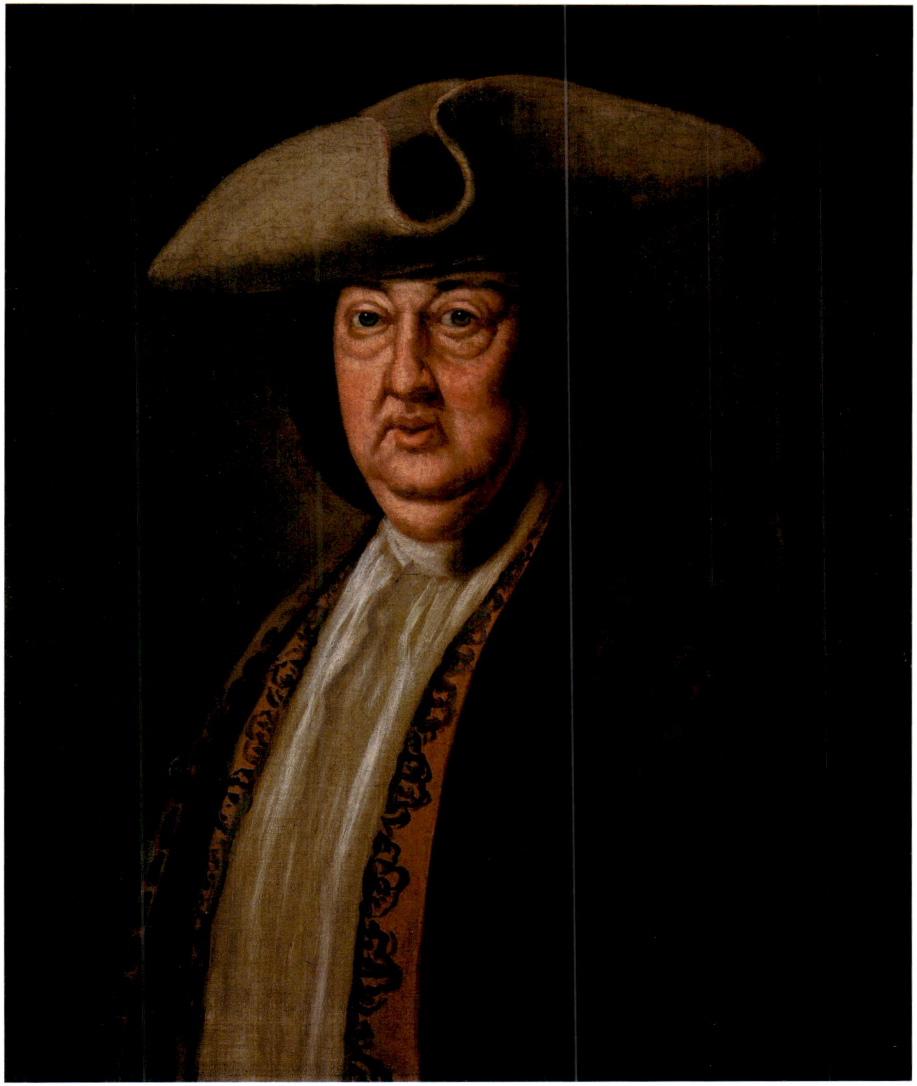

JANE AUSTEN AND BATH

Parents: George Austen (1731–1805), Cassandra Leigh, (1739–1827)
Born: 6 December 1775 Steventon, Hampshire
Died: 18 July 1817 (aged 41) Winchester, Hampshire
Resting place: Winchester Cathedral, Hampshire

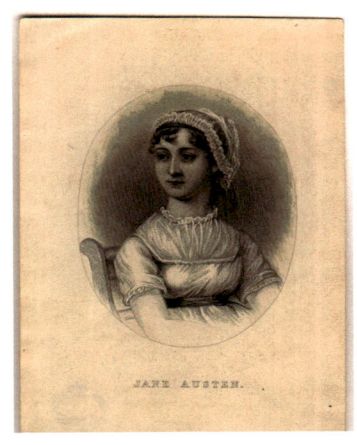

Jane Austen and Bath are intricately connected, though her relationship with the city was complex and, at times, ambivalent. Bath played a significant role in her personal life, family history, and literary works, offering both inspiration and disillusionment. While Austen's novels present contrasting portrayals of Bath, her personal letters reveal a more critical stance towards the city.

JANE AUSTEN'S FAMILY AND BATH

Jane Austen's association with Bath began through her family's connections. Her father, the Reverend George Austen, served as a rector in Steventon, Hampshire, where Jane was born in 1775. However, Bath became an integral part of her life in 1801 when her father retired and decided to move the family there, although the Austens had connections to Bath before the move including the marriage of her parents at St Swithin's church in 1764. Jane also visited and stayed in Bath before the family moved there, which provided early inspiration for her novels.

The Austens resided at various addresses in Bath, including Sydney Place, a fashionable part of the city. However, after her father's death in 1805, the family faced financial strain, forcing them to move to more modest accommodations. This decline in fortunes may have contributed to Jane's mixed feelings about Bath, as it symbolised both genteel society and economic vulnerability.

BATH IN AUSTEN'S NOVELS

Bath serves as a prominent setting in two of Austen's novels: *Northanger Abbey* and *Persuasion*, although all her six books mention Bath. These novels present distinct perspectives on the city, reflecting Austen's dual feelings about Bath.

In *Northanger Abbey*, Bath is portrayed with humour and irony. The novel's heroine, Catherine Morland, arrives in Bath wide-eyed and eager for adventure. The city is depicted as a place of social ambition, where young women seek advantageous marriages, and superficiality abounds. Through Catherine's experiences, Austen satirises the social conventions of Bath's society, portraying it as a realm of gossip, vanity, and fleeting pleasures.

Conversely, *Persuasion* offers a more melancholic view of Bath. The novel's protagonist, Anne Elliot, finds herself in Bath due to her family's financial troubles. Rather than revelling in the city's charms, Anne endures the shallowness of Bath's social scene while longing for deeper, more meaningful connections. This portrayal likely reflects Austen's own disenchantment with Bath, as it represents a place where personal hardship and social pretensions collide.

TOP LEFT: Jane Austen portrait. This engraving is the basis for a late nineteenth-century engraving, commissioned by Austen's nephew, which features on the ten pound bank note. The original was by her sister and closest confidante Cassandra Austen, pencil and watercolour, circa 1810 and is the only reasonably certain portrait from life to show Austen's face. © National Portrait Gallery.

JANE AUSTEN'S HOMES IN BATH

13 Queen Square: Lodged with her mother and sister-in-law here in 1799 while her brother took the waters for his health.

4 Sydney Place: The Austen family lived here for three years, from 1801 to 1804. It is now a guesthouse.

Green Park Buildings: The family moved to lodgings in Green Park Buildings after their lease on 4 Sydney Place expired, in 1804. It was here that her father died in 1805.

25 Gay Street: After her father's death, Jane, her mother, and her sister moved to the first floor of 25 Gay Street with a lodger.

7 Trim Street: Austen's final stay in Bath, from January to July 1806.

PLACES IN BATH JANE AUSTEN KNEW WELL

Sydney Gardens
Holburne Museum
The Pump Room
Sally Lunn's
The Assembly Rooms
Alexandra Park
St Swithin's Church George Austen is buried here

Download an audio tour and a map of Jane Austen locations at *visitbath.co.uk*

Find out more about Jane Austen's House in Chawton, Hampshire, here final home. *janeaustens.house*

See the maps on pages **7** and **89** for the houses that Jane Austen lived in.

RIGHT: scenes from the Jane Austen Festival held each year in September.

JANE AUSTEN'S PERSONAL VIEWS ON BATH

Austen's letters provide further insight into her feelings about Bath. She often expressed dissatisfaction with the city, lamenting its crowded nature and lack of the rural tranquility she cherished. In a letter to her sister Cassandra, she wrote, "It will be two years tomorrow since we left Bath, with what happy feelings of escape." This sentiment suggests that Bath, rather than being a cherished home, felt more like a constraint.

Her dislike may have stemmed from multiple factors. First, the move to Bath signalled an abrupt change from her familiar life in the countryside, which she dearly loved. Second, the city's social expectations and emphasis on wealth and status likely felt stifling to her independent spirit. Lastly, her father's death in Bath and the resulting financial difficulties cast a shadow over her time there.

BATH'S INFLUENCE ON AUSTEN'S LEGACY

Despite her mixed feelings, Bath remains an important part of Austen's literary and historical legacy. Today, the city celebrates its connection to her with institutions like the Jane Austen Centre, which offers insights into her life and works. The annual Jane Austen Festival attracts fans from around the world, demonstrating how Bath, despite Austen's reservations, remains central to her enduring appeal.

MORE INFORMATION

Jane Austen Centre *janeausten.co.uk*. The Jane Austen Centre at 40 Gay Street is a permanent exhibition which tells the story of Jane Austen's Bath experience, and the effect that visiting and living in the city had on her and her writing. Since 2001 it has hosted the annual Jane Austen Festival. **The Jane Austen Festival** is an annual event of tours, lectures, talks, book groups, workshops, a Regency costumed ball and parade, held at various venues around Bath usually in September.

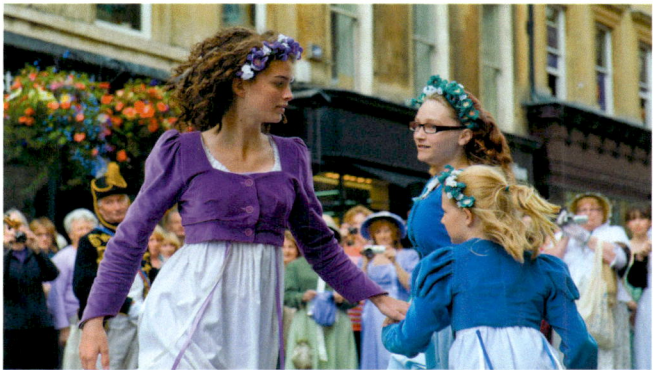
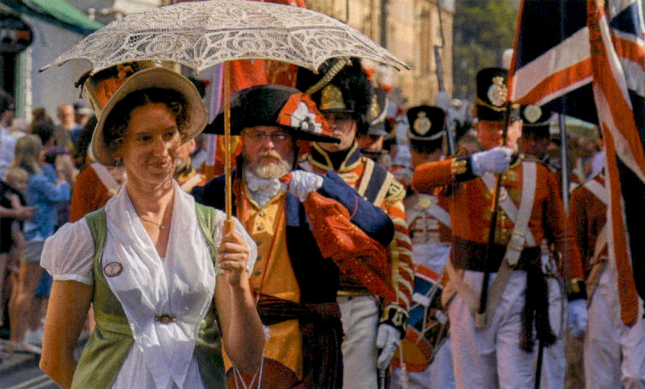
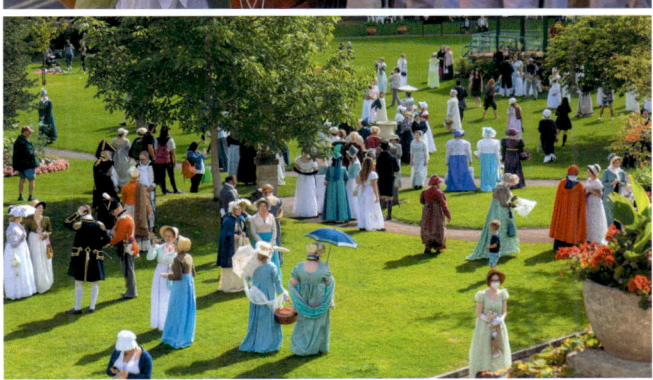

MARY SHELLEY, FRANKENSTEIN AND BATH

Parents: William Godwin (1731–1805), Mary Wollstonecraft (1739–1827)
Born: 30 August 1797, London
Died: 1 February 1851 (aged 53), London
Resting place: St Peter's Church, Bournemouth

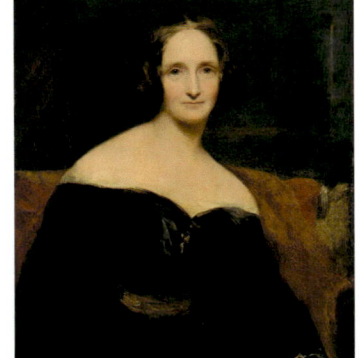

Mary Shelley's connection to the city of Bath is an important yet often overlooked aspect of her life and literary career. Best known for her groundbreaking novel *Frankenstein*, Shelley spent time in Bath during a pivotal moment in her personal life, and the city likely played a role in shaping her creative process.

MARY SHELLEY'S TIME IN BATH

Mary Wollstonecraft Shelley (née Godwin) arrived in Bath, aged 19, in September 1816, seeking refuge from the turbulence of her personal life. She took lodgings at 5 Abbey Church Yard, which was demolished to make way for the Pump Room extension in the 1890s.

At the time, she was deeply involved with the poet Percy Bysshe Shelley, though they were not yet married. Their relationship was marked by scandal, as Percy was still legally married to his first wife, Harriet. Mary and Percy had eloped in 1814, traveling across Europe in a whirlwind romance, and by the time Mary came to Bath, she was pregnant with their second child.

Bath served as a place of retreat for Mary and allowed her a degree of anonymity as she awaited news from Percy, who was frequently in London handling legal and financial matters.

However, her time in Bath was also marked by personal tragedy. In December 1816, she learned that Harriet Shelley had died by suicide. Shortly afterward, Mary and Percy married, legitimising their relationship in the eyes of society. When she left Bath early in 1817 much of the novel had been written

BATH'S INFLUENCE ON FRANKENSTEIN

Frankenstein is associated with the famous 'ghost story contest' that took place at Lord Byron's villa in Geneva during the summer of 1816. 'We will each write a ghost story,' Lord Byron said. 'There were four of us,' Mary Shelley recalled fifteen years later. Herself, the two illustrious poets – Byron and her husband Percy Shelley, and Byron's personal physician, John Polidori. There was a fifth person there, her stepsister, and Byron's lover, Claire Clairmont, but her presence was not mentioned to prevent scandal. Out of this 'competition' not one but two modern horror legends were born, Mary Shelley's *Frankenstein*, and John Polidori's *The Vampyre*, a forerunner of Dracula.

Whilst Mary had begun developing her ideas in Switzerland, it was during her stay in Bath that she continued drafting and refining the manuscript. She attended scientific lectures by Dr Wilkinson in the Kingston Lecture Room where he suggested that one day electricity might be used to bring inanimate matter to life. This idea resonated with Mary, who had recently experienced thunderstorms in nightmares and inspired her to write *Frankenstein*.

MARY SHELLEY PLAQUE

The Mary Shelley plaque is situated outside the Pump Room and Roman baths where Mary lodged above a print shop situated at 5 Abbey Church Yard. Mary lodged in rented rooms upstairs. The building was demolished in the 19th century to make way for a Pump Room extension.

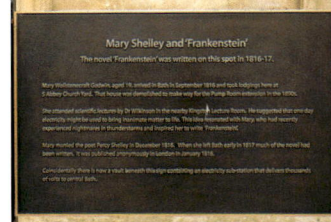

TOP LEFT: Mary Shelley, aged about 40 by Richard Rothwell. circa 1831-1840. © National Portrait Gallery.

Bath, with its elegant Georgian architecture and fashionable society, might seem an unlikely setting for the development of one of the most famous gothic novels of all time.

However, the contrast between Bath's refined surface and the darker realities of Mary's personal experiences – grief, societal pressure, and intellectual ambition – likely fuelled her imagination. The themes of isolation, scientific ambition, and the consequences of unchecked progress in *Frankenstein* may have been shaped, at least in part, by Mary's time in the city.

The novel's protagonist, Victor Frankenstein, embodies the dangers of obsessive intellectual pursuit, something Mary may have contemplated while surrounded by the scientific and philosophical discussions that were common in Bath's social circles. Furthermore, her own experiences of loss and alienation – having lost her first child and suffering societal ostracism – are reflected in the novel's themes of abandonment and suffering.

Frankenstein's first edition of 500 copies was published anonymously in January 1818, soon followed by much longer print runs.

BATH'S ROLE IN MARY SHELLEY'S LEGACY

Bath acknowledges its connection to Mary Shelley through various exhibitions and literary events. The city, often celebrated for its association with Jane Austen, also played a crucial role in the development of *Frankenstein*, a novel that has had a profound impact on literature, science fiction, and gothic storytelling. Though Bath was not where *Frankenstein* was conceived, it was where Mary Shelley brought it to life, making it an essential location in the history of one of literature's most enduring and influential works.

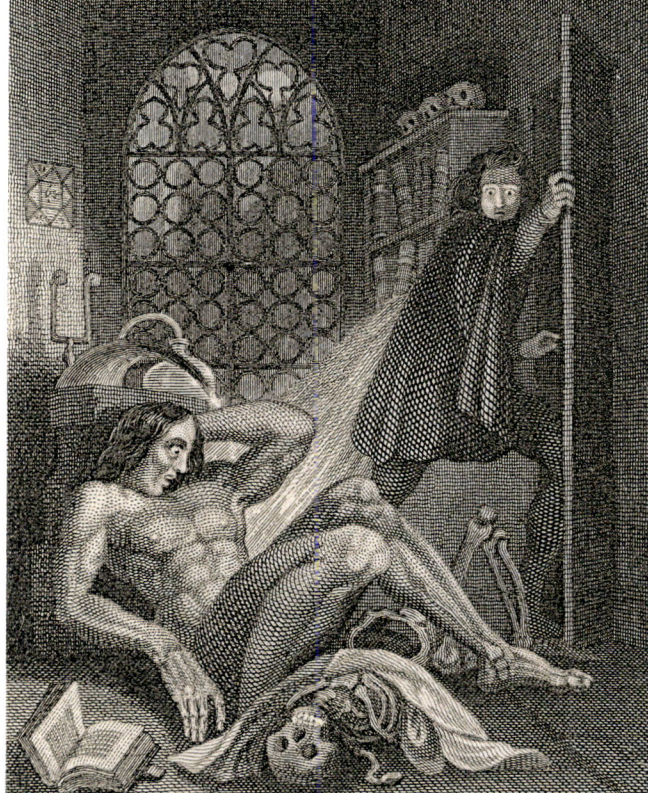

RIGHT: Victor Frankenstein becoming disgusted at his creation. Illustration from the frontispiece of the 1831 edition. Steel engraving for the revised edition of *Frankenstein* by Mary Shelley, published by Colburn and Bentley, London 1831. The novel was first published in 1818.

MORE INFORMATION

Mary Shelley's House of Frankenstein houseoffrankenstein.com
Mary Shelley's House of Frankenstein is an award-winning, multi-sensory, and immersive visitor attraction exploring the life of acclaimed author, Mary Shelley, and her most famous creation, *Frankenstein*.

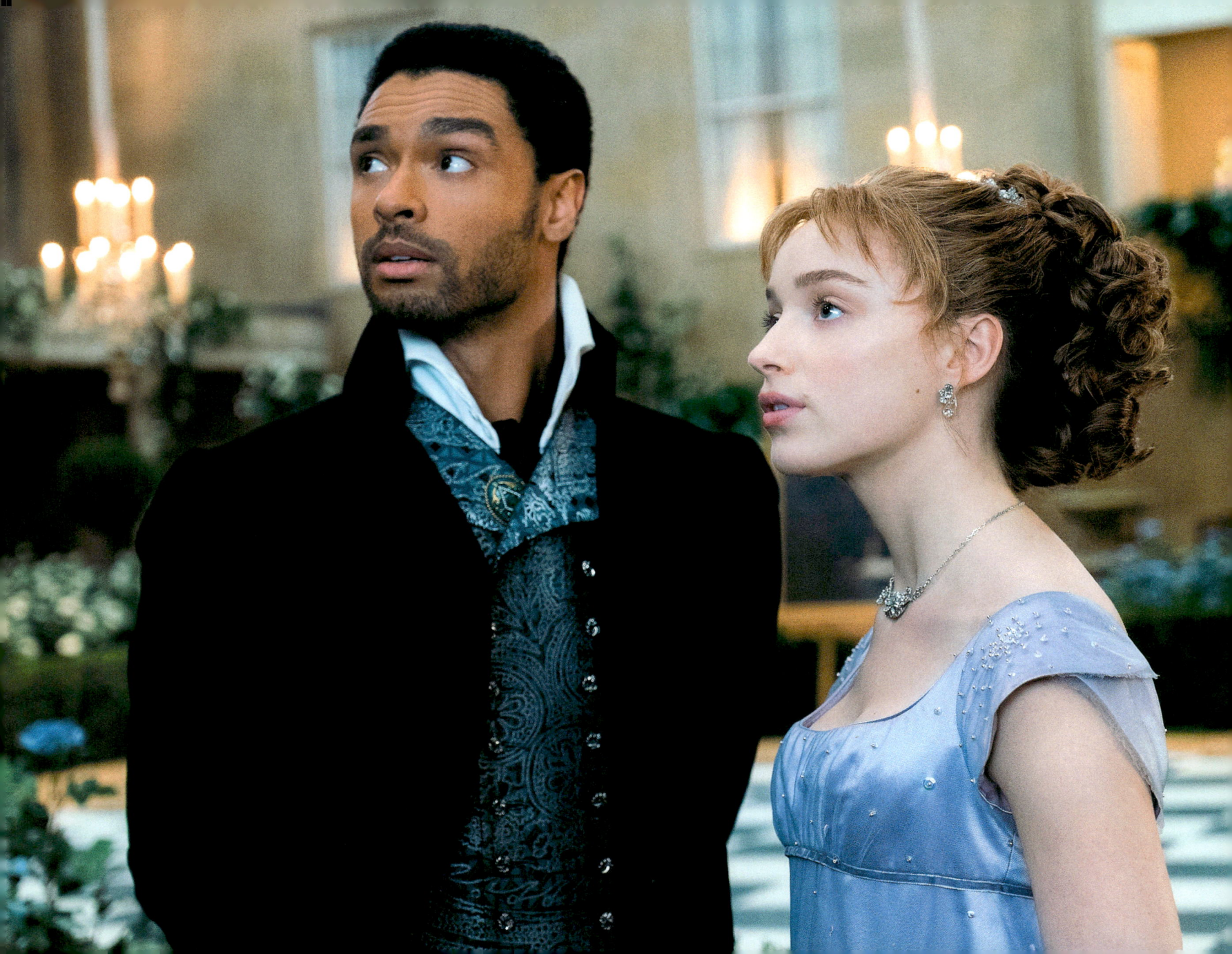

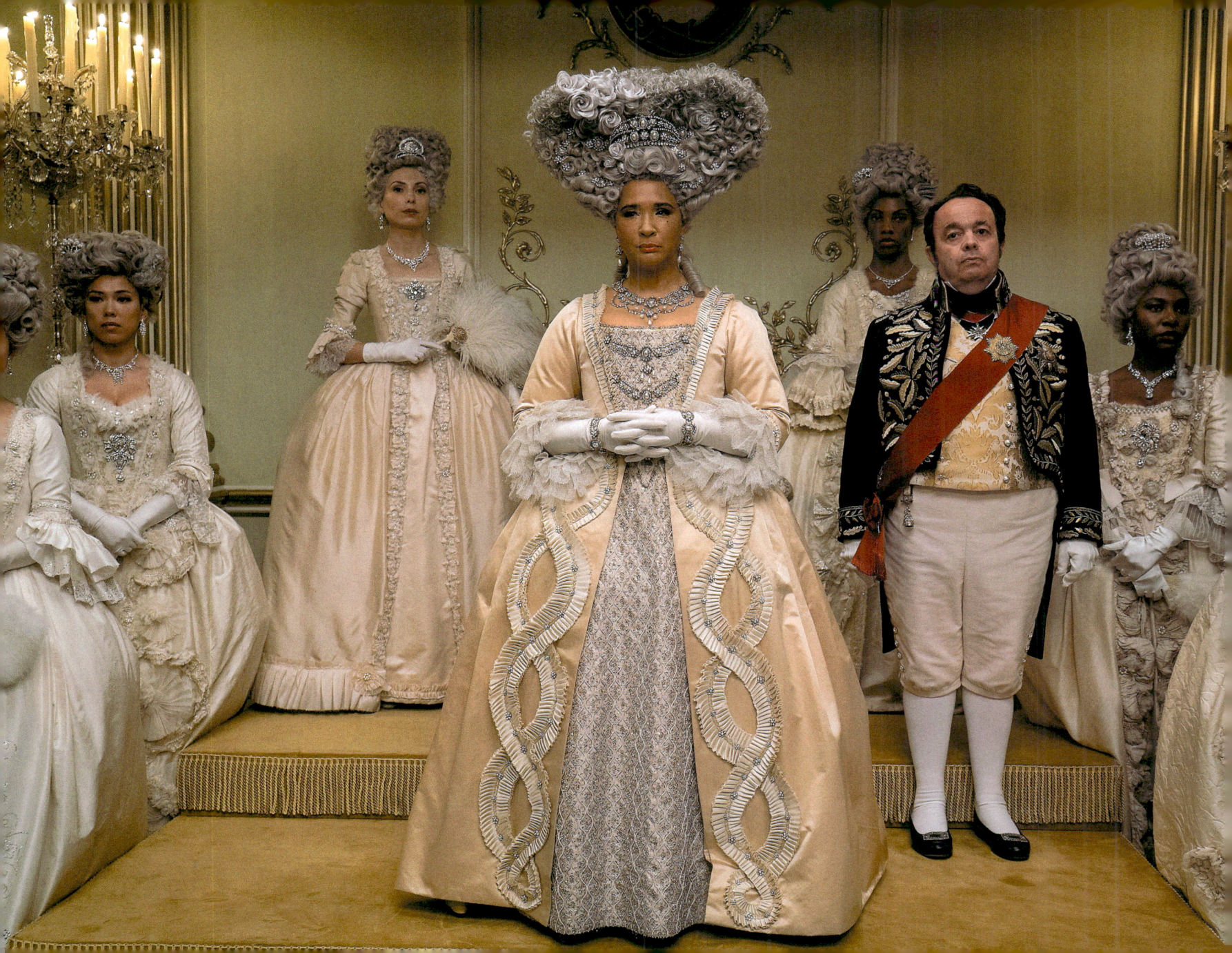

THE USE OF BATH FOR TV AND FILMS – BRIDGERTON

Bath has long been a favoured location for TV and film productions. Its well-preserved Georgian architecture, cobbled streets, and Roman heritage make it a visually stunning backdrop, ideal for period dramas and historical adaptations, especially as it offers a near-perfect representation of Regency-era Britain.

NOTABLE PRODUCTIONS FILMED IN BATH

One of the most famous examples is *Bridgerton*, the hit Netflix series based on Julia Quinn's novels. The series, set in Regency-era London, extensively uses Bath's streets and squares to depict high society. The Royal Crescent, Beauford Square, and the Holburne Museum stand in for grand homes and elegant promenades, bringing the world of *Bridgerton* to life.

Another notable adaptation filmed in Bath is *Persuasion* (1995, 2007, and 2022), based on Jane Austen's novel. Bath held a special place in Austen's life and works, making it a fitting location for her stories. The Pump Room and the Assembly Rooms, both key social hubs in Austen's time, have been used to depict scenes of Regency high society in multiple adaptations of her novels.

Additionally, *Les Misérables* (2018 BBC adaptation) used Bath's streets and landmarks to recreate early 19th-century France. The production utilised locations such as the Guildhall and the Parade Gardens to depict grand European settings, showcasing Bath's versatility as a historical filming site.

For a fuller listing of film and TV locations, including maps visit *visitbath.co.uk*, *bathfilmoffice.co.uk* and *fashionmuseum.cn*

THE LOCATIONS IN BATH USED IN THE NETFLIX SERIES BRIDGERTON

The Netflix series *Bridgerton* whilst set in Regency-era London, much of its filming took place in the city of Bath. Here are some of the locations that you can visit.

The Royal Crescent (p.43)
One of the most recognisable filming locations in *Bridgerton* is the Royal Crescent. The exterior of No.1 Royal Crescent is used as the home of the Featherington family. The Crescent's elegant stone facade and vast lawns make it an ideal representation of the aristocratic lifestyle depicted in the series. Fans of the show will recognise it from numerous scenes featuring high society gatherings and carriage arrivals.

The Holburne Museum (p.121)
The Holburne Museum plays a significant role in *Bridgerton* as the exterior of Lady Danbury's residence. The museum's grand Palladian-style architecture, with its ornate facade and columned entrance, makes for a fitting home for one of the show's most influential characters.

The Assembly Rooms (p.79)
Bath's Assembly Rooms, feature prominently in *Bridgerton* as the setting for several grand ballroom scenes. The elegant interiors, including the magnificent chandeliers and high ceilings, provide a perfect venue for the lavish balls where debutantes and suitors mingle. These spaces capture the essence of Regency high society, reflecting the excitement and tension of the marriage market central to the show's plot.

BRIDGERTON
PREVIOUS SPREAD LEFT: Regé-Jean Page as Simon Basset and Phoebe Dynevor as Daphne Bridgerton.
RIGHT: Golda Rosheuvel as Queen Charlotte and Hugh Sachs as Brimsley.
© Shondaland/Netflix.

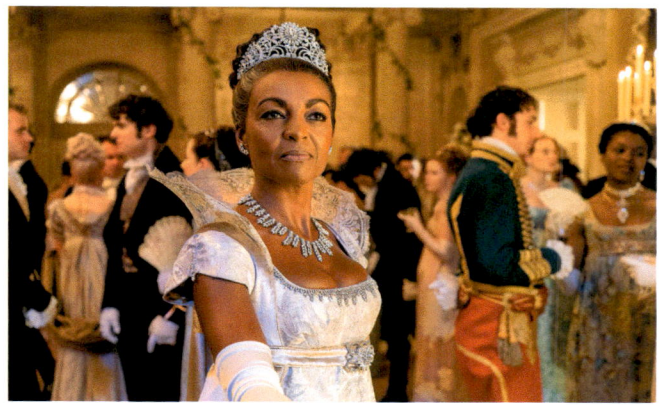
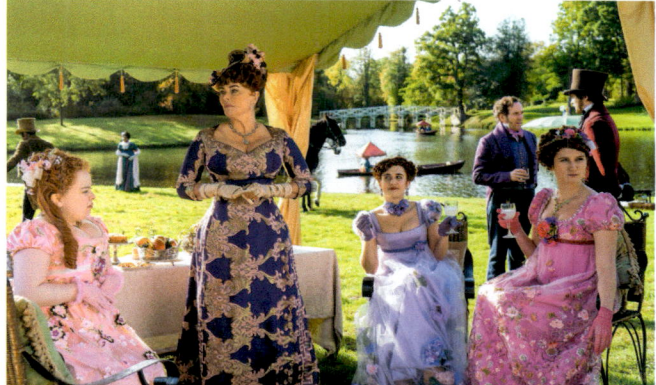
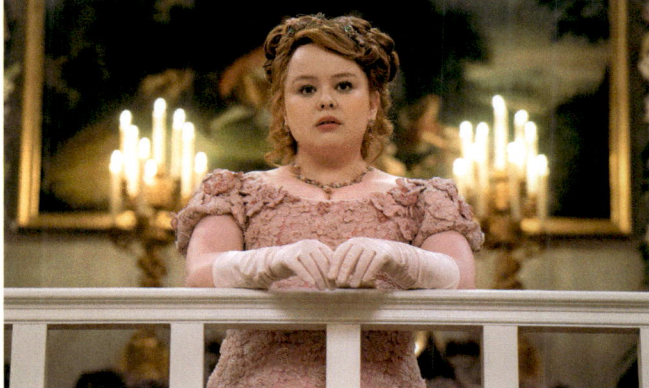

The Guildhall (see map on page 7)
Another significant filming location is Bath's Guildhall, an imposing building that serves as a backdrop for various indoor and outdoor scenes in the series. The building's grand Georgian interiors, including its stunning Banqueting Room adorned with crystal chandeliers and intricate plasterwork, add an air of authenticity to *Bridgerton's* elaborate gatherings and social events.

Bath Street (p.189)
Bath Street, with its striking colonnades and historic charm, was also used for several exterior shots in the series. This picturesque thoroughfare, lined with Georgian buildings, helps create the illusion of Regency London's bustling streets. The symmetry and architectural elegance of Bath Street contribute to the show's immersive historical atmosphere.

Beauford Square and Trim Street (p.196)
Beauford Square and Trim Street, both featuring well-preserved period buildings, also appear in *Bridgerton*. These locations help depict the city streets and marketplaces of London, giving depth to the show's setting with their authentic period features.

Abbey Green (p.165)
Nestled just behind the Roman Baths lies Abbey Green. This picturesque spot is home to The Abbey Deli, which doubled as the Modiste dress shop in the first two seasons of the show. Filming took place both inside and outside the Grade II listed building, known for its classic double-fronted bay windows. Today, visitors can enjoy a delightful afternoon tea at the Deli and explore an array of Modiste-themed merchandise.

Sydney Gardens (p.126)
Sydney Gardens, one of the few remaining Georgian pleasure gardens in the UK, serves as a backdrop for some of the outdoor scenes in *Bridgerton*. These gardens, which were once frequented by Jane Austen, add a touch of historical realism to the series, providing a picturesque setting for promenades and romantic encounters.

BRIDGERTON
TOP: Adjoa Andoh as Lady Agatha Danbury. **TOP RIGHT**: Nicola Coughlan as Penelope Featherington, Polly Walker as Lady Portia Featherington, Harriet Cains as Philipa Featherington, Ben Miller as Lord Archibald Featherington and Bessie Carter as Prudence Featherington. **RIGHT**: Nicola Coughlan as Penelope Featherington.
© Shondaland/Netflix.

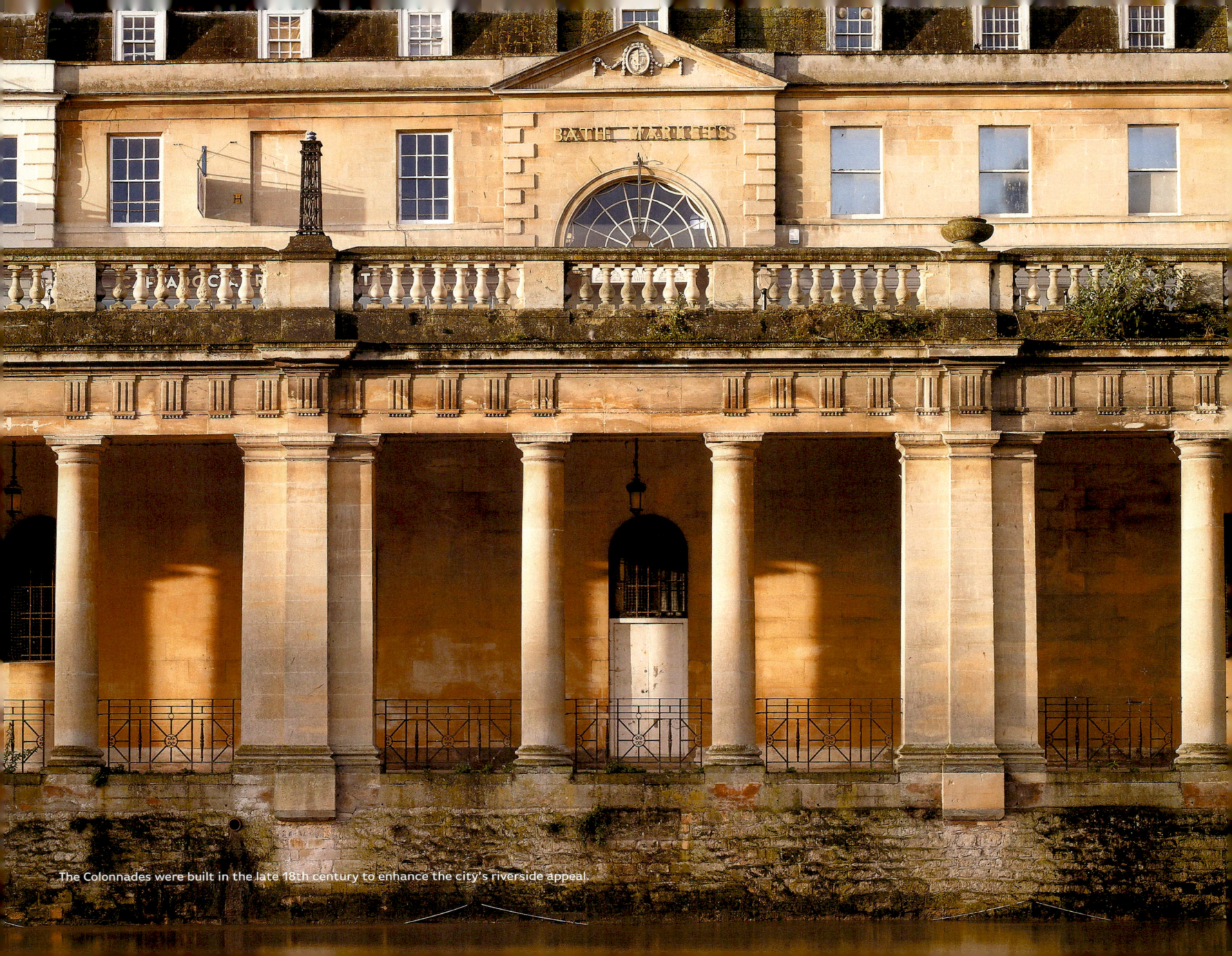
The Colonnades were built in the late 18th century to enhance the city's riverside appeal.

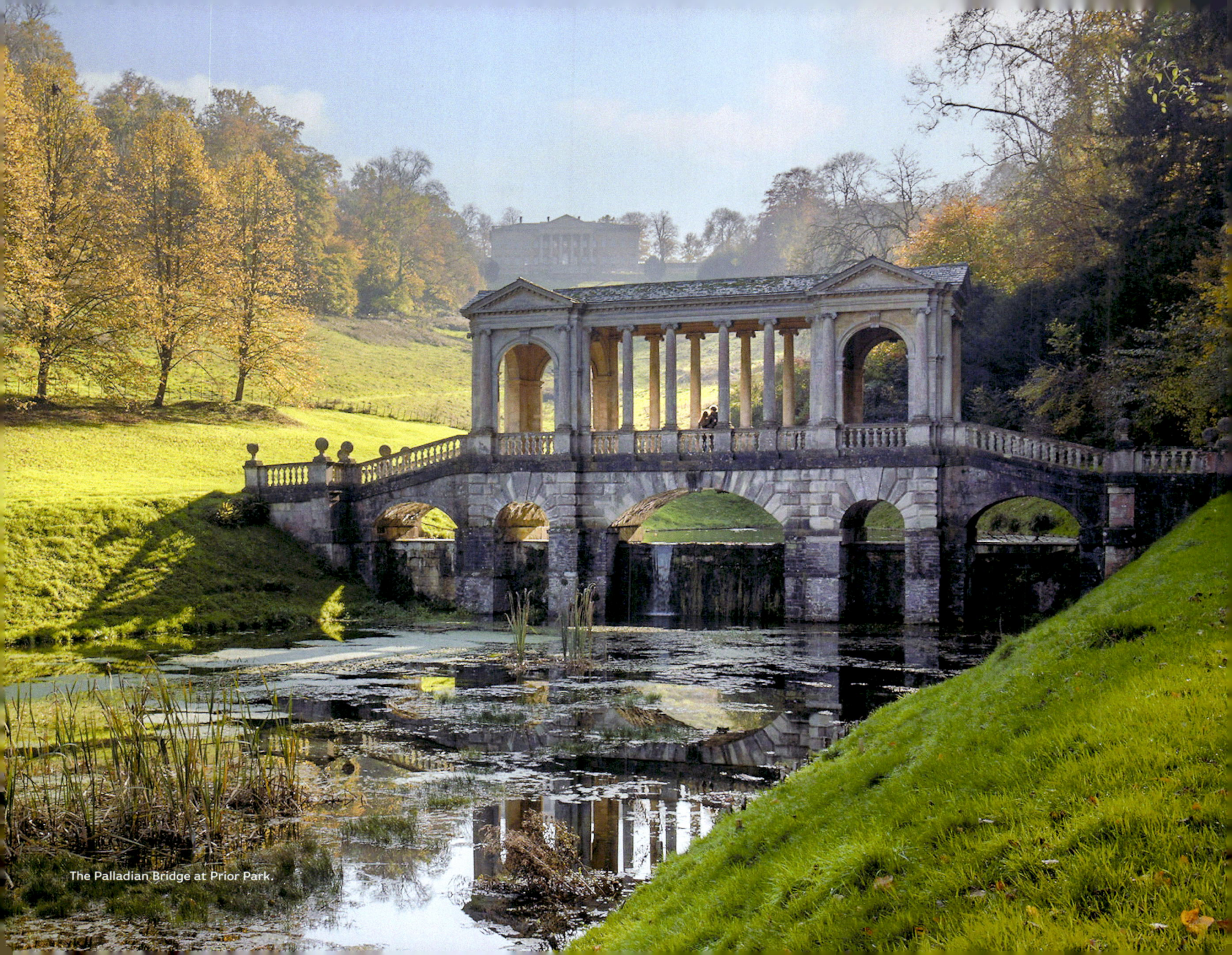
The Palladian Bridge at Prior Park.

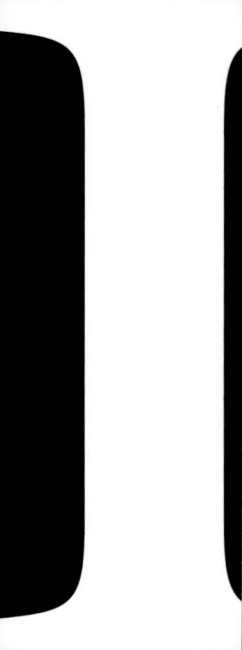

1 THE ROYAL CRESCENT

"The Royal Crescent was designed to display the nobility of architecture, and to offer a view of the open countryside while preserving the elegance of the city."
– Attributed to John Wood the Younger (circa 1770s)

"The Royal Crescent in Bath is one of the great set-pieces of European architecture, and its curve is a gesture of supreme confidence."
– Sir John Betjeman Poet Laureate and Architectural Commentator

The Royal Crescent is arguably the grandest of Baths' famous set pieces. It is an immense building, one continuous terrace of 30 houses formed into an elegant curve that enhances the architectural beauty of the wonderful Palladian style exterior. Built of Bath stone with slate roofs there are 114 Ionic columns along the terraces's 500ft/150m length.

The Crescent sweeps gracefully aloft a natural rise in the landscape, with wonderful views over Bath, and is enhanced further by a bank and ditch 'ha ha' feature, placing the building bold and centred within an open parkland setting.

Built between 1767 to 1775, the Crescent was designed by John Wood the Younger (son of John Wood the Elder, the architect responsible for transforming Georgian Bath). It is one of the finest Georgian buildings in the UK and worthy of its Grade I listed status.

On the eastern approach is Number 1 Royal Crescent, a fabulous museum which perfectly transports visitors back to Georgian times within its immaculately curated rooms. Centrally located in the half moon curve of the building is The Royal Crescent Hotel, a grand opulent place to stay that takes full advantage of a double set of Ionic stone pillars either side of the main entrance. The terrace was home to many notable artists, politicians, musicians and retired army officers in the 18th and 19th centuries, today it is a mix of private residences and flats.

Close by are the Marlborough buildings, the Royal Victoria Park, the Botanic gardens and St James's Square. It is well worth the twenty minute walk from the city centre.

THE ROYAL CRESCENT

Postcode: BA1 2LS
what3words: count.trade.slate

NO.1 ROYAL CRESCENT

Postcode: BA1 2LS
what3words: void.entry.sands

MARLBOROUGH BUILDINGS

Postcode: BA1 2LU
what3words: cattle.effort.serves

ROYAL VICTORIA PARK

Postcode: BA1 3BA
what3words: fear.with.home

THE BOTANIC GARDENS

Postcode: BA1 3BA
what3words: admit.kinks.years

ST JAMES'S SQUARE

Postcode: BA1 2TS
what3words: pounds.moon.claims

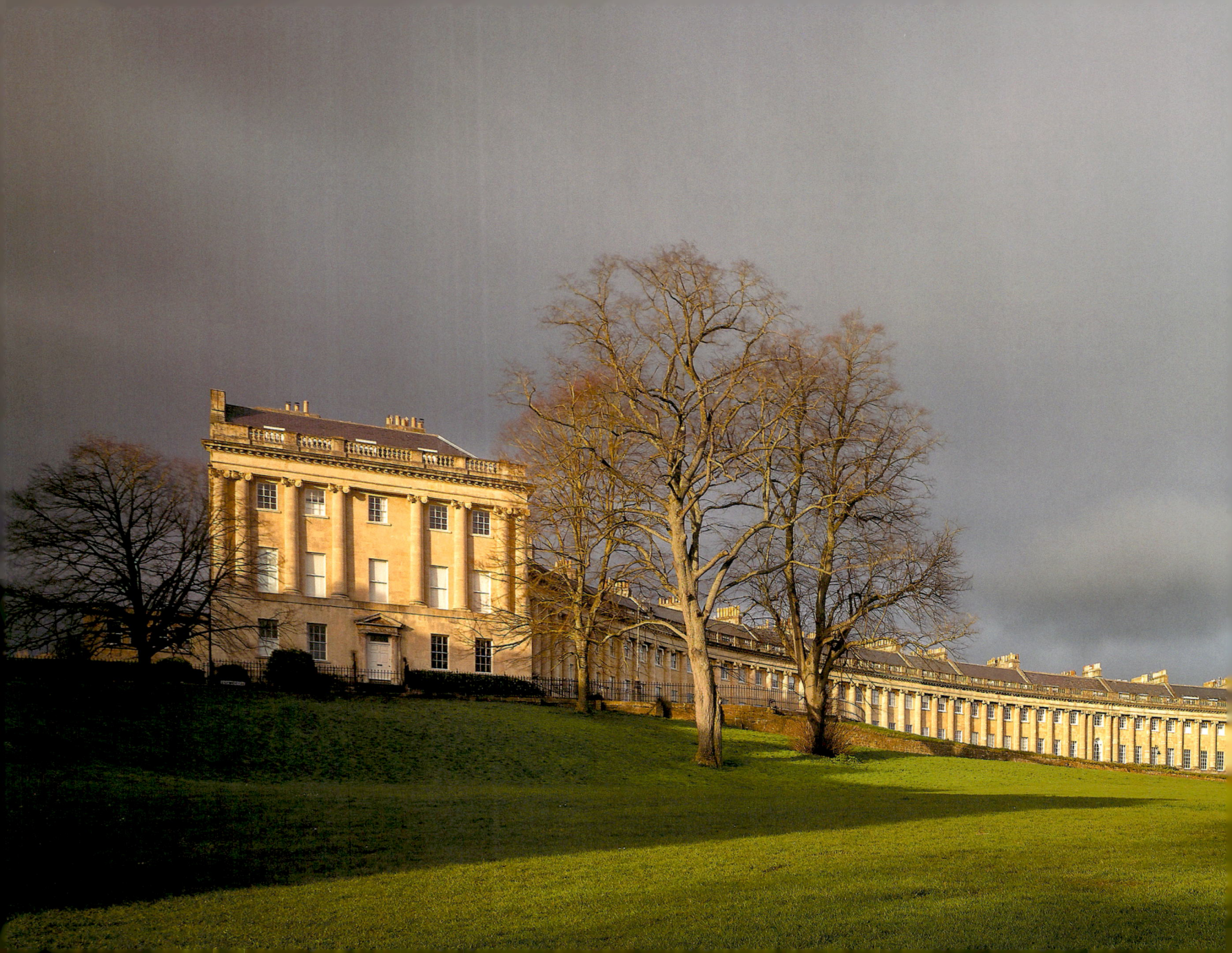

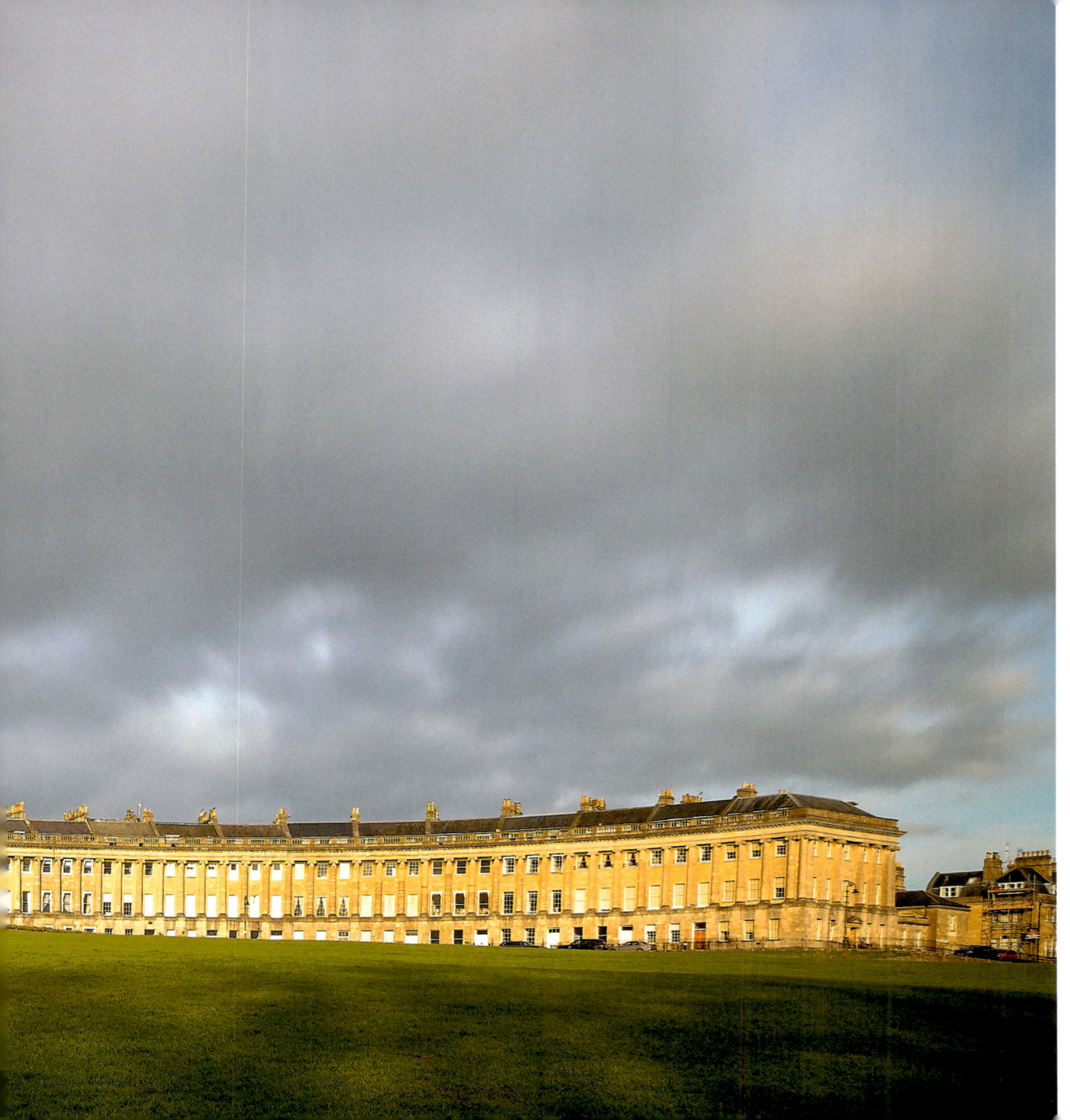

THE ROYAL CRESCENT

Perched on a commanding ridge in Victoria Park, the Royal Crescent, built between 1767 to 1775, faces south and basks in sunlight from dawn till dusk. A timeless d splay of Georgian elegance.

1 THE ROYAL CRESCENT

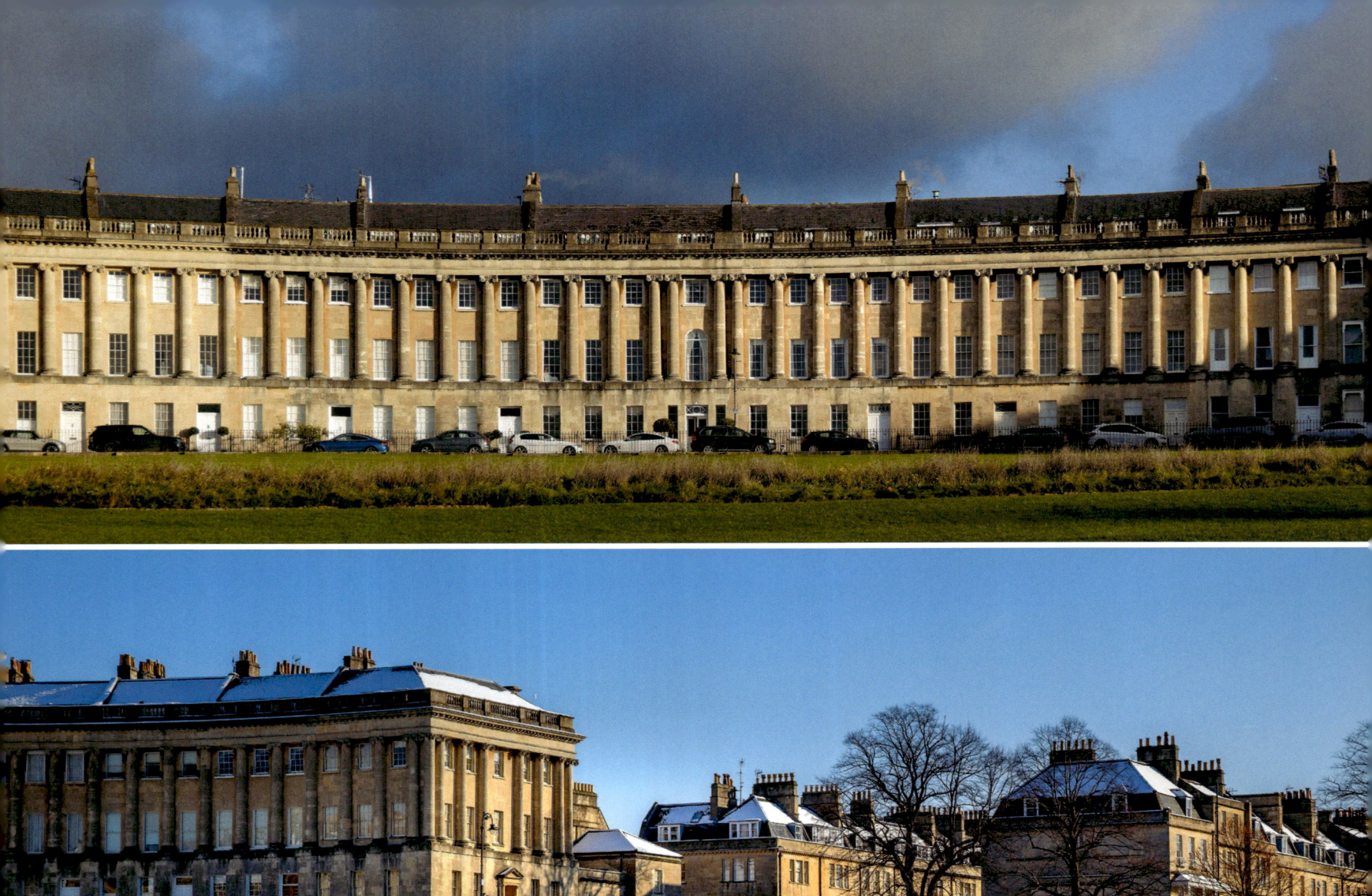

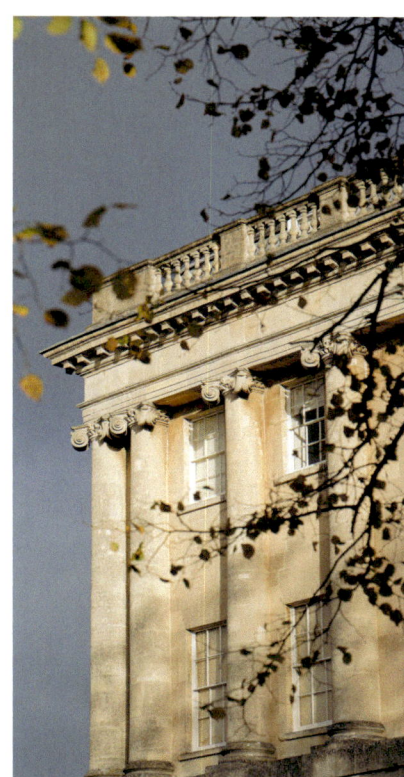

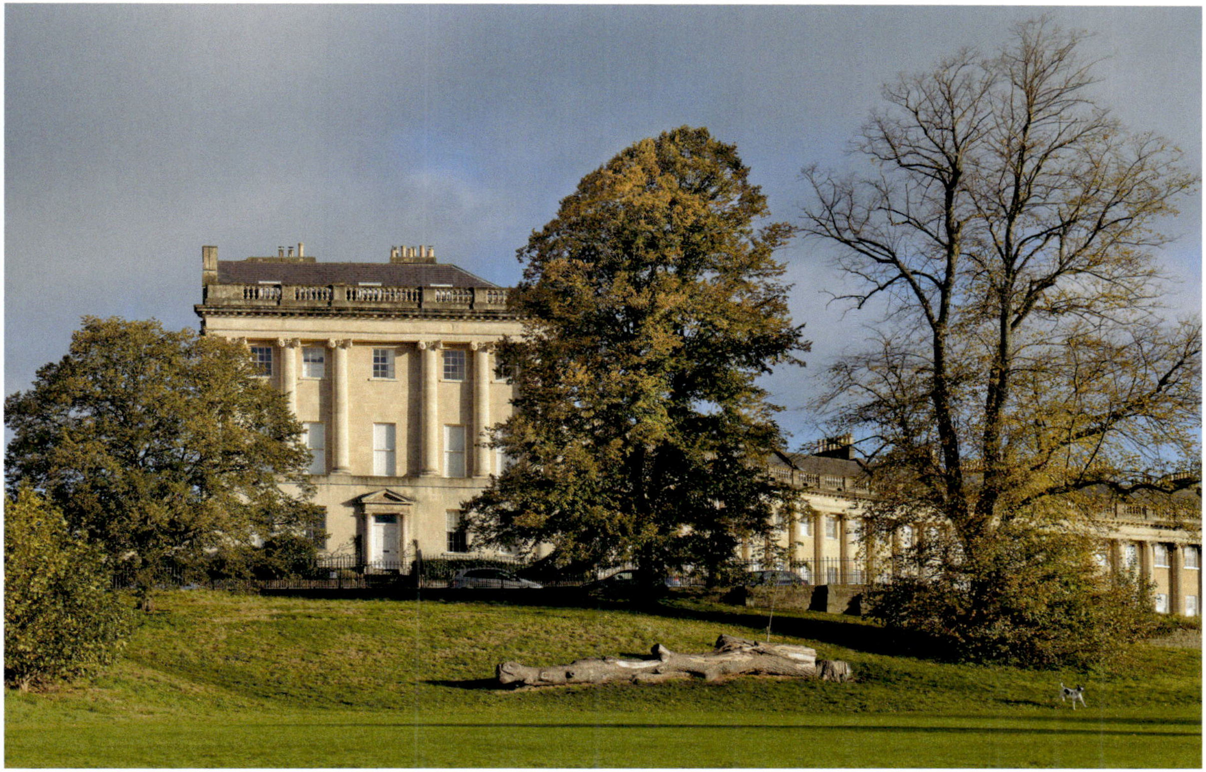

OPPOSITE TOP: thirty stunning townhouses in a perfect curving row with the iconic Royal Crescent Hotel taking pride of place at its centre. Often regarded as one of the most desirable places to live in the country the Royal Crescent has welcomed many notable residents over the years. Among them was the renowned writer Christopher Anstey along with Prince Frederick, Duke of York, who once stayed at No.16 – now home to the Royal Crescent Hotel where a suite proudly bears his name *(commemorative plaques indicate the homes of notable residents)*. To stay at the Royal Crescent Hotel visit *royalcrescent.co.uk*
BOTTOM: a destination for every season, the Royal Crescent overlooks a vast open public parkland, offering beauty year-round.

ABOVE LEFT: the east and west elevations are carefully balanced, with identical facades that emphasise order and proportion.
ABOVE RIGHT: in the soft glow of autumn the Royal Crescent's Bath stone exterior radiates warmth.

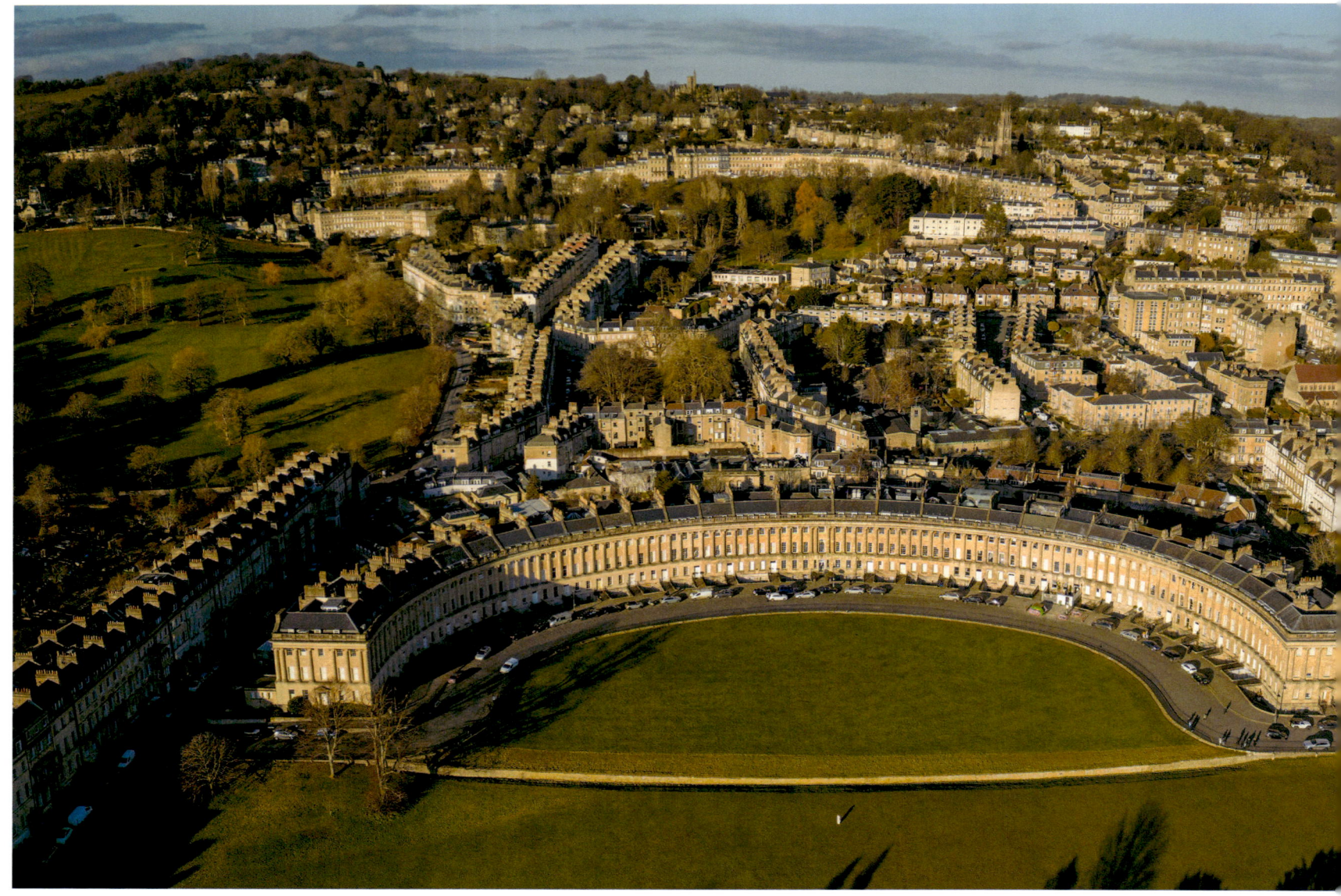

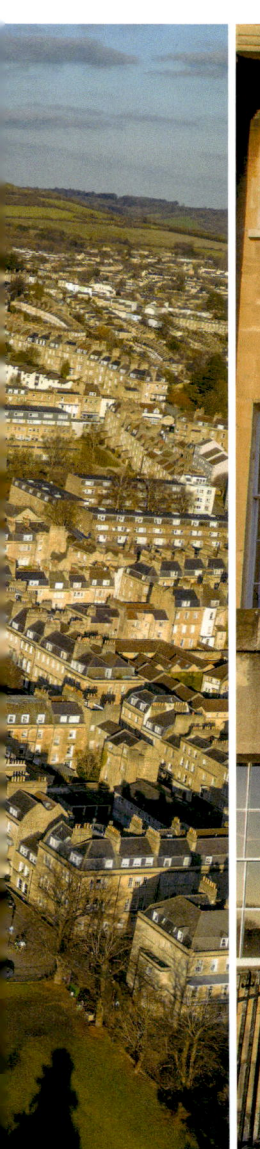

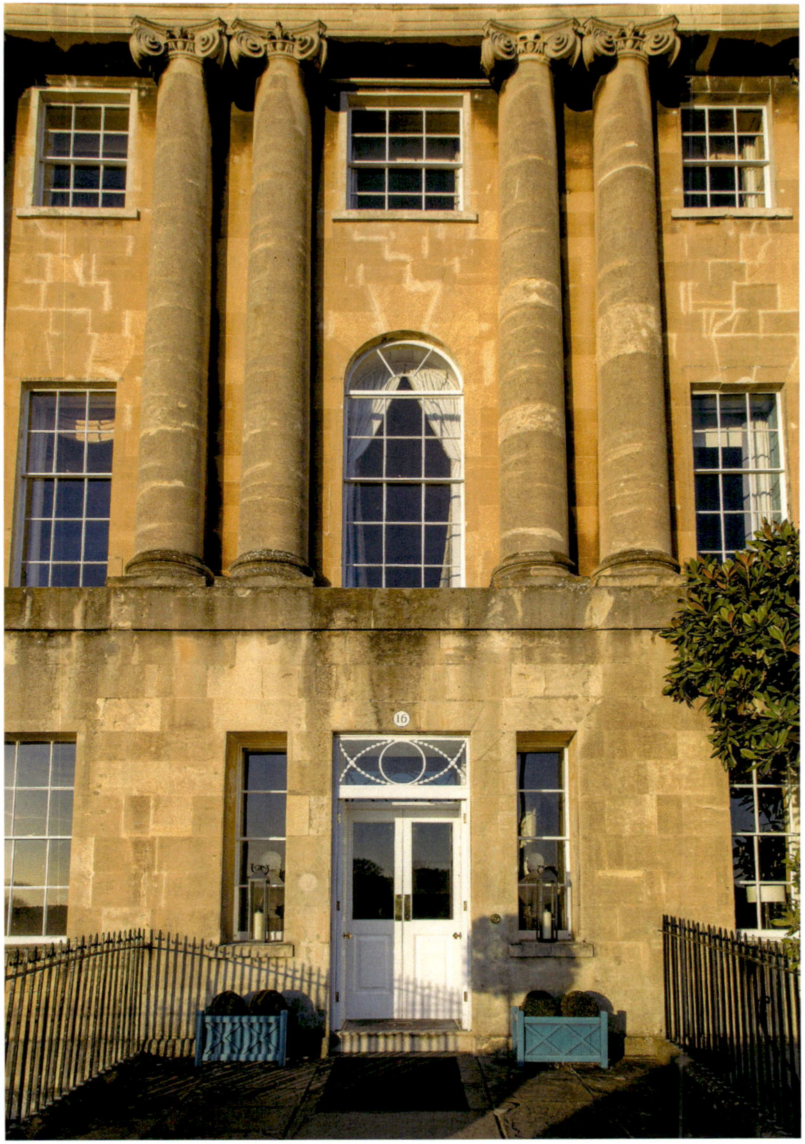

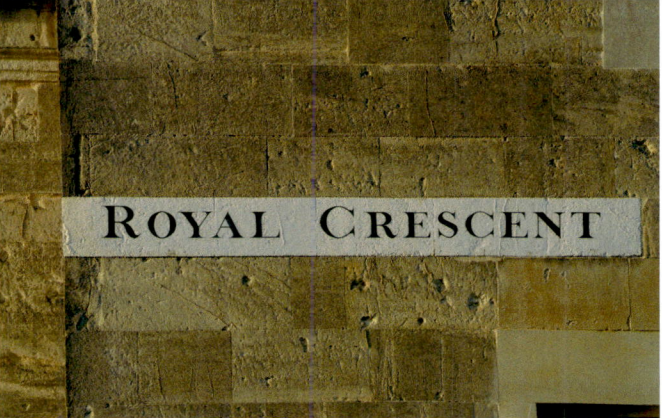

OPPOSITE: The Royal Crescent's graceful crescent shape evokes the form of the moon reflecting the Georgian era's desire for refinement and grace drawing on classical and historical influences.

Separating the residents lawn from the parkland is an intriguing and ingenious feature known as a ha-ha. This sunken ditch and wall serve as both a functional and aesthetic purpose enhancing the property's elegance by preserving an unobstructed view of the landscape beyond.

LEFT: the entrance to the Royal Crescent Hotel reflects the vision of architect John Wood the Younger whose design embodies the harmonious blending of grandeur and symmetry. Influenced by classical ideals the entrance features a refined Palladian entrance that complements the sweeping curves of the Crescent. **ABOVE:** elegant hand-painted signs adorn some of Bath's most prestigious properties.

1 THE ROYAL CRESCENT

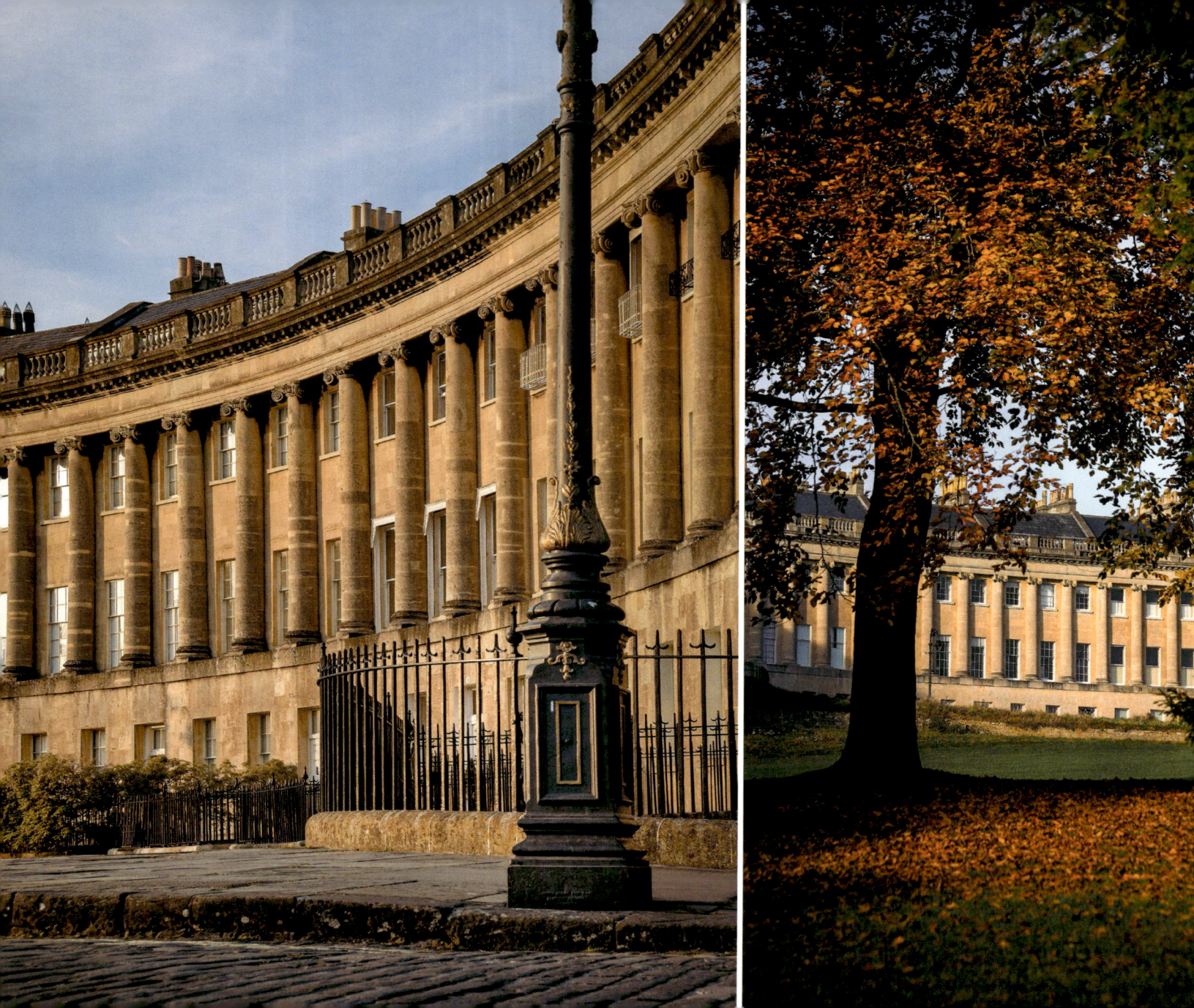

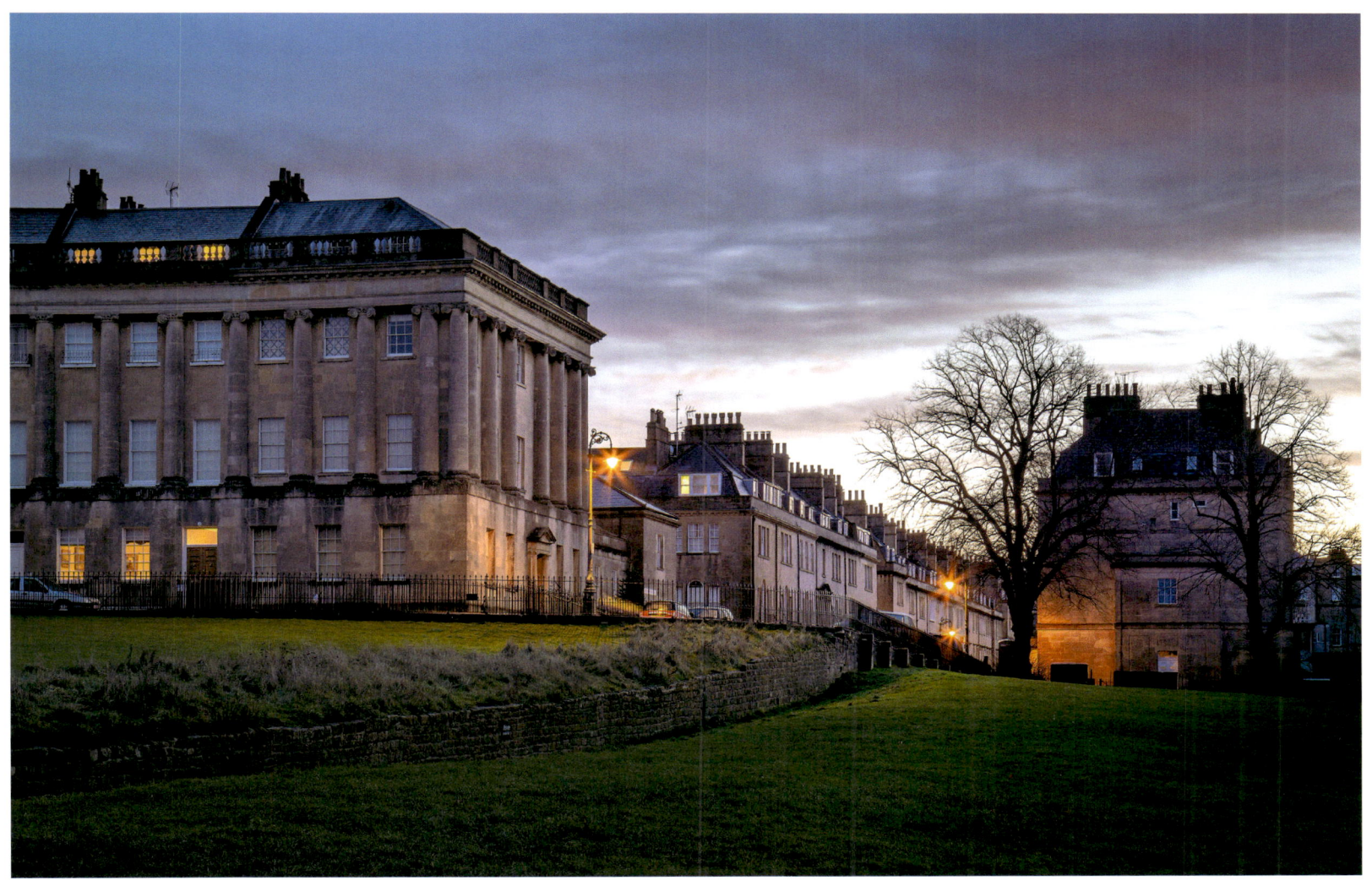

OPPOSITE FAR LEFT: a striking hallmark of Georgian design, the Royal Crescent's 114 elegant Ionic columns sweep across its facade.
OPPOSITE LEFT: The Royal Crescent is beautifully framed by its parkland setting, stretching along Royal Avenue.
ABOVE: as twilight sets in, the softening light subtly changes the hue of the Bath stone.

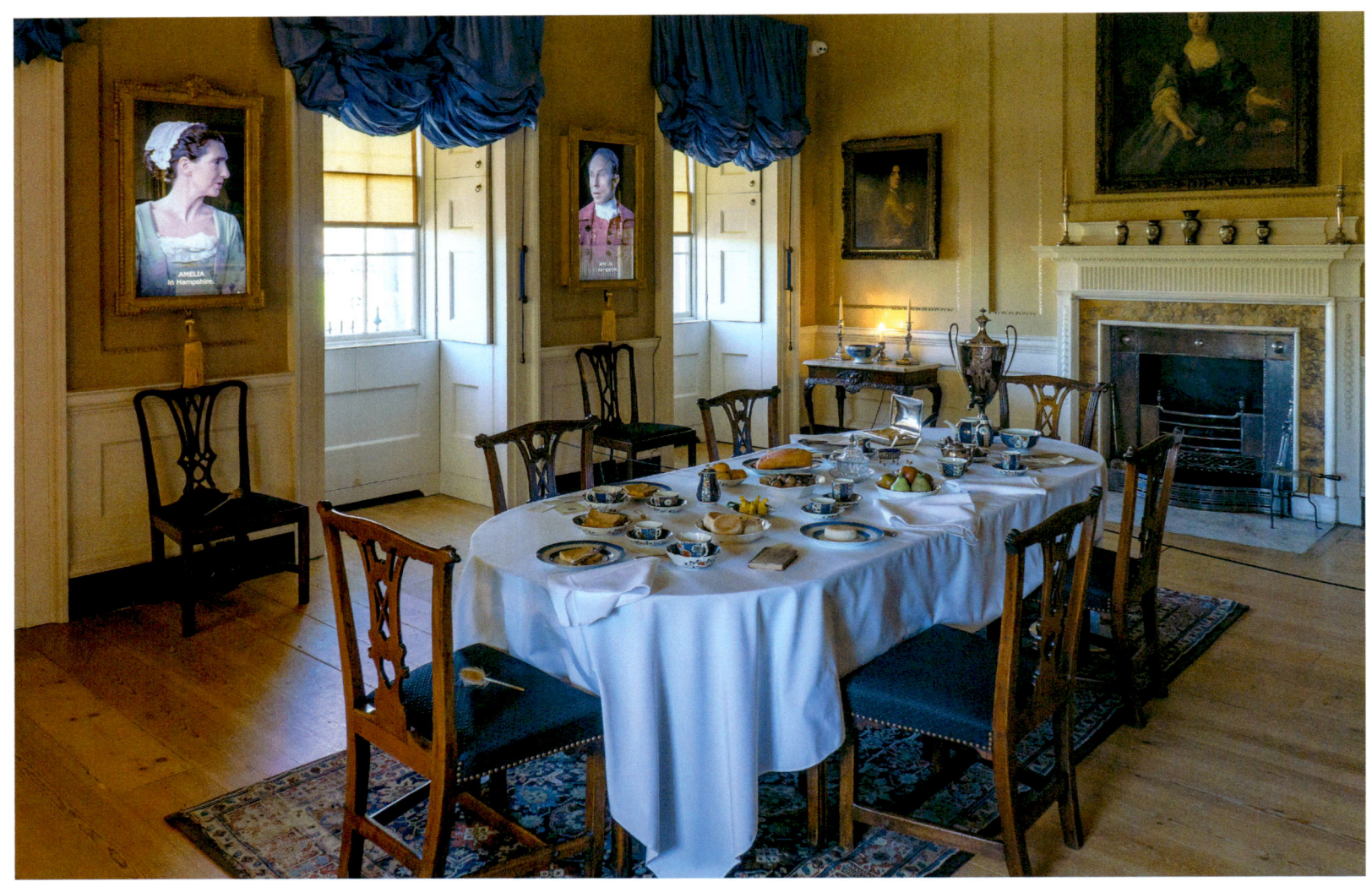

The dining room at No.1 Royal Crescent, set for a Georgian meal, combines period furnishings with immersive portrait screens that bring historical figures to life.

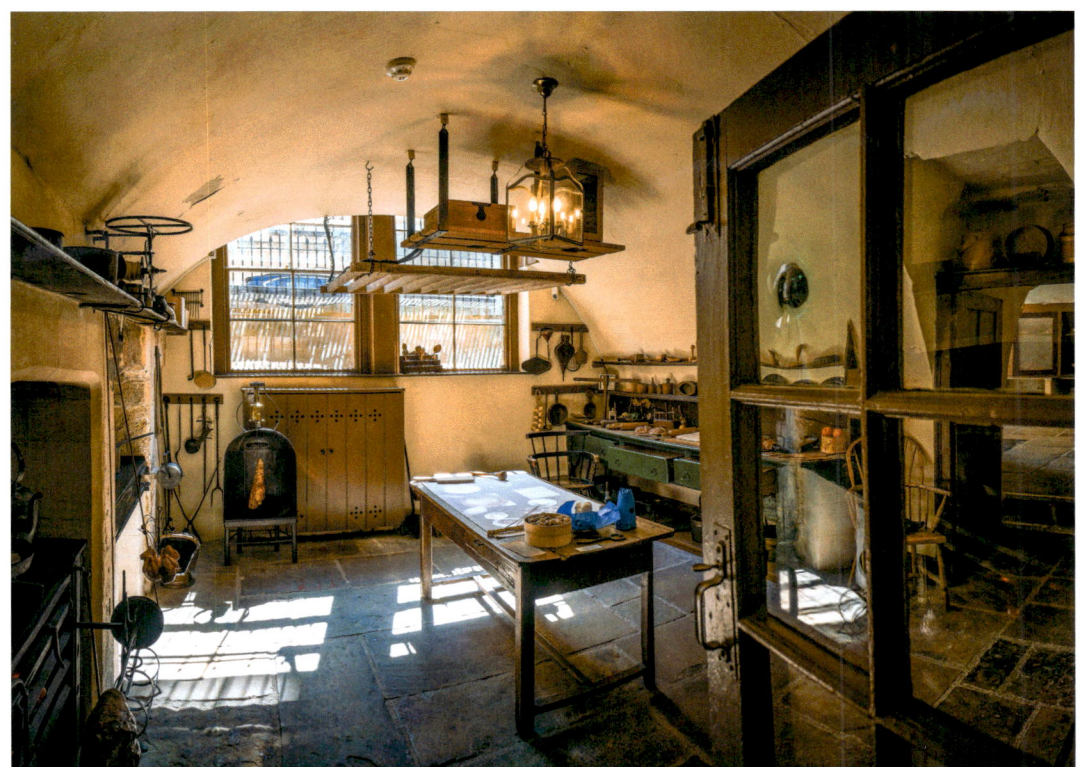

NO. 1 ROYAL CRESCENT

Imagine being able to step back in time and discover how the affluent Georgians lived in Bath. The fascinating No.1 Royal Crescent is an entire townhouse faithfully recreated from top to bottom reflecting a day in the life of a family of high status and the servants that tend to their every need.

The house serves as a museum, showcasing period furniture, artwork and other artefacts that would have been typical of a Georgian home. Visitors can explore the various rooms, including the kitchen, bedrooms, and drawing rooms and learn about the history of the house and its former inhabitants through exhibits and tours.

Accompanied by an immersive audio and visual story system a self guided trail over several floors leads through rooms furnished and decorated depending on usage or cultural pastime allowing visitors to experience life during the mid 18th Century

The faithful recreation of No.1 Royal Crescent as a Georgian home creates a chance to step back in time and experience the elegance and sophistication of this period in British history. It is a fascinating and popular tourist attraction in Bath and a must-visit for anyone interested in architecture or Georgian culture and a perfect place begin or end a trip to this part of the city.

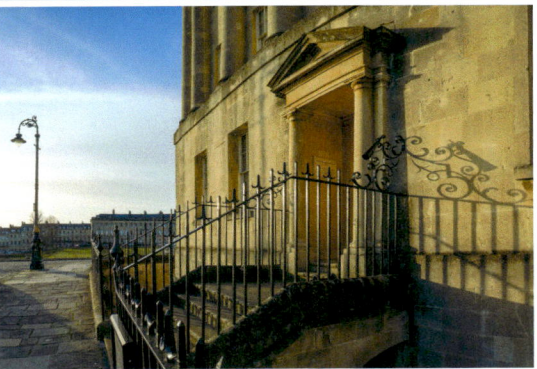

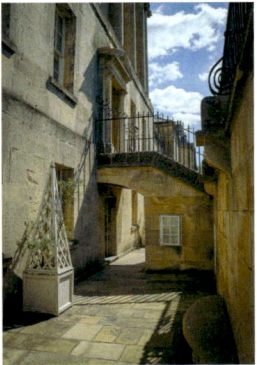

ABOVE: the basement kitchen offers a glimpse into domestic life downstairs. **FAR LEFT**: the entrance to No.1 Royal Crescent features ornate iron railings and a classical pediment and was used in *Bridgerton* series for the exterior shots of the Featherington's home. **LEFT**: set over four floors, additional access to an enclosed courtyard beneath the Royal Crescent offers unique views beneath the building.

MORE INFORMATION

no1royalcrescent.org.uk
Find out the opening times, events, book a ticket and learn about history of No 1 Royal Crescent.

MARLBOROUGH BUILDINGS

Framing the grassy parkland and enclosing the Royal Crescent next door the beautiful terrace of Marlborough Buildings seem to effortlessly 'step' up the hillside, each building rising up just a chimney stack or so higher in turn.

Built in 1788 some 15 years after the Royal Crescent, Marlborough Buildings effectively bisects the once open common land which originally stretched towards the village of Weston. This created a kind of 'book end' to the grandiose Georgian properties on the western edge of the city. It was conceived as a row of beautifully faced townhouses with four storeys that can be seen at road level at the front and an enormous six to eight storeys to the rear. Each property is adorned with decorative details such as sash windows, ornate doorways, and classical pilasters, upon completion the interior designs, walls and layouts were up to each prospective buyer to develop and stylise as they wished.

Explore behind the street and it is remarkable how tall the rear of Marlborough Buildings are. So enormous that they tower over the allotments below. The architectural styling of the front facade in comparison is neat, orderly and regimented where as the rear seems to have had a 'carte blanche' approach. The uniformity replaced with irregular balconies and protruding back porches; it's an amazing view which is worth exploring by following the winding path which edges Victoria park or accessed via Cow Lane which runs to the park adjacent to No. 1 Marlborough Buildings.

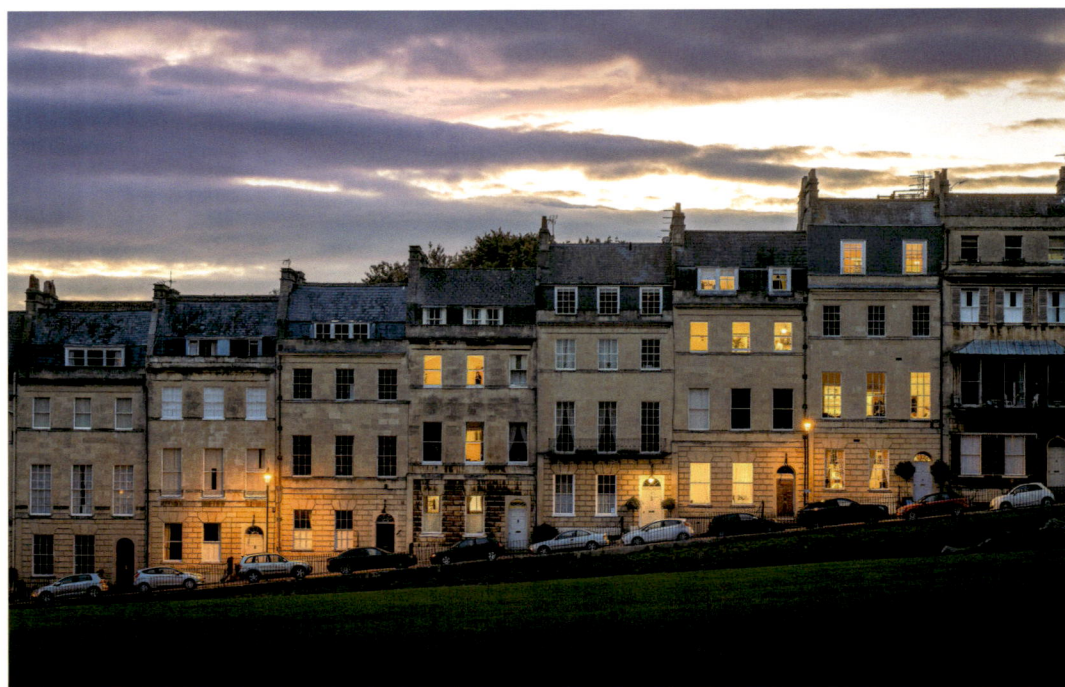

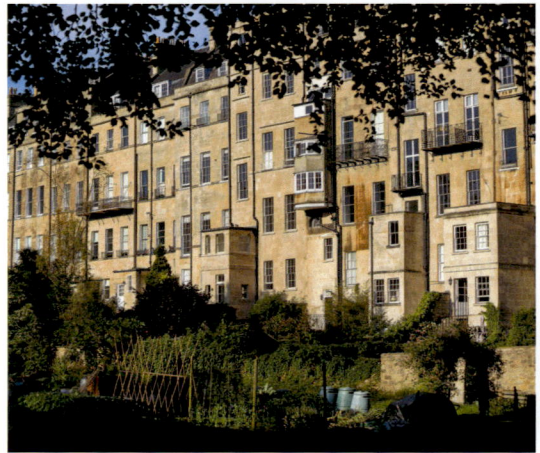

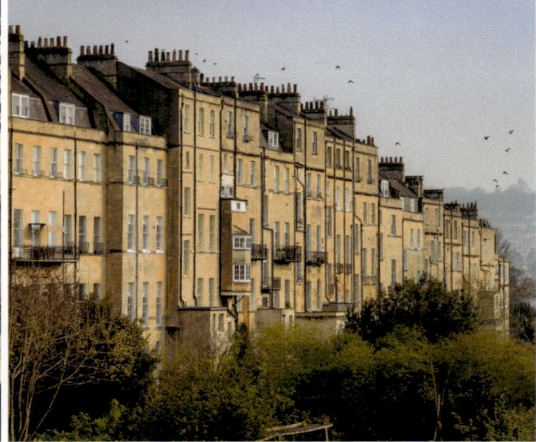

TOP: the main facade ascends the hillside with effortless grace. **RIGHT**: the rear view presents a more relaxed design overlooking residents allotments. **FAR RIGHT**: a remarkable height difference compared to the front elevation reveals an impressive array of additional stories.

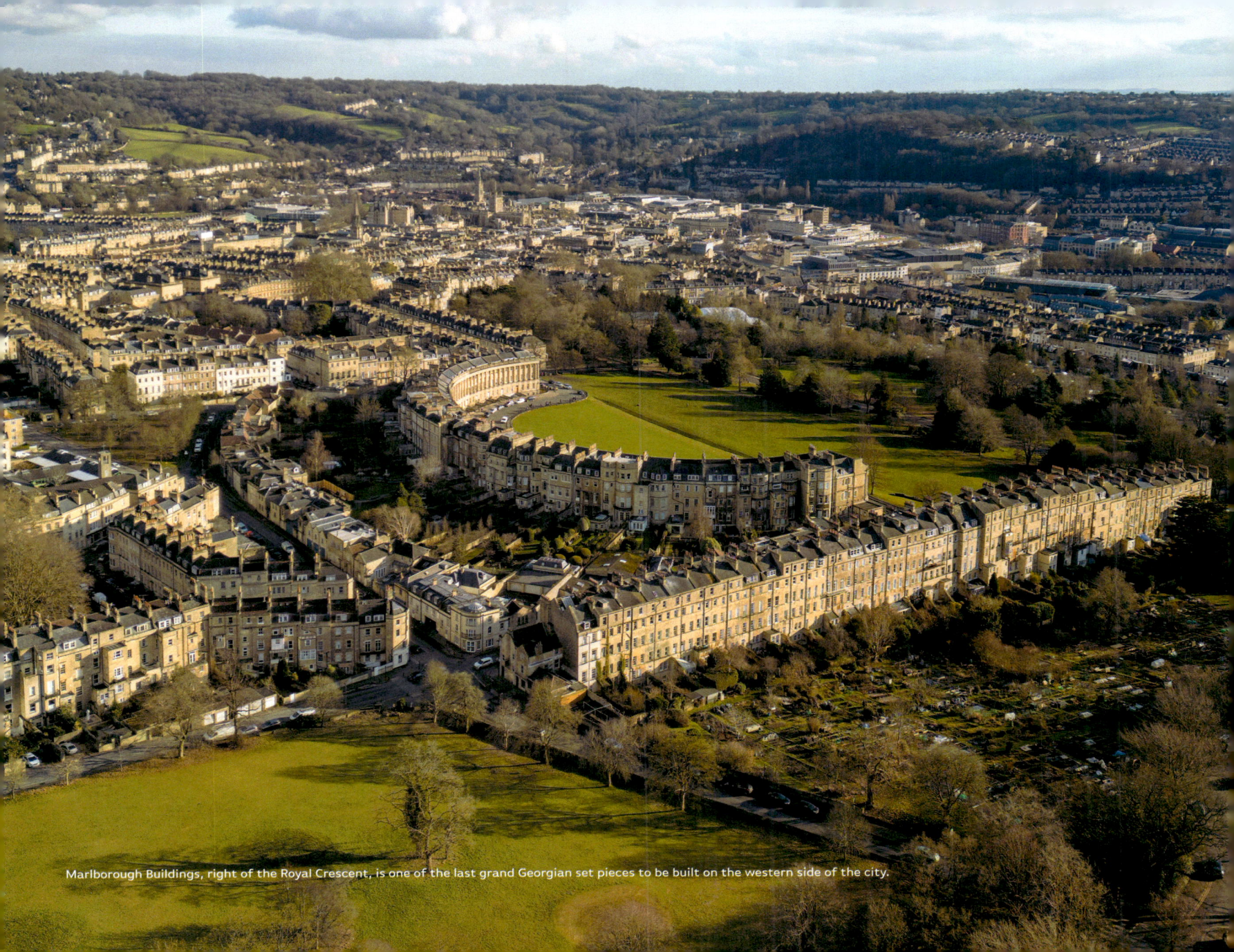

Marlborough Buildings, right of the Royal Crescent, is one of the last grand Georgian set pieces to be built on the western side of the city.

ROYAL VICTORIA PARK

Royal Victoria Park is a beautiful, historic green space with over 57 acres of lawns, flower beds, pathways, a botanic garden and mature specimen trees. The park is also home to tennis courts, a cafe and bandstand and is often used as an outdoor music venue for concerts and theatrical performances. It was the country's first municipal park designed by city architect Edward Davis and opened in 1830 by a young Queen Victoria. The parkland flanking the Royal Avenue is the best location to view both Marlborough Buildings and the Royal Crescent together.

A trip to Royal Victoria Park during each season is unique. Winter time gives the clearest views of the wonderful architecture through trees. In early spring head to Laurel Lawn where thousands of daffodils and crocus flowers emerge and in summer you can enjoy colourful flower beds and neatly trimmed lawns. In autumn russet orange colours appear across the leaves and overhanging branches frame the Georgian landmarks.

Beyond the Royal Avenue the parkland passes beside a quaint historic gothic cottage and a monument dedicated to Queen Victoria before opening out onto a large flat area of ground, a fantastic picnic spot or somewhere to play ball sports, throw a frisbee, feed ducks beside the lake and even a good place to watch hot air balloons inflate before soaring up into the sky over the city. Close by is a vast children's play area crammed with playground equipment and a skate park.

MORE INFORMATION

visitbath.co.uk
Search 'Royal Victoria Park' at the Visit Bath website to find out more about this beautiful parkland. Free to enter.

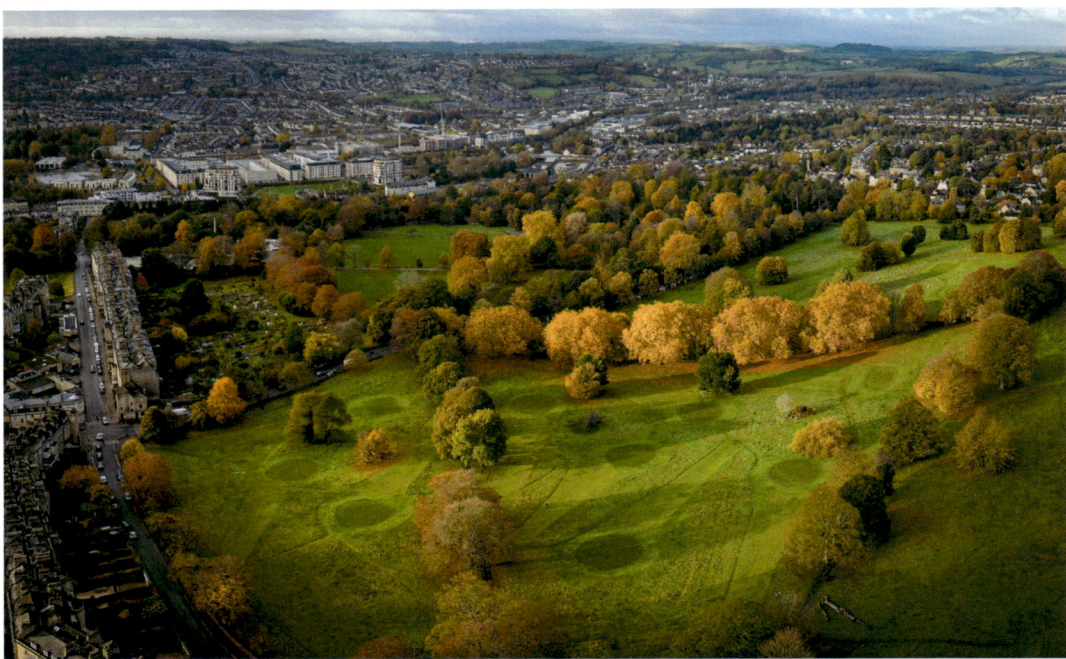

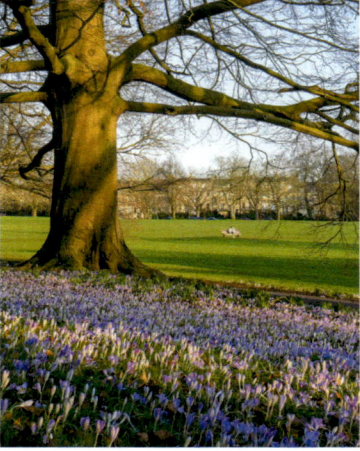

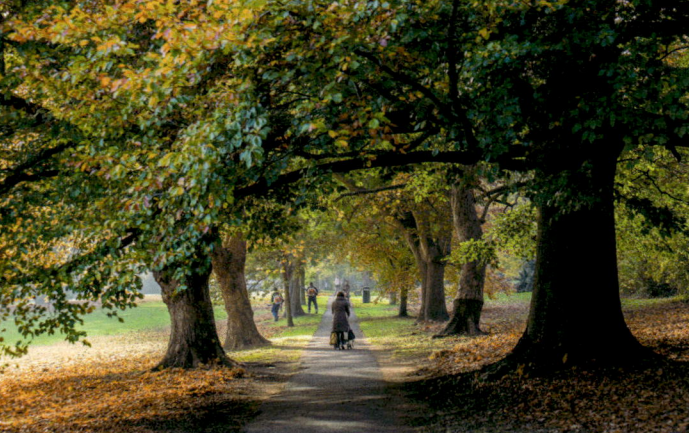

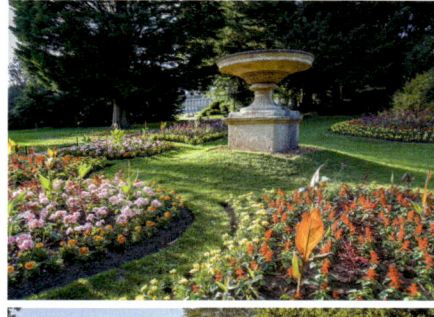
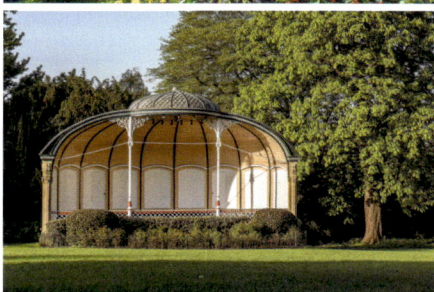
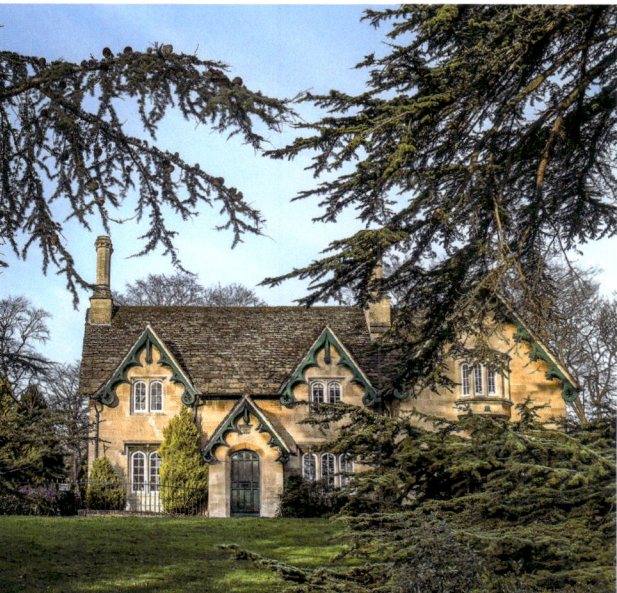

The parklands are marked by a gated entrance featuring carved statues upon stonework pillars and emblem adorned ironwork railings. The Upper Common is located north of the main park and is home to a golf course which also has numerous public pathways that cross the hillside, each lined with veteran trees and offering beautiful views across the city.

OPPOSITE TOP: Upper Common, situated to the northwest of the Royal Crescent offers a scenic viewpoint surrounded by beautiful trees. **FAR LEFT**: crocus flowers in full bloom. **LEFT**: numerous paths crisscross the parkland.
TOP LEFT: well-maintained seasonal flower beds and historic features can be found throughout the main park areas. **MIDDLE LEFT**: a Grade II listed bandstand, built in 1890, also used for concerts and as a wedding venue. **LEFT**: Park Cottages, once home to the park keepers was built in the style of a Gothic farmhouse. **BOTTOM LEFT**: the views from Upper Common across chimney pots and rooftops into the heart of the city. **BELOW**: the parkland is dotted with many mature and interesting specimen trees, such as those along Cavendish Road.

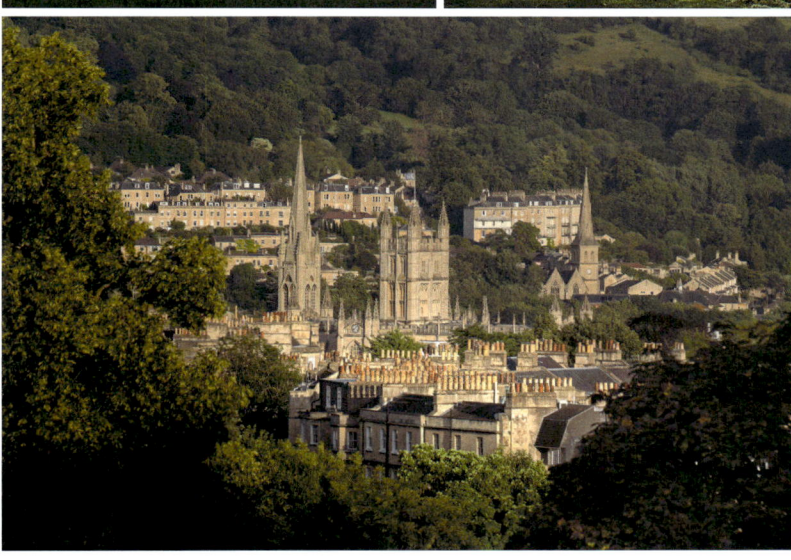
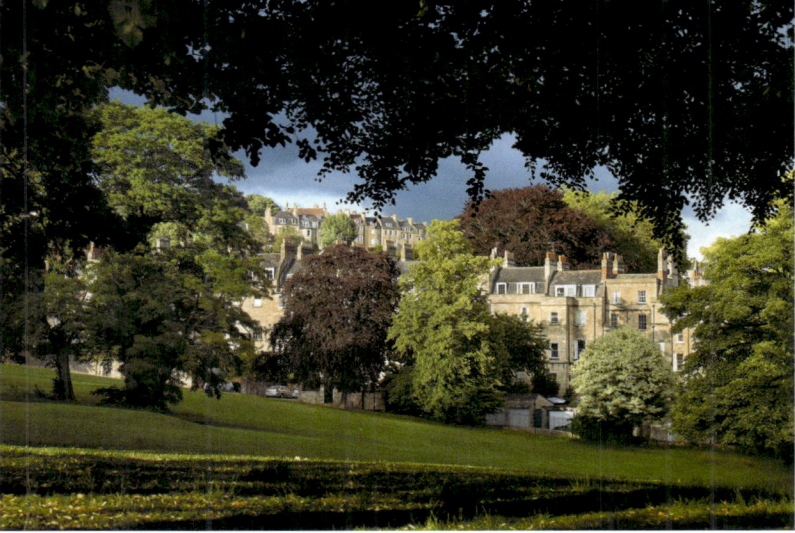

1 THE ROYAL CRESCENT

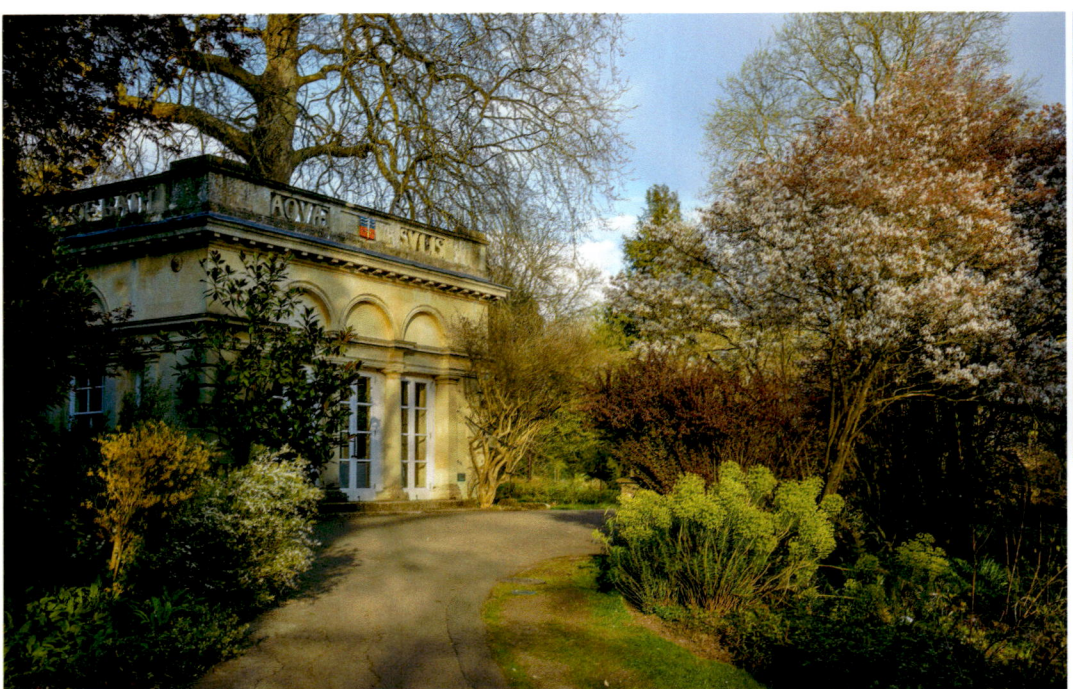

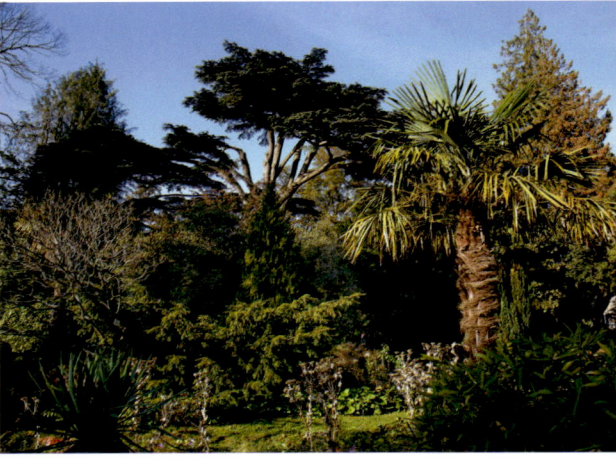

THE BOTANICAL GARDENS

Situated on the furthest fringes of Victoria Park a Botanical Garden has occupied this site since 1840 originally created by WH Baxter as part of the further development of the parkland.

The Botanical Gardens boast a diverse collection of plants from around the world, set amidst beautifully landscaped grounds. Many of the specimens contained within the gardens were grown from seed and are gifted from local horticultural collectors or botanists. Access to the collection is free and in all there are 9 acres to explore housing a vast collection of ornamental and exotic shrubs, scented walks, herbaceous borders and water side features.

TOP: the Temple of Minerva, originally built in 1924 as Bath's pavilion for the British Empire Exhibition, now a wedding venue. **ABOVE**: distinct tree specimens from around the world are scattered throughout the gardens. **LEFT**: seasonal flower beds along with fascinating shrubs and trees are arranged in unique sections.

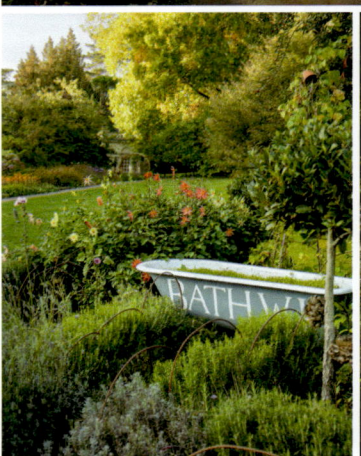
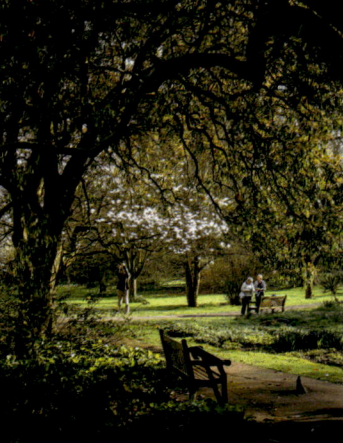
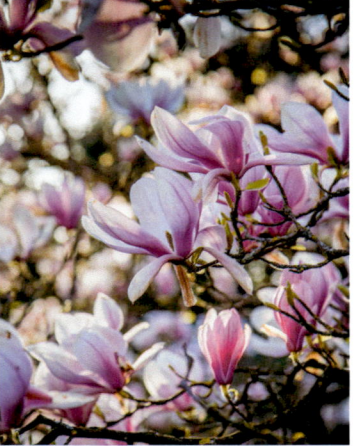

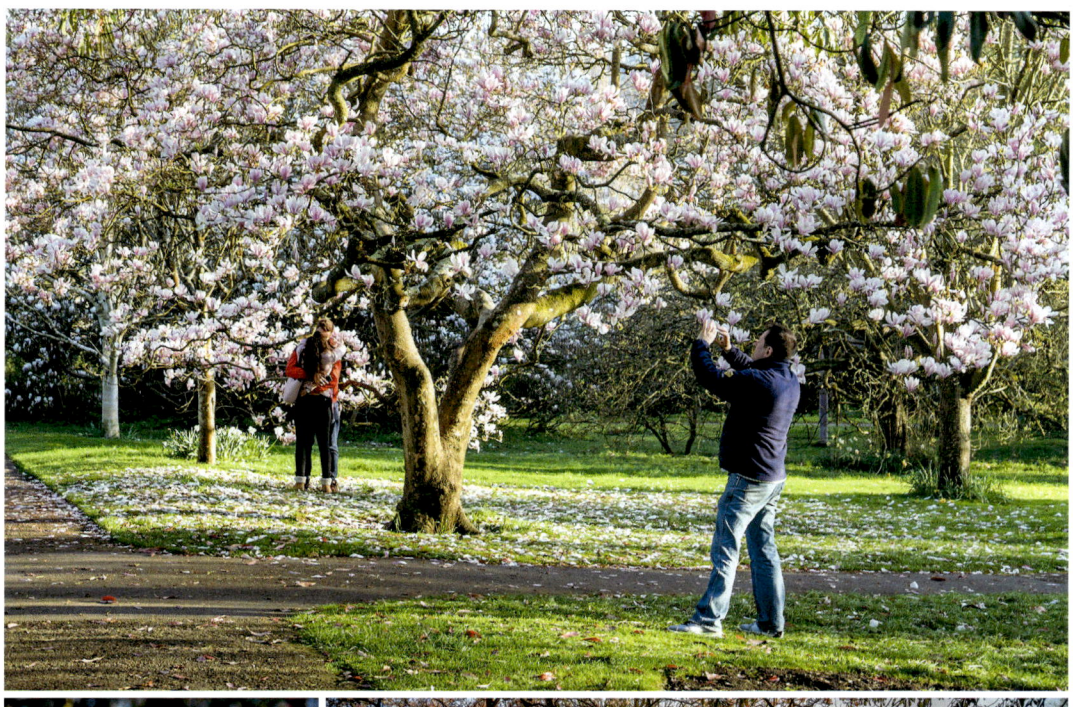

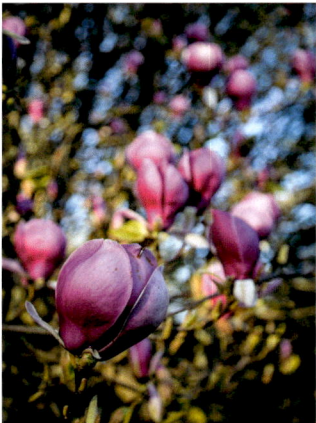

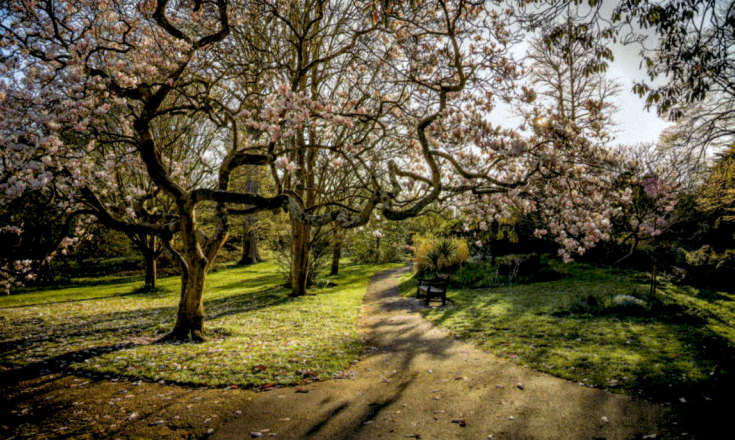

The gardens were extended further in 1987 incorporating the Great Dell situated across the perimeter park road, already planted with North American trees since 1840.

A circular path winds its way through the gardens accessed via two entrances on the north and west boundary. There are plenty of opportunities to veer off course should an interesting tree or flower grab your attention. All times of the year offer a unique experience when visiting, however if possible aim to arrive in spring if only to experience the wonderful magnolias in full bloom.

Parcels of mown lawns also offer moments to pause and linger longer particularly on hot summer days where the trees offer shelter from the sun; its a great spot for relaxing with a picnic or choosing a tasty treat from the seasonal takeaway cafe.

Close to the northern boundary of the garden is the Temple of Minerva, a beautifully proportioned feature of the park relocated here fairly recently in 1926. It was originally designed and built for the 1924 British Empire Exhibition in Wembley as an advertisement for the City of Bath, in particular drawing visitors to the area to enjoy the spa waters. Now a wedding venue it is a charming feature nestled amongst the foliage overlooking an oval shaped pool below lined with Japanese Maple trees.

MORE INFORMATION

 visitbath.co.uk
Search 'Botanical Gardens' at the Visit Bath website to find out more about the botanical gardens. Free to enter.

TOP: mature magnolia trees in full bloom are a major attraction for visitors in spring. **FAR LEFT**: this magnolia radiates beauty with its rich, velvety petals. **LEFT**: the pathways invite exploration, guiding you past fragrant blooms, ancient trees and vibrant seasonal displays.

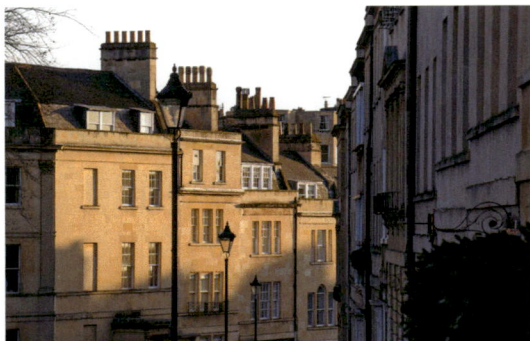
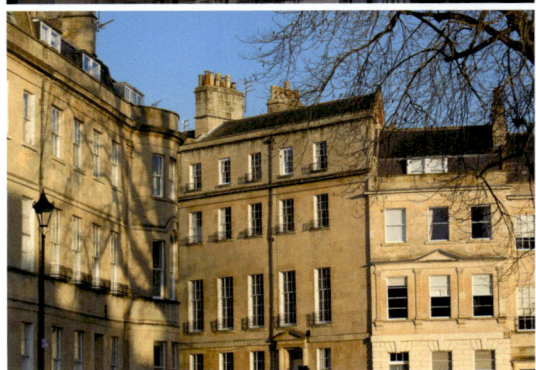
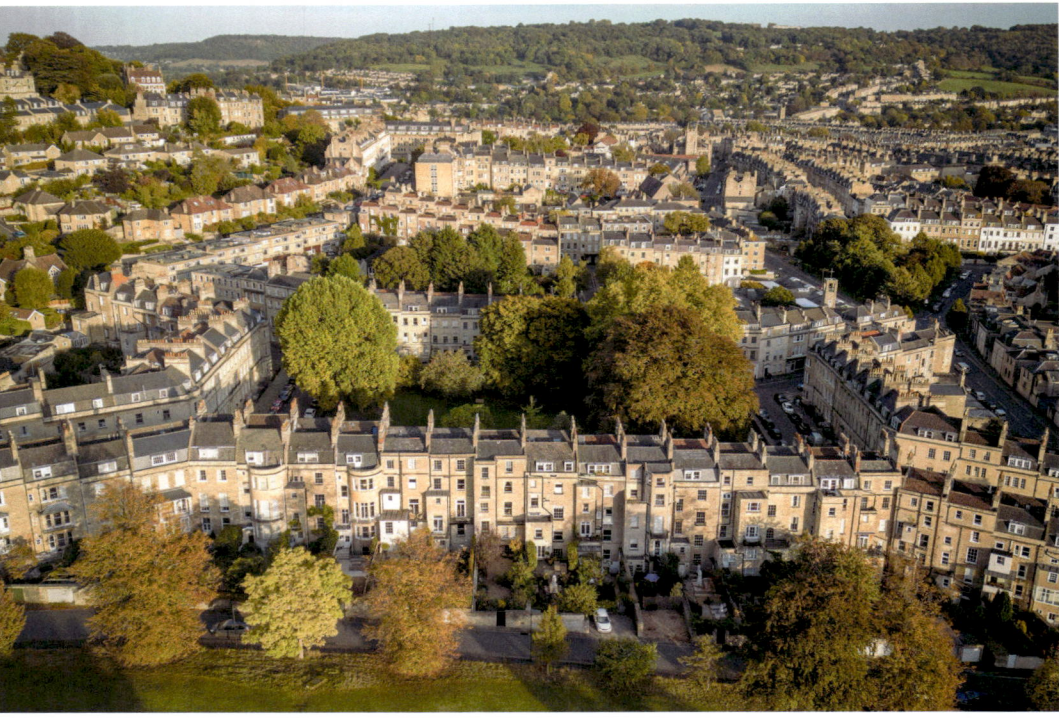

ST JAMES'S SQUARE

St James's Square is a remarkable terrace of 45 residential grade 1 listed houses positioned around and overlooking a large enclosed garden. Built by John Palmer in 1793 the picturesque St James's originally occupied tenanted land associated with the Royal Crescent built around 20 years earlier to the south.

Each of the three storey properties exhibit the finest of Georgian stone craftsmanship complete with tall sash windows and a recognisable symmetrical style that benefit from overlooking the central parkland. Noted as one of the finest Georgian squares outside of London each of St James's central townhouses are topped with a large pediment and Corinthian columns echoing the design of a grand palace, a style also found elsewhere in the city (such as Queens Square).

The gardens are mostly laid to lawn and are planted with informal groupings of early flowering bulbs and cherry blossom in the spring. Autumn brings golden colour from a cluster of large mature broadleaved trees, notably a Tree of Heaven and a collection of impressive plane trees.

On the south eastern corner a curious archway breaks the line of terraced properties leading to the aptly named Curiosity Cottage. A shop front, set back from the road and almost hidden from view set is said to have inspired ones of the Square's most famous occasional residents, Charles Dickens who based his novel The Old Curiosity Shop on the quaint establishment.

TOP LEFT: St James's Square is regarded as one of the finest examples of Georgian residential designs in Britain. **BOTTOM LEFT:** adjacent roads feed into the square, catching the sunlight and highlighting its 18th-century facade. **ABOVE:** located just to the west of the city centre the square offers a peaceful retreat while remaining close to key landmarks.

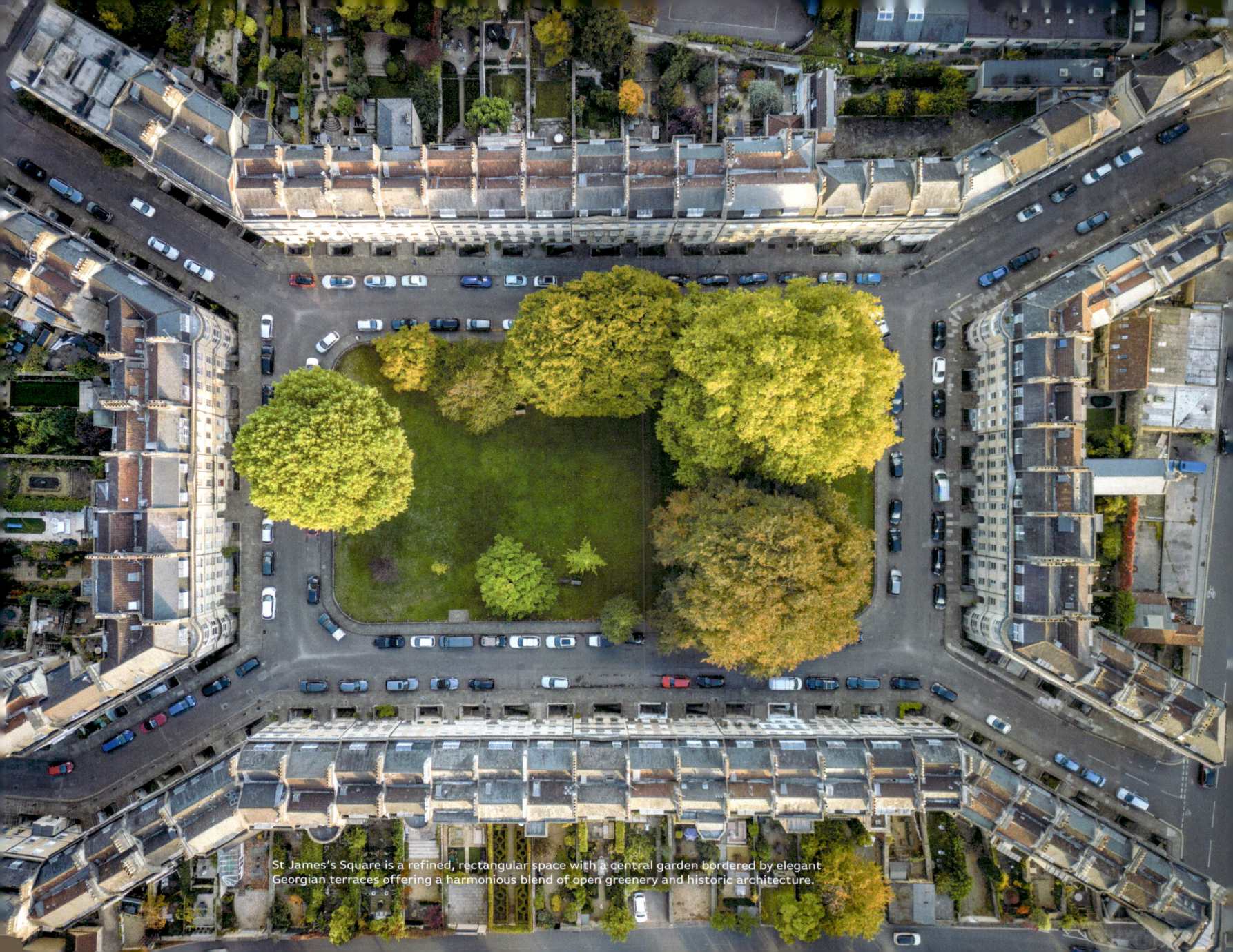

St James's Square is a refined, rectangular space with a central garden bordered by elegant Georgian terraces offering a harmonious blend of open greenery and historic architecture.

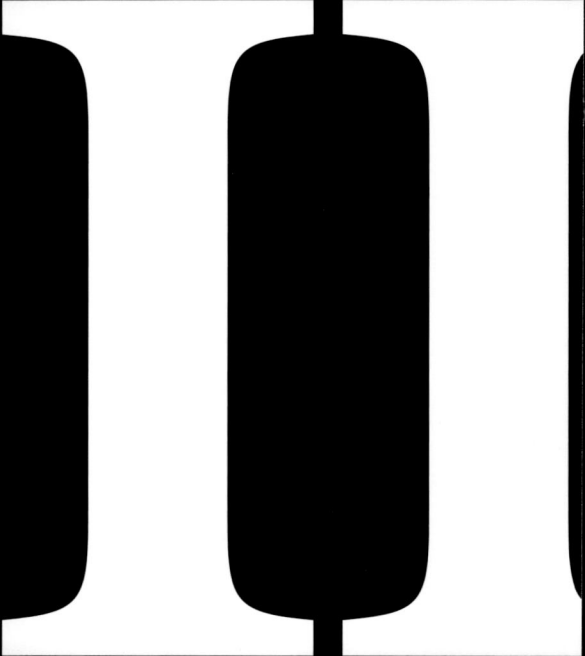

2 LANSDOWN

"The design ensures that the three-storey fronts of the buildings are of uniform height and have matching doors and windows."
– John Palmer, Architect of Lansdown Crescent circa 1789–1793

"Sir Walter had taken a very good house in Camden Place, a lofty, dignified situation, such as becomes a man of consequence…"
– Jane Austen, *Persuasion* (1818)

Lansdown is one of Bath's most picturesque district areas known for its elegant Georgian architecture, parklands and stunning natural surroundings. Perched on the northern hills of the city it offers an escape from the bustling city centre while still being just a short distance away.

One of Lansdown's most distinctive features is the abundance of crescents in the area. Most notably, Lansdown Crescent which stands as a prime example of Bath's iconic Georgian architecture. Designed by John Palmer in the late 18th century it boasts a graceful curve of townhouses with sweeping views over the city and the rolling hills beyond. The crescent, along with neighbouring ones like Somerset Place and Cavendish Crescent in the west to Camden Crescent further on the eastern hillside are beautiful examples of Bath's compelling architecture that appear to glide across the hillside.

The Lansdown area is also one of the best places in Bath to catch a stunning sunset. As the sun dips below the horizon, the sky is often painted in shades of pink, orange and purple creating a magical backdrop against the silhouette of the city and its surrounding hills. Landmarks and honey-coloured buildings emit a golden glow when the light rakes across the city and whether you're enjoying the view from a crescent or one of the many viewpoints, the sunsets here are truly memorable.

LANSDOWN CRESCENT

Postcode: BA1 5EX
what3words: tribes.mixed.safe

SOMERSET PLACE

Postcode: BA1 5AD
what3words: youth.charmingly.model

CAVENDISH ROAD

Postcode: BA1 2UB
what3words: curl.little.form

CAVENDISH CRESCENT

Postcode: BA1 2UG
what3words: rich.nerve.lasted

CAMDEN CRESCENT

Postcode: BA1 5HY
what3words: pump.unity.space

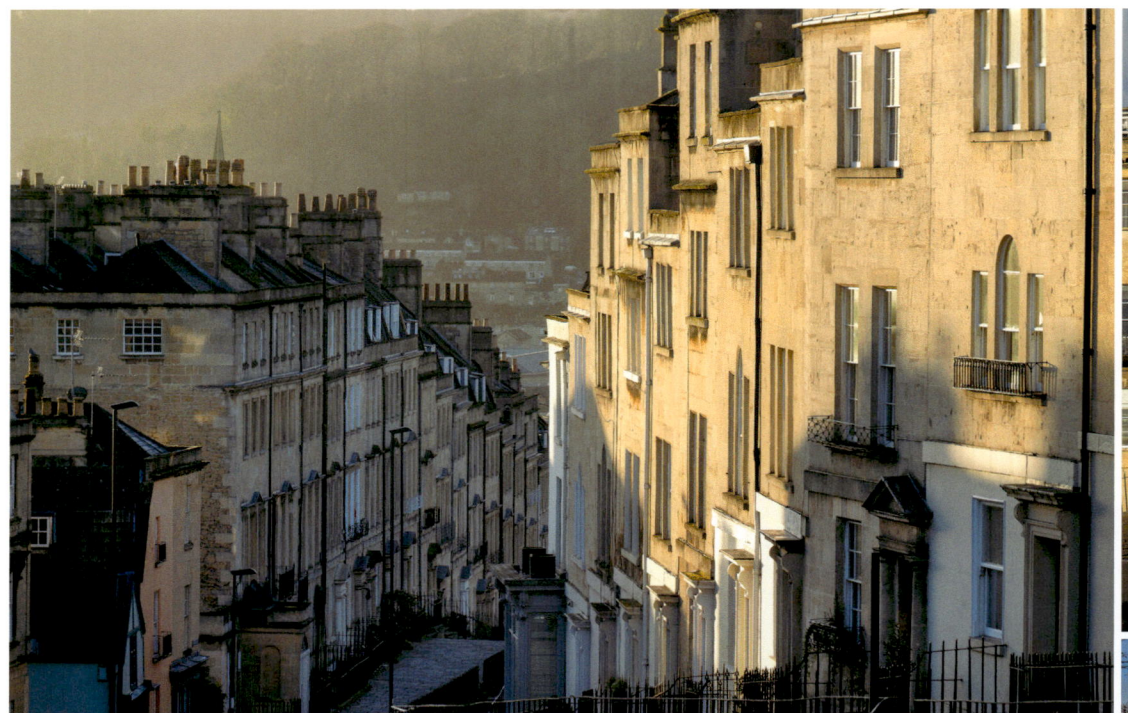

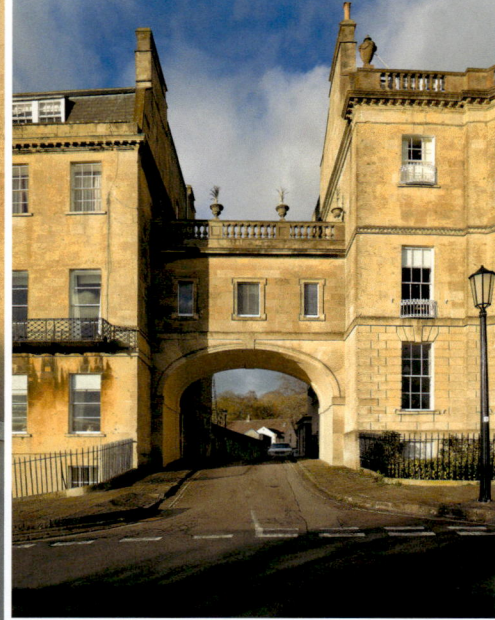

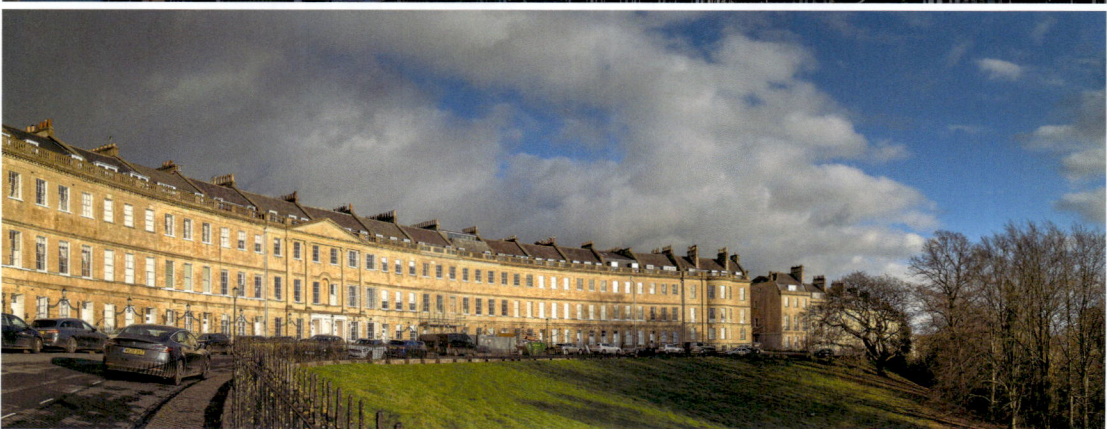

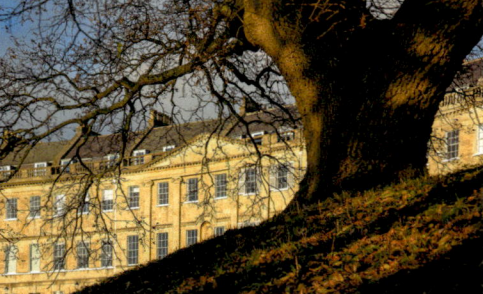

TOP LEFT: Lansdown Road rises dramatically from Bath's city centre to the elegant Lansdown Crescent, offering sweeping views as it climbs. **TOP**: the former home of the wealthy and eccentric novelist, William Beckford. **ABOVE**: perched high above the city centre the crescent offers a serene and desirable retreat with stunning views of Bath. **LEFT**: an open paddock in front of Lansdown Crescent, lined to the south with mature trees.

LANSDOWN CRESCENT

Built between 1789 and 1793, Lansdown Crescent is a prime example of Georgian architecture, renowned for its graceful curves, elegant proportions, and classical detailing. As part of a portfolio of work featuring some of the finest residences in the city such as St James's Square and Kensington Place, Lansdown Crescent was designed by John Palmer who became Bath City Architect during its construction. It is one of the last major properties and crescents to be built on the edge of 18th Century Georgian Bath. The interiors of the houses within the crescent feature spacious rooms, high ceilings, and ornate plasterwork, offering a glimpse into the luxurious lifestyle enjoyed by its affluent residents during the Georgian era.

Lansdown Crescent's most famous and controversial resident was William Thomas Beckford who moved in during 1822. Over a residency spanning 20 years Beckford acquired extra properties which were merged via a 'bridge' that arched across an access road joining together the main crescent with Lansdown Place West. He would often ride northwards to his rural retreat at Beckford's Tower which housed an art collection and library of books, the tower was quite the statement piece for reclusive Beckford whose wealth was attributed to the transatlantic slave trade.

One of the most distinctive features of Lansdown Crescent is its commanding position overlooking the Lansdown hillside offering panoramic views of the southern fringes of the city. An enclosed paddock opposite the crescent brings a rural feel to the Georgian splendour and is often grazed by sheep. A beautiful tree-lined avenue of beech and sycamore trees skirt around the base of the paddock offering glimpses through the canopy to Lansdown Crescent rising up onto the sky line above. A visit here is fantastic at any time of year, summer months bring cool shade and luscious green growth and autumn brings golden hues and a carpet of fallen leaves.

The eastern approach to Lansdown Crescent follows a main thoroughfare up the hillside beyond the centre where glorious views across rooftop chimney pots can be appreciated across the city. At the junction to Lansdown Road, Lansdown Crescent is joined by two additional rows of houses creating a unique and unusual shape. Flanked by Lansdown Place East and West they form of two additional attached crescents that are convex, compared to Lansdown Crescent's more conventional concave appearance. The overall effect is a sinuous meandering terraced row of buildings that ebb and flow across the edge of the hillside.

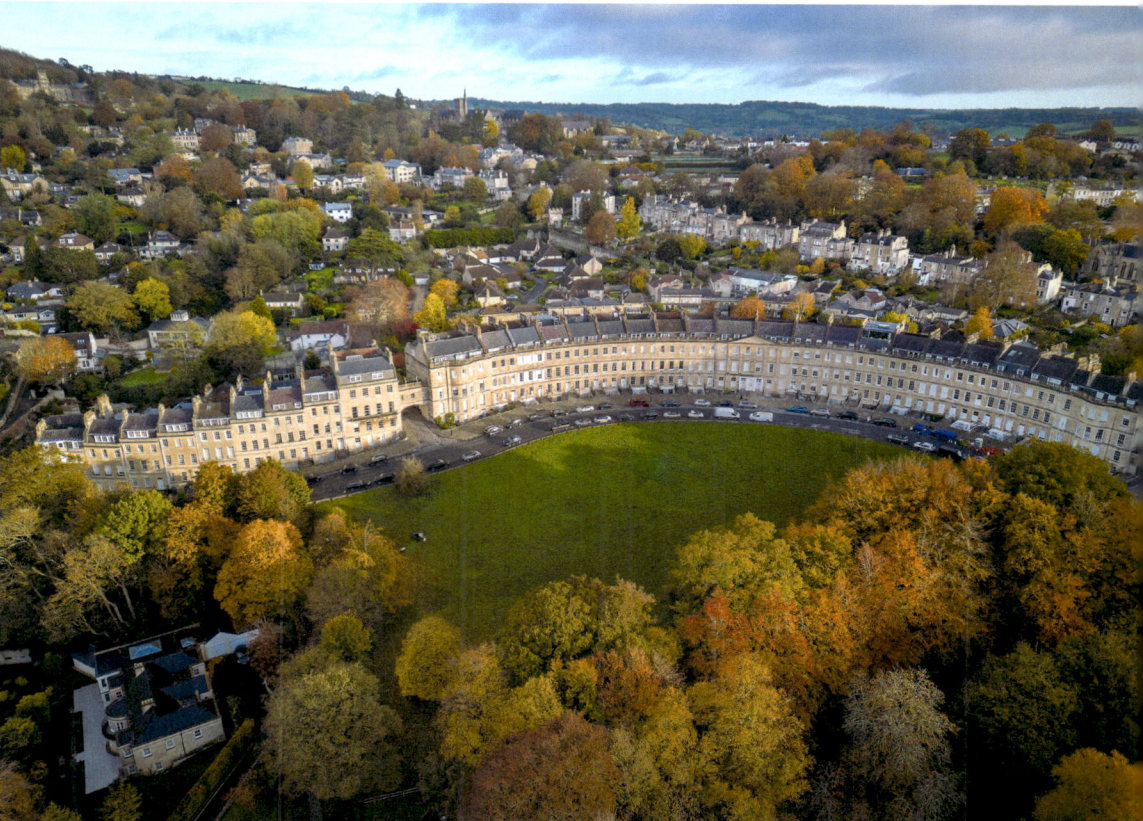

ABOVE: Lansdown Crescent is a highly desirable place to live, with properties reaching up to £5.5 million. It remains one of the city's most prestigious addresses.

SOMERSET PLACE

Somerset Place is a sweeping crescent of Grade 1 listed buildings completed in 1820 and is a prime example of Georgian architecture, characterized by its elegant symmetry, graceful proportions, and use of locally quarried Bath stone. An elevated position on the Lansdown hillside created a landmark that can be viewed from many vantage points across the city.

Designed by the renowned architect John Eveleigh, Somerset Place was commissioned by Thomas Brock to provide upscale housing for the affluent residents of Bath. The development consists of a crescent-shaped terrace of thirty houses, arranged around a central landscaped garden enclosed by iron railings. Each house features four stories above ground level, with a basement below.

A keen eyed visitor may notice that some of the buildings are missing. Originally 20 townhouses were to be built but no's 1 to 4 were never constructed due to less than suitable ground conditions and as a result the crescent has a slightly truncated appearance.

Somerset Place has one of the finest central 'broken' style pediments decorated with discs and cloth swags, a style not seen on the other crescents and notable buildings in the city. Look above the doors to also see a pair of keystones faces made of carved stone icicles peering out onto the street below.

RIGHT: the central pediment at Somerset Place is a distinctive feature that sets it apart from other Georgian terraces in Bath.

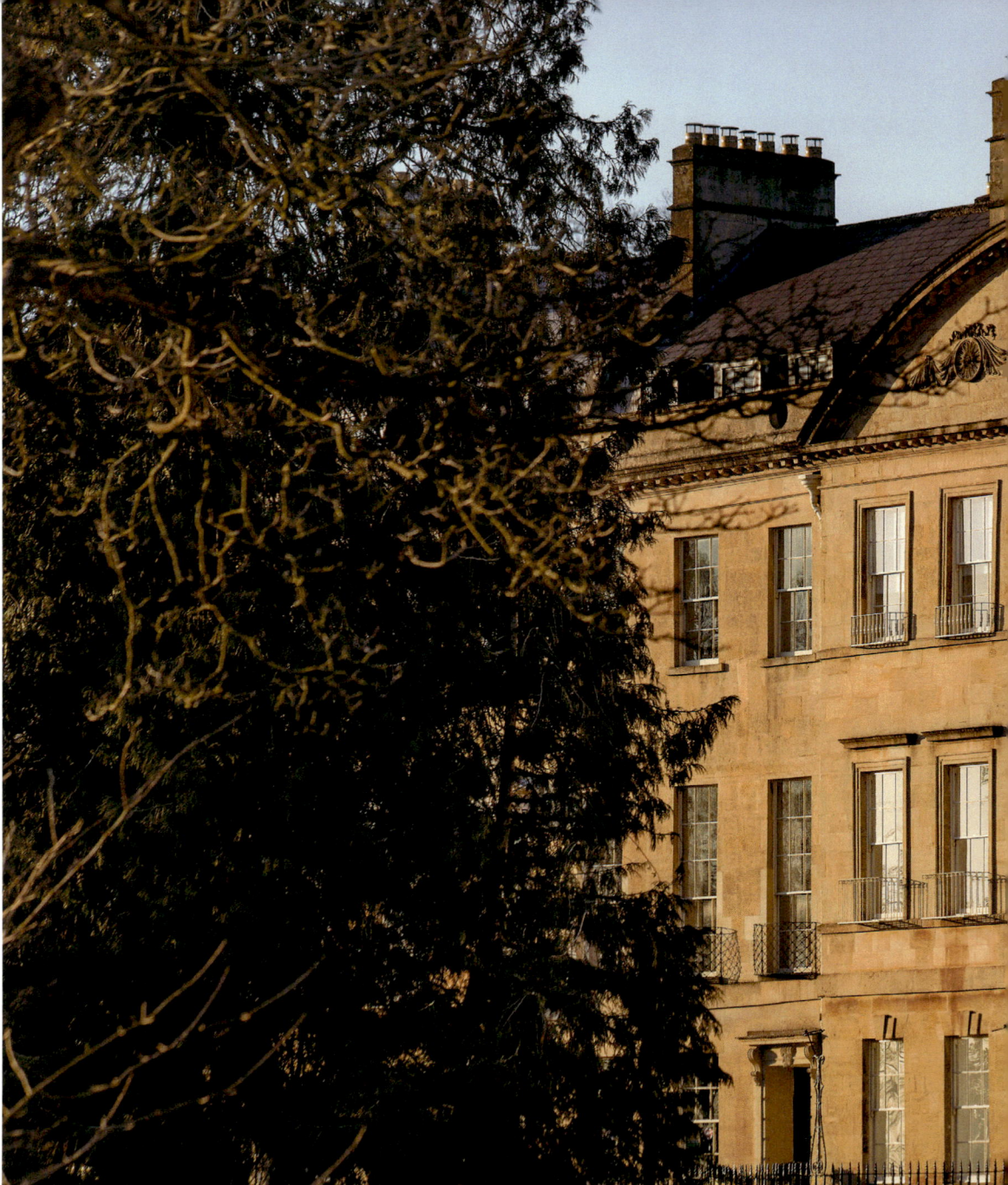

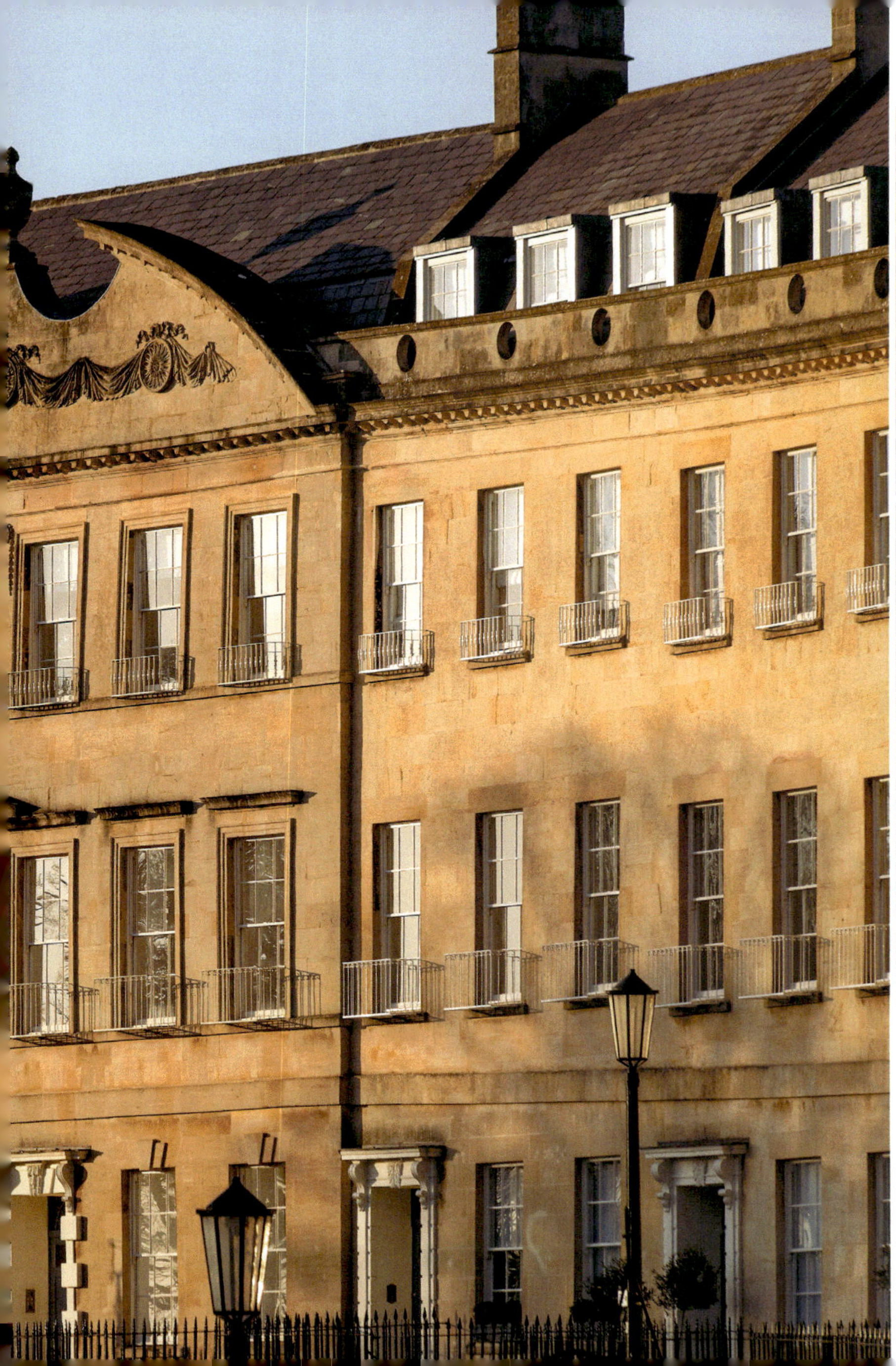

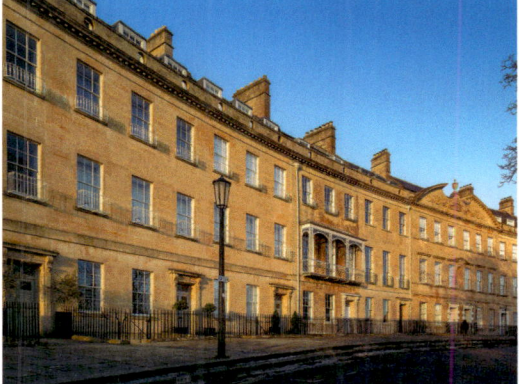

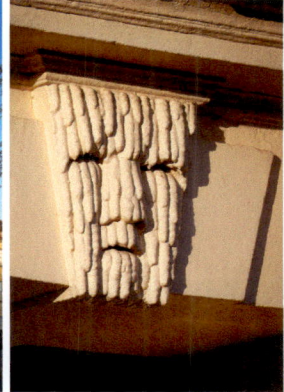

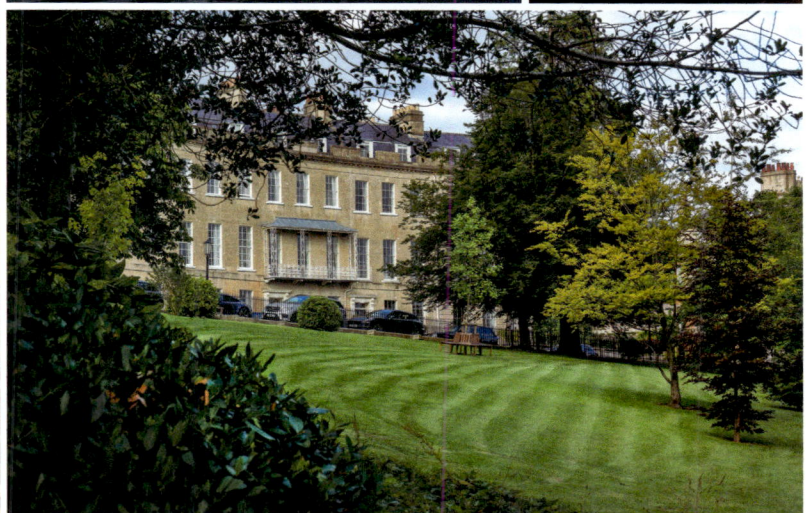

TOP LEFT: one of Bath's later Georgian crescents, Somerset Place was built between the late 18th and early 19th centuries. **TOP RIGHT**: above each door carved stone faces peer out from beneath delicate patterns resembling icicles. **ABOVE**: the residents garden at Somerset Place offers a private sanctuary, located at the front of the crescent.

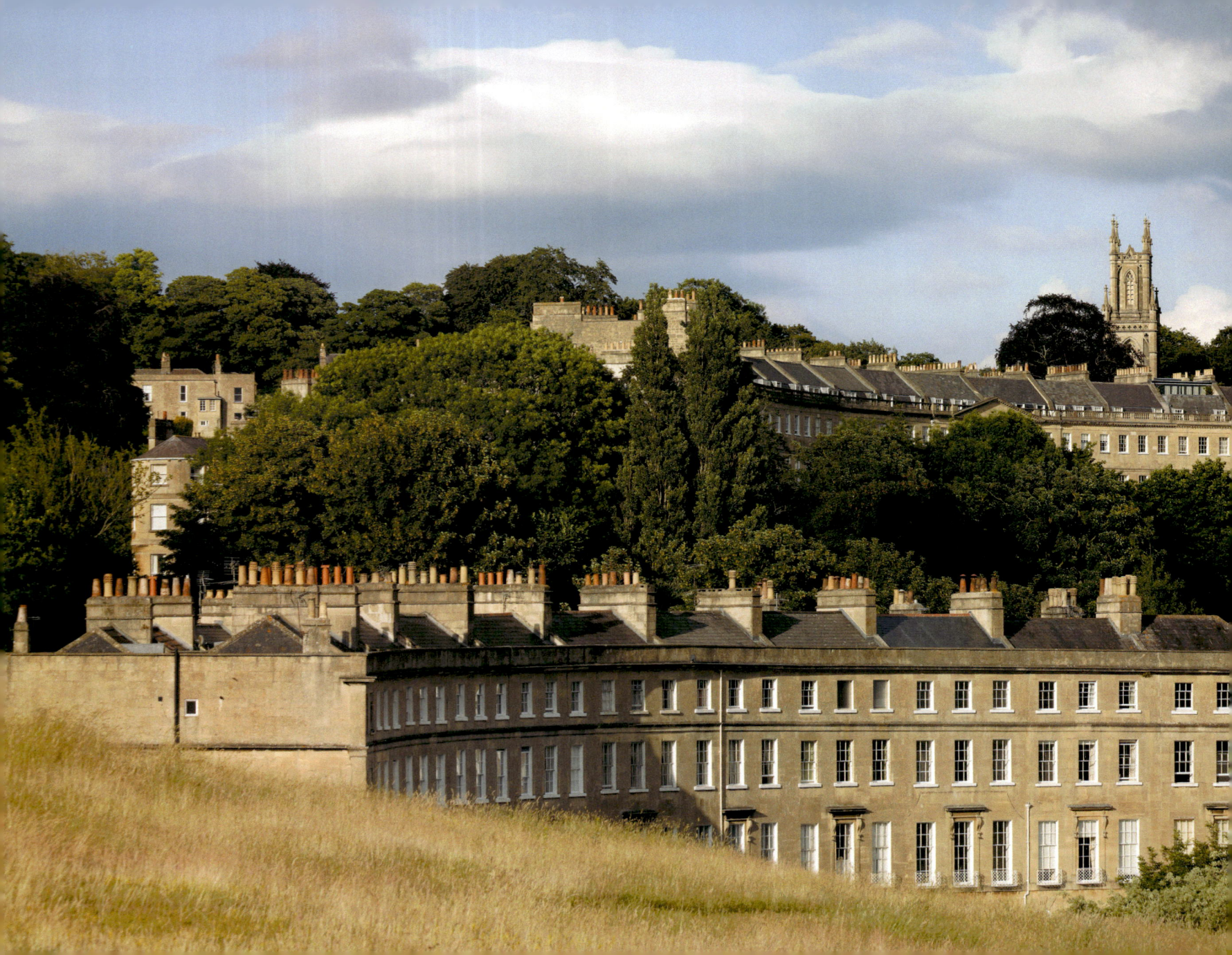

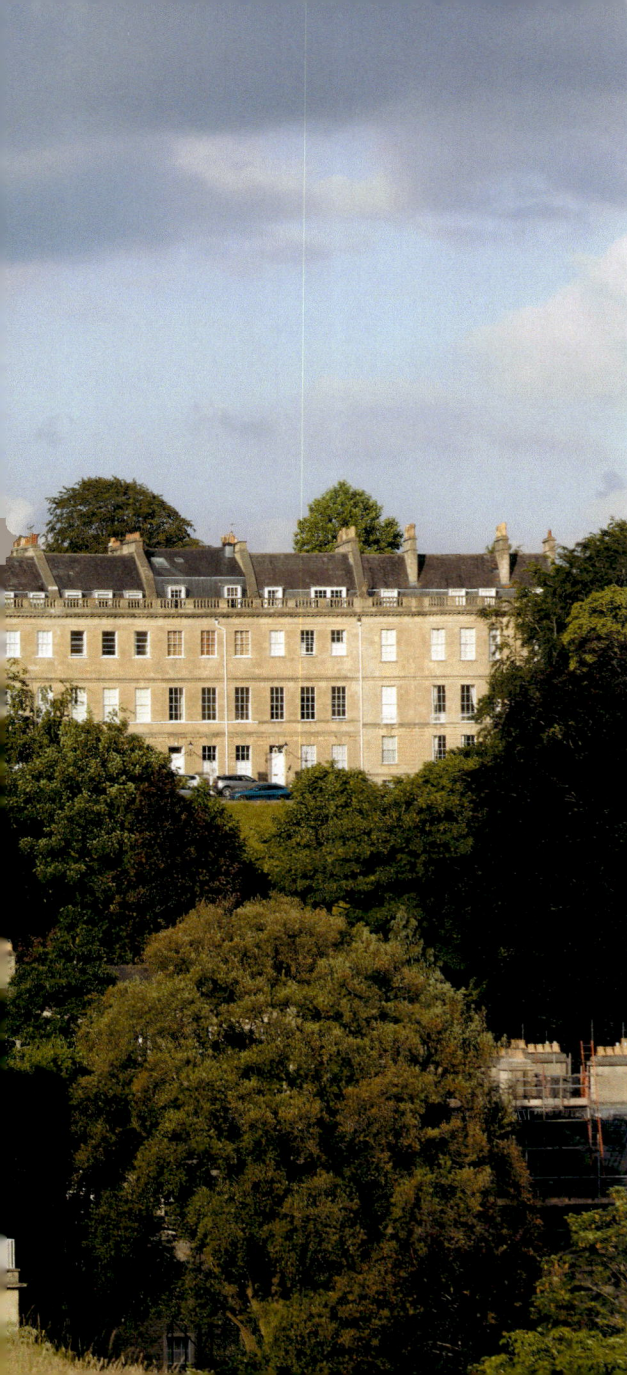

CAVENDISH ROAD & CRESCENT

Skirting the edge of Upper Common, Cavendish Road is a tree-lined street with echoes of leafy London suburbia, a distinct section of Georgian townhouses that are beautifully framed by foliage glimpsed through the boundary of the parkland opposite. The lower section comprises the back view of St James's Square, one street over. Whilst the upper section opens onto Cavendish Place, a terraced row of homes built in 1808 complete with exquisite stonework and ornate ironwork window balconies, the unmistakable stylings of a quintessential Bath street.

The northern end of Cavendish Road reveals a cluster of interesting architectural properties, notably is The Doric House; a bespoke oddity that was conceived as a gallery space for renowned rural life and landscape artist Thomas Barker who used the space to showcase his own works alongside a collection of Old Master pieces. The peculiar design emerged from a growing early 19th century trend for Philhellenism, a love of all things Greek and features a Doric temple plinth and columns.

The slender Somerset House, perched above the road junction was originally planned to be the starting property for a new terrace of houses that was never completed, just this single delightful sentinel remains. Opposite, Ivy House, another slim villa teetering on the edge of the road is a wonderful anomaly. A former shop now a converted guesthouse, its rear elevation is just as fascinating at the front, perhaps even more so. ➜

A striking arrangement showcasing three distinguished landmarks: Cavendish Crescent, Lansdown Crescent and rising above them, the tower of St. Stephen's Church.

2 LANSDOWN

One of the last Georgian set pieces to be built in Bath, Cavendish Crescent takes up a prime location on the wider slopes of Lansdown beneath Sion Hill. It is also the shortest crescent in the city, stretching to just eleven properties and reaching four storeys in height with fine views across historic common land. Designed by John Pinch the Elder under instruction of tradesman William Broom the project was started in 1815 but did not see completion until much later in 1830.

The crescent shape itself is visually striking and as with many similar properties it is the grandeur of the statement piece that shines out onto the public facing side, perfected finished stonework of the front facade that hides the fact that a quick look at the rear of the building will reveal a more modest, basic outer shell and finish. Creating a grand and imposing facade was a clever and common Georgian trait, keeping costs to minimum.

OPPOSITE: elegant Cavendish Road seems to glide effortlessly up the street.
BELOW: Ivy House rear elevation.

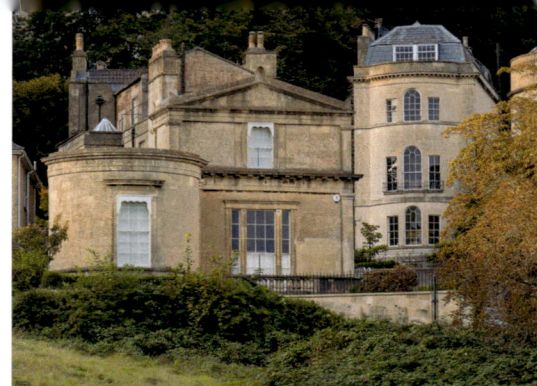

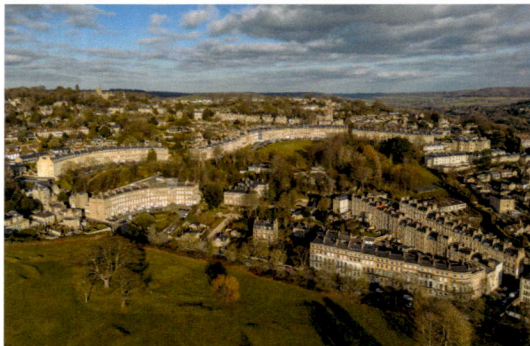

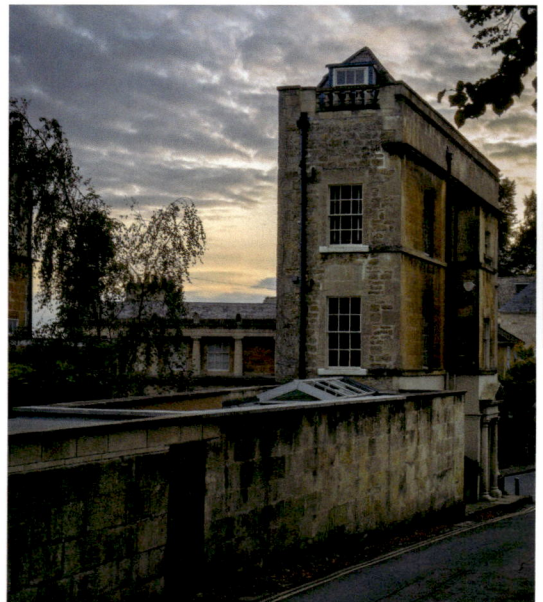

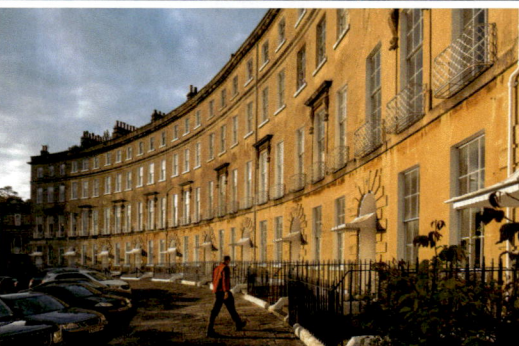

TOP: the Doric House – former residence of landscape artist Thomas Barker and Somerset House beyond.
MIDDLE: from above, it's clear why this area of Bath was a prime location for building grand statement residences.
ABOVE: golden light on Cavendish Crescent.

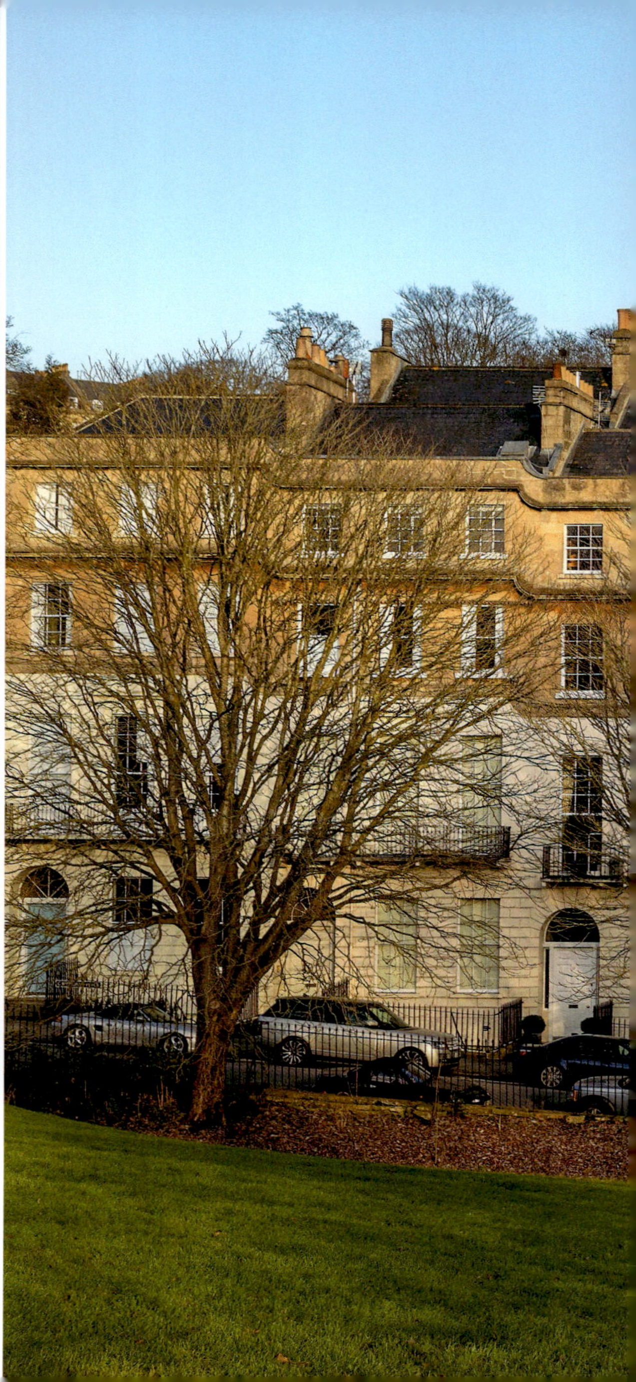

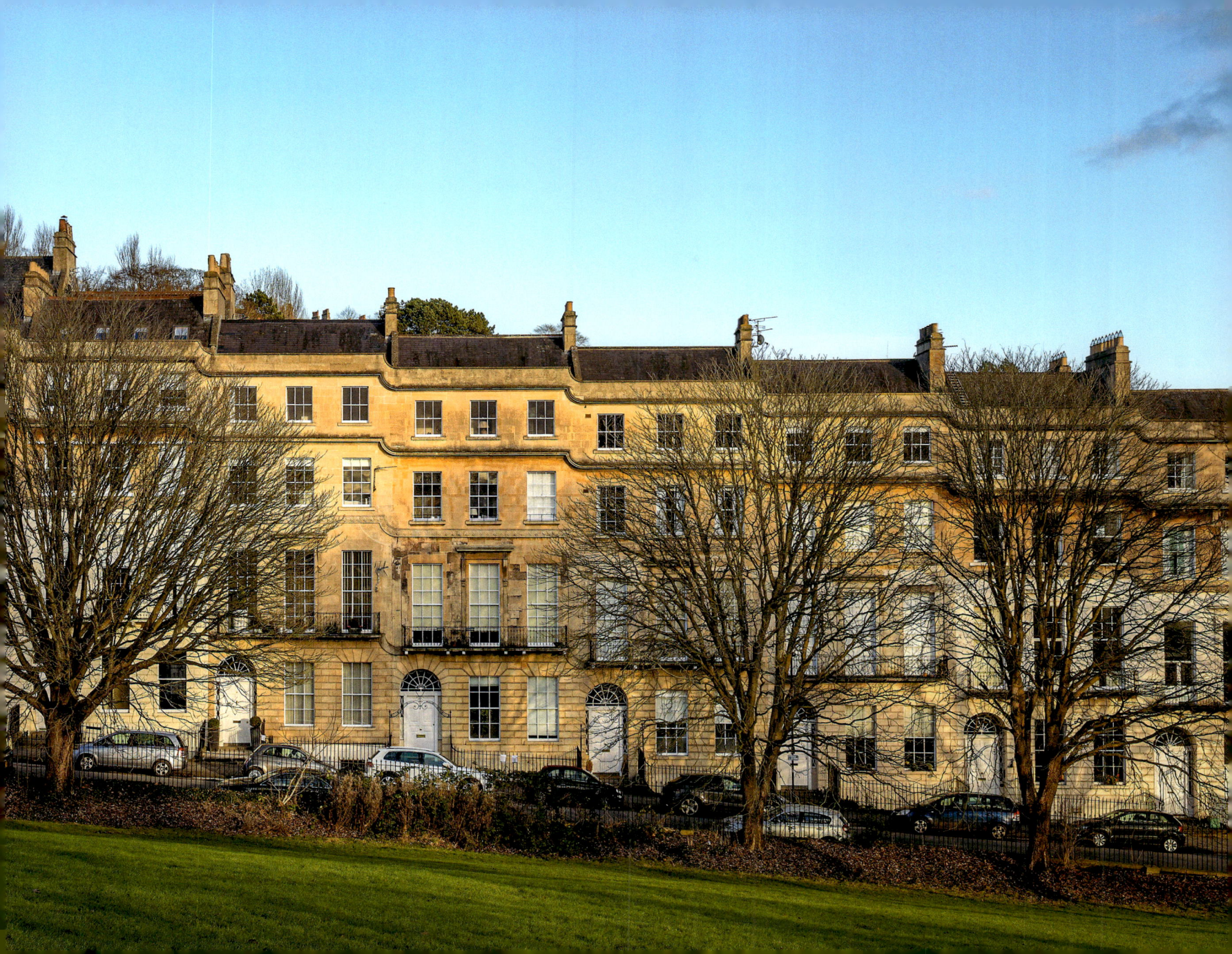

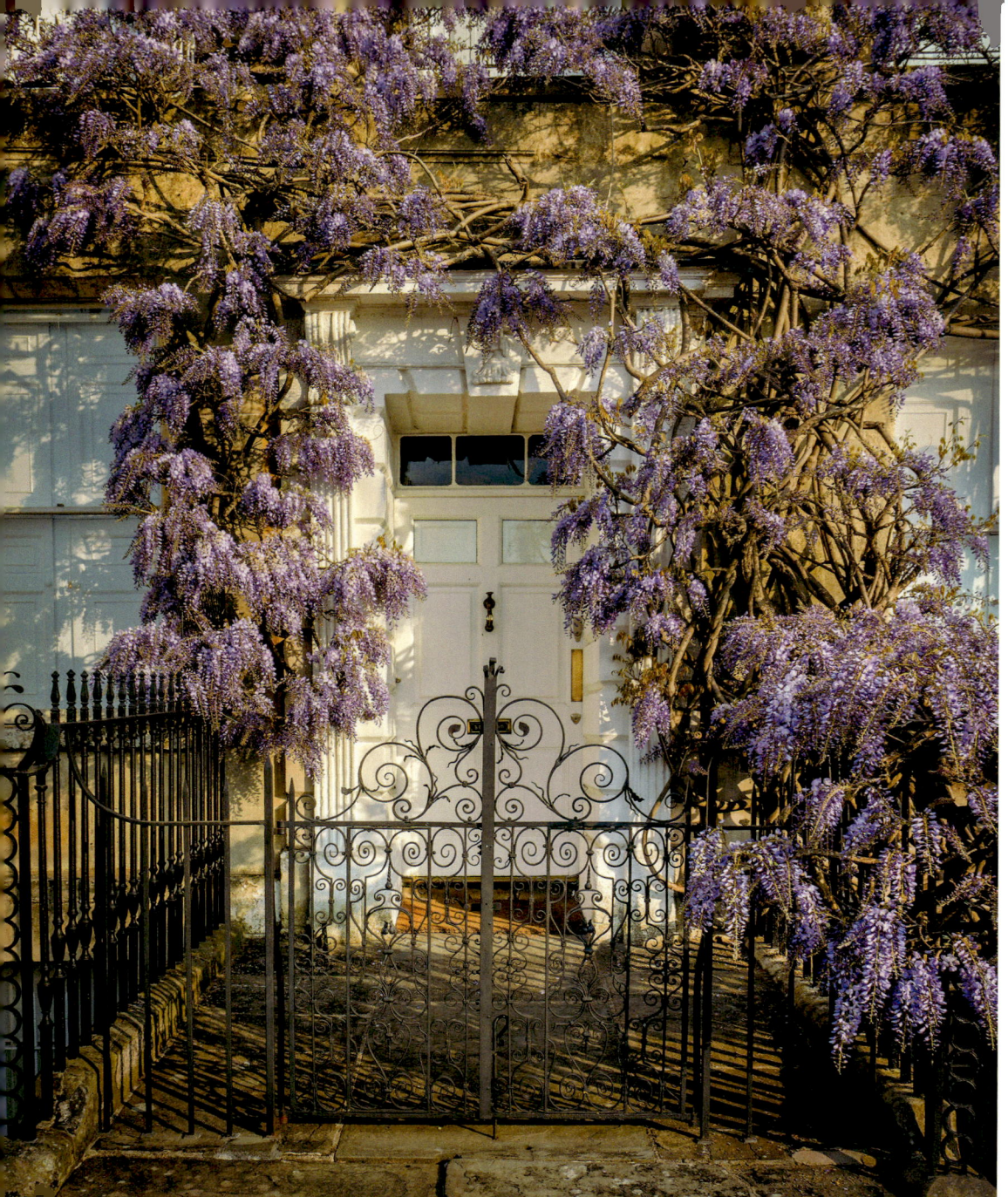

CAMDEN CRESCENT

Camden Crescent must surely be one of the most dramatically situated buildings in Bath. Originally named Upper Camden Place the crescent is perched along the spine of Lansdown Hill and dominates a commanding view on an escarpment overlooking the east and southern slopes of the city. Camden Crescent was originally intended as a perfectly symmetrical crescent of 32 homes built by John Eveleigh and completed in 1793. Standing in front of the building today it's noticeable that this dramatic statement piece was never actually finished. Terrible landslips altered the design of the crescent resulting in a shortened version. Grand columns beneath the middle pediment originally intended as the central feature now stand to one side, a further 9 buildings are missing from the eastern wing.

The full length of the crescent is either Grade I or II listed and was named after the First Earl of Camden, Charles Pratt. His family crest, the carved profile of an elephant is above each door. Another link to Bath's literary past is set here within Camden Crescent as the home lodgings to several characters from Jane Austen's novel *Persuasion*.

In early summer during the months of May and June a spectacular wisteria plant sends it's vibrant purple blooms cascading down the stonework of one of the properties. It's a popular photo, one made for sharing on social media and often features in the top ten lists of places to capture in Bath – and for good reason, it is a glorious display perfectly draped across the doorway.

LEFT: overflowing with wisteria blooms in early summer Camden Crescent has one of the most enchanting doorways in the city.

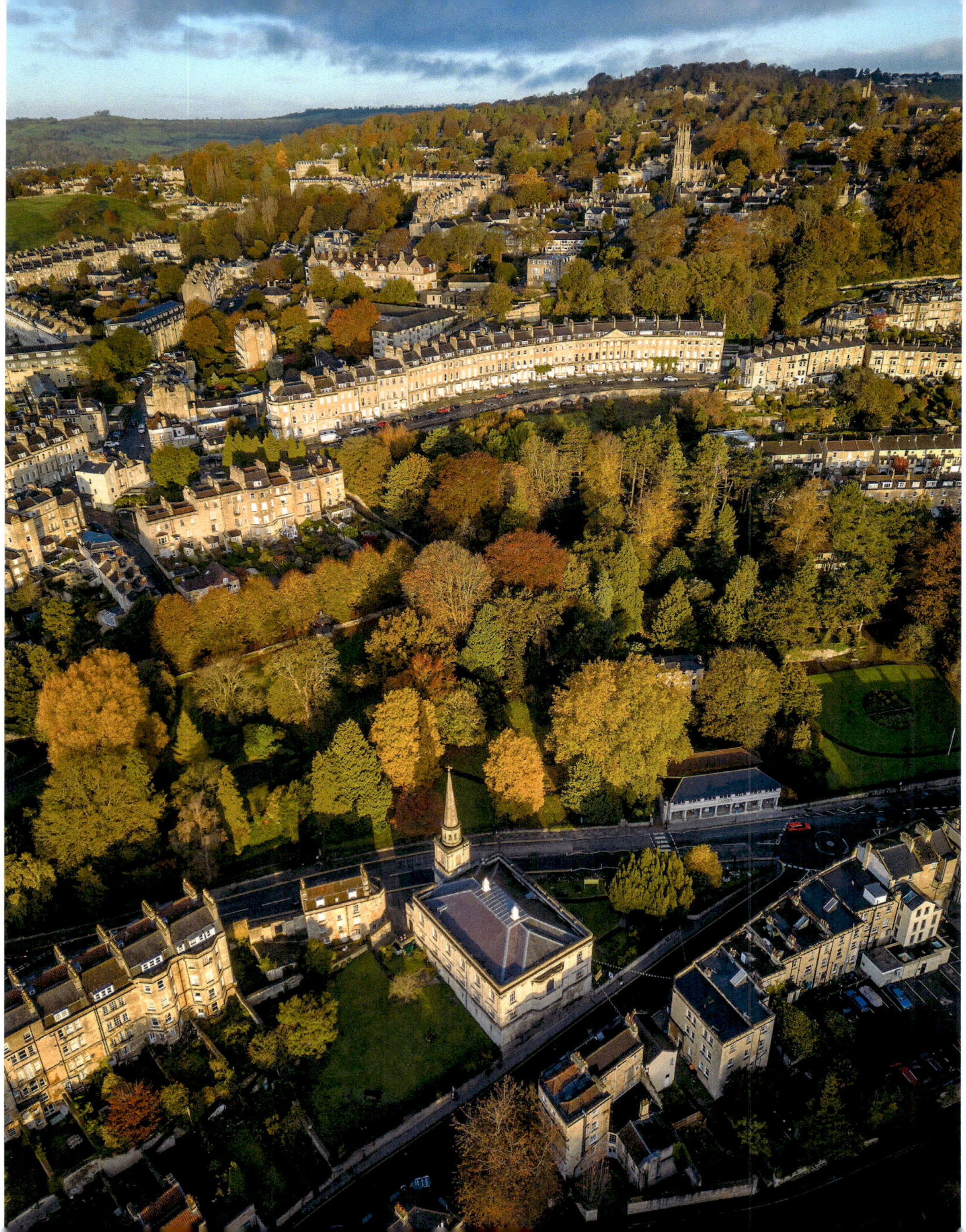

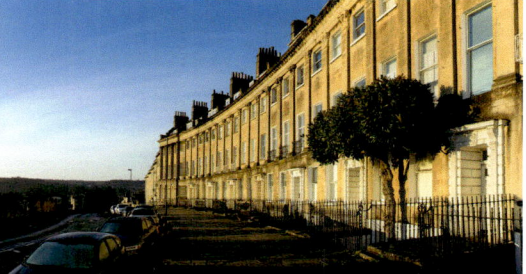

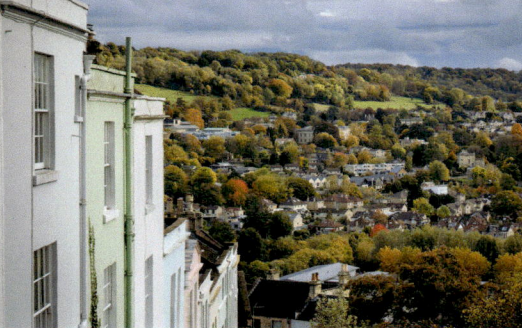

Beneath Camden Crescent lies Hedgemead Park, a grade II listed Victorian five acre pleasure ground built on the site of demolished houses and victims of earlier landslides. Mature flower borders and specimen trees fill the green space which is also home to a band stand, children's playground and dozens of benches, perfect for taking in the views through overhanging trees to the city beyond.

LEFT: Camden Crescent occupies a prominent position on the Lansdown hillside, overlooking St. Swithin's Church and Hedgemead Park. **TOP**: one for the early riser. At dawn, Camden Crescent basks in morning sunlight. **ABOVE**: further along Camden Road, vistas extend across the eastern hillsides of Bath.

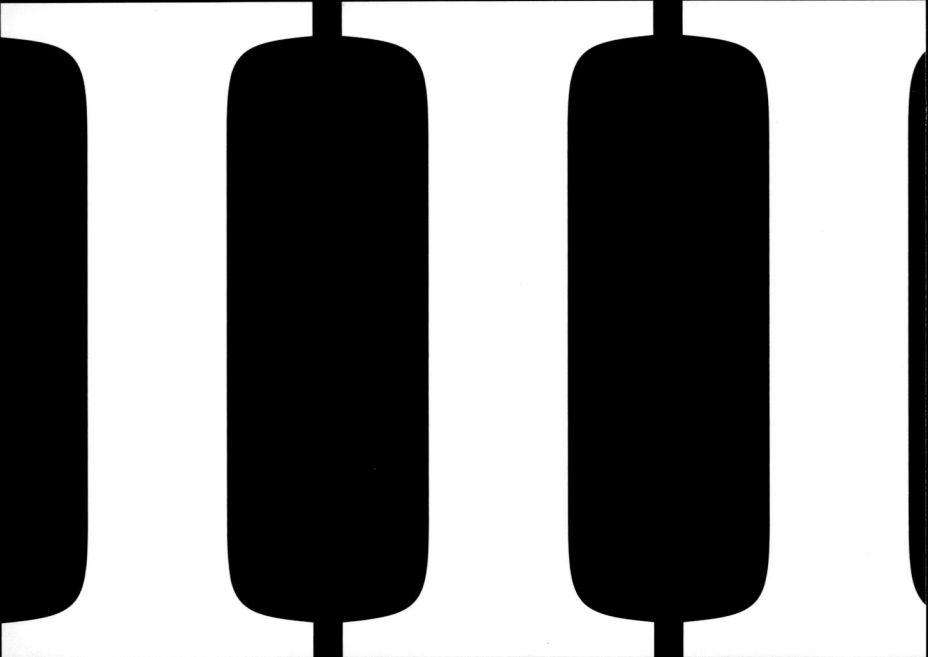

3 THE CIRCUS

> "The Circus was part of John Wood's grand vision to recreate a classical Palladian architectural landscape for Bath."
> – Jean Manco, *The Hub of the Circus: A history of the streetscape of the Circus, Bath*

> "The important evening came which was to usher her into the Upper Rooms."
> – Jane Austen, the Assembly Rooms in *Northanger Abbey* (1817)

Designed by architect, John Wood the Elder, The Circus is a perfect circle of 30 townhouses split into three equal sections with three entry points. In the centre a large expanse of lawn is dominated by enormous plane trees that reach their limbs skyward. Each section of the Circus is cleverly designed so that when seen from any of the three entrance streets you will always face directly onto the classical face of the building, experiencing the facade in its entirety.

John Wood the Elder spent much of his formative years in London absorbing the great set pieces of the capital city. He admired the vast open public spaces, grand raised parades and terraces and sought to bring them to Bath, to create a new concept city, one that would also reflect his other passion for the grandeur of Imperial Rome tinged with Druidic influences.

John Wood took the concept of a grand square and combined it with the Roman amphitheatres of the past. The Circus is a scaled down version of the Colosseum found in Rome, but instead turned inside out. Exhibiting the same styling of Doric, Ionic and Corinthian features detailed in a series of tiered columns completely encircling the design.

The Circus goes further than just a grand statement piece of Georgian architecture, it also has a deeper significance and is supposedly positioned on ley lines which run through this point towards the Royal Crescent in the west. John Wood the elder admired greatly the ancient settlers believing that Bath and its source of healing waters was the heart of Druidic Britain and designed the Circus to match the diameter of Stonehenge in Wiltshire.

The northern side of the Circus started construction in 1754, though barely three months into the build John Wood the Elder died leaving it up to his son John Wood the Younger to complete his father's masterpiece. It wasn't until almost fifteen years later in 1769 when the circle was complete and John Wood the Elder's own elegant vision of Rome could be admired.

THE CIRCUS

Postcode: BA1 2EW
what3words: spoken.tune.shelf

THE GEORGIAN GARDEN

Postcode: BA1 2NR
what3words: diary.rare.olive

THE ASSEMBLY ROOMS

Postcode: BA1 2QH
what3words: intend.venues.wire

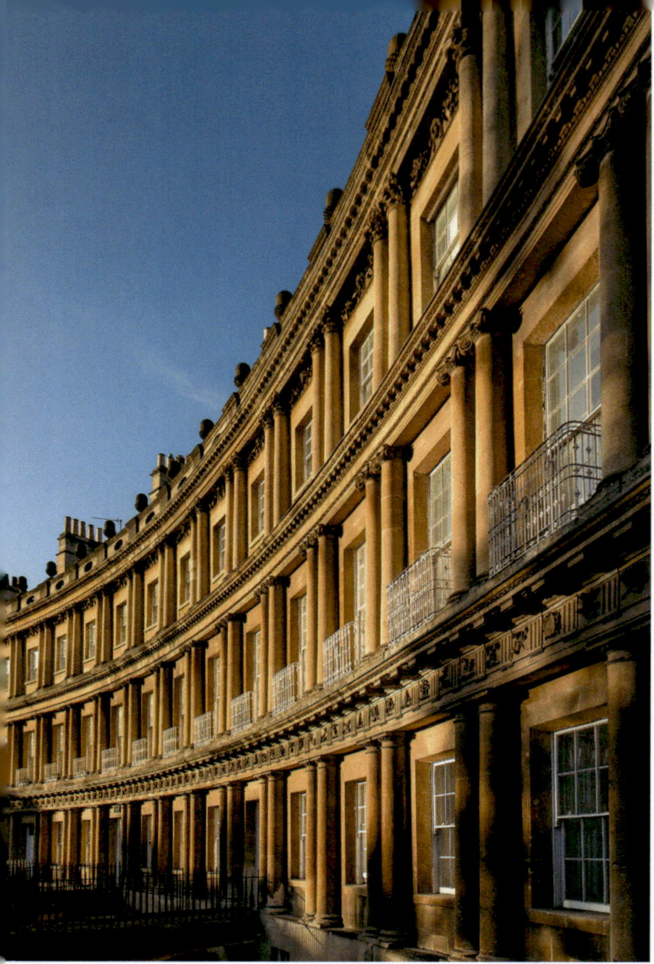

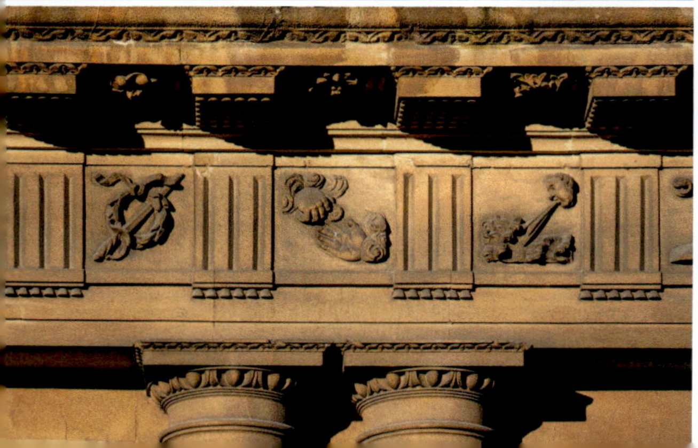

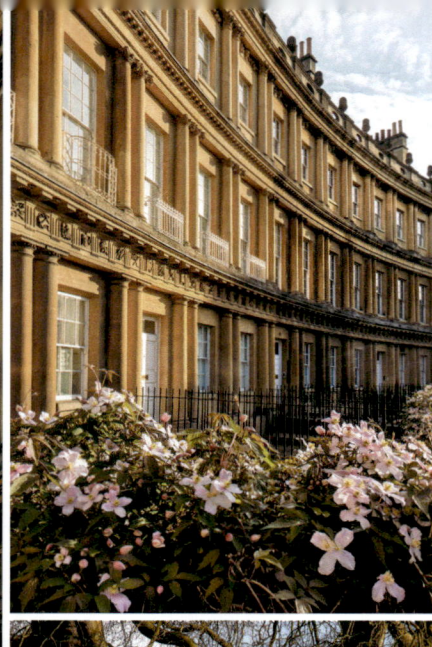
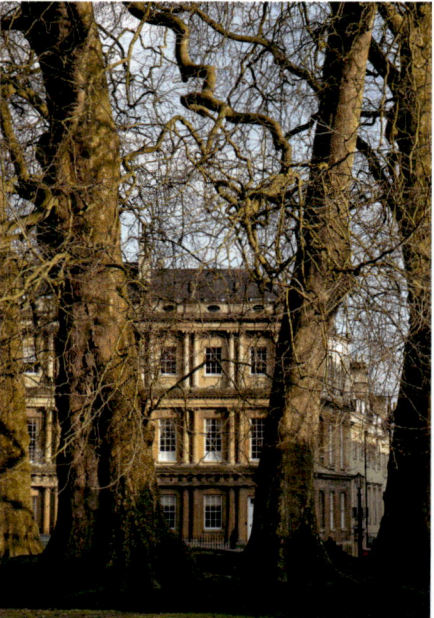
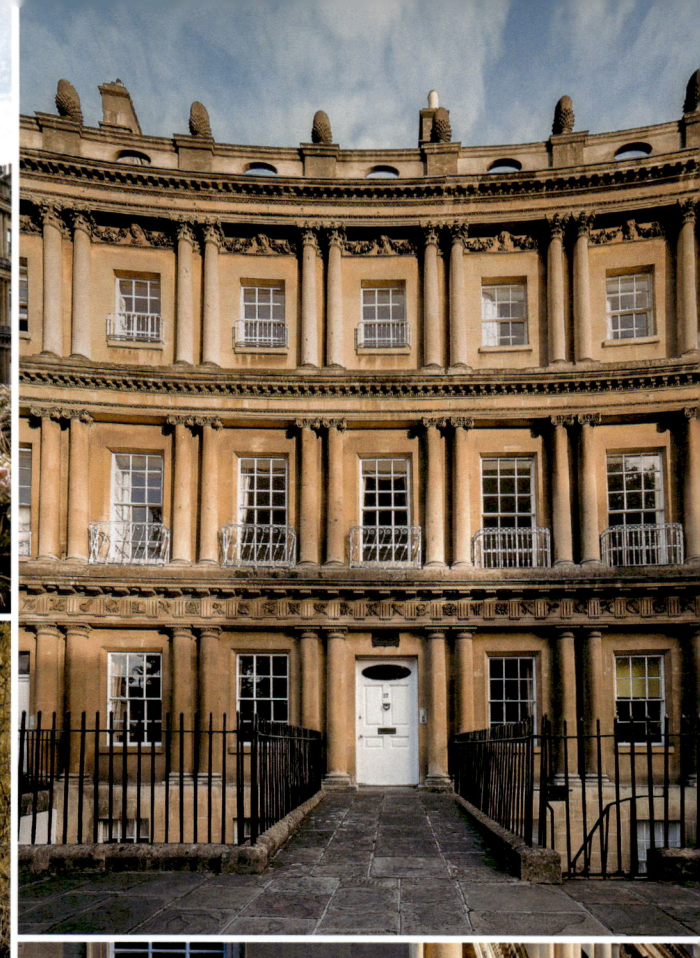
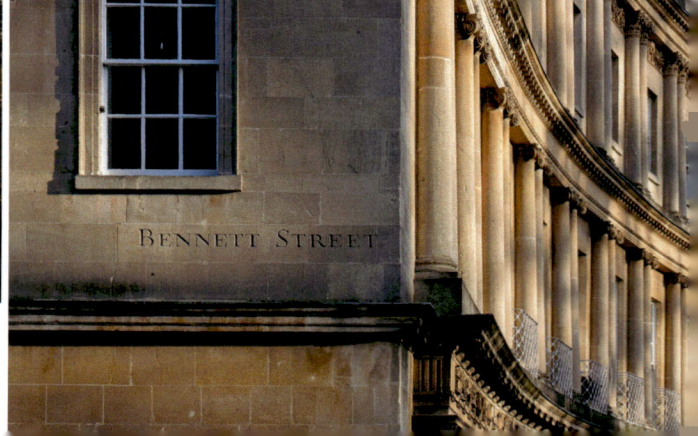

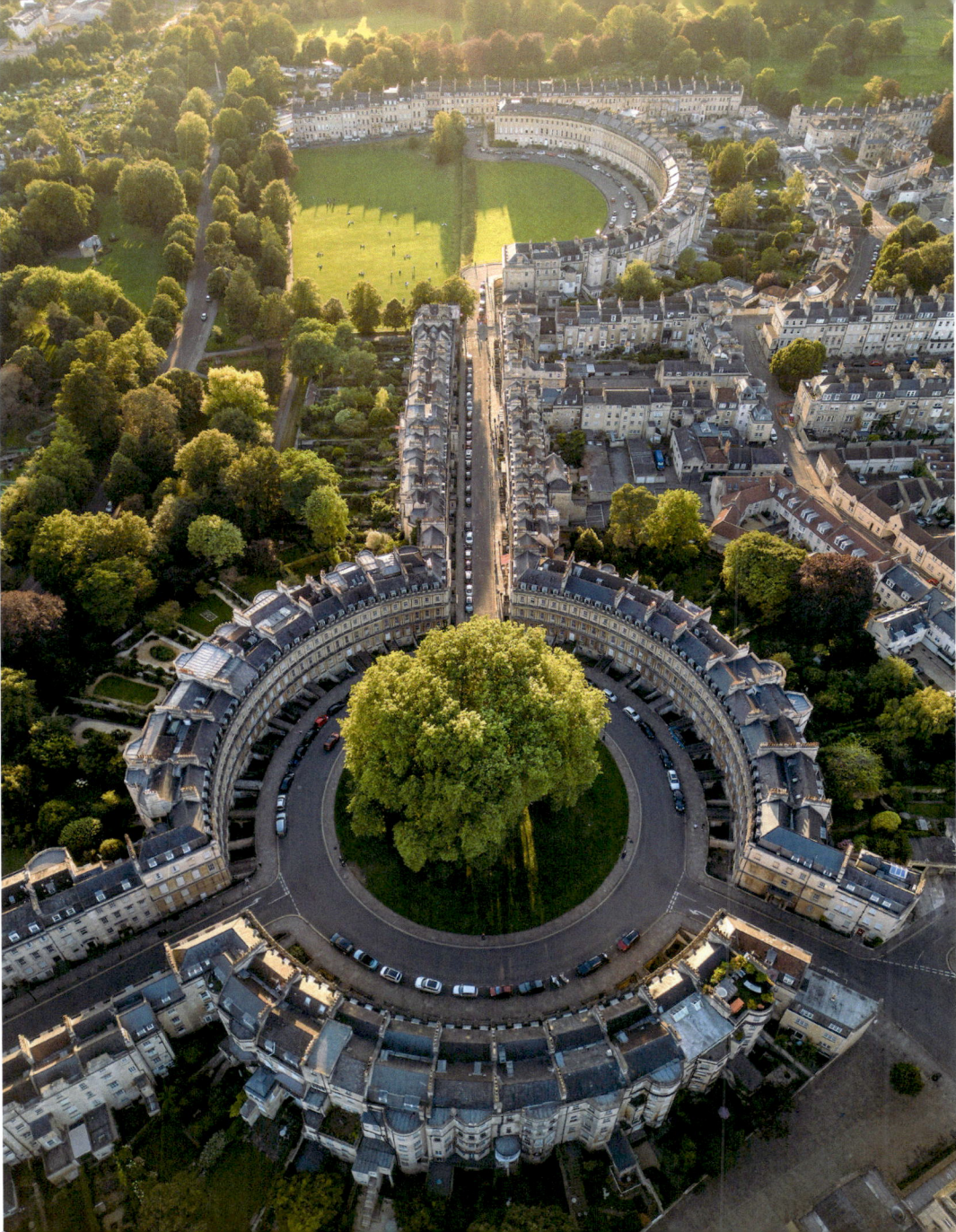

THE CIRCUS

From above a birds eye view of the Circus and the Royal Crescent resembles the shape of a sun and moon symbols that both feature in the rites and rituals of Freemasonry. The outline of the Circus itself is highly significant in that it forms part of a key shape when combined with Queens Square in the south, Gay Street also forming the stem section of the key. The Circus has an incredible collection of carved stone reliefs spanning the entire ground floor. Scenes of art, crafts and scientific imagery along with fantastic creatures form part of 525 unique emblems displayed along a frieze above the doors and windows.

Along the roofline a row of acorns can be seen, 108 in total line the parapet. It is unclear what they represent, though they may depict the acorns eaten by pigs belonging to King Bladud, legendary king of the Britons and original founder of Bath who had discovered the original source of city's healing waters in a spring nearby. Acorns are included on the Bath coat of arms, see page 22.

OPPOSITE TOP LEFT: quintessentially Bath – the graceful sweep of the Circus. **TOP MIDDLE**: clematis flowers cover the railings at the entrances of some properties.
TOP RIGHT: each property is a mansion in its own right, spanning six floors. **BOTTOM LEFT**: carved pictorial emblems depict symbols of science, art and masonic themes.
BOTTOM MIDDLE: the central plane trees are estimated to be over two centuries old. **BOTTOM RIGHT**: the Circus is accessed symmetrically from three sides by adjoining streets.

LEFT: from above the Circus seamlessly connects to The Royal Crescent through Brock Street and is said to symbolise the union of the sun and crescent moon.

3 THE CIRCUS

THE GEORGIAN GARDEN

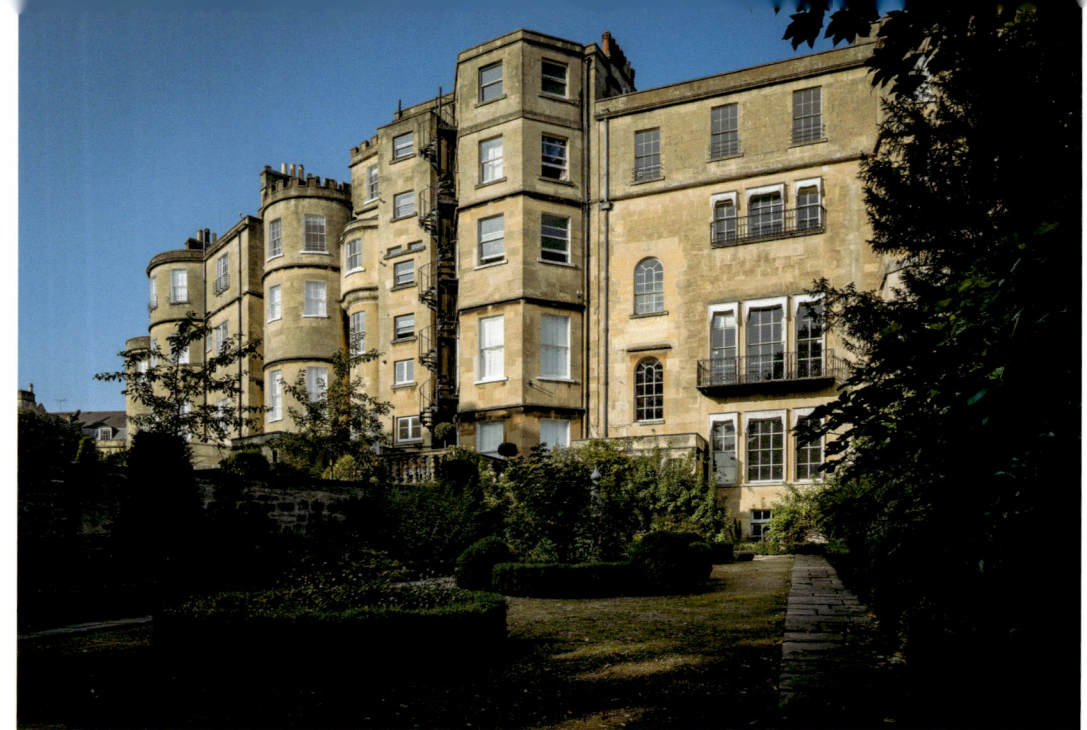

Located directly behind south side of the Circus is a faithfully restored recreation of an 18th Century town garden. Original plans dating from the 1760s reveal that there was a formal outdoor space here. Archaeological excavations in 1985 peeled back the layers initially from a modern garden layout, through to Victorian times and on deeper still to the first formal Georgian garden and the presence of flowerbeds, borders and framework supports.

Access to the garden is from the rear of The Circus along a route called Gravel Walk. The long narrow garden is flanked on each side by long borders crammed full of authentic Georgian plant species gleamed from historic records and mainly comprise of Roses, Geraniums, Rosemary, Holly, Figs and seasonal displays.

MORE INFORMATION

 visitbath.co.uk
Search 'Georgian Gardens' at the Visit Bath website to find out more about the botanical gardens including directions and a map. Free to enter.

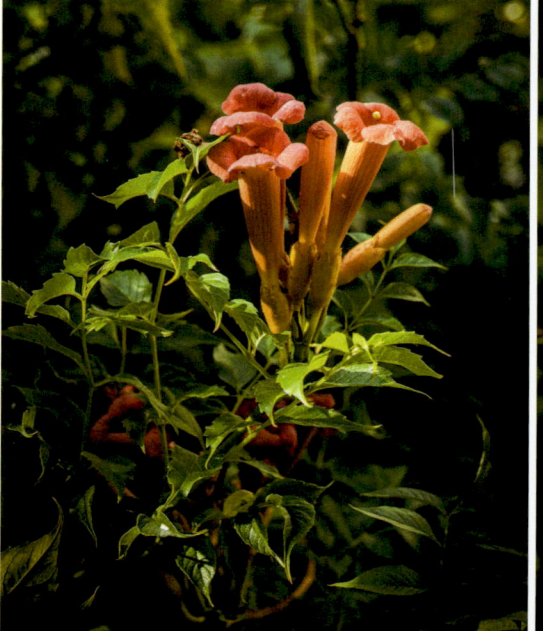 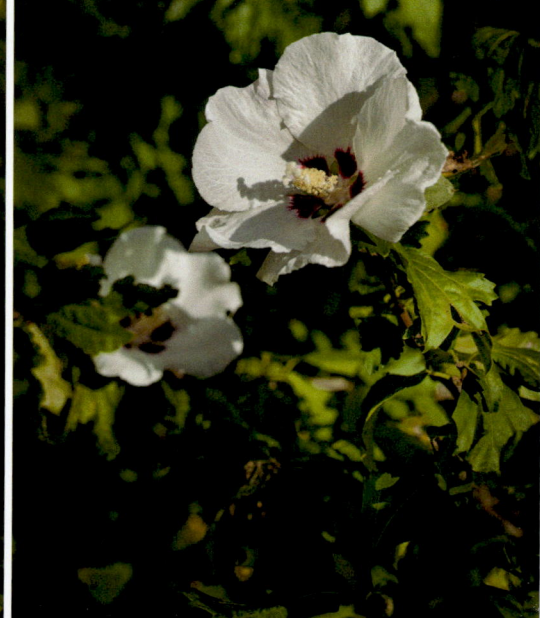

TOP: tucked behind the towering rear facade of the Circus, the Georgian Garden offers a serene and picturesque retreat faithfully reconstructed from original 18th century designs. **RIGHT**: campsis radicans, Trumpet Vine.
FAR RIGHT: malva species flower.

THE ASSEMBLY ROOMS

Located at the heart of fashionable society, the Assembly Rooms were the place to be seen in Georgian Bath. Built in 1771 for music and dancing, each of the four internal rooms hosted exclusive events and socialising.

The name comes from a place where residents could 'assemble' for live musical functions and dances. The largest gatherings accommodated up to 800 guests, where nobility and gentry sought potential suitors, akin to a giant dating service.

All rooms interlocked, allowing guests to move between them for entertainment. The Great Octagon, Ballroom, and two function halls were spaces to enjoy popular trends like tea drinking and playing cards. The ballroom, 30 metres long and 13 metres high, has the largest Georgian interior in Bath – perfect for period gatherings with ample room for wide dresses to flow.

Five intricate crystal chandeliers hang low, the only light source creating an intimate atmosphere during social soirees. These decorative lights were the only surviving part of the Assembly Rooms, removed for restoration before a WW2 bombing in 1942 destroyed the roof and interior.

Each September, the Jane Austen Festival welcomes attendees in full Regency attire to parade through Bath before evening events at the Assembly Rooms. Fans of the novelist and Georgian period visit from across the globe. The Regency era remains popular and the Assembly Rooms have been used in films such as *Persuasion* and *Bridgerton*.

MORE INFORMATION

nationaltrust.org.uk
Search 'Assembly Rooms, Bath' at the National Trust website to find out more.

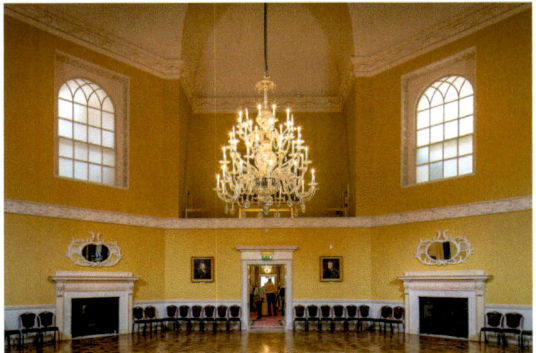
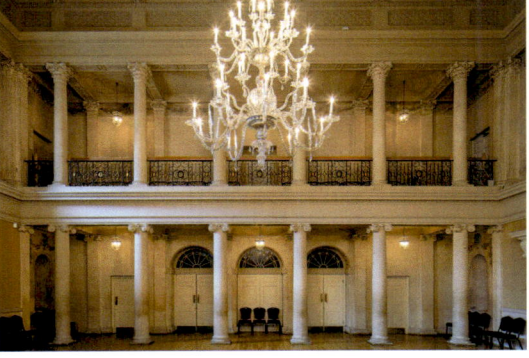

TOP: a highlight of upper-class Georgian society was a visit to the Assembly Rooms. **ABOVE LEFT**: gaming was central to Georgian high society and the Card Room blended social intrigue with high stakes. **ABOVE RIGHT**: the Tea Room complete with Georgian chandelier and upper gallery.

IV

4 THE PARAGON

Jane Austen stayed with her aunt and uncle, the Leigh-Perrots, at No. 1 The Paragon during her visits to Bath in the late 1790s and early 1800s. These experiences influenced her portrayal of Bath in her novels.

"While many pubs have adapted and modernised to stay afloat, Bath's old Star Inn stays gloriously unchanged."
2022, The Guardian

Jane Austen's parents were married at St Swithin's on 26 April 1764 and her father George Austen is buried there.

The buildings of the Paragon are an early example of an architectural concept that was starting to transform Bath beyond straight lines and rectangular buildings, boldly announcing the arrival of the crescent gold rush era to the city.

Built in 1768 and noted as the longest Georgian terrace, it is thought to be the first 'designed' crescent in Britain. Its row of uniform townhouses, symmetrical in design, seemingly disappear into the distance. At street side the townhouses extend to four storeys before dropping steeply over cellar spaces to the rear towering over Walcot Street below.

One of Bath's earliest Georgian terraces is here, branching off the Paragon, the Vineyards faces east upon an enormous raised pavement. The row of townhouses vary in size and shape, each unique with delightful period features. Tucked away on the north side of the Paragon is The Museum of Architecture which houses a complete architectural story of Bath.

A public house has stood at the end of the Vineyards since 1759, pre-dating the Paragon opposite. The Star Inn has an original framed liqueur licence dated 1776 belonging to one of the first landlords still hanging behind the bar. Ordering a drink here retains the 'ways of old' where ale is first dispensed into a large glass jug from barrels on the floor before being tipped into pint glasses at the bar. The interior hasn't altered much since restoration in the mid-20th century, a series of small panelled rooms creating a characterful time capsule.

Located directly behind the Star Inn is the tall imposing Walcot School, a much later addition to the street built in 1841 by architect James Wilson Esq. who incorporated styling hints taken from classic ornamental Italian designs.

THE PARAGON
Postcode: BA1 5NA
what3words: less.silver.stump

THE VINEYARDS
Postcode: BA1 5NB
what3words: locked.expect.rubble

THE STAR INN
Postcode: BA1 5NA
what3words: spoil.certified.cared

WALCOT SCHOOL
Postcode: BA1 5NB
what3words: rewarding.case.aside

ST SWITHINS CHURCH
Postcode: BA1 5LY
what3words: bottle.match.dawn

MORE INFORMATION
museumofbatharchitecture.org.uk
Visit the Museum of Bath Architecture website for opening times, admission and directions.

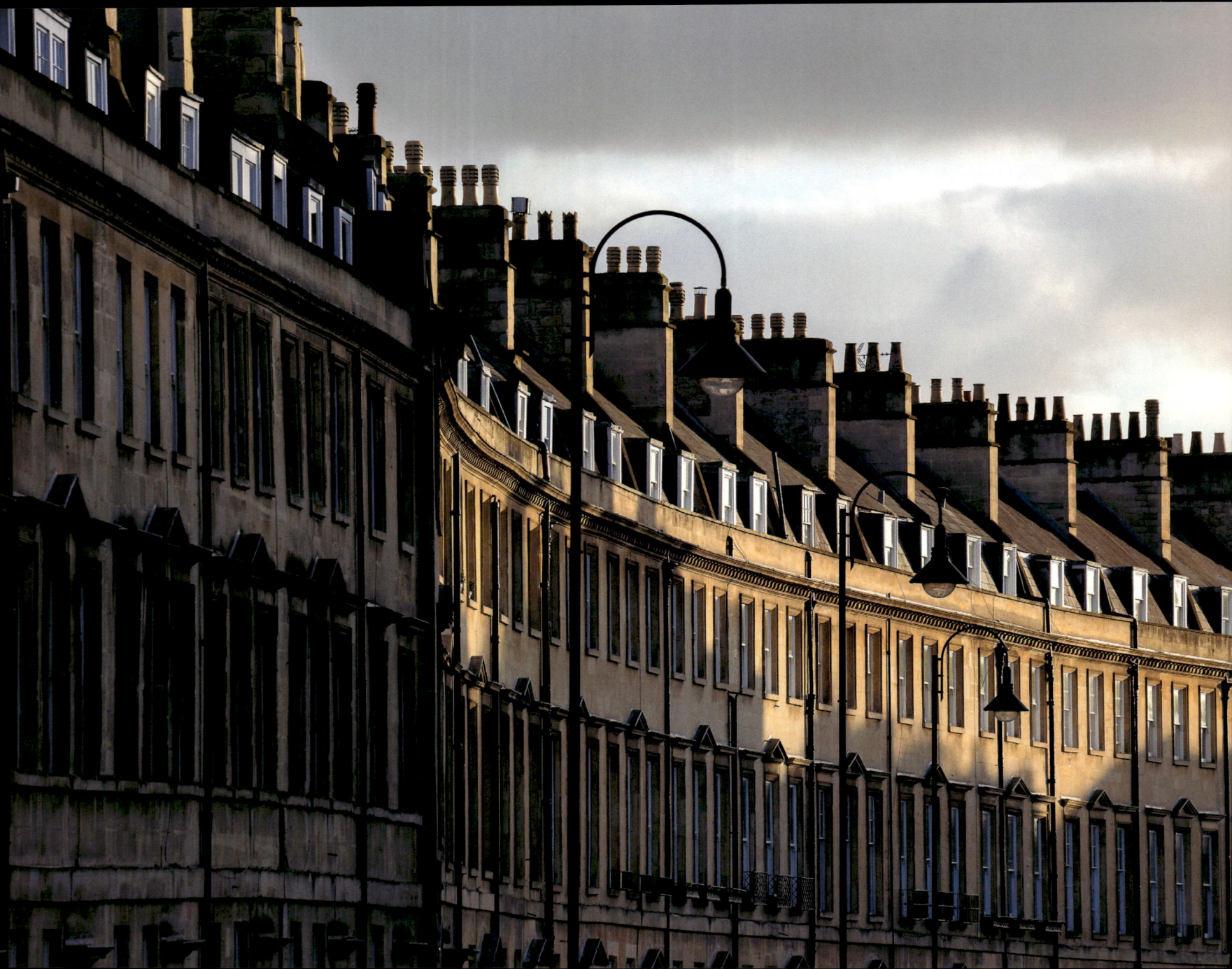

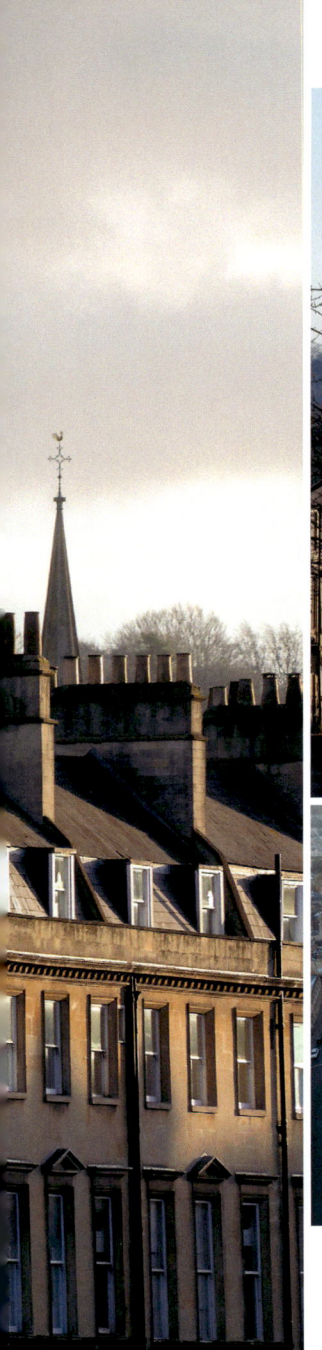
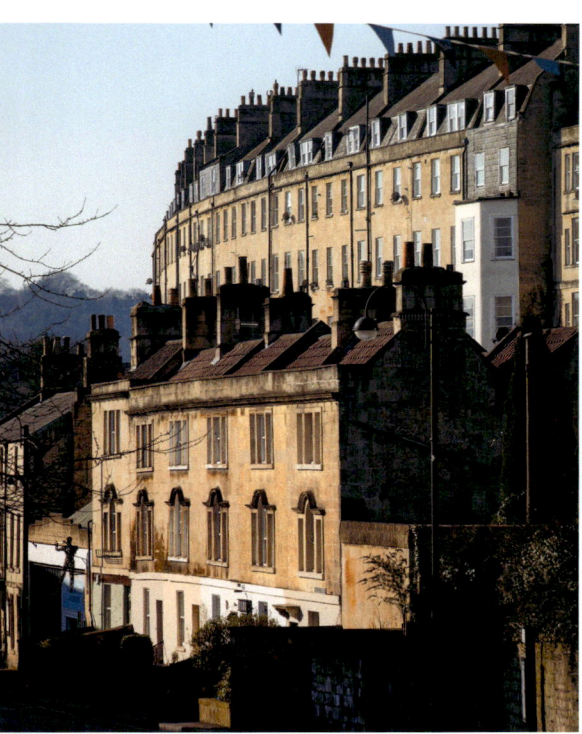
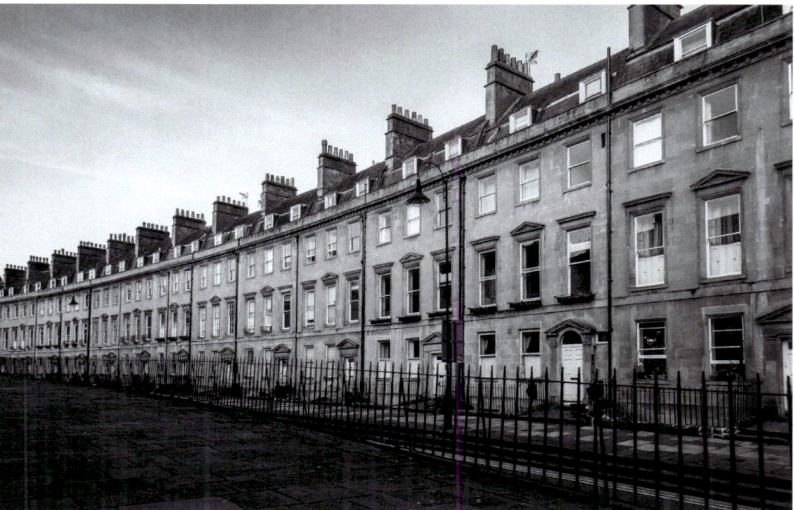

THE PARAGON

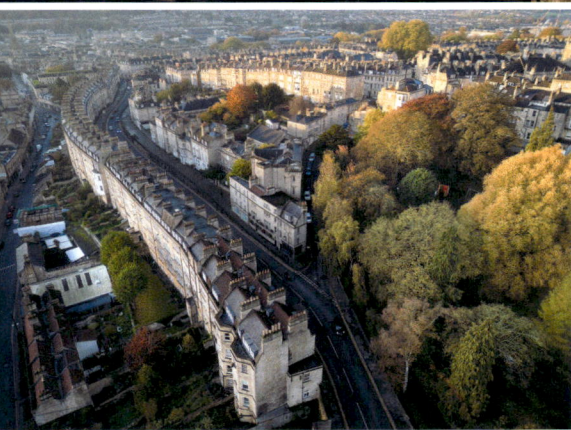

OPPOSITE: one of the longest continuous terraces in Bath, The Paragon is an elegant Georgian row that showcases the city's signature style of architecture.

TOP LEFT: towering over Walcot Street below, The Paragon is an extraordinary feat adapting to the city's undulating terrain. **LEFT:** historically the main route through Bath, The Paragon follows the route of the modern day A4 road. **ABOVE:** in total, 37 Grade I listed buildings form part of Thomas Warr Attwood's original design.

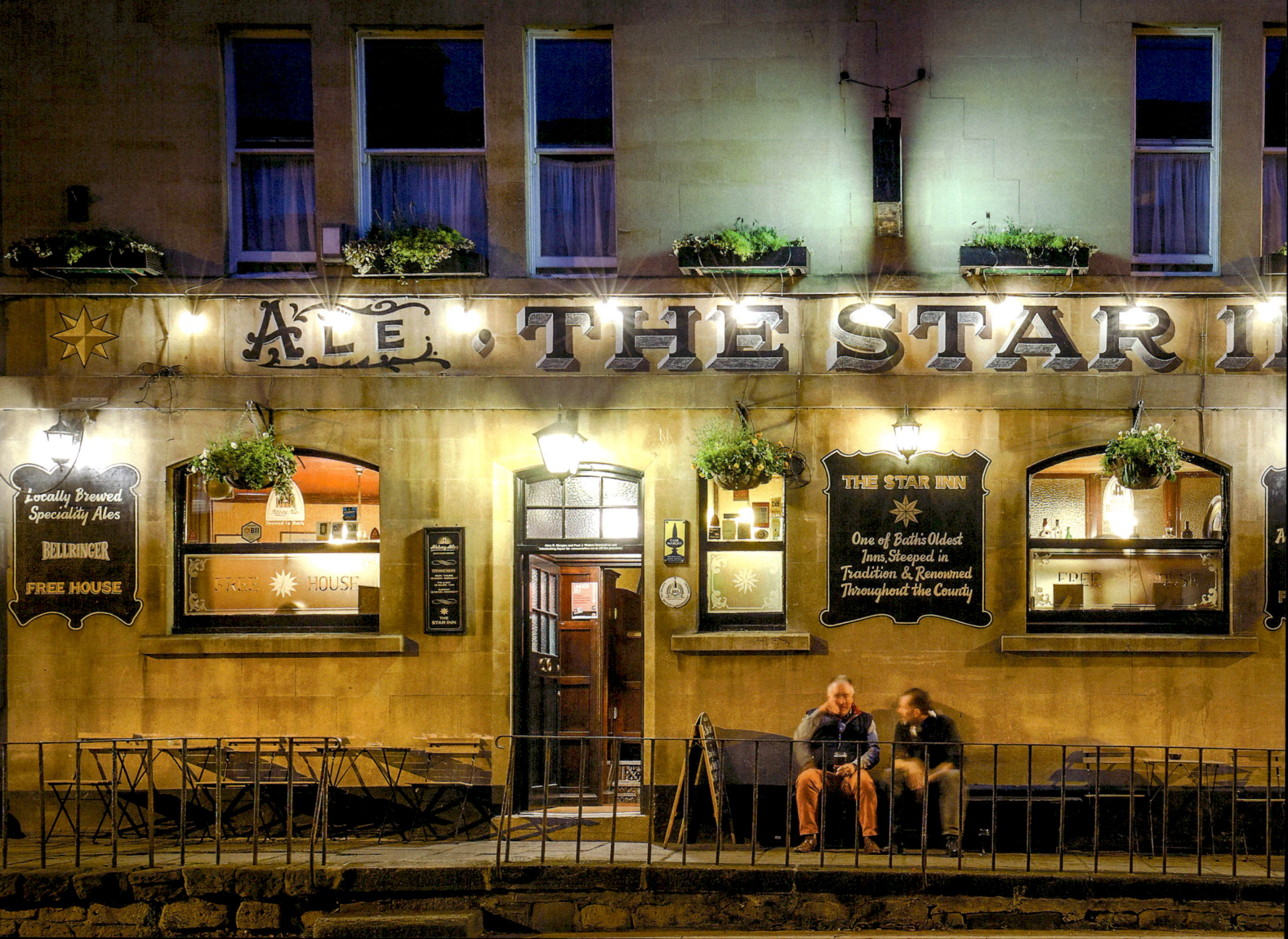

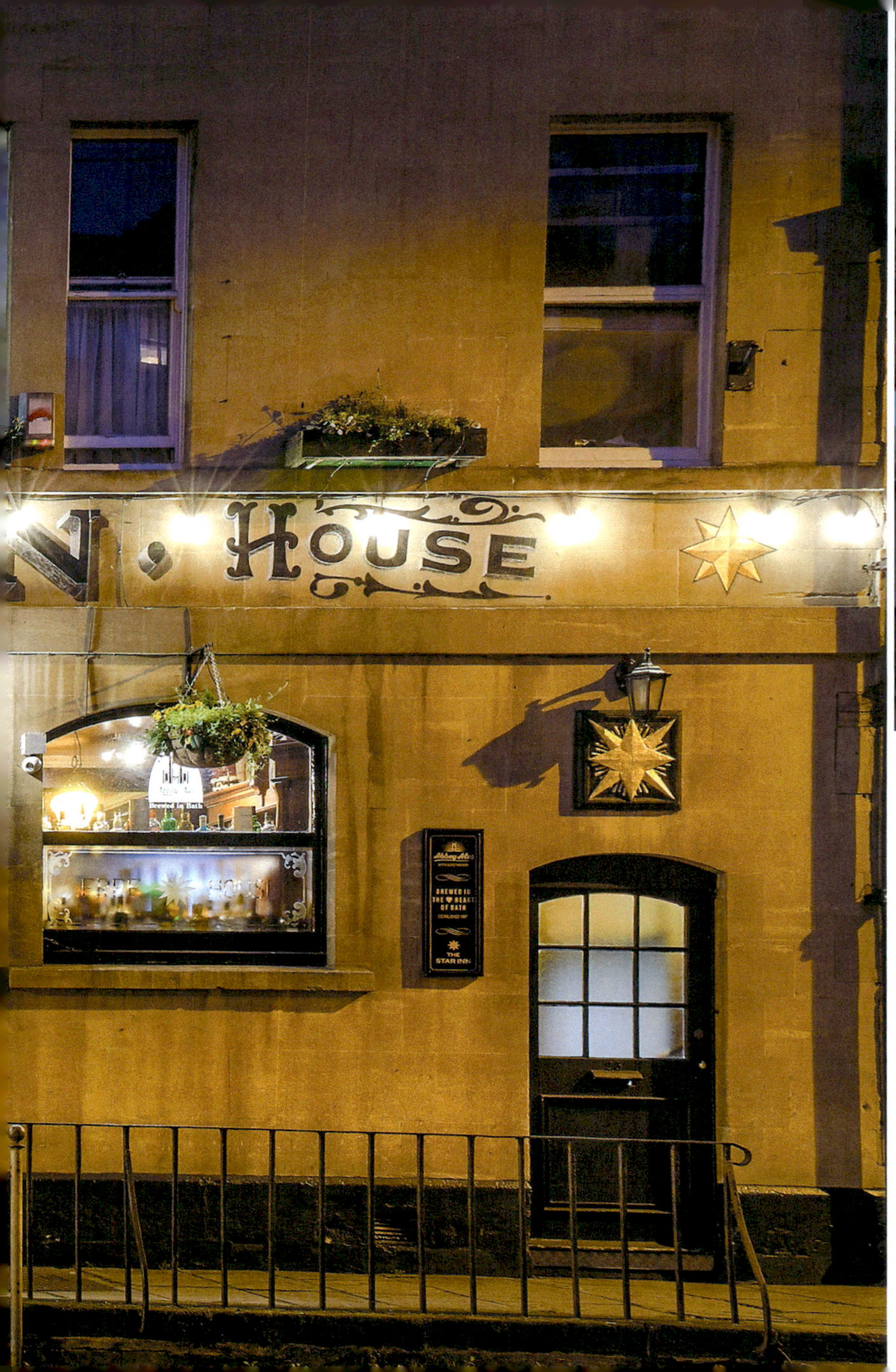

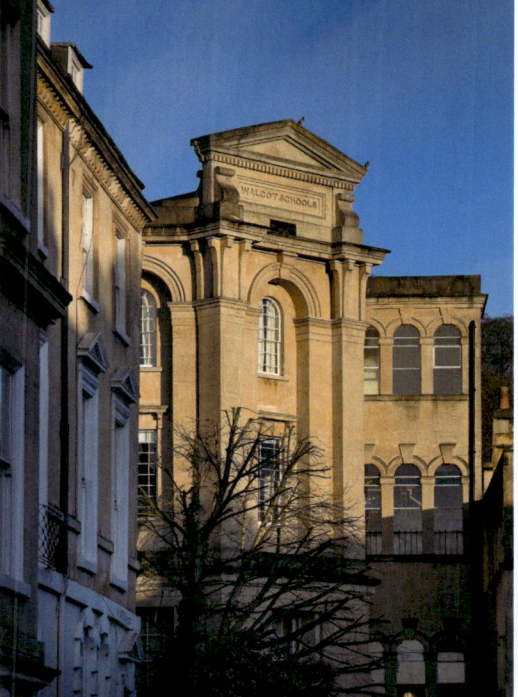

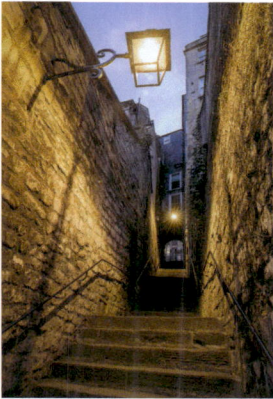

THE STAR INN & WALCOT SCHOOL

MORE INFORMATION

 camra.org.uk
Visit the Campaign for Real Ale website to find out more about the Star Inn.

OPPOSITE: an authentic watering hole, The Star Inn is a timeless example of a traditional English pub, with cosy rooms it preserves many original features including 18th-century bar fittings and beer served from the jug.

ABOVE LEFT: the Walcot School. A prominent building squeezed into the corner of Vineyards and facing Guinea Lane to the rear, this former school and church hall built in 1840 towers over the surrounding buildings. **ABOVE RIGHT:** Walcot Steps – linking the Paragon to Walcot Street below.

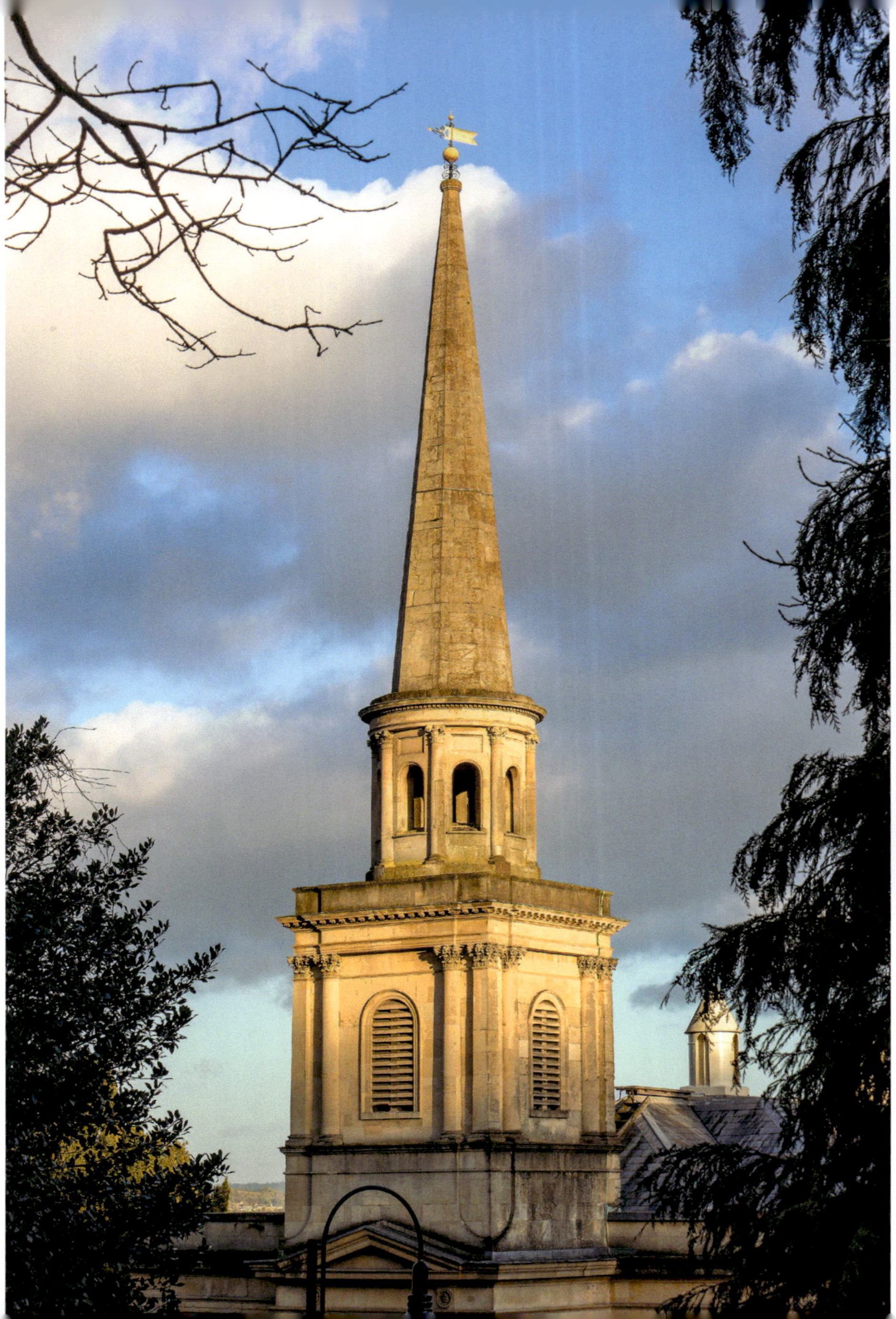

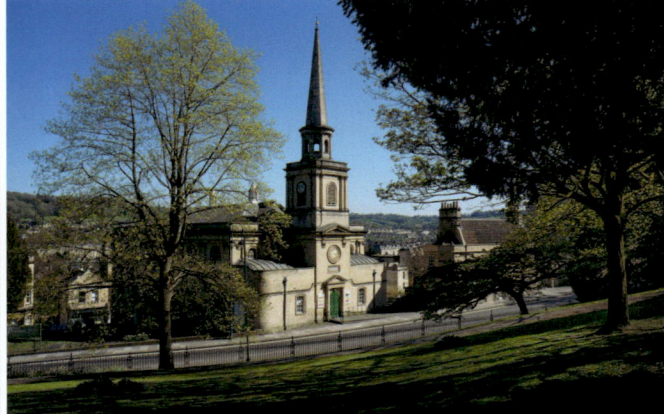

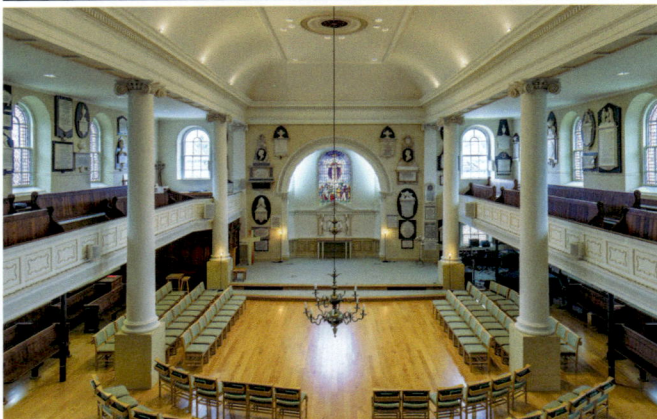

MORE INFORMATION

stswithinswalcot.org.uk

Visit the St. Swithins website for more information.

OPPOSITE: the current and last remaining 18th Century parish church in Bath. There has been a church on this site since 971 AD.

LEFT: a slender spire was added to the church in 1790. **TOP**: St Swithin's main north entrance viewed from Hedgemead Park. **ABOVE**: lives of the rich and famous. The walls feature a collection of distinctive black and white memorials, each dedicated to the worshippers of the era.

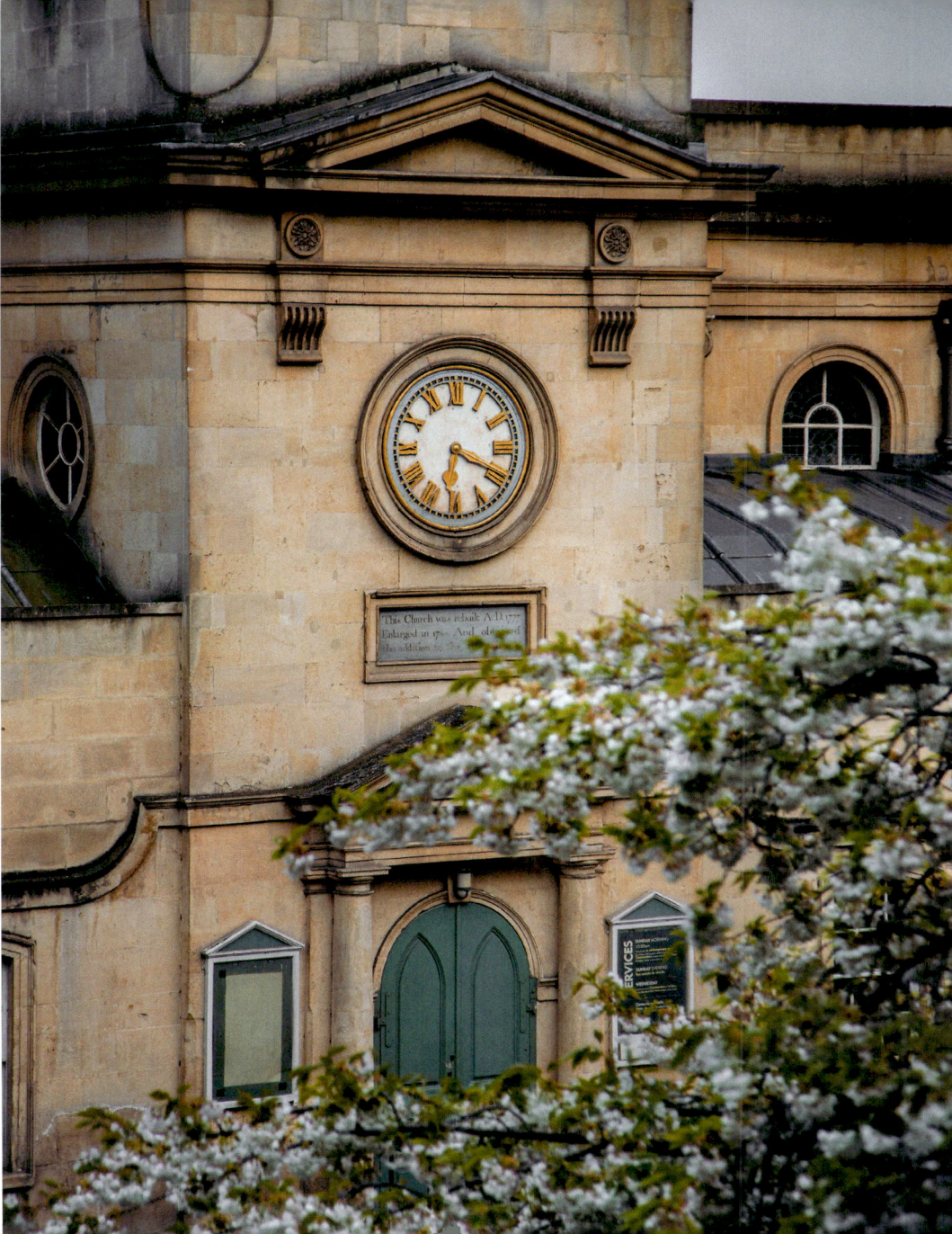

ST SWITHIN'S CHURCH

St Swithin's is a Grade 2 listed Georgian church perched at the intersection to Walcot Street and the Paragon. A single slender spire reaches to the sky. A church has stood at this spot since 971 AD, changing in size and appearance over the centuries, the current building was completed in 1790, designed by John Palmer. Historic remains point to the original Saxon church where stone foundations have been discovered in the crypt.

A beautiful bijou building complete with a unique collection of urns and marbled plaques are contained within. It was a popular place for Bath's high society – the rich and famous flocked to worship here every Sunday. Prominent people such as the architect John Palmer (famed for the Pump Rooms and Lansdown Crescent) are memorialised along with around 163 distinguished residents attributed to this small corner of Bath including the father of novelist Jane Austen, the Rev. George Austen.

George was so deeply fond of this location that he chose the original church of St Swithin's (pre-dating the current structure) as his preferred venue to both marry his sweetheart Cassandra Leigh in 1764 and eventually as a final resting place, his tombstone is located in the small graveyard next to the church.

Separate to Sunday services is an open doors event held annually each September allowing visitors inside to freely explore a surprisingly spacious auditorium. The walls display numerous marble memorials creating a unique monochrome colour palette. A beautifully composed stained glass image of Christ is positioned centrally to the rear of the main public space and glimpses towards the distant city skyline are worth exploring through windows on the upper balcony.

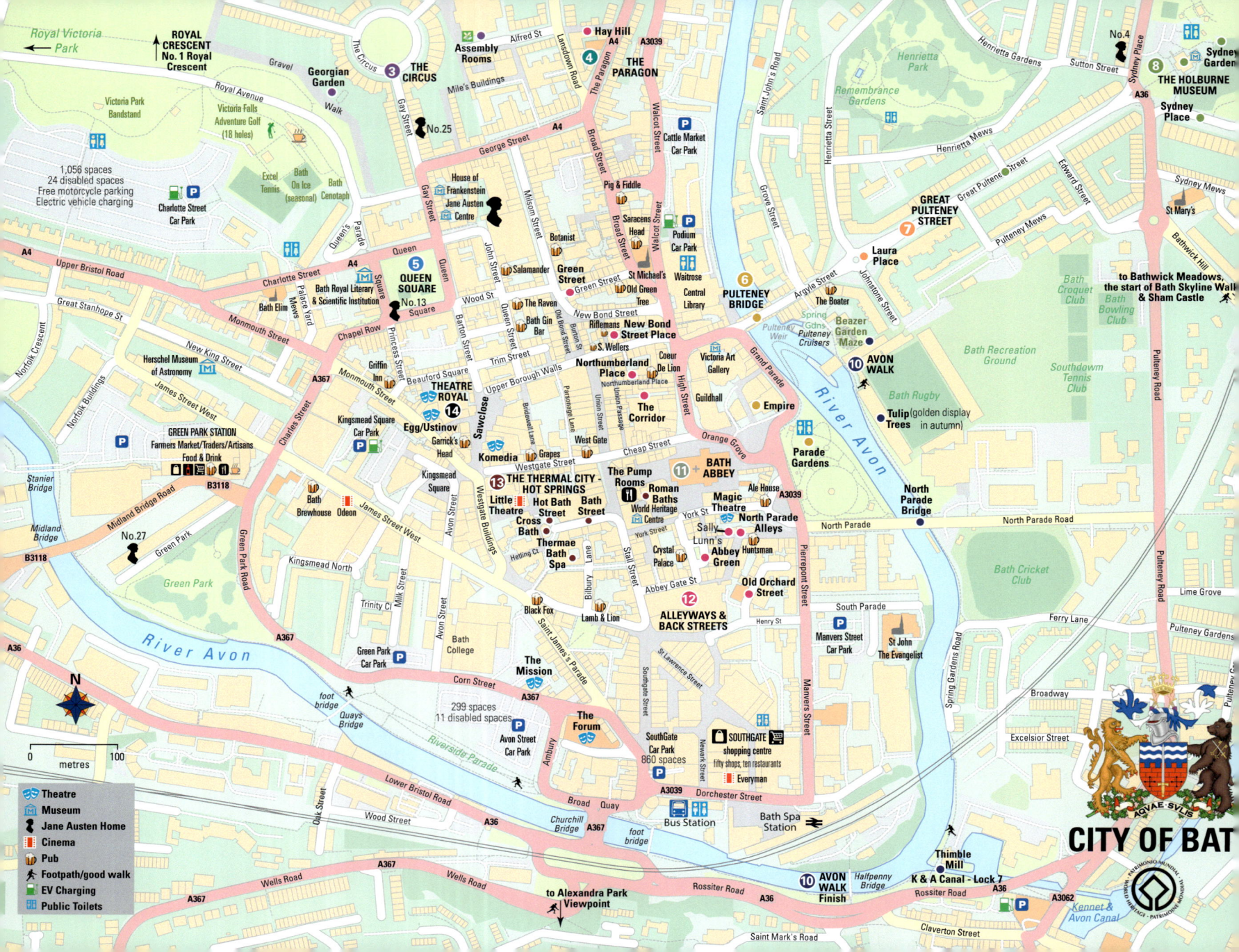

THE HEART OF BATH

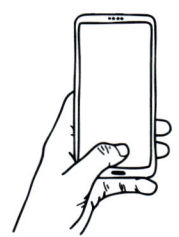

Take a photo of the map for reference.

5 **Queen Square** **91**

6 **Pulteney Bridge** **97**
　The Empire 102
　Parade Gardens 106

7 **Great Pulteney Street** **111**
　Laura Place 117

8 **The Holburne Museum** **121**
　Sydney Gardens 126
　Sydney Place 132

9 **Kennet & Avon Canal** **135**
　Kennet & Avon Canal – Bathampton 137
　Kennet & Avon Canal – Bath Section 138

10 **River Avon** **143**

11 **Bath Abbey** **149**

12 **Bath's Alleyways & Back Streets** **163**
　Abbey Green 165
　North Parade Alleys 168
　Old Orchard Street 172
　Green Street 173
　Hay Hill 174
　The Corridor 176
　Northumberland Place 177
　New Bond Street Place 177

13 **The Thermal City – Historic & Modern Hot Springs** **179**
　The Roman Baths 180
　The Pump Rooms 187
　Bath Street 189
　The Cross Bath &
　Hot Bath Street 191
　Thermae Bath Spa 192

14 **The Theatre Royal** **195**

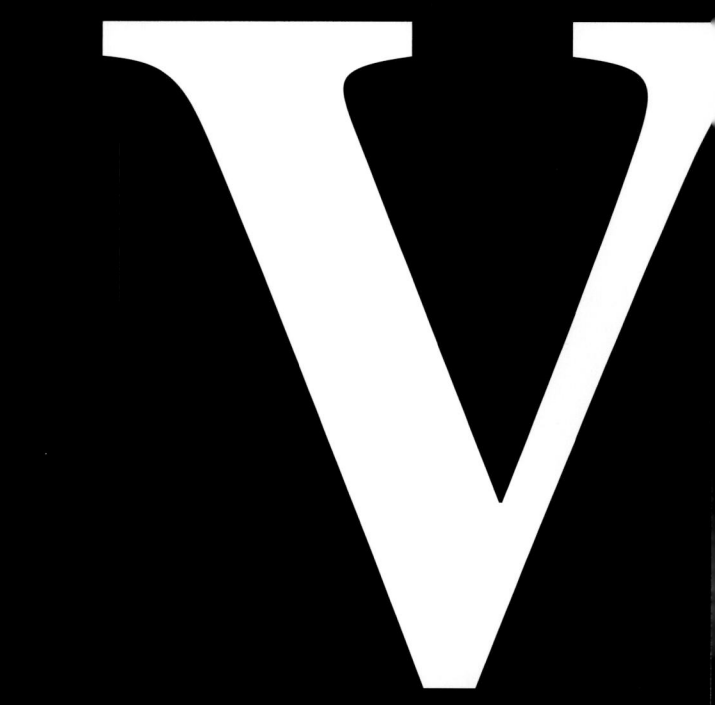

5 QUEEN SQUARE

"The intention of a square in a city is for people to assemble together."
– John Wood the Elder

"I hope we shall be in Bath in the winter; but remember, papa, if we do go, we must be in a good situation: none of your Queen Squares for us!"
– Jane Austen, *Persuasion* (1817)

Queen Square is laid out symmetrically, with a central garden surrounded by uniform buildings. Its architecture reflects the Georgian fascination with Greek and Roman design, resulting in a new interpretation of Palladianism.

Intended as a public space, it allowed visitors to meet and amble in a naturalistic setting away from busy streets. Today, the square remains a green oasis, isolated from traffic, with specimen trees, park benches, and numerous food markets throughout the year, including the annual Bath Boules event.

A tall stone obelisk stands at the heart of Queen Square. Commonly known as *the needle*, it commemorates a visit by Royal Highness Frederick, Prince of Wales. Originally surrounded by a circular pool, it stood 21 metres tall but was truncated by storm damage in 1815.

Architect John Wood the Elder envisioned Queen Square as a palace setting, with the northern building as the main feature, flanked by east and west wings. The southern row was his home, offering the perfect vantage point to admire his creation. Today, Wood's former home is the Francis Hotel.

Queen Square was Wood's first speculative venture, but bureaucratic challenges and opposition from landowners and the local council thwarted his plans. Determined, he moved his project outside the city walls onto open fields leased from MP Robert Gay, owner of the vast Walcot Estate.

Here, Wood finally made his mark, introducing his architectural style and shaping Bath's iconic Georgian identity. As a kind gesture, Robert Gay had a nearby street named after him.

QUEEN SQUARE

Postcode: BA1 2HX
what3words: season.angle.bricks

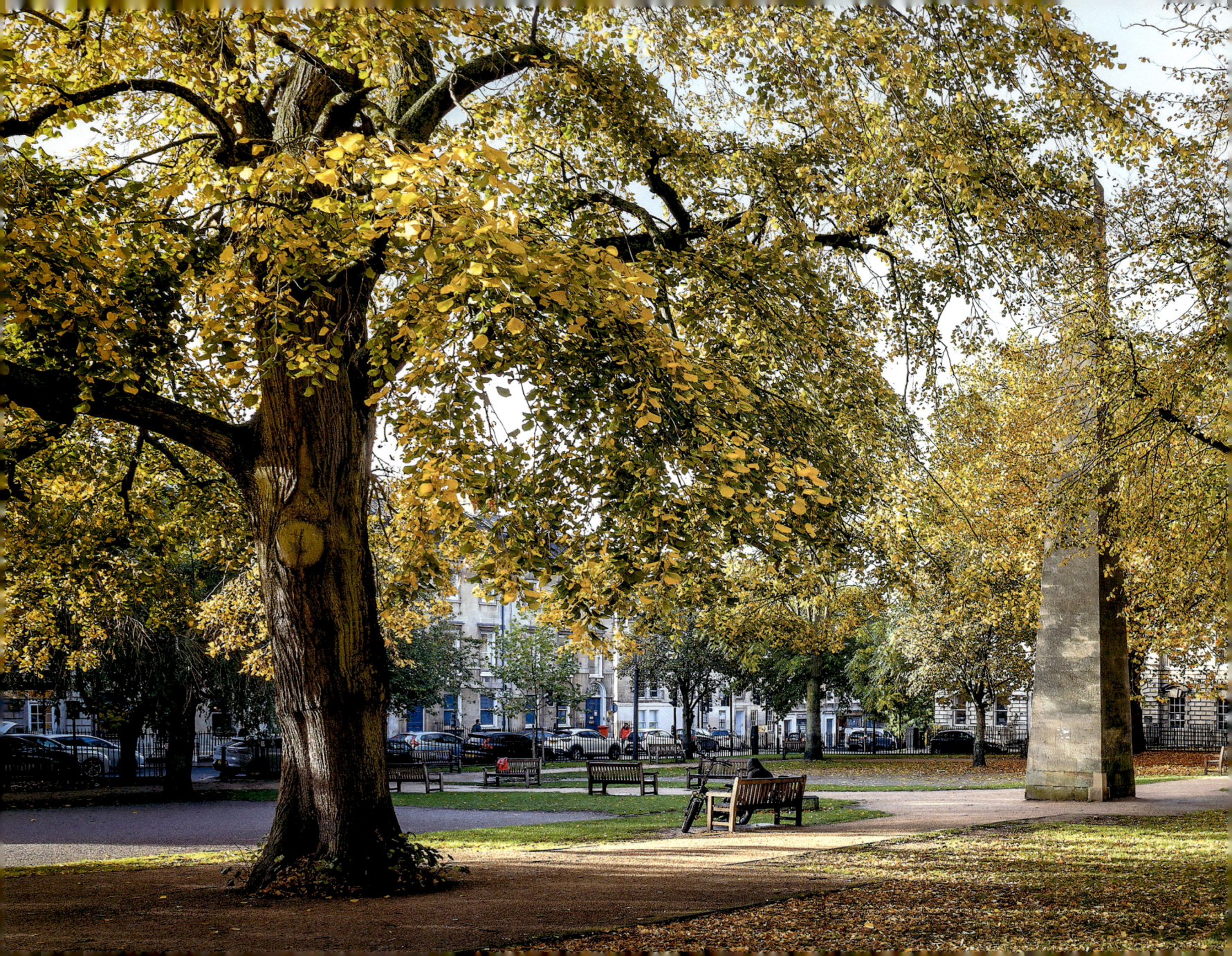

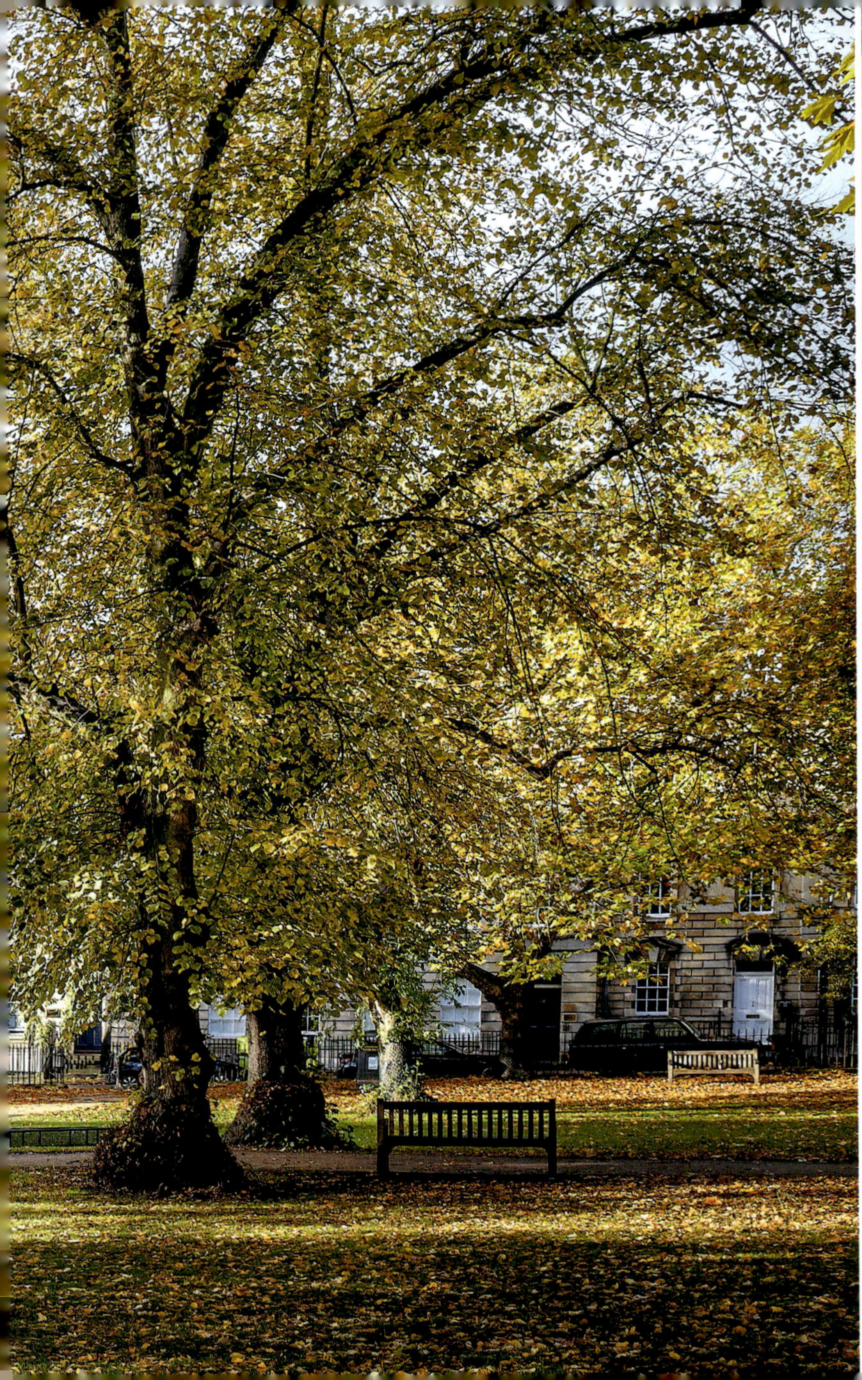

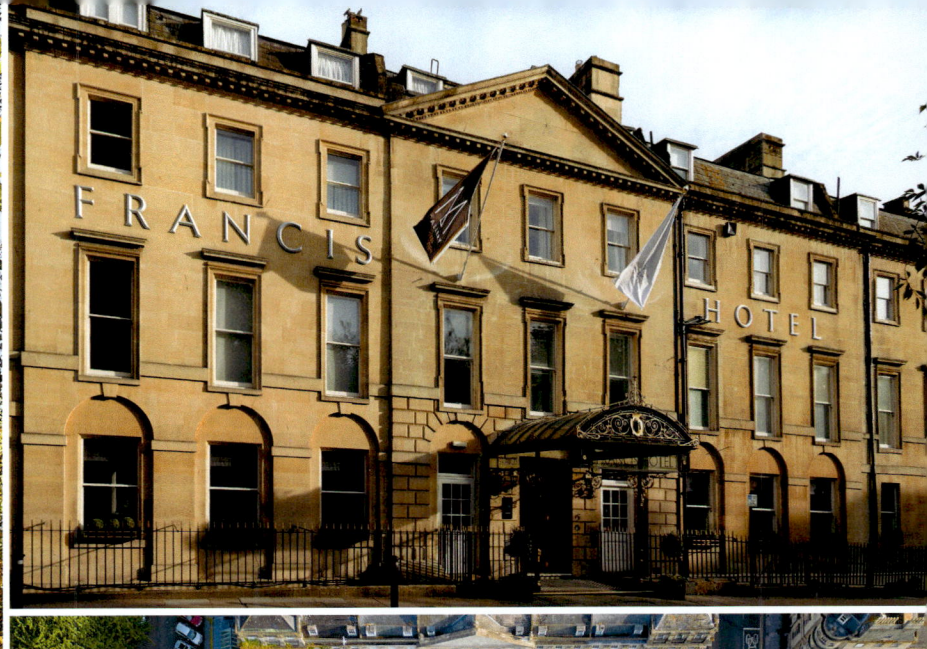
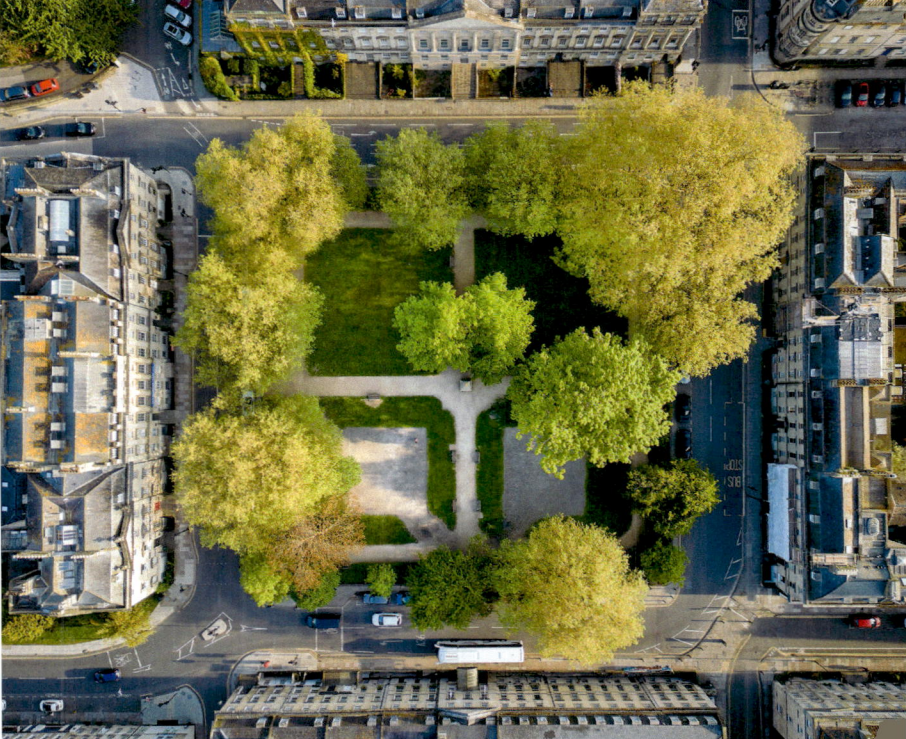

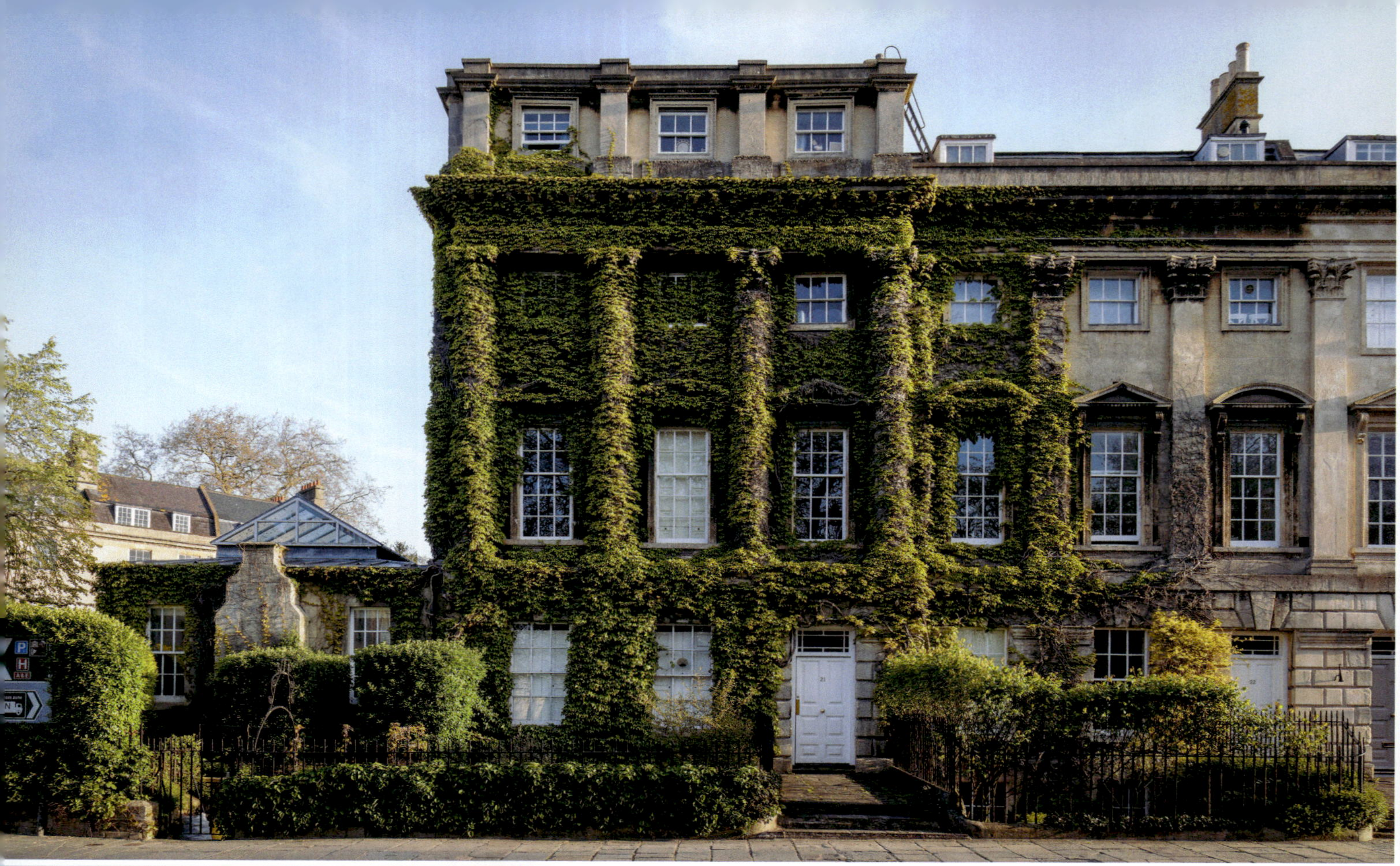

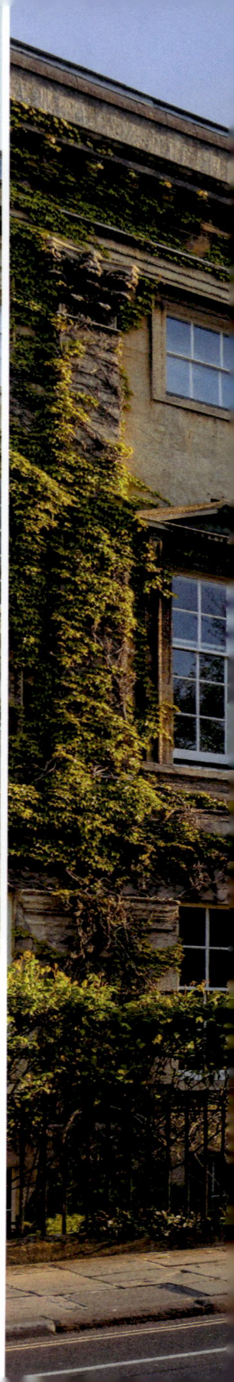

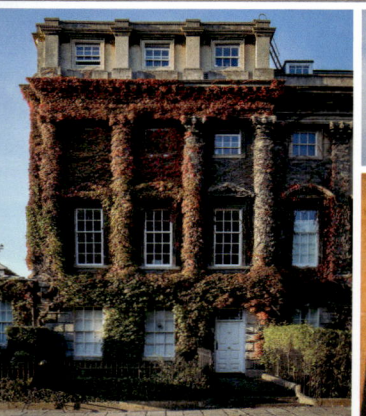
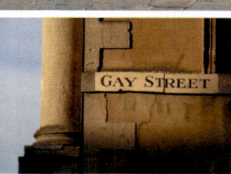
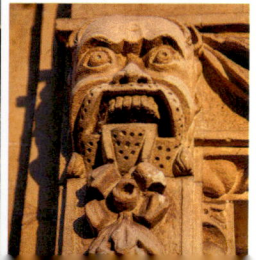

PREVIOUS SPREAD LEFT: in autumn, Queen Square is bathed in a golden glow as stately trees turn vibrant shades of yellow surrounding a central obelisk dedicated to Frederick, Prince of Wales in 1738.
TOP RIGHT: the Francis Hotel stands on the south side of Queen Square. **BOTTOM RIGHT**: from above reveals perfect Georgian symmetry. A neat boundary of townhouses framing a central green, serving as a leafy lung in the heart of the city.
ABOVE: virginia creeper (Parthenocissus quinquefolia) is a striking feature completely smothering one of the townhouses on the northern side. **FAR LEFT**: the same virginia creeper in autumn – its leaves transform into vibrant shades of red. **LEFT MIDDLE**: a street named in honour of Robert Gay, one of John Wood's earliest supporters and a key backer of his bold architectural vision. **LEFT**: baroque-style stone carving adorns one of the doorways.
OPPOSITE: one of the finest Palladian compositions in England, the north side of Queen Square was designed to resemble a grand palace and also served as a striking focal point when viewed from John Wood's former home on the southern edge (now the Francis Hotel).

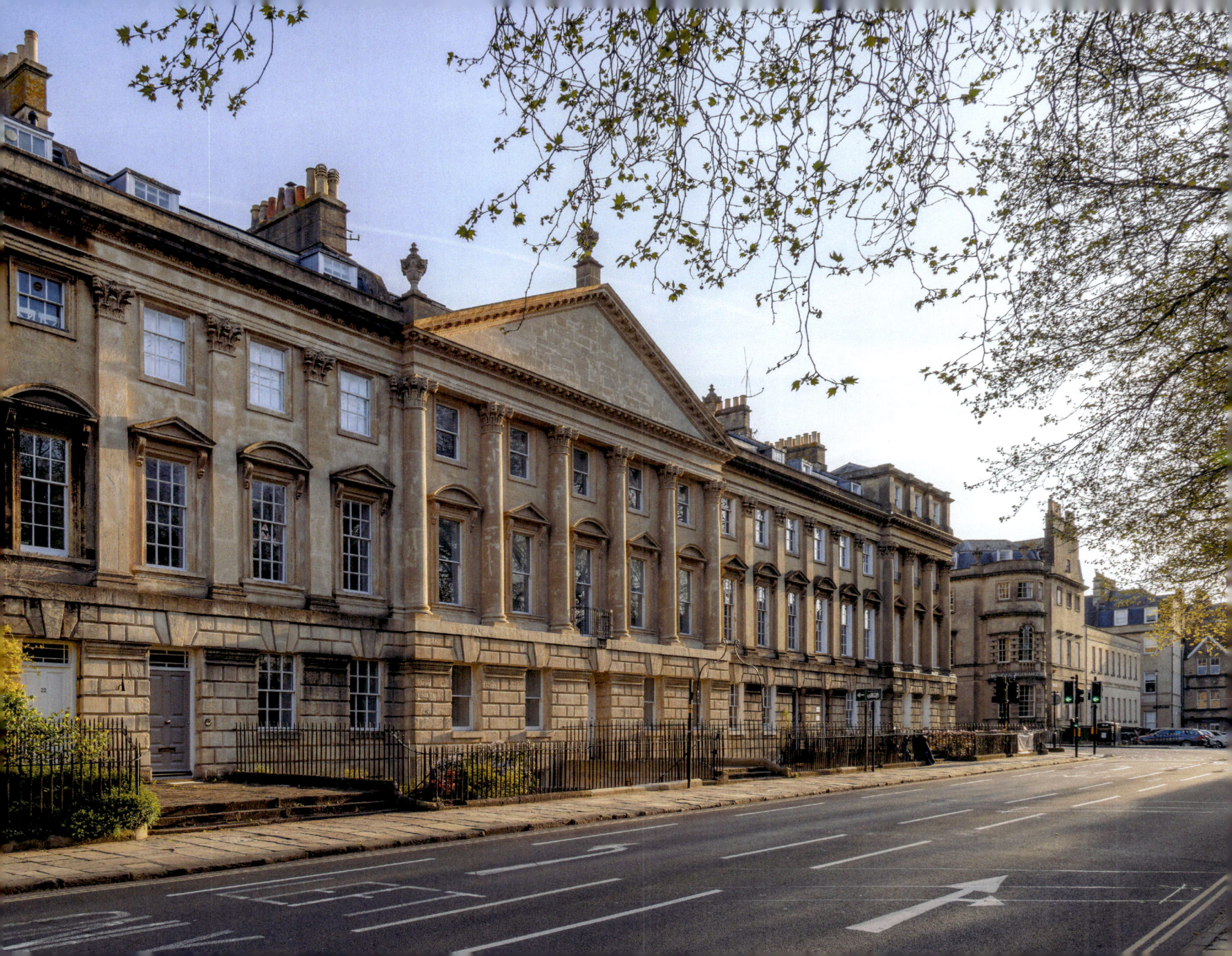

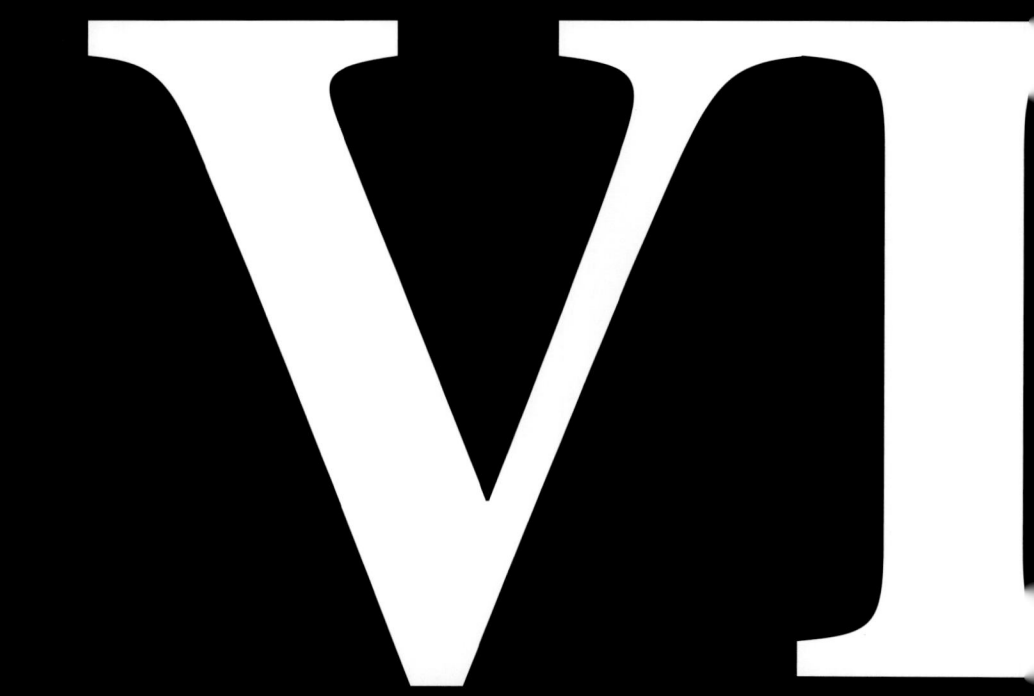

6 PULTENEY BRIDGE

"Pulteney Bridge is one of only four bridges lined with shops in the world, but Robert Adam's creation has more than novelty value. His graceful composition is one of the unqualified successes of English Palladianism and provides the perfect integrating link between two halves of a Palladian city."
– Bath City Life

Pulteney Bridge was designed and built by Robert Adam between 1769 and 1774, and is one of his finest masterpieces. It closely follows unused designs for the Rialto bridge in Venice. The bridge is Palladian in style and spans the river Avon linking the 'new' Georgian town of Bathwick with the rest of the city. It is considered one of the most beautiful and romantic bridges in the world, exhibiting architectural similarities also seen on the Ponte Vecchio in Florence, Italy. The result is an elegant compact bridge, consisting of three arches built from Bath stone and like its European counterparts has the unique feature of supporting a roadway above and shops spreading along each side, one of only four in the world.

These independent shops whilst offering fascinating wares also provide incredible views on each side overlooking the waters below, take a moment in one of the cafes or restaurants to peer down to the weir and remember to choose a window seat.

A short flight of steps accessed on Argyle Street descends below street level taking you within almost touching distance of the bridge and at eye level to the weir. This charming riverside walk opens out onto a small tree-filled area in full view of the bridge and weir, close to a handful of cafes, bars and restaurants (one of which is actually named the Ponte Vecchio). The roar of cascading waters and proximity to the entire span of the bridge is a wonderful experience revealing a unique view of Bath's architecture towering above.

Boat tours start and finish at this location and offer visitors a unique river perspective travelling beneath the arches of the bridge before heading upstream towards the hamlet of Bathampton in the east.

PULTENEY BRIDGE

Postcode: BA2 4AS
what3words: noble.secure.open

THE EMPIRE HOTEL

Postcode: BA2 4AN
what3words: likely.sugars.scarf

PARADE GARDENS

Postcode: BA2 4AL
what3words: spider.loudly.score

MORE INFORMATION

pulteneycruisers.com
For a one hour boat trip starting from Pulteney Pier, visit the Pulteney Cruiser website for details.

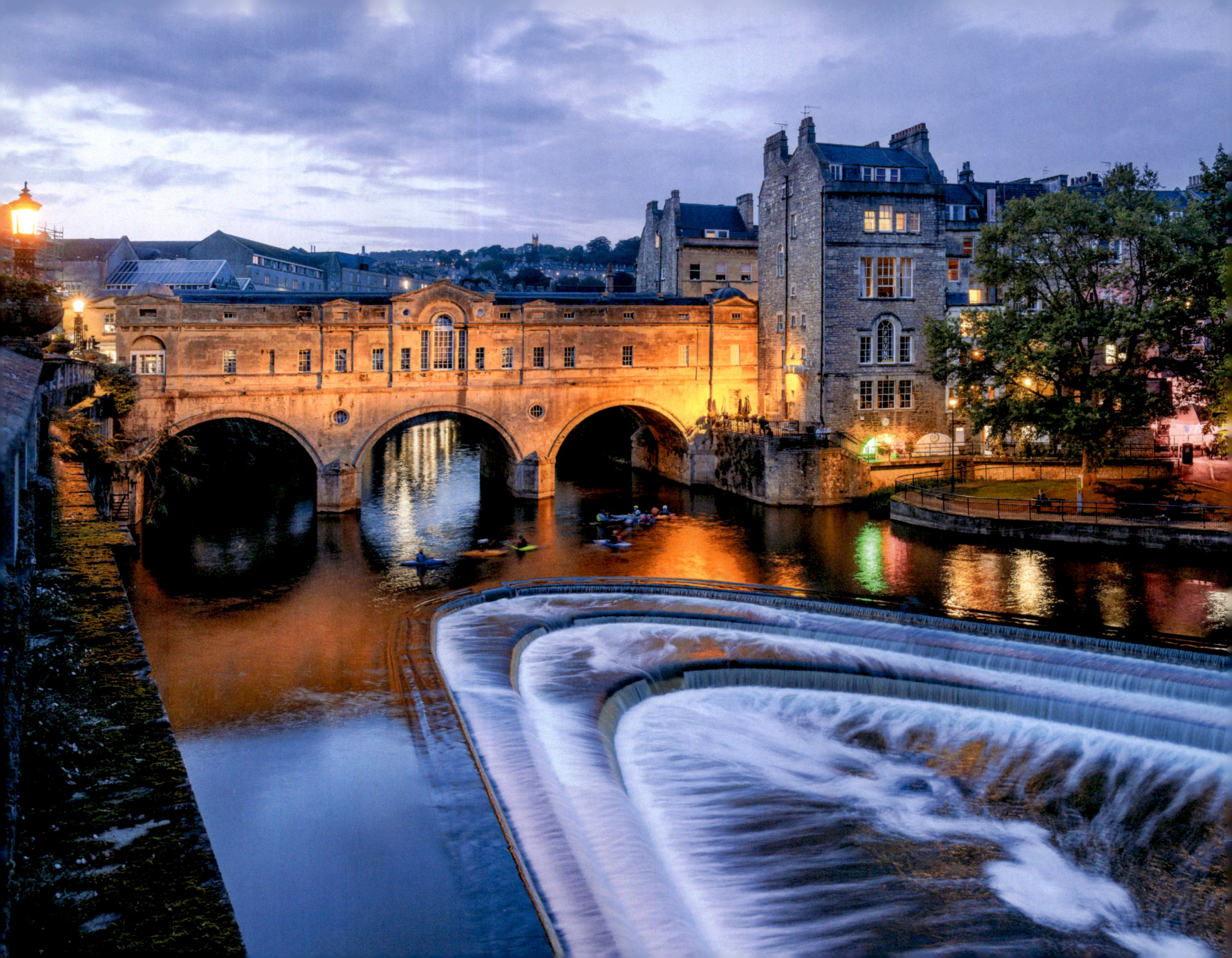

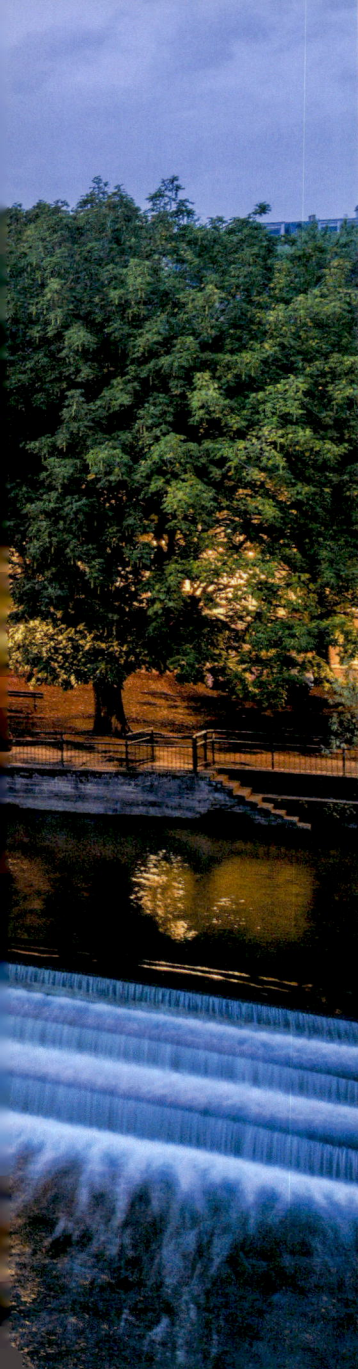

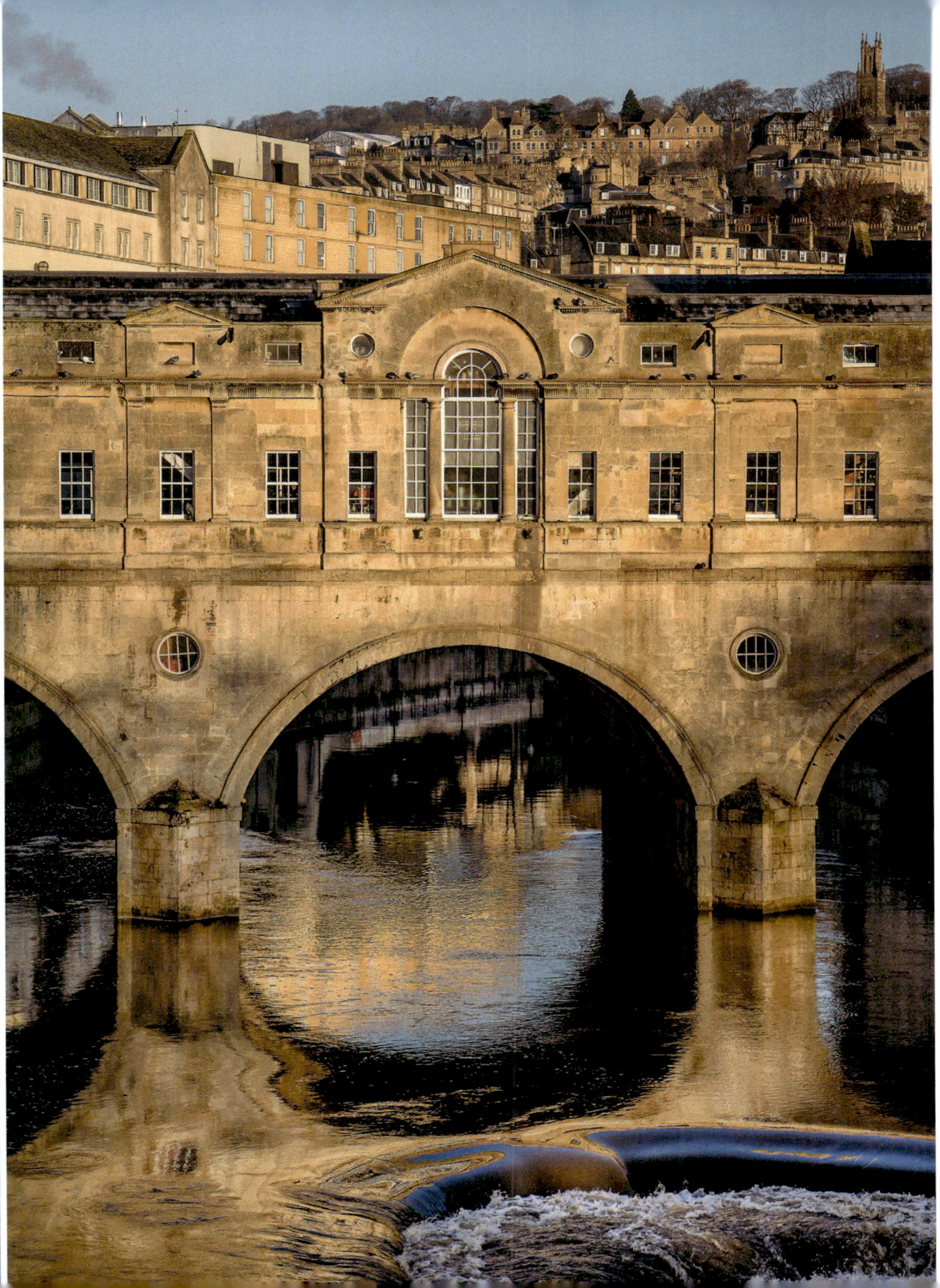

OPPOSITE: dusk is a enchanting time to visit Pulteney Bridge, where the glow of street lamps and illuminations dance on the river's surface.

LEFT: early light highlights the bridge's striking architecture.

6 PULTENEY BRIDGE

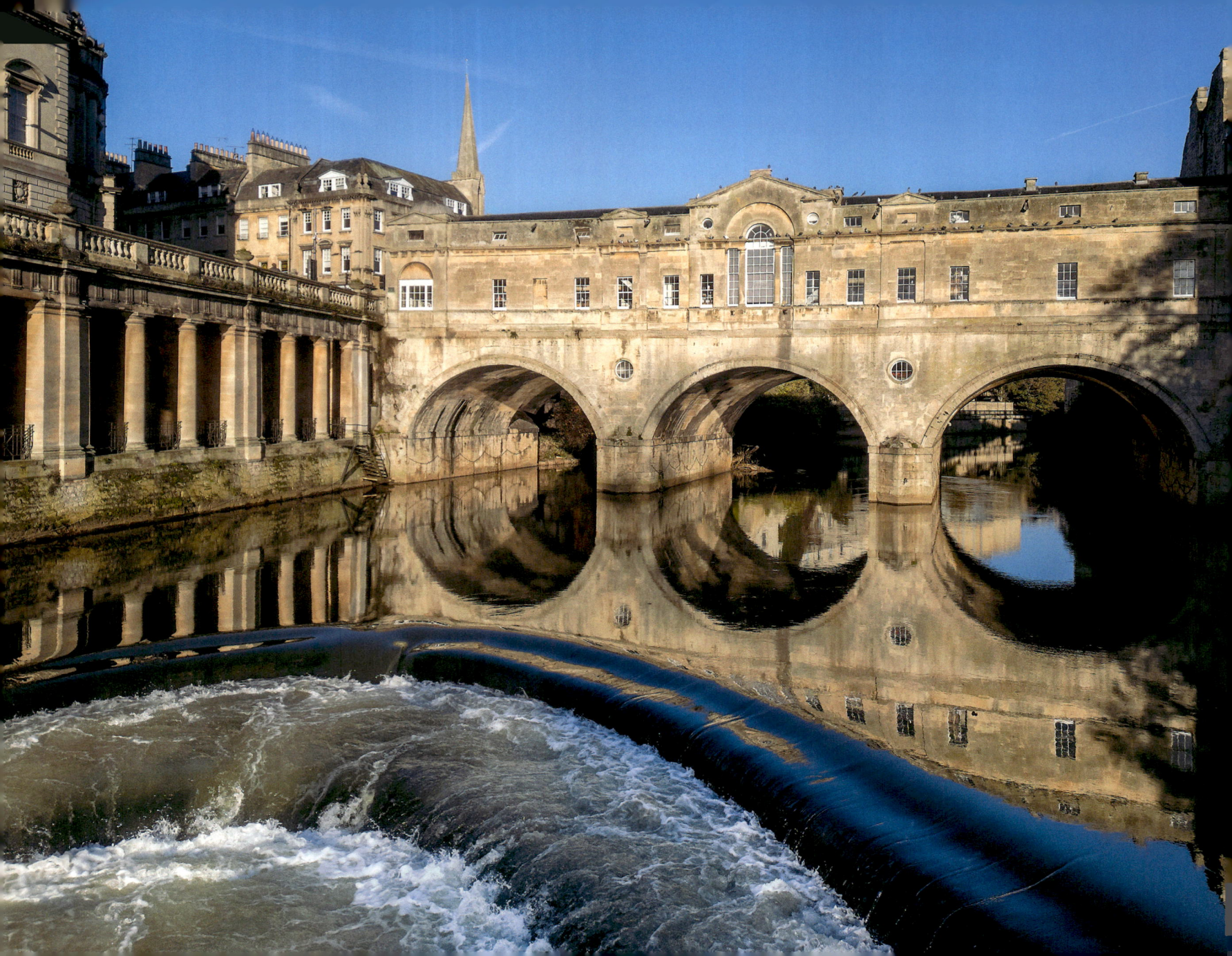

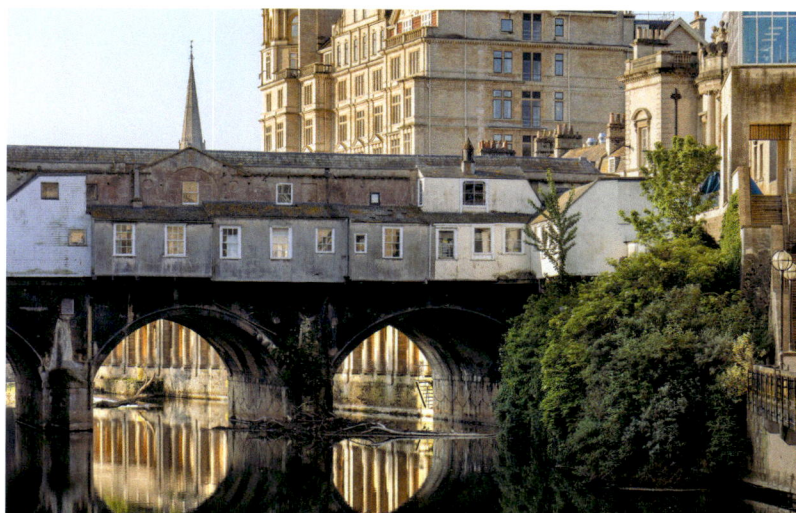

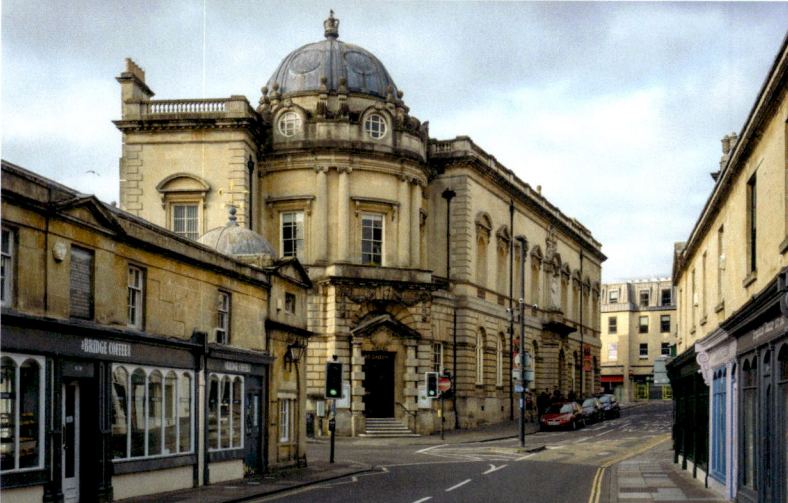

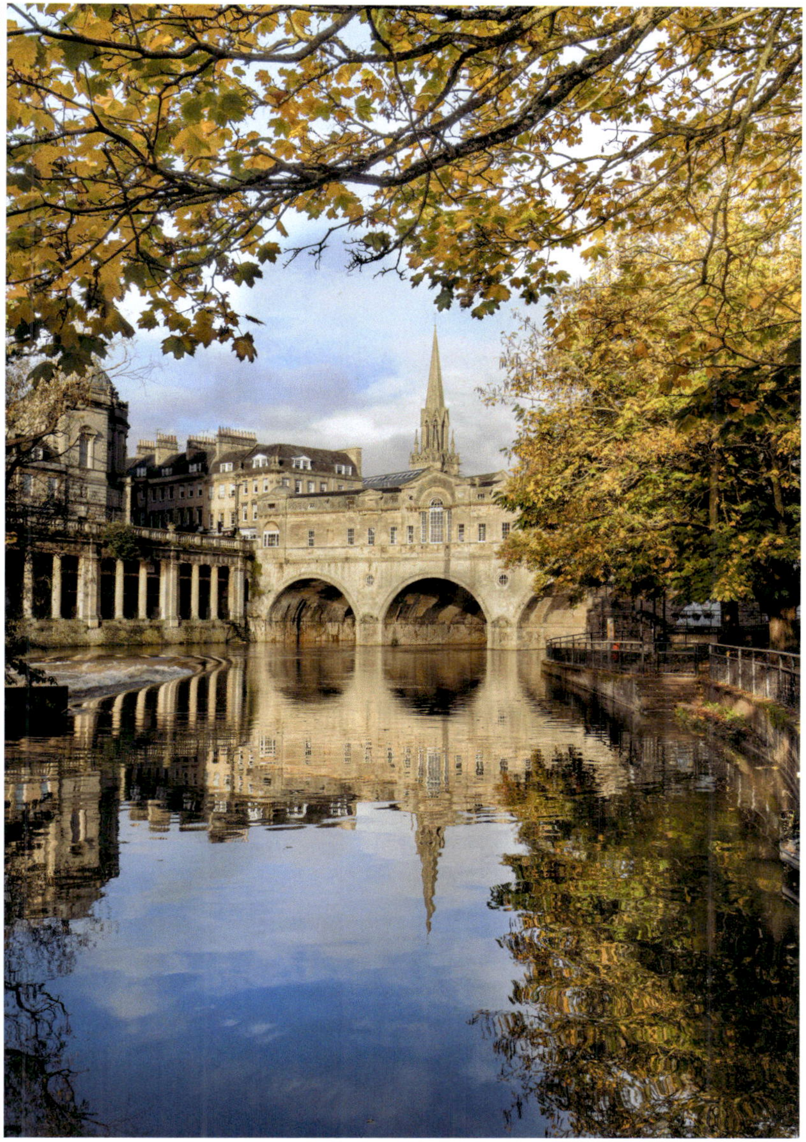

OPPOSITE: one of only four bridges in the world to have shops across its full span on both sides.

TOP: strikingly different, the rear of Pulteney Bridge has a unique charm all of its own.
ABOVE: a double row of shops lines the path of Pulteney Bridge leading to the Victoria Art Gallery. **RIGHT**: beautifully framed by autumn's golden trees, it's said that standing beside Pulteney Bridge is one of the most romantic spots in Britain.

6 PULTENEY BRIDGE

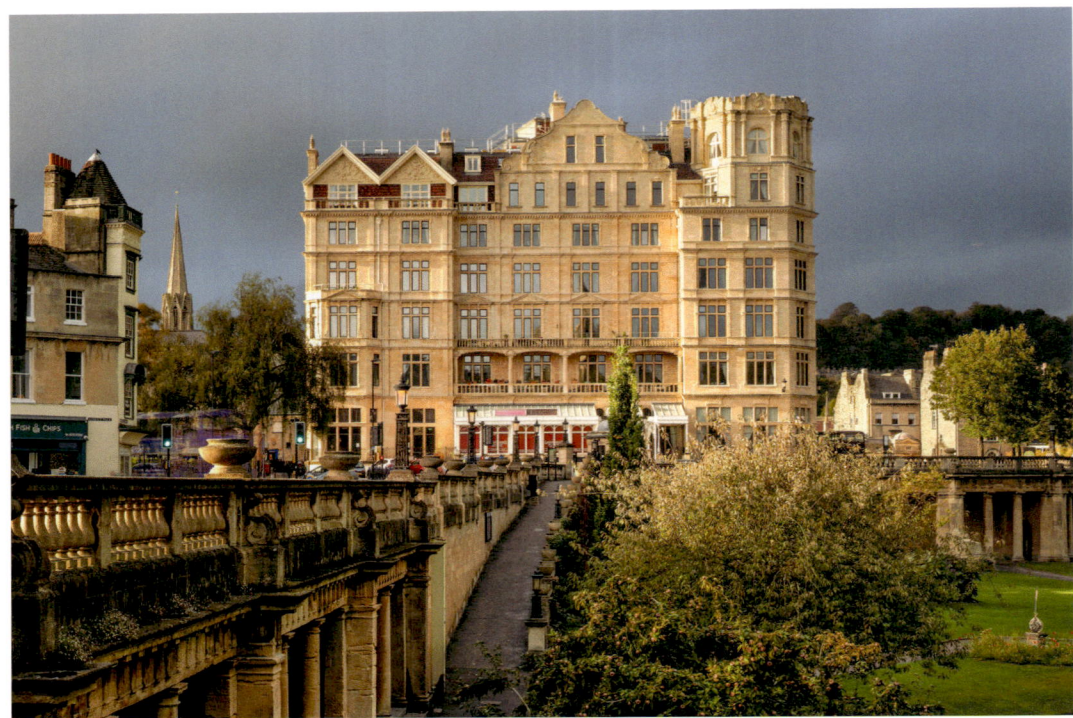

LEFT: the Empire stands proudly over Grand Parade, one of the largest and most impressive Victorian buildings still remaining in the city.

OPPOSITE: seek out Spring Gardens, beside the River Avon, for one of the best vantage points to view the Empire (and Pulteney Bridge).

THE EMPIRE

Described as the last of the great Victorian enterprises in the city the Empire Hotel was a bold and confident architectural statement, as dominant on the city skyline as its nearest lofty neighbour, the Abbey. The structure unashamedly towers above surrounding buildings reaching seven storeys high occupying the corner of Grand Parade and Orange Grove.

The Empire was built for the hotelier Alfred Holland in 1901. The construction of the Empire Hotel was to be the 'final surge of Bath's confidence in its future as a Spa town, designed by architect and Bath City Surveyor of Works Major Charles Davis who adopted the Queen Anne Revival style evident in the arrangement of windows, corner tower structure and tiled exterior partially found on the top floor.

The top floor exteriors of the Empire were actually designed to depict three class types found in Victorian Britain, represented by different building types: Lower class – a cottage, middle class – a house and the upper class – a castle.

Compelling views of the Empire can be explored on the opposite side of the river Avon as it flows under Pulteney Bridge at Spring Gardens. The Empire reflects beautifully in the waters below as they dramatically cascade over the tiered levels of the weir.

The Empire was a hotel until 1939 when it was requisitioned by the Admiralty as a postal sorting office. In 1996 it was refurbished and became apartments and a restaurant

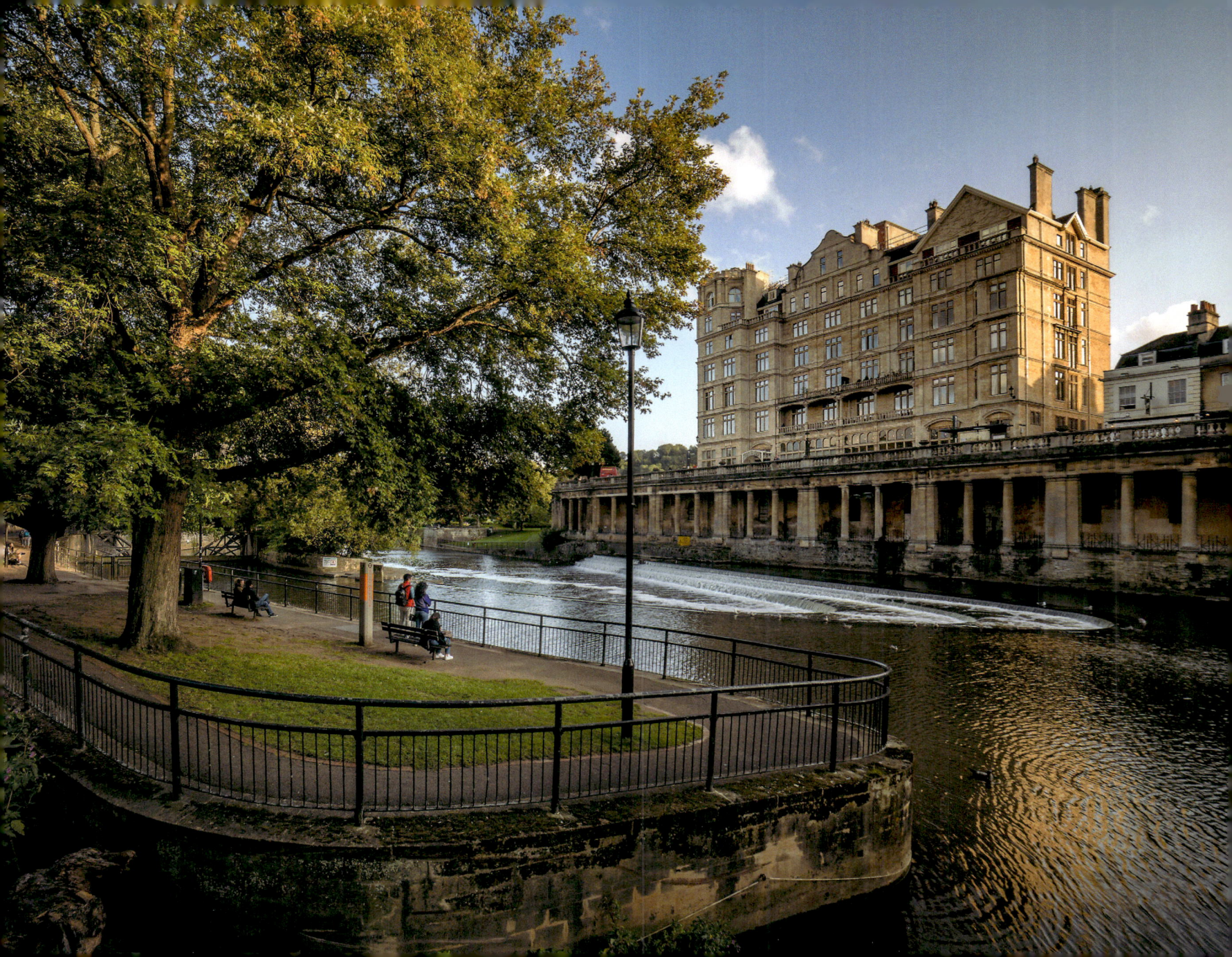

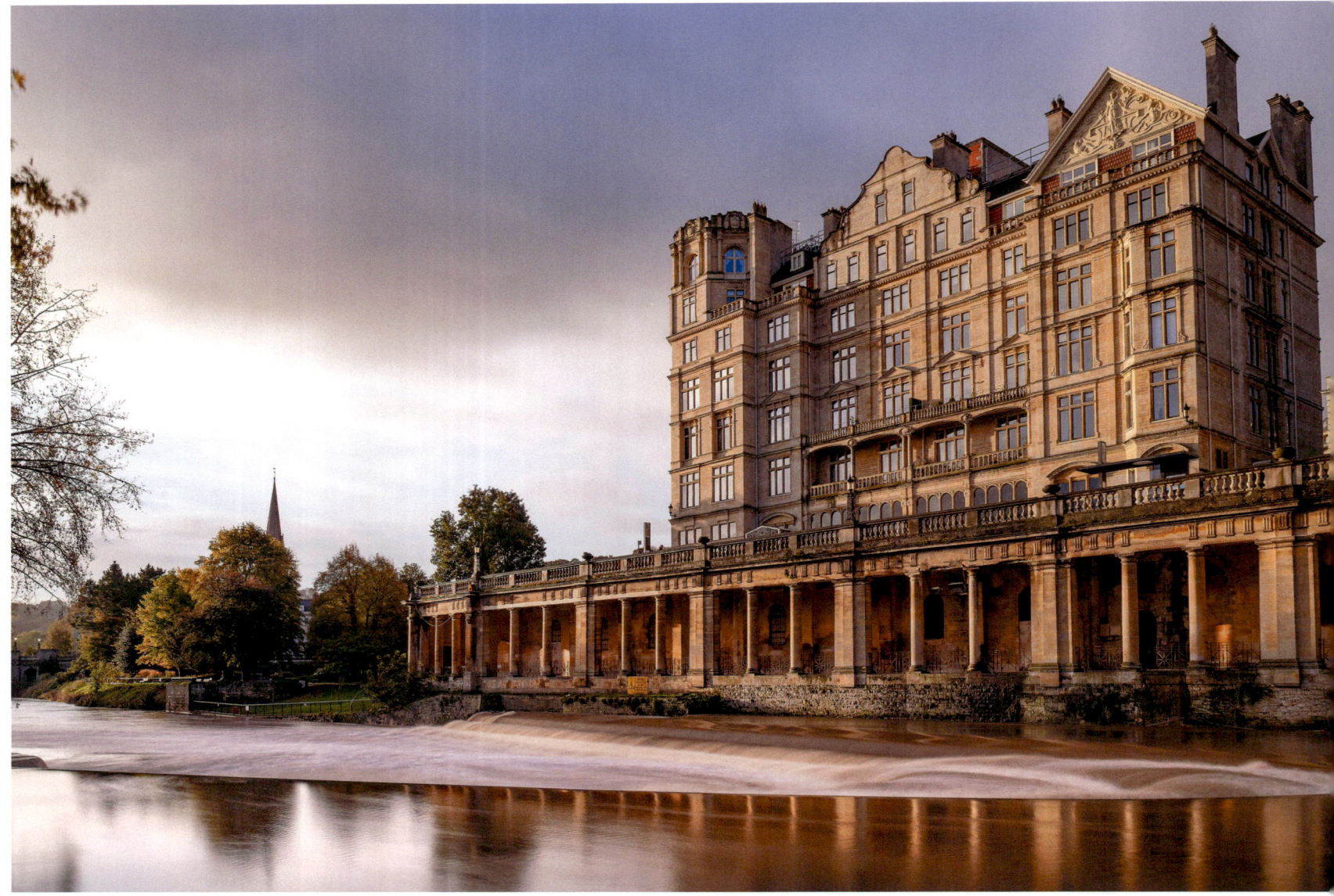

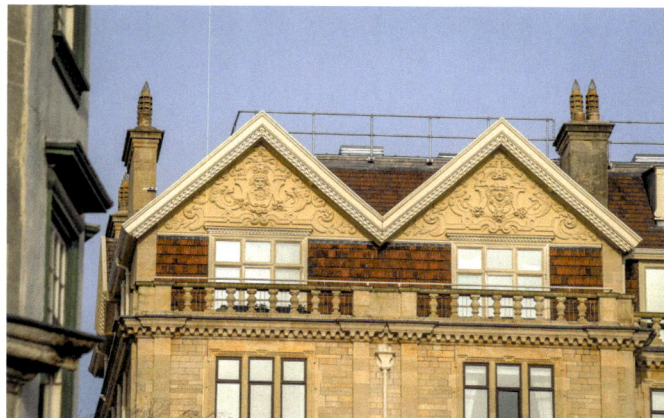

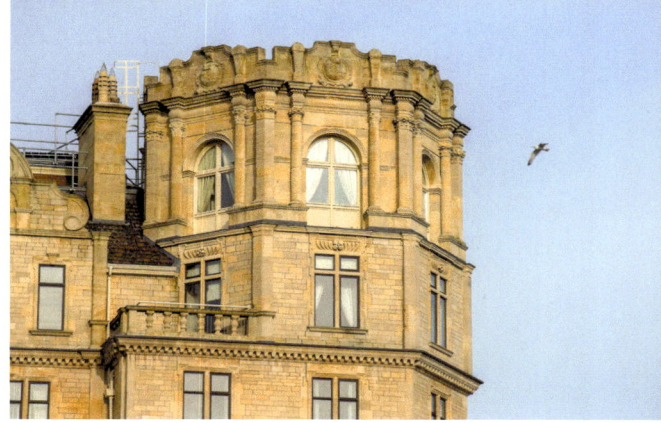

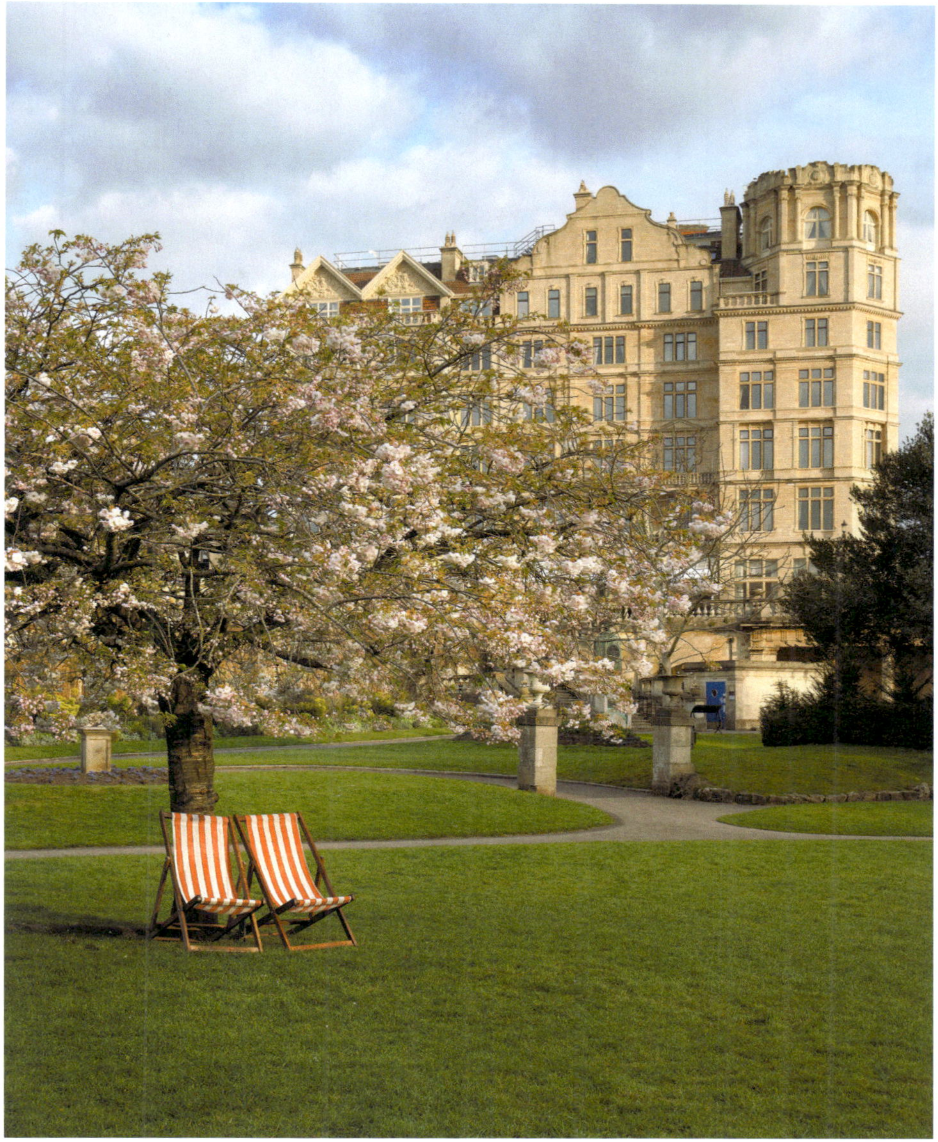

OPPOSITE: the Empire dominates the skyline above Pulteney Weir and the Colonnades below.

TOP: the roof's architecture represents the three social classes, a cottage for the lower class (shown) and a house for the middle class. **ABOVE**: a castle represented the upper class of society. **RIGHT**: the former hotel offers a striking backdrop for visitors to Parade Gardens.

PARADE GARDENS

Located on the lowest banks of the river Avon, Parade Gardens is a Grade 2 listed pleasure ground of two and a half acres packed with seasonal plantings, expansive open spaces and pathways providing spectacular views of Pultneney Bridge and the surrounding city.

Historically associated with Bath Abbey as a fruit orchard, the grounds were once part of the abbey's extended estate before later becoming home to the original Assembly Rooms and later the Royal Literary and Scientific Institution. A road widening scheme saw the gardens landscaped into the setting seen today beneath a long stone balustrade that almost completely encloses the grounds.

Spring sees blossoming trees and flowering bulbs whilst in summertime the gardens really shine with immaculately maintained borders and tightly-clipped grass lawns. Parade Gardens has long been associated with the RHS Britain in Bloom annual competition and is a gold award winner along with many more accolades. During the warmer months concerts are held on the centrally located band stand and circular lawn which was originally a Georgian bowling green.

A cafe provides refreshments to visitors who can also rent deck chairs; a perfect spot to sit back and immerse yourself in a tranquil setting. Entry is free, and in the spring and summer months there are extended opening hours, in the autumn and winter the gardens occasionally close early at dusk.

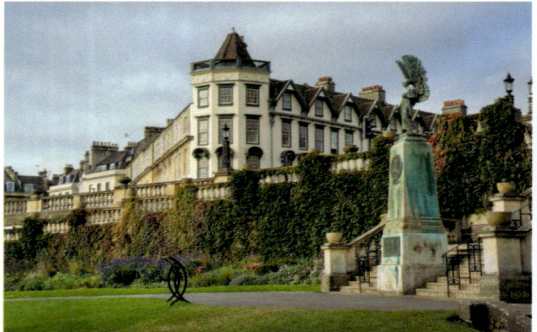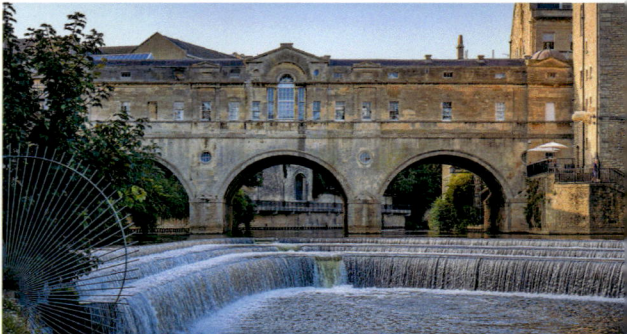

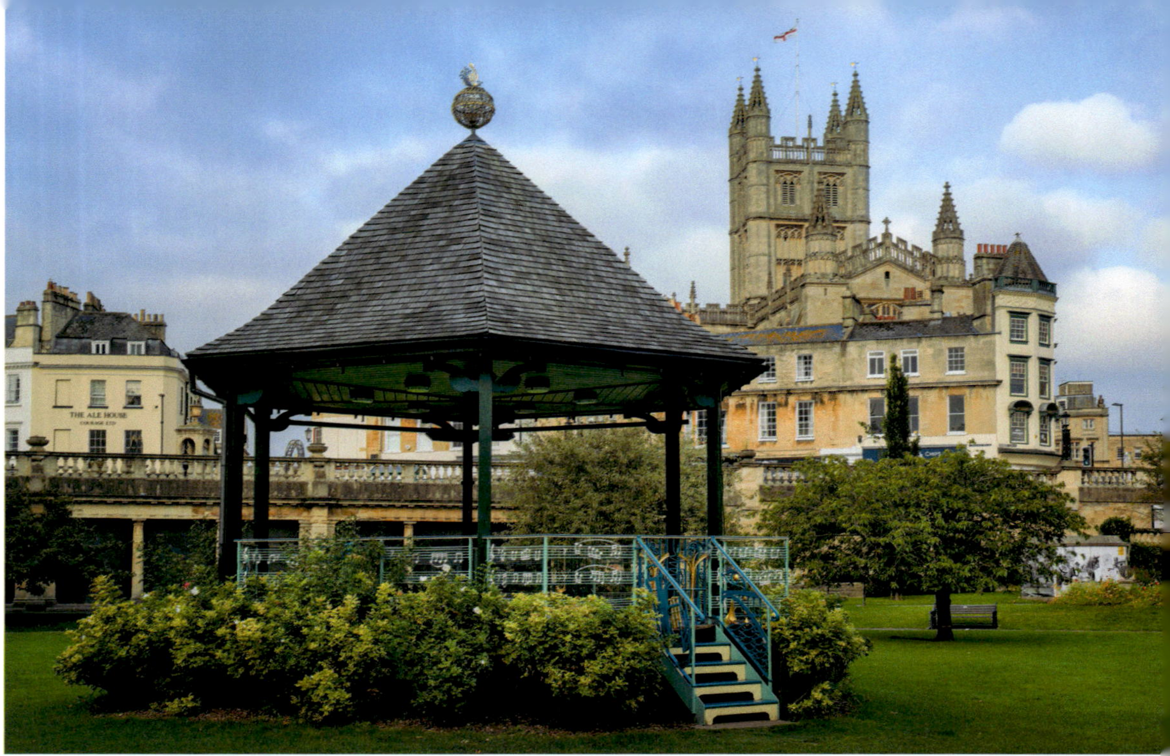

TOP: the Victorian bandstand serves as a focal point for events and performances. **ABOVE LEFT**: the gardens are accessed by steps (and an accessible ramp) via Grand Parade, beside the Orange Grove. **ABOVE RIGHT**: impressive views of Pulteney Bridge and Weir can be enjoyed from a viewing area in the northeast corner of the gardens.

OPPOSITE TOP: manicured lawns and flower beds reflect the seasons. **MIDDLE**: the gardens offer a great spot to unwind, with free deck chairs for relaxing and picnicking. **BOTTOM**: wildflowers overflow the borders in summer time. **FAR RIGHT**: Parade Gardens is a sunken oasis, where the city streets fade away, leaving only a few unique buildings.

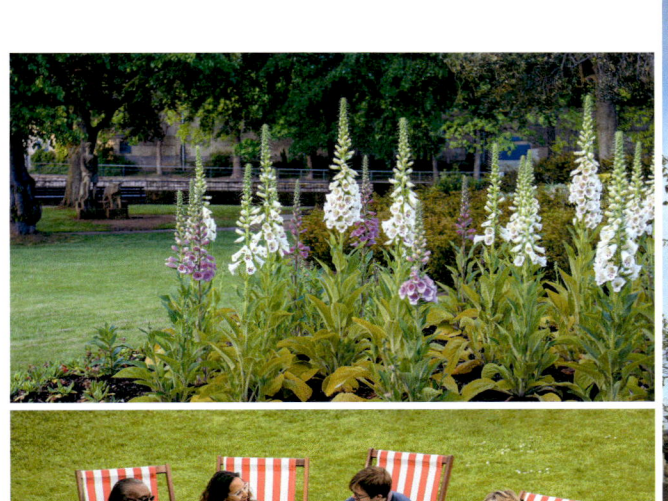
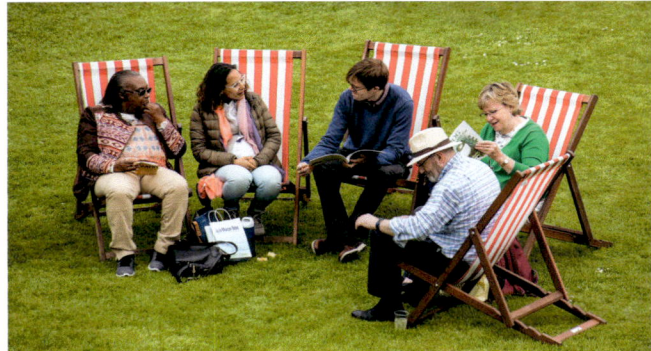
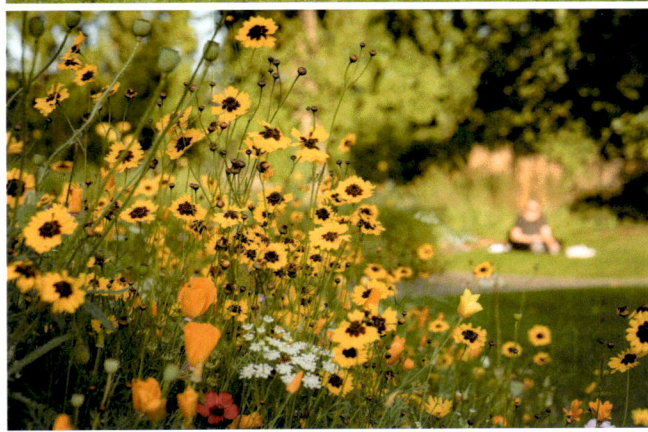

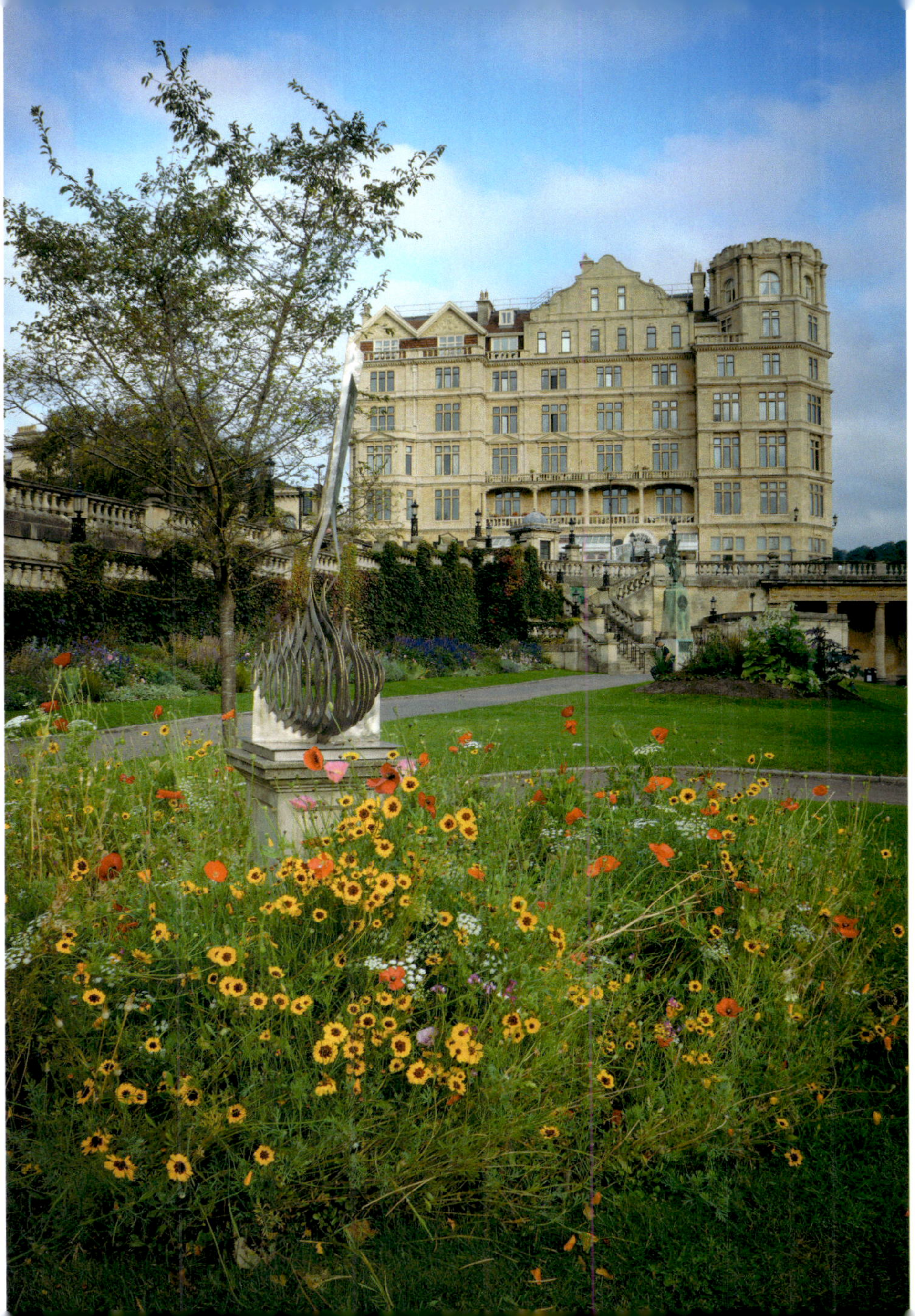

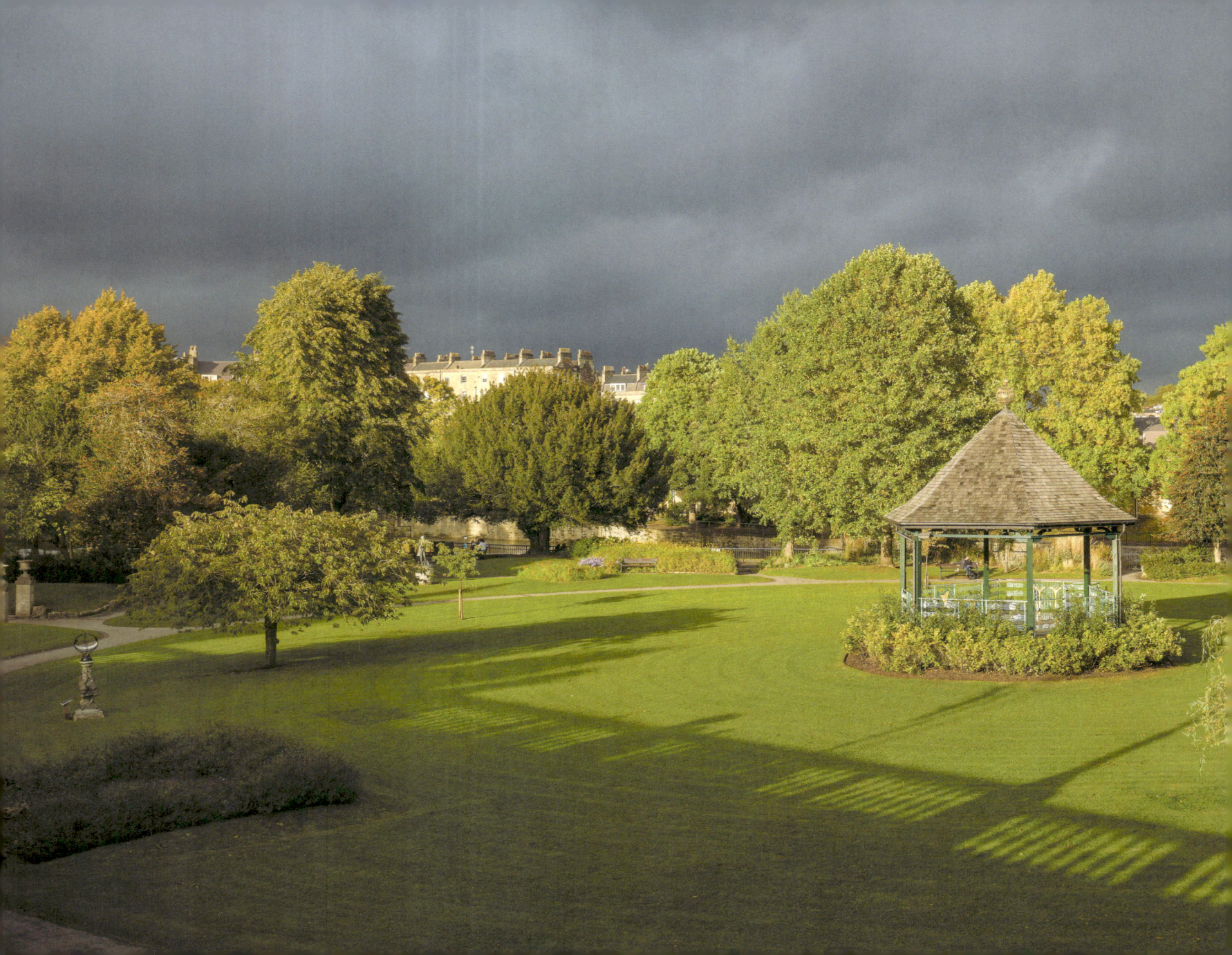

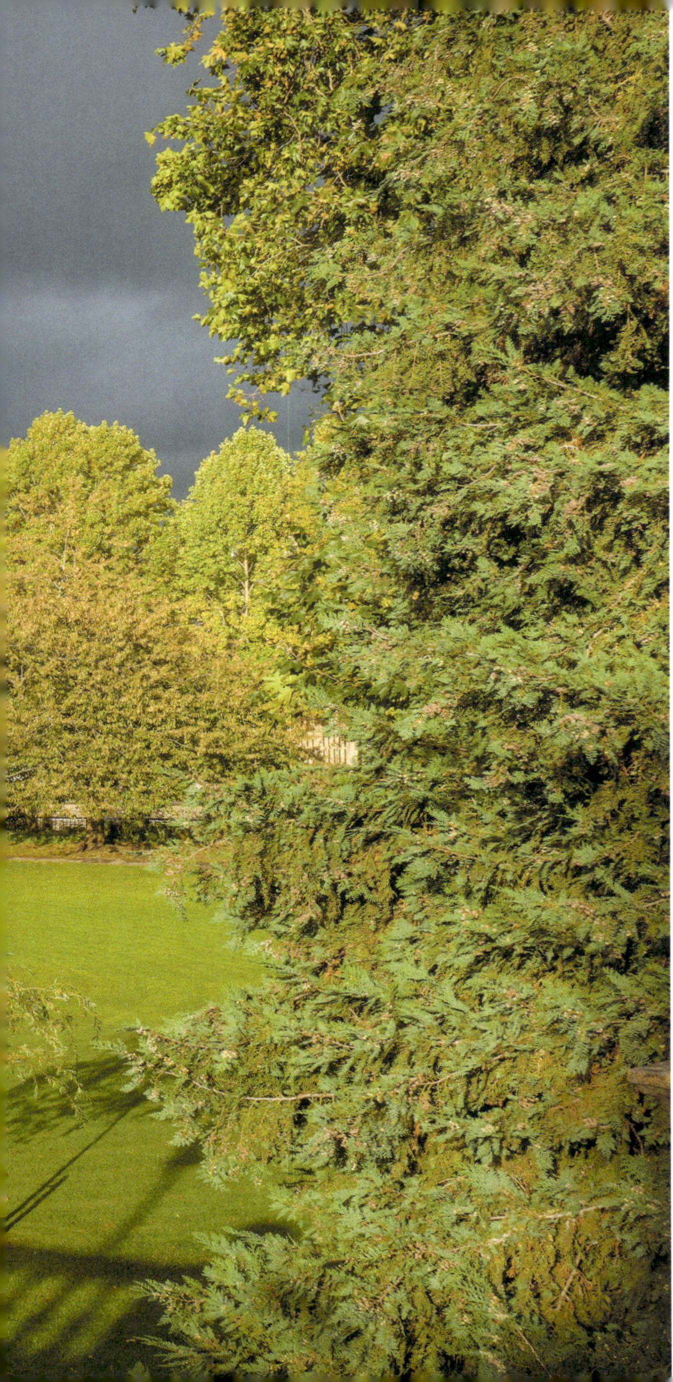

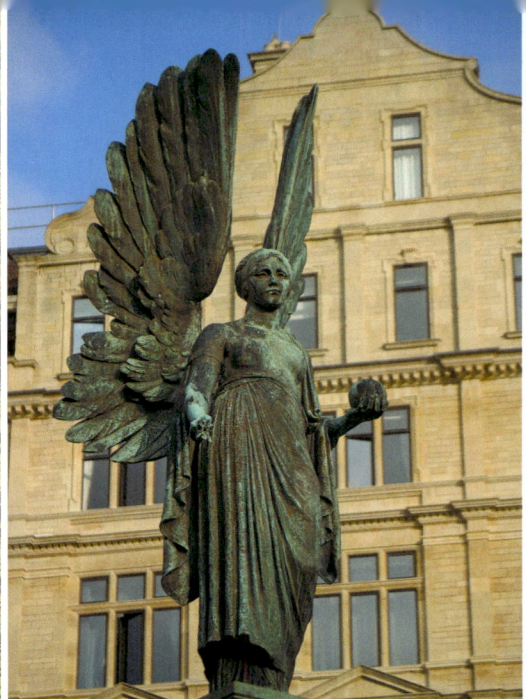
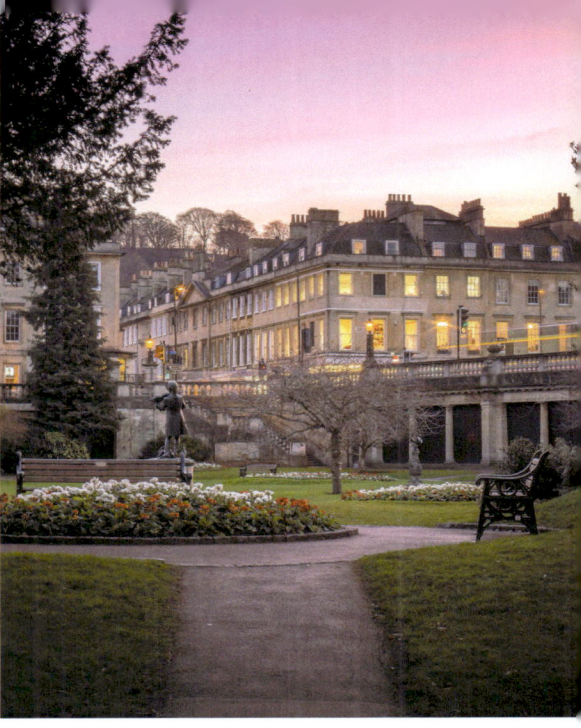
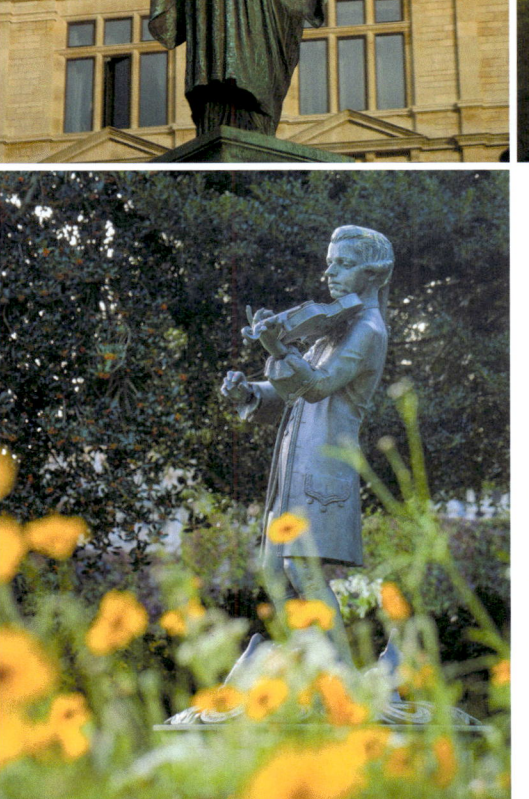

OPPOSITE: one of Bath's earliest public parks, Parade Gardens has been a pleasure ground since 1709. At just over three acres it offers plenty of space among the trees and shrubs for visitors to explore or relax.

TOP LEFT: the Angel of Peace, a memorial to King Edward VII. **ABOVE**: even at twilight, Parade Gardens transforms into an enchanting haven. **LEFT**: a statue of a young Mozart playing his violin stands proudly in Bath, the city hosts the annual Mozartfest Music Festival, celebrating his legacy in a vibrant display of music.

6 PULTENEY BRIDGE

VIII

7 GREAT PULTENEY STREET

William Wilberforce (1759–1833), the renowned British politician and abolitionist, is best remembered for his tireless and successful campaign against the transatlantic slave trade. He lived at 36 Great Pulteney Street in 1802 and 1805. A heritage plaque commemorates his stays at this address.

"Lady Dalrymple had taken a house, for three months, in Laura Place, and would be living in style."
– Jane Austen, *Persuasion* (1817)

Bath's grandest boulevard links the historic city centre beyond the river Avon at Pulteney Bridge to the historic Pulteney family estate at Bathwick. Designed by Thomas Baldwin and completed in 1789 this 'Georgian new town' was intended to become the start of a wider expansion plan commissioned by Sir William Pulteney. Great Pulteney Street is truly an impressive sight at over 1000 feet long and 100 feet wide, a man-made vanishing point stretching eastwards towards the Holburne Museum which sits perfectly symmetrical at its furthermost point.

The street is arranged as a row of two vast terraced Georgian townhouses in the Neoclassical style adorned with Greco-Roman features, imposing doorways and wooden sash windows. Each facade is almost identical in appearance, except for a few slight additional alterations such as balconies or ironwork features. Architect Baldwin's intention was to retain this uniform appearance which allowed each individual property owner to arrange the interior layout as they wished, as such some properties became guest houses stretching wider throughout the row whilst other smaller vertical arrangements became private residences.

The vast majority of the buildings are Grade 1 listed and sit upon seven metres of vaulted cellars below in an effort to prevent flooding from the nearby river Avon, impressively a further two storeys are below the four that can be seen from street level.

Great Pulteney Street is a popular filming location and scenes from cinematic greats such as *Vanity Fair* and the *Duchess* were set here. Local resident Jane Austen also based part of one of her popular novels in this area of Bath dealing with the intricacies of high society in the book *Northanger Abbey*. Seasonal events often fill the wide boulevard with colour and joy as both the Bath Marathon and Bath Carnival routes pass along Great Pulteney Street.

GREAT PULTENEY STREET

Postcode: BA2 4DN
what3words: humid.beast.crowned

LAURA PLACE

Postcode: BA2 4BL
what3words: couches.really.pints

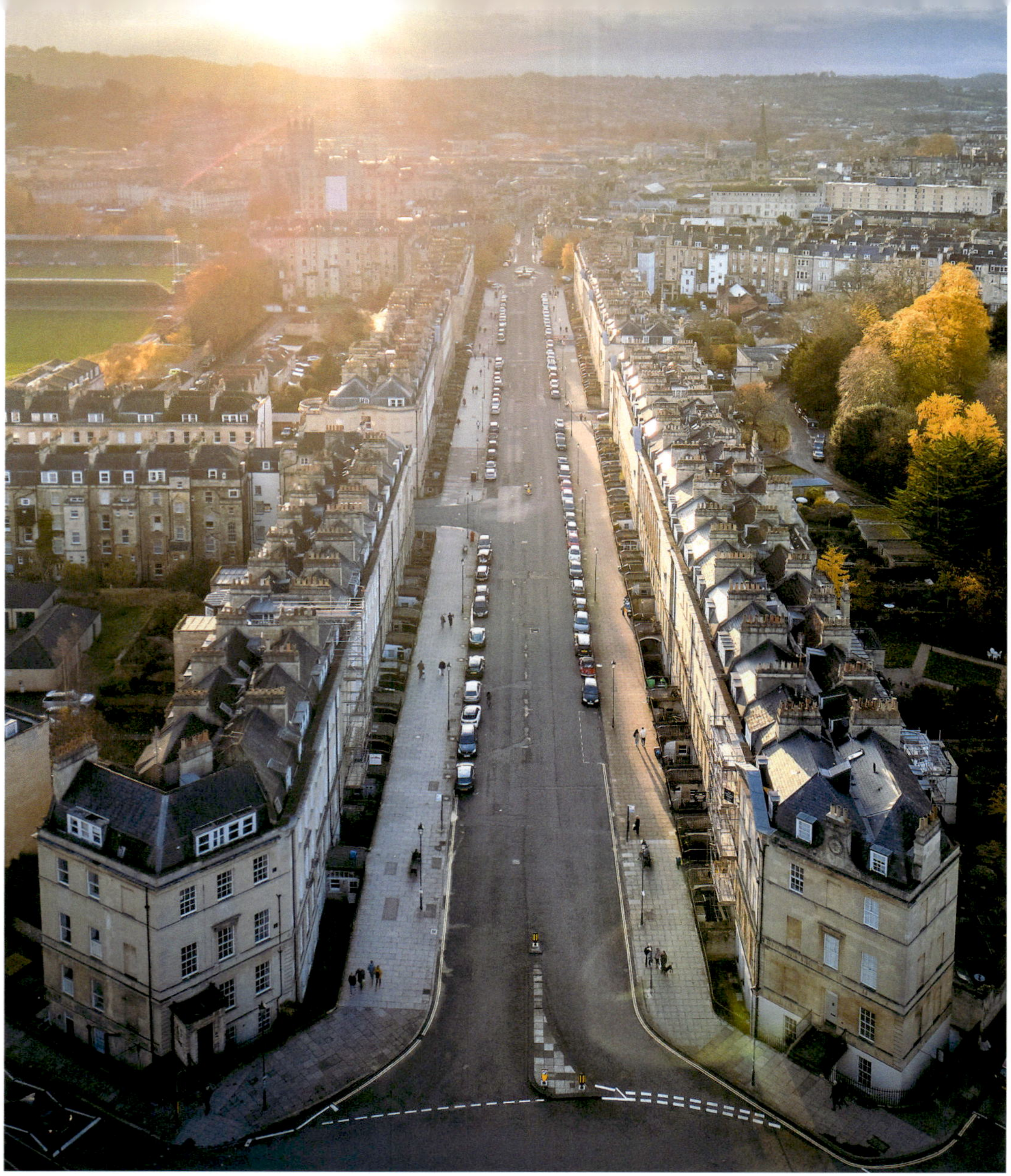

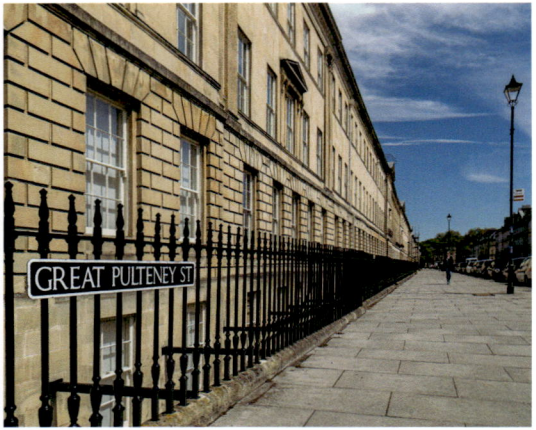

ABOVE: the wide pavements of Great Pulteney Street, designed in Georgian times were made to accommodate the fashionable social life of the era. These spacious walkways provided ample room for leisurely strolls and conversation, allowing people to admire the grand architecture and each other. **LEFT**: Great Pulteney Street, lined with stunning Georgian buildings, stretches over 1,000 feet long and 100 feet wide, making it the grandest, longest and widest street in Bath.

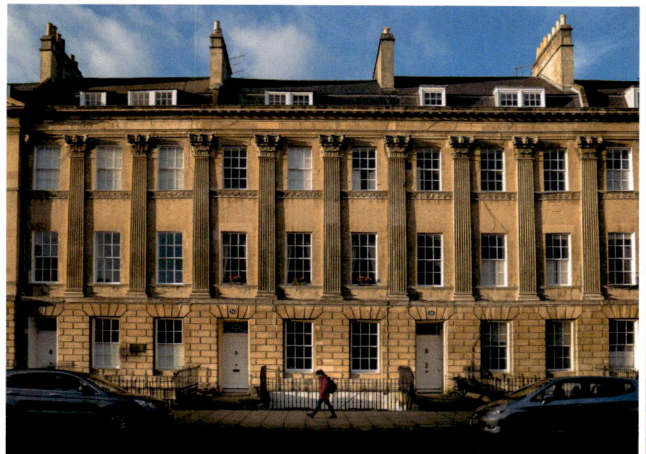
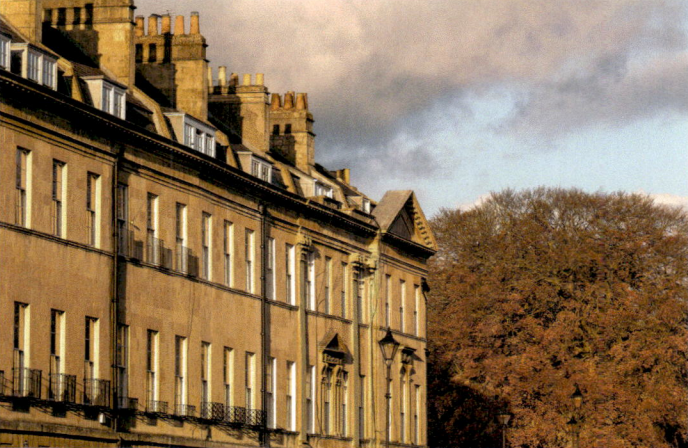

FAR LEFT: the facades of the townhouses along Great Pulteney Street are adorned with striking Corinthian columns. **LEFT**: autumn beautifully complements the stonework. **BELOW LEFT**: stretching from Pulteney Bridge, the street culminates at the entrance lawn of the Holburne Museum. **BELOW**: a prime example of a Bath townhouse.

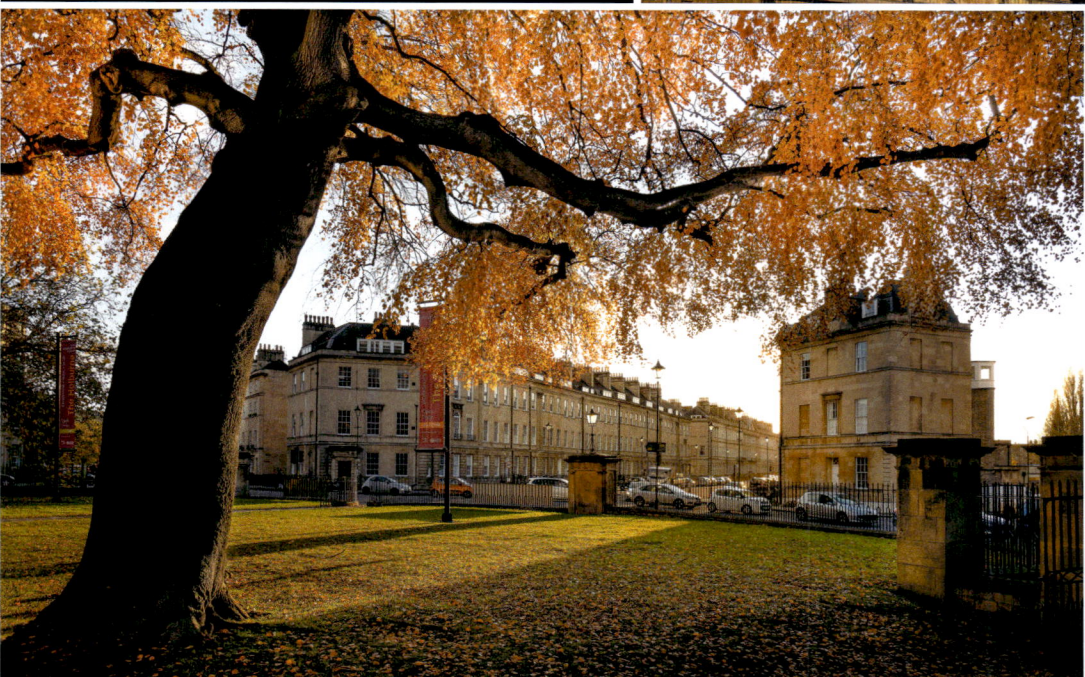
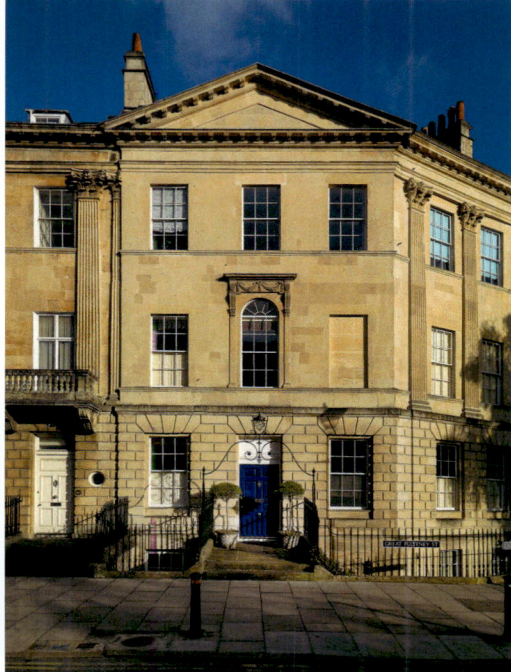

7 GREAT PULTENEY STREET

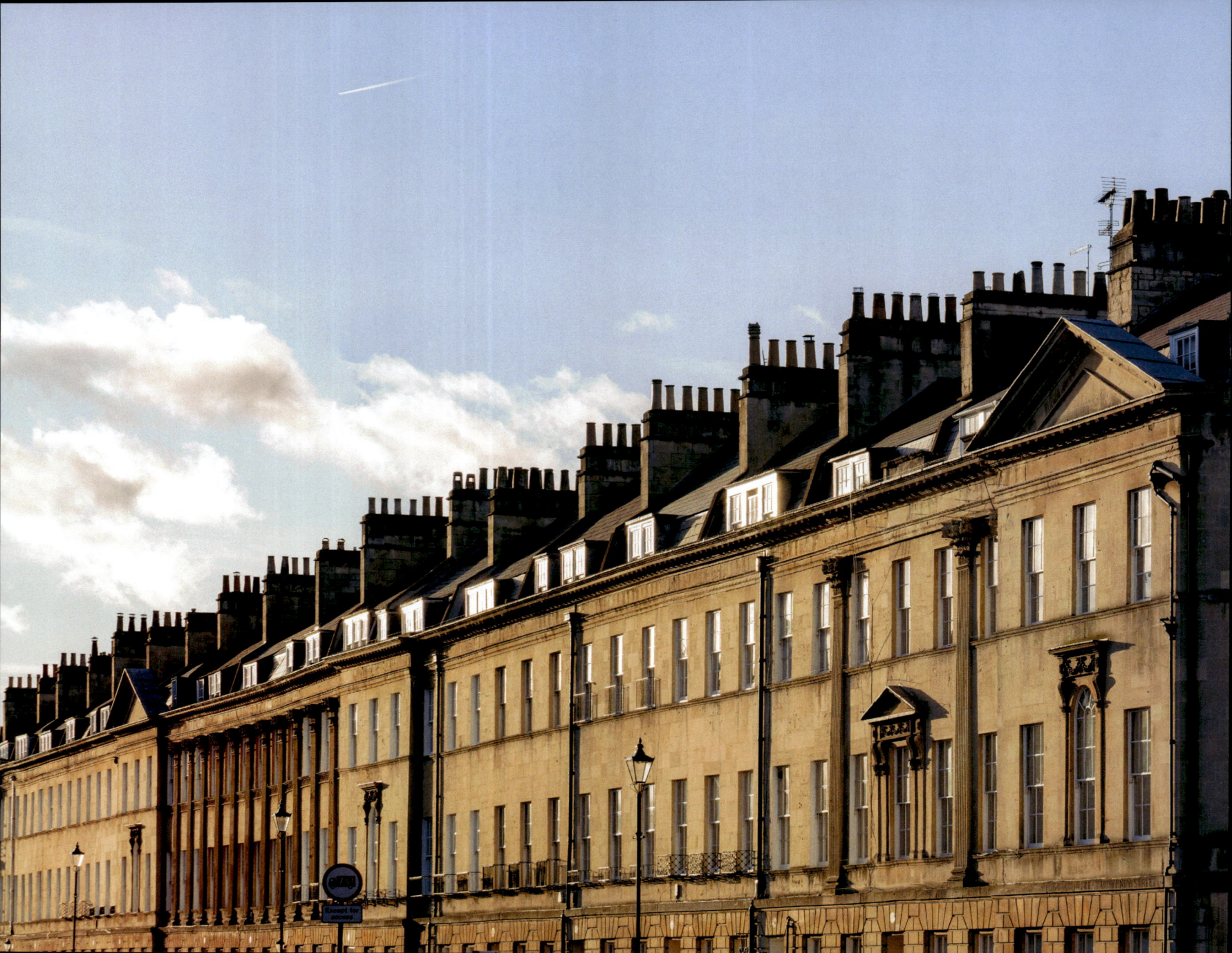

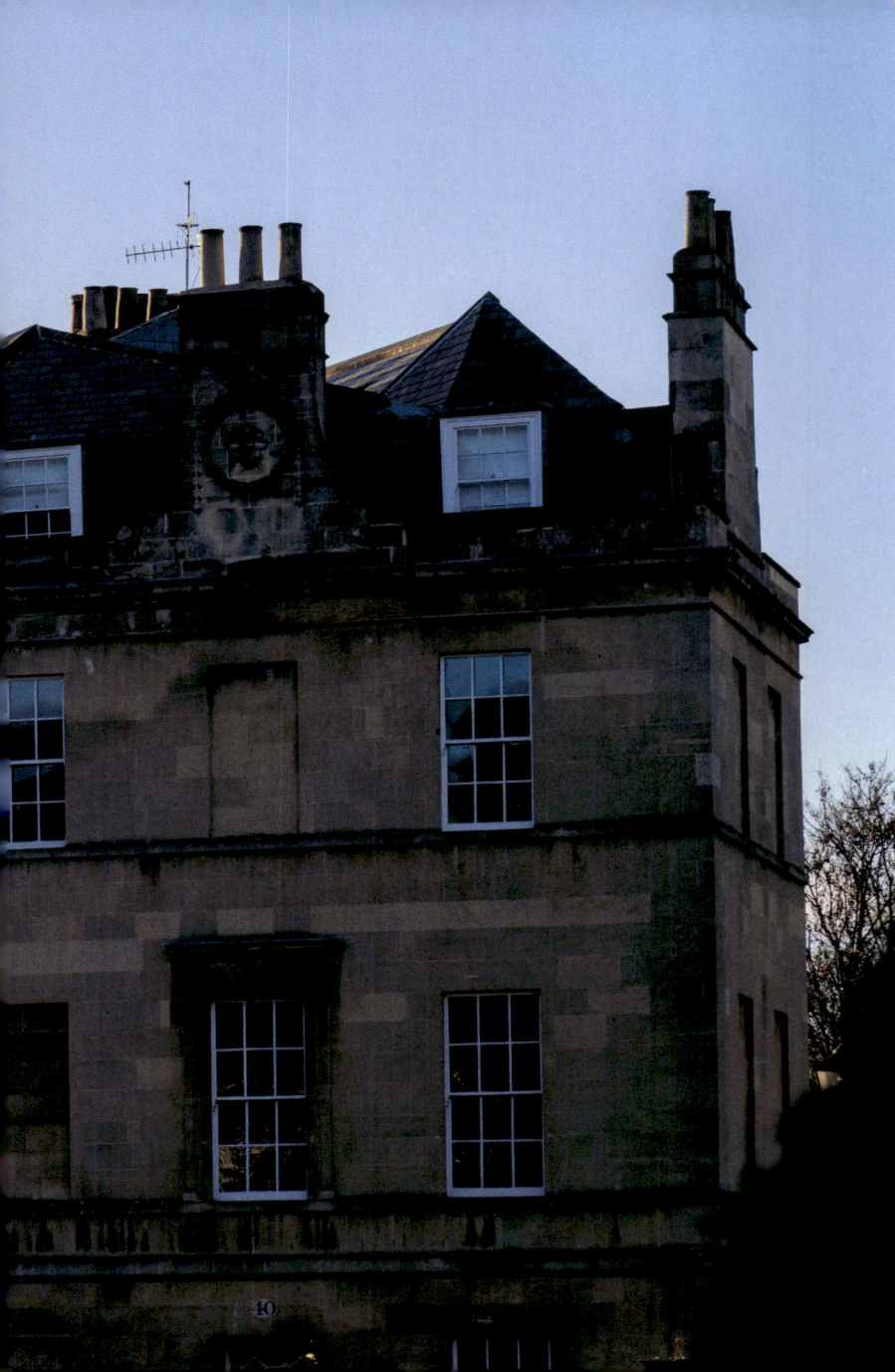

Though Great Pulteney Street appears uniform, many of the houses are beautifully embellished with unique pediments, intricate windows, door carvings and elegant ironwork balconies.

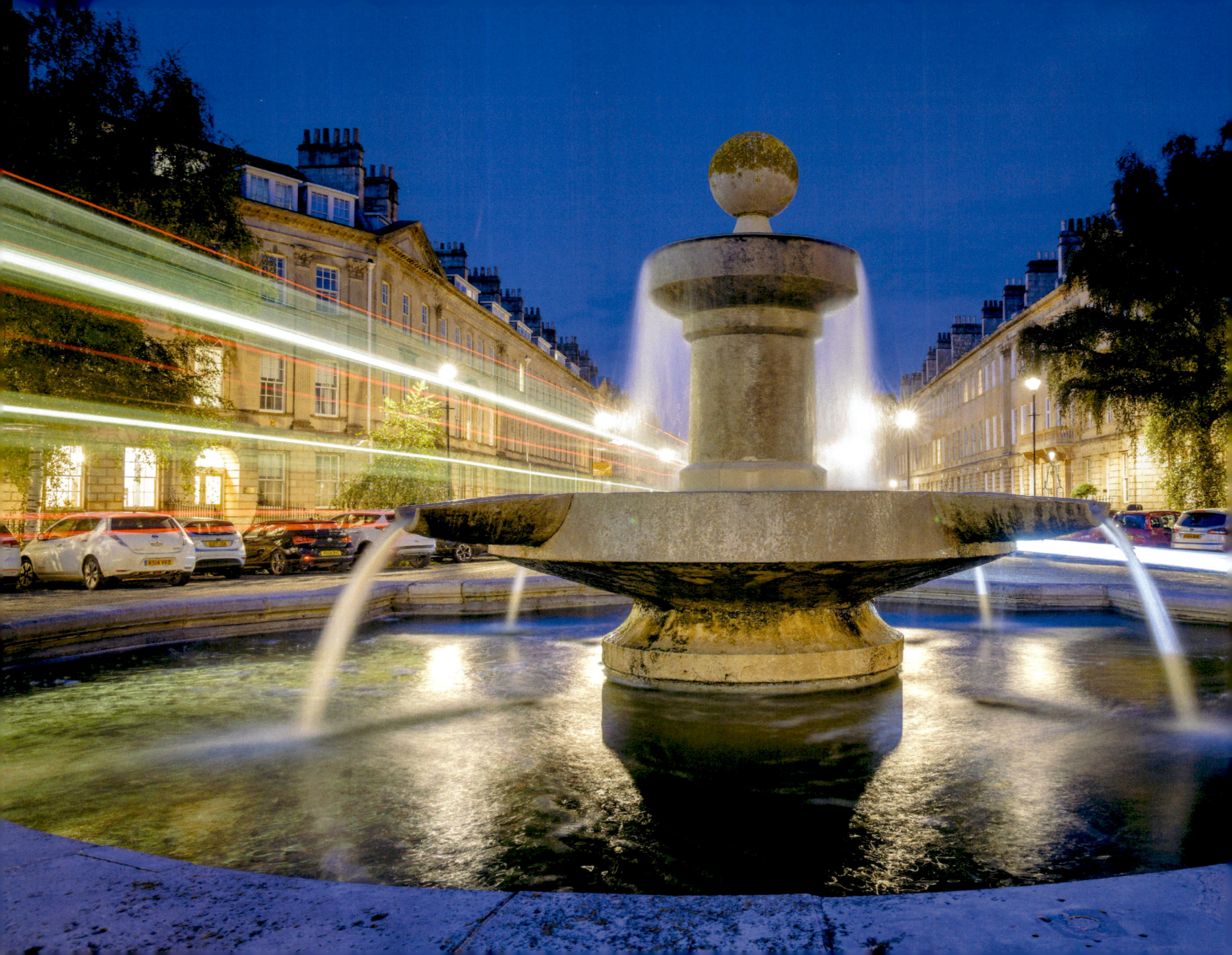

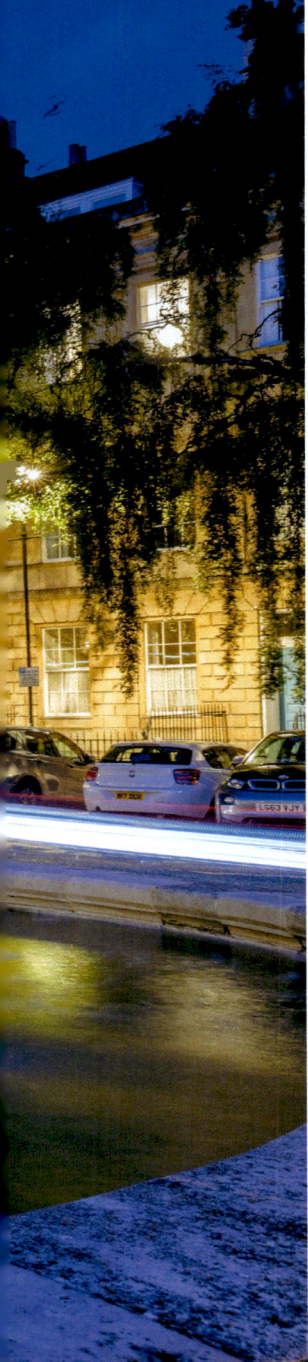

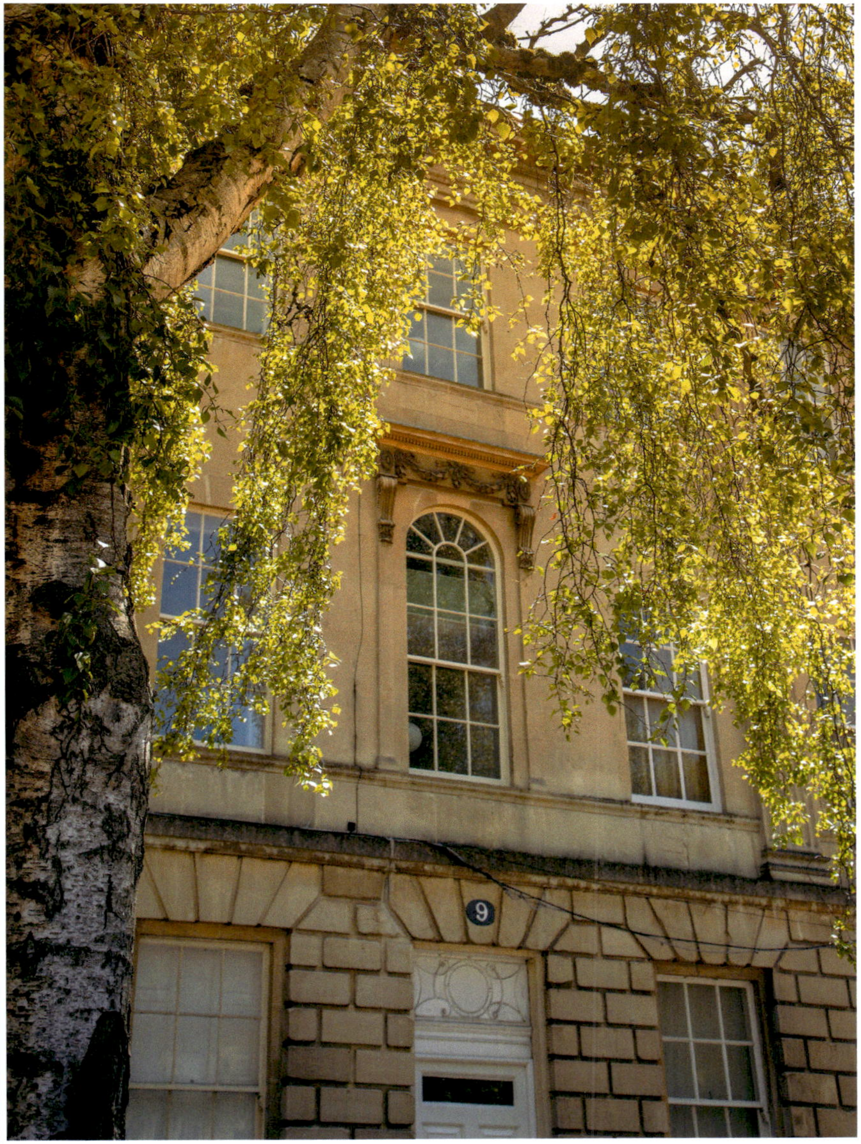

LAURA PLACE

Laura Place was named after Henrietta Laura Pulteney, daughter to Sir William Pulteney, the same wealthy landowner who commissioned Robert Adam to create the architectural wonder of Pulteney Bridge that links the old city to his land beyond the river. She was his only child and was fortunate to not only have Henrietta Street and Henrietta Park named after her but she also inherited her fathers estate when he passed away in 1792.

Designed and built jointly by John Eveleigh and Thomas Baldwin between 1788 and 1794 Laura Place connects the pleasingly wide grand boulevard of Great Pulteney Street to Baldwin's other commission, Argyle Street, creating the long and impressive route from the bridge to the Holburne Museum in the east. Two further routes lead away along Henrietta Street to Henrietta Park in the north and on the southern exit is Johnstone Street overlooking the Recreation Ground, home to Bath Rugby.

This is a beautiful part of Bath with some of the finest Georgian properties in the city and is considered the epitome of Georgian urban planning. Four different streets link up with Laura Place arranged around a quadrangle of townhouses flanked by a collection of beautiful silver birch trees lining each side of the terraced properties, and at the heart of the street stands a bubbling water fountain.

OPPOSITE: a fountain sits at the heart of Laura Place, originally installed in 1877 and altered in the 1970s. It adds a distinctive feature to the street, reflecting Bath's deep connection with water.
LEFT: silver birch trees beautifully frame the exteriors.

OPPOSITE: Laura Place is regarded as one of the most impressive Neoclassical urban set pieces in Britain.

RIGHT: Laura Place leads into Argyle Street, where several historic shop fronts still stand, including A.H. Hale LTD, one of the oldest pharmacies in the UK. Above its entrance a crest of Queen Charlotte can be seen. **BELOW LEFT:** spring blossom at Henrietta Park, located behind Great Pulteney Street and Laura Place to the north. **BELOW RIGHT:** opened in 1897 to celebrate Queen Victoria's Diamond Jubilee, Henrietta Park spans 10 acres and features an impressive collection of ancient trees, including two national champions and several regional ones, the largest or tallest of their kind.

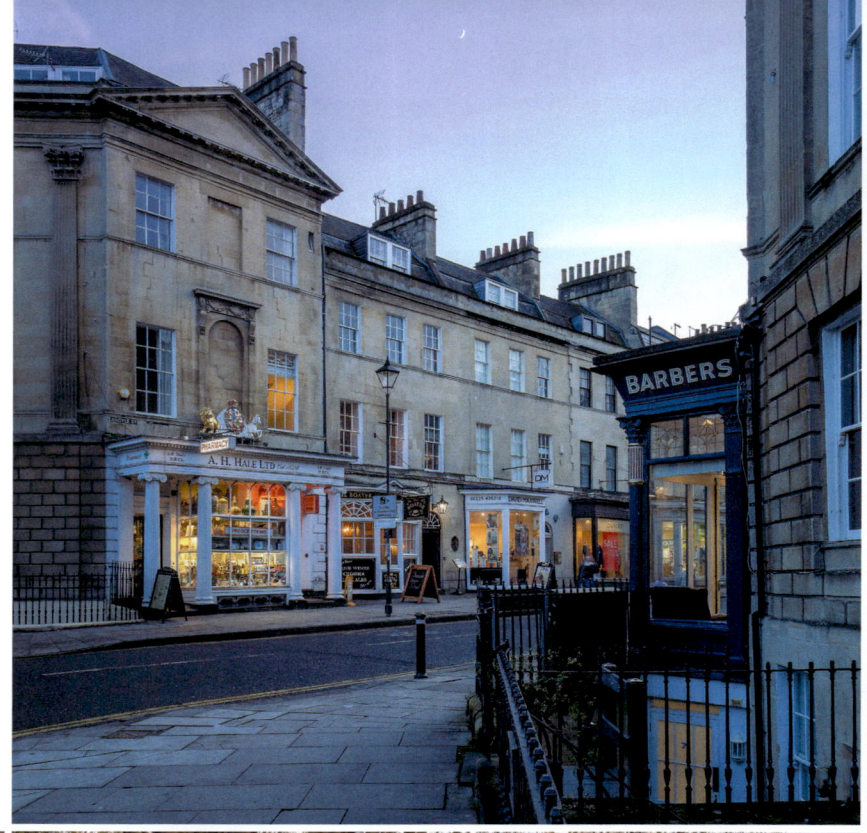

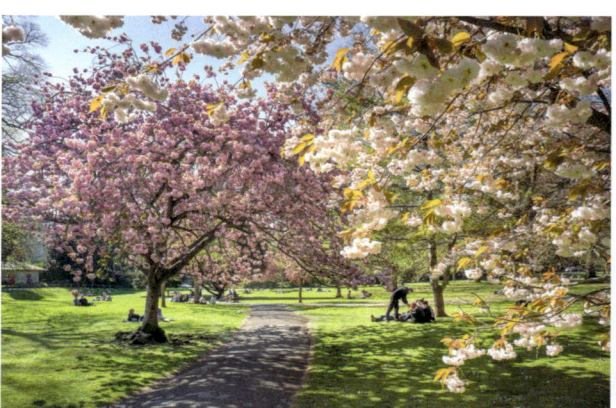

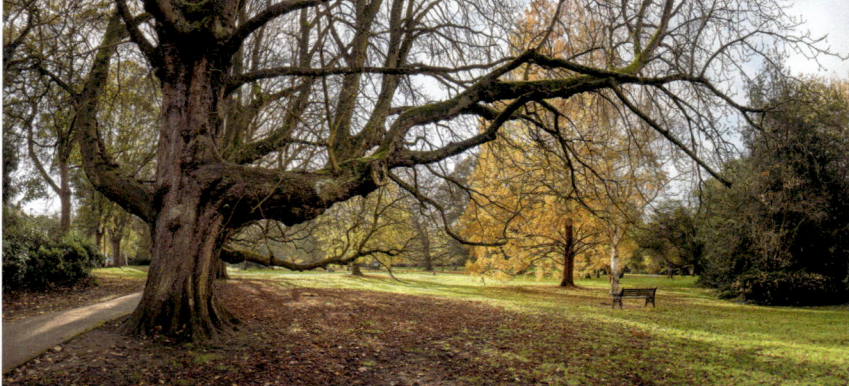

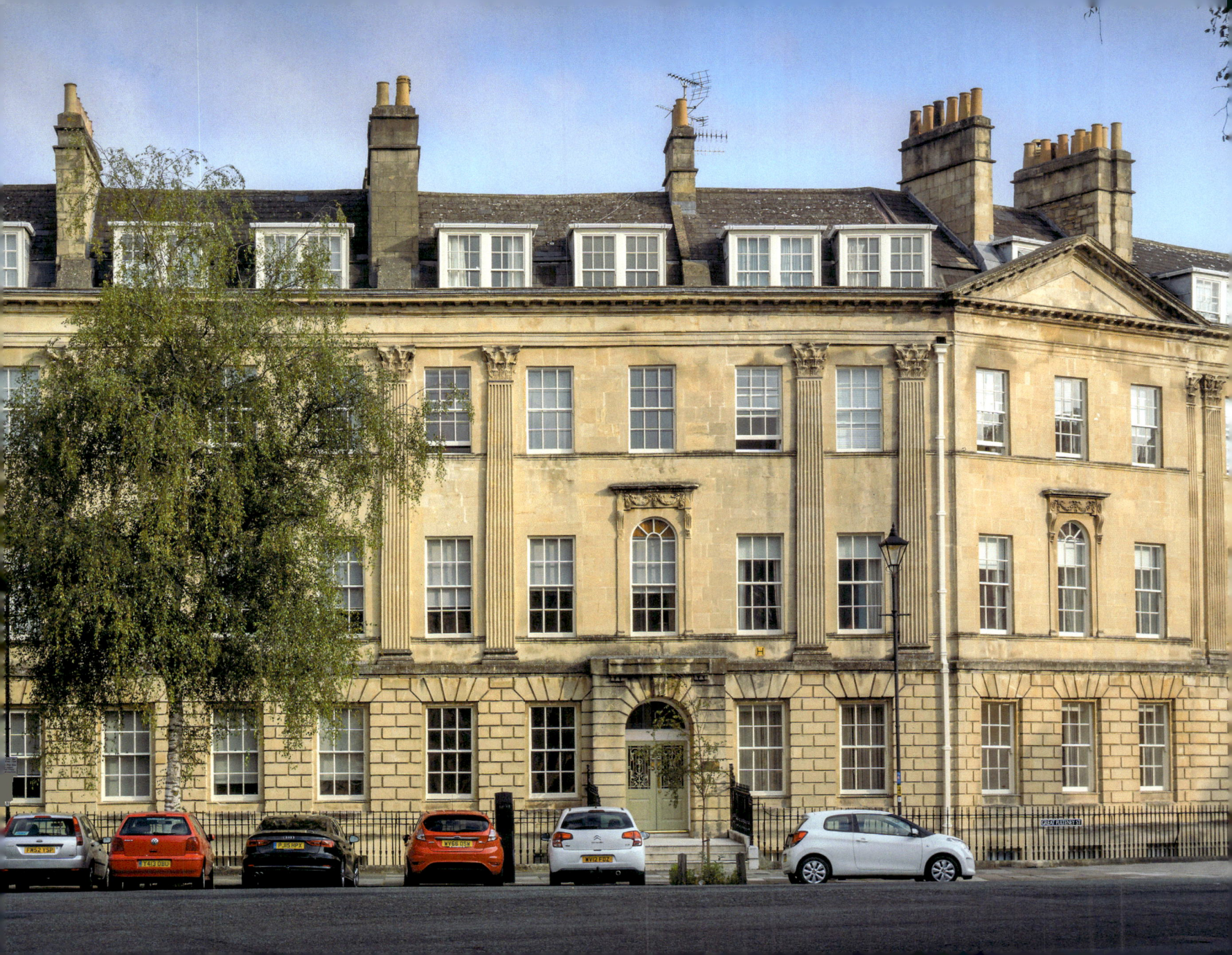

VIII

8 THE HOLBURNE MUSEUM

"Sir William Holburne (1793–1874), fifth baronet of Menstrie, inherited the family title and a modest fortune. He left the navy and embarked on an eighteen-month Grand Tour of Europe, visiting Italy, the Alps and the Netherlands. This sparked a life-long interest in art and his enthusiasm for collecting. Since his death, more than 9,000 items have been added to his collection including portrait miniatures, porcelain, embroideries and portraits by some of the greatest artists of the eighteenth century."
– Holburne Museum

On the eastern side of the city, uniquely placed as the crowning jewel at the end of Great Pulteney Street, the Holburne Museum acts as a gateway to the intriguing public parkland beyond called Sydney Gardens. Built in 1796 and formerly known as the Sydney Hotel, the museums original purpose was to serve the fashionable eighteenth century clientele with its concert hall and ballroom. As the gardens began to wane in popularity during the early 1800's the building became a private lodge which had an additional floor added to accommodate guests.

In 1916 the building became Bath's first public art gallery and museum, changing its name to reflect the vast and eclectic assortment of porcelain, silverware, furniture and portraits collected by ex-naval commander, Sir Thomas William Holburne. After his death in 1874 his sister bequeathed his extensive collection to the city of Bath, laying the foundation for the museum's establishment. Today, the Holburne Collection forms the core of the museum's holdings, offering visitors a glimpse into the tastes and interests of a bygone era. Alongside this treasure-trove of historic delights the museum also houses contemporary exhibitions and hosts educational and summer events.

The beautiful symmetrical front facade has remained relatively untouched thanks to a Grade 1 listing status and in 2011 the museum underwent a major restoration with the addition of a contemporary steel and glass structure at the rear effectively doubling the museum's exhibition space and also housing a book, gift shop and award winning cafe.

To book tickets go to: www.holburne.org

THE HOLBURNE MUSEUM

Postcode: BA2 4DB
what3words: trial.sizes.life

SYDNEY GARDENS

Postcode: BA2 6NT
what3words: bags.linked.remain

SYDNEY PLACE

Postcode: BA2 6NE
what3words: trade.export.stream

MORE INFORMATION

holburne.org
Visit the Holburne museum website for opening times, events, admission, history and directions.

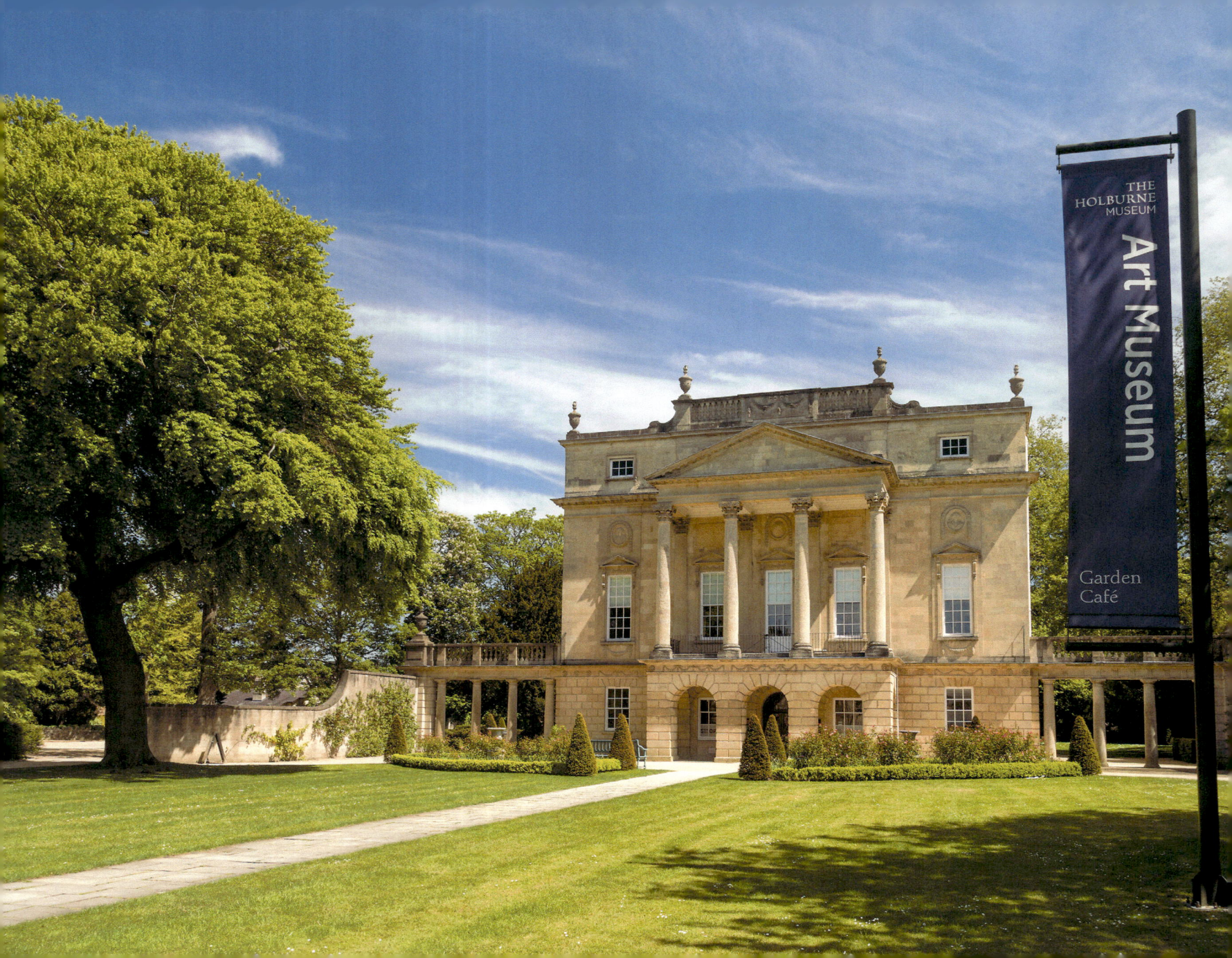

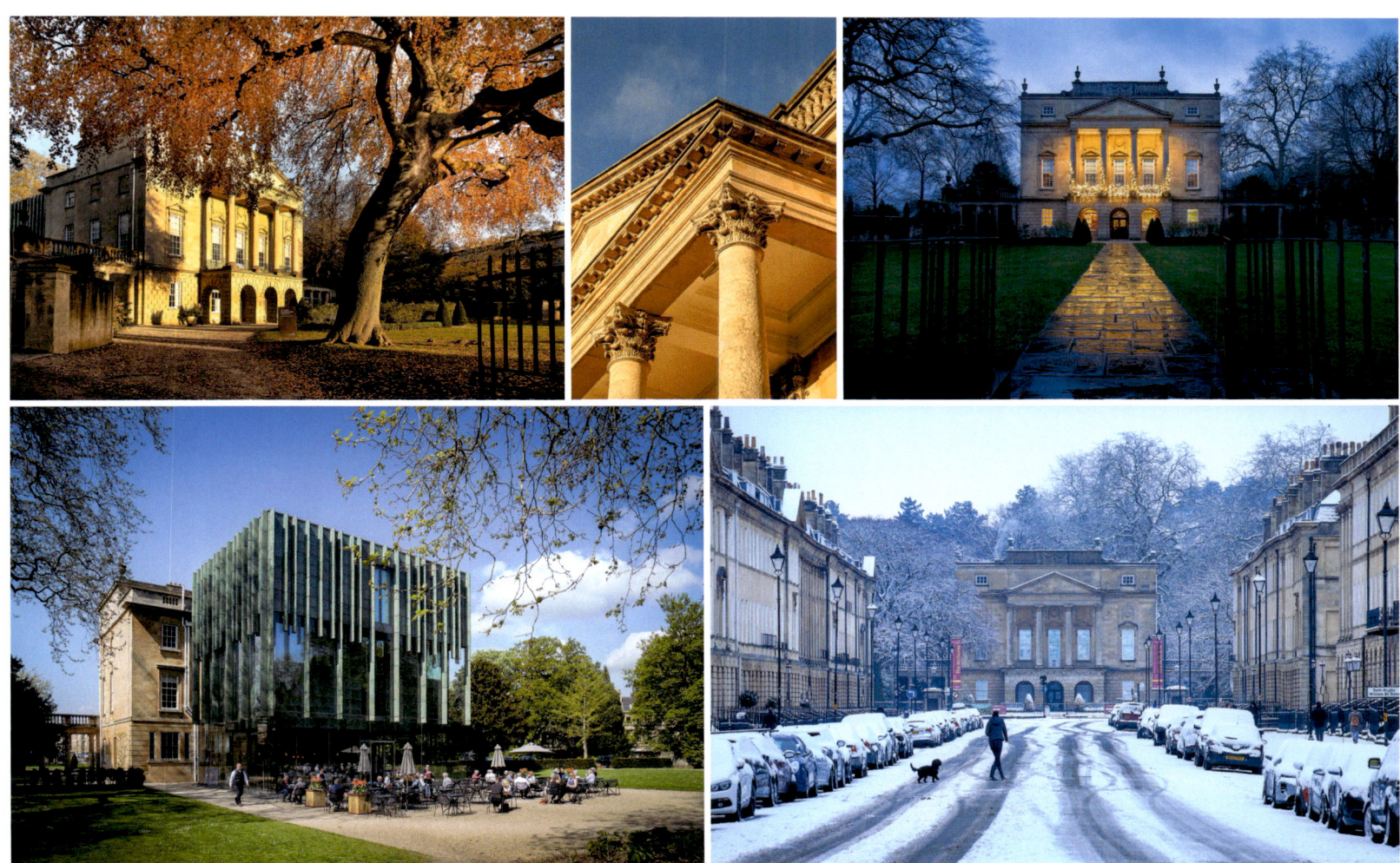

OPPOSITE: instantly recognisable as Lady Danbury's house in the popular Netflix series *Bridgerton*, the Holburne Museum is also home to 9,000 unique artworks. Established as Bath's first public art galleries it contains a fine collection of porcelain, silver and 18th-century British portraiture.
TOP LEFT: an impressive beech tree stands at the entrance to the museum, its leaves casting a golden glow in autumn. **TOP MIDDLE**: the entrance facade of the Holburne Museum features a tetrastyle portico. **TOP RIGHT**: a Light in the Dark. Festive illuminations brighten the Holburne Museum during Christmas time.
ABOVE LEFT: at the rear a new gallery space and coffee shop (free to enter) was added in 2011 extending the museum layout by an additional 800sq metres.
ABOVE RIGHT: the Holburne's symmetrical design is beautifully complemented by Great Pulteney Street.

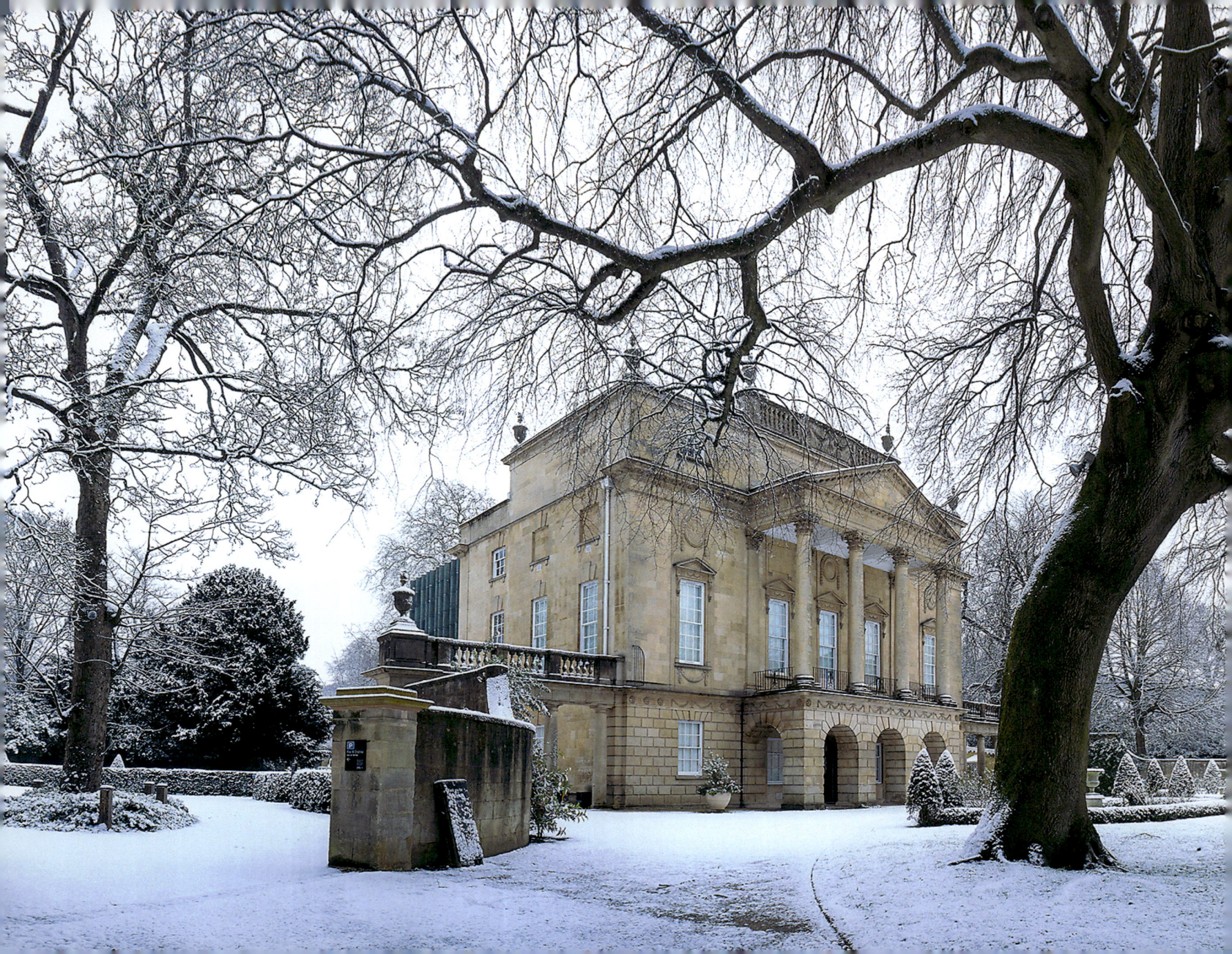

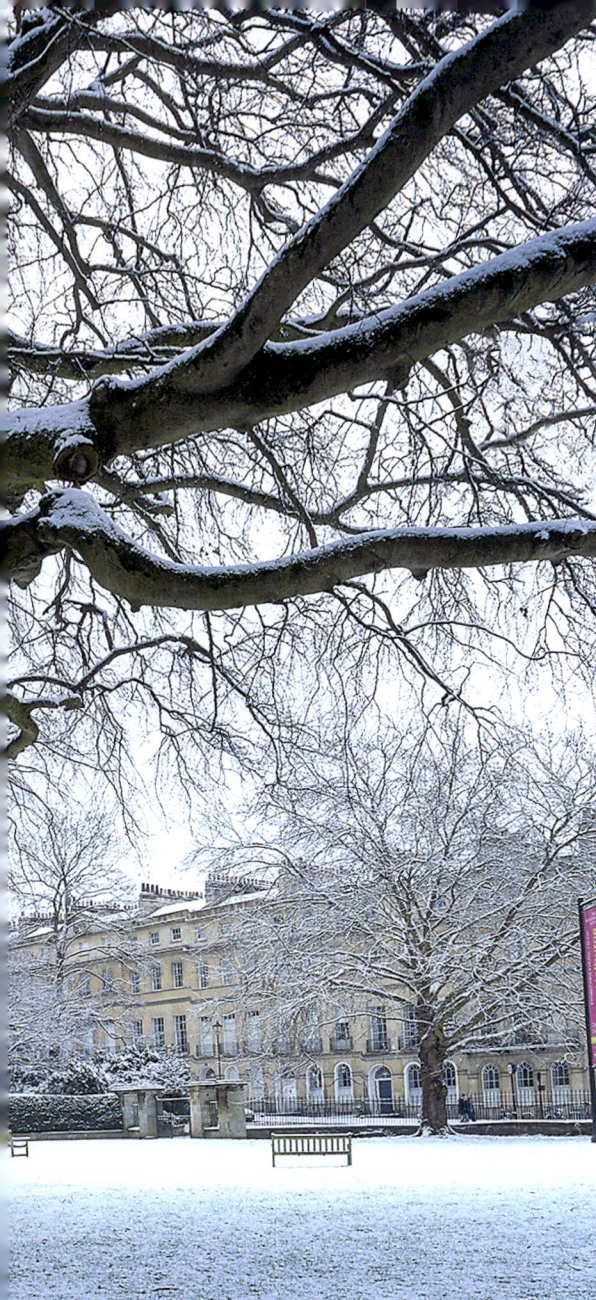

The Holburne Museum stands at the gateway to Bath's first pleasure garden, a spot familiar to Jane Austen. Living opposite, she would have visited to attend garden parties and lavish functions during her time in Bath.

8 THE HOLBURNE MUSEUM

SYDNEY GARDENS

Located 15 minutes walk from Bath city centre, Sydney Gardens has long been referred to as the 'green lungs' of the city and are a popular destination. Here you can relax, take picnics, watch canal boats float by and even dabble in a bit of train-spotting. The gardens are fantastic to visit throughout the year to witness the changing seasons with intense yellow foliage in autumn. This area of the city is the perfect destination when combined with a visit to the neighbouring Holburne Museum. There is a network of paths to explore leading off from a main central route surrounded by open lawns and flanked by beautifully maintained flowerbeds and shrubs.

Opened in 1795 and originally called Bath Gardens Vauxhall they operated as a commercial pleasure ground, originally inspired by and taking the name of the popular Vauxhall Gardens in London. Sydney Gardens are the only remaining intact 'Vauxhall' gardens in the country and have been given a Grade 2 listing, protecting the unique characteristics of the site; even the cast iron public conveniences are listed.

The most scenic part of the gardens is the glorious Kennet & Avon Canal that meanders its way through the heart of the park. Crossing the water are a series of ornate iron bridges allowing for a perfect vantage point above the canal. The view southwards is probably the best, taking in Cleveland House in the distance which sits above the canal with the tunnel running directly beneath. Below the canal is the Great Western Rail route which passes through the park before stopping at Bath Spa Station in the city centre. Elevated bridges give clear views of trains, perfect for spotting unique steam trains that occasionally pass through.

Centrally located is a replica of the ancient Temple of Minerva discovered at the Roman Baths which was used to promote the city and the quality of locally quarried stone during the 1911 Festival of Empire Exhibition at the Crystal Palace in London; it was later relocated to the gardens.

The gardens are open throughout the year and contain numerous activity trails, play areas for children with playground equipment and open spaces for outdoor activities and games, sport courts, a small cafe and picnic benches.

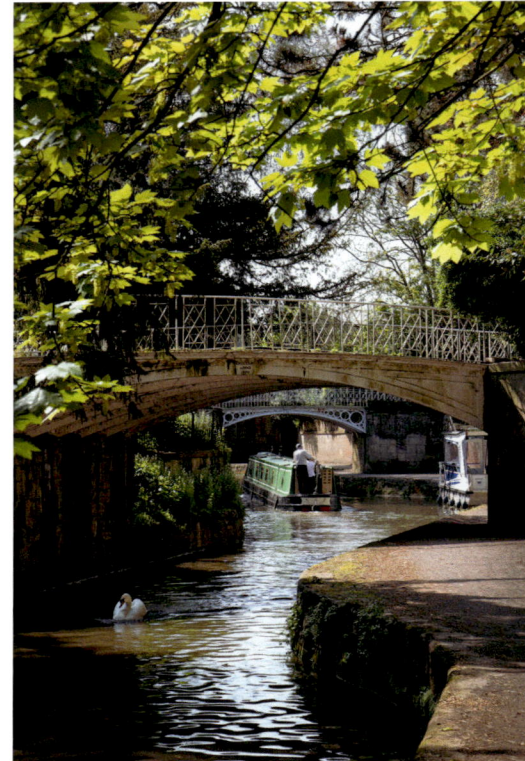

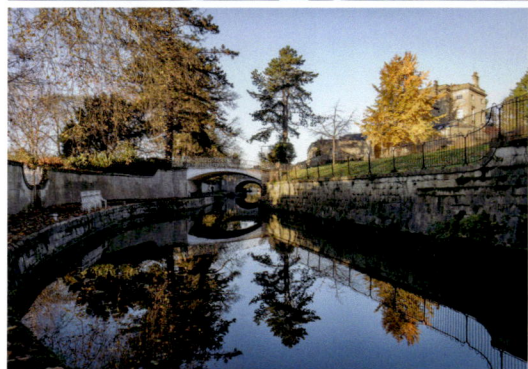

OVERLEAF LEFT: Sydney House stands at the top of the gardens, where seasonal plantings surround trees and pathways. **MIDDLE TOP & MIDDLE**: elegant columns, a hallmark of Bath's styling can be seen throughout. The Corinthian style, used in Roman, Renaissance and Neoclassical architecture is often seen in grand public spaces. **MIDDLE BOTTOM**: springtime crocus bulbs emerge providing early season interest. **RIGHT**: even on misty days the beauty of the gardens is revealed, perhaps even more so, creating atmospheric scenes along the canal.

TOP RIGHT: the charming Kennet & Avon Canal flows through the gardens, crossed by elegant ironwork footbridges. **RIGHT**: the canal towpath can be accessed from the gardens, offering a scenic route to explore the waterway through the city.
OPPOSITE: wide pathways and ample space invite visitors to leisurely stroll beneath the boughs of mature trees.

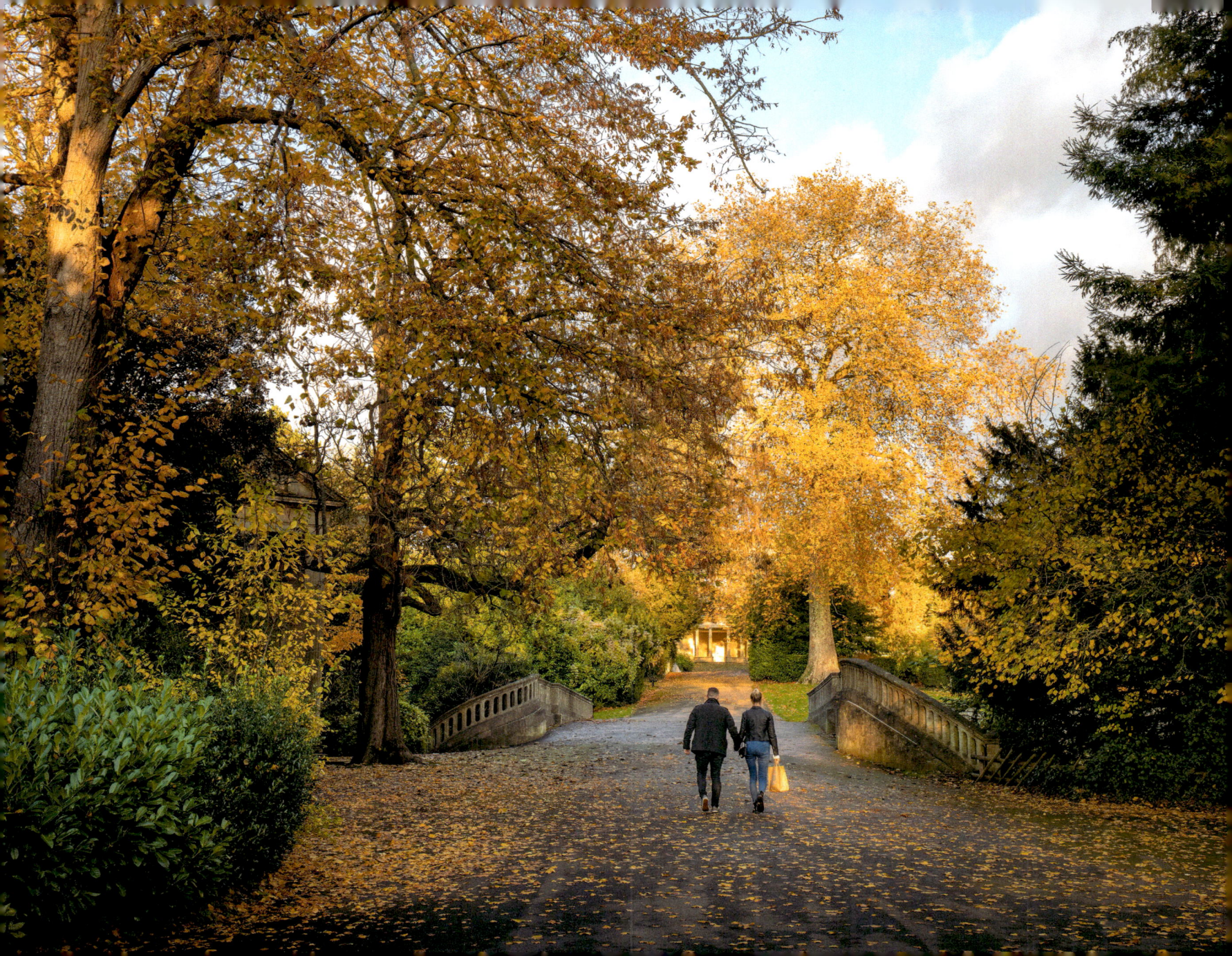

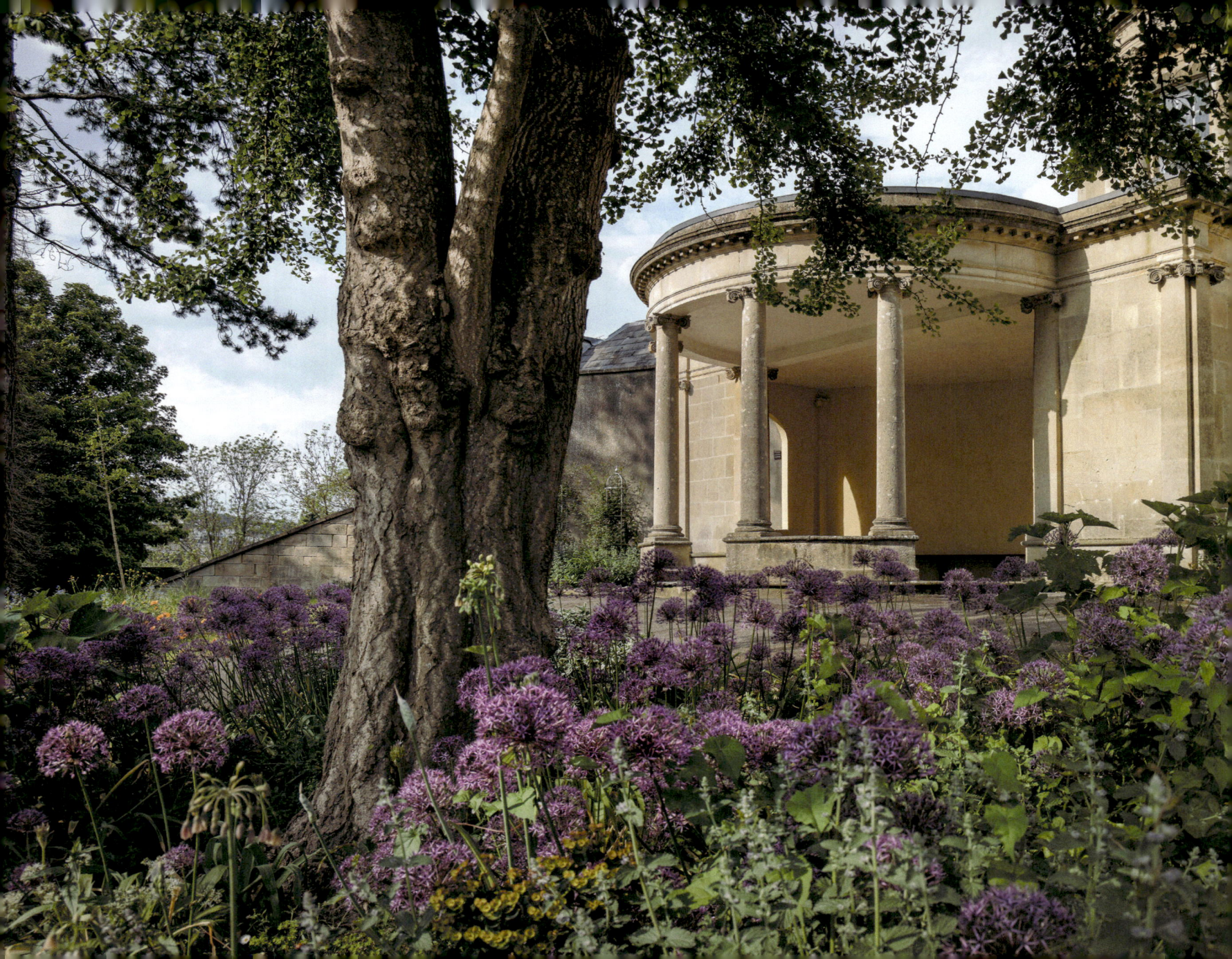

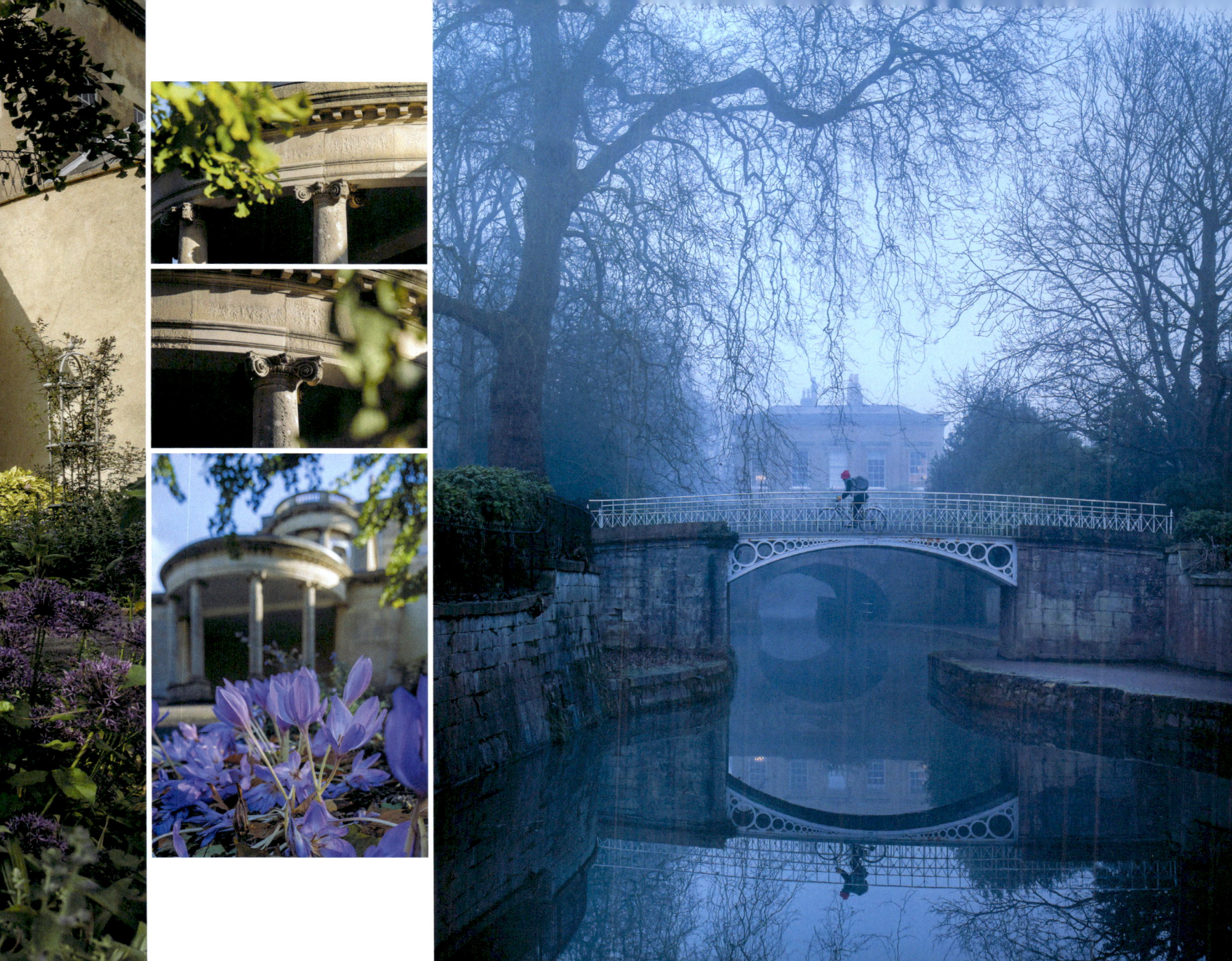

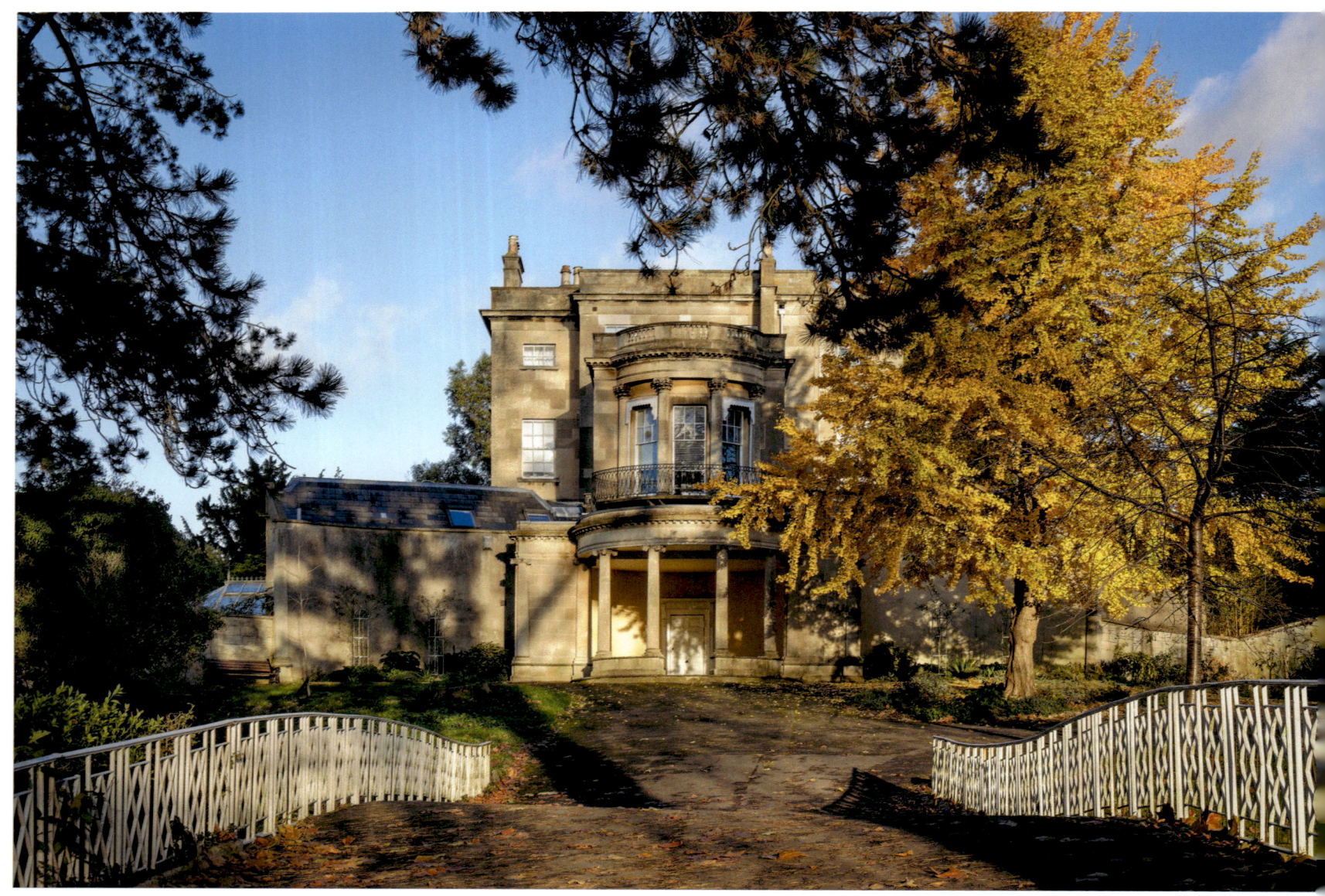
Sydney House stands on the north-eastern edge of the park, perfectly aligned with the Holburne Museum at the south-east of the park.

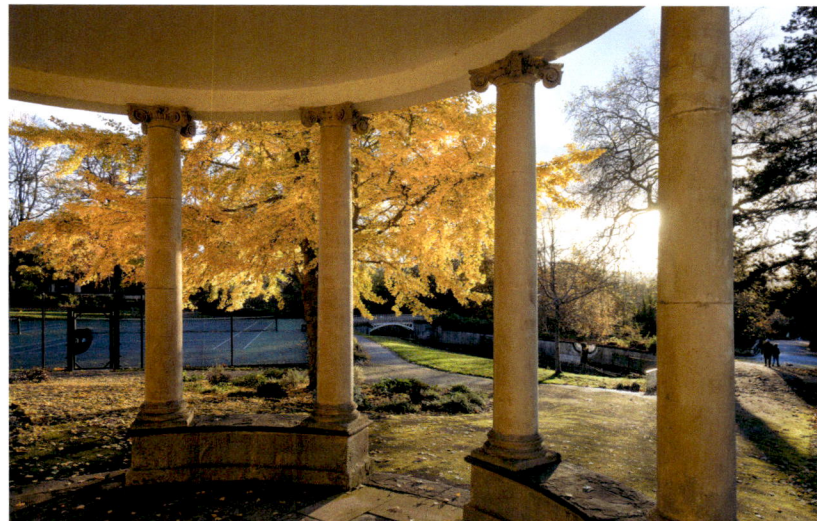
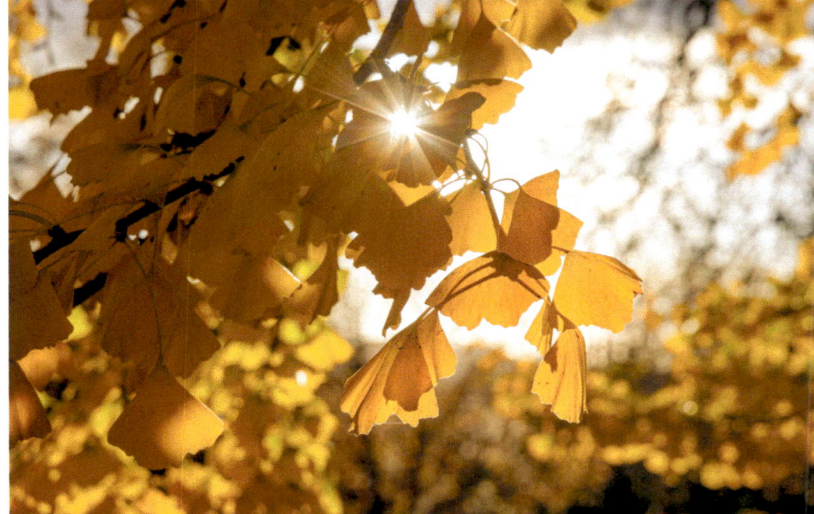

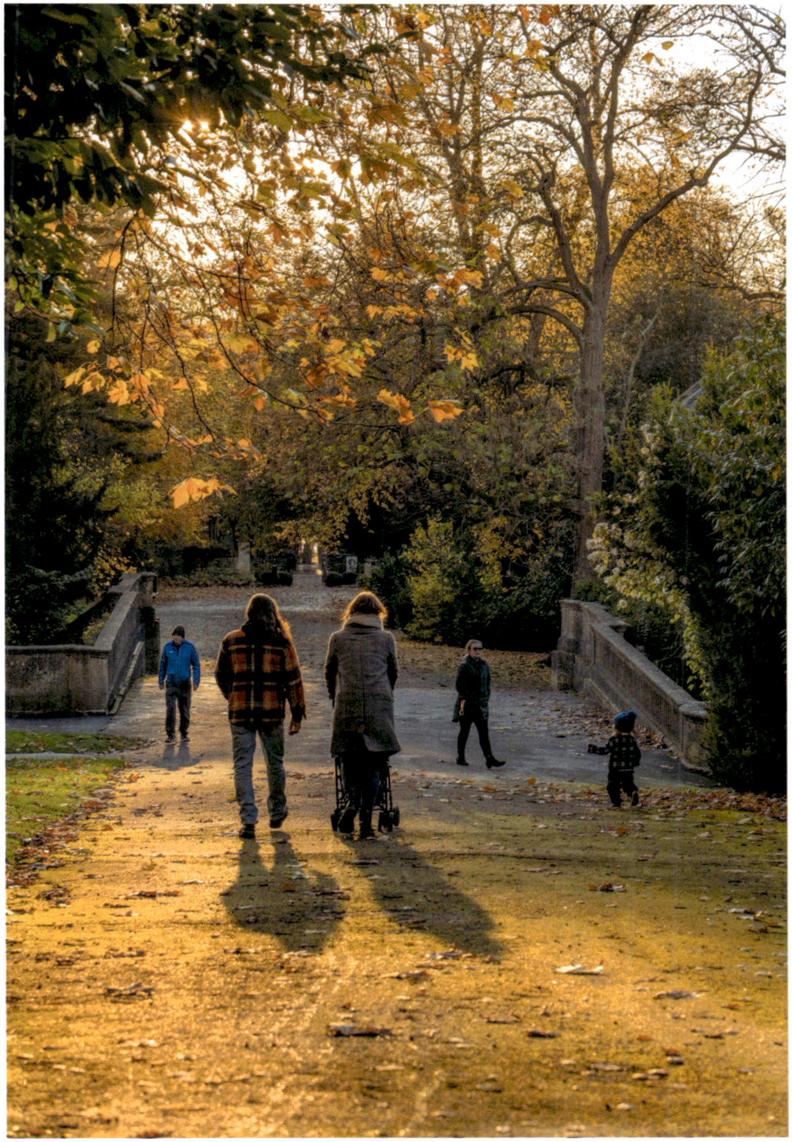

TOP: a covered seating area offers shelter and a perfect viewpoint. **ABOVE**: the leaves of a ginkgo tree, one of many fine specimens found in the park. **RIGHT**: autumn brings the best colour to the changing leaves — a perfect time to explore.

SYDNEY PLACE

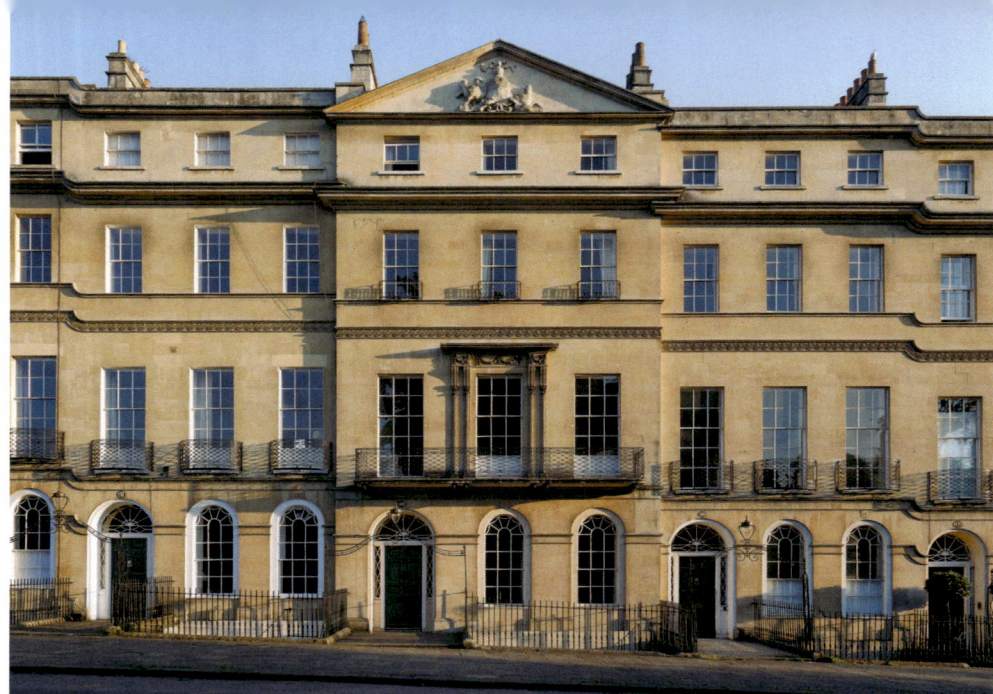

Sydney Place is a good example of Bath's famous Palladian architectural style. Built in the late 18th and early 19th centuries, it features classic Bath stone facades, symmetrical proportions, and grand sash windows, typical of the city's development during the Georgian era. One of Sydney Place's most famous residents was Jane Austen, who lived at No. 4 from 1801 to 1804. During her time there, she frequented the nearby Sydney Gardens, a scenic retreat for Bath's upper class.

TOP: the graceful Palace fronted exterior of Nos. 93 to 103 Sydney Place were designed by John Pinch the Elder in 1808.
RIGHT: each townhouse gently follows the slope of the hill.
FAR RIGHT: a house fit for a queen. No. 93 Sydney Place was once the Bath home of Queen Charlotte, wife of King George III who came to the city to 'take the waters,' a popular treatment that utilised the areas natural springs.

OPPOSITE: Sydney Place borders the Bathwick area of Bath, once considered the centre of fashionable life in the city during the Regency period.

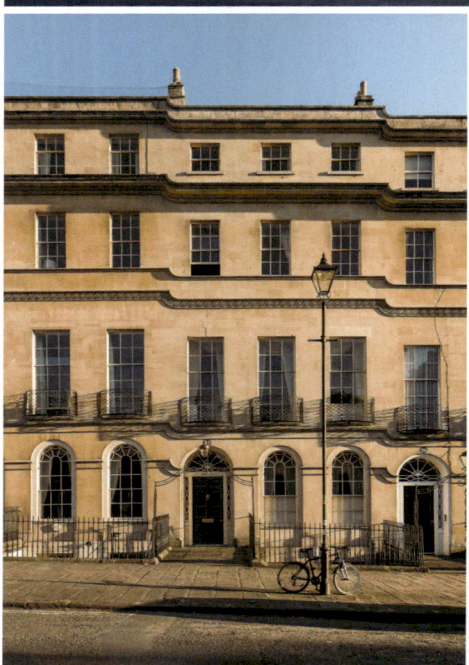
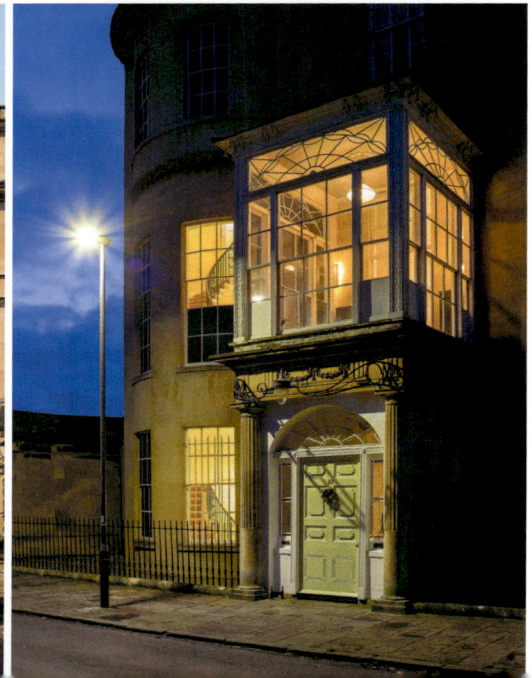

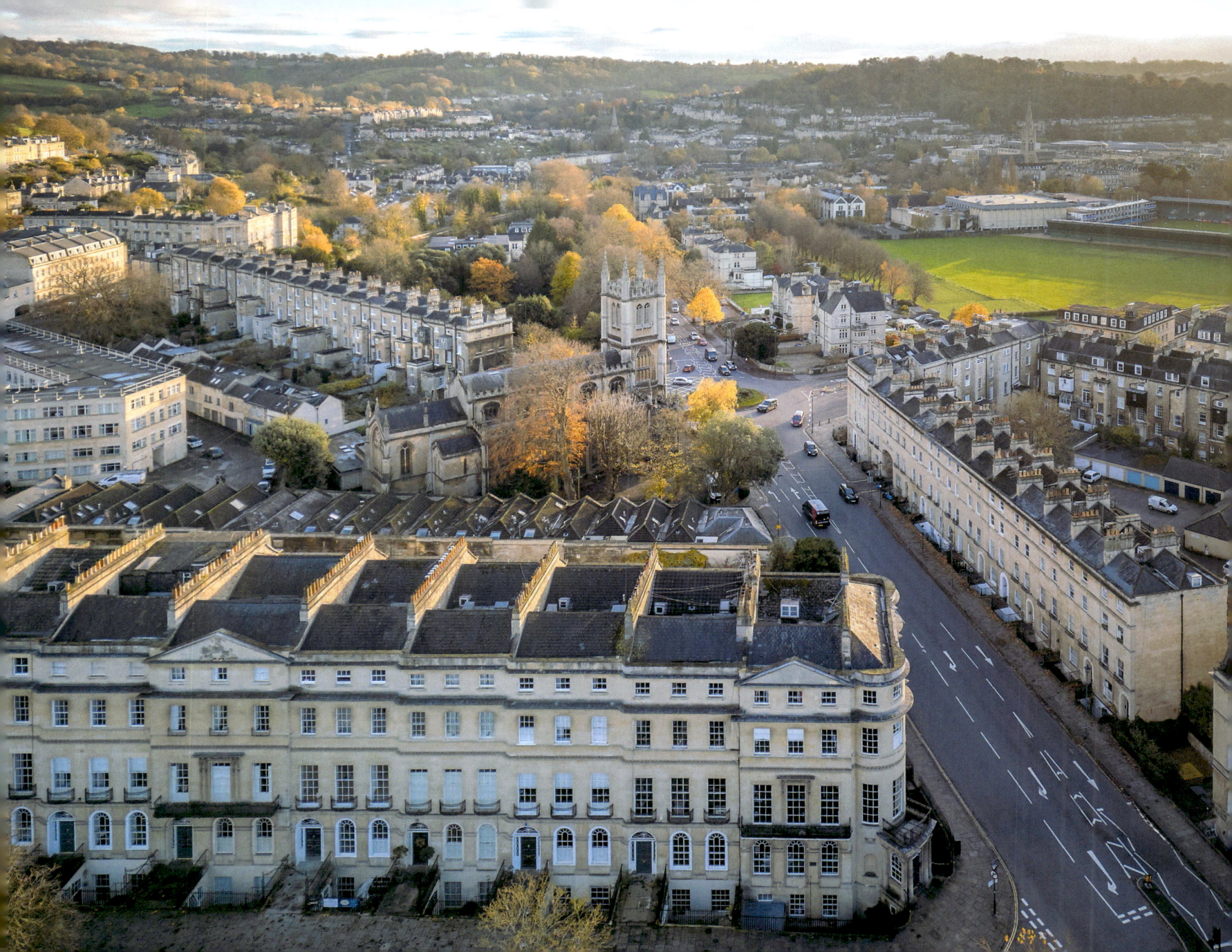

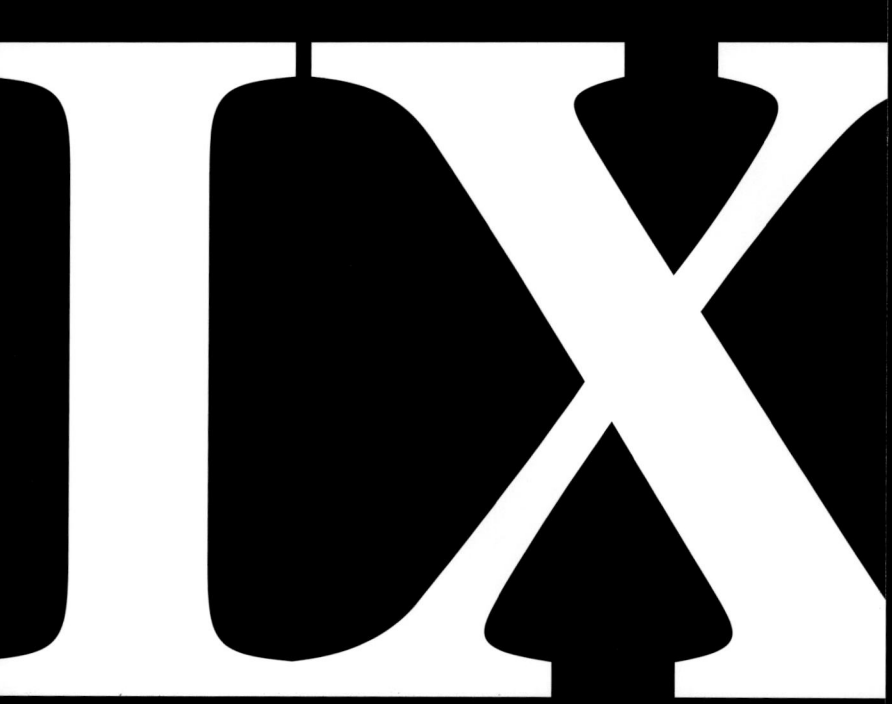

9 KENNET & AVON CANAL

The canal was engineered by John Rennie, one of the leading civil engineers of the day (also known for London's Waterloo and Southwark Bridges). Rennie's designs blended functionality with classical Georgian elegance, in keeping with Bath's style. Locks, bridges, and aqueducts were built using local Bath stone, helping them harmonise with the city's iconic architecture.

The Kennet and Avon Canal is one of the longest navigable waterways in the country, starting at Bristol in the west before passing through Newbury along the Kennet river and ending at Reading on the river Thames. The main section is a traditional canal cruiseway which runs from Bath to Newbury and contains over one hundred locks.

There are many fabulous sections of the canal to explore along its 87 mile length, especially as it winds through the enchanting Wiltshire landscape with its beautiful mix of small towns and chalk downs. Though for pure atmosphere and presence, the section that runs through Bath is the most picturesque, with walks starting at the pretty hamlet of Bathampton in the east to Bath (a 1.5 mile walk) or a shorter version in Bath itself starting at Sydney Gardens (just short of an half-mile walk).

The Kennet and Avon Canal has a rich history dating back to the late 18th century when it was constructed to facilitate transportation of goods between London and Bristol. The canal played a vital role in the industrial development of Bath and the surrounding region, serving as a major trade route for coal, timber, and other commodities. Although the canal fell into disuse with the advent of rail transport it was later restored in the late 20th century as a recreational waterway attracting visitors and boaters from around the world.

The canal features several locks and bridges as it winds its way through Bath with the tree lined route from Bathampton to Sydney Gardens containing the longest section between locks.

BATHAMPTON START

Postcode: BA2 6TR
what3words: ozone.having.sport

BATH START: SYDNEY GARDENS

Postcode: BA2 6NT
what3words: bags.linked.remain

BATH END: THIMBLE MILL

Postcode: BA2 4JP
what3words: origin.chest.bulb

MORE INFORMATION
THE KENNET & AVON CANAL TRUST

katrust.org.uk
The Kennet & Avon Canal Trust is the charity that restored the canal running from Bristol to Reading into the thriving waterway that can be enjoyed today

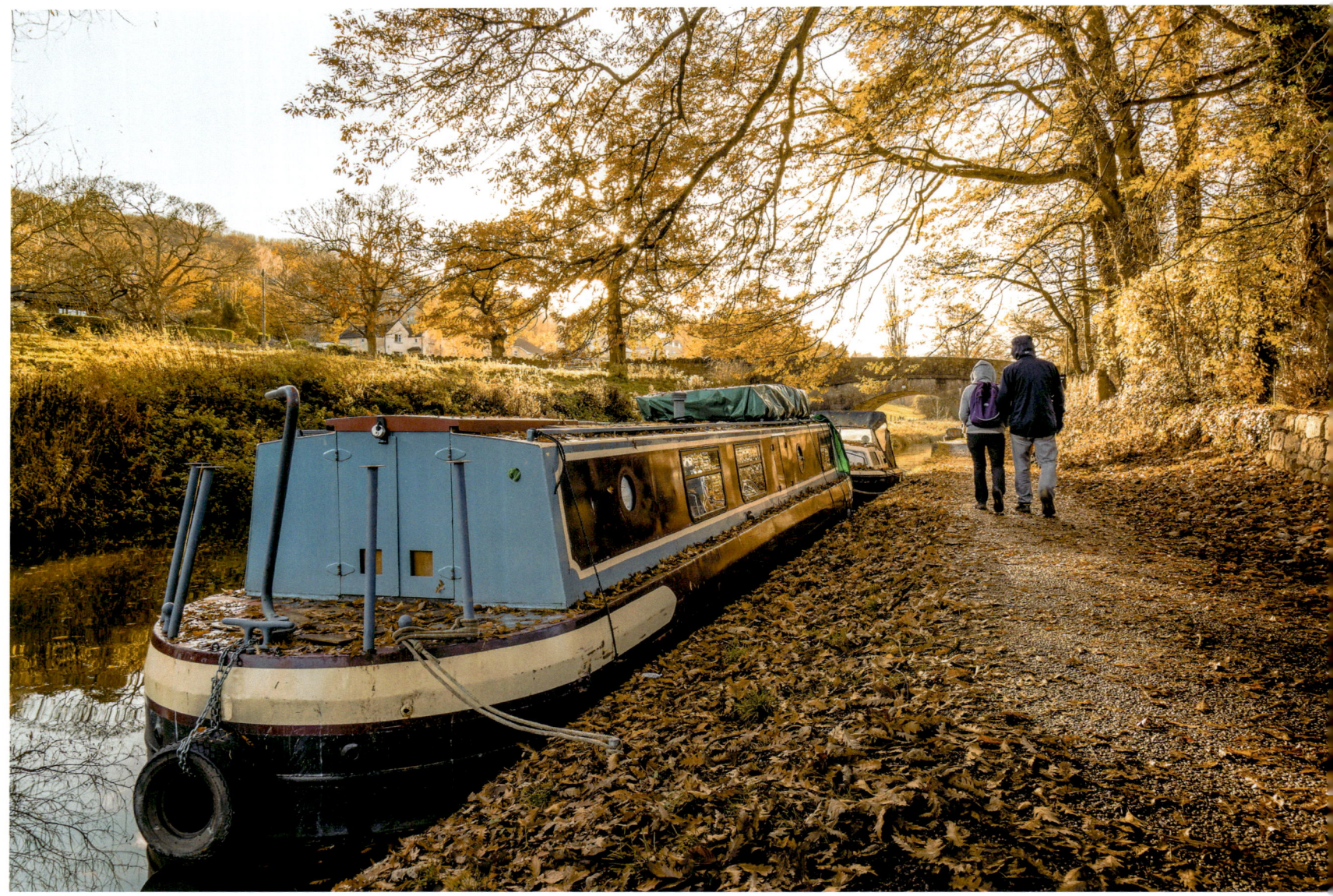

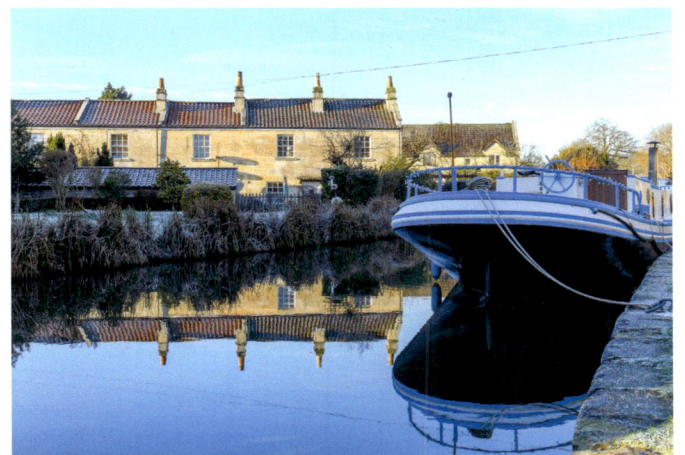

KENNET & AVON CANAL – BATHAMPTON

Ideal for hikers, cyclists and boaters, a rewarding journey begins in Bathampton just 1.5 miles from central Bath leading through the city's scenic suburbs. This leafy stretch of the canal passes by a charming assortment of narrow boats moored along the towpath, some of which have been converted into shops selling drinks and tasty treats.

DIRECTIONS

This canal walk starts at the George Inn in Bathampton which can be reached by bus from Bath. Walk along the canal to Bath, roughly a 1.5 mile walk. Finish at Pulteney Bridge or continue along the Bath section of the canal – an extra half-mile to Thimble Mill (see overleaf).

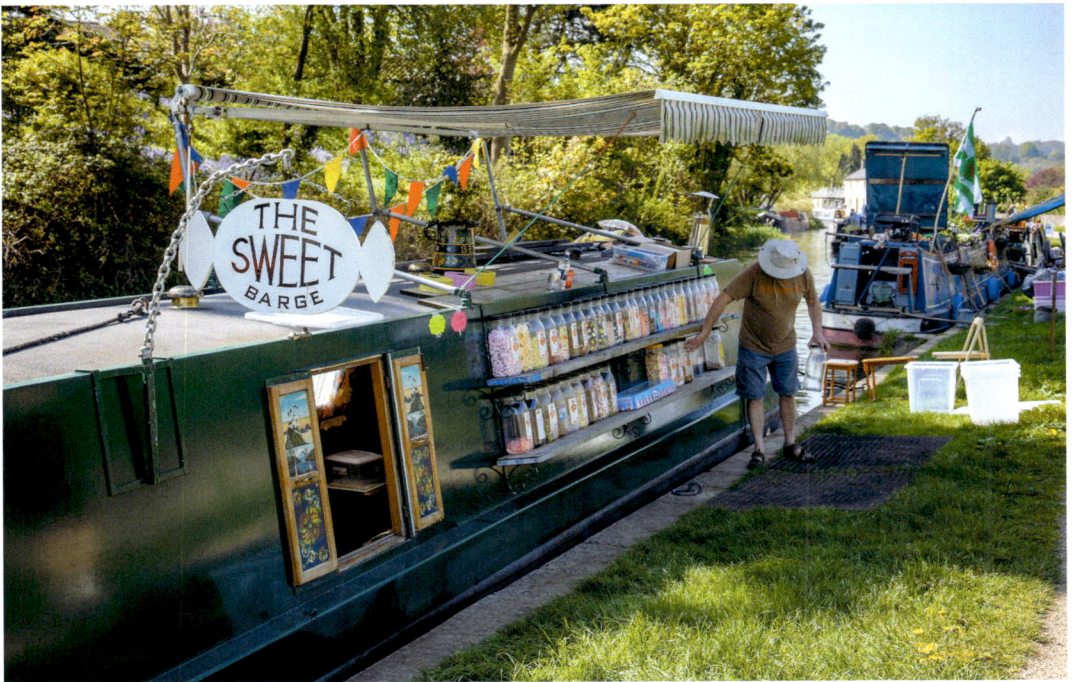

OPPOSITE: walking along the canal from Bathampton feels as though you're immersed in a charming countryside village.
TOP: canal-side cottages lead down to the waters edge.
LEFT: a Floating Fayre is held at Bathampton on select dates throughout the year, with boats offering wares during the spring and summer seasons.

KENNET & AVON CANAL – BATH SECTION

This shorter section (a half mile walk) is perfect if you prefer a more leisurely stroll. Start your journey at Sydney Gardens and follow the well maintained towpath as it passes elegant townhouses leading you through a landscape rich in history and beauty. Along the way explore historic locks, experience seasonal wildlife, watch narrowboats glide through the water or simply pause to soak in the peaceful atmosphere.

The section of the canal at Sydney Gardens was created to reflect the beautiful pleasure grounds that it passes through. Ornate white ironwork footbridges are a key feature and the high sided walls bordering the towpath are as unique a setting as any that have ever been created on a stretch of water in the country. One of the canal's most iconic buildings Cleveland House is perched directly above Cleveland Tunnel. Once the headquarters of the canal company, the waterway passes beneath a 173 foot tunnel where a historic letter hatch remains, a relic of a time when messages were exchanged between passing boats and the office above.

Beyond the tunnel the towpath follows the curve of Sydney Wharf, where narrowboats cluster at a small marina beneath elegant villas and terraces on Bathwick Hill.

Follow the towpath onto the hill to continue your journey where the canal glides through the southern edge of Bathwick. This stretch is bordered by a mix of residential buildings, historic industry and greenery offering views of Bath's skyline through gaps in the trees. Waterside properties along this route have some of the most charming back gardens that cascade down towards the banks of the canal. ➔

BELOW LEFT: once an industrial hub, the canal through Bathwick is now one of the most peaceful and scenic stretches. **BELOW**: at Sydney Wharf, the water's edge is right outside your back door. **BOTTOM**: the back gardens in the Bathwick area seamlessly blend into the canal.

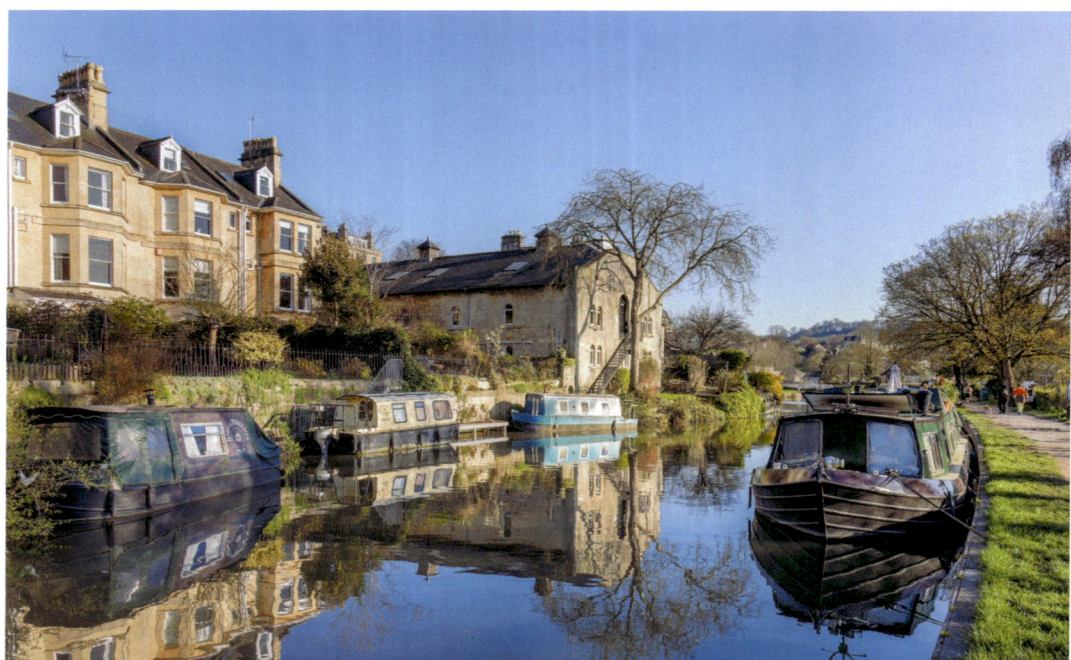

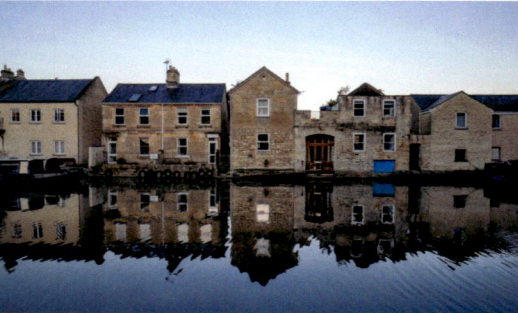

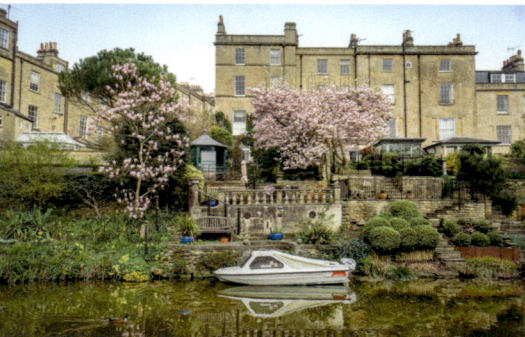

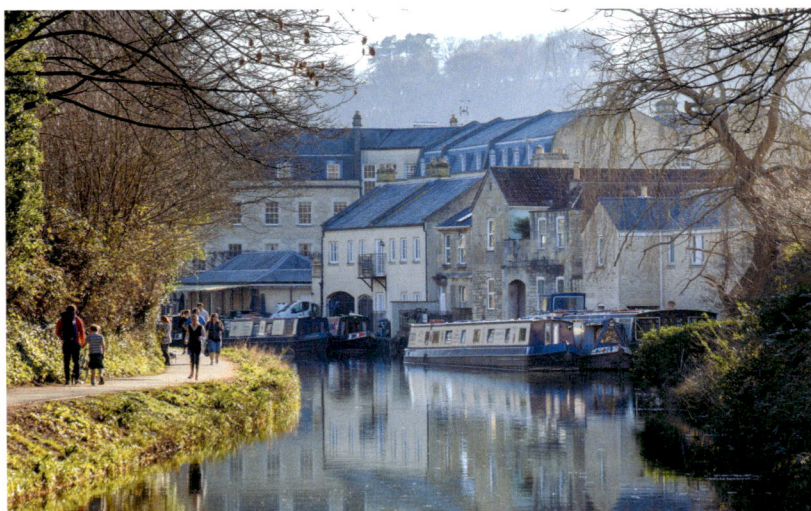

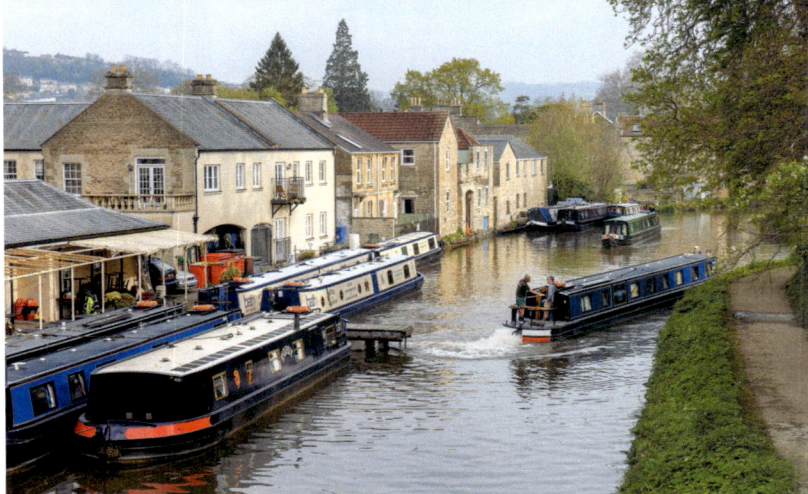

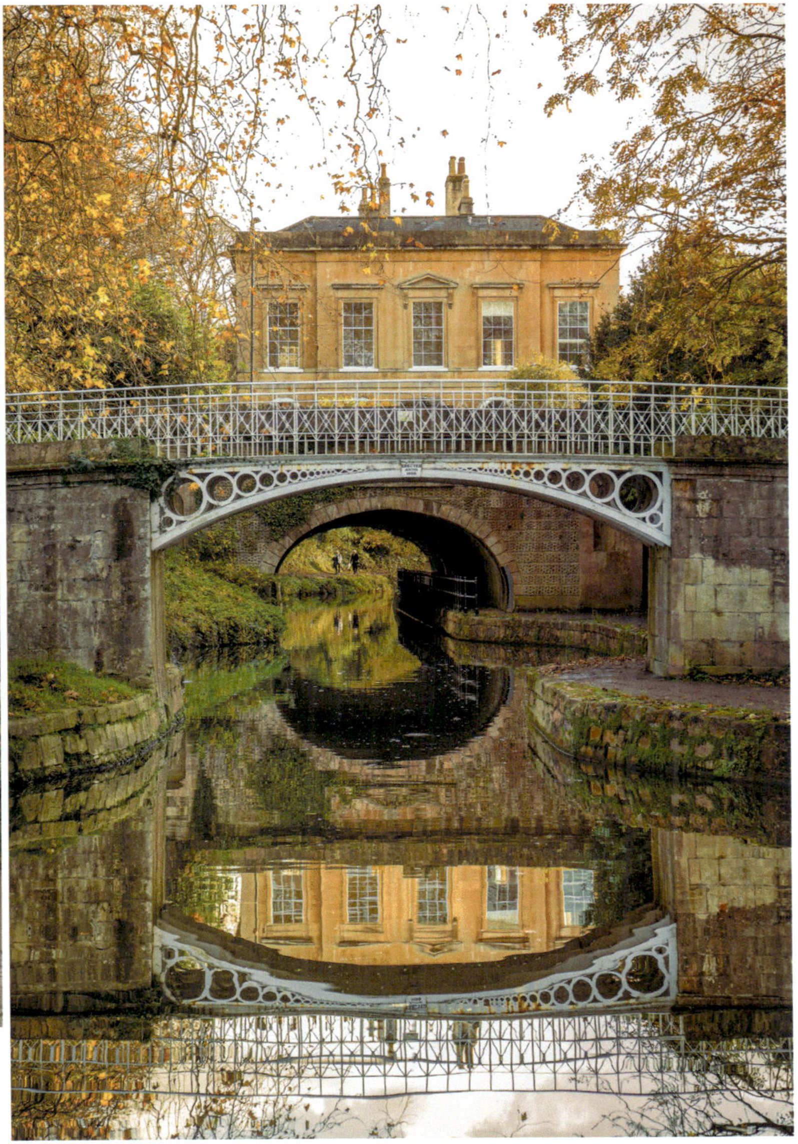

TOP: the towpath is a perfect alternative route through the city – taking visitors past some charming properties. **ABOVE**: Bath Narrowboats, operating from Sydney Wharf offers pleasure trips for visitors, including day trips, longer canal holidays, bike hire and electric boat hire.
RIGHT: Cleveland House is one of the canal's most striking buildings. Formerly the K&A Canal head office, it stands above a tunnel, overlooking the water.

As you approach Widcombe, you'll pass a beautifully restored lock keeper's cottage, Top Lock Cottage, at Sydney Buildings. Further along this flight of the canal additional locks are connected by iron footbridges. At the end of this stretch the canal widens into Widcombe Basin where a series of locks gradually lower it towards the river Avon. Most notably is Lock No.10 'Deep Lock' one of the deepest locks on the canal and in the country.

Once a working watermill, Thimble Mill stood near the point where the canal descends into the river, a crucial junction for goods and cargo moving between the canal and the Avon's wider trade routes. The lock system here engineered by John Rennie in the early 19th century allowed boats to navigate the changing levels with precision. Just beyond, the canal merges with the river at a point where cargoes of stone were transferred.

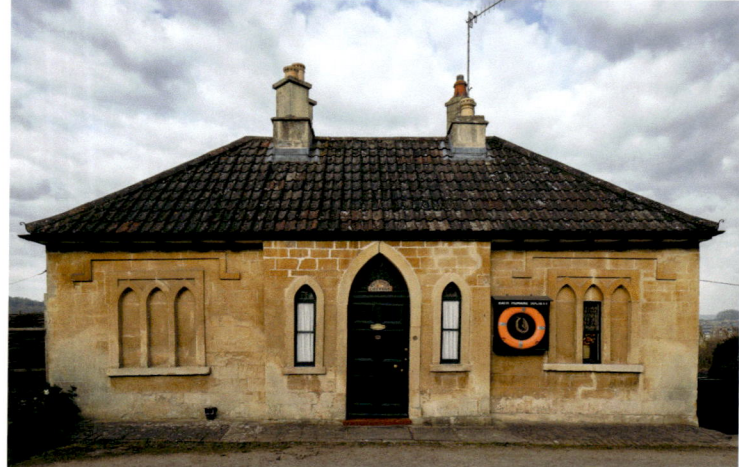

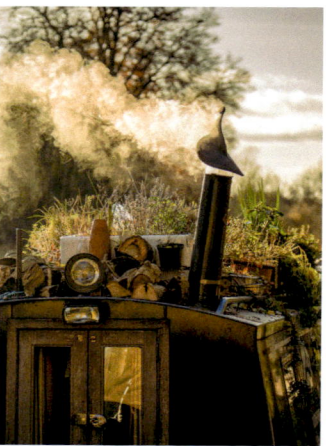

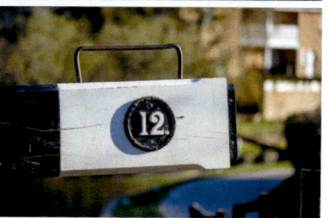

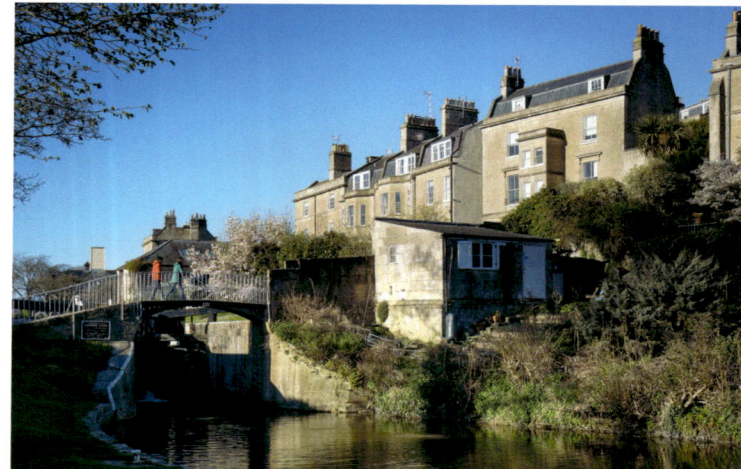

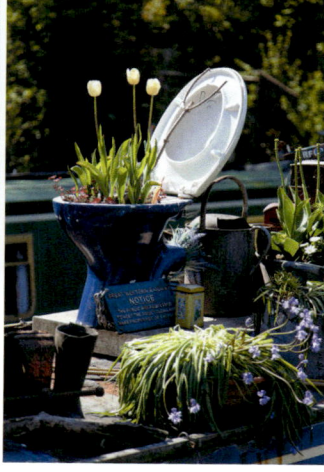

OPPOSITE TOP LEFT: beyond Lock 12, the canal continues into Widcombe. **TOP MIDDLE**: the majestic Sydney Buildings seem to float above the water. **TOP RIGHT**: Thimble Mill is located where the canal meets the river Avon. **BOTTOM LEFT**: beyond Bathwick, the canal drops into Widcombe Basin. **BOTTOM MIDDLE**: the spire of St Matthew's Church. **BOTTOM RIGHT**: the view towards Widcombe from Horseshoe Walk Bridge.

TOP: Top Lock Cottage. **ABOVE**: Bath Top Lock Footbridge leads to Sydney Buildings. **TOP RIGHT**: Taking the world with you, characterful residential narrowboats line the route. **MIDDLE**: each lock is numbered along the route, serving both boat navigation and as helpful waymarkers for walkers on the towpath. **RIGHT**: a loo with a view, each boat has its own distinctive charm, decorated to the owner's design.

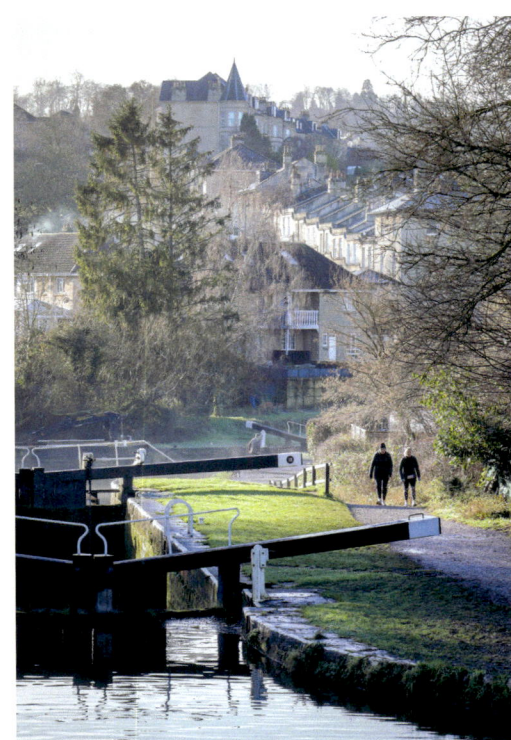
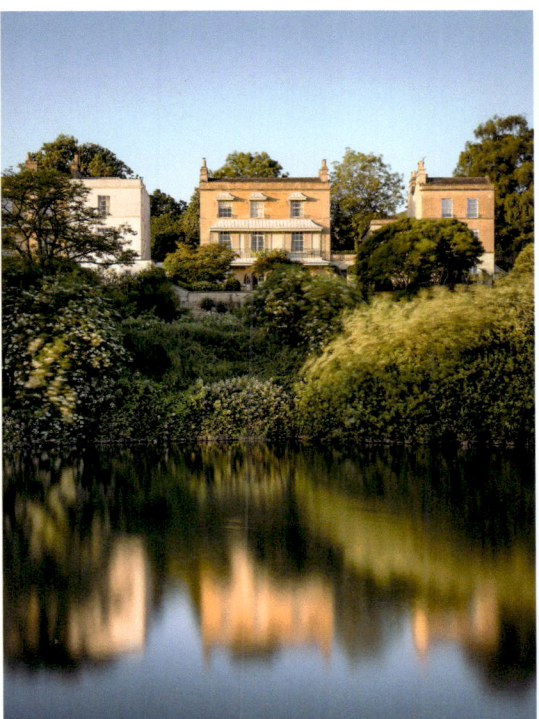
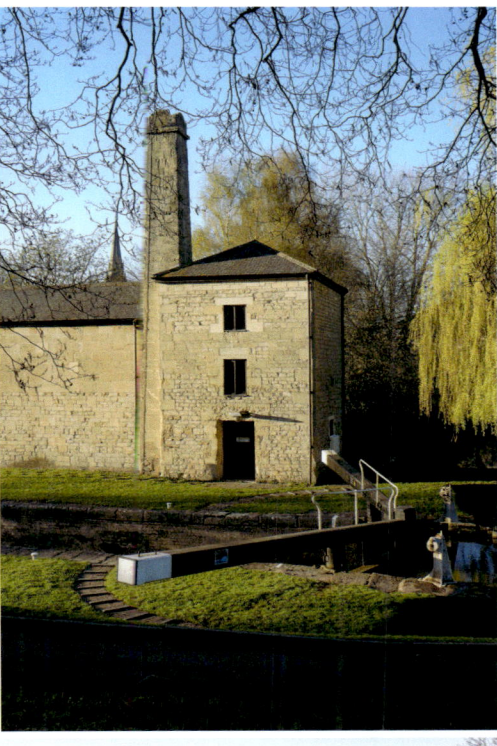
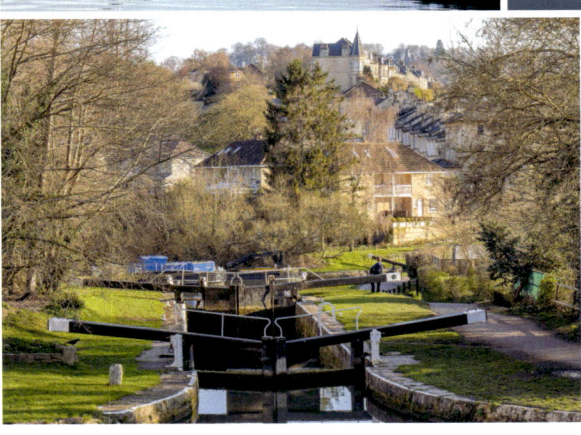
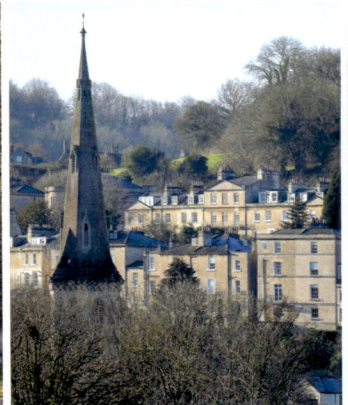
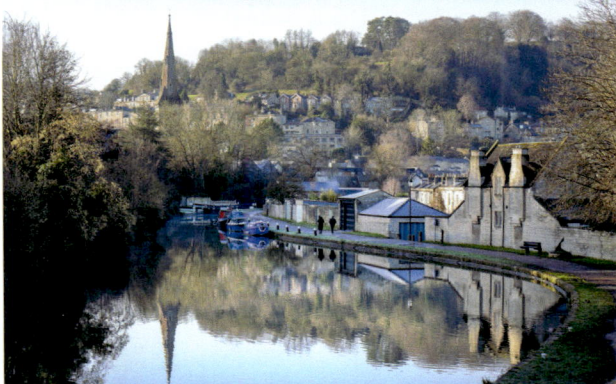

10 RIVER AVON

"Avon" comes from the Welsh word afon, which literally means "river." So "river Avon" actually means "river river". There are several river Avons in the UK – this one is specifically the Bristol Avon. The Avon through Bath is home to kingfishers, otters, herons, and swan colonies.

Located close to a selection of cafes and restaurants a walking route follows the river Avon south offering a tranquil and scenic journey starting from Spring Gardens beside Pulteney Bridge before passing by several historic landmarks, to Widcombe Lock; a walk just short of half-a-mile. There are compelling views across the water to the Empire Hotel, Parade Gardens and the impressive tower of Bath Abbey in the distance. On the opposite side of the river is the Colonnade, a beautiful row of columns beneath Grand Parade and the Guildhall Market above.

Cross Pulteney Bridge to the east of the river and take an immediate right onto the riverside path. A unique feature garden lies tucked away in a corner beside Pulteney Weir and is a quirky detour from the river. Beazer Garden Maze is a labyrinth comprising of a single paved pattern branching outwards from a central Roman themed mosaic depicting the head of a Gorgon. Much loved by adults and children alike who enjoy following the small series of paths. It's a maze you can never really get lost in as all routes return to the same starting point.

Then follow the river path south by a bank of tulip trees that line the river Avon adjacent to the grounds of Bath Rugby. These magnificent specimens are transformed into a glorious golden display each autumn and are a magnet for visitors. Beyond here is North Parade Bridge, the perfect vantage point looking north towards Pulteney Bridge and up the hillside to Camden Crescent. Views on the opposite side of North Parade Bridge overlook the south side of Widcombe and under the right conditions lingering morning mists hug distant tree lines and the tall spire of St. Matthews Church.

PULTENEY BRIDGE START

Postcode: BA2 4AX
what3words: jams.leaves.cattle

SPRING GARDENS

Postcode: BA2 4BQ
what3words: added.fields.patch

BEAZER GARDEN MAZE

Postcode: BA2 4BL
what3words: reply.twins.kind

WIDCOMBE LOCK

Postcode: BA2 4DG
what3words: action.dragon.layers

MORE INFORMATION
BRISTOL AVON RIVERS TRUST

bristolavonriverstrust.org
Bristol Avon Rivers Trust (BART) is a charity which delivers education, land and river management advice and practical river restoration work throughout the Bristol Avon catchment.

Situated on the riverbank, St. John's Church is a beautiful example of decorated Gothic style architecture. Built in 1863 its elegant spire rises above the surrounding buildings, creating a picturesque backdrop against the river's serene waters.

Follow the path under the railway bridge to Halfpenny Bridge that links the village of Widcombe to the main city centre via Bath Spa Train Station, aptly named after a toll of one half-penny it cost pedestrians to cross. The small former tollhouse at Halfpenny Bridge only appears as one room at street level but is in fact a three-storey tower supporting the bridge which also hides a fascinating account of history inscribed into the walls beneath. Water level markers carved into the brickwork beside the towpath reveal the incredible peak of the river Avon during major flooding events from 1866 to 1960.

Widcombe Lock provides a fascinating glimpse into the canal heritage of Bath where it merges into the river Avon. Visitors can observe boats navigating the lock and learn about the operation of these historic waterway features.

Beyond Widcombe it is possible to loop back into the city centre at Southgate or continue westwards to pass by rows of Georgian townhouses and through the former industrial heart of the city at Bath Quays and Green Park, a former railway station now home to cafés and seasonal markets.

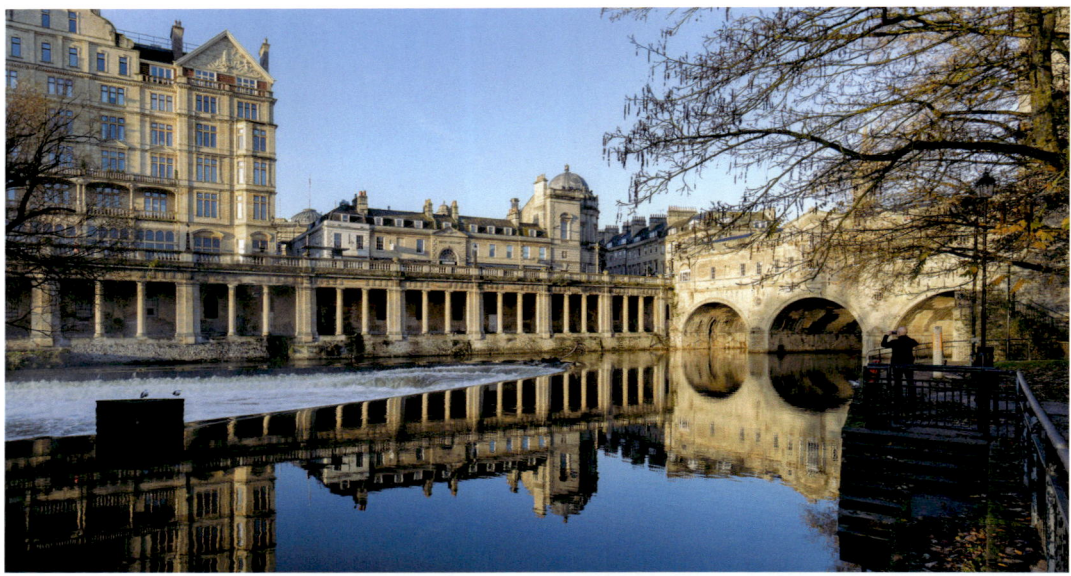

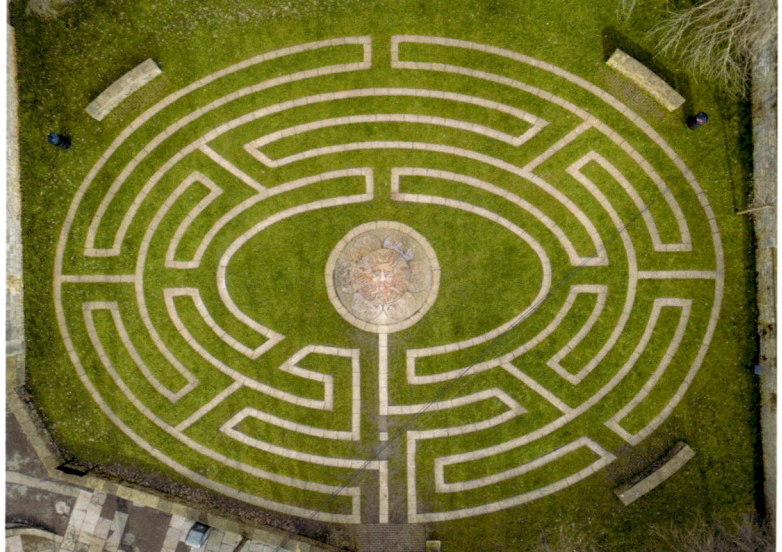

TOP: the riverside walk begins at Pulteney Bridge and Weir, where waterside buildings stand in all their reflective beauty. **RIGHT**: Beazer Maze, close to Pulteney Bridge in Spring Gardens, is a fun novelty to explore. The paving stone maze, weaving around a mosaic centre, is a favourite with younger children.
OPPOSITE: the river Avon meanders through the city centre, originally marking the boundary of the old city. It was later, after Pulteney Bridge was built in 1774, that the bridge linked the old city to the newly developed Bathwick estate.

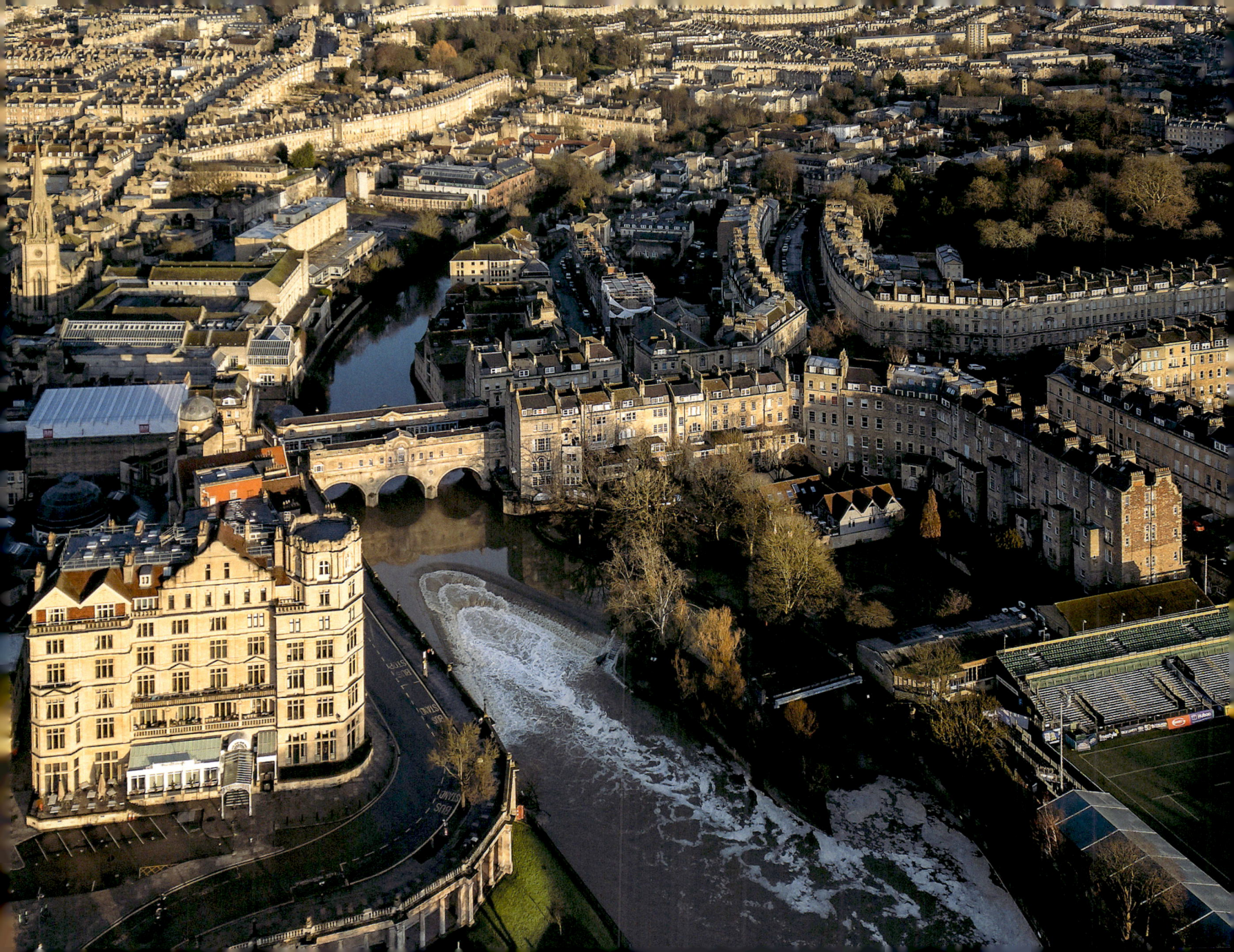

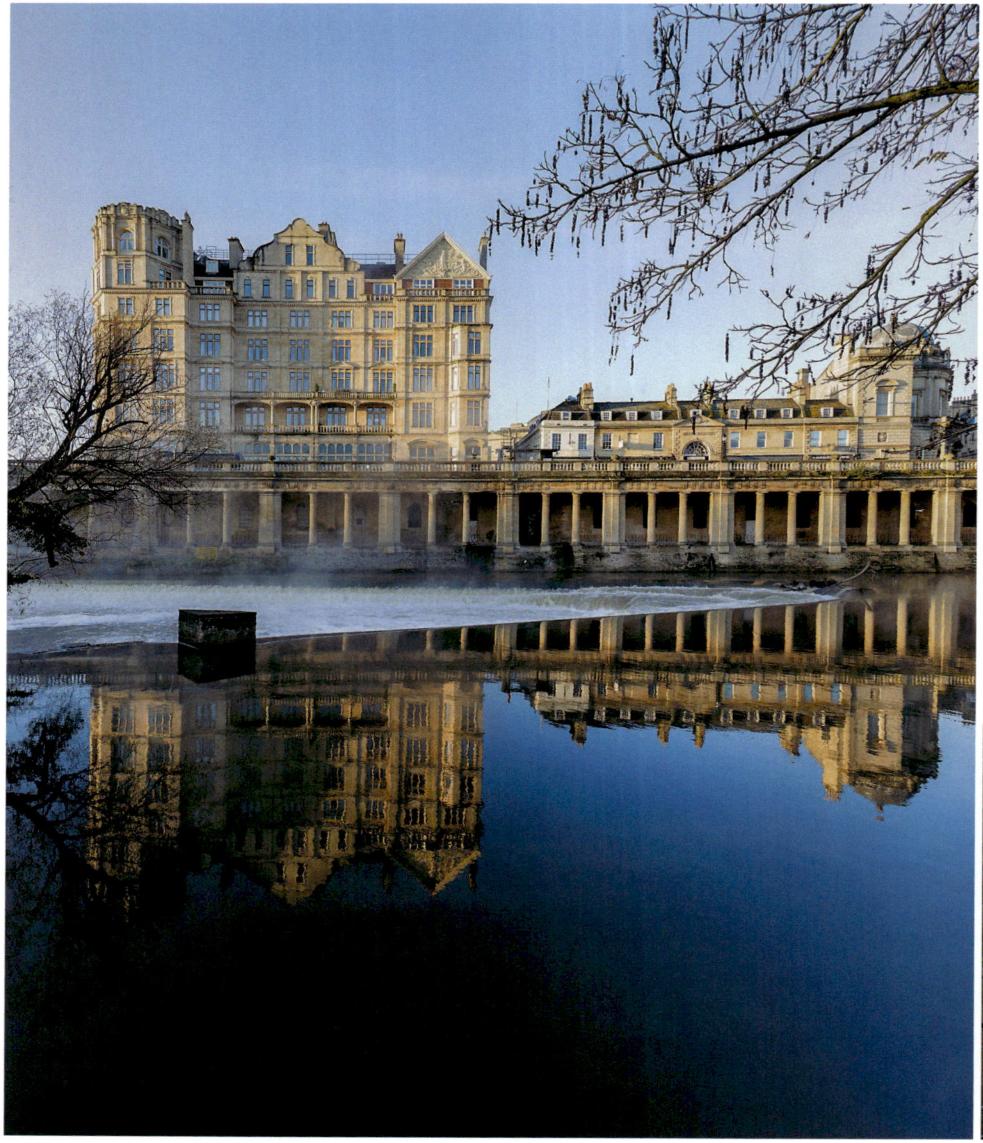

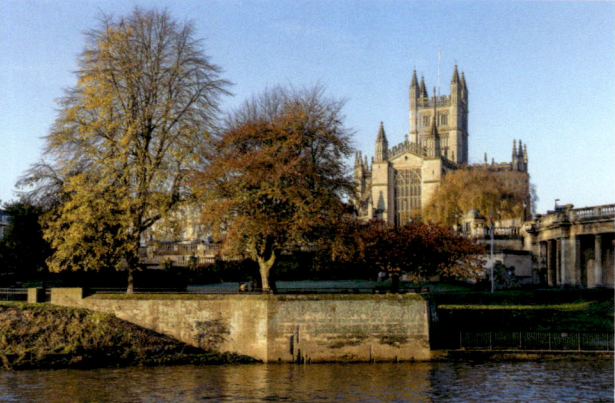
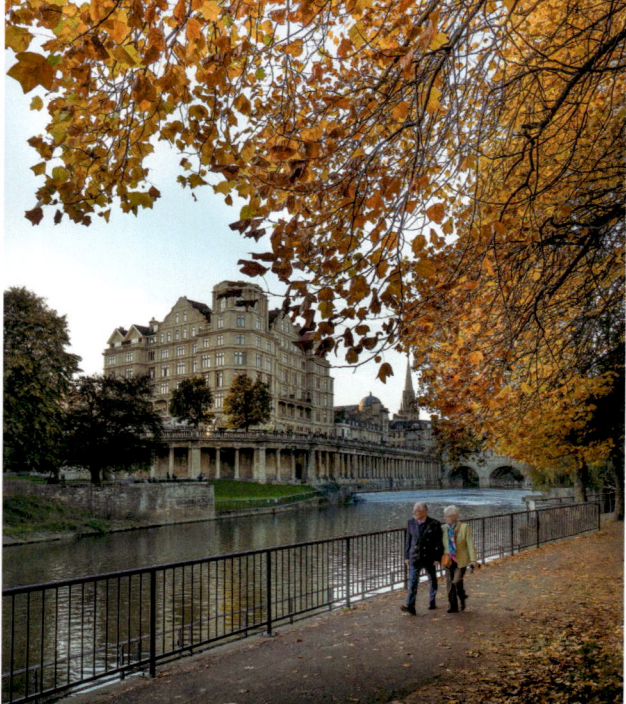

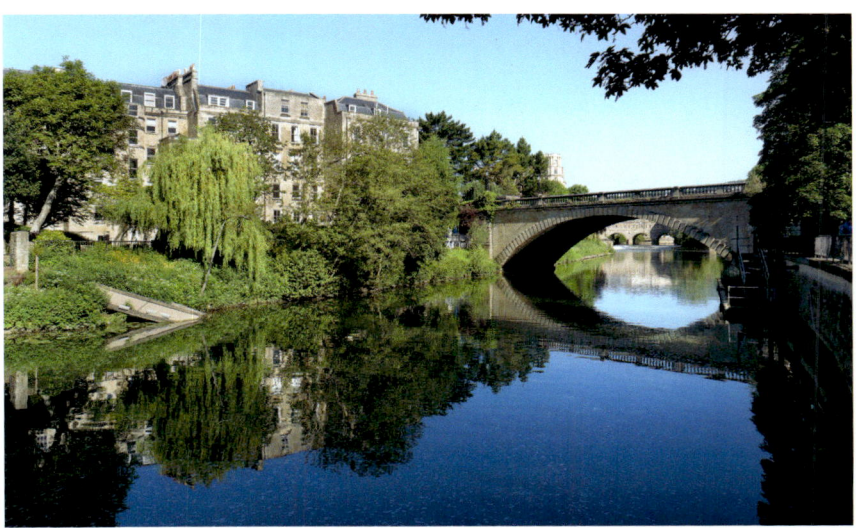
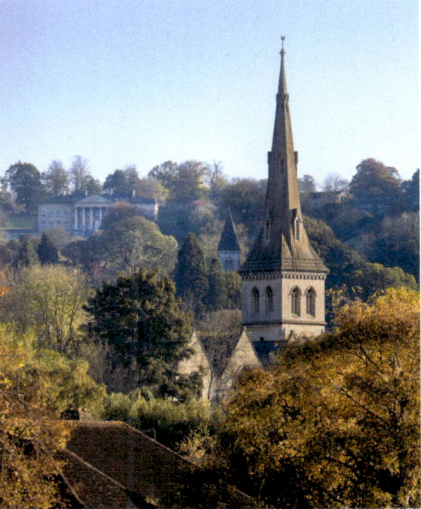
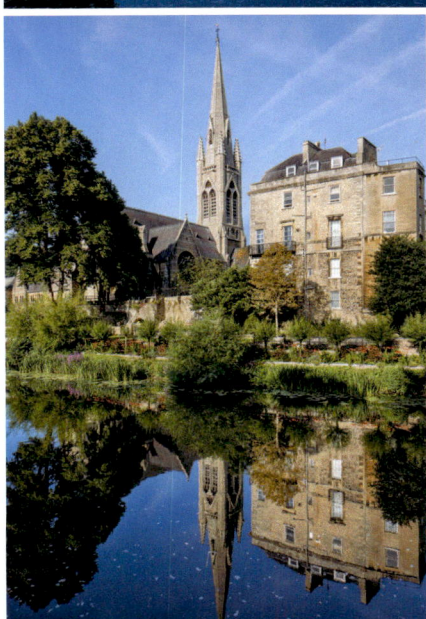
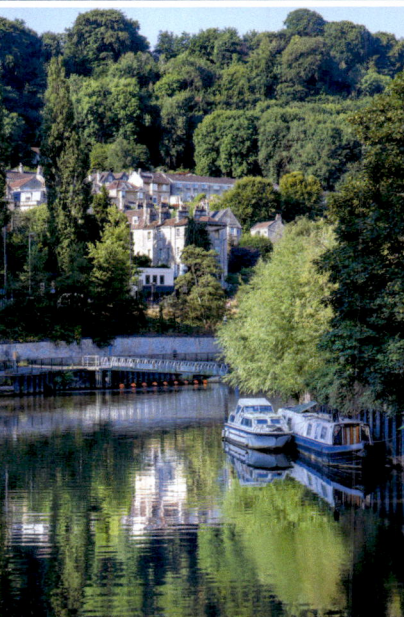
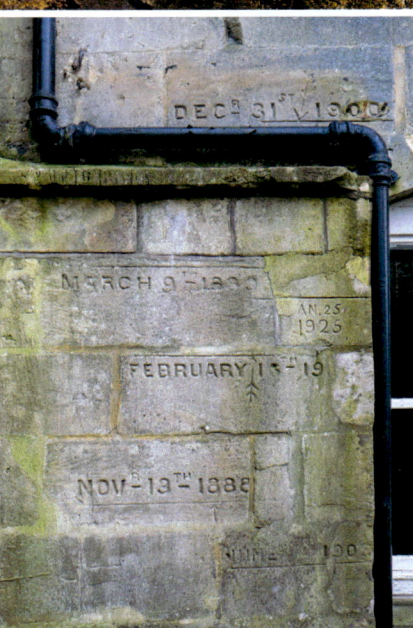

OPPOSITE FAR LEFT: the Empire and Colonnades viewed from Spring Gardens. **TOP**: seen from the opposite side of the river, the sunken Parade Gardens reveal Bath Abbey in the distance. **BOTTOM**: glorious tulip trees line the river walk in autumn, their vibrant colours a sight to behold, a perfect photo spot.

TOP LEFT: North Parade Bridge crosses the river Avon, beside the rear elevations of Duke Street and South Parade. **TOP RIGHT**: St Matthew's Church and Prior Park College nestled in the hillside beyond. **FAR LEFT**: the spire of St John's church is the tallest structure in the city **MIDDLE**: the river passing beside Widcombe reveals how much of the city is enveloped in lush greenery. **LEFT**: markers reveal the extent of past flooding, with waters rising to 13 feet on New Year's Eve in 1900.

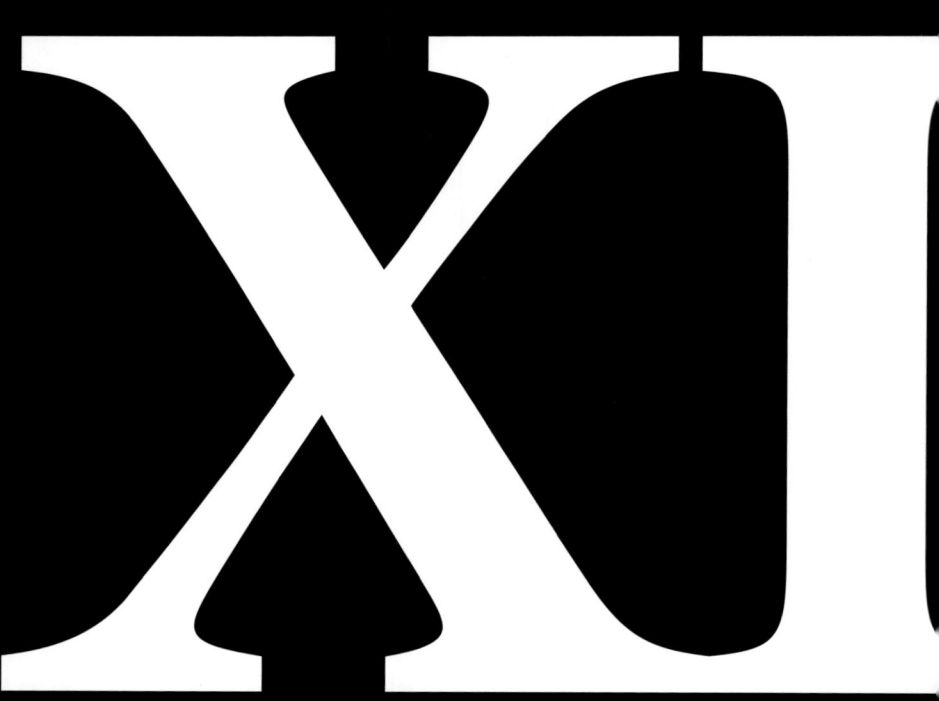

11 BATH ABBEY

In 1539, Bath Abbey was dissolved under Henry VIII. The roof was removed, windows broken, and it lay abandoned for decades. It wasn't fully restored and completed until the early 1600s, and again in the Victorian era by architect Sir George Gilbert Scott.

There has been a place of worship at this spot in the city for over a thousand years with a history reaching back to the Anglo Saxon period. Once a former monastery founded in the 7th century the Abbey has endured many changes; it has been rebuilt twice, suffered damage from a fire, structural changes were added in the mid 1800s to finally surviving the falling bombs of the Second World War. The current structure was built in the 12th and 16th centuries, with renovations and additions over the years. It has served various religious and civic purposes throughout its history and is dedicated to Saint Peter and Saint Paul as a place of Christian worship. It holds regular services, including holy communion, evensong, and choral performances. The Abbey also hosts special events, concerts, and educational programs.

The Abbey boasts an impressive Perpendicular Gothic style, characterised by its pointed arches, elaborate vaulting, and intricate stone carvings. The exterior features striking flying buttresses and large stained glass windows, while the interior is adorned with elegant columns and detailed decorations. Created in the 1500's (with later Victorian restorations) the Abbey has one of the finest fan vaulted ceilings in the country and is immensely strong whilst appearing weightless.

Within the Abbey, there are numerous monuments, tombs, and around 635 wall memorials stones dating from the 1700s and 1800s dedicated to notable figures from Bath's history, including politicians, military leaders, and dignitaries. These memorials provide insights into the city's past and commemorate the lives of those who contributed to its development.

BATH ABBEY

Postcode: BA1 1LT
what3words: spared.strain.clay

MORE INFORMATION
BATH ABBEY WEBSITE

bathabbey.org

Check the Abbey website for opening times admission charges (general £8, tower £16), events and its history.

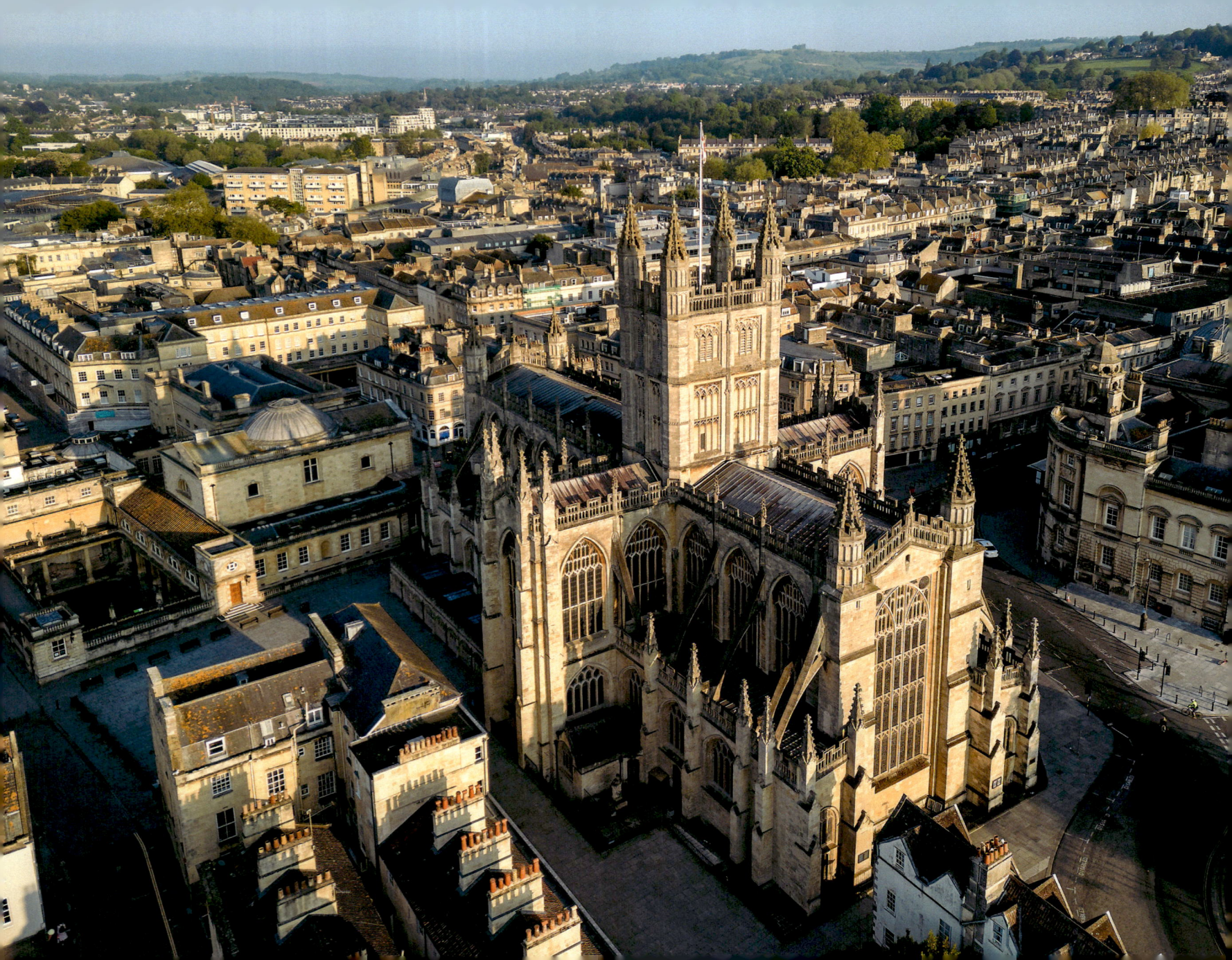

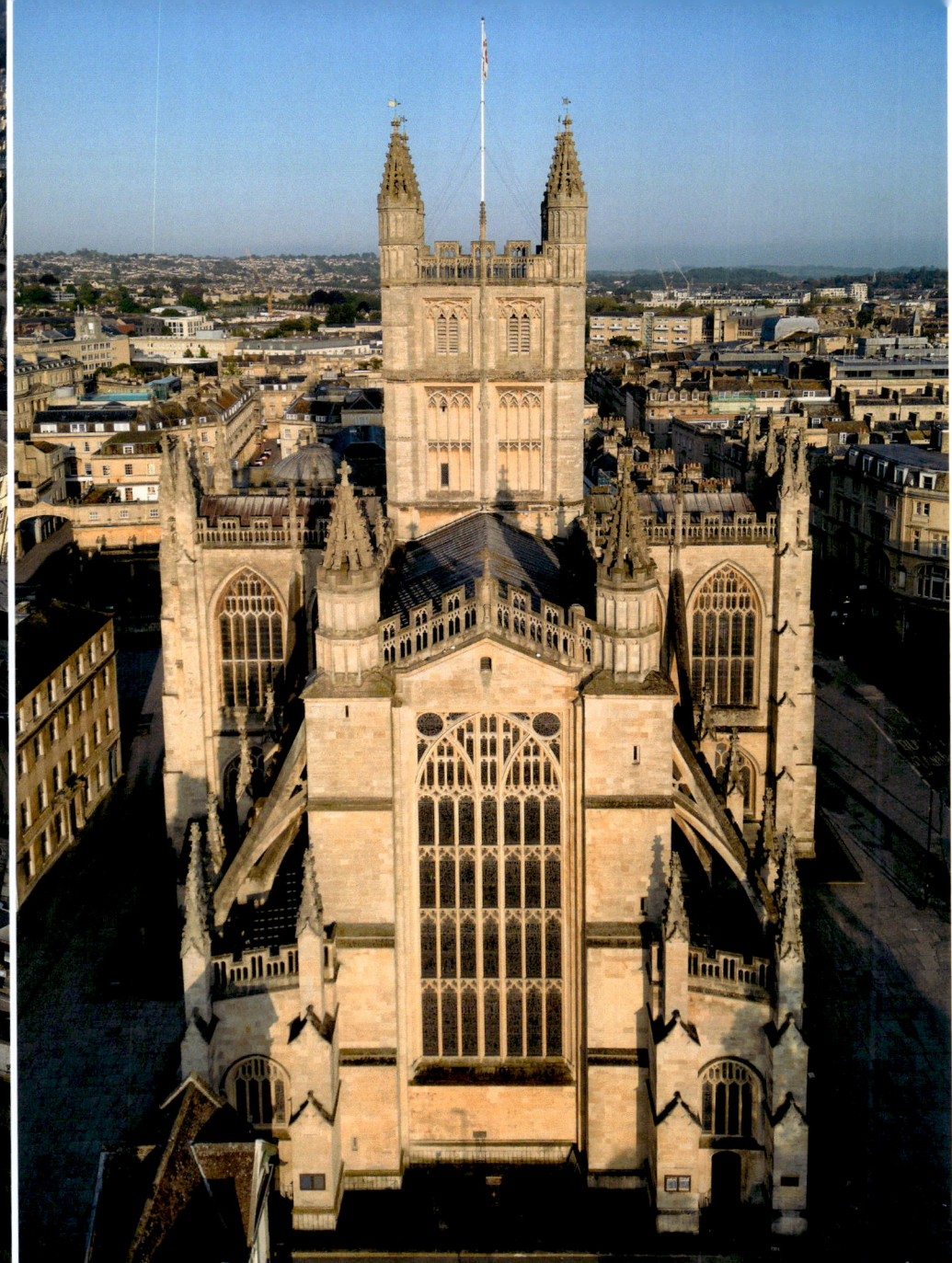

One of the most recognizable features of Bath Abbey is its tower, which stands at over 49 meters (161 feet) tall. Visitors can climb the 212 steps to the top for breathtaking panoramic views of the city and surrounding countryside, it is one of the tallest structures in the city, seen for miles around. Standing at this location as part of a later tour will ensure you could experience the warming glow of a sunset as the light dramatically envelopes the city streets below.

The main courtyard outside the Abbey is also historically known as the churchyard; a vast paved area lined with beautiful and unique styles of architecture housing restaurants, gift shops and craft wares. Close to the Abbey's west doors are the distinctive entrances to the Roman Baths and also the Pump Rooms which both open out onto Abbey Churchyard. Part of the former replaced a series of townhouses where the famous author Mary Shelley once lived and was the very spot in which she composed most of the classic Gothic novel, *Frankenstein*.

OPPOSITE: with its history spanning over 1,200 years, Bath Abbey is a significant religious site and parish church. The earliest mention of a monastery on the site dates back to 757 AD.
LEFT: Bath Abbey's east front.
OVERLEAF LEFT: Arrive at daybreak to enjoy Bath Abbey all to yourself. Accessed from all sides, the entrance on Stall Street is especially dramatic. **RIGHT**: the stone bridge spanning York Street once carried water from the Victorian spa to its laundry across the road. It now offers a wonderful framing point for the Abbey.

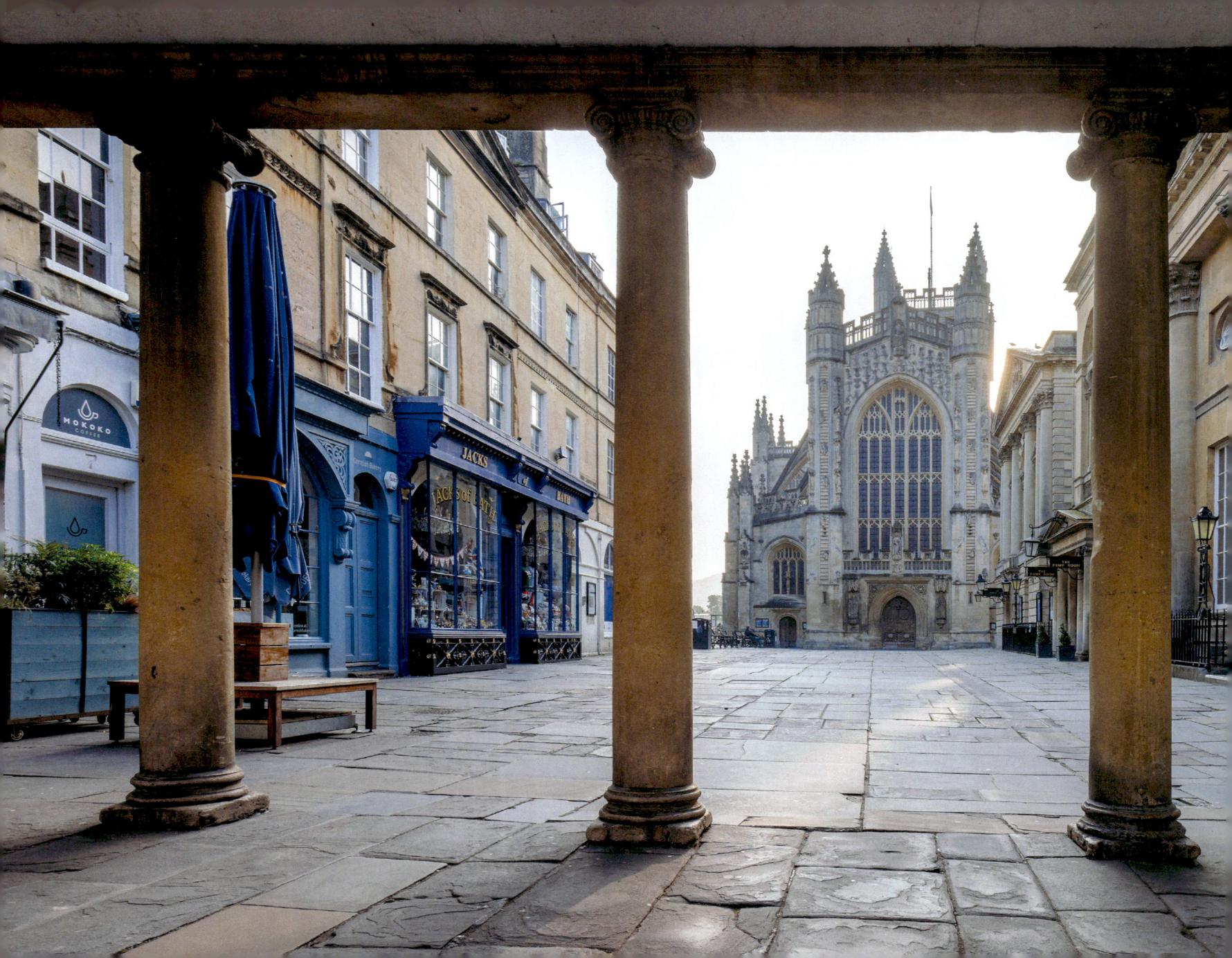

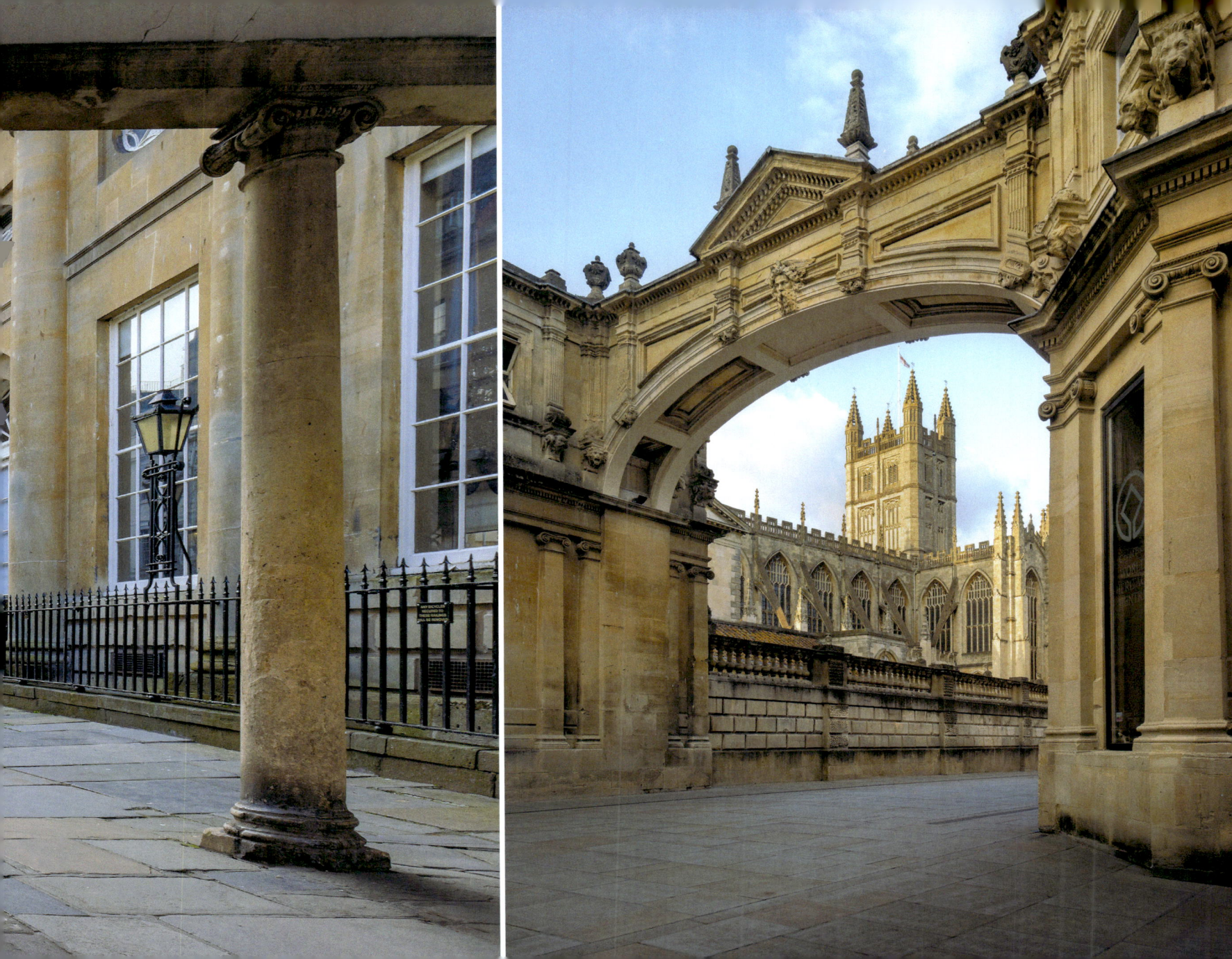

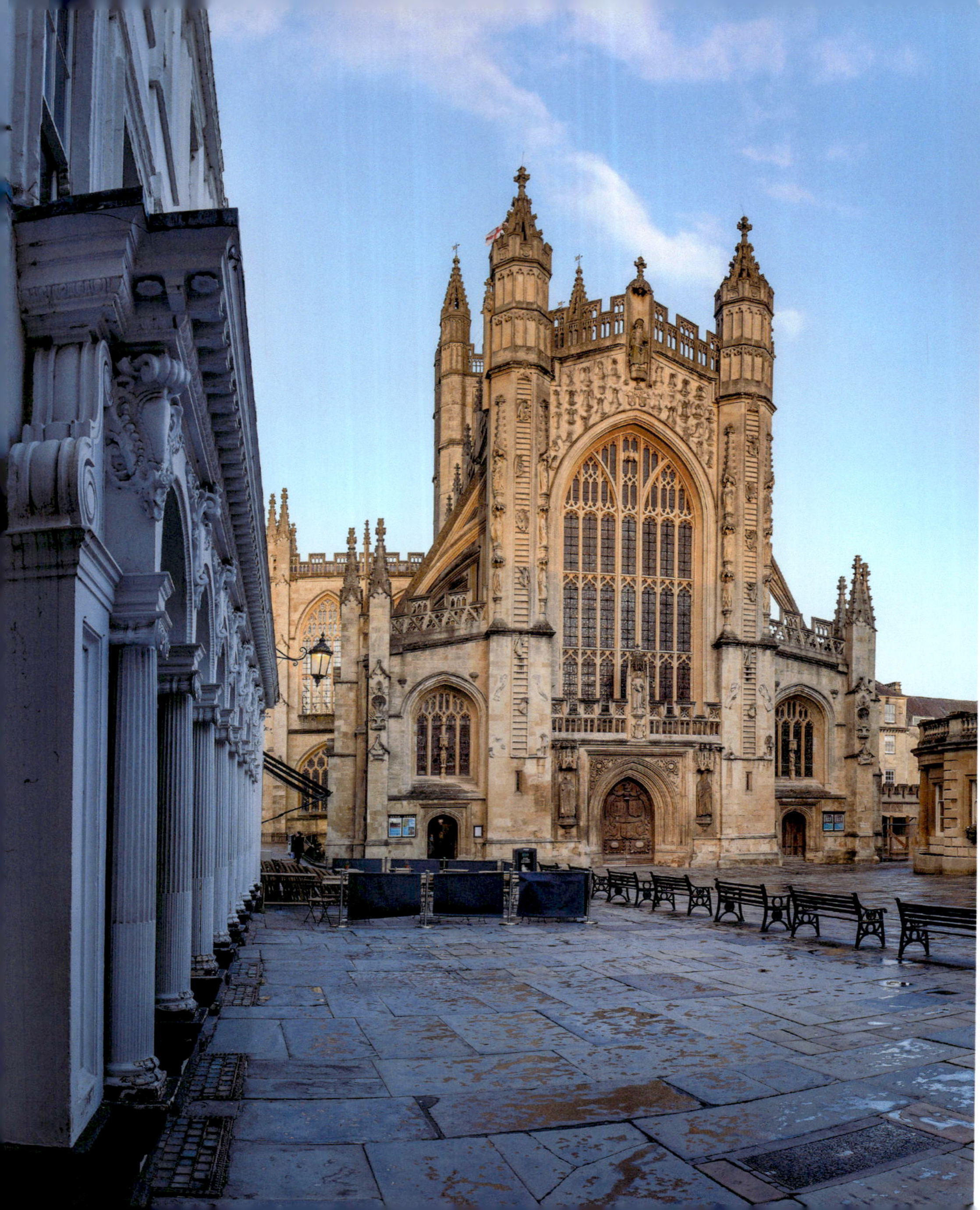

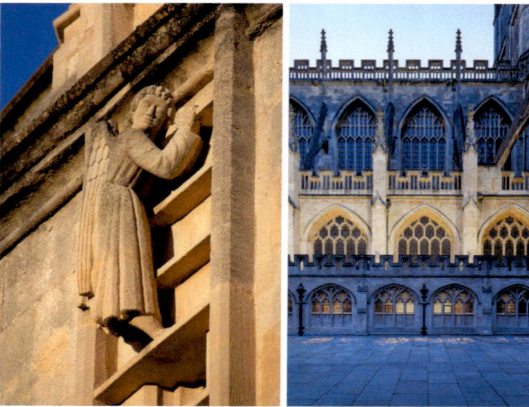
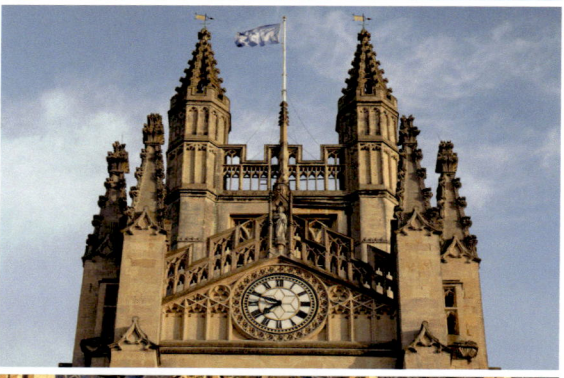
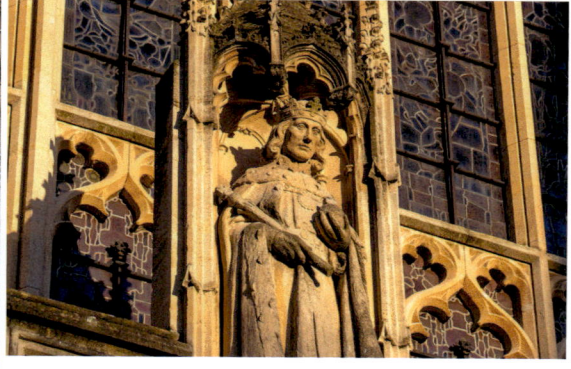

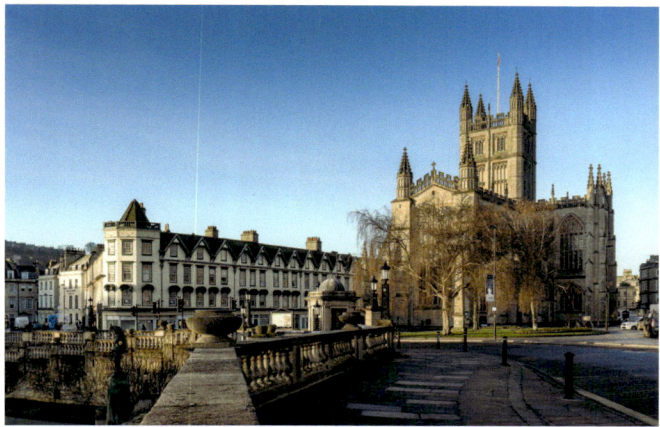

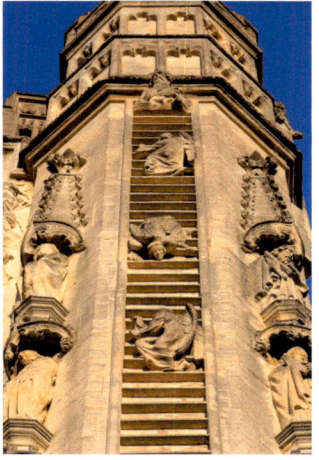

TOP: the Abbey stands beside Orange Grove and Grand Parade. **LEFT**: sculptures of angels climbing to heaven on two stone ladders, representing Jacob's Ladder; note one climbing in the wrong direction. **RIGHT**: seen from across the city, the tower stands 161 feet (49.1 m) high and is accessed by a staircase of 212 steps.

OPPOSITE FAR LEFT: most visitors' first view of Bath Abbey is the West Front, originally constructed in 1520 it features a large arched window and intricate carvings. **TOP LEFT**: the Abbey is renowned for its unique sculptures of angels climbing Jacob's Ladder. **TOP RIGHT**: a later addition, flying buttresses support the nave on the exterior. **MIDDLE**: Bath Abbey tower tours take visitors behind the clock face, offering a glimpse of its interior. **BOTTOM**: a statue of King Henry VII stands over the west door.

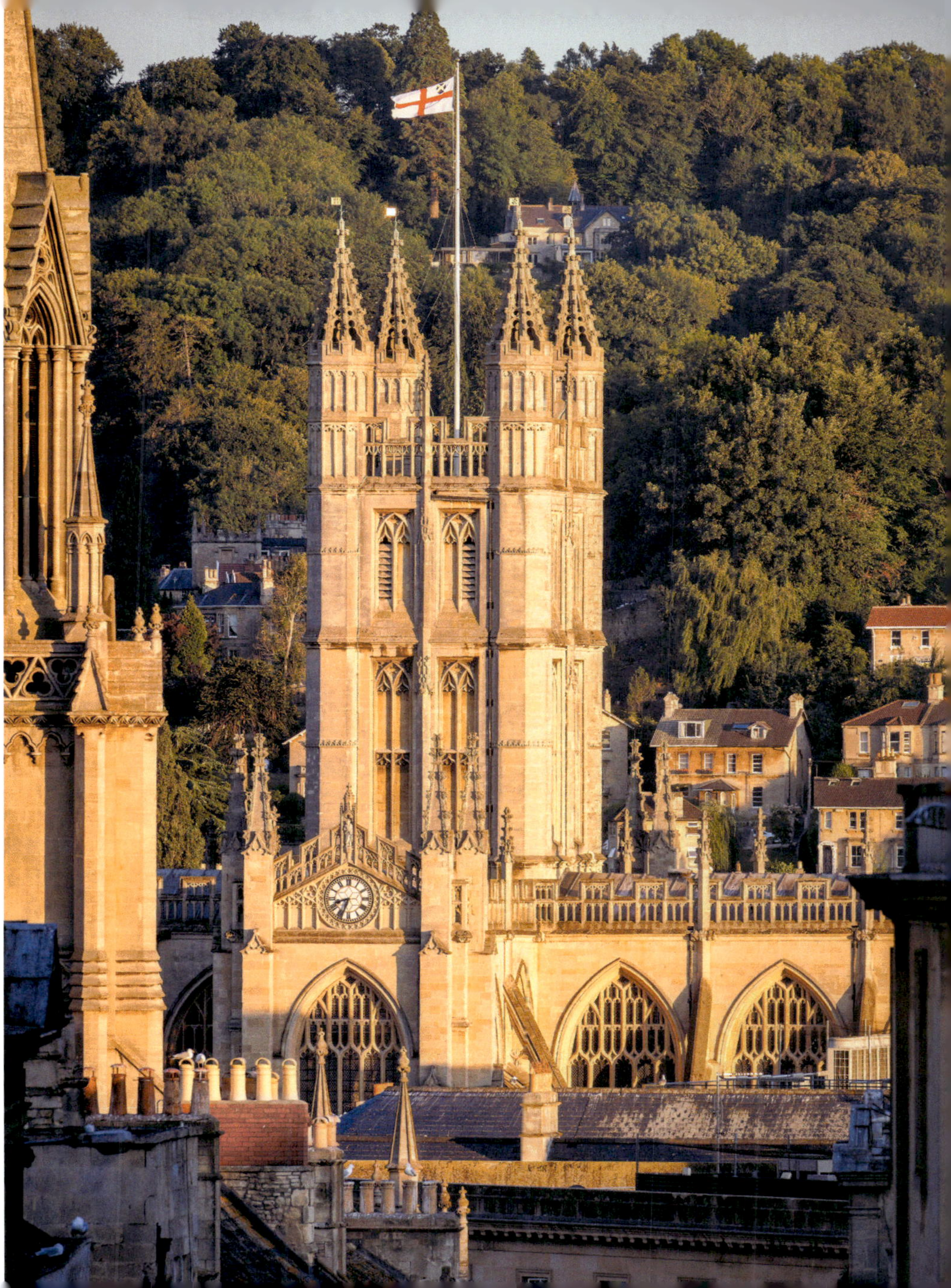

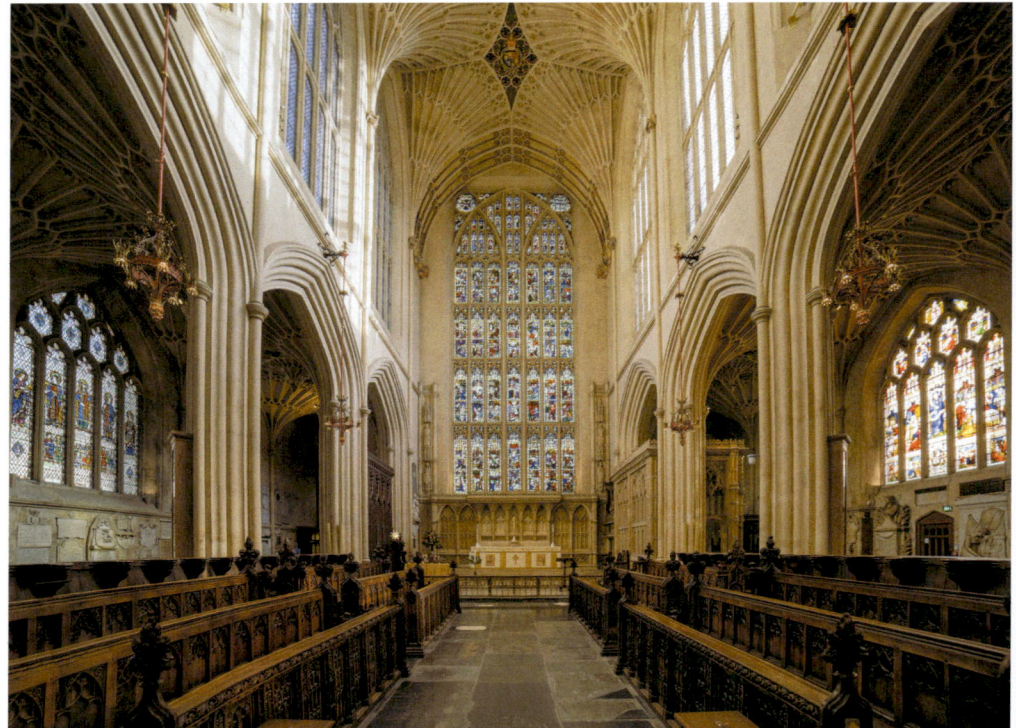
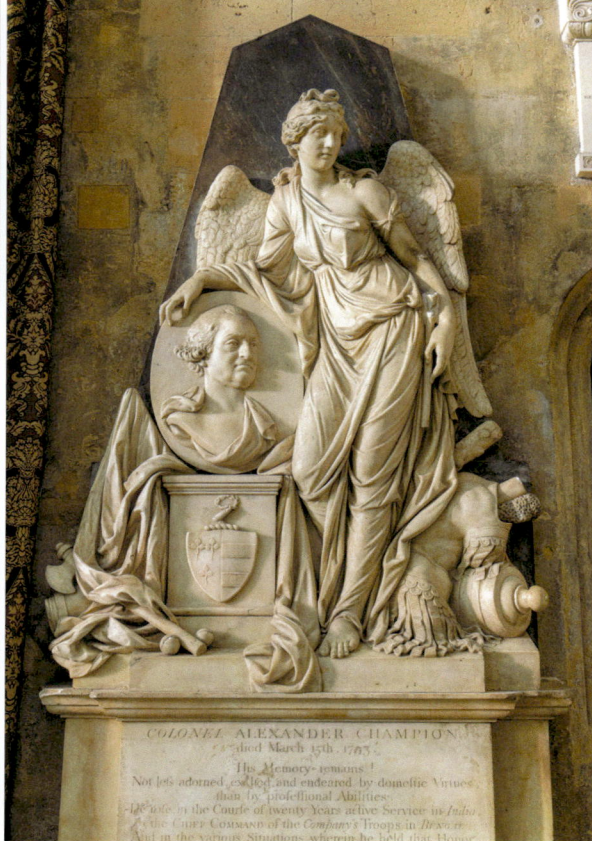
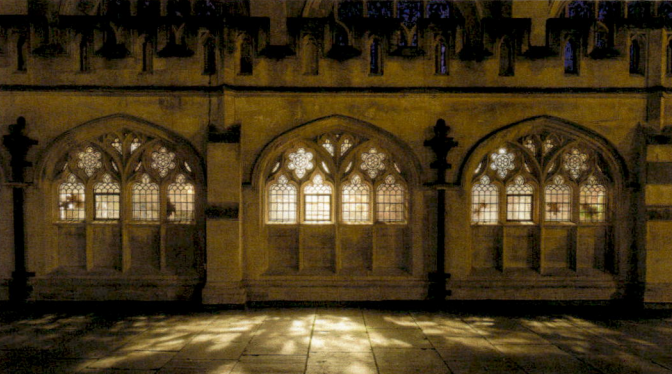
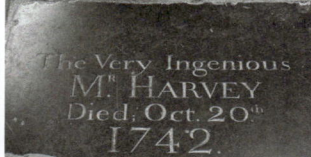
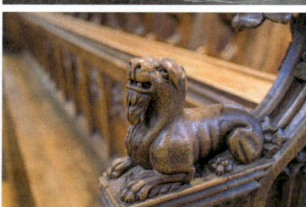

TOP LEFT: the eastern side of the Abbey, where the choir performs. **ABOVE:** many intricately carved memorials adorn the walls. **FAR LEFT:** visit at night to experience the atmospheric glow of the inner lights reflecting on the pavement outside. **MIDDLE:** aAn intriguing memorial to the ingenious Mr. Harvey. **LEFT:** a carved pew end in the form of a lion.

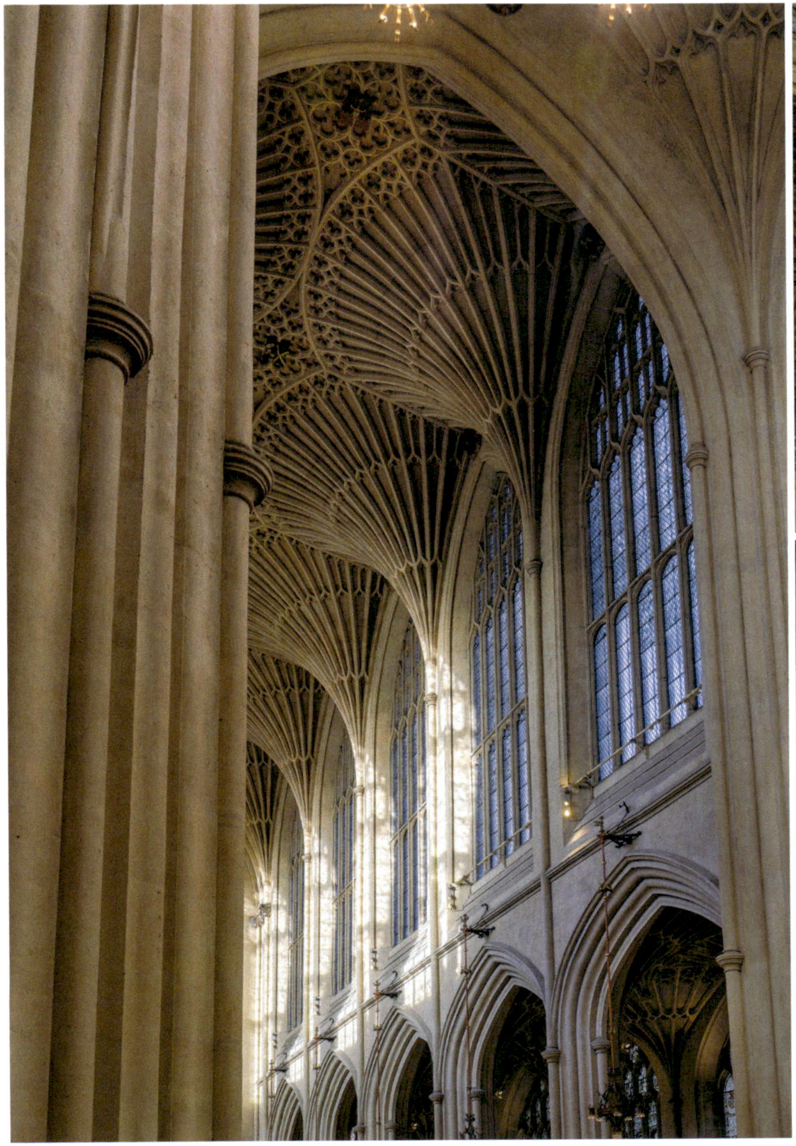

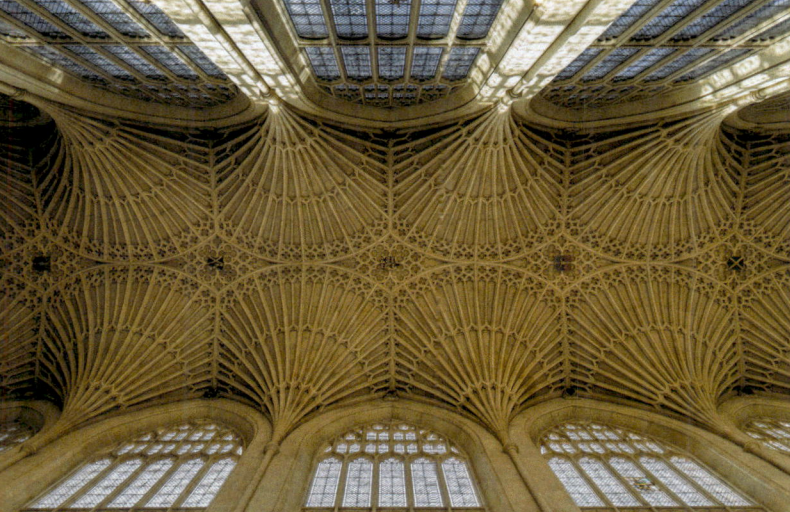

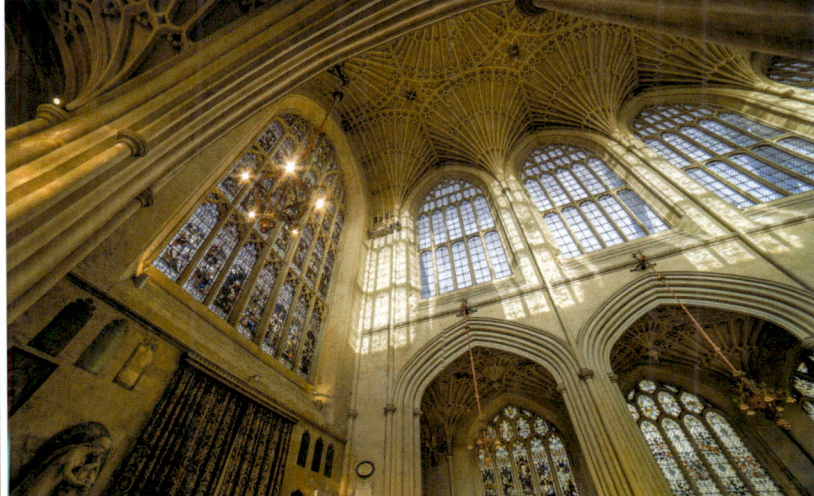

LEFT: The Abbey features an impressive fan vaulted ceiling held up by slender columns.
TOP: Built by master architects Robert and William Vertue, it is considered one of the finest examples of fan vaulting in the country. **ABOVE**: The original wooden ceiling was replaced by stone in 1863 AD.

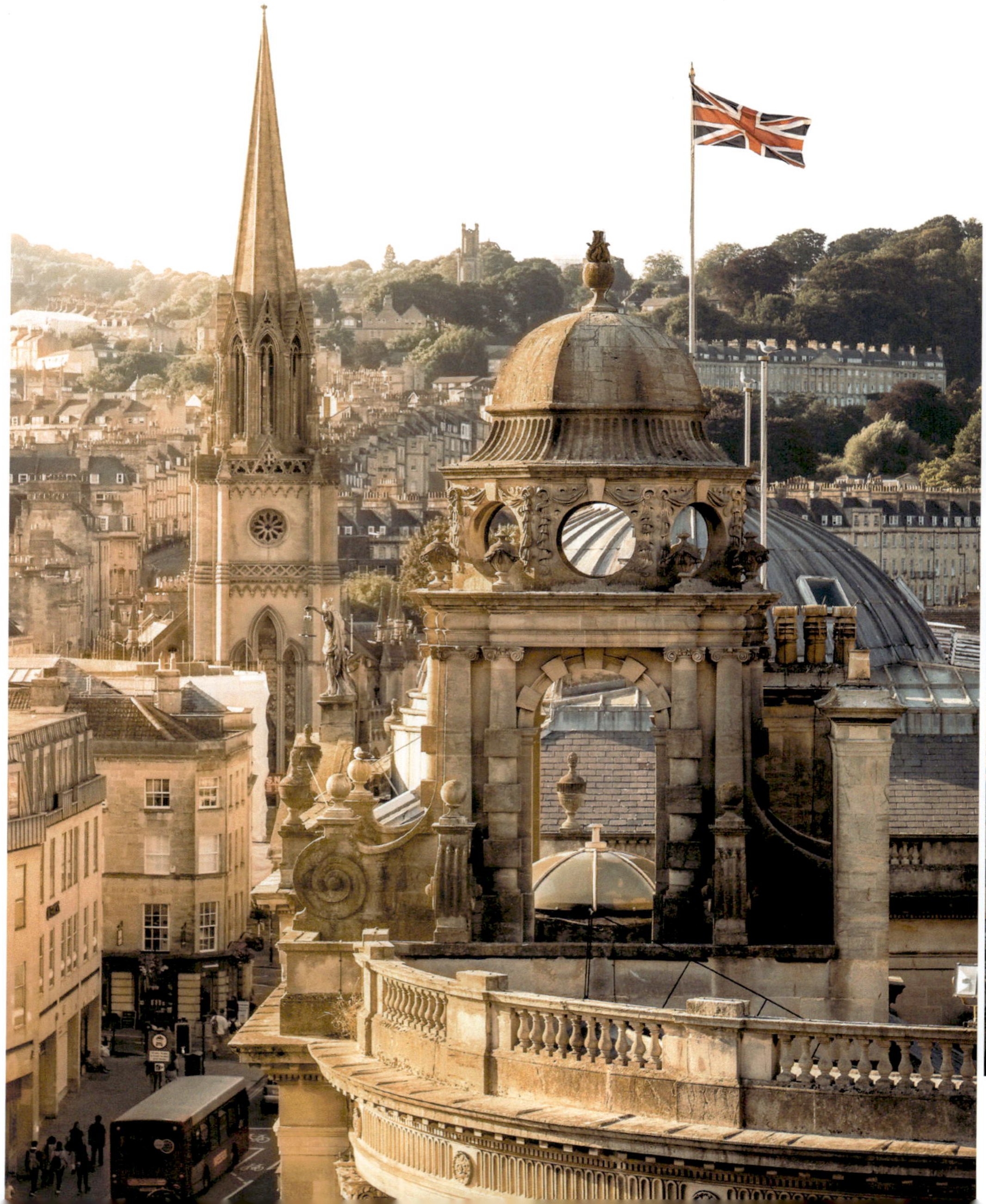

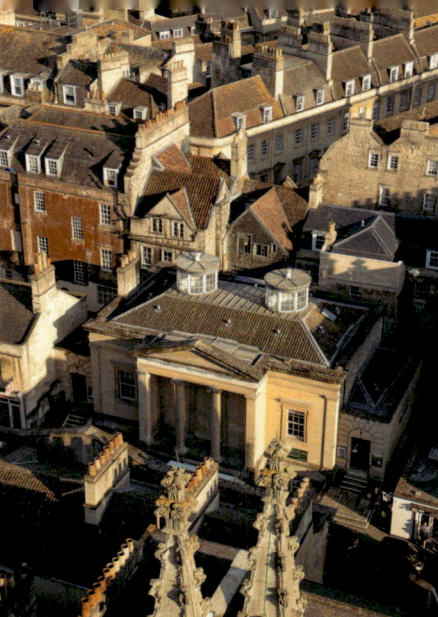
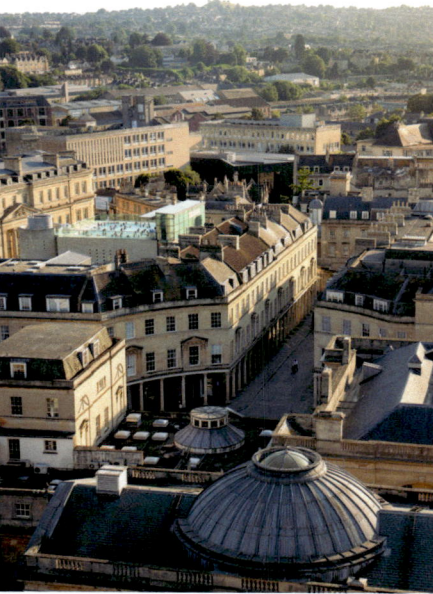

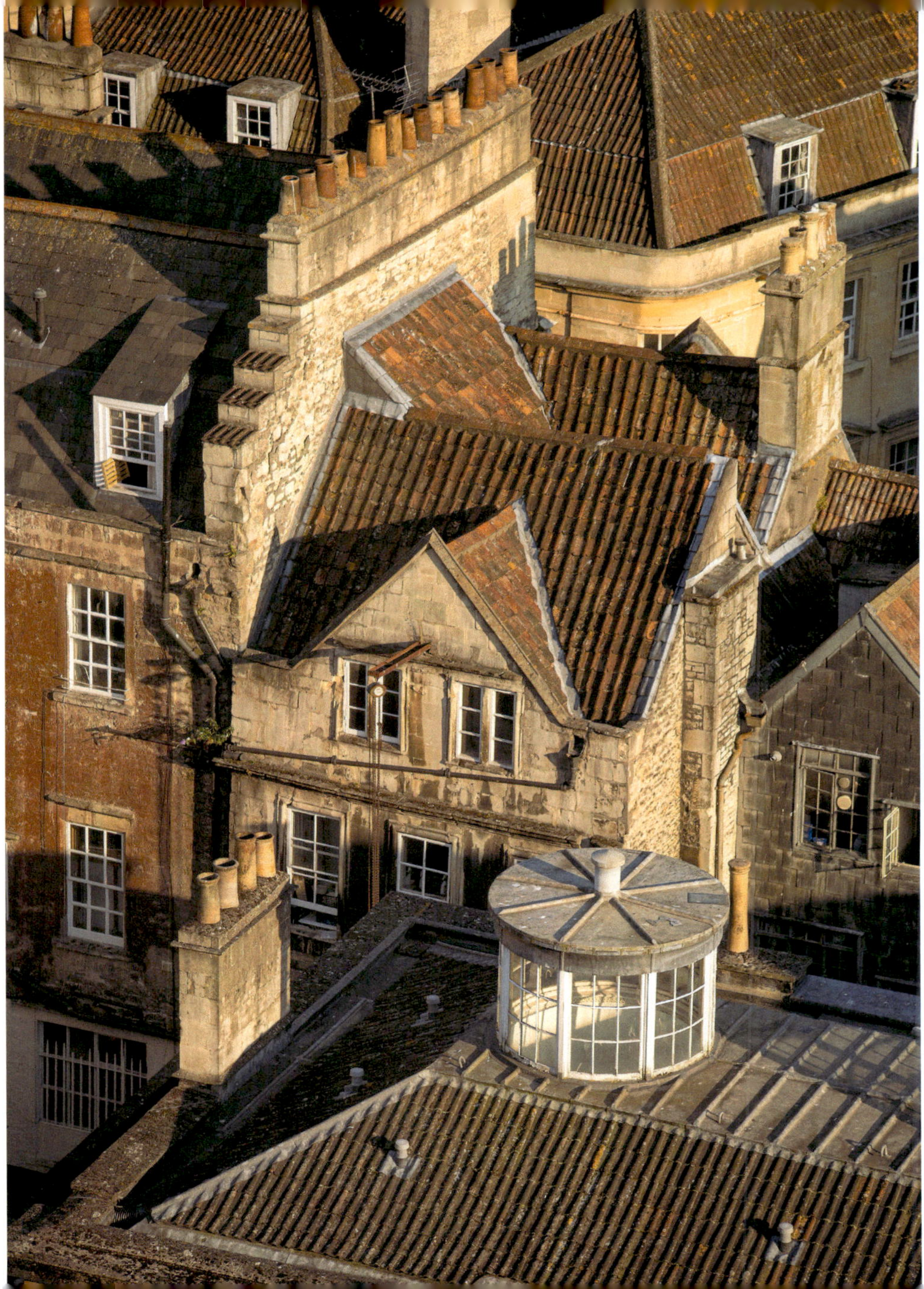

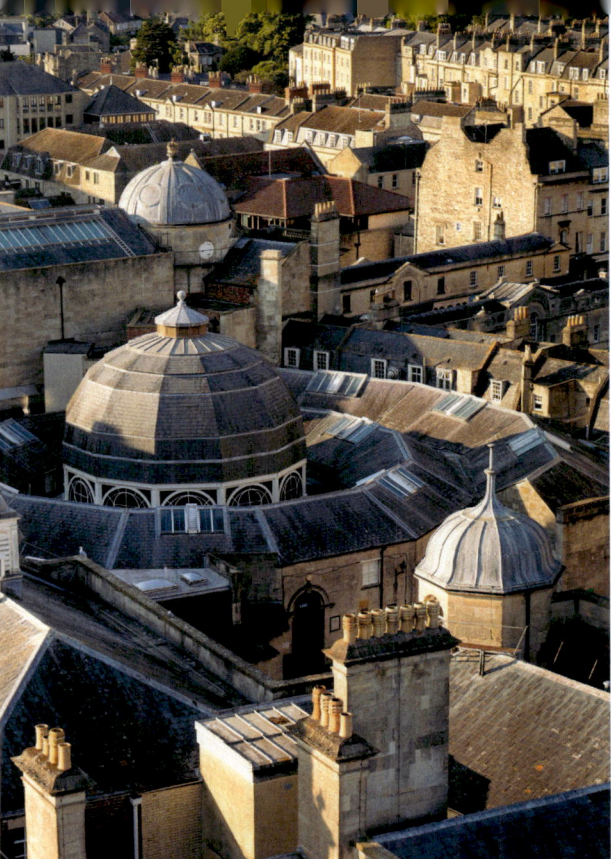

VIEWS FROM THE ABBEY TOWER

OPPOSITE FAR LEFT: stunning views of Bath's rooftops, featuring the Guildhall and St Michael's Church. **TOP LEFT**: the Abbey Tower offers a unique vantage point, providing a view into one of Bath's oldest districts. **BOTTOM LEFT**: looking westward, you can see Bath Street and the rooftop pool of Thermae Spa.

LEFT: the circular rooftop lantern of the former Friends Meeting House (now Topping & Company Booksellers) alongside the existing medieval buildings at the rear. **ABOVE**: the unique circular roof design of the Guildhall Market, the oldest shopping venue in the city.

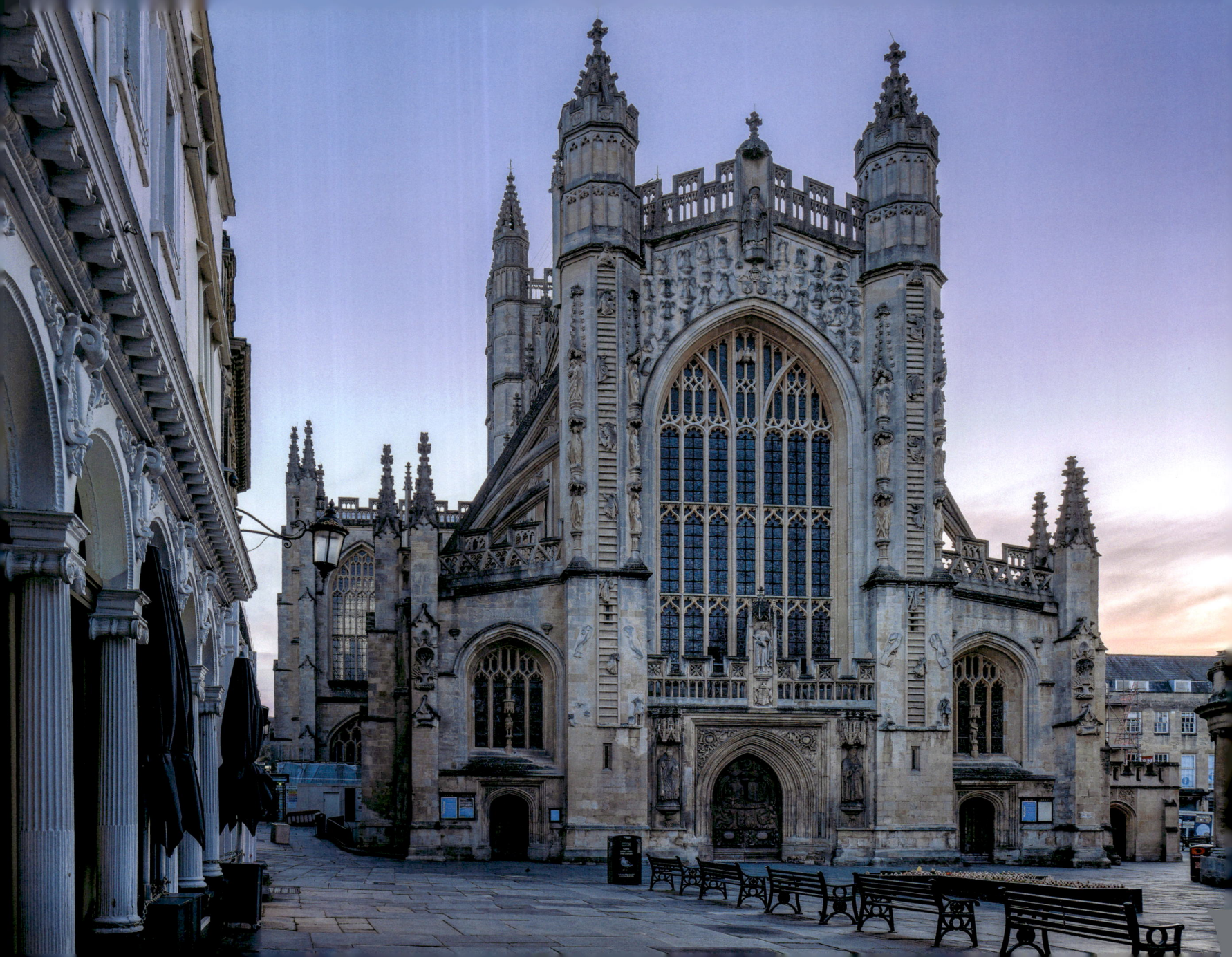

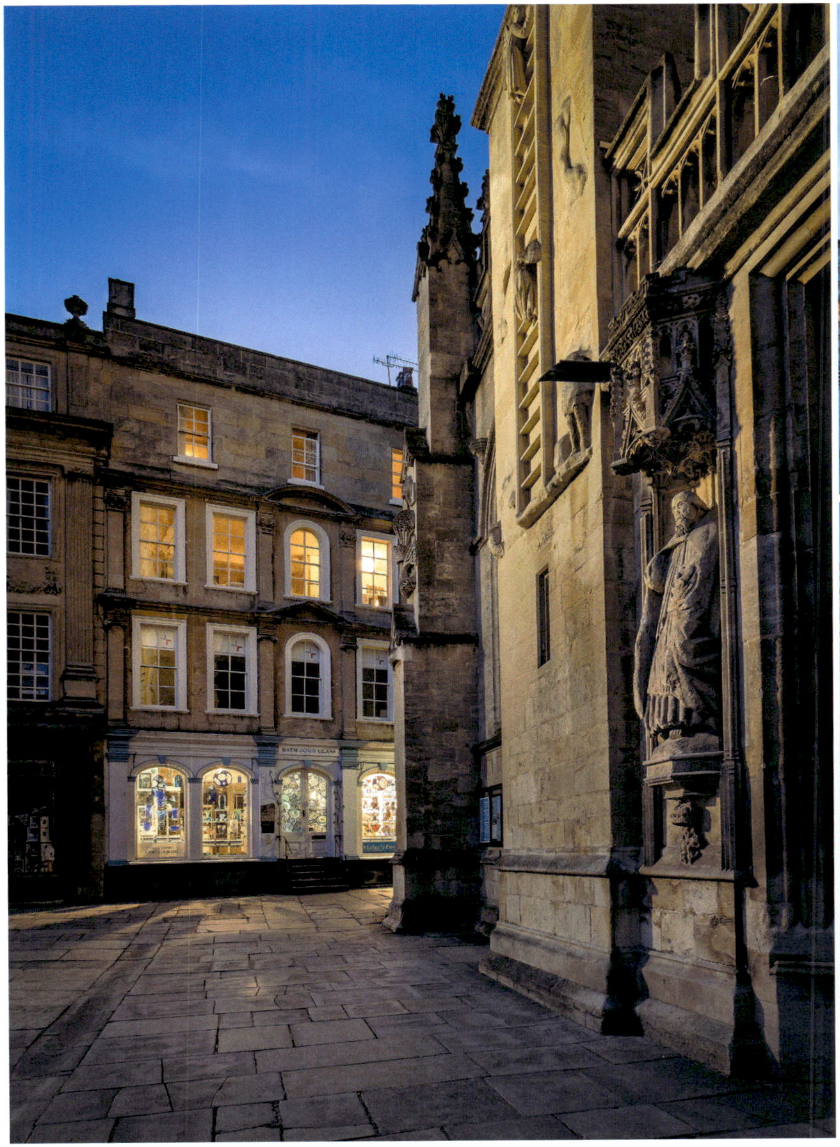

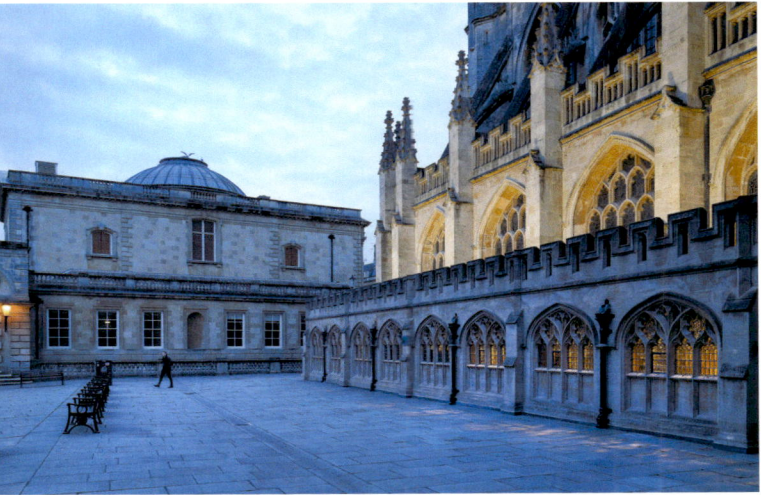

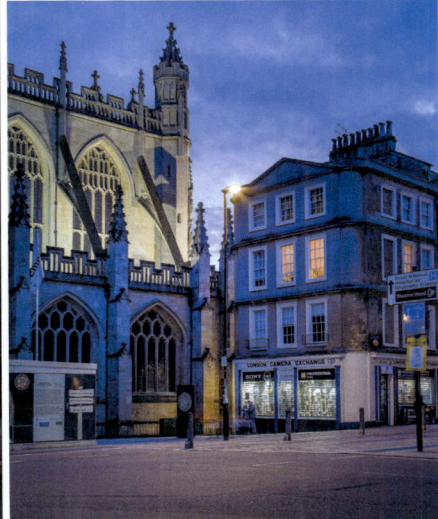

OPPOSITE: the west front opens onto the former churchyard, now home to dining establishments and restaurants offering a full view of the Abbey.

LEFT: statues of St. Peter and St. Paul stand beside the doorway of the west front.
TOP: Kingston Parade is a large open public space located beside the Abbey.
ABOVE: the Abbey as seen from the junction of Cheap Street and High Street.

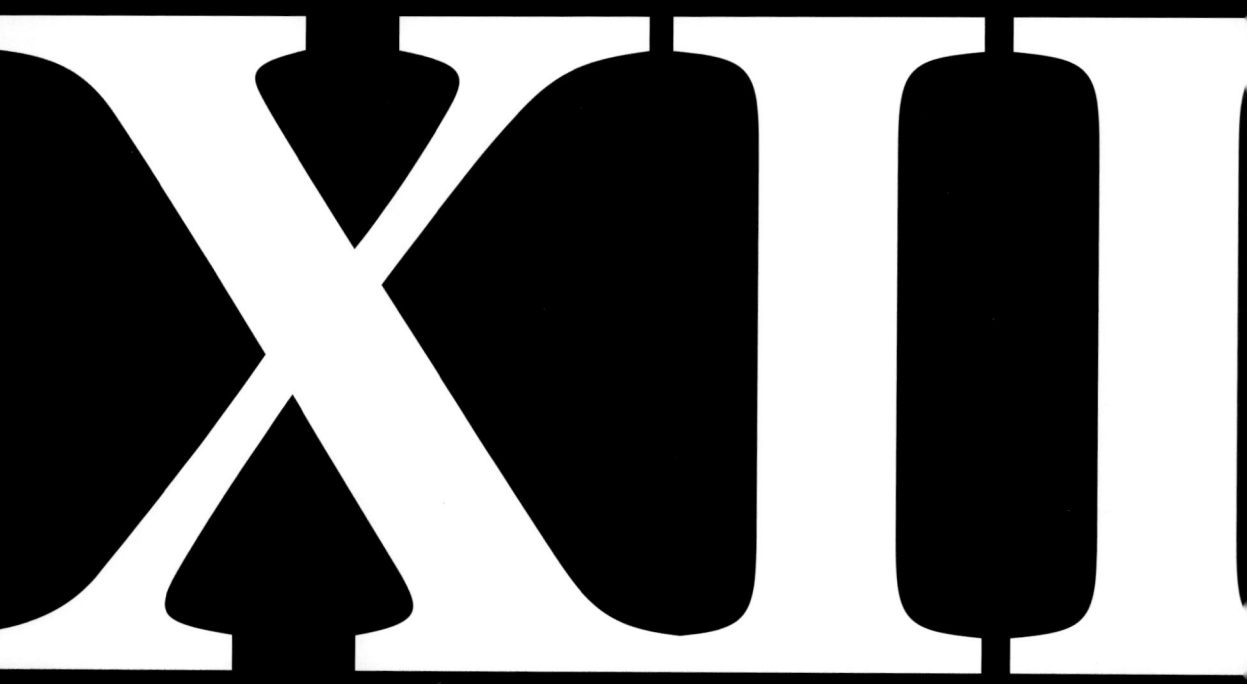

12 BATH'S ALLEYWAYS & BACK STREETS

A Glimpse into Medieval Life

The narrow lanes near Bath Abbey harken back to the city's earlier layout before 18th-century developments. These streets, with their smaller shopfronts and modest buildings, contrast sharply with the grandeur of Georgian avenues.

A JOURNEY THROUGH HISTORY

Beyond Bath's grand Georgian facades and landmarks lies a maze of enchanting alleyways, each brimming with history. These hidden passageways reveal tucked-away gems many visitors overlook.

One atmospheric area is **North Parade Alleys**, narrow walkways once used by traders navigating Bath's markets. Today, they lead to independent boutiques, cafés, and historic buildings.

Nearby, **Old Orchard Street** holds a fascinating past. Home to Bath's first Theatre Royal in the 18th century, it later became a Masonic hall and Catholic chapel. Walking here, you can almost hear echoes of actors and worshippers.

For a mix of shopping and history, **Green Street** and **The Corridor** are must-visit spots. **Green Street** offers independent shops and charm, while **The Corridor**, one of England's earliest shopping arcades (1825), features boutique stores and elegant architecture.

Tucked behind grand thoroughfares, **Hay Hill** descends elegantly between streets, providing a scenic shortcut along paved paths with historic appeal.

No visit is complete without stopping at **Sally Lunn's**, one of Bath's oldest houses, tucked in a quiet passage. Famous for its iconic Sally Lunn buns – part bread, part cake, and entirely delicious.

Exploring these alleyways, with a stop for pint or a pot of tea lets you uncover Bath's true essence. Whether seeking history, hidden treasures, or a quiet retreat, these secret corners promise a journey through time unlike any other.

ABBEY GREEN

Postcode: BA1 1NW
what3words: second.after.began

NORTH PARADE ALLEYS

Postcode: BA1 1NX
what3words: vocab.festivity.back

OLD ORCHARD STREET

Postcode: BA1 1JU
what3words: follow.rabble.strict

GREEN STREET

Postcode: BA1 2JY
what3words: moon.firm.slams

HAY HILL

Postcode: BA1 5LZ
what3words: noted.things.stuck

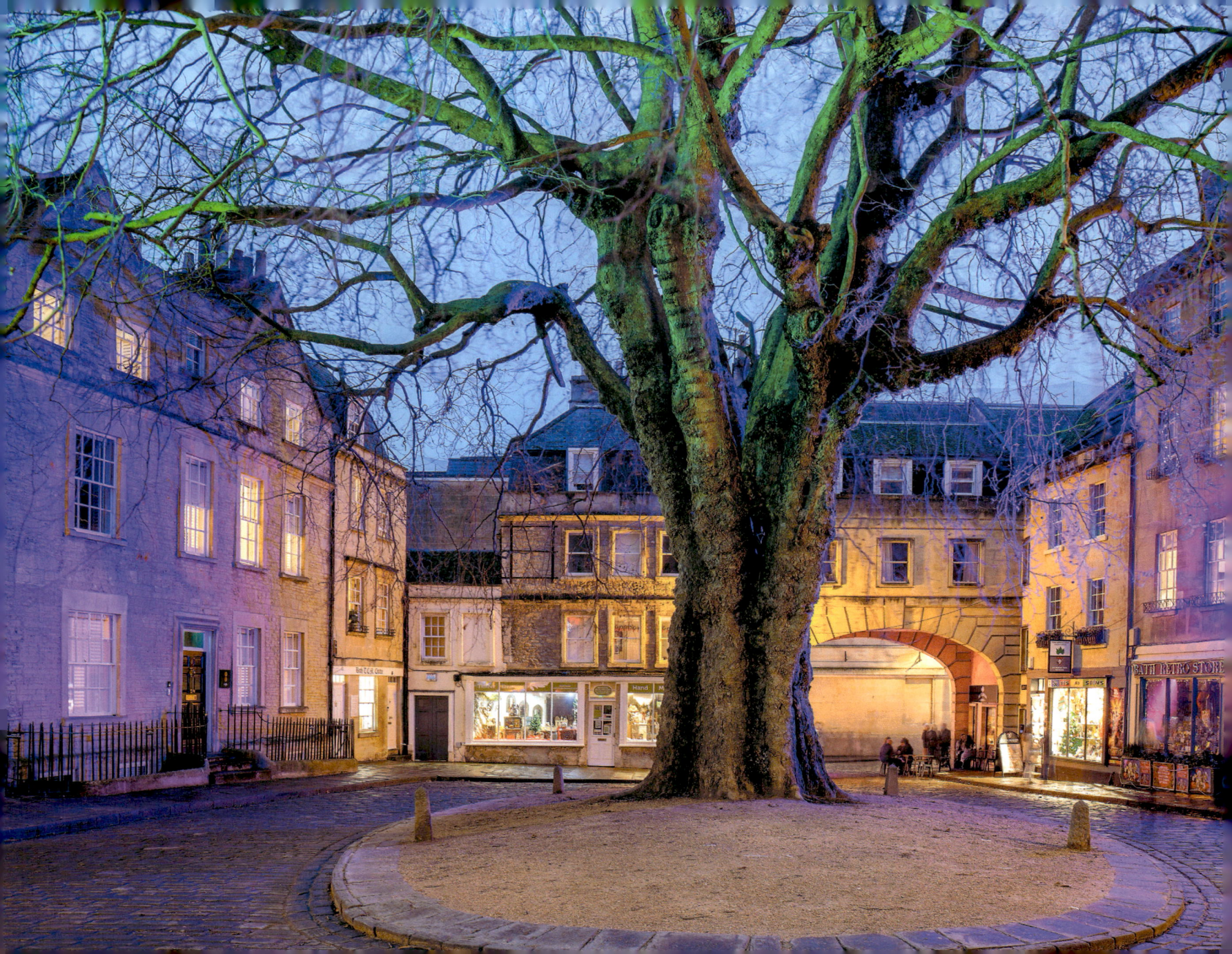

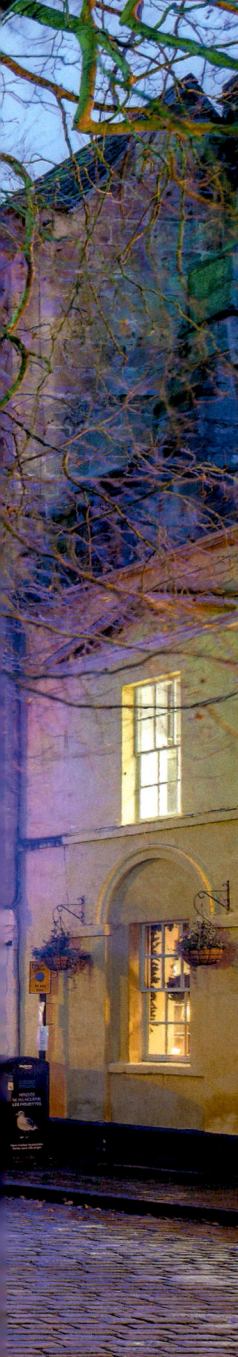

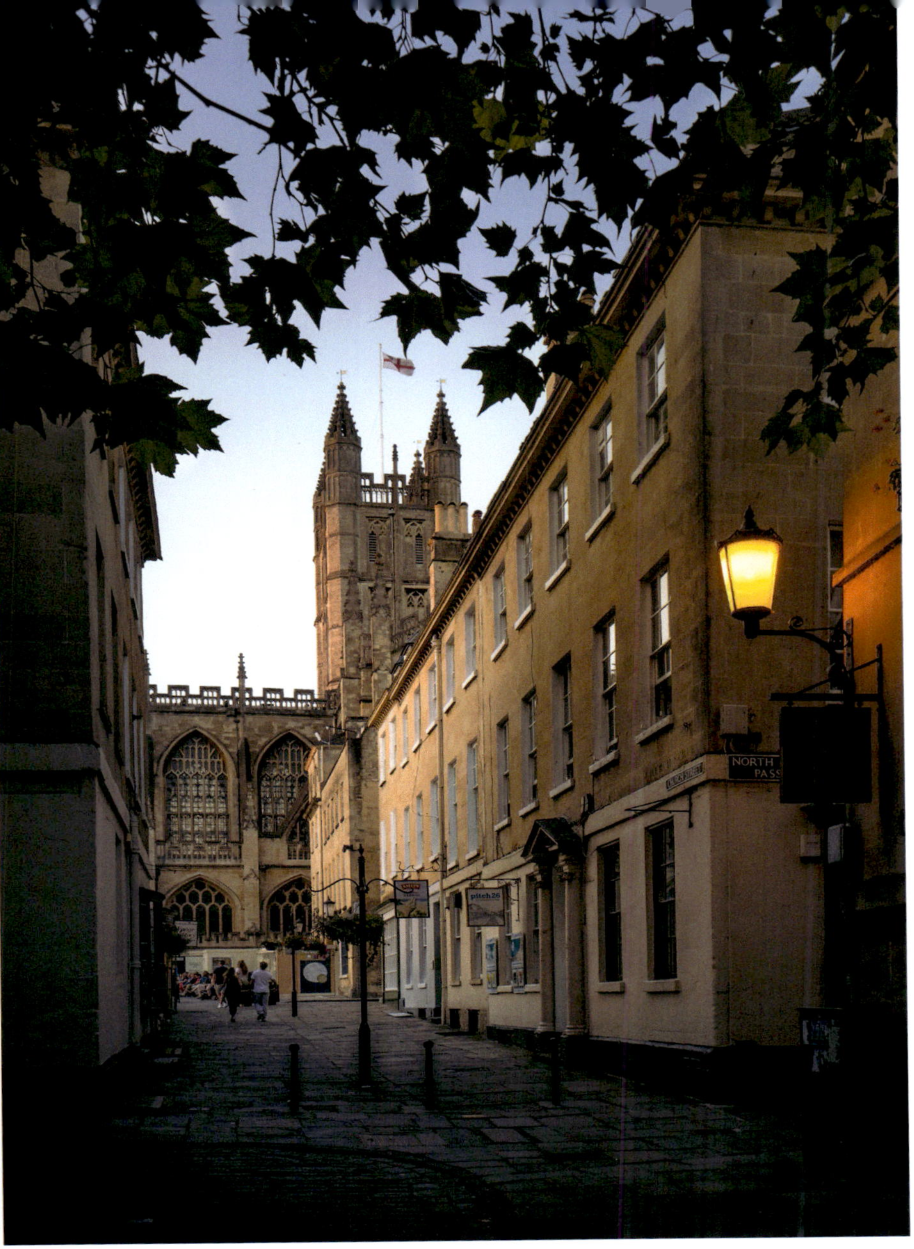

ABBEY GREEN

A visit to the alleyways surrounding Abbey Green is the closest we can come to stepping back into Bath's Medieval past, narrow streets fan out from the central courtyard each concealing their own fascinating mix of historic shops and eateries. At the heart of Abbey Green is an impressive plane tree which has stood here for over 220 years.

Once part of a larger complex surrounding Bath Abbey the 'Green' in the latter part of the 17th Century was an open natural space including a series of enclosed gardens within the boundaries of the city walls. On the western side, the church of St James used to stand where the Crystal Palace pub is now located and on the southern edge, Abbey Gate Street once led to an arched entrance large enough for horse and carts to pass through. Today, the only clue remaining is one single iron hinge bracket fixed into the wall.

Abbey Green is a beautiful destination, tucked away from the bustling city streets offering a rich sense of history set amongst some of the oldest properties on Bath. The atmosphere of Abbey Green is often described as quaint and tranquil, despite its central location. Numerous artisan shops, restaurants and cafes surround the Green and seasonal markets line the cobbled streets. During November and December the Bath Christmas Market is an especially magical time to visit when the entire courtyard glows with a myriad of colours from the stalls and Christmas decorations and the mighty plane tree is bathed in a rainbow illumination.

OPPOSITE: an enormous plane tree has stood here for over two centuries, beautifully lit up at Christmas and filling the entire space.

LEFT: Church Street, located in the top right corner, leads to Kingston Parade and Bath Abbey.

12 BATH'S ALLEYWAYS & BACK STREETS

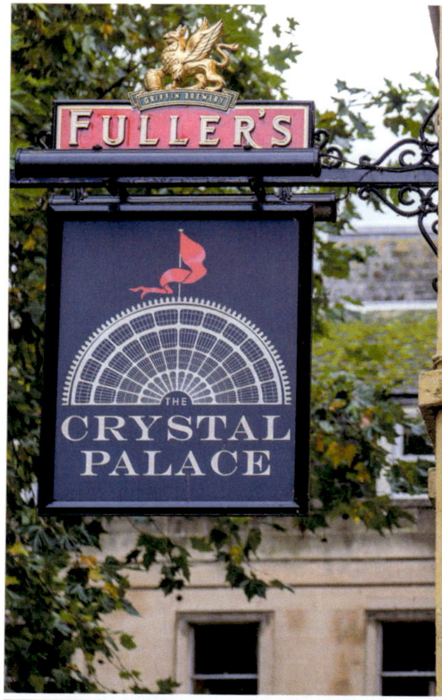

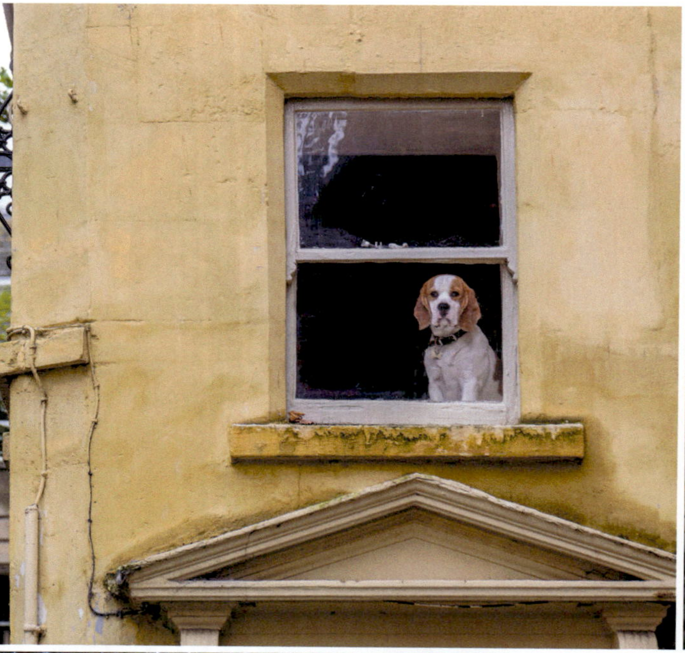

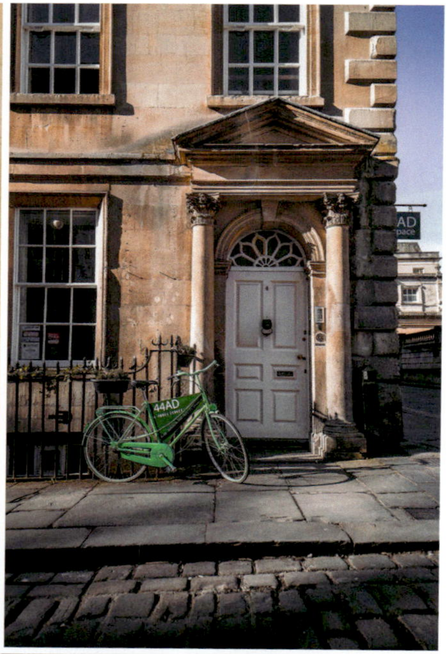

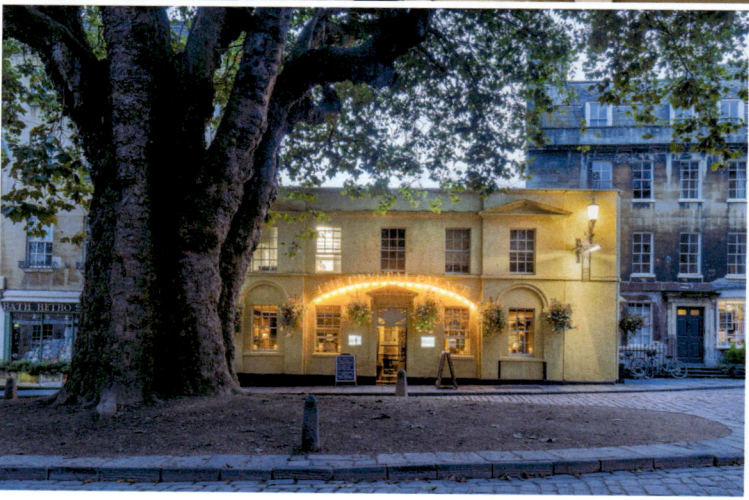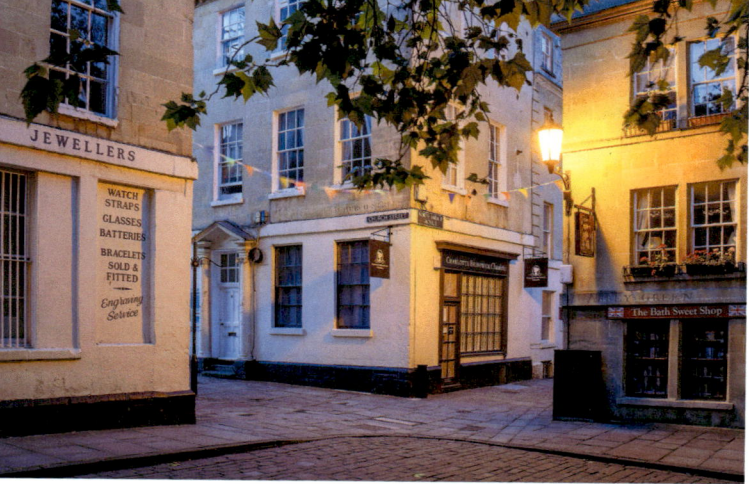

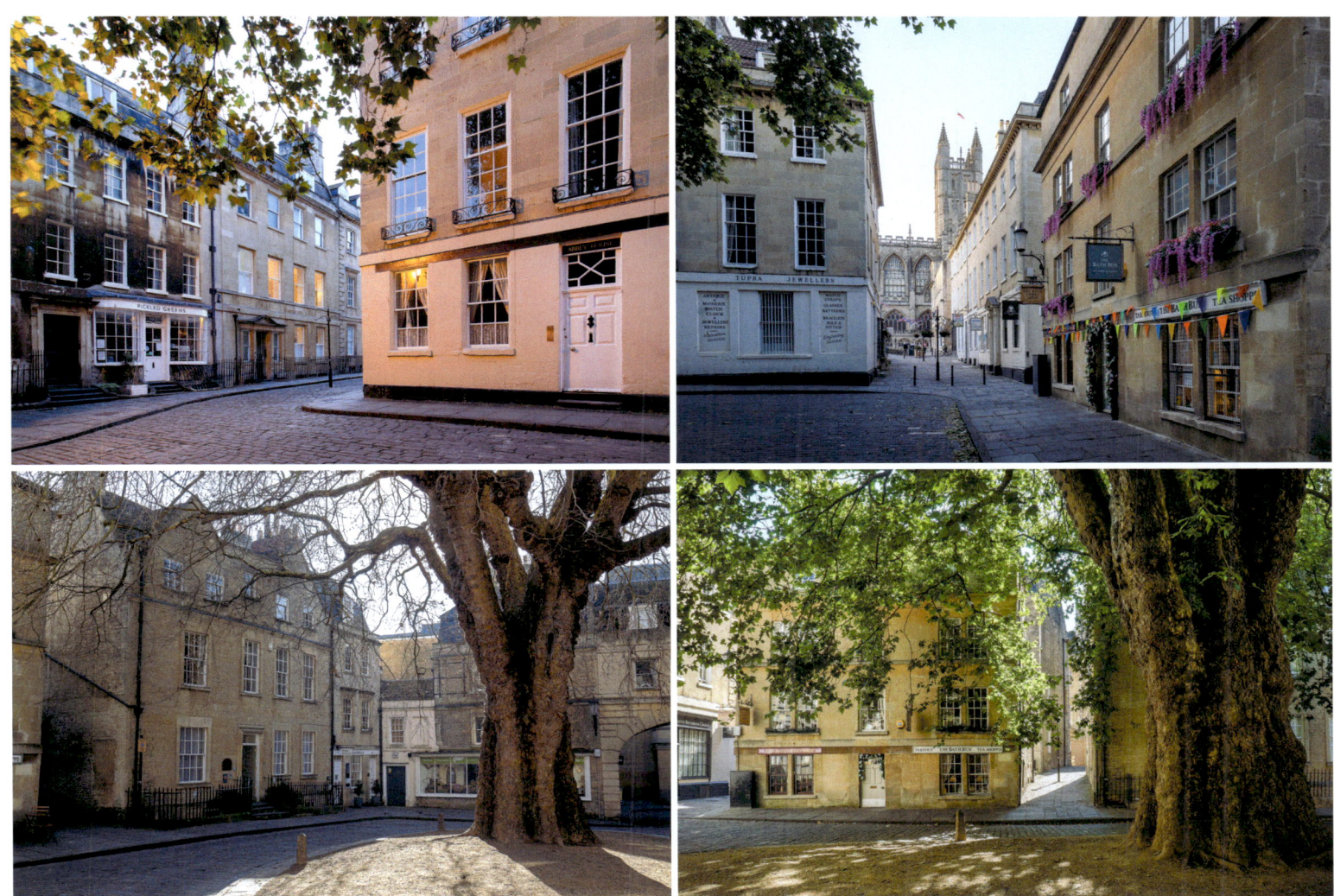

OPPOSITE TOP LEFT: keeping an eye on things, one curious resident. **TOP RIGHT**: 44AD Artspace, featuring an art gallery and artist studios.
BOTTOM LEFT: the Crystal Palace public house. **BOTTOM RIGHT**: Bath's iconic and charming alleyways lead to Abbey Green.

TOP LEFT: cobbled streets create a timeless atmosphere, as if stepping back into the past. **TOP**: many independent shops and eateries line Abbey Green.
BOTTOM LEFT: many buildings are granted protected listed status. **ABOVE**: the tree canopy provides welcome shade during the summer months.

NORTH PARADE ALLEYS

The hidden back-alleys of Bath don't come more charming than this. North Parade Alley is a narrow passageway located in one of the oldest districts of Bath with some of the original structural elements of the buildings dating to the Medieval period. It connects North Parade, Abbey Green and York Street beyond and is renowned for its picturesque pedestrian friendly pathway, lined with curved shop fronts, quaint bars, boutiques, and restaurants.

One of the most famous establishments along North Parade Alley is Sally Lunn's Eating House. This iconic restaurant is housed in one of Bath's oldest buildings, dating back to the late 15th century. Sally Lunn's Eating House is famous for its namesake delicacy, the Sally Lunn Bun. This legendary bun is a cross between a bread roll and a sweet bread, with a rich history dating back to the 18th century. It is typically served warm with a variety of toppings, including butter, jam, or even savoury fillings like ham and cheese.

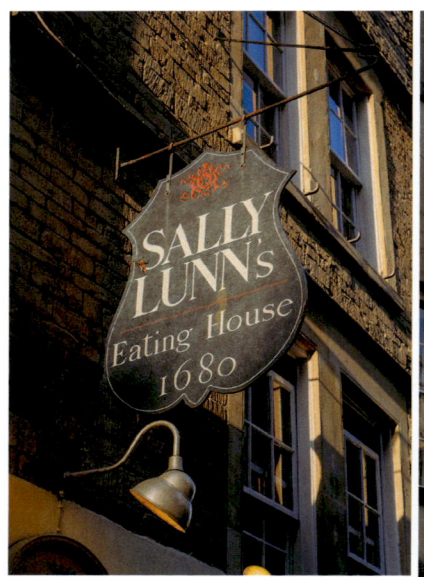

The interior of Sally Lunn's Eating House is cosy and inviting, with low ceilings, wooden beams, and rustic decor that harkens back to its historic roots making it a popular spot for both locals and visitors alike. Inside a small museum reveals in greater detail the varied past of this fascinating place. From within you can view the bakery range as it would have existed at the original street level, now much lower than the paved area above which was raised considerably in the 1700s as part of the Georgian redevelopments in the area.

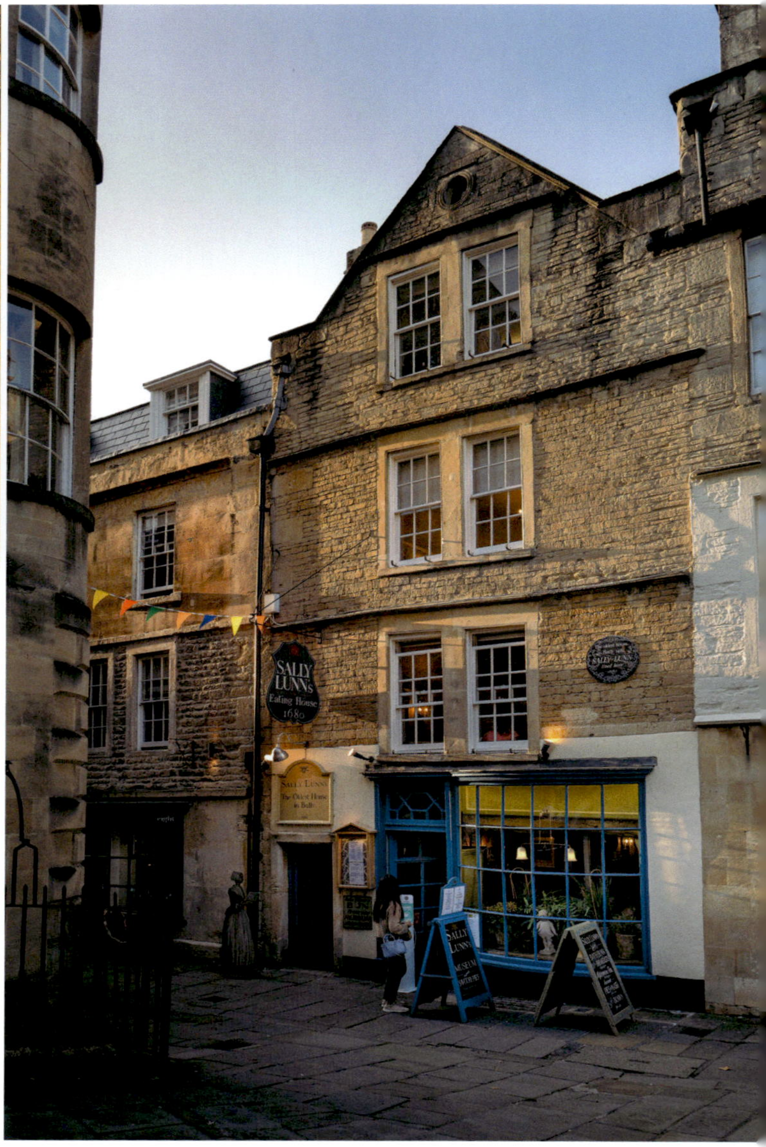

TOP: the bun's origins are unclear, but legend says it was introduced by French refugee Sally Lunn in the 1680s.
RIGHT: today, Sally Lunn's is a historic site and cafe, serving its famous buns and afternoon tea.
OPPOSITE: North Parade is an enchanting spot to wander historic streets at dusk, charming and timeless.

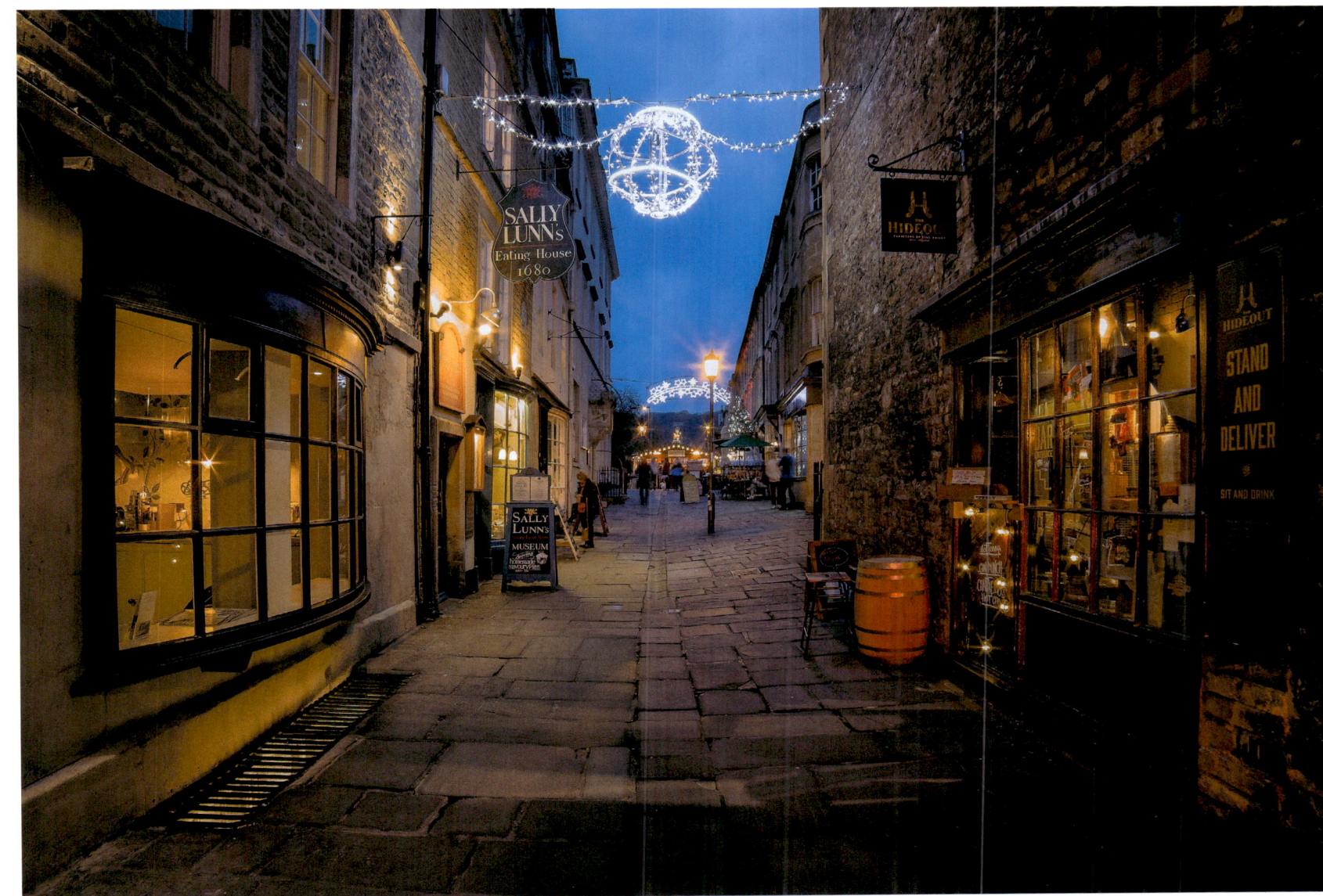

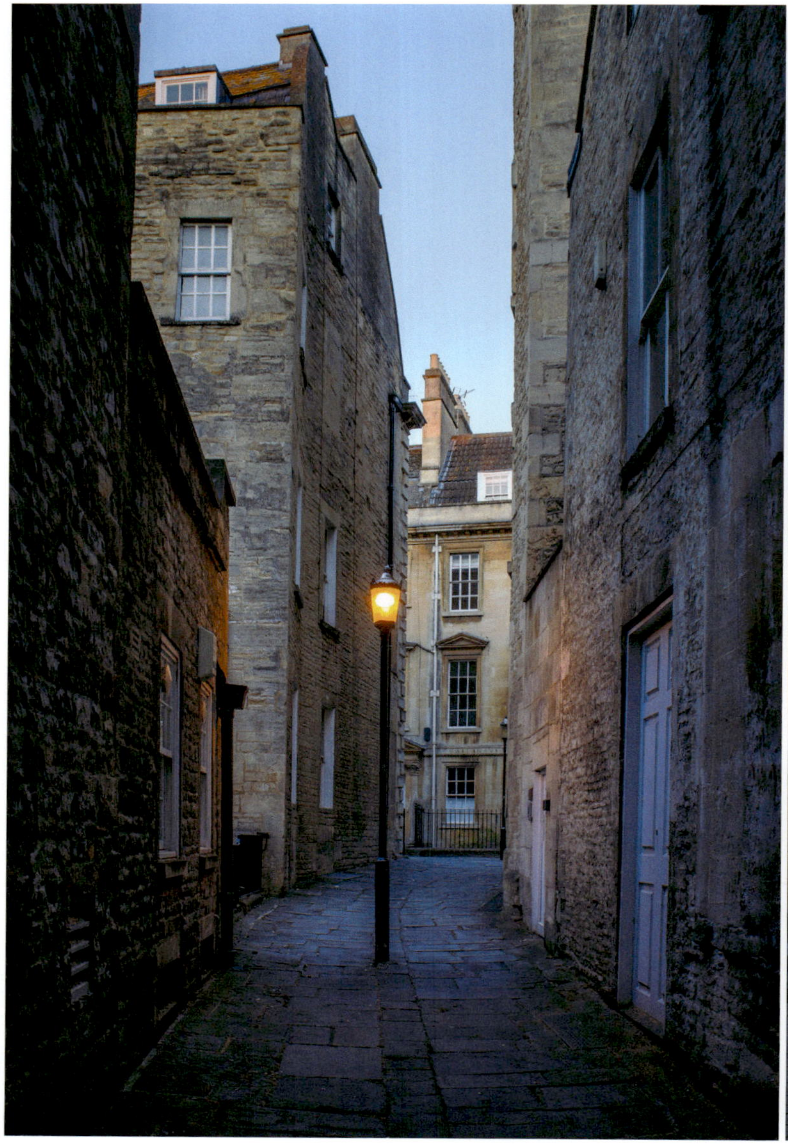

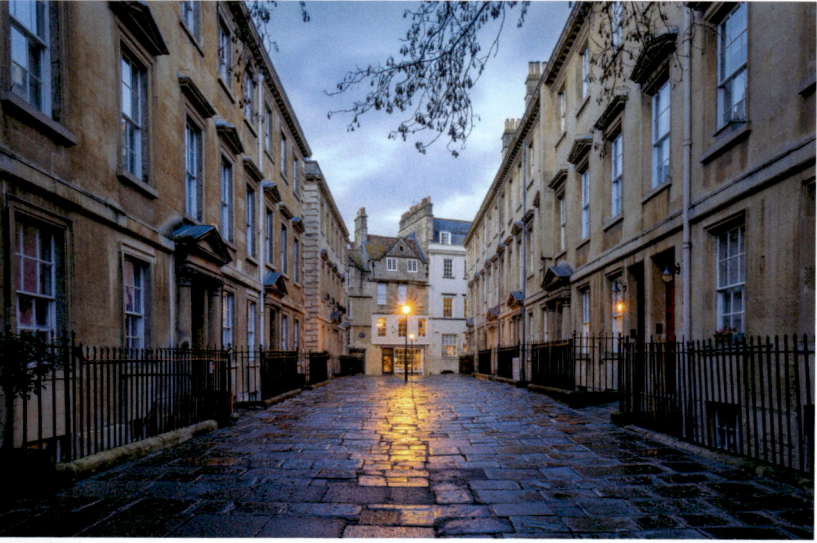
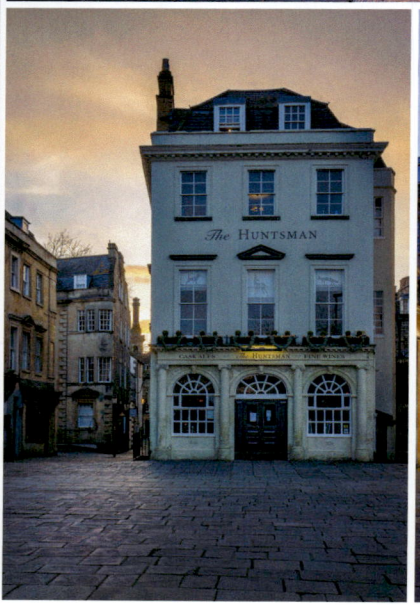
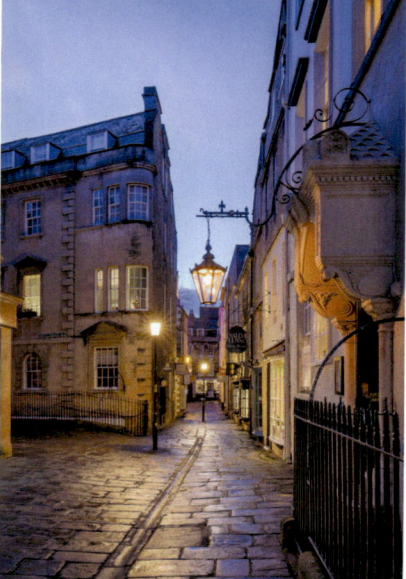

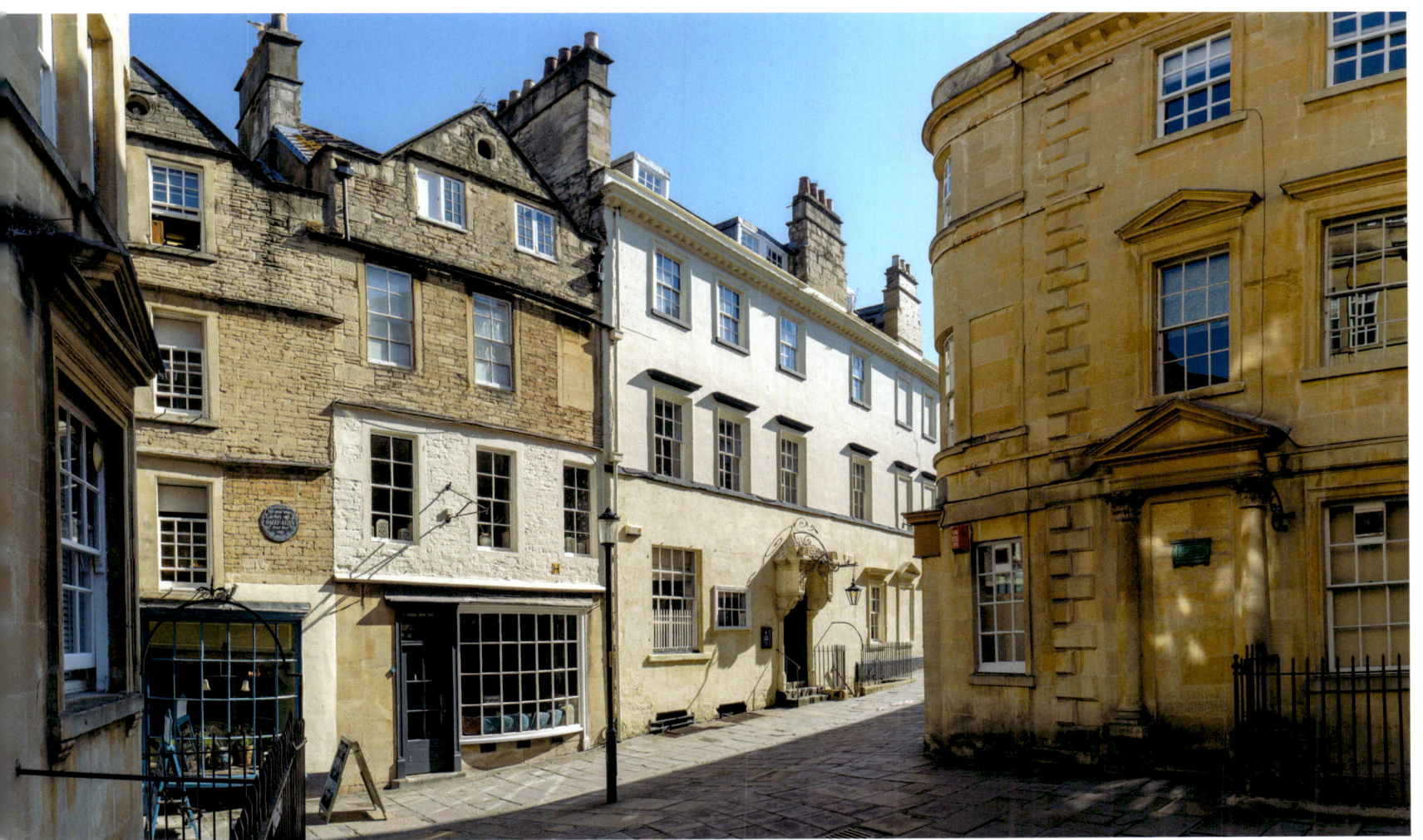

OPPOSITE LEFT: narrow alleyways offer a glimpse of what Bath's streets were like before the Georgians arrived. **TOP**: the arrival of the Georgians brought grander pavements and boulevards lined with terraced townhouses. **BOTTOM LEFT**: the Huntsman Pub. A public house has served locals and visitors alike at this spot for centuries. **BOTTOM RIGHT**: a captivating corner of Bath, ideal for those who admire the city's rich history and tranquil atmosphere.

ABOVE: a blend of building styles cluster together in this part of the city, with gabled medieval-style buildings mingling with opulent Georgian splendour.

OLD ORCHARD STREET

Located a short walk from Bath Spa Train Station to the south and North Parade in the north, Old Orchard Street instantly transports you to a setting that would seem very familiar to Bath's Georgian residents. The surrounding area has seen a huge change in building design and urban sprawl; historic buildings lost to either the Blitz or modern town planning schemes have encircled Old Orchard Street leaving it as a Georgian time capsule.

The charming cobbled side street takes its name from the fruit orchard that was planted in the grounds of Bath Abbey and underwent major development before becoming the 'place to be seen' during early Georgian social gatherings. The area particularly grew in popularity in 1750 when the (then named) St James Theatre arrived in town. Master planner John Wood the Elder, responsible for much of Bath's re-imagined street designs, chose this location to establish the first dedicated theatre venue in the city where popular performances reigned supreme for the next 55 years.

BELOW: a quiet cobbled back alley, Old Orchard Street is accessible from Monmouth Street. **RIGHT**: once home to two pubs and a public theatre venue, it was a bustling, thriving part of the city.

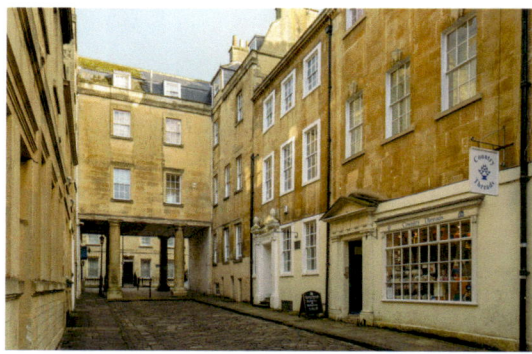

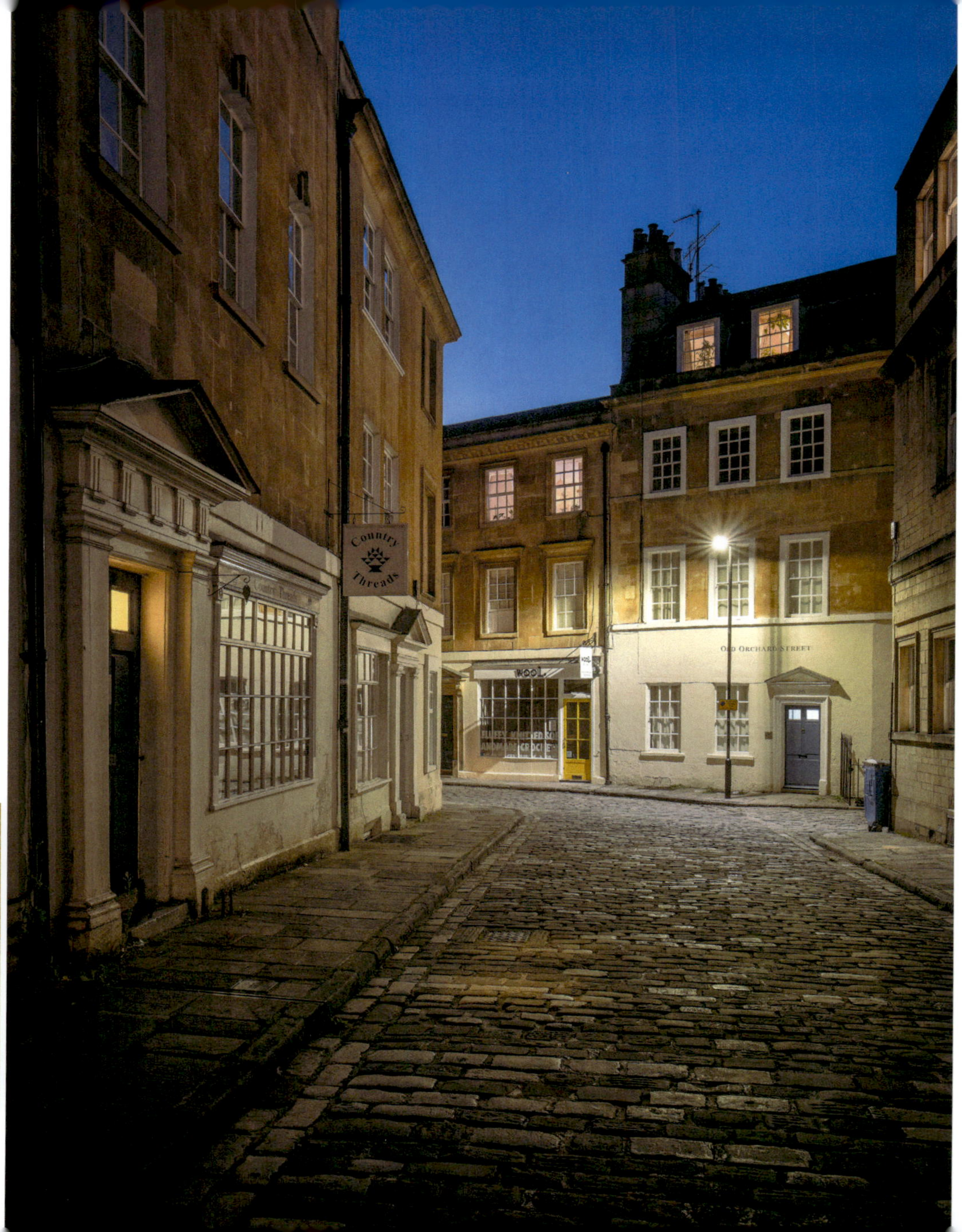

GREEN STREET

Tucked away and located close to one of Bath's premiere shopping streets is an array of businesses and vintage shop fronts on Green Street that have an unchanging and ageless quality; the only give away clue to the current decade would perhaps be varying trends in fashion or types of goods on display in the store windows.

Originally the street was the local bowling green and as development expanded residents had to share existing rights of way with livestock that continued to be driven between buildings and onto grazing pastures outside the Medieval city walls. As the city expanded in 1715 the street became inhabited by a range of gable-fronted properties some of which were adapted into all manner of businesses. Some of the earliest 18th century buildings in Bath can still be seen on the street, the upper storeys revealing clues to the past whilst at street level, a bakers shop, silversmiths and tobacconists are all recorded as occupying the narrow lane during this period and echo a similar line of independents that can be found today.

At the furthest end stands St Michaels Church, occupying the full width of the street with its majestic spire piercing the sky, at 180 feet, one of the highest landmarks in the city. Partially based on the Lady Chapel at Salisbury Cathedral the Victorian church was built by George Manners in 1835 and is a fine piece of ecclesiastical architecture. This is the fourth church to occupy the site as each previous building could no longer accommodate a growing congregation.

One of the quirkier establishments and one the smallest pubs in Bath is the Old Green Tree, a northerners style pub in the heart of the South West complete with wonderful wood paneled walls and small rooms depicting their licensed usage, such as the smoke room.

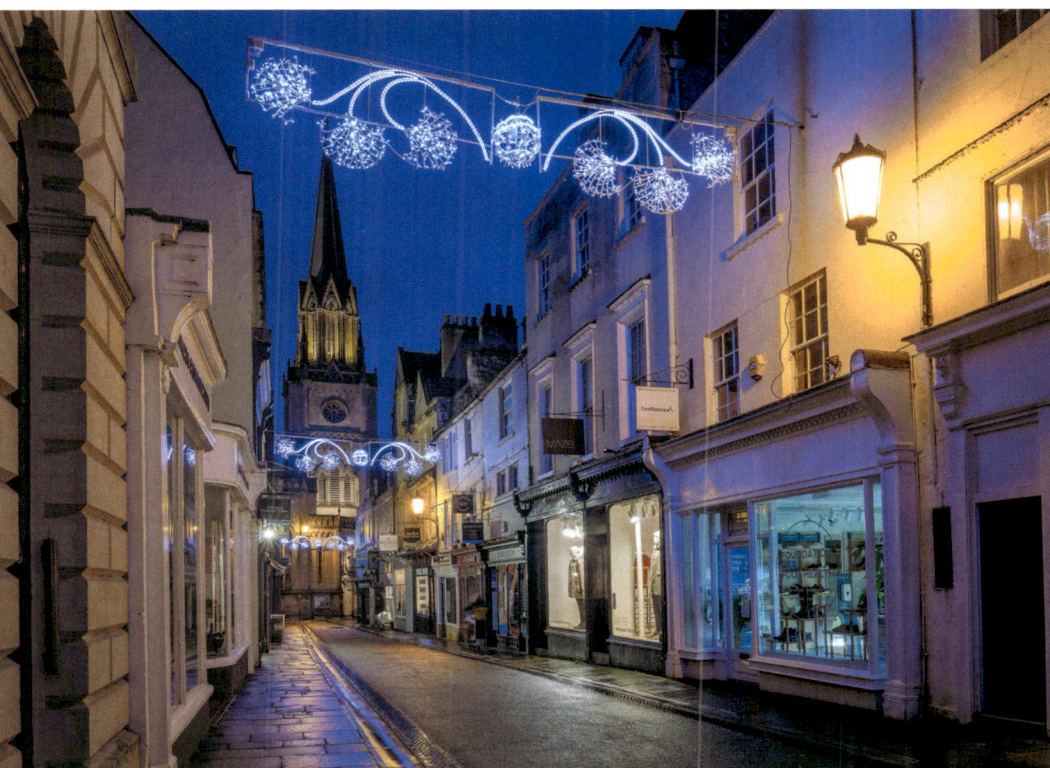

Although originally built in 1770 many of the alterations here date back to 1926 and with its quaint shop-like exterior creates a 'proper pub' feel indicative of that time.

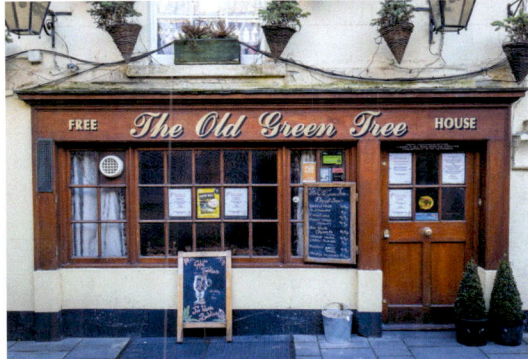

TOP: the tall, slender spire of St Michaels's Church contrasts with the surrounding buildings, framed by the narrow shop lined street. **RIGHT**: the Old Green Tree — one of the smallest pubs around.

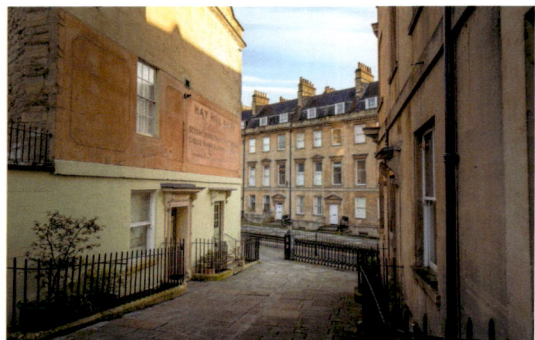
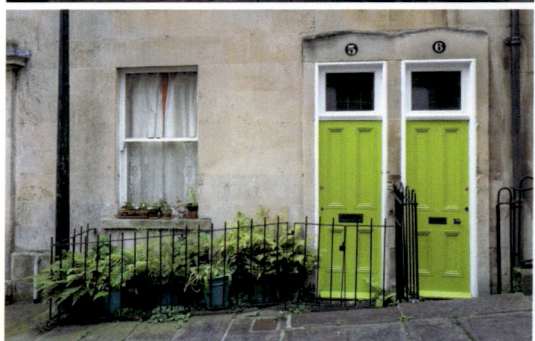
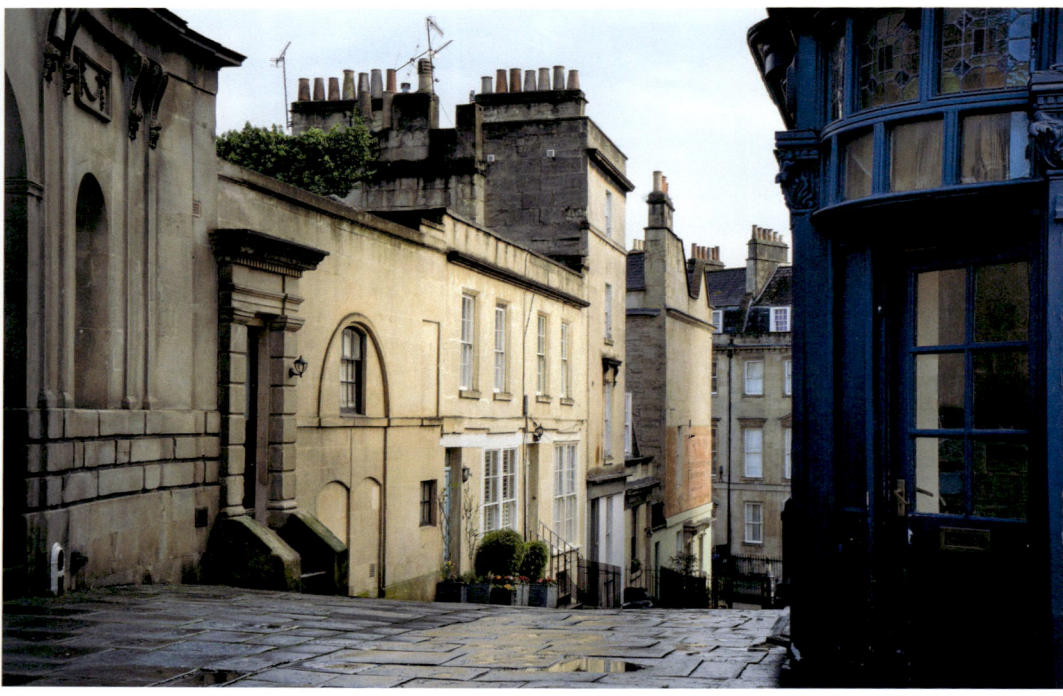

HAY HILL

This intriguing alleyway is a real hidden gem set away from the main thoroughfares of the city. Hay Hill is a short delightful flagstone route that links the steep upper slope of Lansdown Road to the impressive Paragon below. Terraced houses dating from the late 19th Century line the street and consist of mainly private residences although there are a few clues remaining of tiny shop fronts which are interesting to spot. A jumble of differing property sizes make up part of a miniaturised version of this intriguing Georgian side street which has some of the smallest doorways in Bath.

A ghostly remnant of the past can be seen on the wall above the first property at the entrance to Hay Hill. A faint painted sign for the Hay Hill Dairy which used to occupy this site in 1888 advertises a range of products, such as cream and bacon fresh from the fields of Devon and Dorset.

TOP LEFT: a ghost sign remains at the bottom of Hay Hill, advertising a dairy that once stood here. **BOTTOM LEFT**: two of a kind; compact and bijou house entrances. **ABOVE**: Hay Hill drops gradually from Lansdown Road to the Paragon below.

OPPOSITE: the small alley is now a mix of private residences and holiday lets, an intriguing detour from the grand Georgian streets, tucked betwixt the buildings.

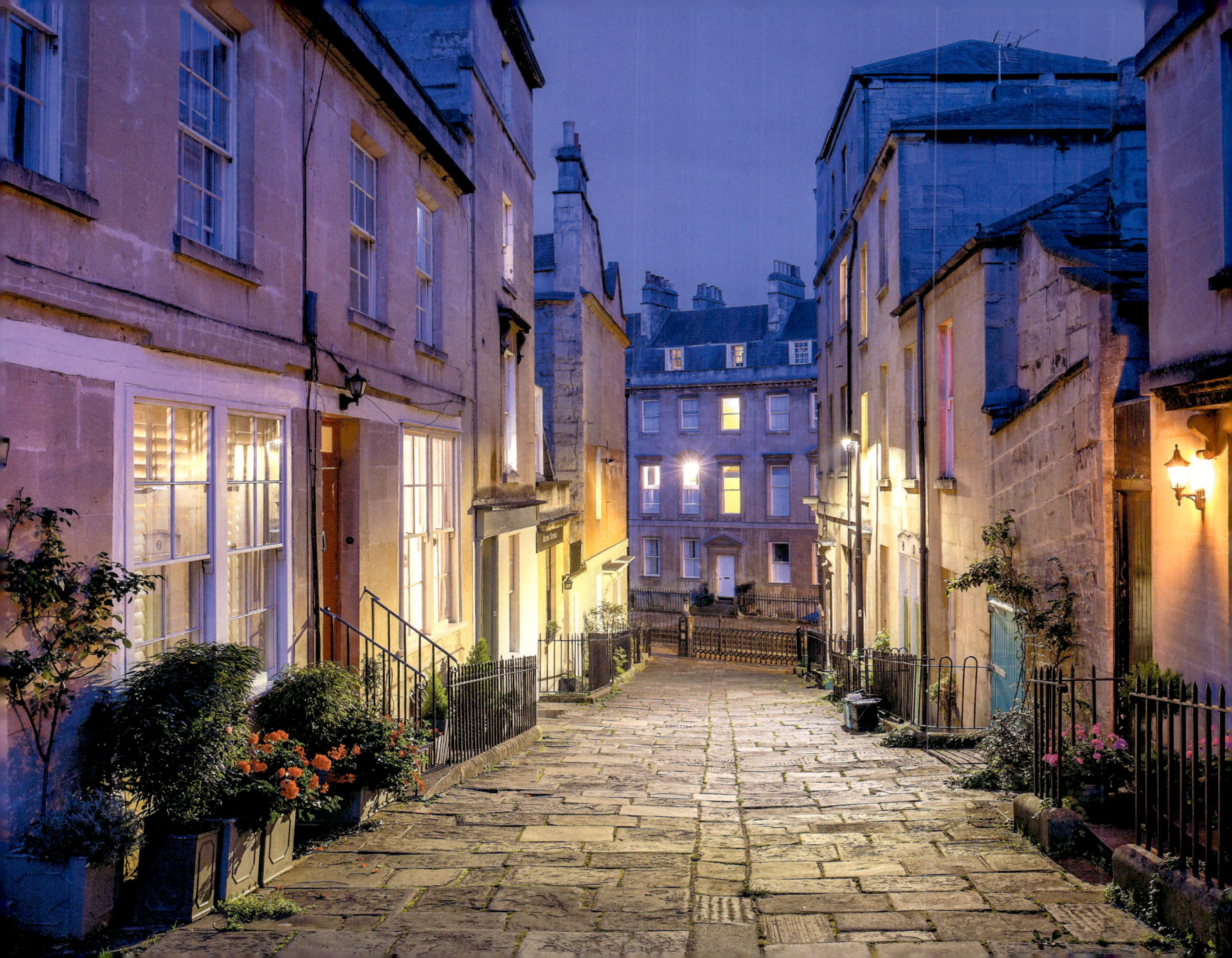

Away from the main shopping streets are a series of small alleys that filter from Union Passage, a long narrow pedestrian side route that runs parallel to Union Street. It is a maze-like setting full of characterful properties and charming shop fronts that collectively create an atmospheric place to spend some time exploring, each passageway slightly different from its neighbour.

THE CORRIDOR

Opened in 1825 the Corridor was one of Britain's first covered indoor shopping arcades, the only other one being the Burlington Arcade in London. Built by Henry Goodridge in a neo-classical style that reflects his take on Roman and Greek architecture featuring embellishments with a bit of Italian flair thrown in for good measure. Designed to provide a whole new shopping experience primarily to entice the wealthy away from filthy crowded streets and into the relative clean and exclusive surroundings of a Parisian style shopping mall.

It is a short, covered passageway flanked by shops on either side of equal size and appearance, fronted by elegant slightly-arched plate glass windows, polished brass and a cornice of golden garlands and gilt lions. An arched glass roof follows much of the route along with large orbed lighting hanging down at intervals. At the halfway point the roof height changes to reveal the musicians gallery where performers once accompanied shoppers below as they browsed the stores.

THE CORRIDOR

Postcode: BA1 5AR
what3words: latest.knots.gains

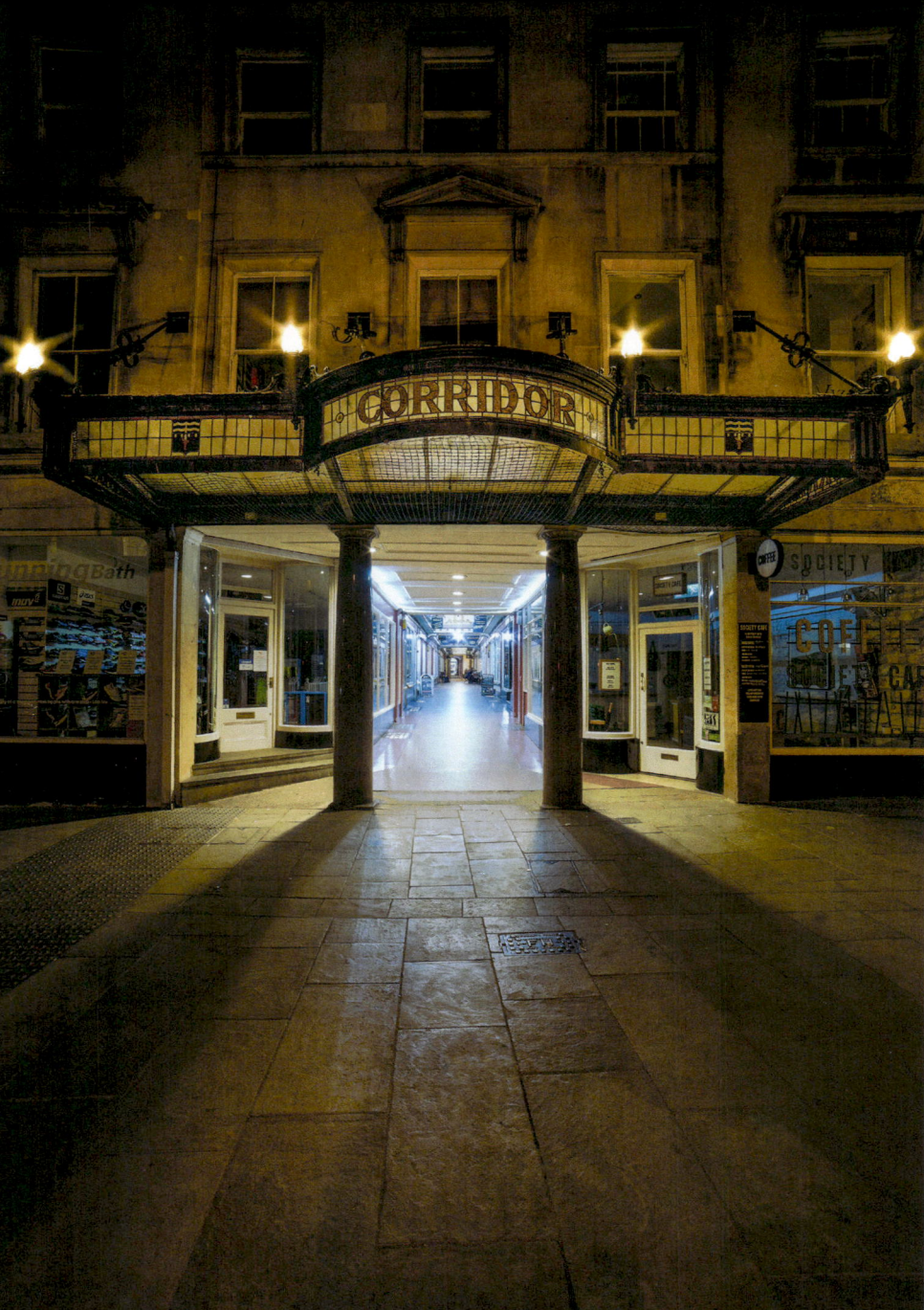

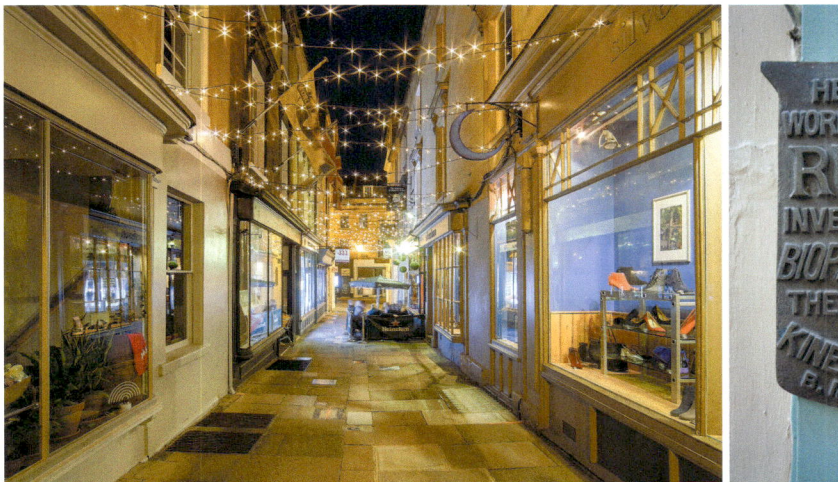
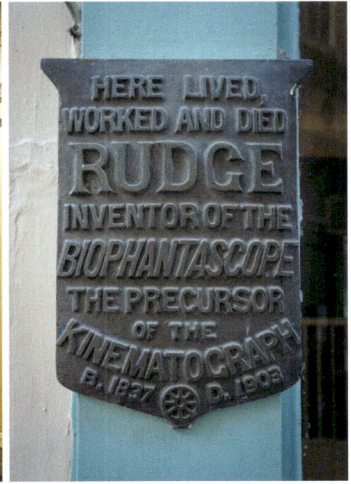

NORTHUMBERLAND PLACE

Home to independent shops, eateries and one of Bath's smallest pubs, the Coeur De Lion, Northumberland Place resembles the tightly packed streets of yesteryear, although transformed in the Georgian style and dates as far back to 1694 when it was originally a Medieval street known as Marchant's Court. This is a shoppers paradise, colourful shop fronts offer a wild array of goods and fascinating products. Cafes and restaurants are plentiful along the narrow streets which exit at the eastern end under an archway leading onto the High Street

NORTHUMBERLAND PLACE

Postcode: BA1 5AR
what3words: thinks.silks.once

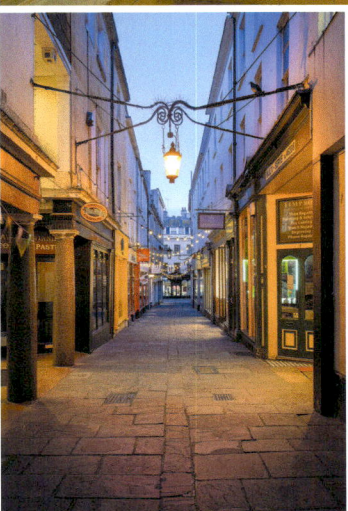
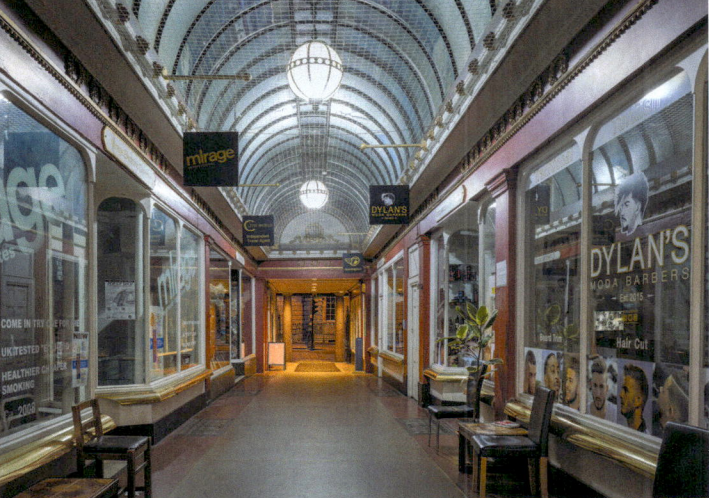

NEW BOND STREET PLACE

Bath's back alleys were once home to a prolific and resourceful hive of small independent business owners – the first marketable type of permanent hair dye was created here along with the pioneers of early cinema, William Friese-Green and John Rudge who invented the Magic Lantern, a revolutionary invention used to marvel crowds with moving images, the first of it's kind and heralding a new type of film creation.

NEW BOND STREET

Postcode: BA1 1BA
what3words: stages.famous.voice

OPPOSITE: one of the earliest examples of a shopping arcade outside London, the glazed canopy was added in 1927.
TOP LEFT: New Bond Street Place, leading to the Volunteer Riflemans Arms. **TOP RIGHT**: memorial plaque to the pioneer of film and moving pictures. **ABOVE LEFT**: at the intersection of Union Passage and Northumberland Place.
ABOVE RIGHT: inside the Corridor, where shoppers were once serenaded by live music.

XIII

13 THE THERMAL CITY – HISTORIC & MODERN HOT SPRINGS

"To the goddess Sulis, Lucius Marcius Memor, soothsayer, gave (this) as a gift."
– Inscription found on a Roman statue base during a 1965 excavation underneath the Pump Room (1st century AD)

"Come and be cured by the steaming elixir of life."
– Beau Nash (Master of Ceremonies, 18th century)

The hot springs of Bath originate from rainfall that percolates through limestone bedrock, where geothermal heating raises its temperature to about 69°C (156°F). The water ascends through faults, becoming rich in minerals like calcium, sulphate, and sodium, contributing to its perceived medicinal qualities. It emerges at several springs at 46°C (115°F).

Bath's healing reputation stems from the semi-mythical tale of Prince Bladud around 863 BCE. According to medieval accounts, Bladud, son of King Lud, contracted leprosy and was banished. While tending pigs in the Avon valley, he noticed that those wallowing in warm, mineral-rich mud had clear skin. Inspired, he bathed and was miraculously cured. Returning, he ascended the throne, founded Bath, and established its first baths.

Regardless of legend, Romans in the 1st century CE recognised the springs' therapeutic and religious significance. They built a grand bathing complex and a temple to Sulis Minerva, merging Celtic and Roman beliefs. Constructed around 70 CE, the Great Bath was an engineering marvel with lead-lined pools, hypocaust-heated rooms, and a sophisticated drainage system. The town, named Aquae Sulis, became a major pilgrimage site for physical and spiritual renewal.

Bath's rise as an elite spa peaked in the 18th century. Architects John Wood the Elder and John Wood the Younger designed iconic buildings, including the Royal Crescent and Pump Room, attracting aristocrats seeking therapeutic bathing.

Today, Bath's thermal waters remain a cultural and economic asset. The Roman Baths are a major heritage site, meticulously preserved. In 2006, the Thermae Bath Spa opened, allowing visitors to experience the restorative waters. Scientific analysis confirms their rich mineral content, supporting their reputation for therapeutic benefits.

THE ROMAN BATHS
ABBEY CHURCHYARD

Postcode: BA1 1RB
what3words: throw.flame.stand

THE PUMP ROOMS
SEARCYS AT THE PUMP ROOM, STALL STREET

Postcode: BA1 1LY
what3words: alien.region.tile

BATH STREET

Postcode: BA1 1SB
what3words: report.harsh.vibes

CROSS BATH & HOT BATH STREETS

Postcode: BA1 1SL
what3words: hulk.raced.ranged

THERMAE BATH SPA
THE HETLING PUMP ROOM, HOT BATH STREET

Postcode: BA1 1SJ
what3words: stick.loves.melon

THE ROMAN BATHS

The Roman Baths are a well preserved historic site built over 2,000 years ago during the Roman occupation of Britain and is one of the city's premiere visitor attractions.

The Romans found the hot springs to be a valuable resource choosing to establish a town here naming it Aqua Sulis translated to 'Waters of Sulis'. The baths are centred around a natural hot spring, believed by the Romans to be sacred to the goddess Sulis Minerva. The hot water still flows from the spring to this day, at a rate of around 1,170,000 litres (307,000 gallons) per day, with a temperature of about 46°C (115°F).

The Roman Baths, built around 70AD are a significant testament to the architectural and cultural achievements of the ancient Roman Empire. Designed around a large courtyard and temple complex the baths are an impressive feat of engineering.

The Great Bath is the largest and most iconic pool. It is lined with lead and stone, and was used for communal bathing and socialising. Adjacent to the Great Bath is the remains of a Roman temple, dedicated to Sulis Minerva, where offerings and prayers were made. The complex also includes various rooms and chambers associated with the bathing ritual, such as the tepidarium (warm room), caldarium (hot room), and frigidarium (cold room). These rooms were designed to provide a sequence of heat experiences for bathers along with other practices using massage and exercise.

MORE INFORMATION

romanbaths.co.uk
Visit the Roman Bath's website to learn more about the Roman Baths and buy tickets.

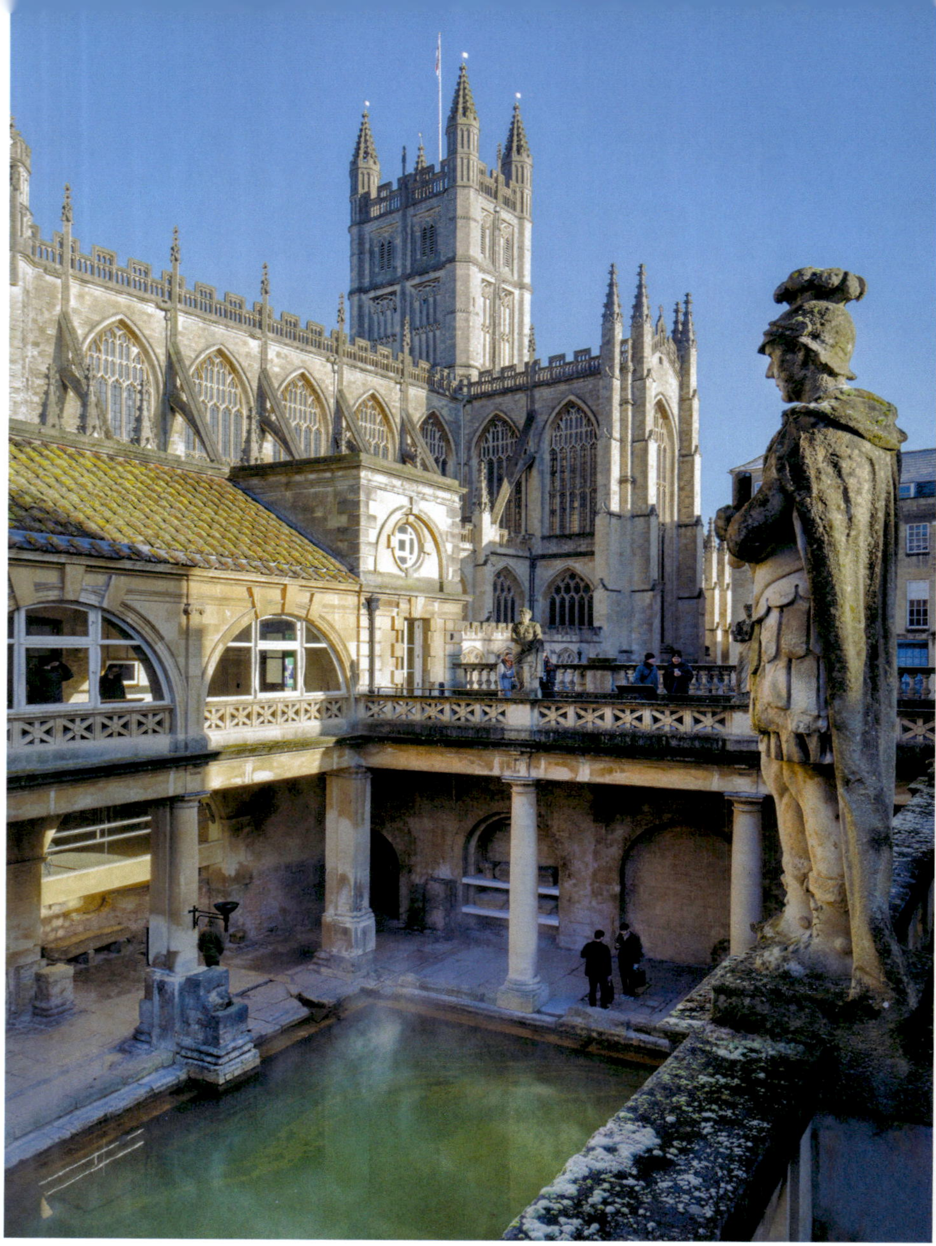

ABOVE: standing guard, Roman statues line the perimeter of the Great Bath.

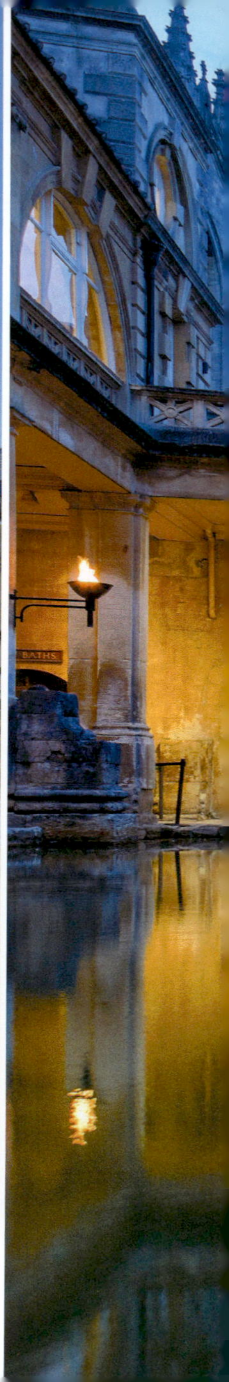

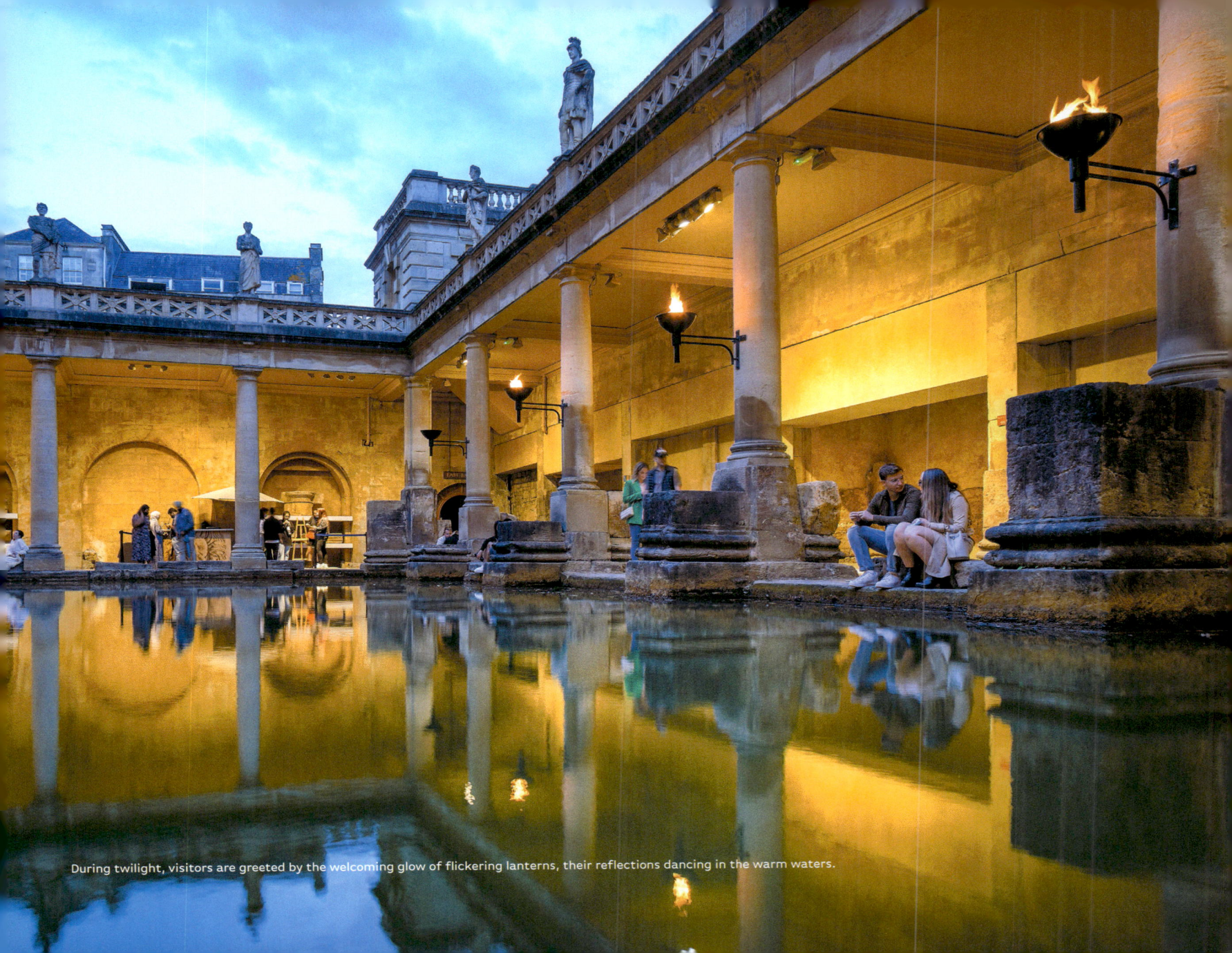

During twilight, visitors are greeted by the welcoming glow of flickering lanterns, their reflections dancing in the warm waters.

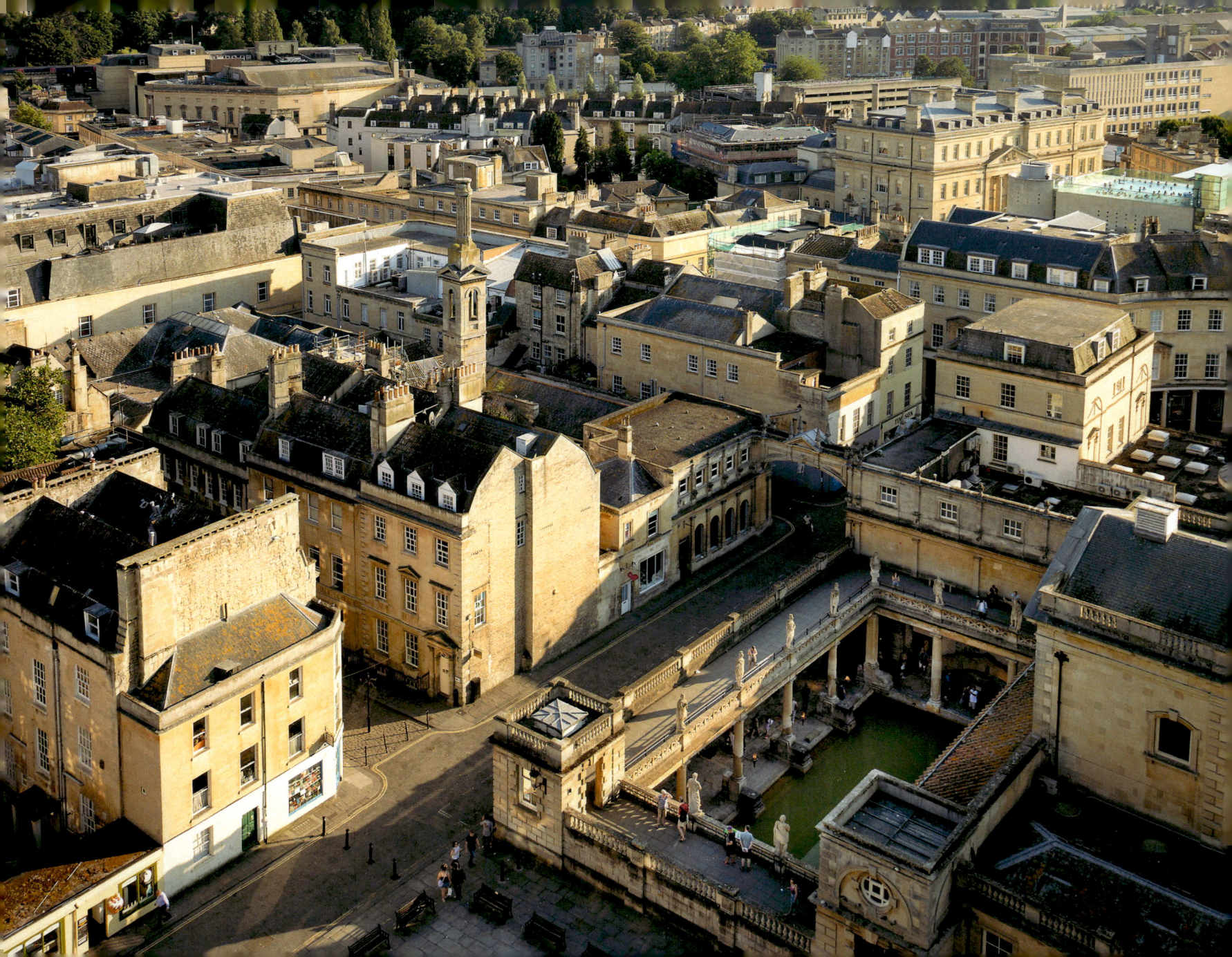

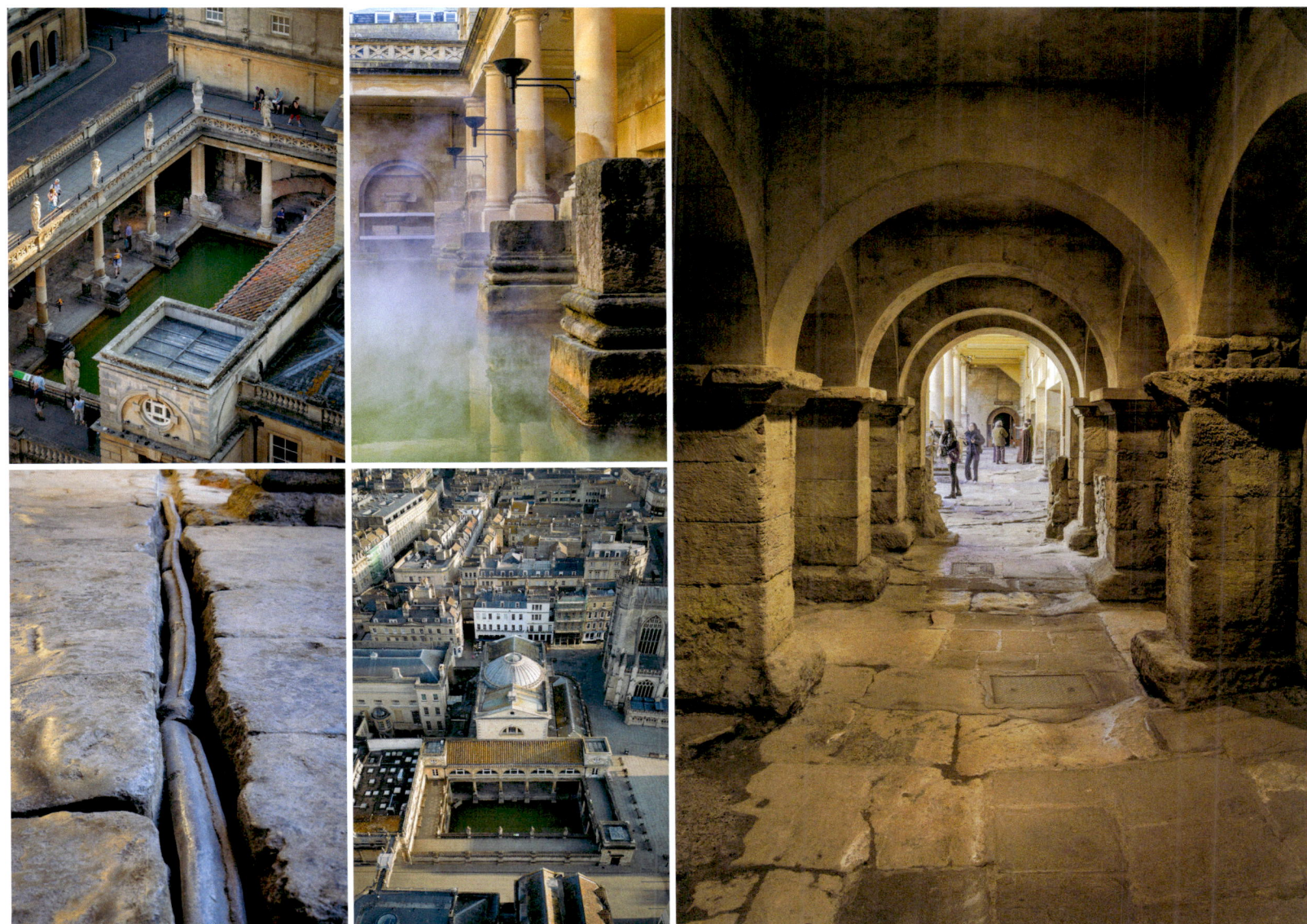

13 THE THERMAL CITY – HISTORIC & MODERN HOT SPRINGS

It is incredible how much of the Roman Baths remain. Rediscovered much lower than the modern street level by Victorian archeologists it is possible to walk on the very same pavements that the Romans once used beside the Great Bath and also on raised walkways above the original temple courtyard. An extensive and fascinating museum explores the entire timeline of the Roman Empire's occupation of Britain and documents the arrival to Bath with a vast collection of sculptures, dioramas and artifacts reflecting the artistic and cultural values of the Romans. Visitors to the Roman Baths can explore the complex, learn about its history through audio guides or guided tours, and even taste the mineral-rich water from the spring.

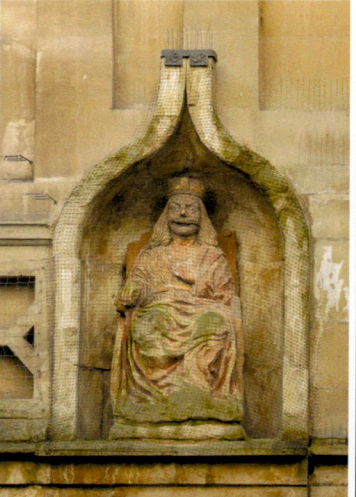
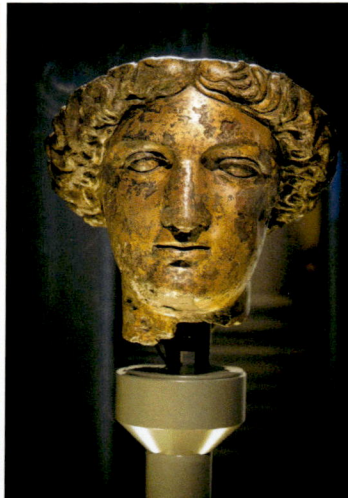
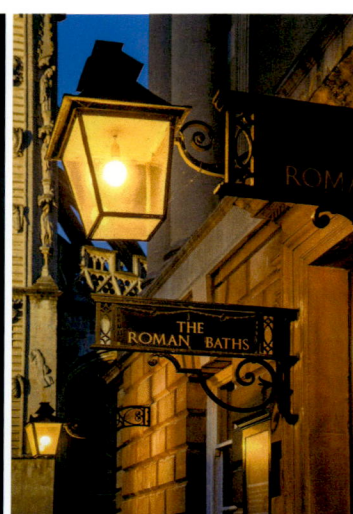
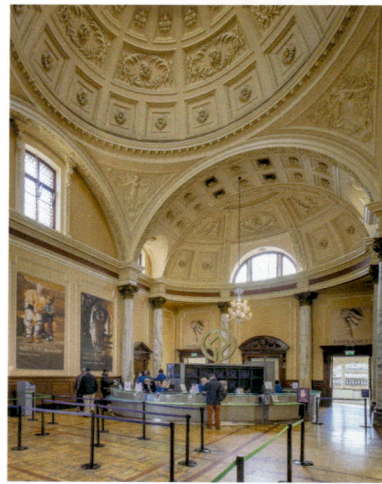
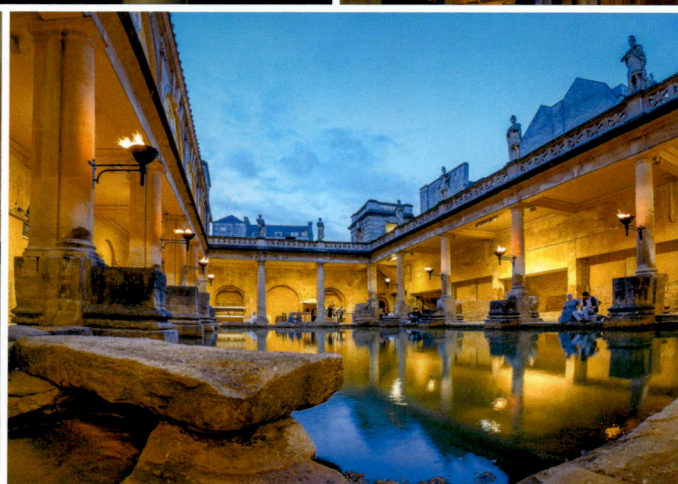

PREVIOUS SPREAD LEFT: over the centuries, Bath has evolved from a Roman settlement into a vibrant city, with the historic baths at its core. **TOP LEFT**: the Great Bath is the largest of all the baths, measuring 12 meters (39 feet) by 9 meters (30 feet). **TOP MIDDLE**: morning mists create magical scenes at the Great Bath. **BOTTOM LEFT**: the original Roman lead piping remains remarkably still in place. **BOTTOM MIDDLE**: the Roman Baths remains a central and iconic part of the city's identity. **RIGHT**: beneath the city streets, visitors can walk where the Romans once stood.

TOP LEFT: the statue of King Bladud overlooks the King's Bath. **TOP MIDDLE**: the gilt bronze head of the goddess Sulis Minerva. **TOP RIGHT**: the Roman Baths entrance is located beside Bath Abbey. **ABOVE LEFT**: Immersive audio guides take visitors through the museum, while reenactors bring the historical wonder of the attraction to life. **ABOVE RIGHT**: the Great Bath's water naturally stays at a steamy 46°C (115°F).

OPPOSITE: the Abbey provides a dramatic backdrop to the Baths, showcasing the city's rich blend of architectural styles spanning centuries.

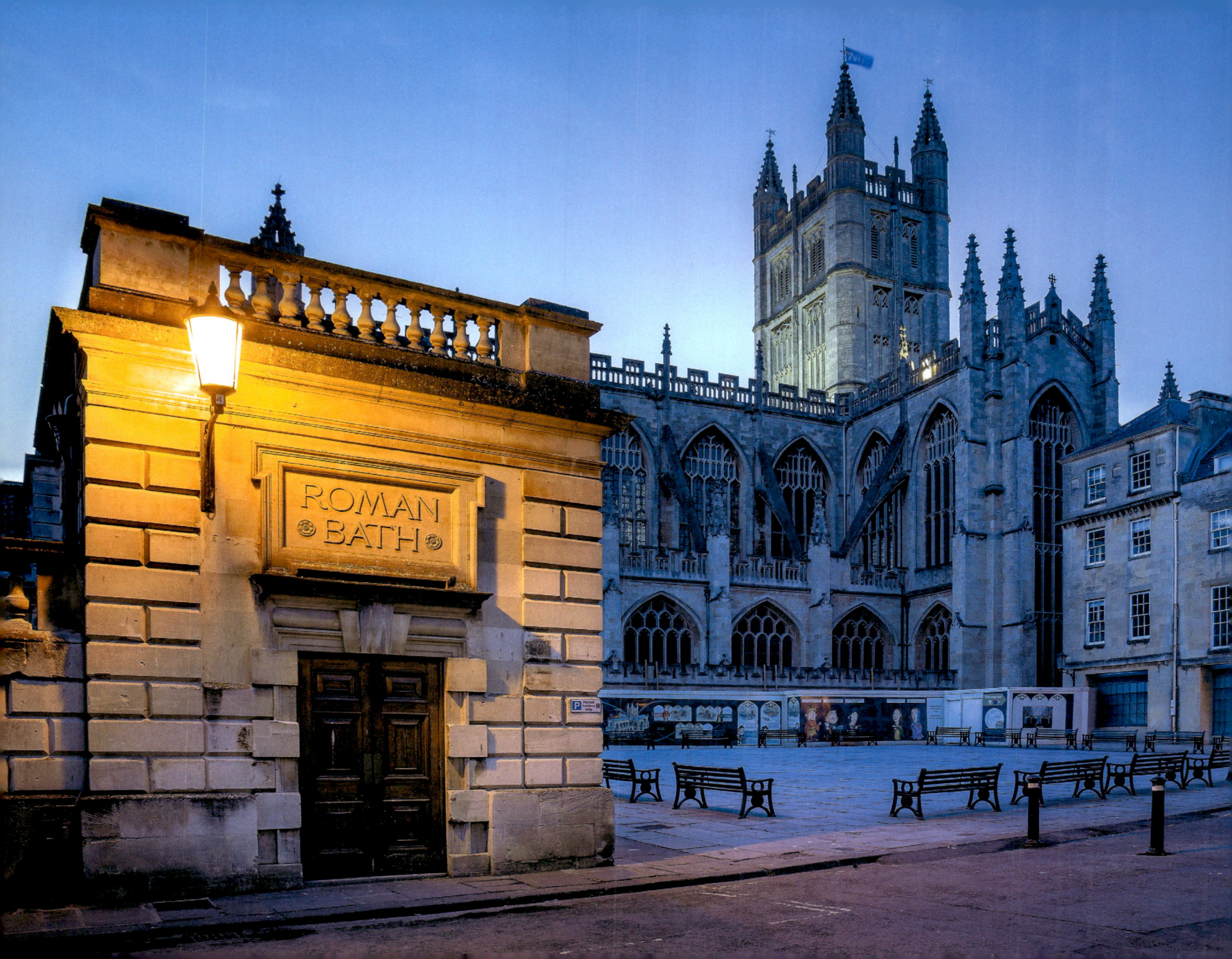

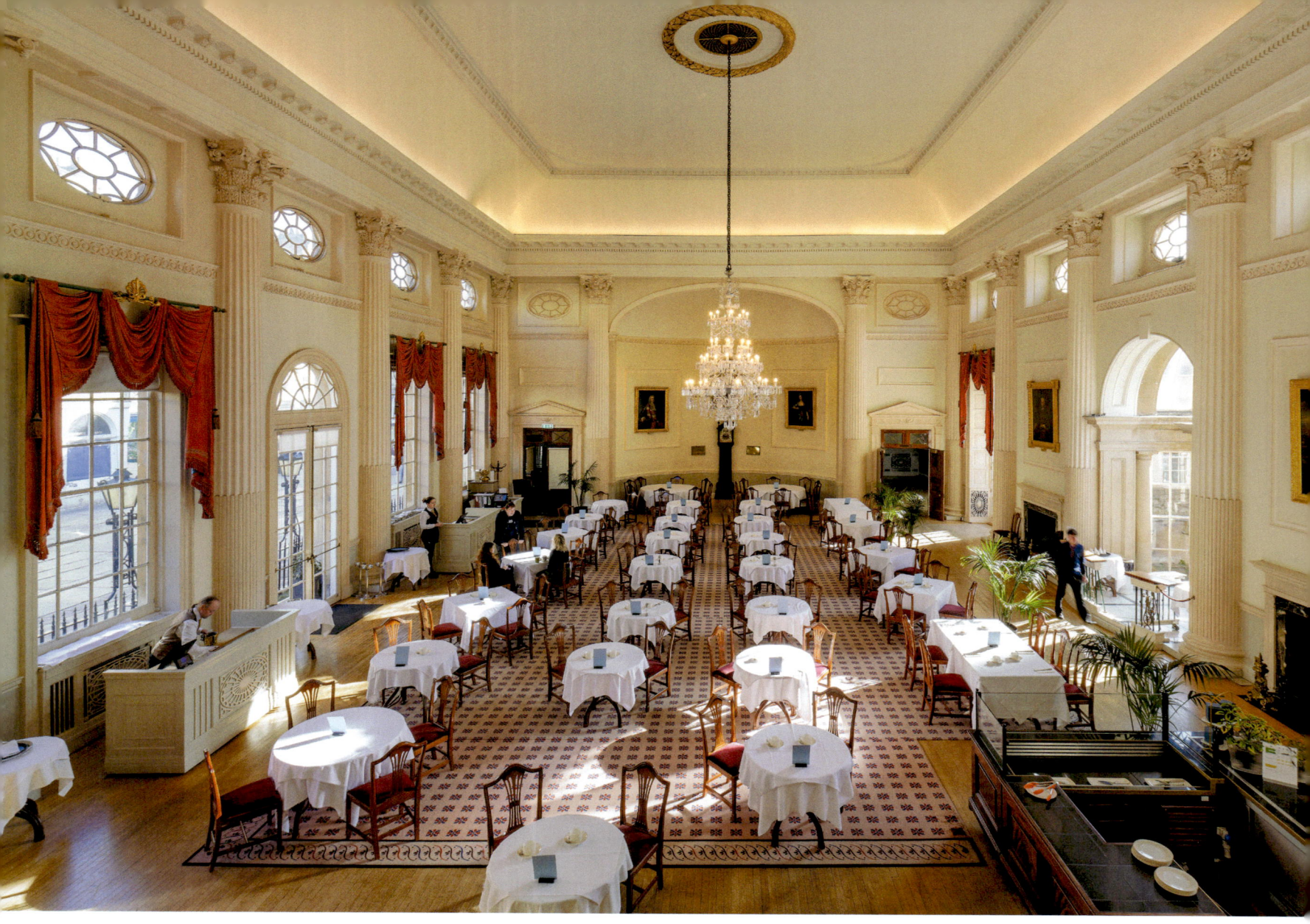

THE PUMP ROOMS

During the Georgian era (1714–1837), the city of Bath was a centre of high society, attracting aristocrats, politicians, and fashionable elites from across Britain. Known for its healing waters and elegant social scene, Bath became a place where the wealthy could seek health treatments while indulging in leisure and entertainment. At the heart of this refined society was the Pump Room – adjacent to the Roman Baths – a grand assembly room where visitors drank the mineral-rich spa water, believed to cure ailments such as gout and rheumatism. However, beyond its medical benefits, the Pump Room became a vital meeting place where members of the upper class could socialise, exchange gossip, and arrange advantageous marriages.

The first Pump Room was built in 1706 by John Harvey as a modest structure to accommodate Bath's growing number of visitors. However, as the city's reputation flourished, the need for a larger and more elegant building became apparent. In 1789, architect Thomas Baldwin was commissioned by Beau Nash to design a grander Pump Room, but after his dismissal due to financial mismanagement, John Palmer completed the project in 1799. The new neoclassical building, with its high ceilings and grand columns, embodied the sophistication of the Georgian elite and became a symbol of fashionable life in Bath.

The Pump Room attracted many notable visitors during this period. Jane Austen, who lived in Bath from 1801 to 1806, featured the Pump Room in her novels *Northanger Abbey* and *Persuasion*, capturing the essence of the city's social scene. Other distinguished guests included the Prince of Wales (later George IV), Admiral Lord Nelson, and the Duchess of York. Even after the Georgian era, the Pump Room remained an iconic venue, drawing visitors such as Charles Dickens and Queen Victoria.

Today, the Pump Room continues to be a major attraction, offering visitors the chance to sample the famous spa water from the fountain, which are warm and contain 43 different minerals, though it has to be said that it is an acquired taste! The building now houses an elegant restaurant serving traditional English fare, accompanied by live classical music from the Pump Room Trio or a resident pianist creating a dining experience akin to a lavish Georgian event.

The Pump Room has also been featured in numerous period dramas and films, adding to its cultural significance. It has appeared in adaptations of Jane Austen's novels, including *Persuasion* and *Northanger Abbey*, as well as in historical TV series such as *Bridgerton*. Its timeless elegance makes it a favoured location for filmmakers seeking to recreate the refined world of Georgian society. Today, it stands as a testament to Bath's rich history, attracting visitors eager to experience the city's golden age.

MORE INFORMATION

thepumproombath.co.uk
Book a table, peruse the menus and find out what's on.

OPPOSITE: a visit to the Pump Room restaurant is recommended for live music, Jane Austen Afternoon Tea, breakfast or brunch.

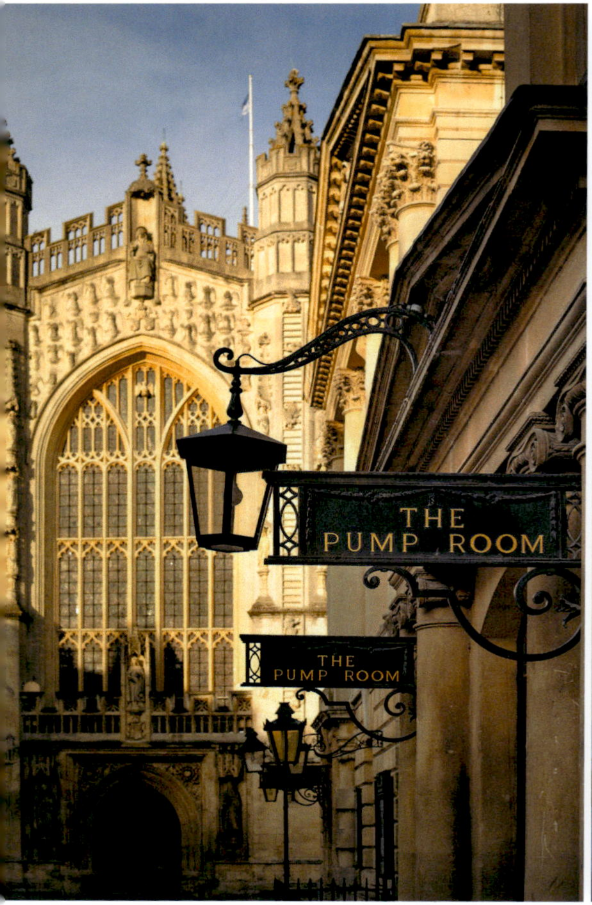

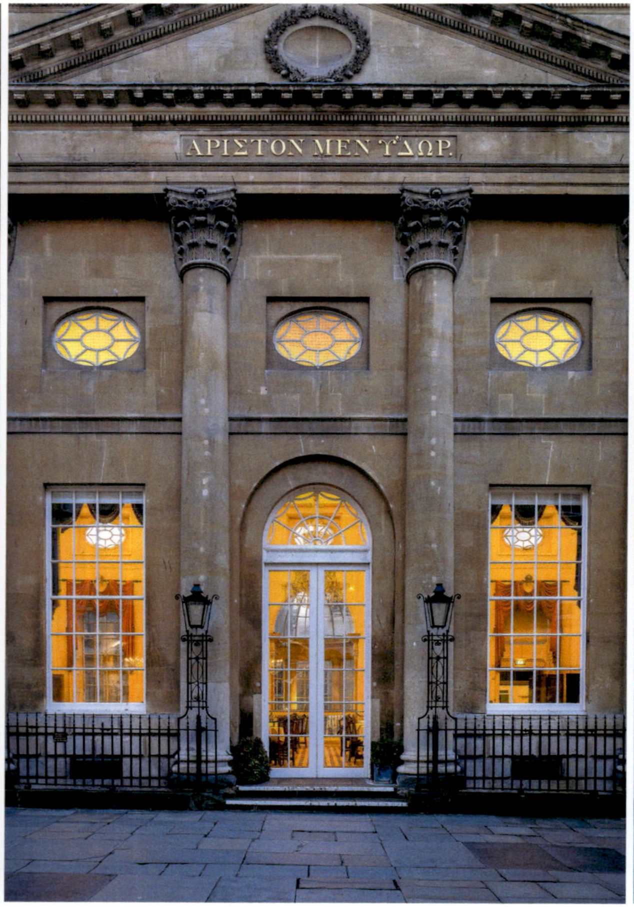

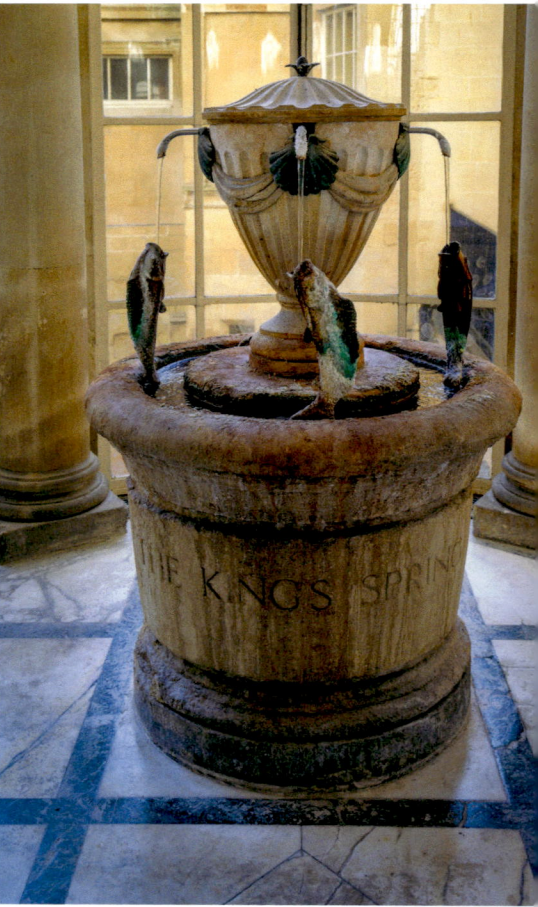

ABOVE: the Pump Rooms embodies the heart of the Georgian social scene, when high society gathered in the city. **MIDDLE**: corinthian pillars frame the stunning exterior of the Pump Rooms. **RIGHT**: the Georgians came to bathe in and drink the waters, where you can still sample the taste today.

OPPOSITE RIGHT: Bath Street has a charming symmetry and a tranquil atmosphere, with its cobbled route linking both historic and modern spa baths. **FAR RIGHT**: a unique feature of the city, it is the only street to feature covered columned walkways along its entire length.

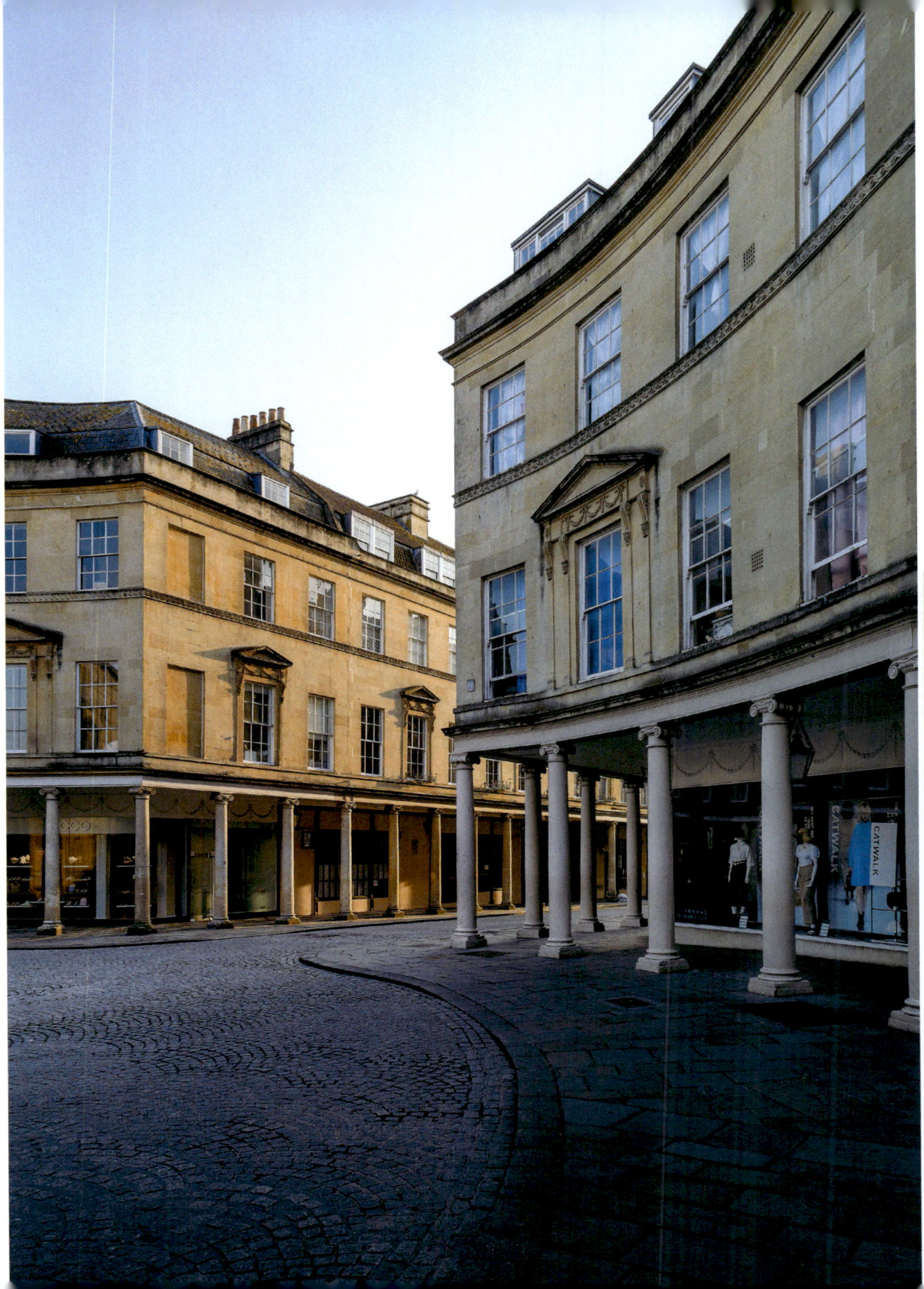

BATH STREET

Designed and built in 1791 by Thomas Baldwin the aptly named Bath Street links the popular King and Queens Bath on Stall Street to the Grade 1 listed Cross Bath on the western side. A double row of pale limestone pillars on opposing sides run parallel to the street backed by a terrace of beautifully constructed three storey houses. It is one of the finest examples of 18th Century Neoclassical street designs in the country and a unique feature in Bath which takes inspiration from French Parisian retail districts, the elegant covered columns that line Bath Street are designed to keep wandering shoppers safe from the elements.

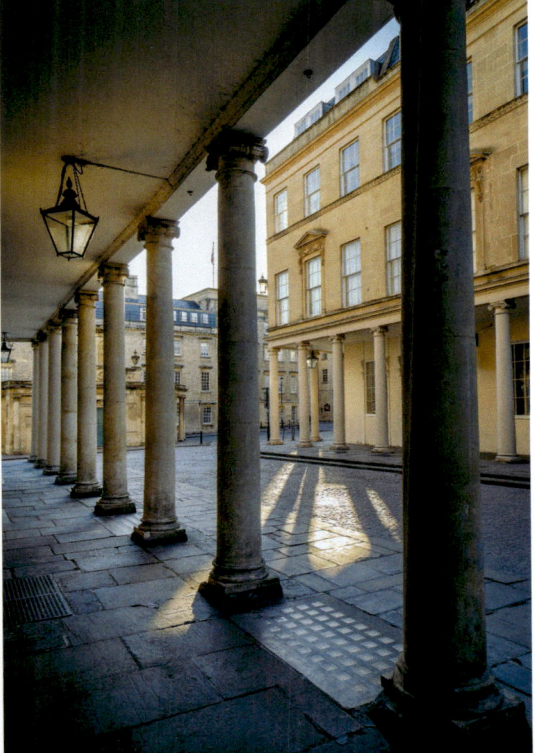

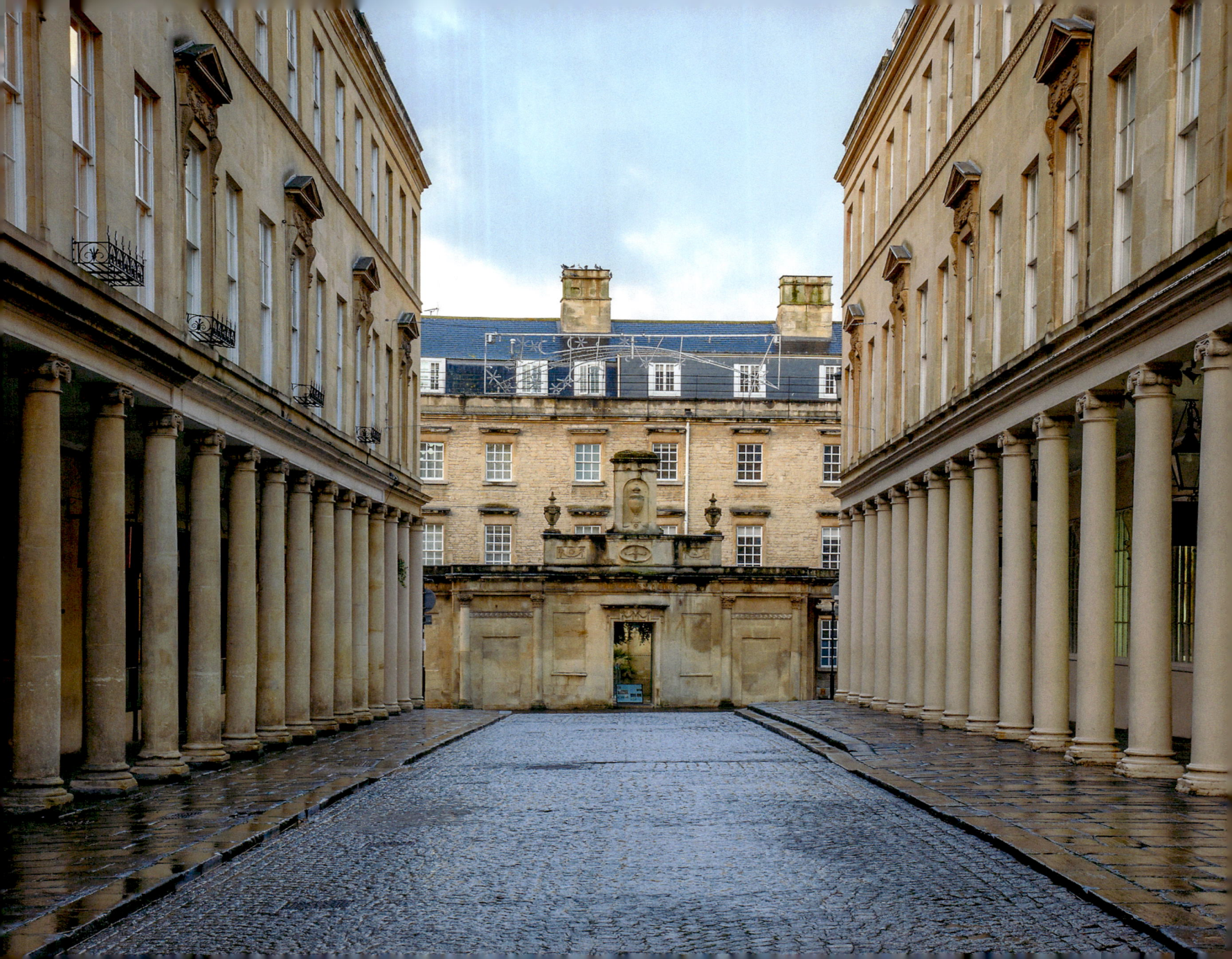

THE CROSS BATH
& HOT BATH STREET

Located a stones throw from the modern main spa Cross Bath is a tiny building enclosing the site of an ancient bathing pool. The source of subterranean thermal waters known as the Kings Spring emerged into the landscape in this area. Previous structures that once surrounded the pool during the Medieval period were simpler in design allowing bathers a discrete environment complete with arches in the perimeter walls offering shelter from inclement weather. The current design adapted from Thomas Baldwin in 1784 is a single storey ornate structure open to the sky with no roof that stands at the junction of Bath Street and Hot Bath Street.

OPPOSITE: the Cross Bath lies at the end of the aptly named Bath Street.
RIGHT: The Cross Bath is modelled in the style of Robert Adam, who designed Pulteney Bridge. **BELOW**: the Cross Bath stands next to the hospital of the St John's Foundation, one of the oldest almshouses in England.
BELOW RIGHT: Hetling Court; a charming pedestrian pathway.

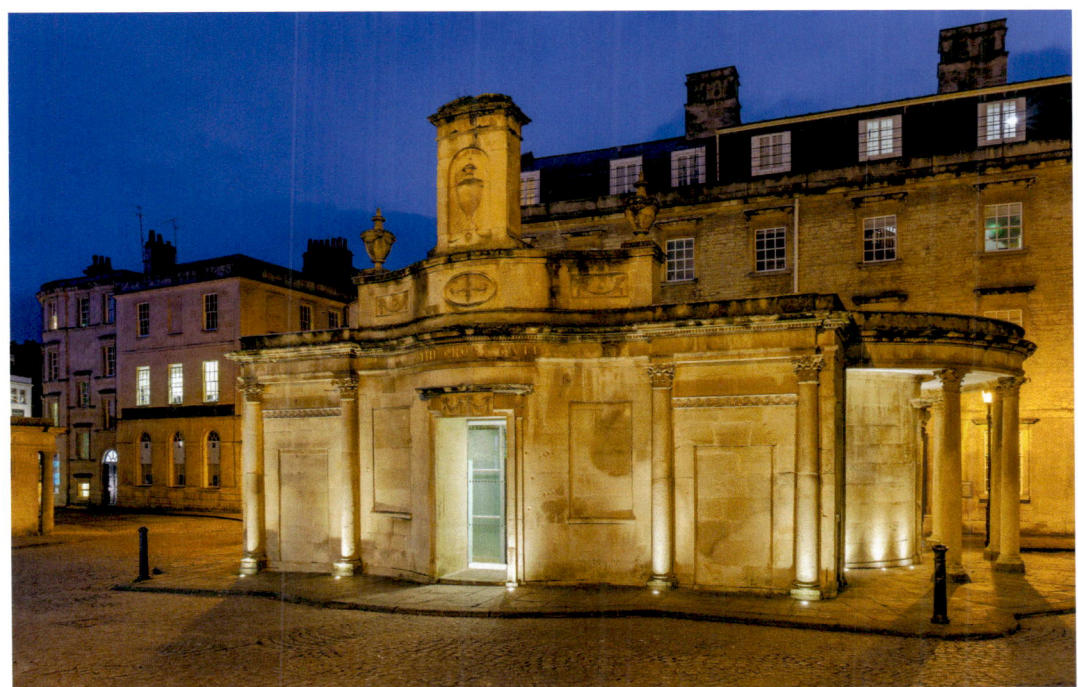

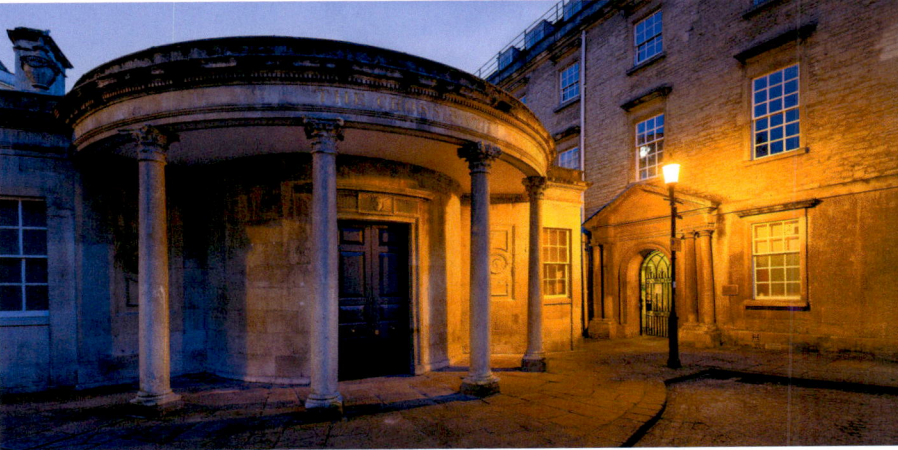

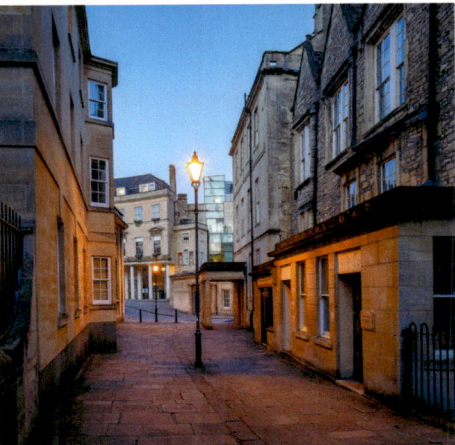

THERMAE BATH SPA

Visitors to Thermae Bath Spa can enjoy a day of relaxation and pampering, immersing themselves in the healing waters and taking in the tranquil ambiance of the spa environment. The spa utilises the city's natural thermal waters, which are rich in minerals and known for their therapeutic properties and are sourced from the same thermal spring that feed the ancient Roman Baths.

The main entrance and reception is housed in the historic part of Bath Street within Thomas Baldwin's curved facade built in 1791. A contemporary designed glass structure houses two large mineral-rich thermal baths, wellness suite, sauna, ice chamber and a pair of Georgian and astronomy themed relaxation rooms. One of the most iconic features of Thermae Bath Spa is its rooftop pool, offering panoramic views of the city's skyline. The rooftop pool allows guests to relax and soak in the warm waters while enjoying stunning views of Bath's historic architecture, including the nearby Bath Abbey and surrounding hills. You can also enjoy a dip in the smaller Cross Bath which is housed in separate building. Cross Bath is the location where the Celts revered their goddess Sul, in whose honour the Romans named their spa town, Aquae Sulis.

MORE INFORMATION

thermaebathspa.com
Visit the website to book the Rooftop Pool, the Minerva Bath or Cross Bath.

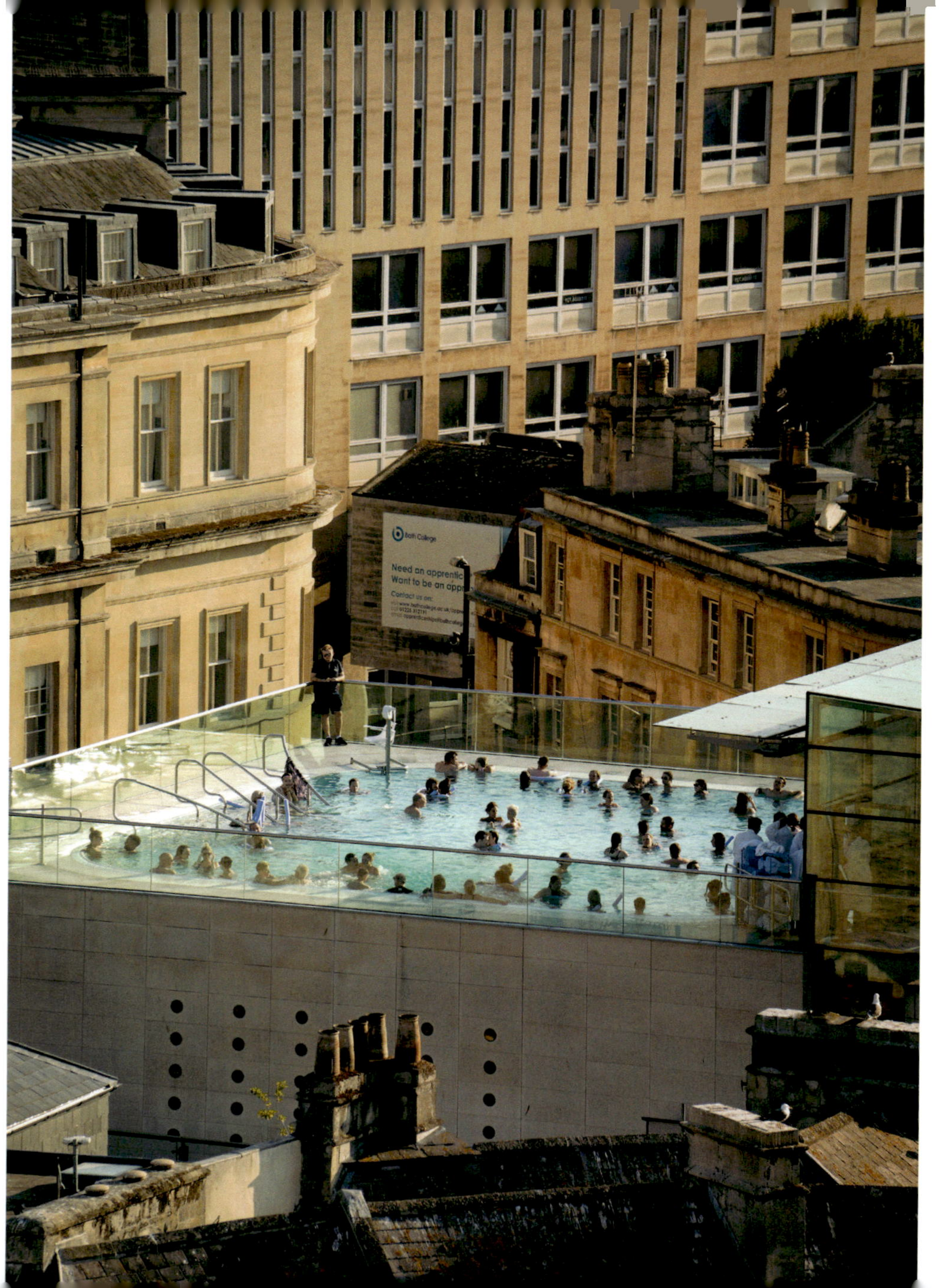

Taking bathing to new heights at Thermae Bath Spa's rooftop pool.

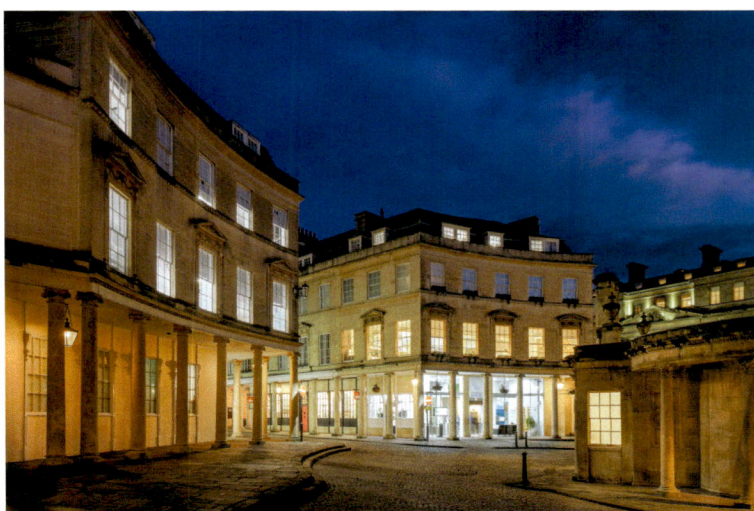

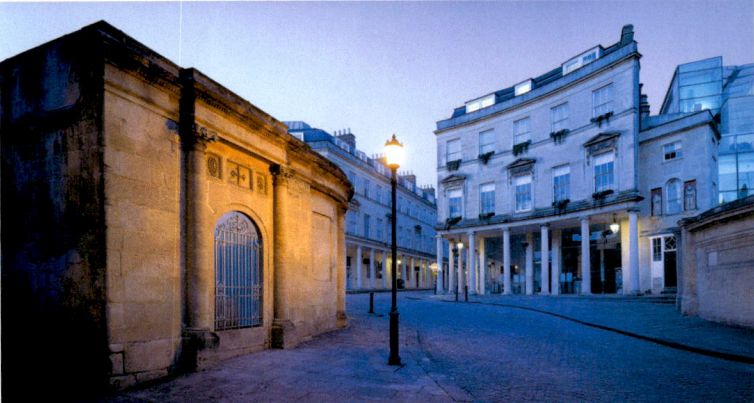

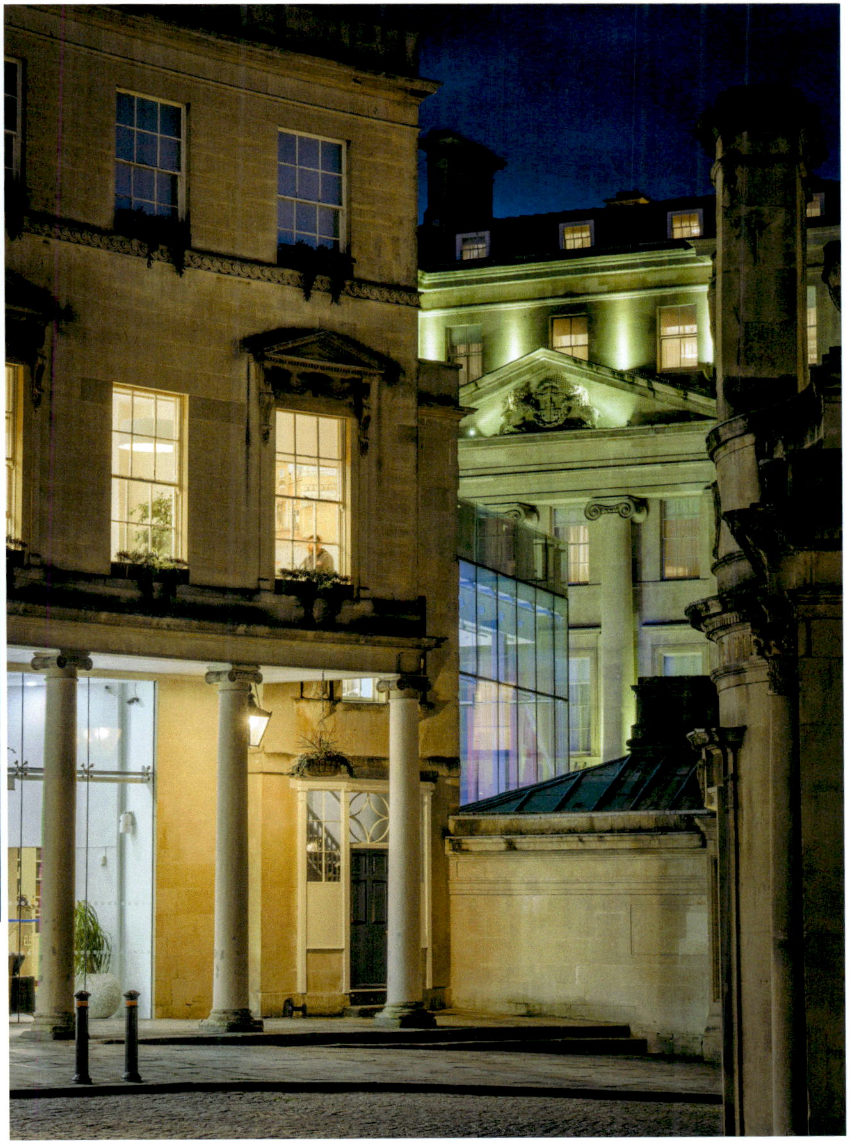

TOP: the spa offers a range of invigorating treatments and experiences, including special twilight packages that let you unwind and bathe into the evening. **ABOVE**: the Cross Bath, part of the Thermae Bath Spa but in separate building, houses an intimate pool behind historic walls and is where the Celts revered their goddess Sul, in whose honour the Romans named their spa town, Aquae Sulis **RIGHT**: the area around the spa perfectly balances Georgian elegance with contemporary design.

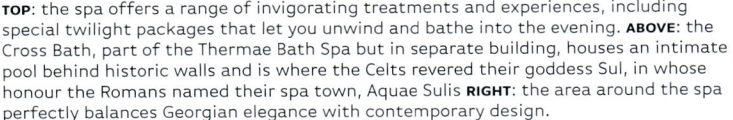

XIV

14 THE THEATRE ROYAL

Recognised as "one of the most important surviving examples of Georgian theatre architecture," the Theatre Royal is a Grade II listed building*, highlighting its historical and architectural significance.

"This theatre is like a jewelled box – small, exquisite, and absolutely right for serious theatre."
– Sir Peter Hall, founder of the Royal Shakespeare Company

The Theatre Royal is one of the oldest and most prestigious theatres in England, renowned for its elegant architecture and vibrant cultural scene. Highly regarded within the theatrical community and among audiences alike it holds a prominent place in British theatre history and is often considered one of the country's leading regional venues.

The Theatre Royal has welcomed numerous renowned artists over the years, including actors, singers, dancers, and musicians. Many celebrated and well known performers have graced its stage, showcasing their talents in iconic roles and acclaimed productions. The annual pantomime performance in particular is a seasonal highlight and a fantastic addition to a festive visit to the city.

A theatre has stood on this spot for over 200 years though its history as a royal institution began at its original location tucked away down an unassuming back alley on Old Orchard Street. Conversion to a Catholic church closed the doors at the original Theatre Royal who relocated across the city to its brand new, larger premises.

The 'New' Theatre Royal, designed by architect George Dance opened its doors with a maiden performance of Shakespeare's *Richard III* in 1805 and saw an ebb and flow of theatre goers during the initial years. Disaster struck in 1862 when a fire ravaged the entire building leaving only the exterior stone walls standing, all the internal staging and seating galleries were completely destroyed. Reaction was swift and decisive and miraculously just one year later after the accident the newly re-built theatre was opened again, designed by CJ Phipps.

THE THEATRE ROYAL

Postcode: BA1 1ET
what3words: plant.work.ears

THE THEATRE ROYAL WEBSITE

theatreroyal.org.uk
Find out what's on and buy tickets.

The original entrance of the Theatre Royal is actually found around the corner on Beauford Square. It is a delightful grand facade flanked by smaller two storey townhouses surrounding an open green and wrought iron railings. Designed by John Strahan in 1730 the square originally enclosed a communal garden created for polite society to amble through.

The secluded setting and relatively untouched nature of the architecture make this a desirable place for filming. The phenomenally popular romantic period drama *Bridgerton* used this location as part of its series depicting life in Regency era London.

The modern main entrance opens out onto Saw Close, a large pedestrianised area which was once a hub of industry. Originally a timber yard this could be considered the beating heart of operations where wood was sawn and sorted to supply the city during its Georgian building phase, quite the opposite to the vast array of restaurants and public houses that line the streets today.

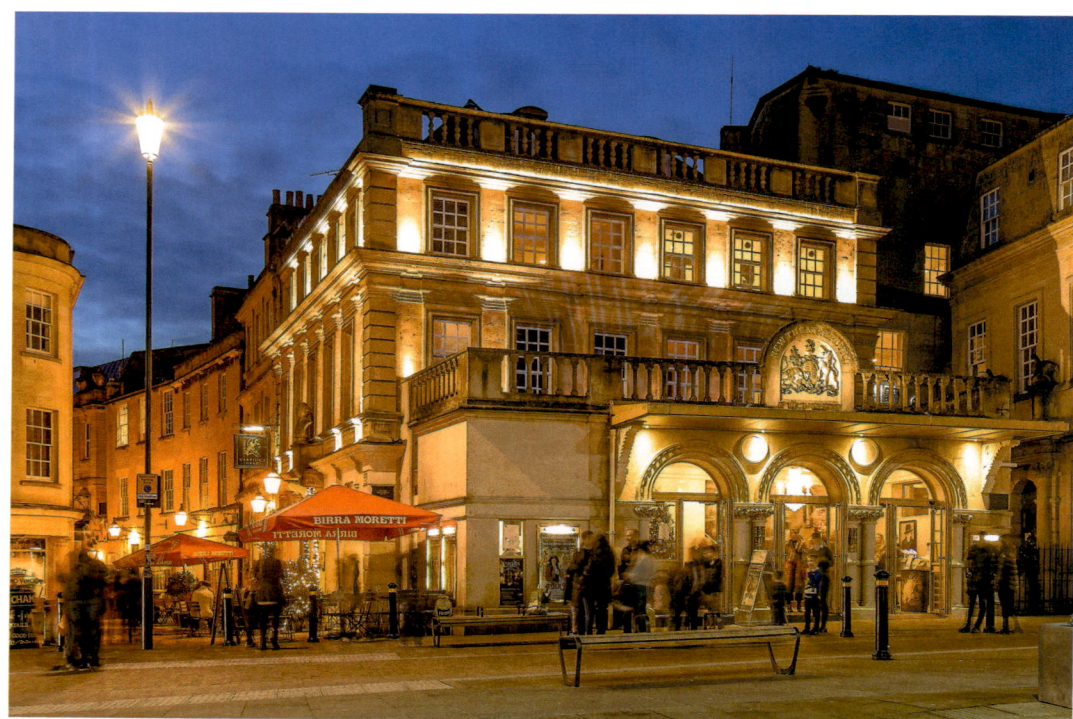

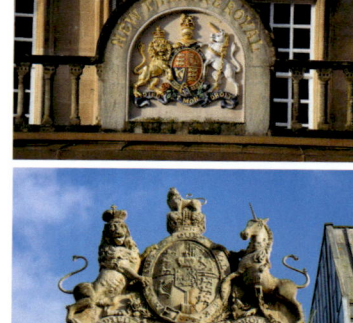

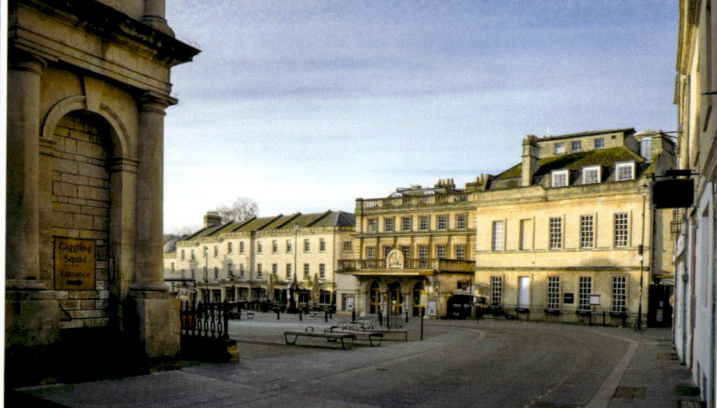

TOP: the perfect way to end a day exploring Bath; unwinding with a captivating theatre performance. **RIGHT MIDDLE**: the Royal Crest above the main entrance. **RIGHT**: the same carved stone crest graces the original entrance on Beauford Square. **FAR RIGHT**: the theatre stands at the heart of Saw Close, a vibrant pedestrianised area.
OPPOSITE TOP: Beauford Square, quintessentially Georgian and like a time capsule is also a popular filming location for the hit TV series *Bridgerton*. **RIGHT**: the original theatre entrance relocated to Saw Close after a fire in 1862.
BOTTOM: the former site of the Bluecoat Charity School, rebuilt in 1860.

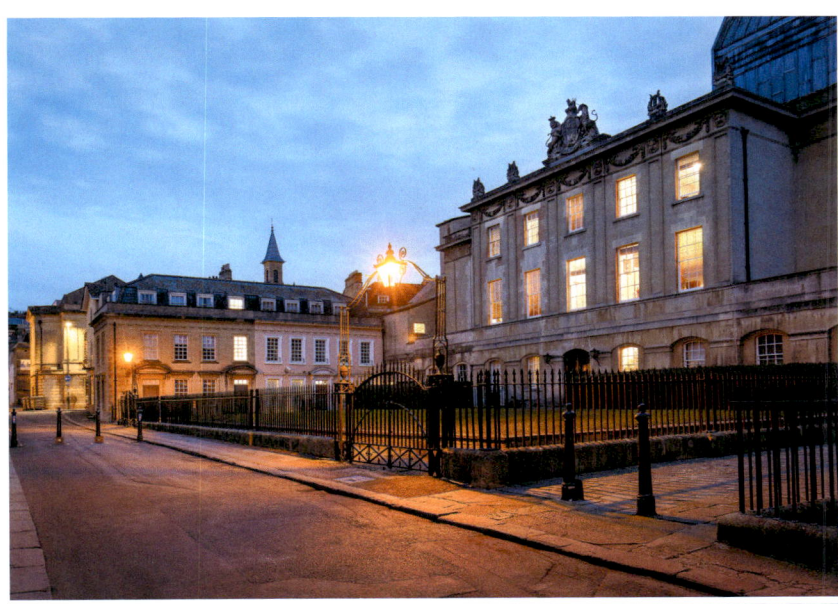
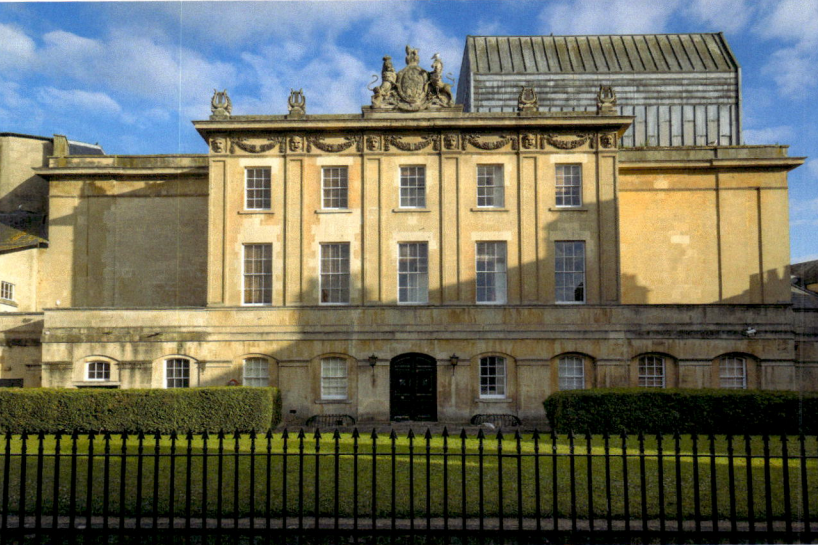

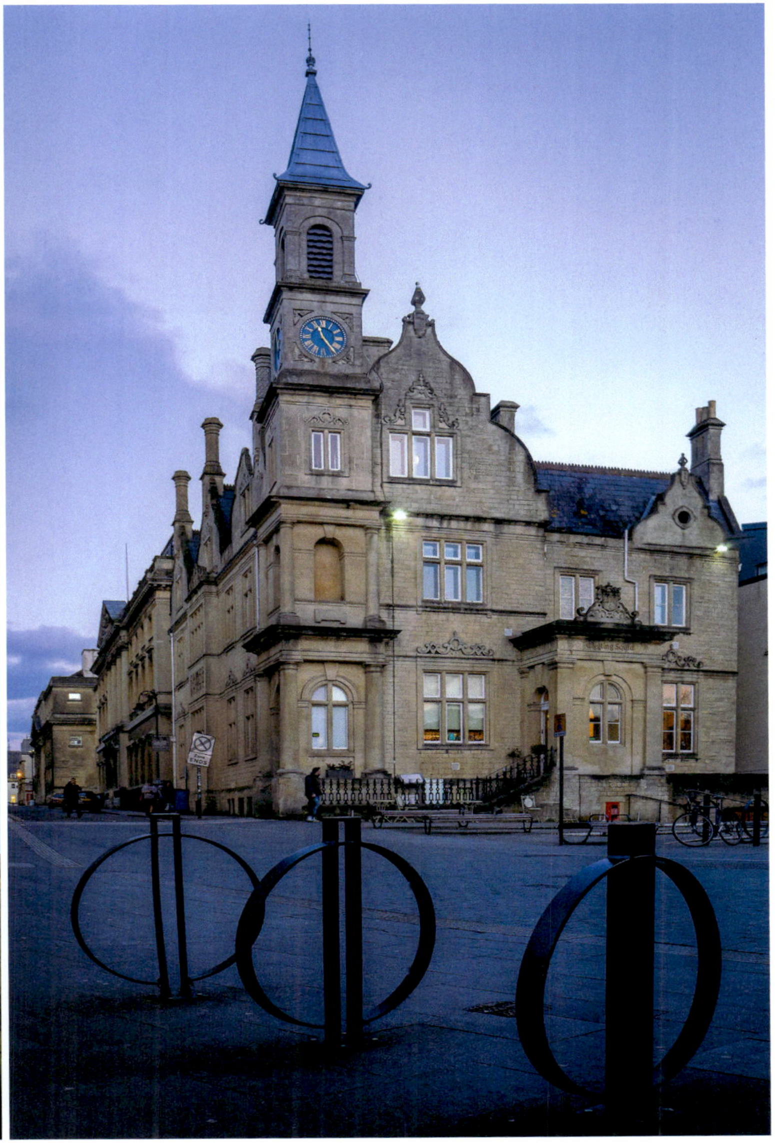

XV

15 BATH SKYLINE & VIEWPOINTS

The city of Bath, like Rome, is surrounded by seven hills, adding to its historic charm. These hills – Southdown, Kelston Round Hill, Lansdown, Solsbury Hill, Bathford Hill, Bathampton Down and Beechen Cliff – offer stunning views and shape the city's landscape. Lansdown and Bathampton Down are known for their sweeping vistas. Bath's seven hills parallel Rome's, reinforcing its classical connections. Their wooded slopes and limestone formations contribute to Bath's unique beauty.

Bath sits in the Avon valley surrounded by a series of limestone hills and high meadows where you can gaze down on Bath's stunning Georgian architecture and lush greenery backed by rolling hills.

These accessible viewpoints that surround the city can be enjoyed individually as described in this chapter, or collectively by walking the Bath Skyline, a 6-mile walking route that surrounds the city.

The Skyline walk takes a well-maintained path that meanders through varied landscapes from semi-rural to pastoral farmland, thickly wooded slopes and glades to hidden clusters of cottages and estates. Each area offers sweeping vistas of the city or intimate glimpses through trees that frame famous landmarks beyond. Visit the National Trust website and search Bath Skyline walk, for a map and detailed directions.

BATH SKYLINE VIEW WALK MAP

nationaltrust.org.uk
Search for Bath Skyline Walk

The viewpoints and locations described in this chapter can all be accessed by walking, car or bus. Use the map QR-codes on this page, the map at the beginning of this book and the directions in this chapter to get to each location. Whilst spectacular at any time of the day, if you can, visit them when the cloud cover is slight at the golden hours just after sunrise or before sunset for a spectacular sight.

OVERLEAF: the Skyline Walk offers elevated views over the city, just a short distance from Prior Park.

ALEXANDRA PARK

Postcode: BA2 4PP
what3words: woof.just.clever

BATHWICK MEADOWS

Postcode: BA2 6DB
what3words: bumpy.loud.photo

SHAM CASTLE

Postcode: BA2 6HT
what3words: agree.shark.hush

PRIOR PARK LANDSCAPE GARDEN

Postcode: BA2 5AH
what3words: submit.hang.bits

ABBEY VIEW GARDENS

Postcode: BA2 6DQ
what3words: third.online.reform

WARMINSTER ROAD

Postcode: BA2 6SG
what3words: crisis.next.galaxy

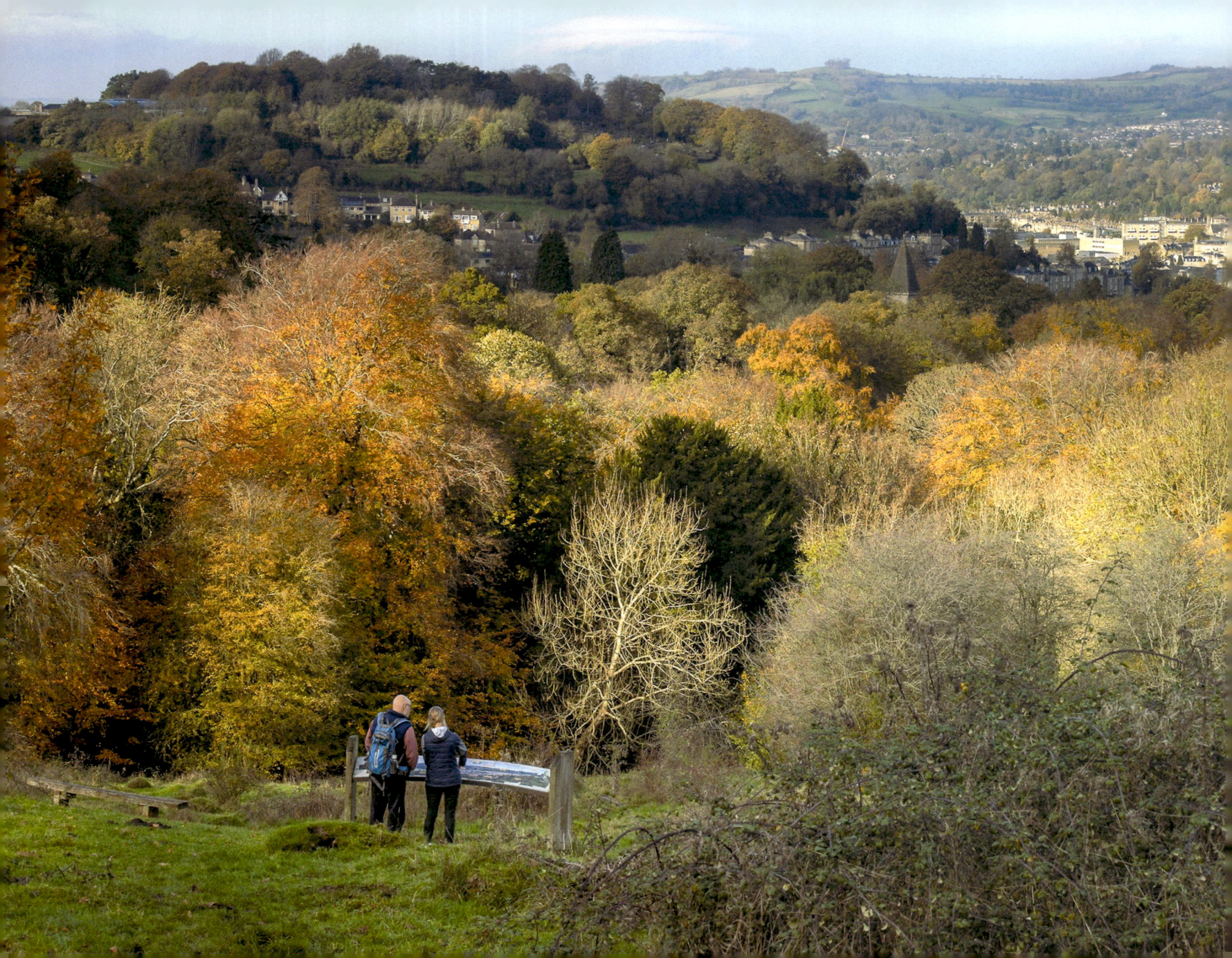

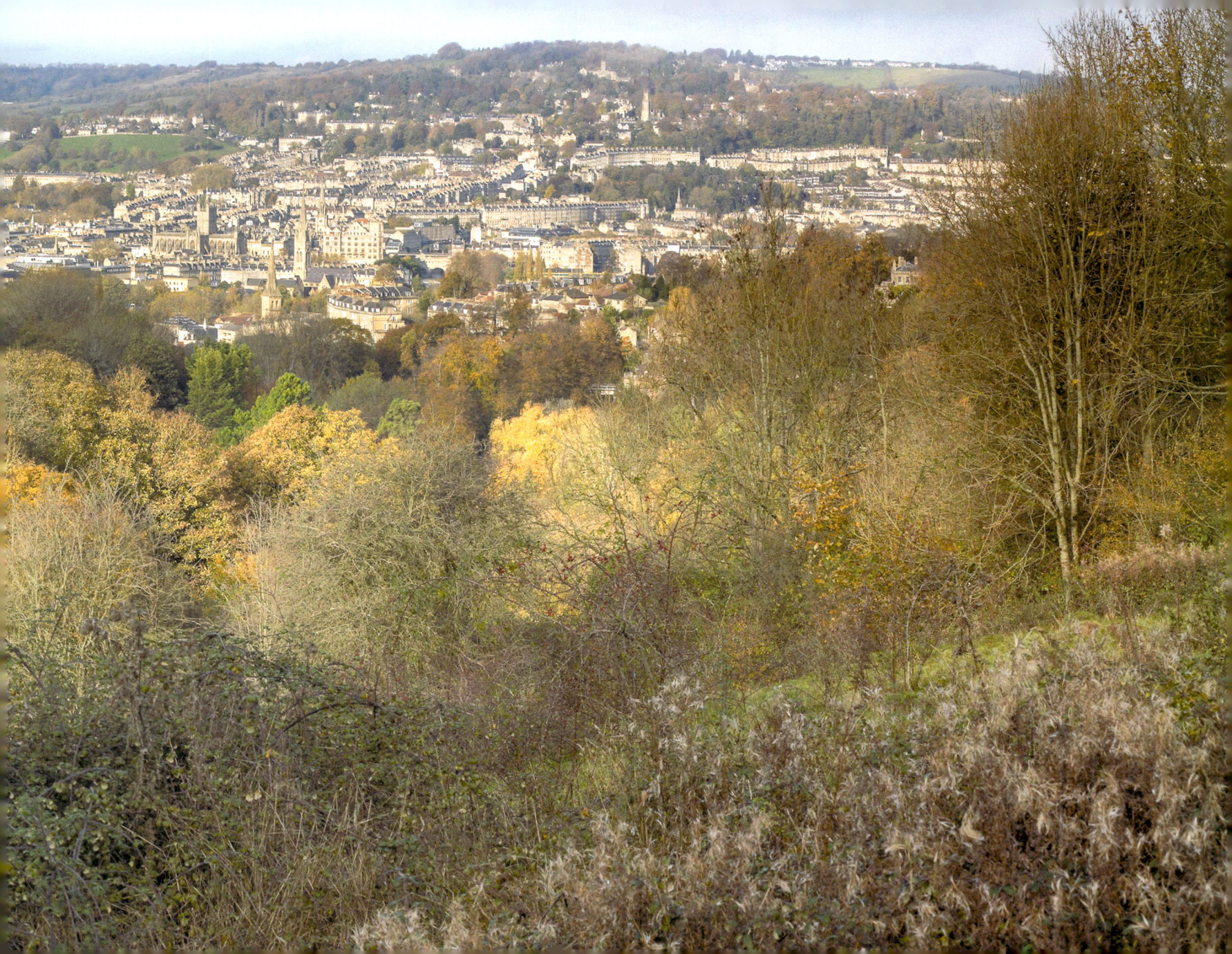

ALEXANDRA PARK

If you only have time to visit one location Alexandra Park is a must. Located closest to Bath's architectural delights the park forms the peak of Beechen Cliff, a steep rocky outcrop found immediately south of the city and is one of the most accessible and impressive places to experience almost the entire city laid out in front of you. Prominent architectural landmarks such as the Royal Crescent, the Circus, and Pulteney Bridge contribute to the city's iconic skyline and a useful diorama at the viewpoint helps to identify each and every graceful curve and grand facade. A spot especially worth experiencing at sunset or sunrise.

DIRECTIONS

On Foot: Cross the river Avon at Churchill bridge (not far from the railway station) and walk up Holloway then take the Jacob's Ladder steps up to the park (a 20 min, steep climb). Alternatively, from Widcombe at Lyncombe Hill follow pathway from Calton Gardens, crossing at Alexandra Road to follow narrow footpath that curves south west to the brow of the hill.

Public Transport: Take First Bus U2 (University Bus) or No.174 service (bay 10, Southgate Bus Station) to Bear Flat, then walk for 5 minutes up Shakespeare Avenue.

MORE INFORMATION

visitbath.co.uk
Search for Alexandra park for a detailed map.

RIGHT: Camden Crescent in the distance, one of many beautiful landmarks waiting to be discovered.

OPPOSITE: the entire world at your feet, almost all of Bath is visible from Alexandra Park.

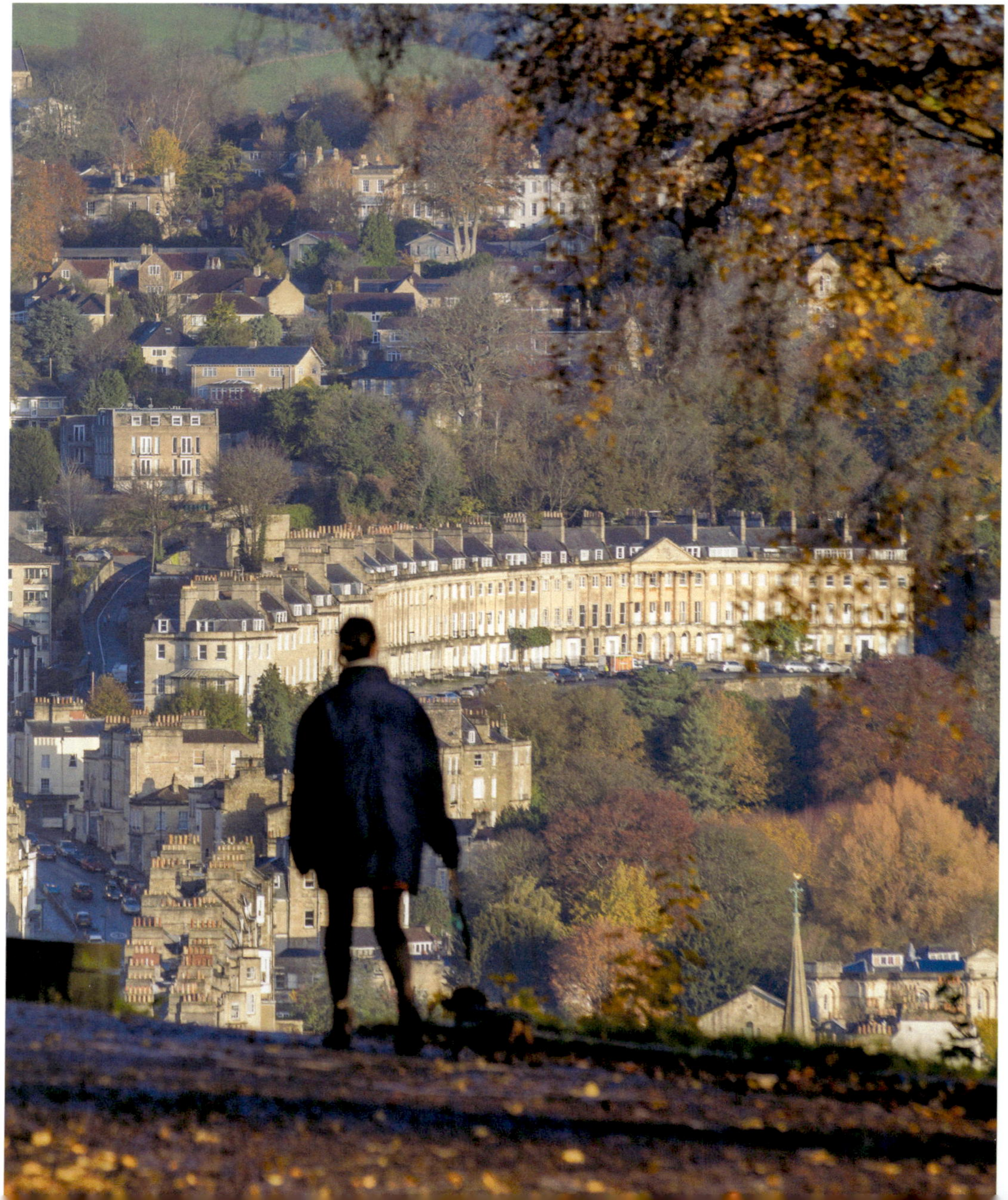

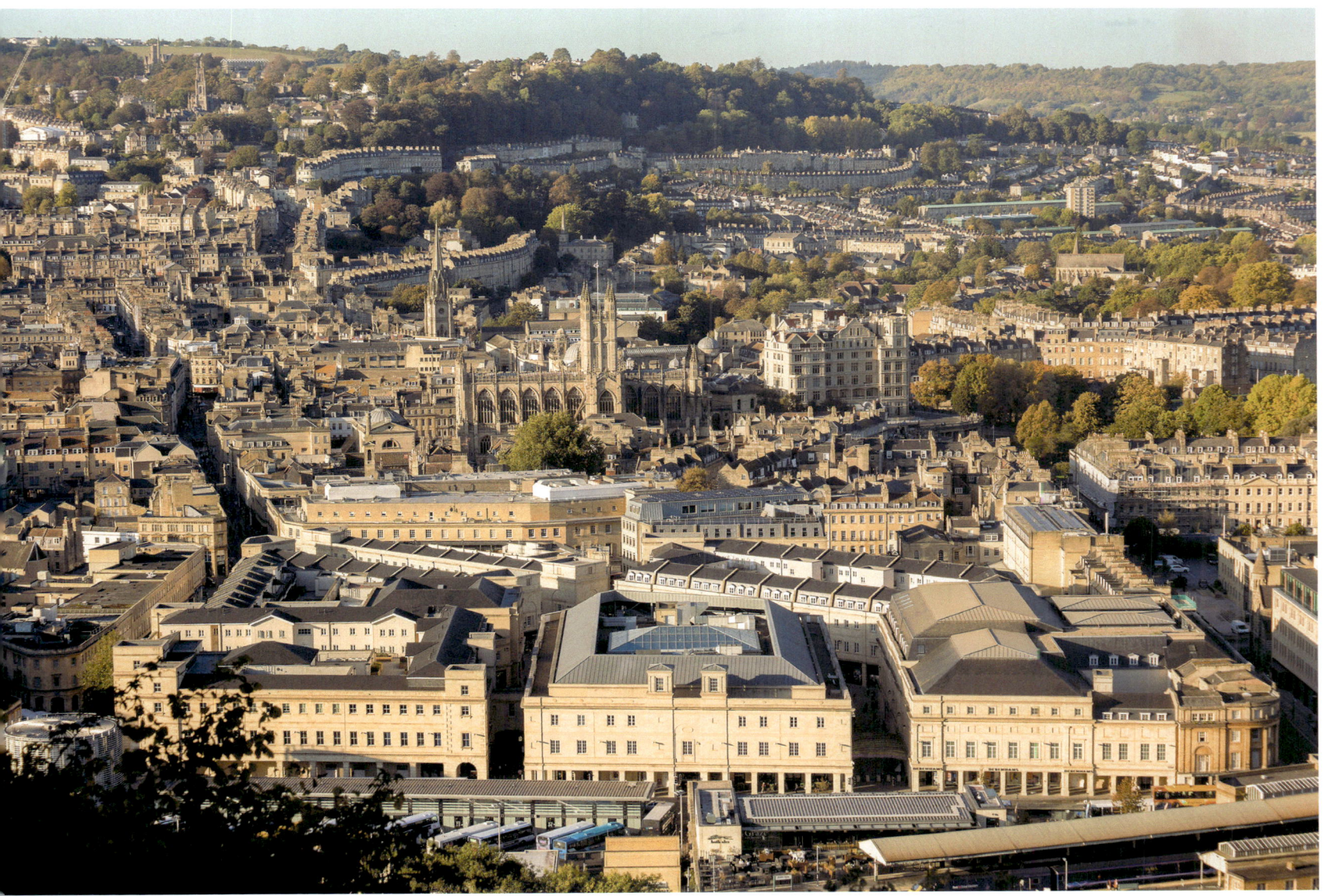

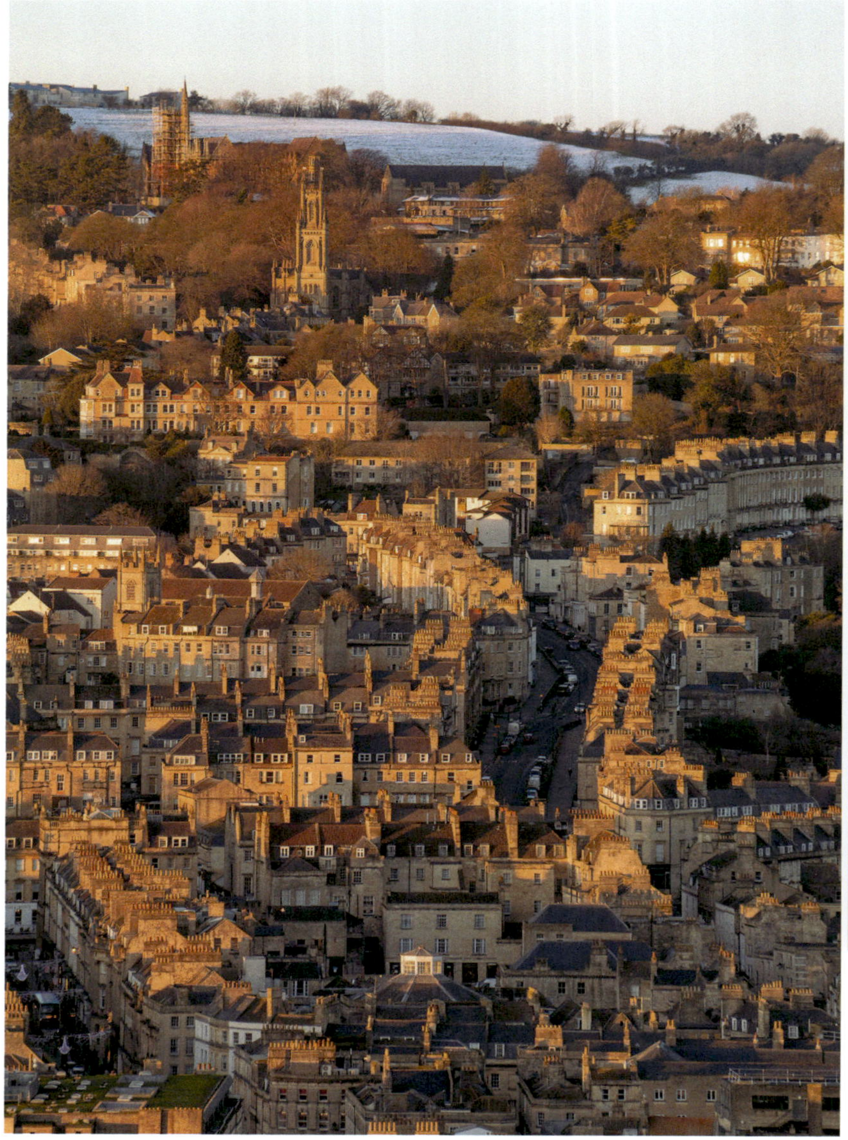

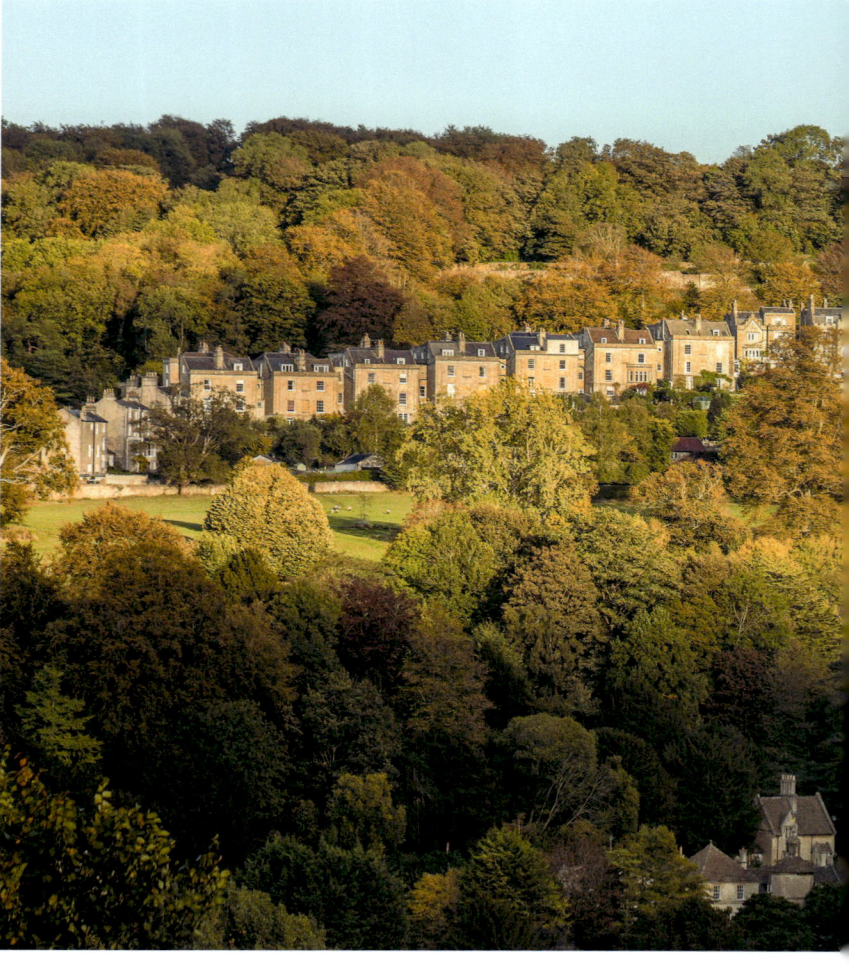

LEFT: Lansdown Road guides the eye towards the northern hillsides of the city.
ABOVE: the Skyline Walk winds behind Macaulay buildings, taking you through leafy paths that lead towards Prior Park and Rainbow Woods.

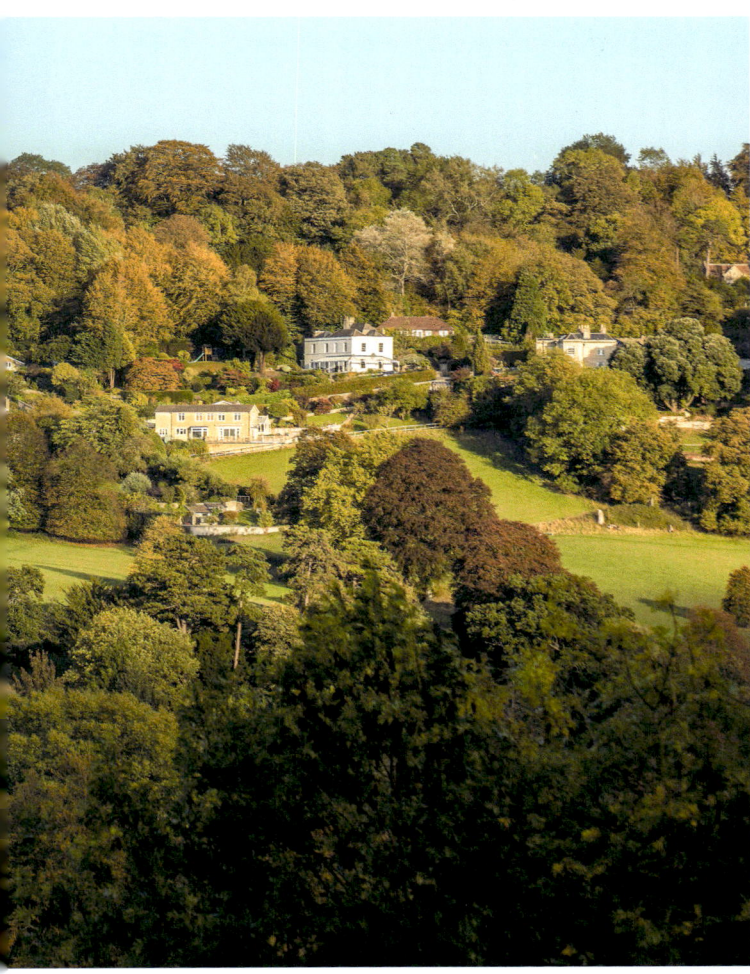

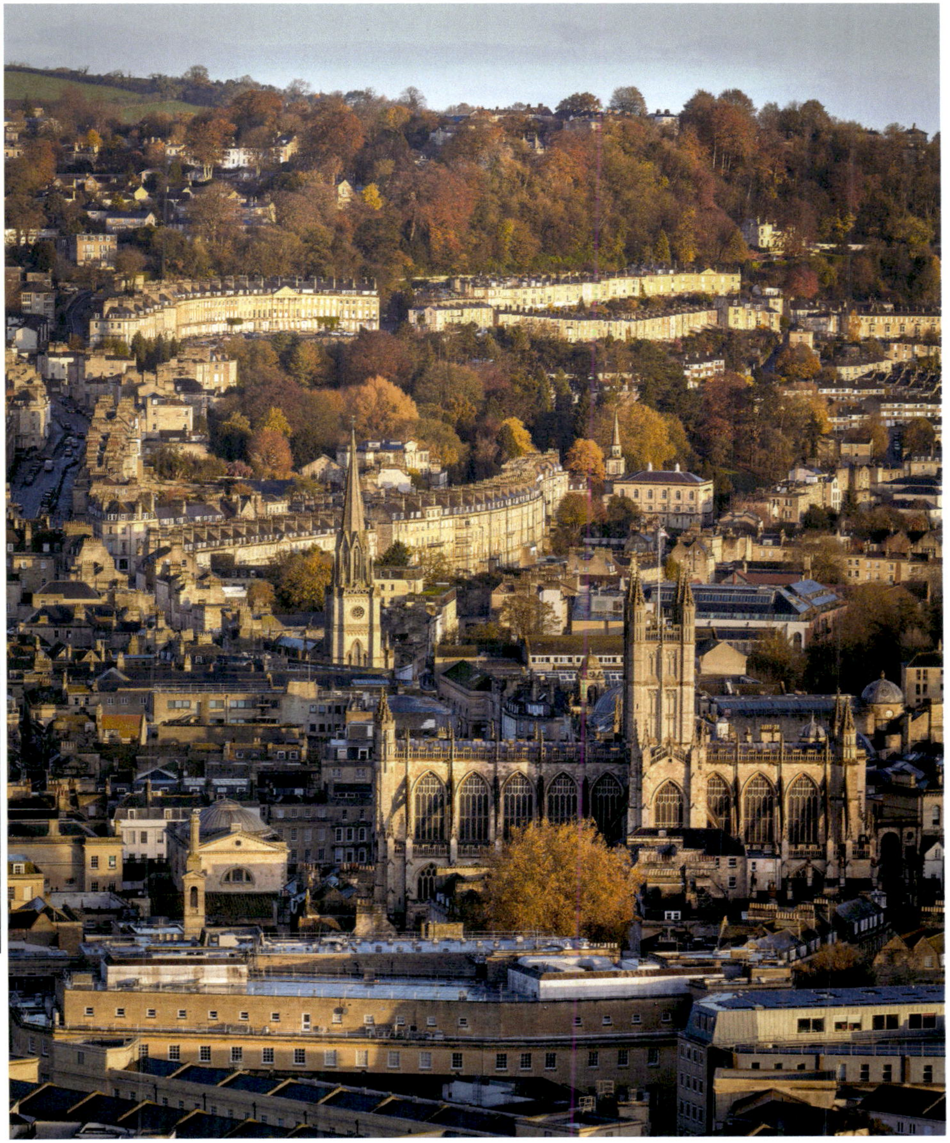

RIGHT: autumn brings a stunning array of colours, perfectly complementing Bath's beautiful golden architecture.

BATHWICK MEADOWS

Bathwick Meadows (aka Bathwick Fields) is a grassland rich with wildflowers and teeming with insect and human life in the summer months. It's a fantastic place to walk or simply relax with breathtaking panoramic views of the surrounding countryside and the historic city centre.

The Meadows are an idyllic setting for picnics, with ample space to spread out a blanket and soak in the beauty of the natural surroundings. From first light at daybreak to the low light of evening this is one of the best places in Bath to watch the sun slowly rise and set over the city's skyline including Bath Abbey, the Georgian crescents, tall church spires reaching into the sky, set against a backdrop of gently rolling hills.

Bathwick Meadows is a popular destination for dog walking, offering plenty of space for dogs to roam, play, and explore.

DIRECTIONS

On Foot: Walk east across Pulteney Bridge, then follow Great Pulteney Street (two thirds of its length) to Edward Street, cross the road at St Mary's Church and follow Raby Place onto Bathwick Hill. Cross over the bridge above the Kennet & Avon canal and continue up the road to the entrance of Bathwick Meadows opposite Cleveland Walk (a 25 minute, uphill walk).

Public Transport: Take First Bus U1 or U2 (University Bus) to Bathwick Hill, bus stop is directly opposite the entrance to Bathwick Meadows, adjacent to the junction of Cleveland Walk.

MORE INFORMATION

bathscape.co.uk
Search for Bathwick Meadows/Fields for a detailed map.

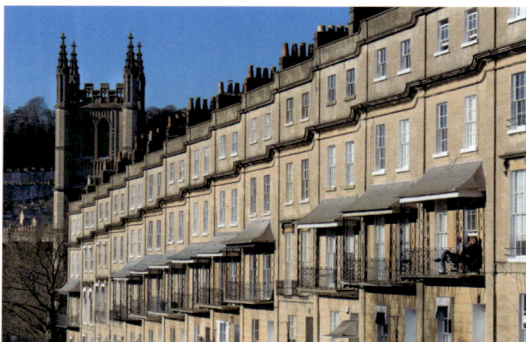

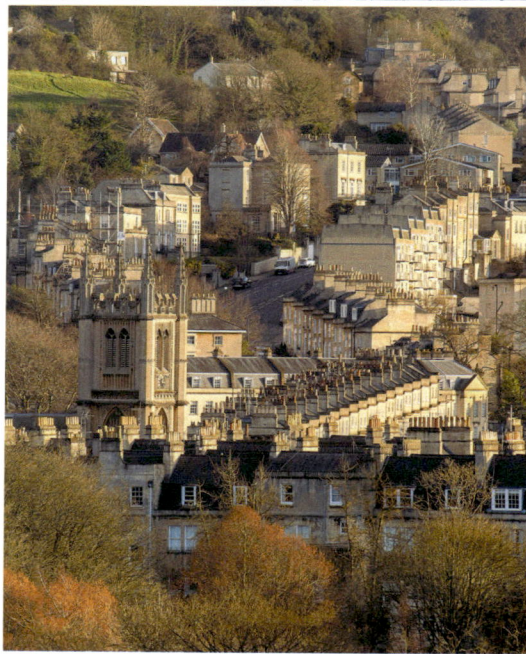

TOP: balconies on Raby Place, Bathwick Hill. **ABOVE:** Bathwick Hill rises to the east, starting from St Mary's Church.

OPPOSITE: bringing a countryside vibe into the city, the meadows are the perfect spot to experience summertime bliss watch the world go by and catch glimpses of hot air balloons drifting overhead.

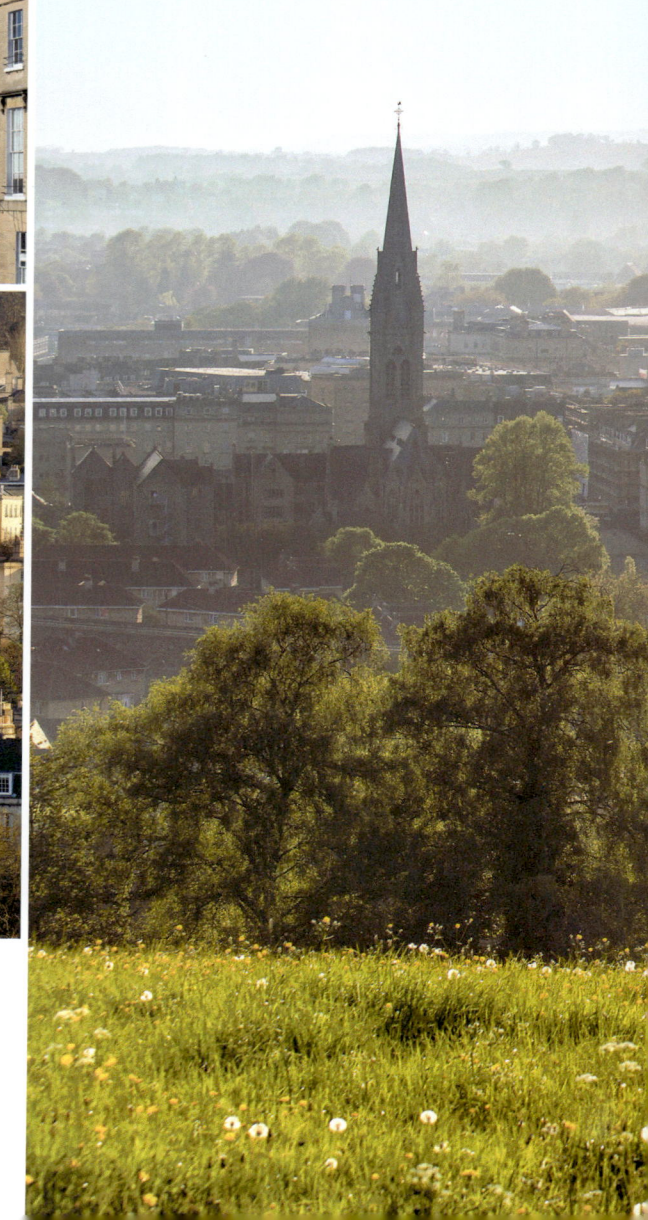

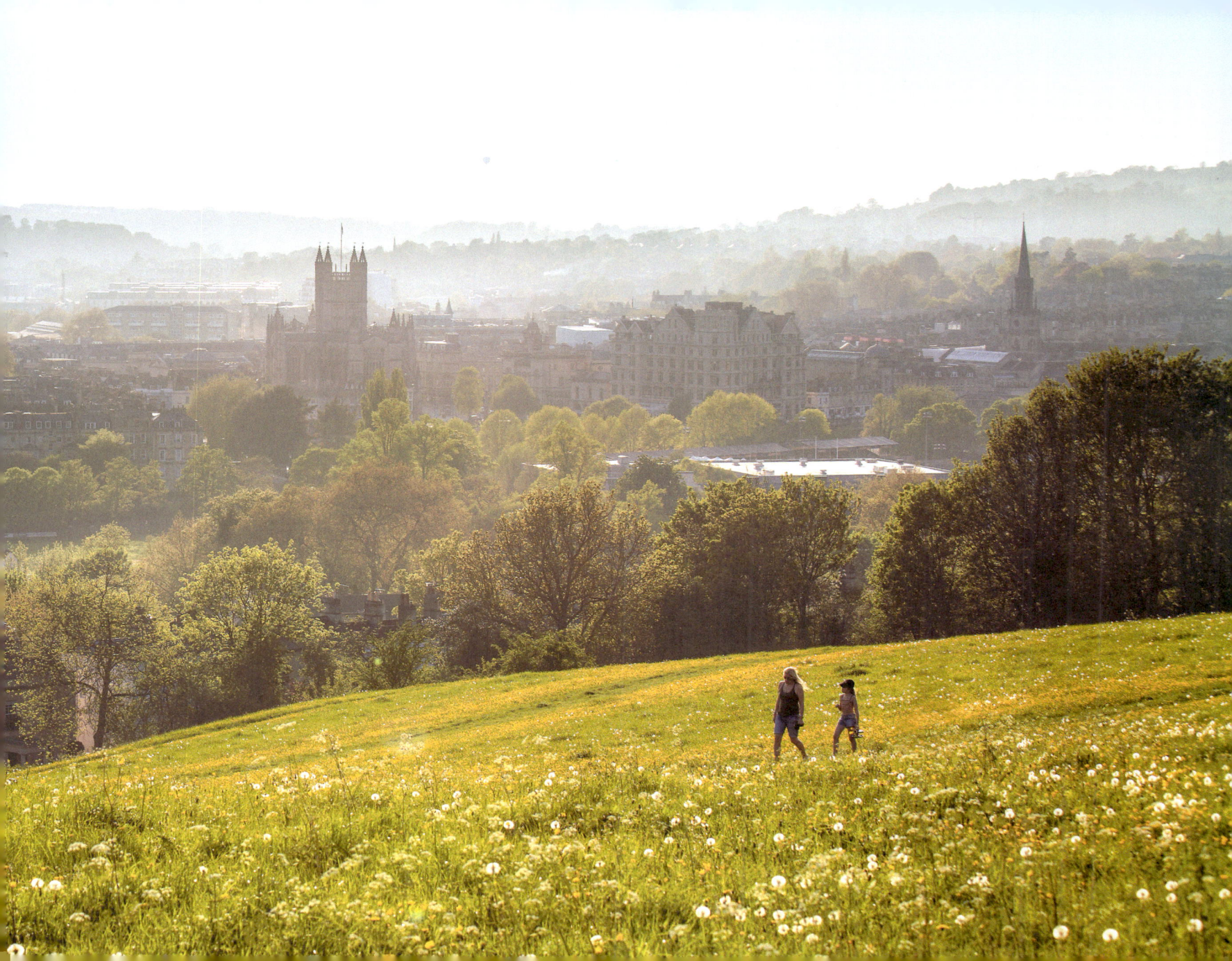

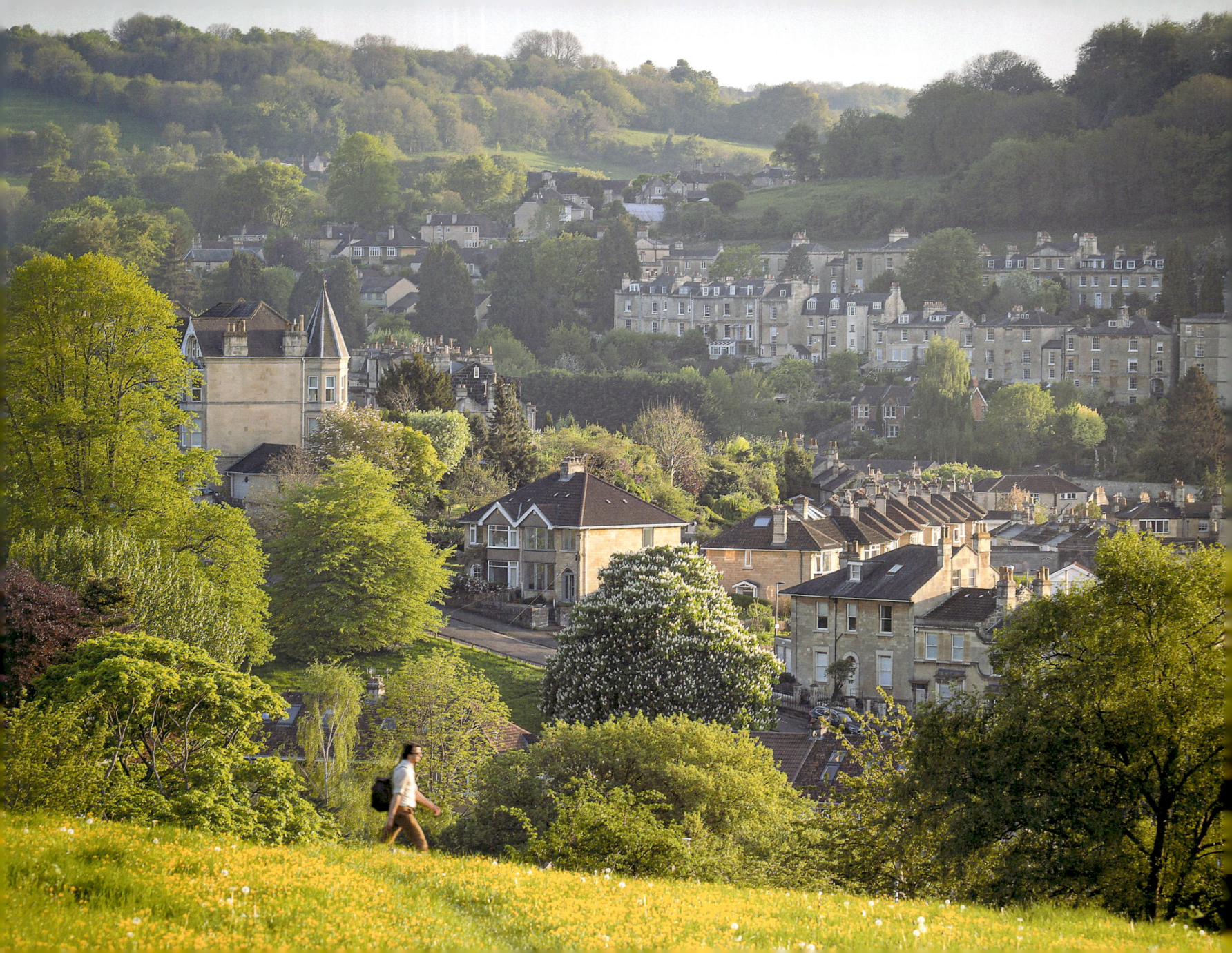

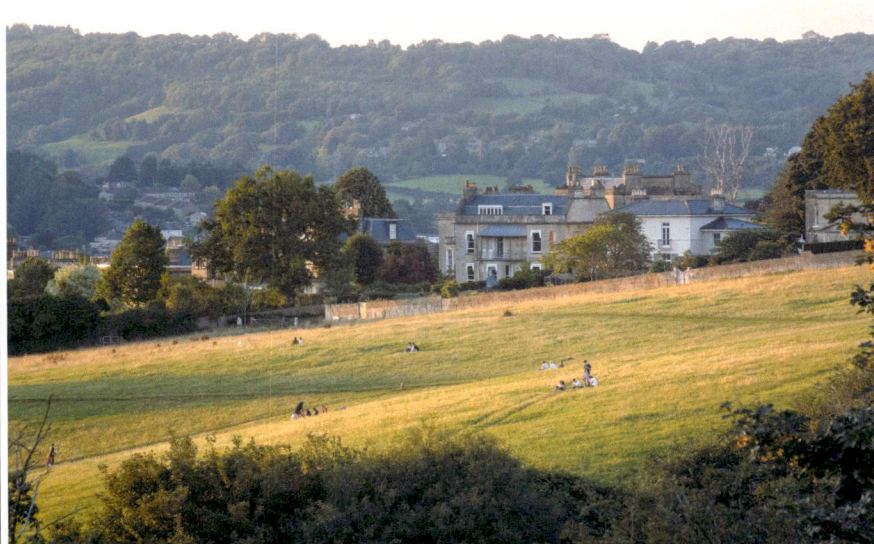

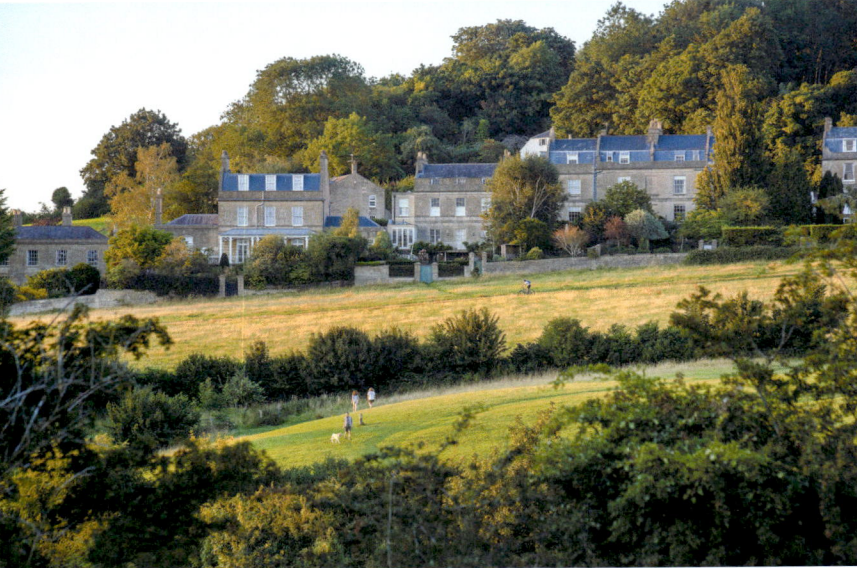

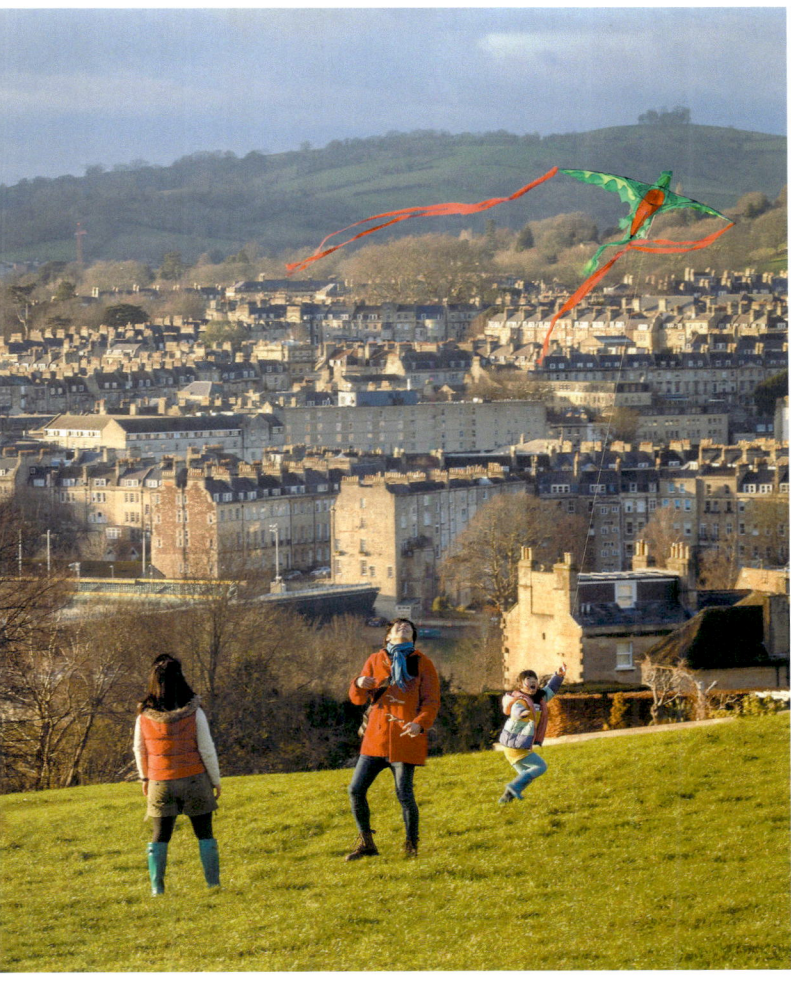

OPPOSITE: buttercups blanket the meadows, as nature gently embraces the city's suburbs.

TOP LEFT: Bathwick Meadows one of the best spots to watch the sun set over the city, casting a golden glow across the landscape. **LEFT**: forming part of the Bath Skyline Walk, it's the perfect spot to begin or conclude your journey. **ABOVE**: plenty of space to catch the breeze and soak in the fresh air.

SHAM CASTLE

Perched on the edge of Claverton Down, Sham Castle is one of Bath's most distinctive landmarks forming part of the city's celebrated skyline circular walk. Though it appears to be a fortified Medieval building this striking structure with its four symmetrical towers, arched openings and battlements create the illusion of a grand stronghold but is actually an 18th century folly designed purely for decorative effect rather than defence.

Commissioned in 1762 by Ralph Allen, a prominent Bath philanthropist and quarry owner, Sham Castle was built to "improve the prospect" from his city centre home. Constructed from locally quarried Bath stone ashlar the folly exemplifies Allen's ambition to enhance both the landscape and his own legacy. Positioned high above the city next to the Bath Golf Club it commands sweeping panoramic views to the west making it a popular spot for walkers and photographers alike.

Open 24 hours and lit up at night the castle can be accessed via a steep but short walk up the hill via a wooded pathway from North Road to admire its dramatic silhouette against the sky. Though the structure itself cannot be entered its commanding presence and historic charm make it an unmissable stop for those exploring the area.

DIRECTIONS
The Bath Skyline Bus Tour route stops at Quarry Road (No.8) which is around a 3 minute walk to Golf Course Road which leads to Sham Castle (or follow a footpath west of Bath University to follow Bath Skyline walking route NW to Sham Castle).

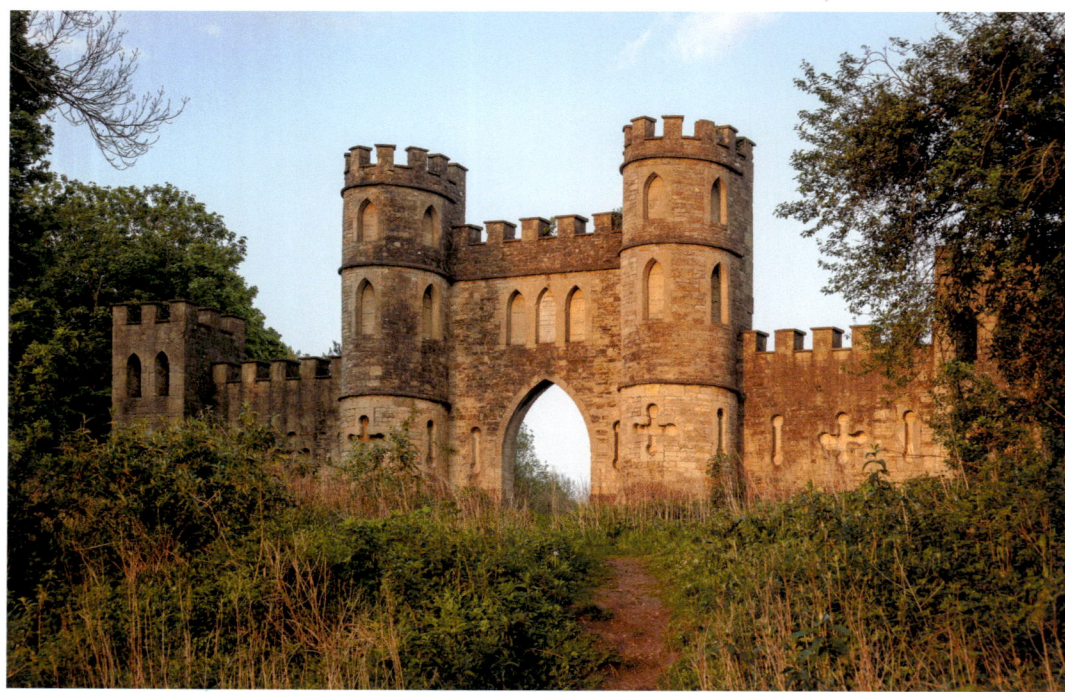

MORE INFORMATION

 bathscape.co.uk
Search for Sham Castle for a detailed map.

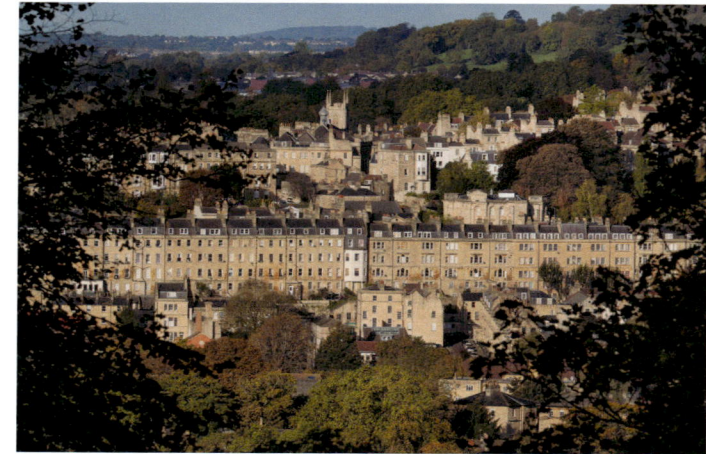

TOP: what a sham! Not everything is as it seems at the castle. **RIGHT**: the rear terraced view of The Paragon.

OPPOSITE: Sham Castle offers a stunning perspective of a unique, alternative side of the city.

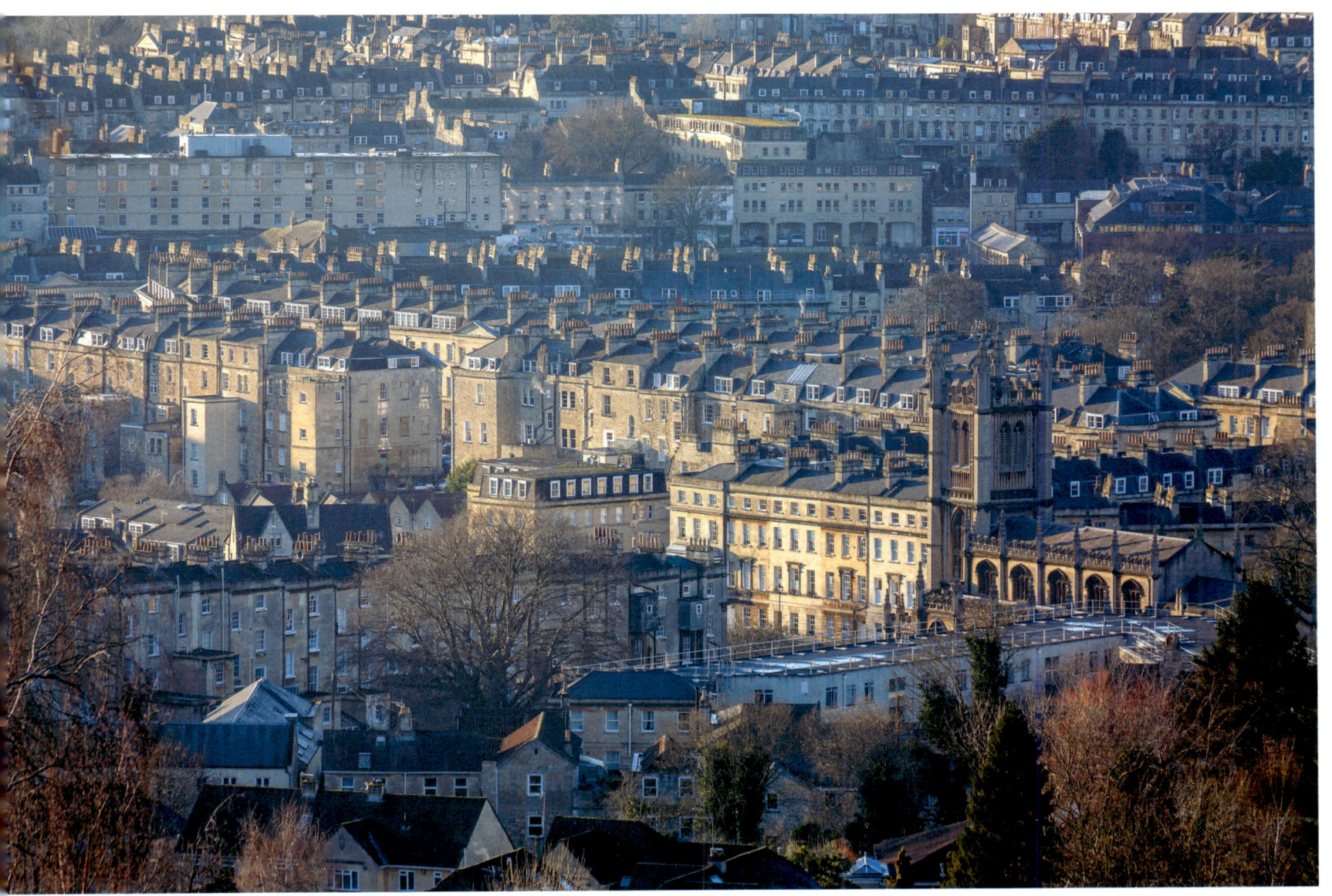

PRIOR PARK LANDSCAPE GARDEN

Prior Park is a picturesque 18th century garden designed by Capability Brown and the poet Alexander Pope, it is owned and managed by the National Trust. Nestled in a valley on the edge of the Combe Down escarpment, south of Bath, the grounds cover 28 hectares of steeply sloping terrain. The original formal gardens were re-imagined following the Georgian trend of creating naturalistic areas comprising of open meadows and pockets of trees designed to 'lead the eye' into the scene, the park is considered one of the finest examples of English landscape gardening.

A high ridge surrounding the city forms part of the Bath Skyline offering spectacular panoramic views over the countryside and also skirts round the edge of Prior Park College. A network of pathways lead through woodlands revealing hidden features such as a Serpentine lake, grotto, wildflower meadow and a timber frame hermitage. One of the most notable features of the park is its Palladian bridge, which spans a small lake at the bottom of the valley. Built in 1755 and one of only four in the world, this elegant bridge, with its classical design, adds a sense of grandeur to the landscape and is a popular spot to enjoy this unique setting amongst beautiful shrub and flower beds.

The mansion and gardens were home to local entrepreneur Ralph Allen who was instrumental in shaping Bath into what we see today. Wealth generated from a stone mining enterprise funded the land and the commission of the architect John Wood the Elder to construct the impressive Palladian style mansion not just as a residence but also as an advert for the qualities of the stone as a building material.

The main house is joined on either side by an additional pair of wings that extend broadly outwards occupying a

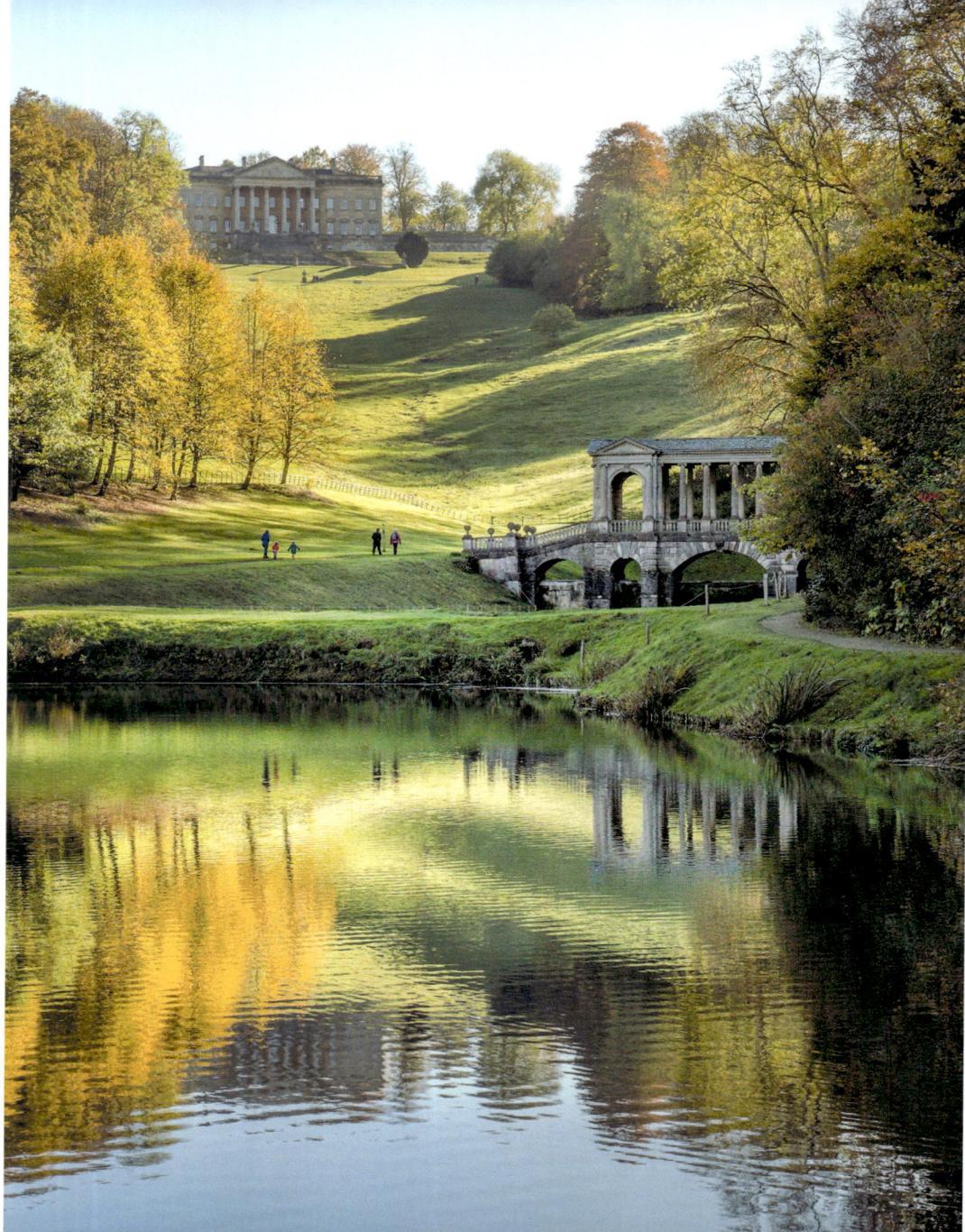

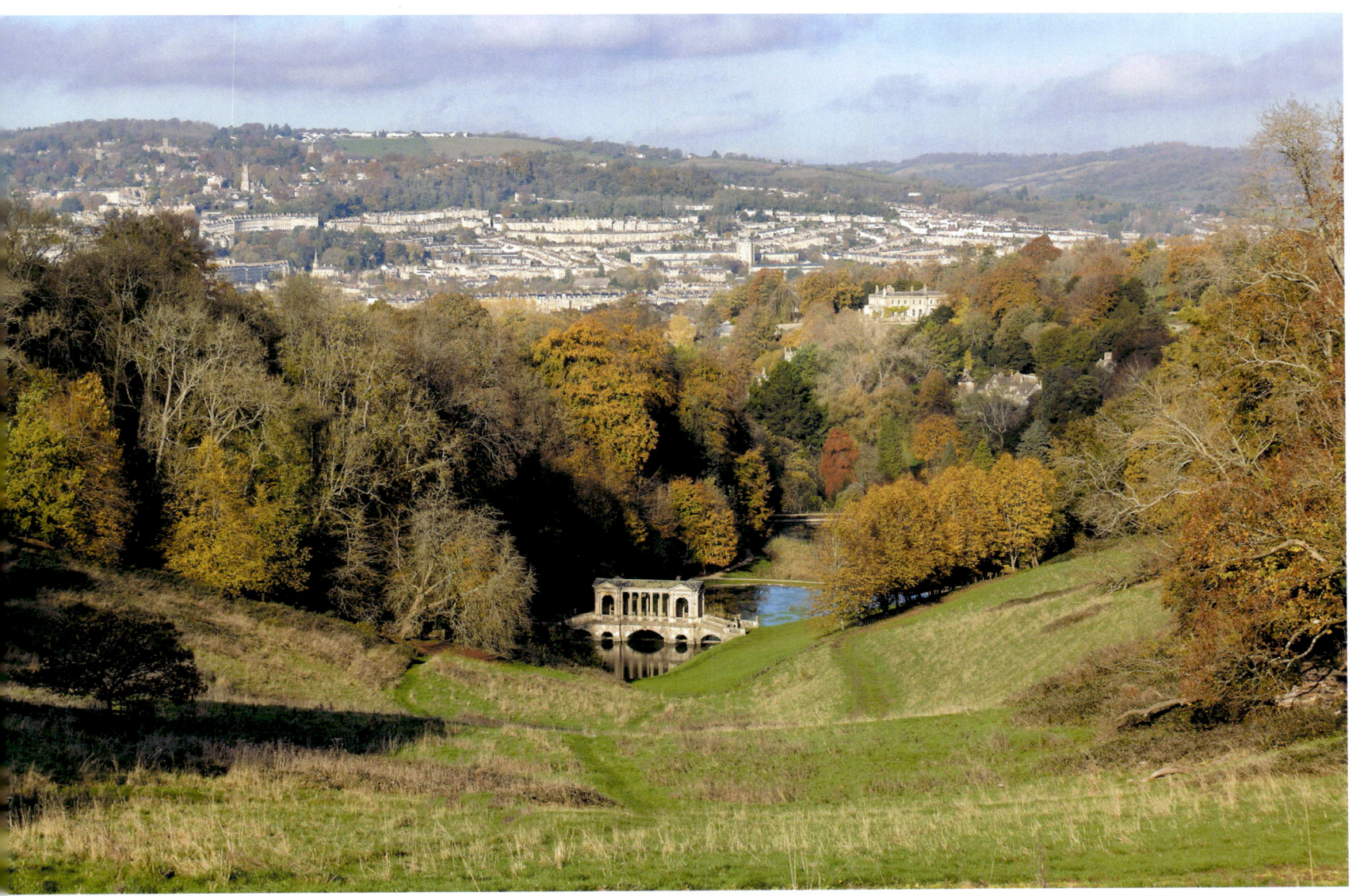

ABOVE: the 18th-century Capability Brown designed landscape garden offers breathtaking views across the city.
OPPOSITE: the landscaped gardens here are breathtaking and particularly so in autumn.

vast stretch on one of the highest slopes overlooking the city. It was designed to impress and certainly would have caught the eye of all those that visited the centre of Bath in the late 18th century. The mansion is now home to Prior Park College, a co-educational public school.

The grandest viewpoint is located beneath the main house, wide reaching views across the parkland reach into the city and the hillside of Lansdown beyond. In the middle distance the Palladian Bridge occupies the central ground creating a wonderful place to linger and enjoy the views. Any time of year provides beautiful scenes though during autumn months the changing colours of the landscape really come into their own and add a touch or magic to the landscape.

DIRECTIONS

On Foot: Walk south via Widcombe, then follow Prior Park Road for approximately 20 minutes past the garden centre. At the junction with Perrymead and Church Street continue south west on Ralph Allen Drive passing Bath Abbey Cemetery on your right to the parkland entrance further up the hill through a set of iron gates. A walk of half-an hour (30 minutes).

Public Transport: Take the First Bus (No.2) from Southgate central station (BK Stop) to Ralph Allen Drive, then walk brief distance to the entrance. Buses run every 30 minutes in peak times (March to October). Alternatively catch the Bath Skyline Bus, alighting at stop Q (next to Prior Park) – city centre pick ups include, Manvers Street, Terrace Walk, North Parade and Great Pulteney Street.

MORE INFORMATION

nationaltrust.org.uk
Search for Prior Park Landscape Garden for more information and a detailed map.

RIGHT: straddling a series of lakes, the Palladian Bridge is one of only four of this design in the world.

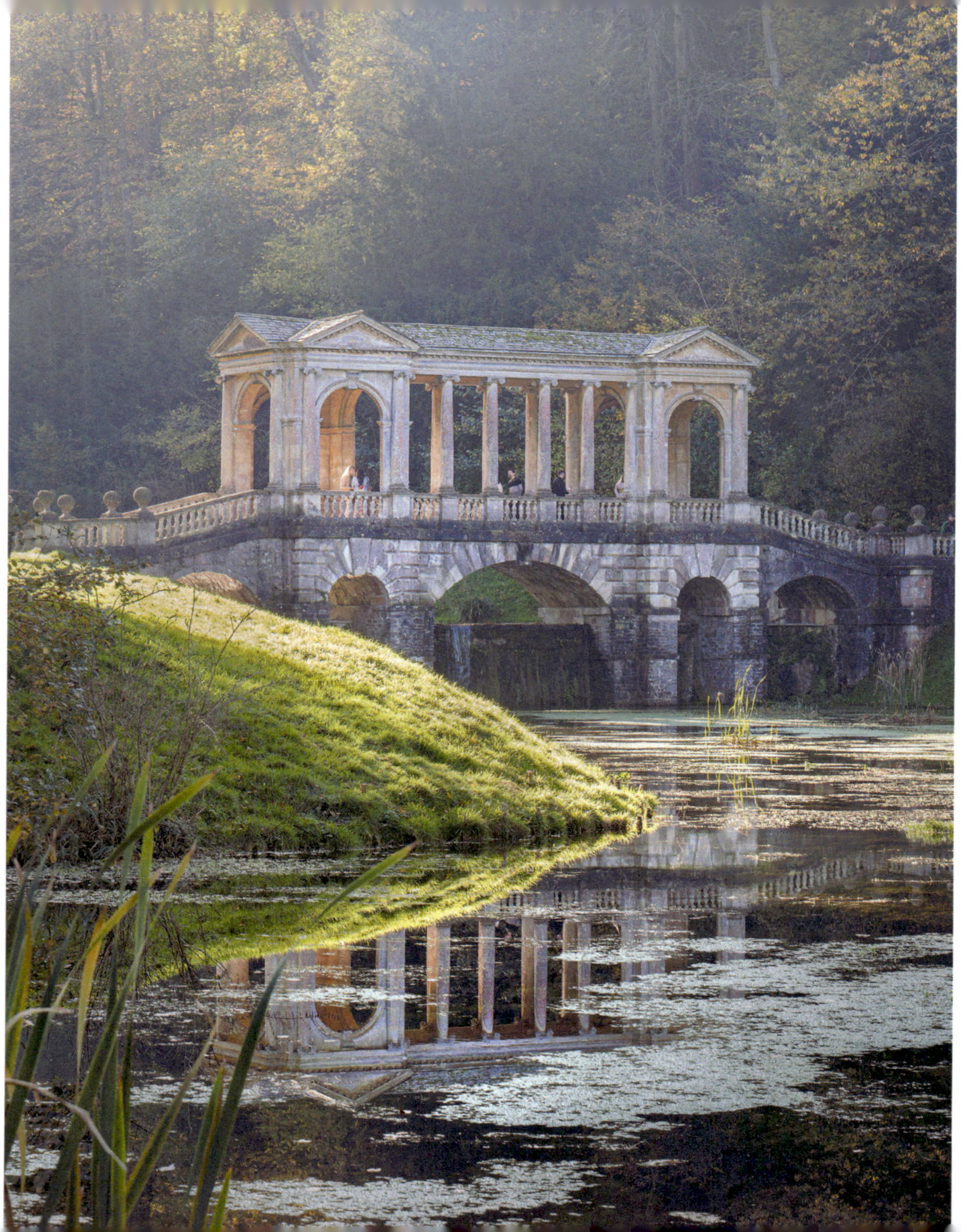

214

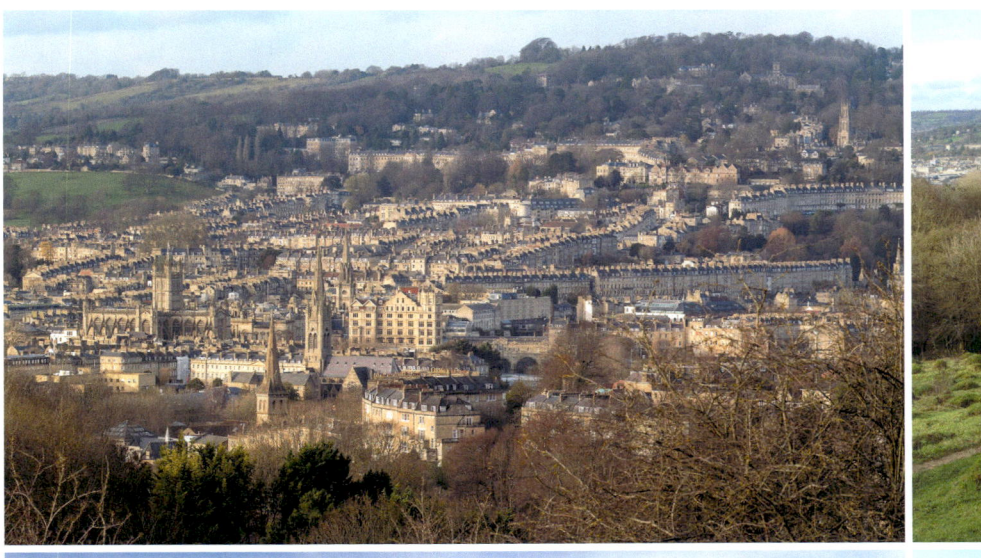
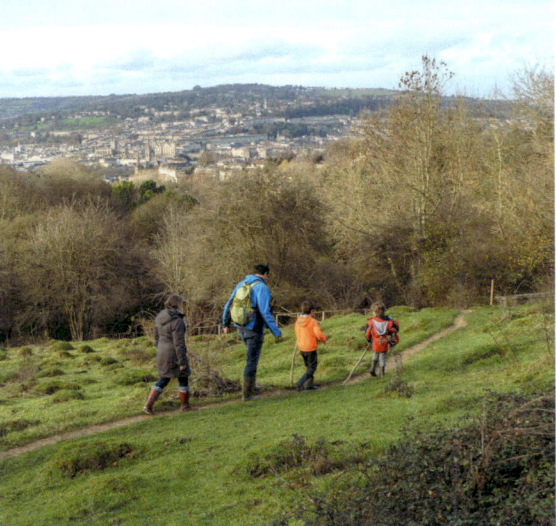
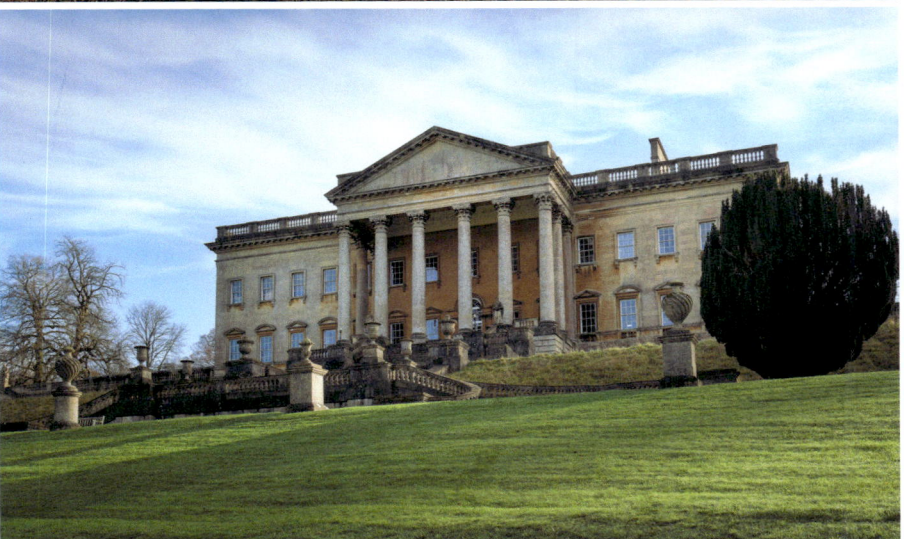
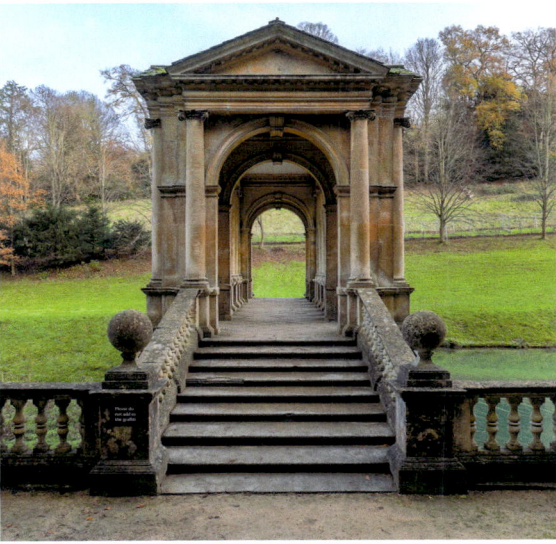

TOP LEFT: the beauty of Bath from its panoramic viewpoints; every angle reveals more to see. **TOP RIGHT**: set in amongst hillsides above Bath, visitors can enjoy magnificent views, making it a perfect place to explore. **ABOVE LEFT**: Ralph Allen, a local businessman commissioned the construction of Prior Park and its mansion in the mid-18th century. Today it is a school, Prior Park College. **ABOVE RIGHT**: the bridge, built in 1755 was inspired by a similar design at Wilton House in Wiltshire.

ABBEY VIEW GARDENS

Abbey View Gardens is located close to the Kennet and Avon Canal and makes a good detour from the tow path at Pulteney Gardens. A small bridge at Lock No. 11 (Pump House Chimney) carries the lane south onto Abbey View.

The road (a cul-de-sac) is only around 100 metres in length but offers an enormous opportunity to experience the most spectacular panoramic views of Bath. Due to its aspect, running parallel to the city, almost the entire collection of tallest landmarks are on display. This is one of my favourite views of Bath. I adore how the architecture is positioned at eye level with an almost oblique angle allowing church spires and the tower of Bath Abbey to majestically rise above everything else.

During summer the scene is awash with bright, blinding light creating hazy layers and outlines between streets and prominent buildings, various parts cast into shadow balanced by the sun. As the day progresses landmarks become backlit as the great orange orb slowly sinks beyond Kelston Hill in the middle distance, its tiny clump of trees an obvious feature to spot perched like a cherry on a cake. This is a place made for evening strolls and early dawn walks; with no traffic and enough time and space to slowly absorb the scene without the hub of busy city streets.

DIRECTIONS

On Foot: A picturesque walk heads along the river Avon from Pulteney Bridge southwards beneath North Parade Bridge – continue beside the cricket ground eastwards along Ferry Lane to Pulteney Gardens. Cross Horseshoe Lock Bridge (over the Kennet & Avon Canal) and follow the road as it forks left onto Abbey View, then Abbey View Gardens. (For an accessible route, missing out the steps at Pulteney Bridge instead start your journey from Terrace Walk on North Parade, eastwards over North Parade Bridge to Pulteney Road South and then follow same directions as above from Pulteney Gardens).

Public Transport: Take University Bus U2 from Southgate bus station (Dorchester Street) through Widcombe to Pulteney Court. Cross the road (safely) and follow Pulteney Avenue to Pulteney Grove, then follow Pulteney Gardens (south east) over the canal at Horseshoe Lock Bridge and follow the road as it forks left onto Abbey View, then Abbey View Gardens.

RIGHT: only the tallest buildings catch the light: St John's Church, Bath Abbey, and The Empire.
OVERLEAF: with sweeping panoramic views, Abbey View Gardens offers one of the finest ways to experience the beauty of Bath.

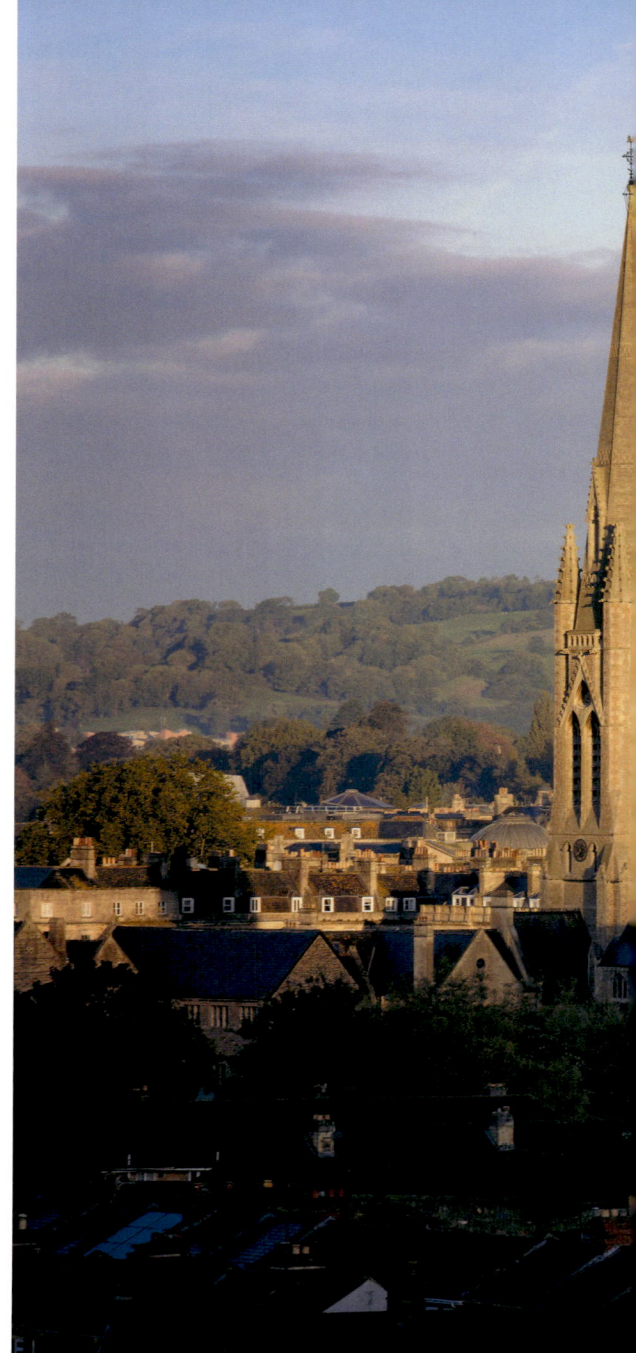

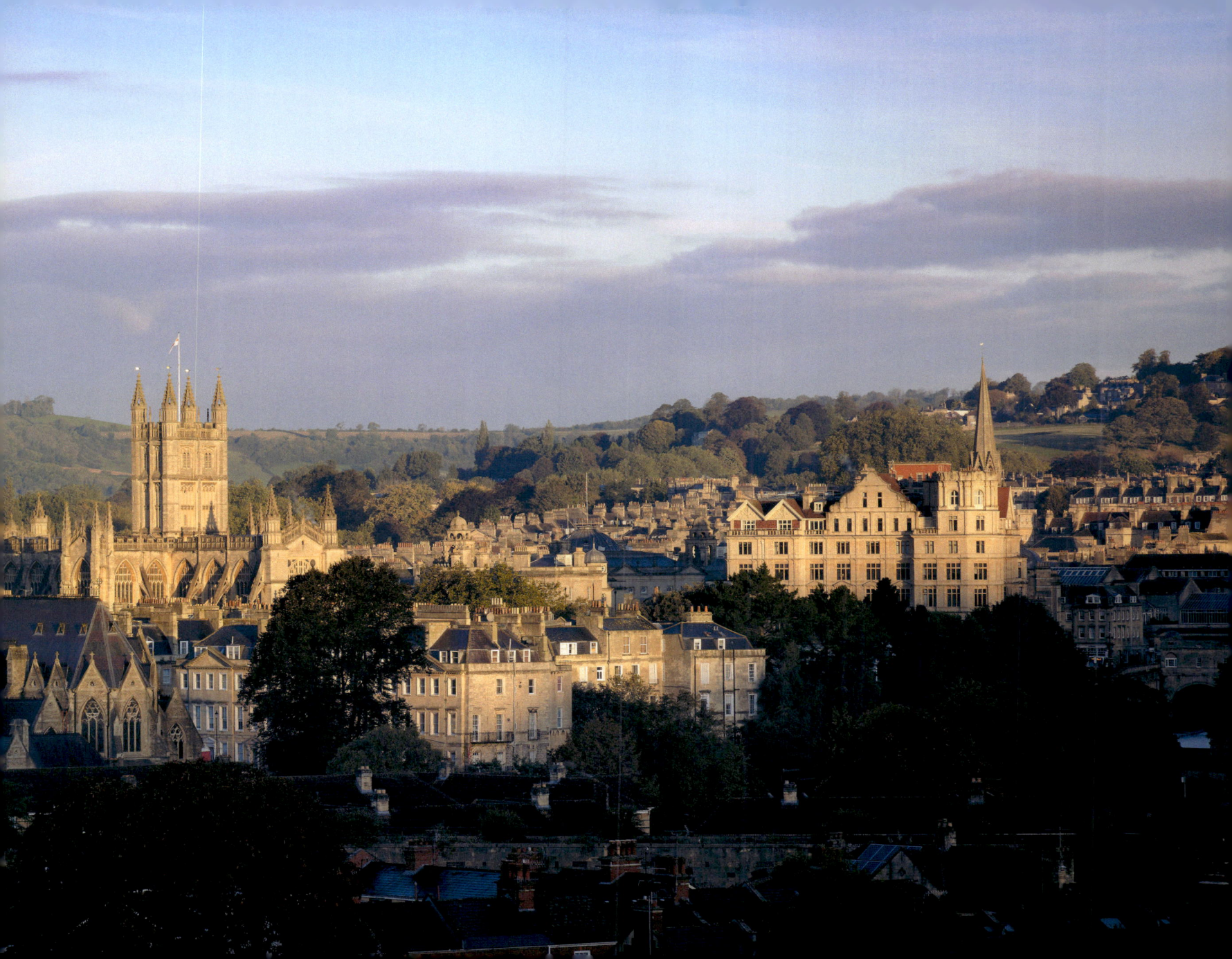

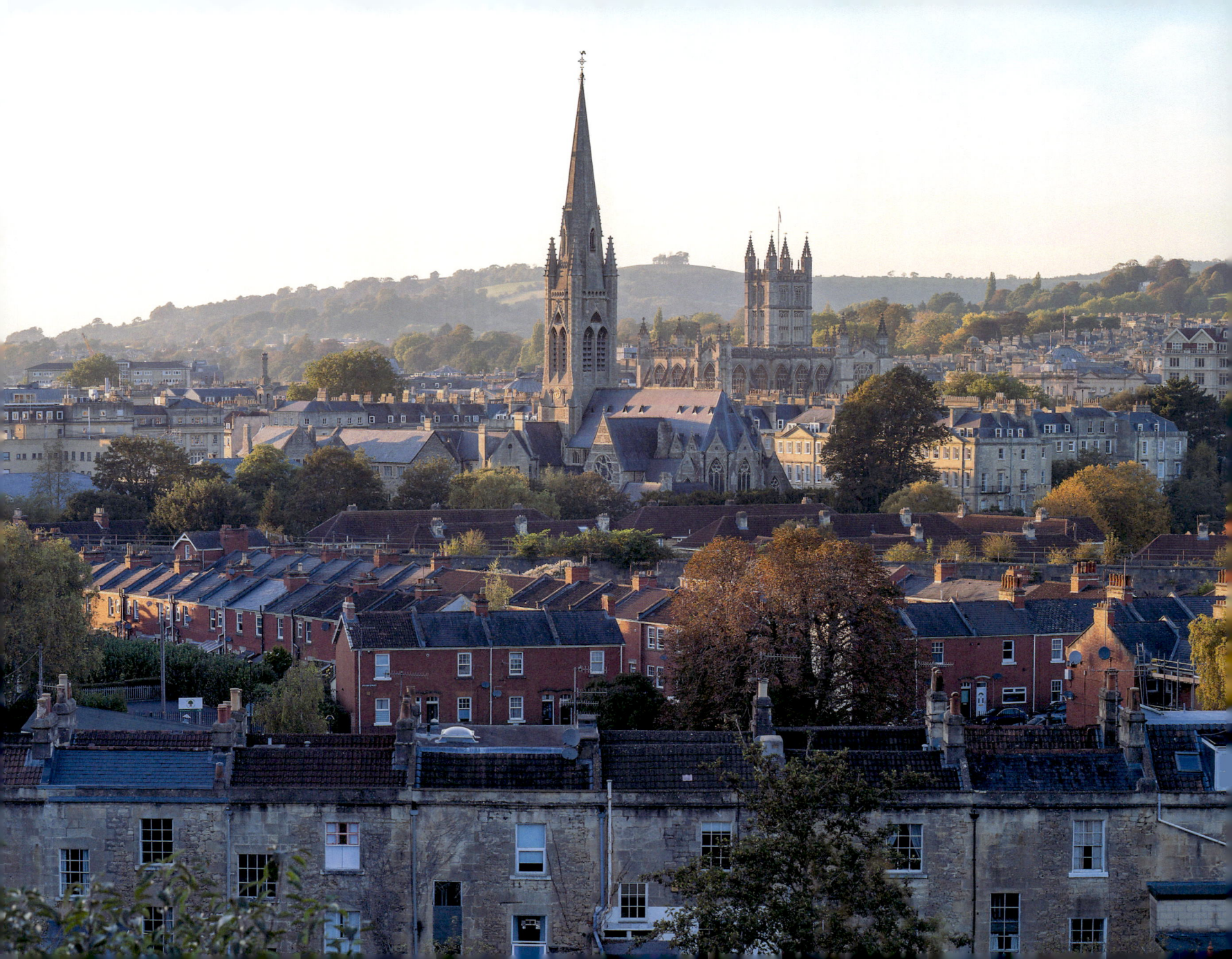

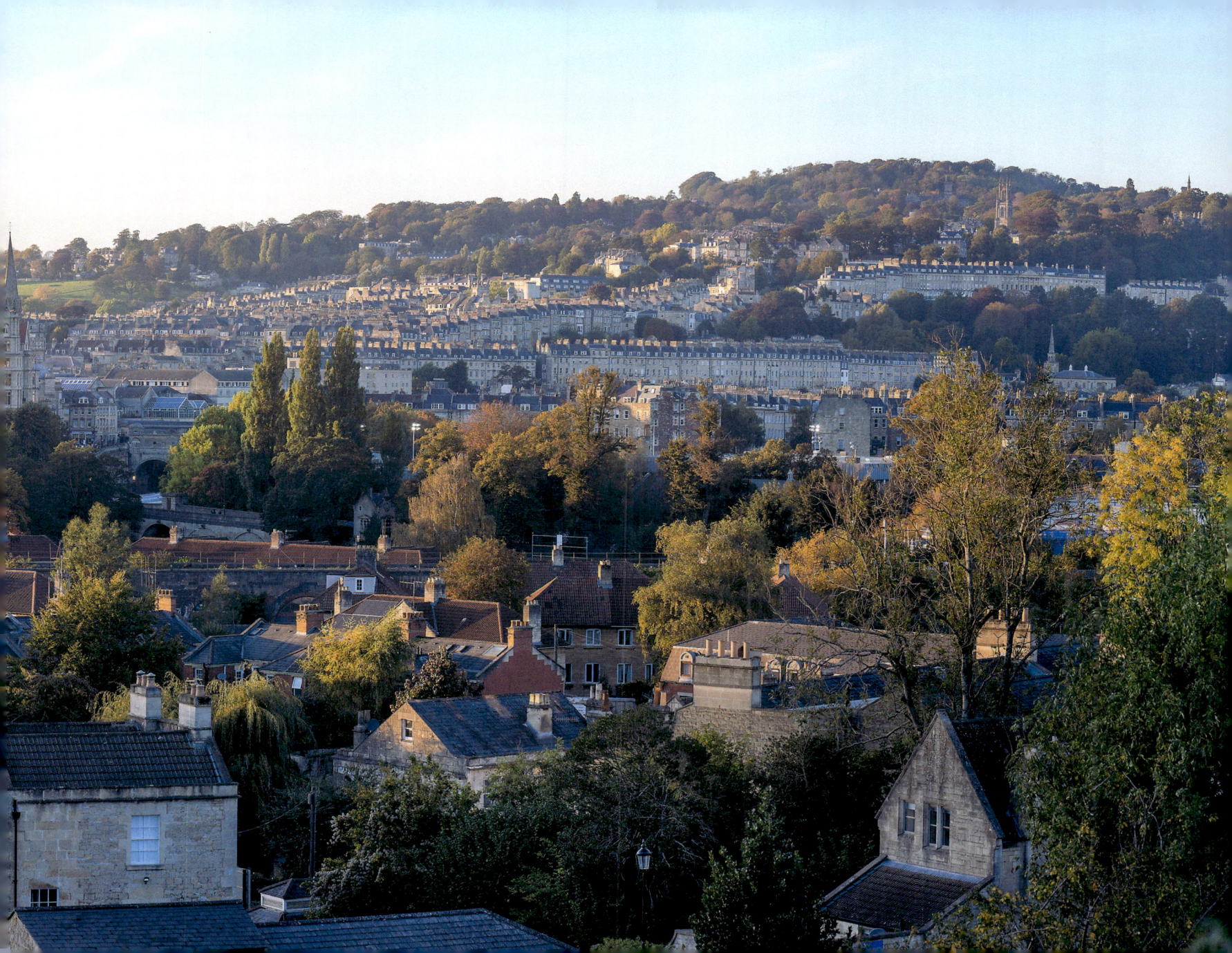

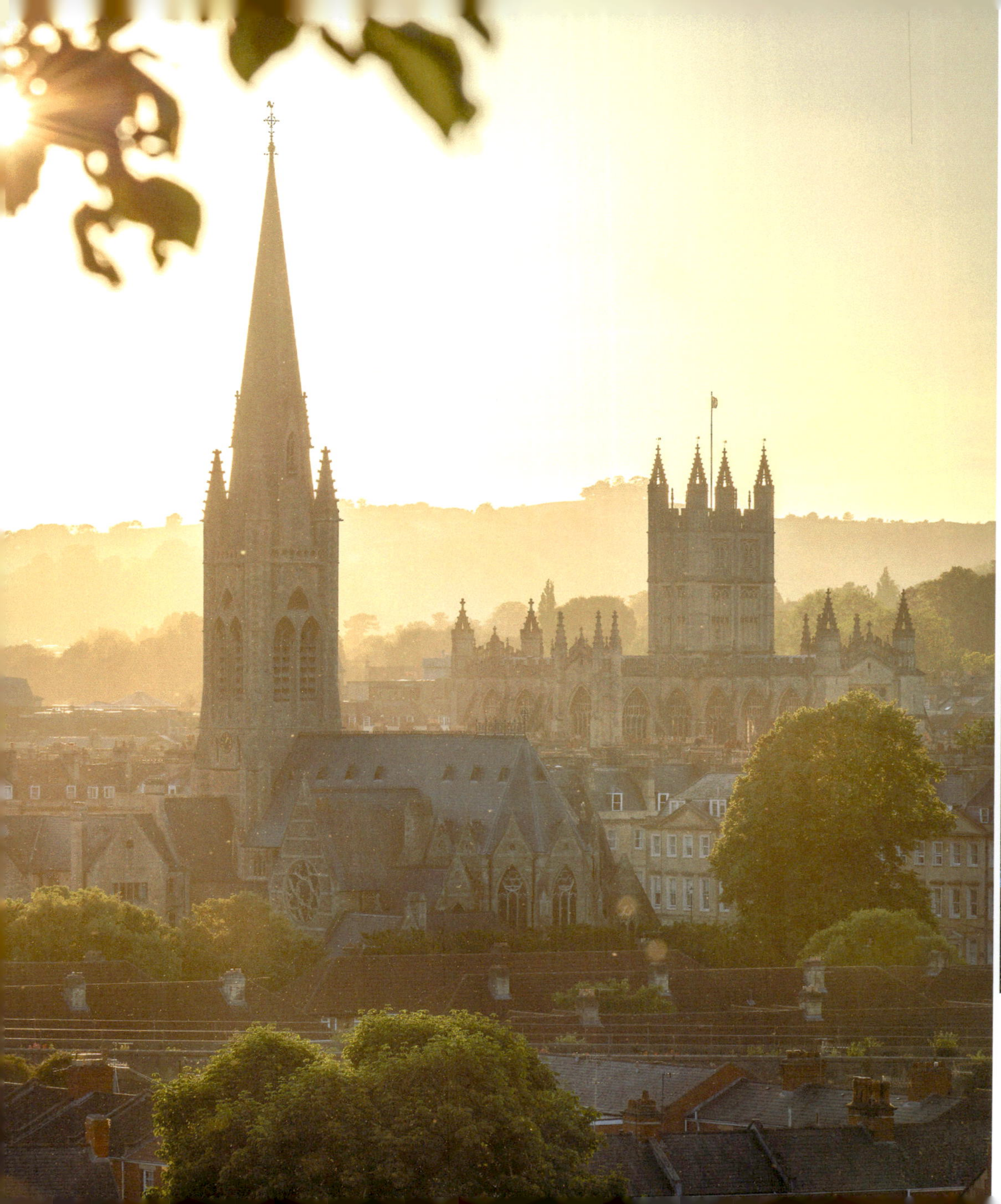

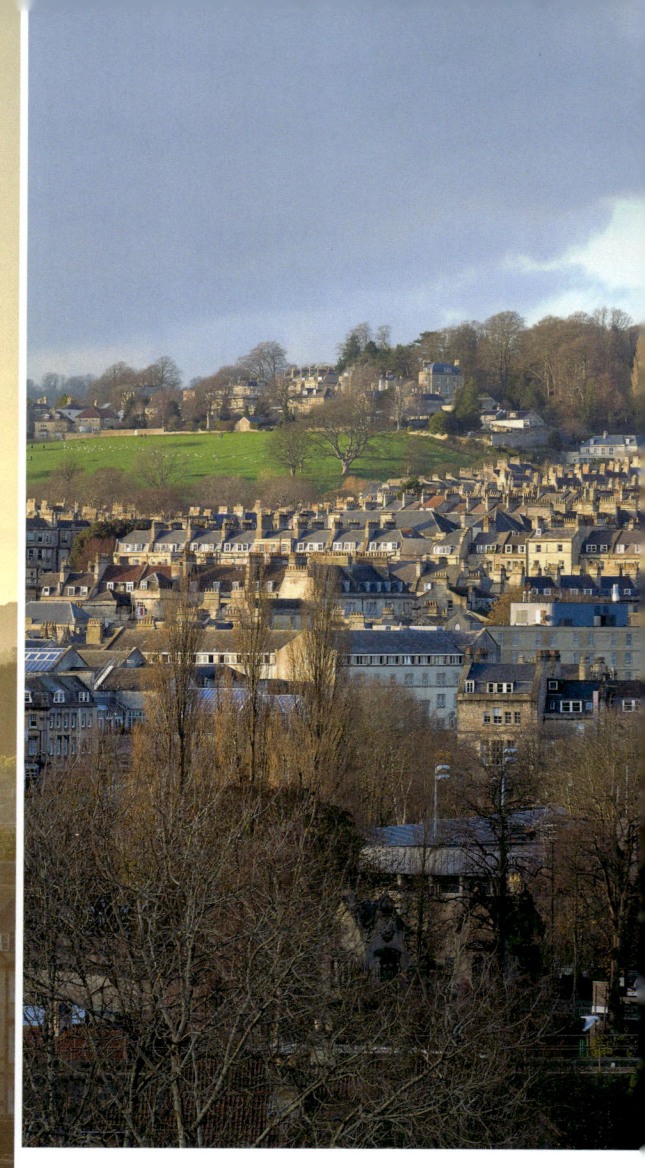

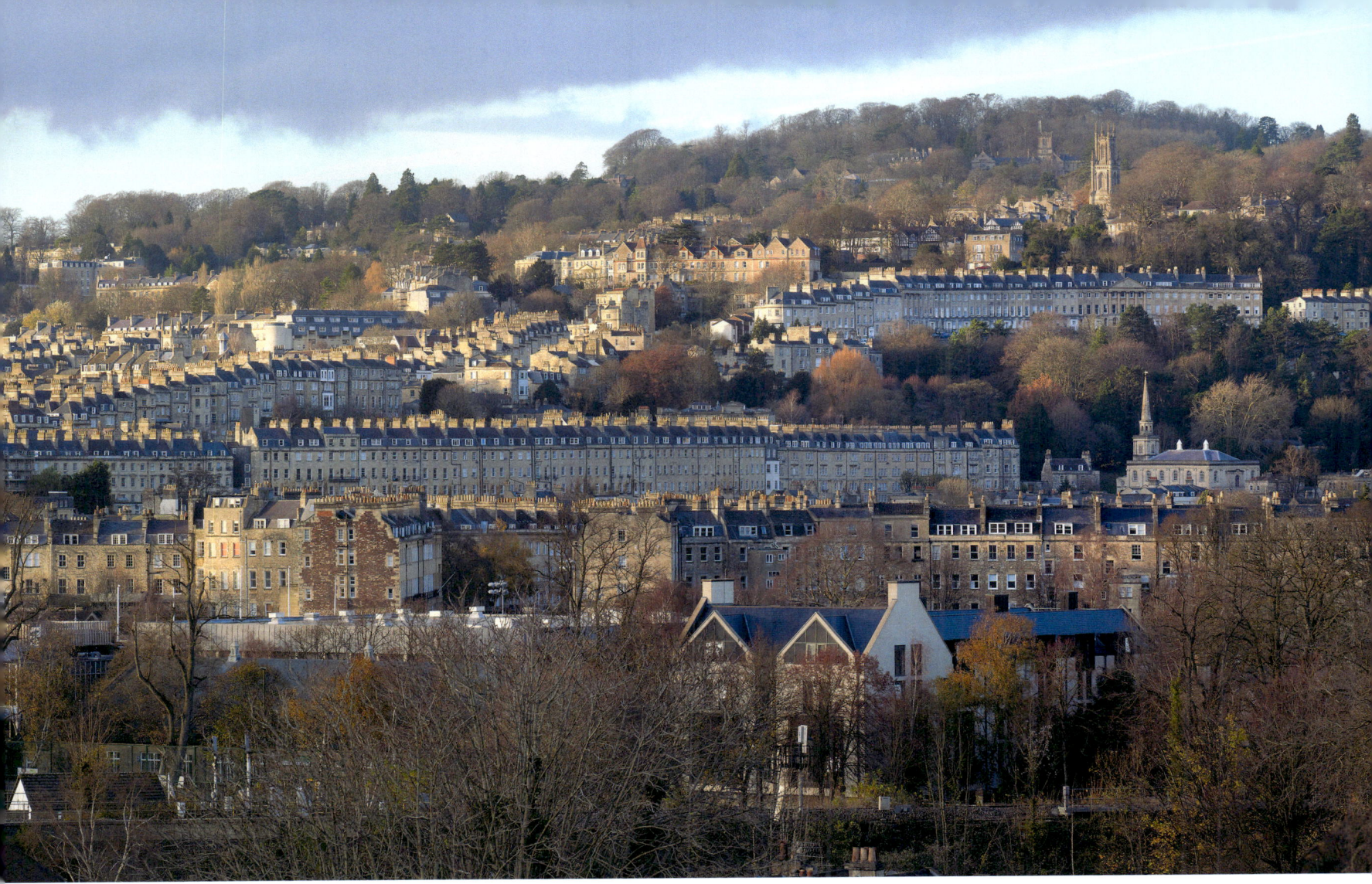

ABOVE: the Paragon stretches gracefully below, while Lansdown Hill climbs skyward to meet the curve of Camden Crescent.
OPPOSITE: St John's Church and Bath Abbey bask in the sunlight.

WARMINSTER ROAD

Located a short walk from Sydney Gardens, Warminster Road provides exceptional views over the eastern fringes of Bath. A small paddock above the Kennet and Avon Canal reveals a gap in the street providing the perfect place to stand and admire the wide ranging vista. This view extends from Camden in the west to the charming residential districts of Larkhall and Charlcombe rising up the hillside beyond.

The long stretch of buildings before you is the rear elevations of Grosvenor Place, a magnificent terrace of 42 tall dwellings built in 1790 by John Eveleigh. On the other side is the main entry route into Bath, the London Road and beyond stands the tall tower of St Saviour's Church, built in a gothic revival style and completed in 1832 and is well regarded for its high quality of architectural detailing.

DIRECTIONS

On Foot: Walk east across Pulteney Bridge and continue along Great Pulteney Street, then turn right onto Sydney Place following the edge of Sydney Gardens northwards. Cross the road at the traffic lights on Warminster Road and walk uphill until you reach the viewpoint located on the northern edge of Holburne Park.

Public Transport: Take First Bus No. 11 or University Bus U1 & U2 to Warminster Road (Holburne Park stop), then walk 2 min uphill to the viewpoint.

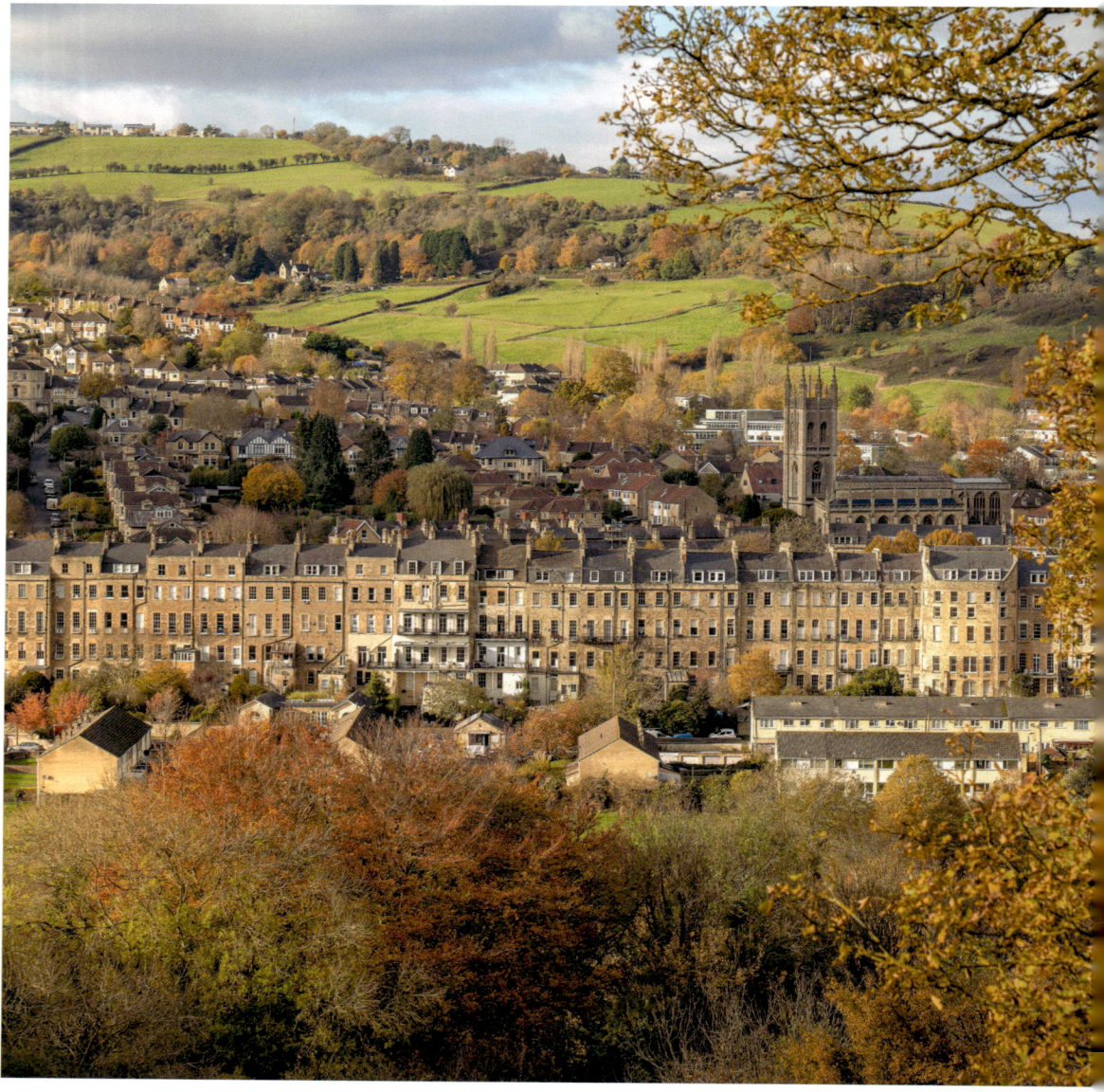

RIGHT: Grosvenor Place traces the line of London Road as it heads past St Saviour's in Larkhall.

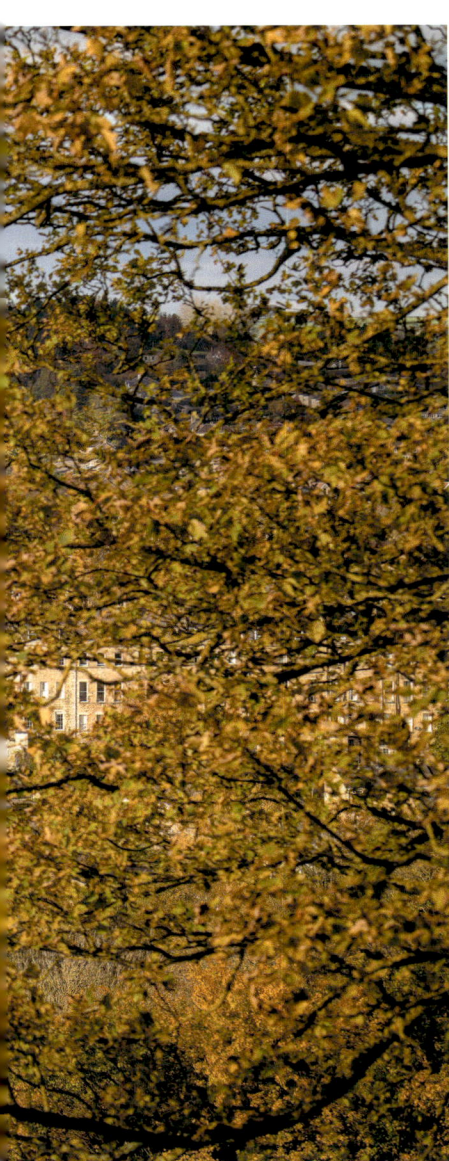

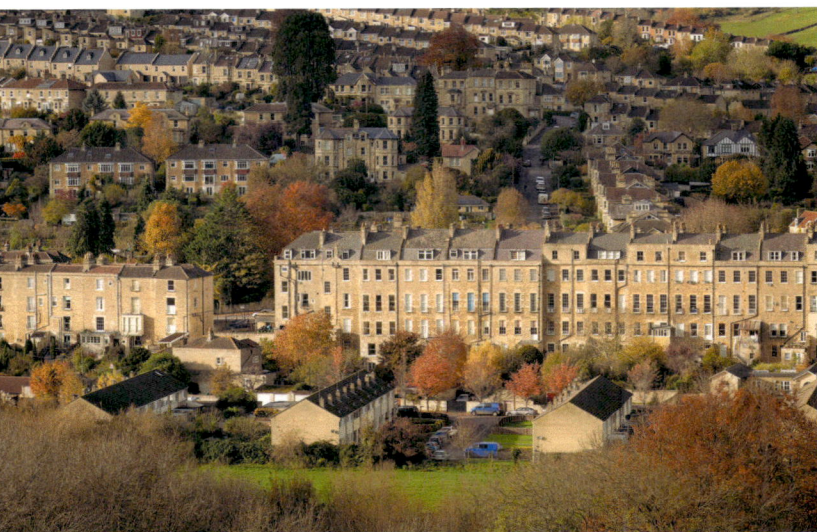

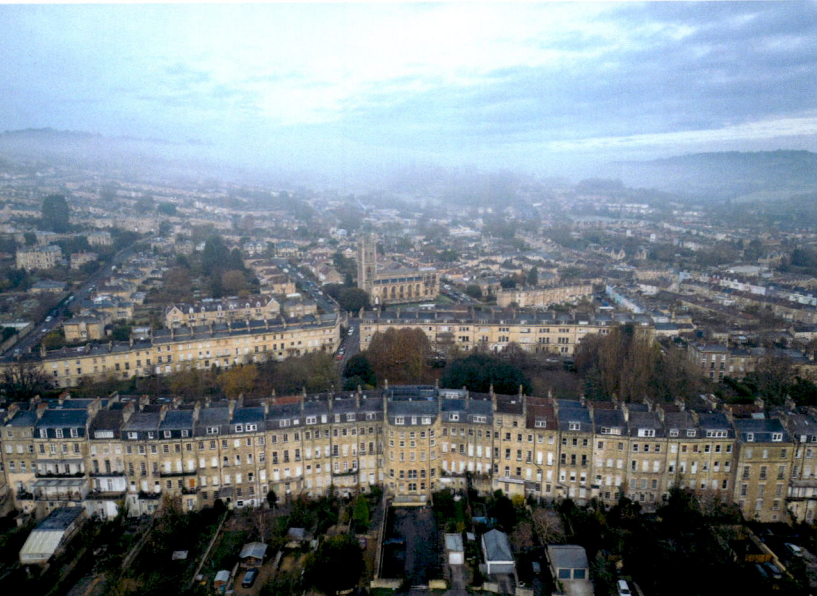

TOP: Bath is one of those unique cities where the backs of buildings are just as attractive as the fronts.

LEFT: the old Grosvenor Hotel sits at the centre, completing the symmetry of the terrace of Grosvenor Place.

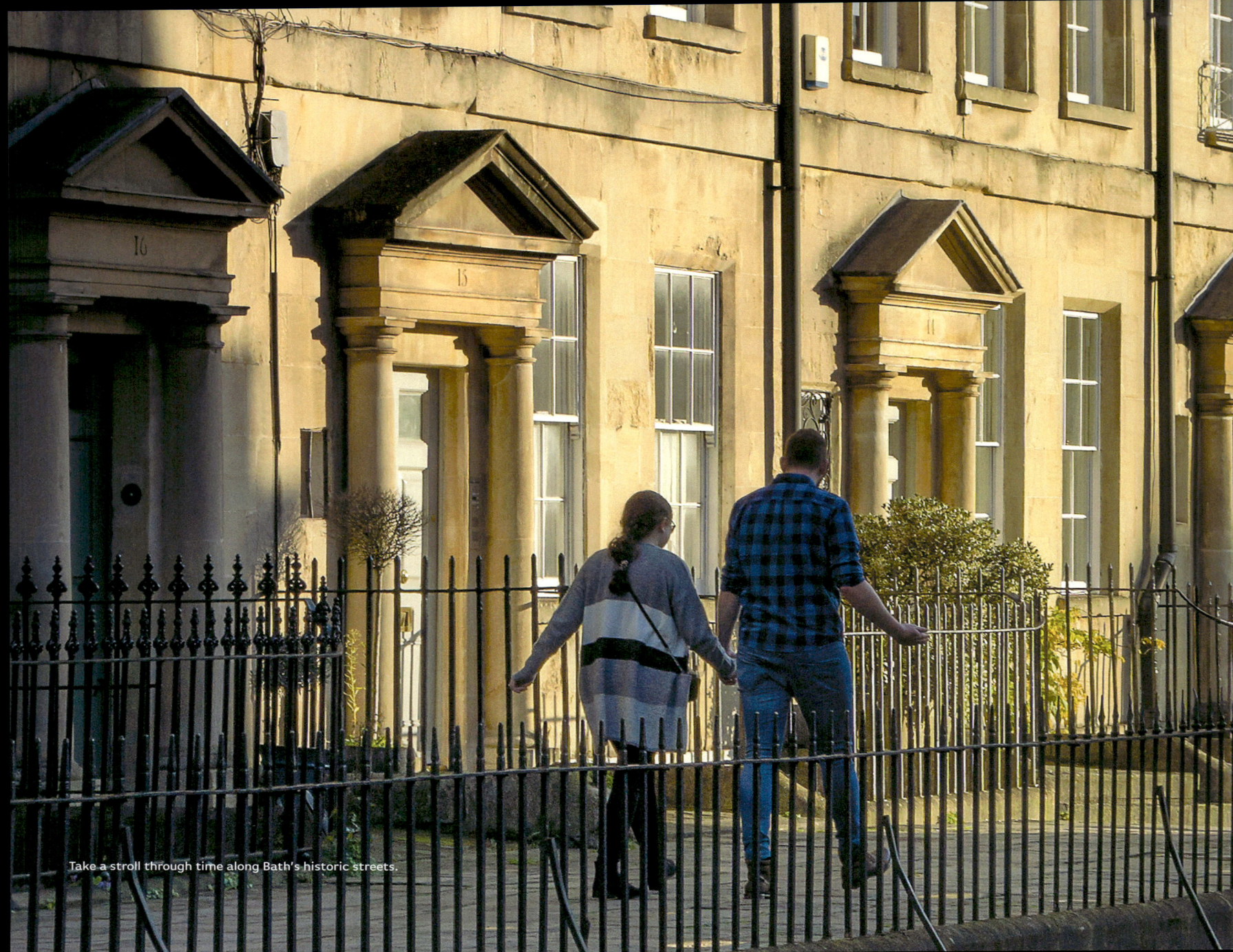
Take a stroll through time along Bath's historic streets.

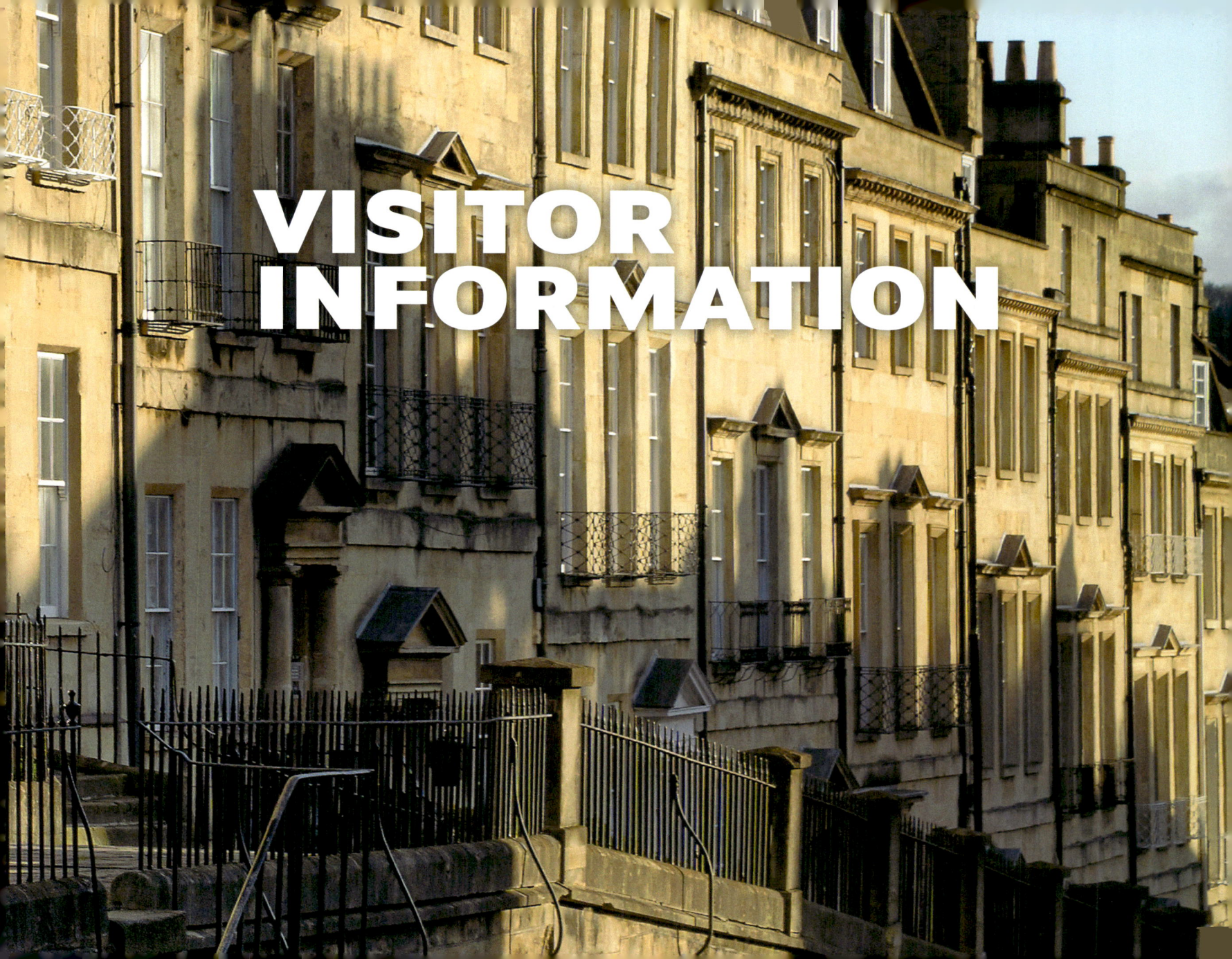

VISITOR INFORMATION

GETTING TO AND AROUND BATH

The City of Bath is located in the county of Somerset, in the southwest of England. It is 115 miles (185 km) west of London and 12 miles (19 km) southeast of Bristol. It is well-connected and accessible from all corners of the UK via train, bus, air, and car.

CAR

Bath is located just off the M4 motorway (Junction 18), making it easy to access by road.

Approximate driving distances and times:

- London – 115 miles / 185 km – 2.5 hours
- Birmingham – 100 miles / 160 km – 2 hours
- Manchester – 175 miles / 280 km – 3.5 to 4 hours
- Cardiff – 60 miles / 96 km – 1.5 hours
- Edinburgh – 370 miles / 595 km – 7 to 8 hours
- Glasgow – 370 miles / 595 km – 7 to 8 hours

PARKING
PARK-AND-RIDE

Be aware that Bath has narrow streets and limited parking, so using a park-and-ride service is recommended. There are three park-and-ride sites around the city: Lansdown, Newbridge, and Odd Down, open every day. Parking is free for those using the bus service which leave every 15 minutes and take 10 minutes to arrive at the centre of Bath.

Bath has multiple car parks within the city centre, catering to both short and long stays (see the map on page 89). The main car parks are Charlotte Street: one of the largest and suitable for long stays, and city centre car parks: Manvers Street, Avon Street, SouthGate and Kingsmead Square. There is also limited on-street parking.

Bus lanes: Bath has several dedicated bus lanes which are clearly marked, use of bus lanes can result in penalties.

RAIL

Bath Spa railway station is in the city centre and served by Great Western Railway. Regular direct trains run from:

- London Paddington – about 1 hour 20 minutes, with multiple services per hour.
- Birmingham New Street – around 2 hours, usually with a change at Bristol Temple Meads.
- Manchester Piccadilly – about 3.5 hours, typically changing at Bristol Temple Meads.
- Cardiff Central – direct trains take 1 hour 10 minutes.
- Edinburgh Waverley – around 6.5 hours, with at least one change.
- Glasgow Central – approximately 6.5 to 7 hours, with connections at Birmingham or Bristol.

BUS

National Express and Megabus operate routes to Bath, often requiring a change in Bristol or London.

- London Victoria Coach Station – about 3 to 3.5 hours.
- Birmingham – around 3.5 to 4.5 hours.
- Cardiff – roughly 2 to 2.5 hours.
- Manchester – about 5 to 6 hours.
- Edinburgh and Glasgow – expect journeys of 9 to 11 hours, usually with changes.

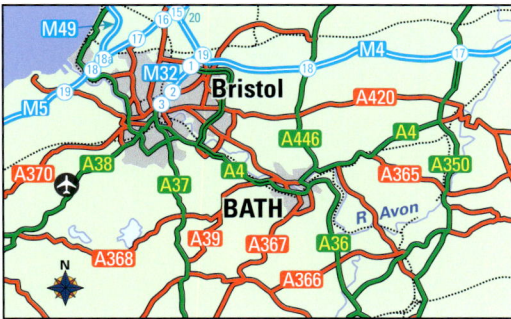

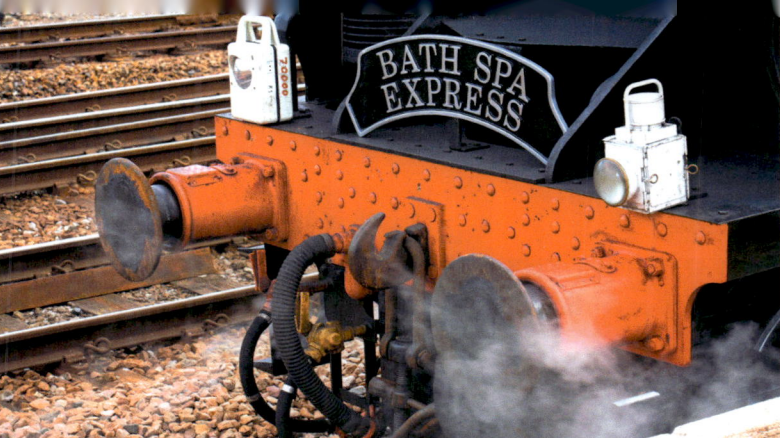

AIRPORTS

Bath is easily accessible from several major airports:

- Bristol Airport (20 miles / 32 km)
- Heathrow Airport (100 miles / 160 km)
- Gatwick Airport (130 miles / 210 km)
- Birmingham Airport (100 miles / 160 km)
- Cardiff Airport (55 miles / 88 km)

GETTING AROUND BATH
ON FOOT

Bath is generally very walkable, and many key attractions are close together in the city centre – but for people with low mobility or wheelchair users, there are a few things to consider.

Bath's compact layout makes it great for walking, especially around the central area, including: Bath Abbey, The Roman Baths, Pulteney Bridge, Royal Crescent and the Circus. Most of the city centre is pedestrian-friendly, and the shopping/restaurant zones are relatively flat.

However cobblestones and uneven pavements are common in older parts and hills and slopes exist – especially north of the city centre toward the Royal Crescent and Lansdown. Some historic sites have steps or limited accessibility.

WHEELCHAIR ACCESSIBILITY

Bath is working to become more accessible, but it's a historic city, so there are challenges:

- The Roman Baths have step-free access, lifts, and free admission for carers.
- Bath Abbey has step-free entry via the south door and internal ramps.
- Thermae Bath Spa has lifts and accessible changing rooms, but some treatments may not be suitable for everyone.
- Buses are generally low-floor and wheelchair-accessible.
- City centre pavements vary – some areas can be tight or uneven.

The *Visit Bath website* and *AccessAble* provide accessibility guides for specific attractions, venues, and routes.

BY BUS

Bath has an excellent bus service operated by First Bus, very useful if you are exploring beyond the heart of the city. Routes and timetables can be found at the First Bus website *firstbus.co.uk*

Bath has several taxi services and you will find e-scooters at designated parking areas around the city centre.

BATH CLIMATE, WEATHER & SEASONAL HIGHLIGHTS

Bath experiences a temperate maritime climate, which is characterised by mild temperatures and moderate rainfall throughout the year. Due to its location in the southwest of England, Bath is influenced by the Atlantic Ocean, leading to relatively stable weather patterns with no extreme seasonal variations. The city's changing seasons make each part of the year distinct.

SPRING (MARCH–MAY)

Spring in Bath is a transitional season marked by gradually increasing temperatures, longer daylight hours, and blossoming nature. March remains relatively cool, with average high temperatures around 11°C (52°F) and lows near 4°C (39°F). As the season progresses, April and May bring warmer days, with highs reaching around 14°C (57°F) and 17°C (63°F), respectively.

Rainfall is moderate in spring, with April often being one of the drier months, averaging around 39 mm of precipitation. However, showers remain frequent, particularly in March and May. Despite occasional wet weather, spring sees an increase in sunshine hours, with May averaging about 5.7 hours of sunshine per day.

Bring a warm jacket, gloves, rain coat and umbrella.

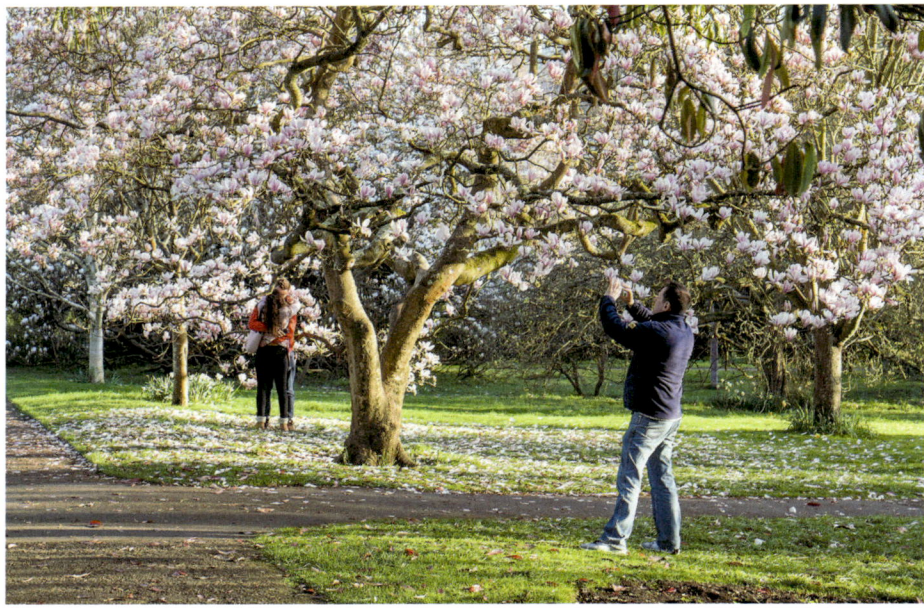

Magnolia flowering in the Botanical Park.

RECOMMENDED

Spring is a magical time in Bath – when the flowers bloom and the city's honey-colored Georgian architecture is framed by fresh greenery. Here are some lovely spots to visit during springtime for floral blooms and blossoms: Royal Victoria Park and the Botanical Gardens, and Sydney Gardens in Bath and further afield Smallcombe Cemetery and vale, Alexandra Park, Prior Park Landscape Garden, Bathampton Down and Bathwick Meadows.

SUMMER (JUNE–AUGUST)

Summer in Bath is typically warm and pleasant, with occasional periods of hotter weather. June marks the beginning of warmer days, with average highs of around 20°C (68°F) and lows near 12°C (54°F). July and August are the warmest months, with daytime temperatures reaching up to 22°C (72°F), though heatwaves can occasionally push temperatures higher.

Rainfall remains moderate, with June and July averaging around 44 mm, while August sees slightly more at 56 mm. The city experiences its highest sunshine levels during summer, with July averaging about 5 hours of sunshine per day. While humidity can increase during warmer spells, Bath rarely experiences the extreme heat seen in other parts of the UK. The pleasant summer weather makes it a popular time to visit Bath's historic sites, enjoy outdoor dining, and explore the surrounding countryside.

RECOMMENDED

Summer in Bath is warm, vibrant, and full of energy – perfect for lounging in green spaces, riverside walks, and soaking up history in the sunshine. Here's a list of places to enjoy when the temperature rises: picnics on the Royal Crescent Lawn, Parade Gardens, Henrietta Park or Bathwick Meadows. Cool walks along the Kennet & Avon Canal, or River Avon. ➜

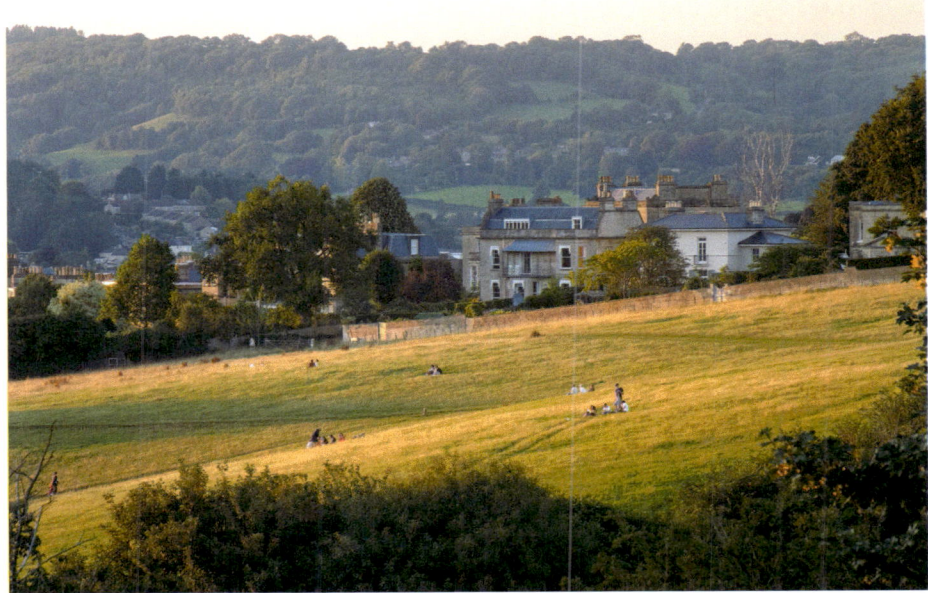

Bathwick meadow on a summer evening.

AUTUMN (SEPTEMBER–NOVEMBER)

Autumn in Bath is characterised by cooling temperatures, shorter days, and increased rainfall. September starts with mild conditions, averaging highs around 19°C (66°F) and lows near 11°C (52°F). By November, daytime highs drop to about 11°C (52°F), with nighttime lows around 5°C (41°F).

Rainfall becomes more frequent in autumn, with October often being one of the wetter months, averaging around 80 mm of precipitation. Wind speeds also tend to increase, bringing crisp autumn air Despite the rain, the season showcases stunning autumn foliage, particularly in Bath's parks and along the river Avon, making it a picturesque time of year. Wrap up again and bring a raincoat and umbrella.

RECOMMENDED

Autumn in Bath is absolutely stunning – golden leaves, crisp air, and the buildings glowing even warmer in the soft autumn light.

Visit any of the local Bath parks, the Kennet & Avon Canal Towpath for reflections of colourful leaves in the canal and further afield for great views of the city over autumn foliage visit viewpoints of the Bath Skyline Walk and Prior Park Landscape Garden.

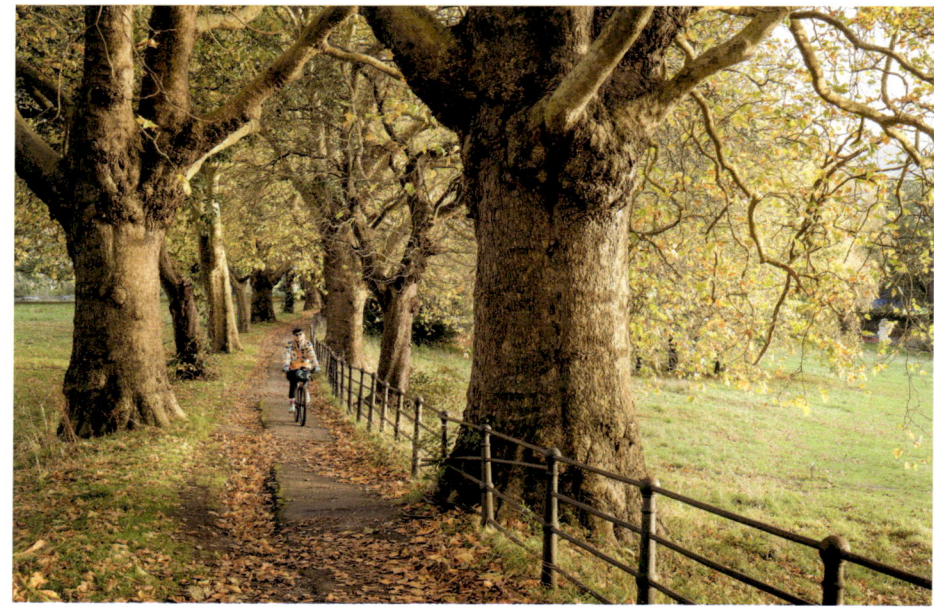

Upper Common above Royal Victoria Park. Bath is blessed with several accessible parks to explore in autumn.

WINTER (DECEMBER–FEBRUARY)

Winters in Bath are generally cold but not extreme, with average high temperatures around 7°C (45°F) and lows near 2°C (36°F). Frost is common, but heavy snowfall is rare, occurring only occasionally. Rainfall remains steady, with December and January receiving around 90 mm of precipitation each.

Despite the shorter days and cooler temperatures, Bath's winter charm is highlighted by festive markets and cozy atmospheres in historic buildings. The city's Roman Baths provide a warm retreat during the colder months, making winter an enchanting time to visit.

RECOMMENDED

Bath Christmas Market is a must-visit if you're here during the season with over 150 wooden chalets selling gifts, food, and mulled wine. Bath Abbey hosts carol services and a beautiful nativity. Thermae Bath Spa will be very special with steam rising from the warm waters. Short walks around the town especially along the river Avon are recommended, and if it snows head up to Alexandra Park for spectacular views across the city.

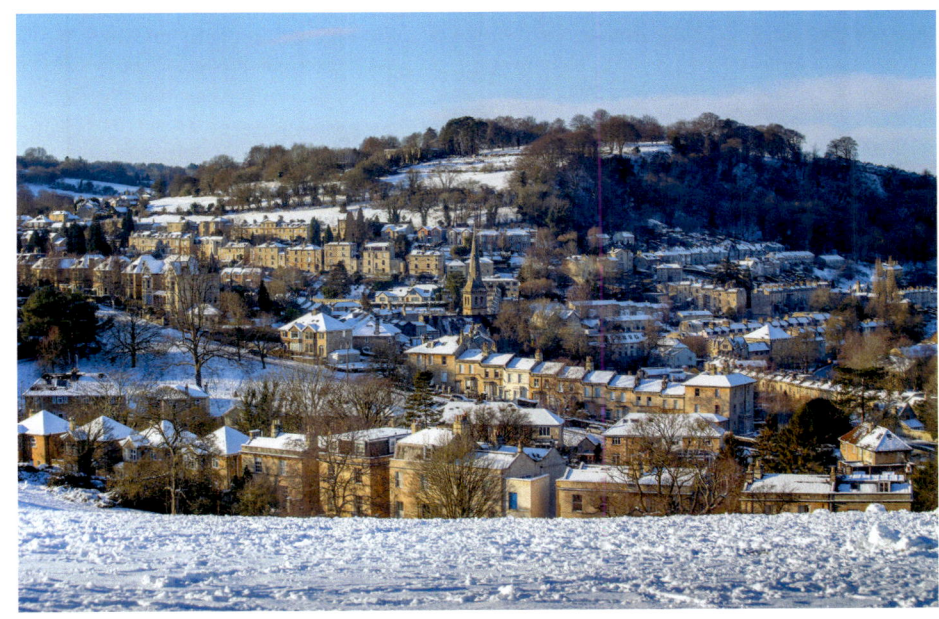

Widecombe in winter. Snow is rare, but if you are lucky, head to one of the viewpoints above Bath.

WHERE TO STAY, EAT, DRINK AND SHOP

Bath is a city that perfectly balances historic elegance with modern sophistication, making it an ideal destination for travellers seeking charm, culture, and comfort, with options to suit every taste and budget. Whether you're visiting for a weekend getaway or a longer stay, the city offers plenty of options for places to stay, dine, drink, and shop – each experience steeped in the city's distinctive character.

Whilst we offer some recommendations here to get you started, the online listings and reviews at the *Visit Bath*, and *The Bath Magazine* websites, and *Bath Life* magazine, are locally produced, current, extensive, authoritative and we recommend that you visit them when making a decision as regards where to stay, dine, drink, and shop.

ACCOMMODATION

Accommodation in Bath caters to a wide range of tastes and budgets. From grand Georgian townhouses converted into chic hotels, to cozy guesthouses and stylish serviced apartments, you can choose to immerse yourself in the city's rich architectural heritage while enjoying contemporary amenities. The city centre is ideal for those who want to be close to the Roman Baths, Bath Abbey, and other key landmarks, while the outskirts offer peaceful retreats with views of the surrounding countryside. If you can, book direct or from StayinBath.org which is owned and run by BIHA, the Bath Independent Hospitality Association.

HOTELS

Queensberry Hotel (5 star, and home to Bath's only Michelin Star restaurant)
The Royal Crescent Hotel (5 star)
The Bath Priory (5 star)
The Gainsborough Bath Spa (Beau Street) (5 star)
The Roseate Villa Bath (Henrietta Road) (5 star)
Macdonald Bath Spa Hotel (Sydney Road) (5 star)
The Francis Hotel (Queen Square) (4 star)
DoubleTree by Hilton Bath (Walcot Street) (4 star)
Hotel Indigo (2–8 South Parade) (4 star)
Abbey Hotel (North Parade) (4 star)
Eight (boutique townhouse at 3 North Parade Passage)
No. 15 (15 Great Pulteney Street) (4 star)
The Bird (18–19 Pulteney Road south) (4 star)

B&B'S & SELF CATERING (AIR BNB ETC, QUIRKIER ACCOMMODATION)

Pulteney House (14 Pulteney Road)
Bath Narrowboats (Sydney Wharf)
Dukes Bath (53–54 Great Pulteney Street)
Grays Boutique B&B (9 Upper Oldfield Park)
Brindleys (14 Pulteney Gardens)
Chestnuts House Boutique B&B (Henrietta Road)
2 Crescent Gardens Guest House
Lock Lodge (Canal side property Widcombe)
Bath Backpackers (13 Pierrepont Street)

BATH BOUNDARY ALTERNATIVE STAYS

The Oakhouse (2 Beechwood Cottages – Oak cabin amongst the trees)
The Straw Bale Lodge (Hilltop Little Solsbury)

For budget options there are Travelodge, Premier Inn, Holiday In Express, Z Hotel and YHA Bath which is set in an 18th-century villa surrounded by private gardens.

EATING

Dining in Bath is a true pleasure, thanks to its diverse and evolving food scene. The city is home to everything from elegant fine dining restaurants to casual cafés and lively bistros. Many establishments emphasise seasonal, locally sourced ingredients, reflecting the region's agricultural roots. Visitors will find a mix of traditional British cuisine and international influences, with plenty of vegetarian and vegan options available. Whether you're after a long, luxurious lunch or a quick bite between sightseeing stops, Bath has something to satisfy every palate. Again check *Visit Bath* and *The Bath Magazine* websites, and *Bath Life* magazine, for reviews and recommendations.

Tea rooms and coffee shops also abound, offering a slower pace and the chance to savour a pot of loose-leaf tea or expertly crafted coffee in a picturesque setting.

RESTAURANTS

The Scallop Shell (22 Monmouth Place) – Seafood
Noya's Kitchen (7 St James's Parade) – Vietnamese
Cote Brassiere (27 Milsom Street) – French
The Elder (2–8 South Parade) – British wild food
The Ivy (39 Milsom Street) – Modern British cuisine
Cosy Club (Southgate Place) – Grill and Tapas
The Botanist (46a Milsom Street) Grills and hearty roasts
The Bath Stable (1–3 Westgate Buildings) – Pizza
Yak Yeti Yak (12 Pierrepont Street) – Nepalese
The Olive Tree (Russell Street beneath Queensbury Hotel) Michelin Star
Corkage (5 Chapel Row – near Queen Square) – Casual dining

CAFES

The Abbey Deli (2 Abbey Street)
Wild Cafe (10a Queen Street)
Walcot House (90B Walcot Street)
Pulteney Bridge Coffee Shop (16 Pulteney Street)
Society Cafe (19 High Street & 5 Kingsmead Square)
The Kingsmead Kitchen (1 Kingsmead Street)
Cafe au Lait (12–14 Dorchester Street)
Treetop Cafe (Royal Victoria Park)

AFTERNOON TEA

The Pump Room Restaurant (Stall Street)
The Mad Hatter's Tea Party (5 Orange Grove)
Sally Lunn's Eating House (4 North Parade Passage)
Sweet Little Things (5 Old Bond Street)
Montagu's Mews (Royal Crescent Hotel)

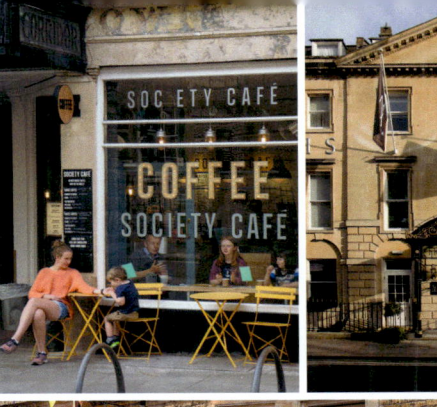
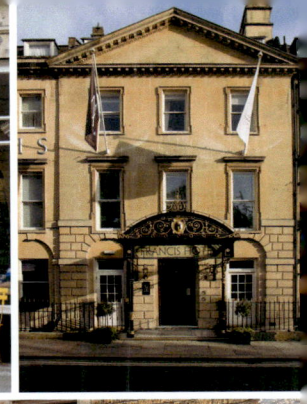
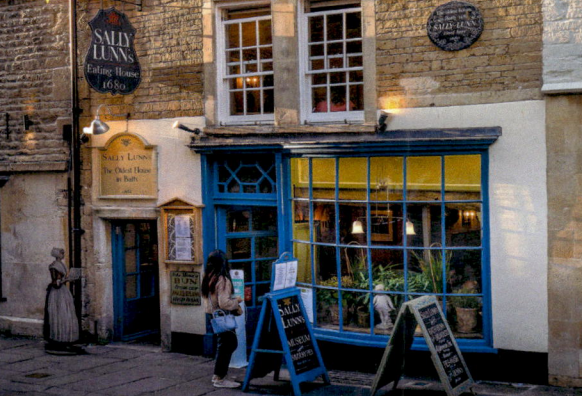
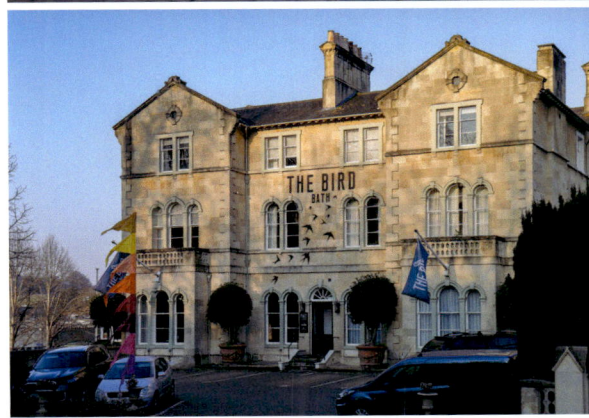

DRINKING

When it comes to drinking, Bath offers an eclectic mix of venues to enjoy a relaxed beverage or a vibrant night out. Historic pubs with characterful interiors and cozy corners sit alongside contemporary cocktail bars and artisan breweries.

BARS & PUBS (TRAD AND GASTRO)

The Star (23 Vineyards, near The Paragon)
The Bell (103 Walcot Street)
The Huntsman (1 Terrace Walk, North Parade)
The Old Green Tree (12 Green Street)
The Grapes (14 Westgate Street)
The Salamander (3 John Street)
The Raven (7 Queen Street)
Pig & Fiddle (2 Saracen Street)
The Bath Brew House (14 James Street West)
The Griffin (Monmouth Street)
Coeur De Lion (17 Northumberland Place)
Marlborough Tavern (35 Marlborough Buildings)
The Bath Distillery Gin Bar (2–3 Queen Street)
Volunteer Riflemans' Arms (3 New Bond St Place)
The Old Green Tree (12 Green Street)
The Crystal Palace (10-11 Abbey Gardens)
See more detailed information about pubs on page 261.

SHOPPING

Shopping in Bath is just as rewarding, with its elegant streets home to a variety of retail experiences. The city combines the best of big-name brands with independent boutiques, artisan stores, and vintage markets. You'll find everything from fashion and homeware to handcrafted gifts and gourmet produce. Bath's layout makes it especially pleasant to explore on foot, with beautiful streets and lanes leading to hidden gems and charming storefronts.

AREAS

Milsom Street – High end and boutique
SouthGate – Familiar high street clothing outlets
Walcot Street – Artisan crafts and independents
Union Street – Central shopping hub

INDEPENDENT SHOPS

The Yellow Shop (72 Walcot Street) – Vintage clothing
Bath Aqua Glass (Main shop at 15 Abbey Churchyard/Glass; Blowing Workshop at 105 Walcot Street)
Always Sundays (9 Broad Street) – Homewares
Toppings Booksellers (York Street)
My Small World Toy Store (19–21 St Lawrence Street)
Mr B's Emporium Bookshop (14–15 John Street)
The Silver Shop of Bath (25 Union Passage) – Jewellery and gifts
Rossiters of Bath (38–41 Broad Street) – Home furniture
Magalleria (5 Upper Borough Walls) – Fine, Independent and Specialist Magazines
Beaux Arts (12–13 York Street) – Contemporary art
Bath Old Books (9C Margaret's Buildings)
Waterstones (4–5 Milsom St)
George Bayntun (23 Manvers St)
The Beaufort Bookshop (1 Beaufort Pl)
Persephone Books (8, Edgar Buildings)
The Oldfield Park Bookshop (43 Moorland Rd)
Skoobs Books (40–42 Guildhall Market)
BookLovers of Bath (12 Bath Rd)
The Jane Austen Centre (40 Gay St)

MARKETS

Walcot Market (Saturdays) – Antiques, arts and collectables
Bath Art Fair (Seasonal) The Pavilion – Original contemporary artwork
Bath Farmer's Market (9am – 1:30pm Saturdays) Green Park Station
Bath Independent Market (3rd Sunday of the month) Green Park Station – Art, craft, vintage and retro wares

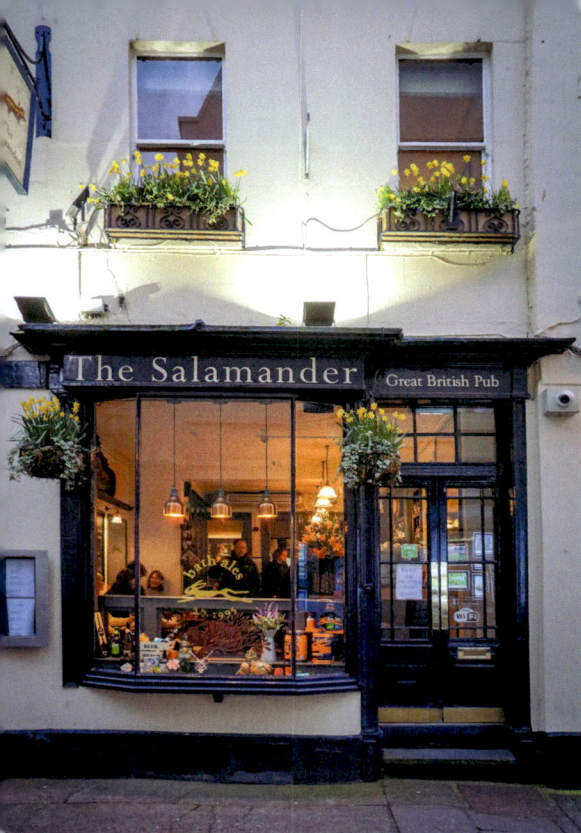
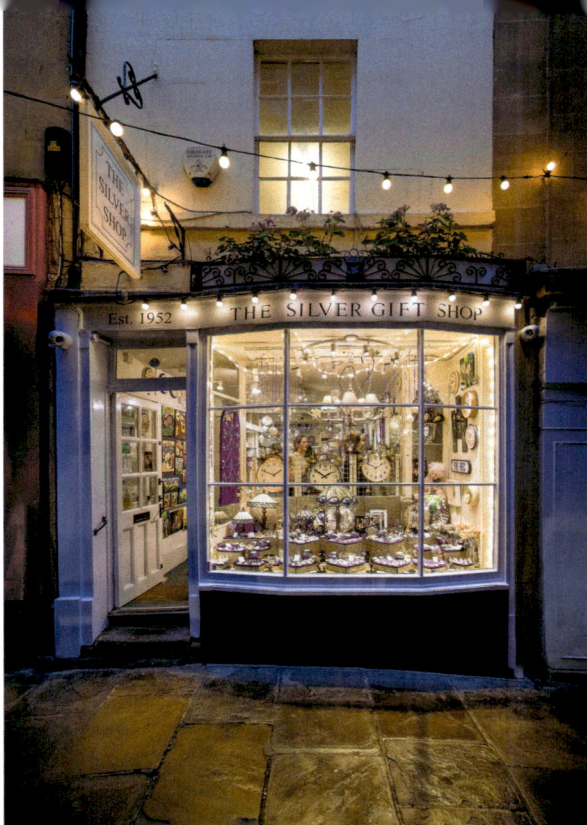
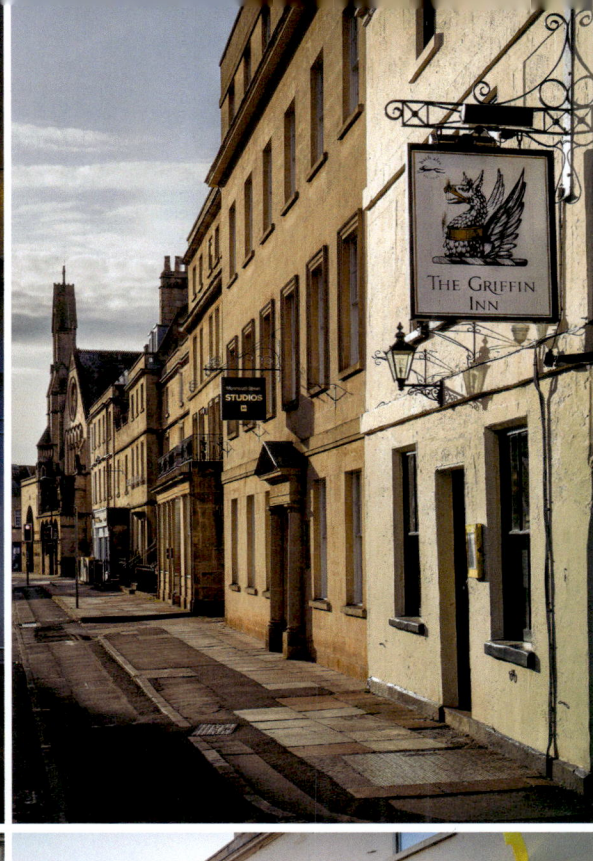
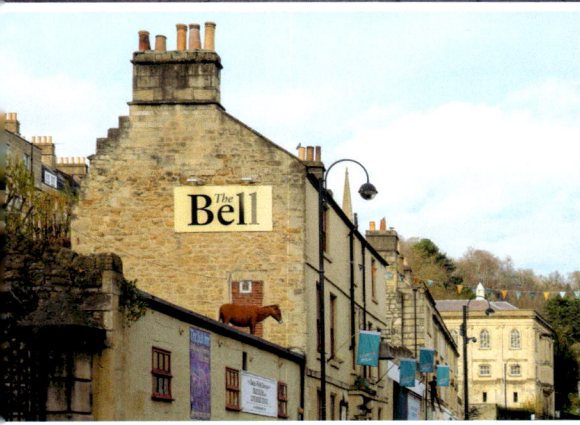
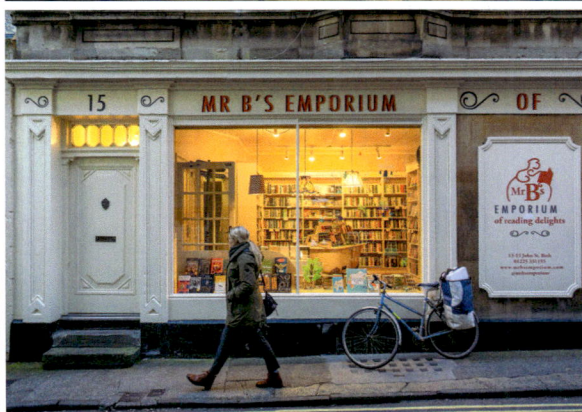
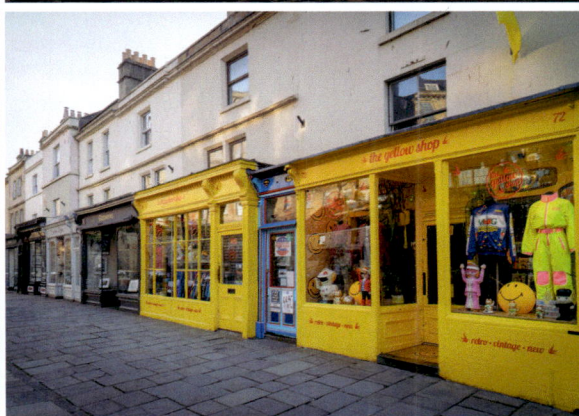

WHERE TC STAY, EAT, DRINK AND SHOP

BATH'S MUSEUMS, AND ART GALLERIES

Bath and its surroundings are home to a rich array of museums and art galleries, each offering unique insights into the city's cultural and historical heritage.

MUSEUMS

No. 1 Royal Crescent .... *1 Royal Crescent, BA1 2LR*
Offers a glimpse into Georgian life, with rooms decorated and furnished as they would have been in the late 18th century.

The Roman Baths .... *Abbey Church Yard, BA1 1LZ*
One of the best-preserved Roman remains in the world, offering a glimpse into ancient bathing rituals and Roman life.

The Holburne Museum .... *Great Pulteney Street, BA2 4DB*
Bath's first public art gallery, housing a collection of fine and decorative arts, including works by Gainsborough and Stubbs.

Jane Austen Centre .... *40 Gay Street, BA1 2NT*
Offers insights into Jane Austen's life and her time in Bath, featuring exhibits and costumed guides.

Museum of Bath at Work .... *Camden Works, Julian Road, BA1 2RH*
Presents the commercial development of Bath over the last 2,000 years, including reconstructions of local businesses.

Herschel Museum of Astronomy .... *19 New King Street, BA1 2BL*
Located in the former home of astronomer William Herschel, who discovered Uranus; the museum showcases his work and achievements.

Bath Royal Literary and Scientific Institution .... *16–18 Queen Square, BA1 2HN*
Houses an antiquarian library and hosts various exhibitions and lectures on scientific and literary topics.

Museum of Bath Architecture .... *The Countess of Huntingdon's Chapel, The Paragon, Bath, BA1 5NA*
Explores the city's architectural history, featuring models, maps, and reconstructions of Georgian buildings.

Beckford's Tower and Museum .... *Lansdown Road, BA1 9BH*
Built in 1827, this tower houses a collection related to William Beckford, reflecting his interests and collections.

Museum of East Asian Art .... *12 Bennett Street, BA1 2QJ*
Houses a collection of ceramics, jades, bronzes, and bamboo carvings from China, Japan, Korea, and Southeast Asia.

American Museum & Gardens .... *Claverton Manor, Bath, BA2 7BD*
Dedicated to Americana, featuring period rooms and folk art, complemented by gardens with replicas of George Washington's Mount Vernon garden.

Fashion Museum Bath
Reopening in 2030. The new museum will be located in the Grade II listed Old Post Office in the heart of the city. Houses a world-class collection of contemporary and historical dress, offering insights into fashion evolution.

ART GALLERIES

Victoria Art Gallery .... *Bridge Street, BA2 4AT*
Bath's public art museum housing paintings, sculpture, and decorative arts, with a mix of historic and contemporary exhibitions.

Beaux Arts Bath .... *12–13 York Street, BA1 1NG*
The city's longest-established independent gallery, showcasing contemporary paintings, sculptures, and ceramics by both established and emerging artists.

44AD artspace .... *4 Abbey Street, BA1 1NN*
A dynamic contemporary art space hosting exhibitions, workshops, and events, supporting local and emerging artists.

Adam Gallery .... *13 John Street, BA1 2JL*
Features contemporary paintings and sculptures from British and international artists.

Rostra Gallery .... *5 George Street, BA1 2EH*
Offers a range of contemporary art, including paintings, prints, sculpture, and jewelry from both established and emerging artists.

The Bartlett Street
Antiques Centre .... *8 Bartlett Street, BA1 2QZ*
Hosts a collection of antiques and artworks from various dealers, providing a diverse range of pieces.

The Francis Gallery .... *3 Fountain Buildings, BA1 5DU*
Focuses on contemporary art with an emphasis on minimalism and Eastern aesthetics, representing international artists.

Walcot Chapel Gallery .... *Walcot Gate, BA1 5UG*
A unique arts venue set in a historic chapel, hosting contemporary art exhibitions and events.

The Edge & Andrew Brownsword
Gallery .... *University of Bath, Claverton Down, Bath, BA2 7A*
A contemporary arts centre hosting exhibitions, performances, and workshops, with a focus on visual arts and interdisciplinary practices.

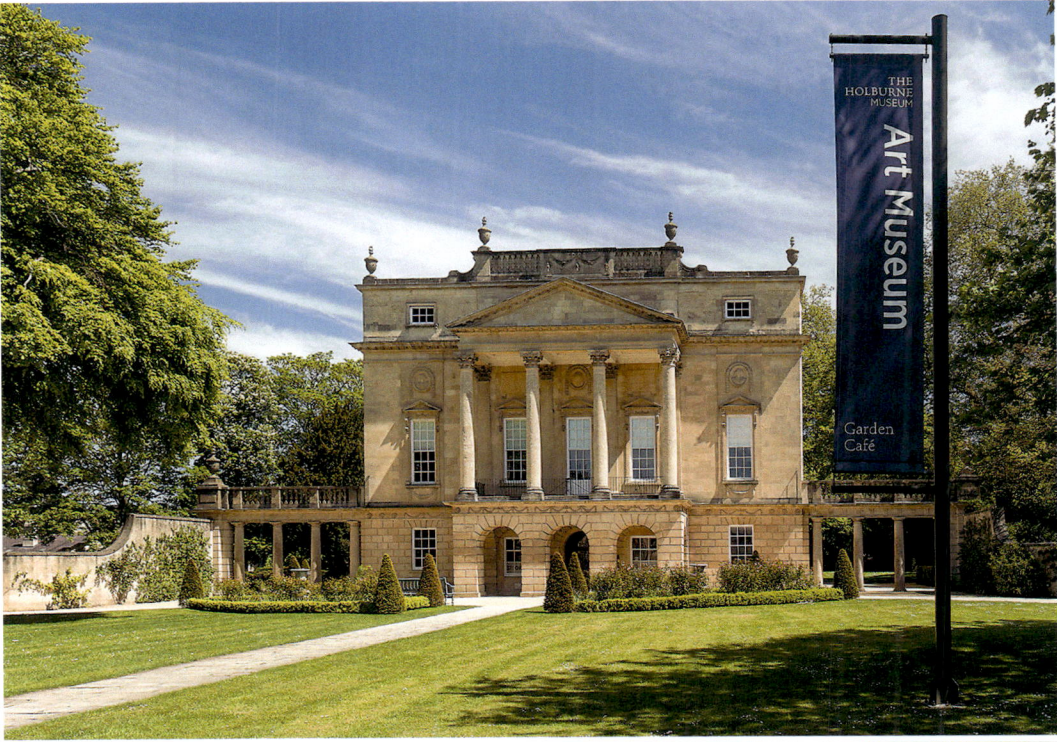

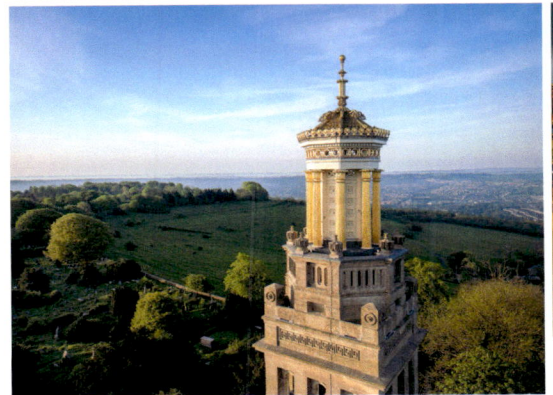

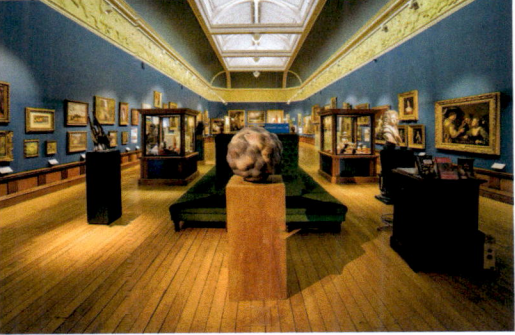

TOP: the Holburne Museum. **ABOVE**: the Victoria Art Gallery. **LEFT**: Beckford's Tower and museum.

BATH'S CINEMAS, THEATRES AND LIVE MUSIC

For an an evening's entertainment, Bath has a great selection of cinemas, theatres, comedy venues, and live music venues. Do a search of a venue to find out what is on.

CINEMAS

Picture House: The Little Theatre Cinema .... *St. Michael's Place, Bath Street, BA1 1SF*
A charming two-screen cinema offering a mix of blockbuster and arthouse films.

ODEON Bath .... *Kingsmead Complex, James Street West, BA1 2BX*
An 8-screen cinema featuring the latest films, complete with a Costa Coffee café.

Everyman Cinema Bath .... *6–8 Dorchester St, BA1 1SS*
Everyman provides a boutique cinematic experience with four screens, a stylish bar, and in-seat dining options, including cocktails and gourmet burgers.

THEATRES

Theatre Royal Bath .... *Sawclose, Bath, BA1 1ET*
A historic Georgian theatre hosting a variety of performances, including plays, musicals, and operas.

The Egg Theatre .... *St. John's Place, BA1 1ET*
A dedicated children's theatre offering innovative performances and workshops for young audiences.

Ustinov Studio .... *Monmouth Street, BA1 1ET*
A studio theatre known for presenting innovative works.

The Mission Theatre .... *32 Corn Street, BA1 1UF*
A 100-seat theatre and arts centre hosting a range of performances and community activities.

The Rondo Theatre .... *St. Saviours Road, BA1 6RT*
A venue known for daring and enjoyable performances, including theatre, comedy, and music.

The Old Theatre Royal .... *12 Old Orchard Street, BA1 1JU*
A historic building with a rich 265-year history, now serving as a Masonic Museum and performance space.

COMEDY VENUES

Komedia Bath .... *22–23 Westgate Street, BA1 1EP*
An award-winning venue presenting the best in comedy, live music, and cinema.

Krowd Keepers: Magic Theatre .... *1 York Street, BA1 1NG*
An intimate venue showcasing some of the world's finest magicians every Friday and Saturday.

The Jesters Comedy Club .... *7 Alfred Street, BA1 2QU*
Bath's underground comedy club hosting regular events.

LIVE MUSIC VENUES

The Forum .... *The Forum, 1A Forum Buildings, BA1 1UG*
As one of Bath's largest venues, The Forum hosts a variety of live music events, including concerts by well-known artists and bands

The Bell Inn .... *103 Walcot Street, BA1 5BW*
A historic, cooperative, free house and music pub offering free live music three times a week, featuring genres like jazz, blues, and folk.

Chapel Arts Centre .... *St. James's Memorial Hall, Lower Borough Walls, BA1 1QR*
A contemporary arts venue hosting live music, theatre, film, and dance events.

Green Park Brasserie .... *6 Green Park Station, BA1 1JB*
A restaurant and bar offering live jazz performances alongside its dining service.

The Cork .... *11–12 Westgate Buildings, BA1 1EB*
Lively bar with karaoke, pub quizzes, bingo and fun. A former debtors prison.

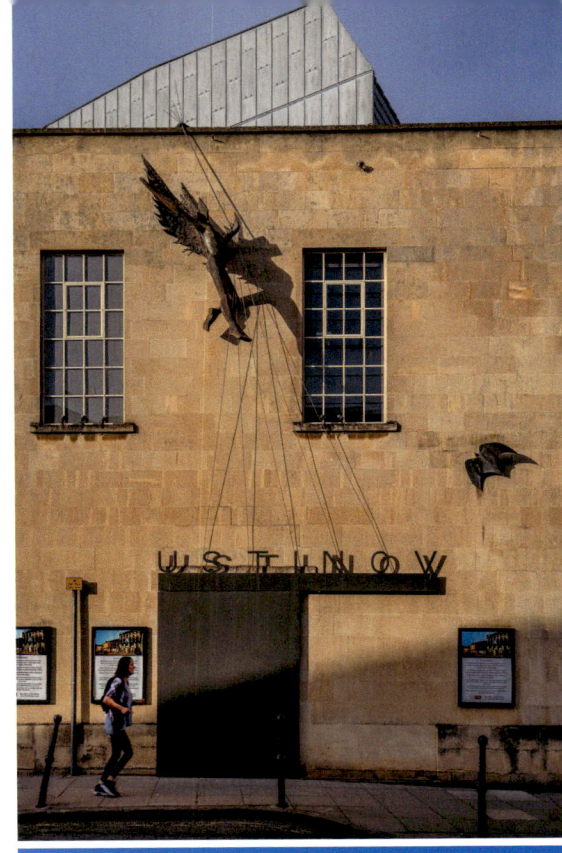
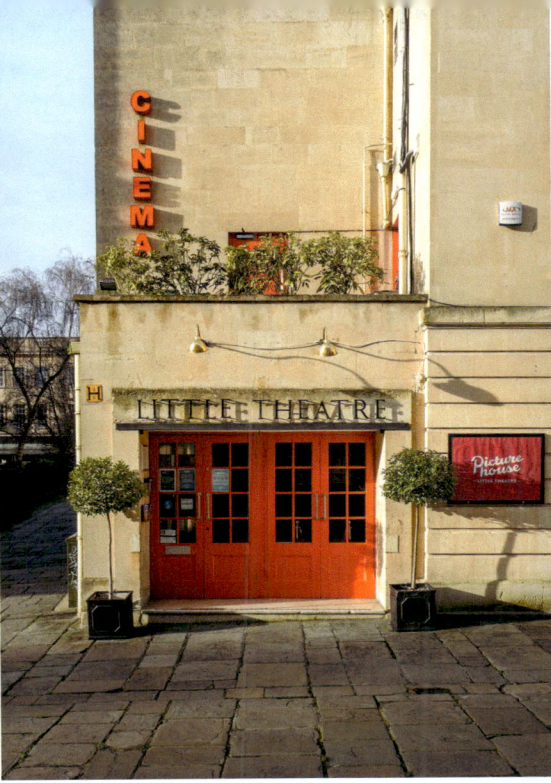
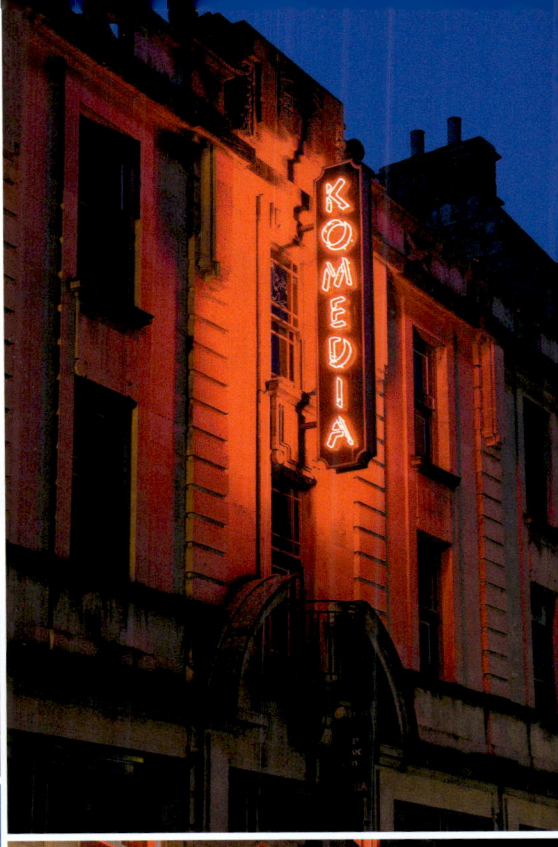
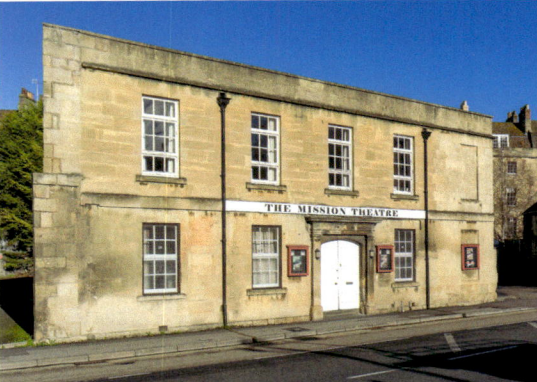
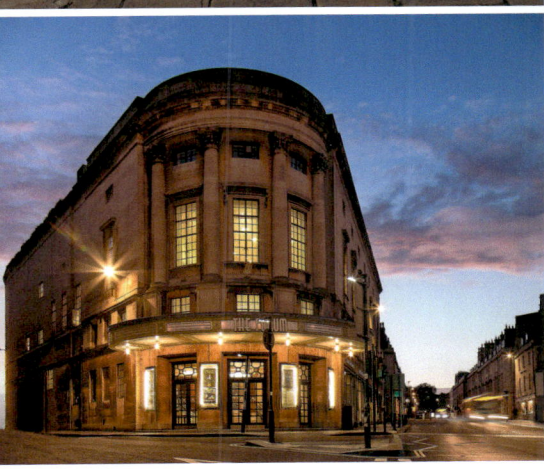
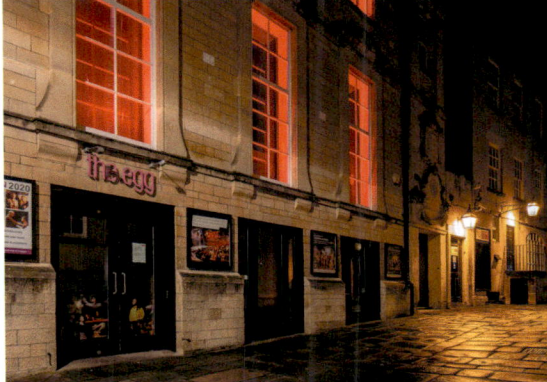

BATH'S CINEMAS, THEATRES AND LIVE MUSIC

BATH'S PARKS AND GARDENS

Bath and its surroundings offer a variety of beautiful gardens, each with its own unique charm and history.

Royal Victoria Park and Botanical Gardens .... *Marlborough Lane, BA1 2NQ*
Established in 1830 and opened by Princess Victoria, this 57-acre park features expansive lawns, a children's play area, and various recreational facilities. Within the park, the Botanical Gardens, created in 1887, house an impressive collection of plants on limestone, including a replica Roman Temple.

Prior Park Landscape Garden .. *Ralph Allen Drive, BBA2 5AH*
Designed in the 18th century with input from poet Alexander Pope and landscape gardener Capability Brown, this garden is renowned for its Palladian bridge – one of only four of its design worldwide. The garden offers sweeping views of Bath and features serene lakes and wooded areas.

Sydney Gardens .... *Sydney Road, BA2 6NT*
As the only remaining 18th-century pleasure garden in the UK, Sydney Gardens boasts historic structures, winding paths, and connections to the Kennet and Avon Canal. Notably, Jane Austen frequented these gardens during her time in Bath.

The Bath Priory Gardens .... *Weston Rd, BA1 2XT*
Covering four acres, the gardens of The Bath Priory hotel encompass a kitchen garden, meadow, and manicured lawns. They provide a peaceful retreat and are meticulously maintained to offer seasonal displays.

Parade Gardens .... *Orange Grove, BA1 1EE*
Located in the city center along the River Avon, Parade Gardens provide fine views of Pulteney Bridge and the weir. The gardens are adorned with vibrant floral displays and offer a serene spot to relax.

Henrietta Park .... *Henrietta Road, BA2 6LP*
Opened in 1897 to commemorate Queen Victoria's Diamond Jubilee, this 7-acre park features ornamental gardens, a pergola, and a sensory garden, making it a delightful spot for leisurely walks.

Alice Park .... *Gloucester Road, BA1 7BL*
A community-focused park offering open spaces, a children's play area, and a café, Alice Park is ideal for families and those seeking a relaxed outdoor environment.

The Georgian Garden .... *The Circus, BA1 2EW*
Located behind The Circus, this restored 18th-century garden reflects the typical layout and planting of the Georgian era, providing insight into historical horticultural practices.

Iford Manor Gardens .... *Iford Manor, Bradford-on-Avon, BA15 2BA*
Located near Bath, these Grade I listed gardens were designed by Edwardian landscape architect Harold Peto. They seamlessly blend Italian, Byzantine, and Oriental styles, featuring terraces, sculptures, and tranquil water features.

American Museum & Gardens .... *Claverton Manor, Claverton Down, Bath, BA2 7BD*
Situated on the outskirts of Bath, this museum is dedicated to Americana and is complemented by gardens that include replicas of George Washington's Mount Vernon garden and a Lewis and Clark trail. The hilltop location offers panoramic views of the Limpley Stoke Valley and River Avon.

Dyrham Park .... *Dyrham, Chippenham, SN14 8ER*
A grand baroque mansion set within an ancient deer park, Dyrham Park offers formal gardens, expansive parkland, and stunning views over the Gloucestershire countryside.

OPPOSITE TOP LEFT: Parade Gardens. **TOP RIGHT**: Alice Park. **BOTTOM LEFT**: Sydney Gardens. **BOTTOM MIDDLE**: Royal Victoria Park. **BOTTOM RIGHT**: Dyrham Park.

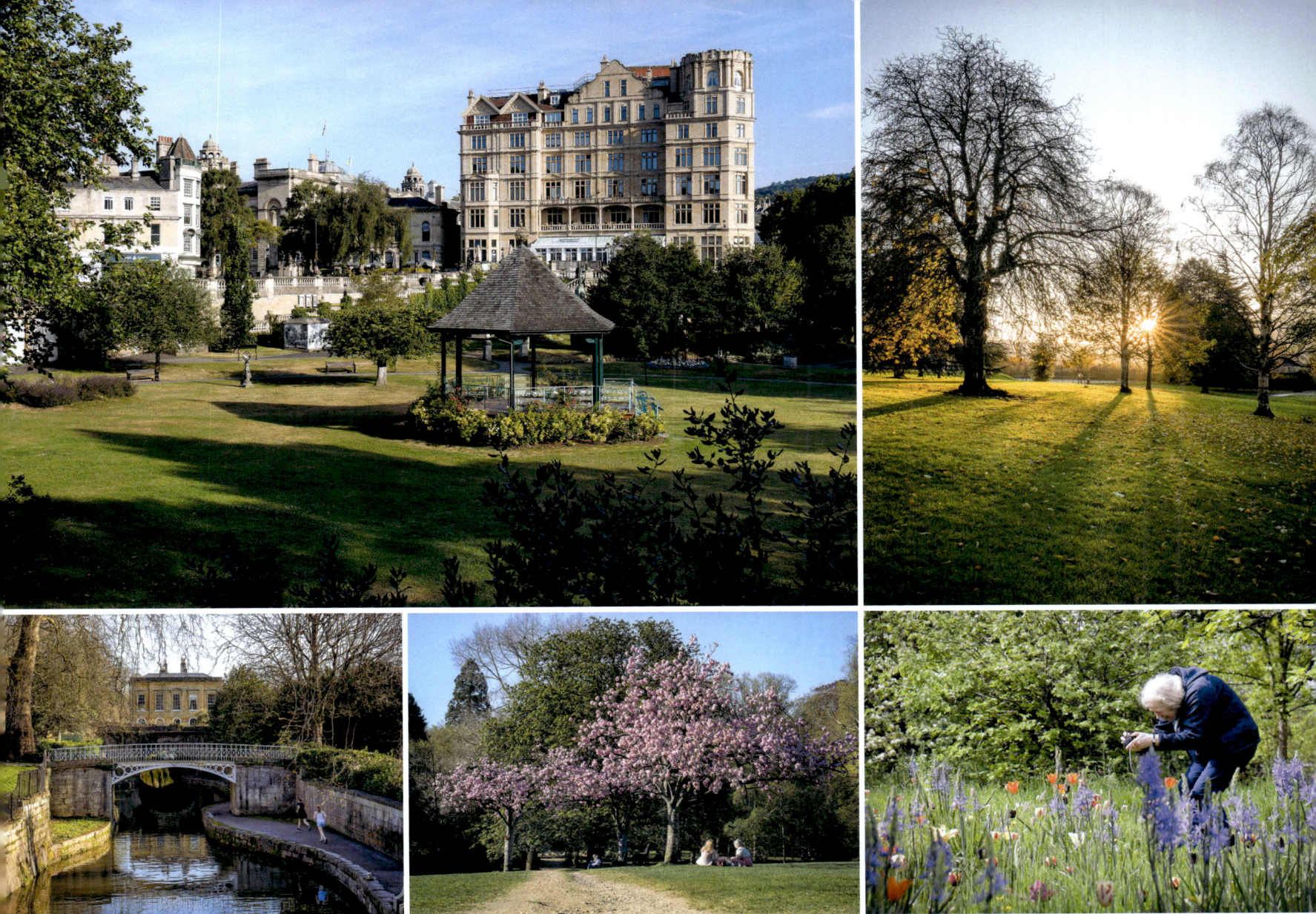

BATH'S PARKS AND GARDENS

SPAS AND WELLBEING

Bath is a haven for spa and wellness retreats. Surrounded by rolling countryside and historic architecture, it offers a perfect setting for relaxation and rejuvenation. Wellness centres here blend traditional healing with modern therapies, providing treatments like hydrotherapy, massages, aromatherapy, and holistic health experiences. Many retreats are set within elegant Georgian buildings or tranquil rural estates offering spa days or a weekend escapes.

Thermae Bath Spa .... *The Hetling Pump Room, Hot Bath Street, BA1 1SJ*
Britain's only natural thermal spa, offering an open-air rooftop pool with panoramic city views, along with a variety of spa treatments and wellness facilities. Incorporates the Cross Bath where the Celts revered their goddess Sul.

The Spa & Bath House at The Royal Crescent Hotel .... *16 Royal Crescent, BA1 2LS*
Situated within the historic Royal Crescent Hotel, this spa features a 12-meter heated relaxation pool, sauna, and a range of holistic treatments in a serene setting.

The Garden Spa by L'OCCITANE at The Bath Priory .... *Weston Road, BA1 2XT*
A tranquil spa offering L'OCCITANE treatments, featuring an indoor pool, sauna, and aroma steam room set within beautiful gardens.

The Spa at No.15 by GuestHouse .... *15 Great Pulteney Street, BA2 4BS*
An intimate spa with bespoke therapies using eco-luxury products, including unique treatment rooms and a focus on mood-boosting treatments.

The Gainsborough Bath Spa .... *Beau Street, BA1 1QY*
A luxury spa hotel with exclusive access to Bath's natural thermal waters, offering Asian-inspired therapies and a serene spa village.

Macdonald Bath Spa Hotel .... *Sydney Road, BA2 6NS*
A 5-star hotel featuring a luxurious spa with a hydrotherapy pool, thermal suite, and a range of rejuvenating treatments.

The Soul Spa .... *2 Hetling Ct, BA1 1SH*
Tucked away in the heart of the Spa Quarter of Bath, the Soul Spa is a space dedicated to mind-body health and fitness.

Lush Spa Bath .... *8 Union St, Bath BA1 1RW*
Lush Spa Bath is a calming retreat above the Lush store, offering tailored treatments using fresh, handmade products in a cosy, cottage-style setting.

OUTSIDE OF BATH

Homewood Hotel & Spa .... *Abbey Lane, Freshford, Bath, BA2 7TB*
Located just outside Bath, this country house hotel offers a boutique spa with an outdoor heated pool, sauna, steam room, and treatment rooms.

The Spa at Lucknam Park .... *Lucknam Park, Colerne, Chippenham, SN14 8AZ*
A luxurious spa set within a country house hotel, featuring a 20-meter indoor pool, hydrotherapy pool, and extensive thermal cabins.

Aqua Sana at Longleat Forest .... *Center Parcs, Longleat Forest, Warminster, BA12 7PU*
Situated a short drive from Bath, this spa offers 24 nature-inspired experiences, including a forest cavern and moonlight steam room.

Babington House .... *Charity Lane, Frome, BA11 3RW*
A Georgian manor offering a members-only spa with a range of treatments, set within the Somerset countryside

OPPOSITE: the Gainsborough Bath Spa.

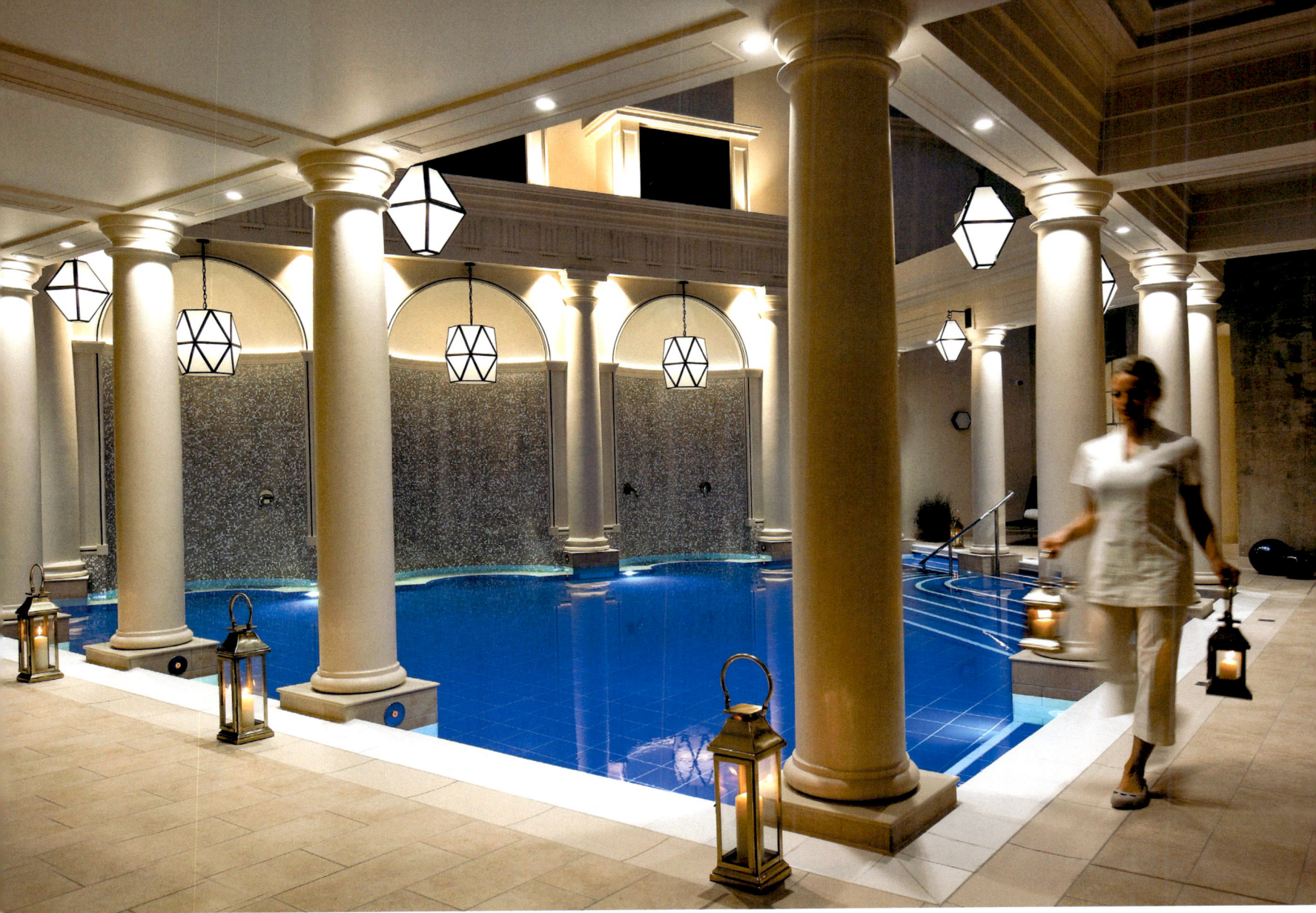

FAMILY FRIENDLY ACTIVITIES AND SPORTS

Whilst the city's attractions, parks, open spaces, and riverside paths offer plenty of opportunities for active days out together, here are some other options for both the sporty and the young.

Bath Sports & Leisure .... *North Parade Road, BA2 4ET*
Bath Sports & Leisure Centre features a 120-station gym, swimming pools, fitness studios, a sports hall, a trampoline park, bowling alleys, and a soft play area.

Royal Victoria Park .... *Marlborough Lane, BA1 2NQ*
As well as a place to enjoy beautiful parkland, the park features an extensive adventure playground equipped with climbing frames, zip lines, a skatepark, and a sandpit, catering to children of various ages.

Bath City Farm .... *Kelston View, Whiteway, Bath, BA2 1NW*
Bath City Farm offers a variety of engaging activities for children. The farm features a playground designed with wood and tyres to inspire imaginative play, and children can interact with various animals, including pigs, sheep, goats, chickens, and ducks.

The Egg Theatre .... *Sawclose, Bath, BA1 1ET*
The Egg Theatre is the Theatre Royal's dedicated venue for children, young people, and families. It offers a diverse program of performances and workshops tailored for audiences from toddlers to teenagers

The Bird of Prey Project .... *Newton St Loe, Bath, BA2 9BT*
The Bird of Prey Project offers engaging children's wildlife workshops designed for ages 6 to 11, focusing on education, teamwork, and compassion for animals.

Yuup Bath
Yuup Bath is an online platform that offers a variety of local experiences in and around Bath, including activities suitable for children. Families can book workshops and adventures such as pottery classes, foraging excursions, and craft sessions. Visit yuup.co/cities/bath

Horse Riding at Lucknam Park .... *Lucknam Park, Colerne,* .... *Chippenham, Wiltshire, SN14 8AZ*
Lucknam Park Equestrian Centre offers a range of horse riding experiences tailored for children. The centre provides pony hire for young riders aged three and above, who must be accompanied by a parent or guardian, allowing them to enjoy escorted hacks around the estate.

Bicycle Hire
Bath offers several bicycle hire providers to help you explore the city and its surroundings: Bath Bike Hire, Bath Boats & Cycles, Bath Ebike Hire and Julian House Bike Workshop

Narrowboats
Bath has several narrowboat hire options for those looking to explore its scenic waterways: Bath Narrowboats, Bath Canal Boat Company, Narrow Escape, Starline Narrowboats and Bloomsbury Canal Boats.

Paddleboard (SUP)
Several paddleboarding providers catering to various skill levels: Bath Outdoors, LiveFree Adventures, Original Wild, Bath Paddleboard Centre and City SUP Adventure.

River Avon Cruises
Both Pulteney Cruisers and River Adventures offer boat trips along the river Avon, both do private groups, with Pulteney Cruisers also serving individuals and smaller groups. Pulteney Cruisers run several trips a day, with two boats running at weekends and you can board at Pulteney Weir, accessed from the Pulteney Bridge steps, on a first come first served basis.

Watch a game
Rugby enthusiasts can attend Bath Rugby's home games at the Recreation Ground, centrally located along the River Avon. Football fans can visit Twerton Park to watch Bath City Football Club and cricket enthusiasts can enjoy matches at Bath Cricket Club's North Parade Ground.

OPPOSITE TOP LEFT: Stand Up Paddleboarding on the river Avon through Bath. **TOP RIGHT**: the Pulteney Cruisers leave from Pulteney Weir several times a day. **BOTTOM LEFT**: Bath Cricket Club, founded in 1859, play in the summer at their North Parade Ground by the river Avon. **BOTTOM RIGHT**: you can hire a canal narrowboat to cruise along the Kennet & Avon Canal.

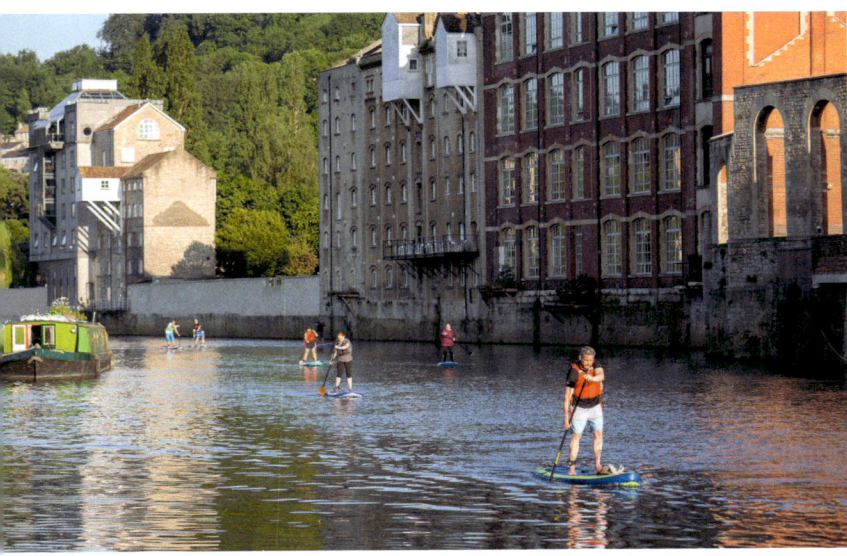
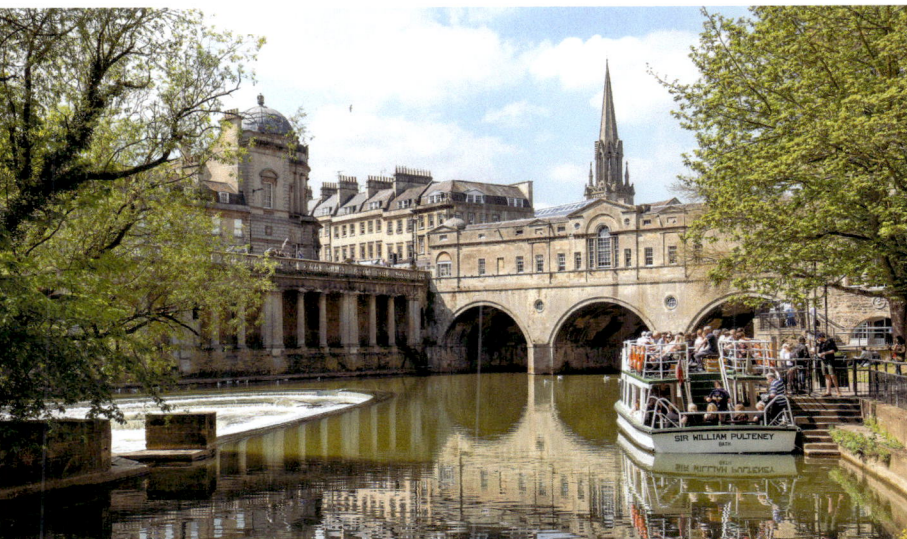
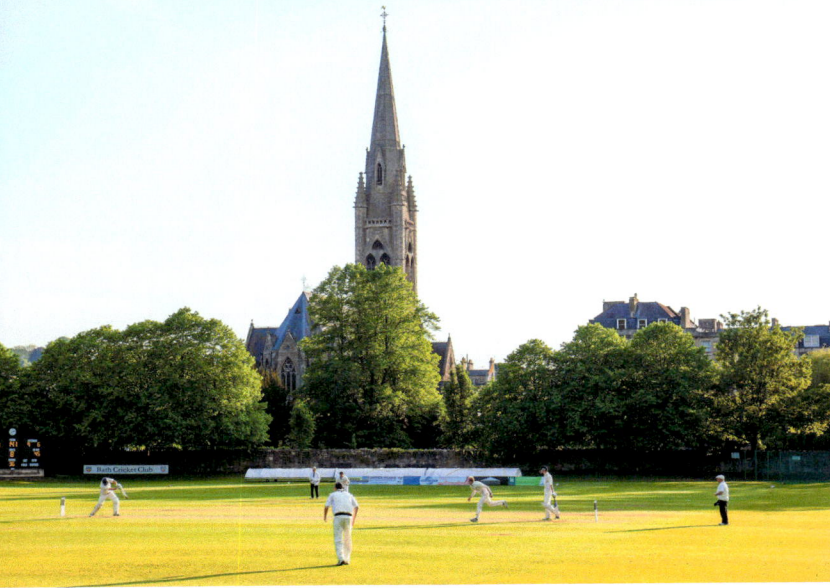
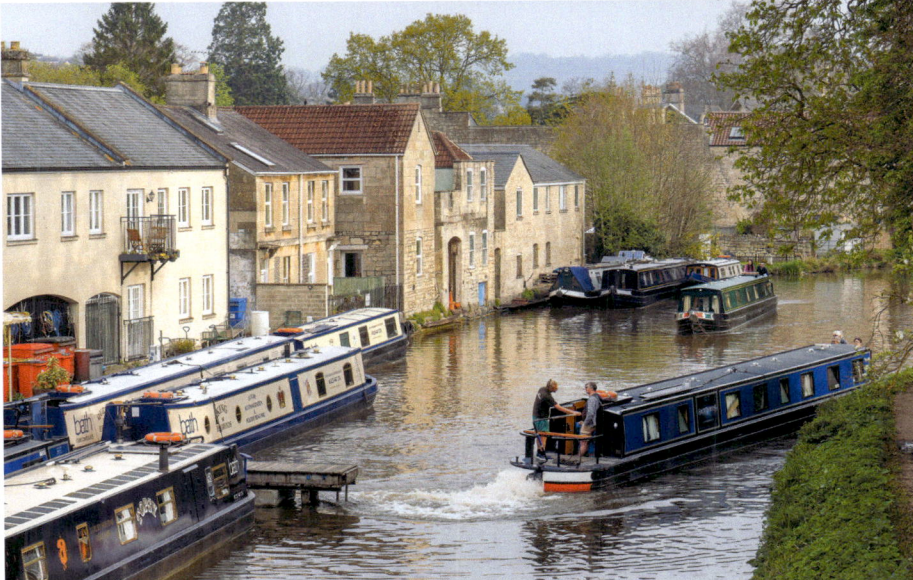

FAMILY FRIENDLY ACTIVITIES AND SPORTS   **245**

BATH GUIDED TOURS

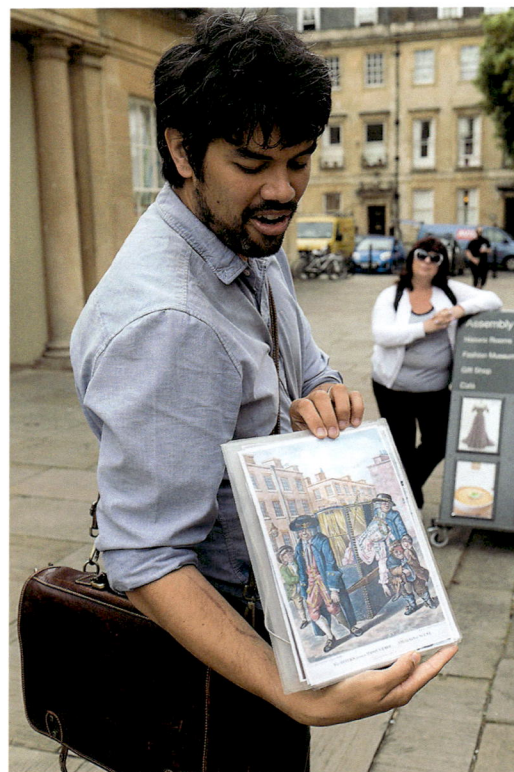

Bath offers a variety of guided tours that showcase its rich history, stunning architecture, and cultural significance. Most guides include Bridgerton Filming Locations Tour (see page 38).

The Mayor of Bath's Honorary Guides
bathguides.org.uk
This organisation provides free historic walking tours led by knowledgeable volunteers, offering insights into Bath's development, architecture, and UNESCO World Heritage status. Tours depart daily from outside the Roman Baths.

Footprints Tours
footprints-tours.com
Led by university students, Footprints Tours offers engaging walking tours that blend historical facts with entertaining anecdotes. Their offerings include free walking tours and specialised options like the Roman Baths & City Tour.

In & Beyond Bath
inandbeyondbath.com
In & Beyond Bath provides themed walking tours such as "Jane Austen's Bath" and "Bath's Favourite Filming Locations," delving into the city's literary connections and its role as a backdrop for various films and series.

Bath Walking Tours
travel-buddies.com
Offering comprehensive explorations of Bath's landmarks, these tours cover iconic sites like the Roman Baths, Royal Crescent, and Bath Abbey, providing a deep dive into the city's history and architecture.

City of Bath Guides
cityofbathguides.com
This group offers a range of tours with experienced guides, including options by coach, walking, or private car, catering to diverse interests and providing in-depth knowledge of Bath's heritage.

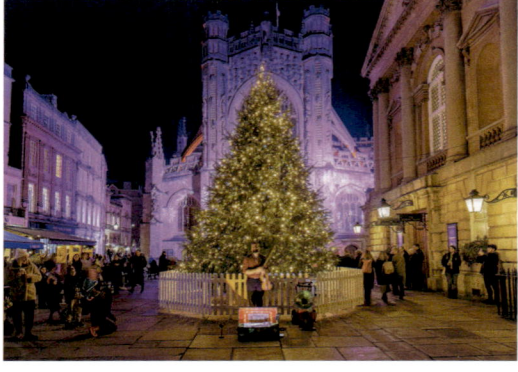

TOP: going on a guided tour will enhance your understanding of Bath. **RIGHT:** the Bath Christmas Market is held late November to mid-December.

BATH EVENTS

Bath hosts a vibrant array of annual and occasional events that celebrate its rich cultural heritage, arts, literature, and community spirit.

For the most current information, it is advisable to check the official event websites or the *Visit Bath* events calendar and *bathfestivals.org.uk*

February
Bath Bachfest
A festival dedicated to the works of Johann Sebastian Bach and his contemporaries, featuring performances by renowned classical musicians in historic venues.

March
Bath Half Marathon
One of the UK's most popular city centre road races, the Bath Half Marathon is a fast, flat course straddling both sides of the River Avon, attracting thousands of runners and spectators.

FilmBath Festival
An annual film festival presenting a diverse selection of films, including previews, documentaries, and shorts, often accompanied by director Q&As and panel discussions.

March/April
Bath Comedy Festival
A celebration of comedy featuring stand-up performances, workshops, and shows across various venues in the city, showcasing both established and emerging comedians.

May
Bath Music Festival
This festival features a curated collection of concerts in some of Bath's most beautiful venues, showcasing internationally renowned artists performing classical pieces from composers like Beethoven, Bach, Mozart, Haydn, and Brahms.

Bath Literature Festival
The Bath Literature Festival is an annual celebration of literature, ideas, and creativity, featuring a diverse lineup of authors, speakers, and events.

September
The Jane Austen Festival
Celebrating Bath's most famous literary resident, this festival includes the Regency Costumed Promenade, where over 500 participants dress in period attire, along with guided walks, costumed balls, theatrical performances, and talks inspired by Jane Austen's works.

September/October
Bath Children's Literature Festival
The largest dedicated children's literature festival in Europe, offering over 80 live events featuring authors, illustrators, and storytellers aimed at inspiring young readers.

October
Bath Oktoberfest at Royal Victoria Park
Experience traditional German beer, food, and music in a festive atmosphere, bringing a taste of Bavaria to Bath.

November
Bath Mozartfest
A celebration of Mozart's music, along with works by other composers, performed by international artists and ensembles in various locations around Bath.

Late November to mid-December
Bath Christmas Market
A festive market featuring chalets selling handcrafted goods, local produce, and seasonal treats, set against the backdrop of Bath's historic streets.

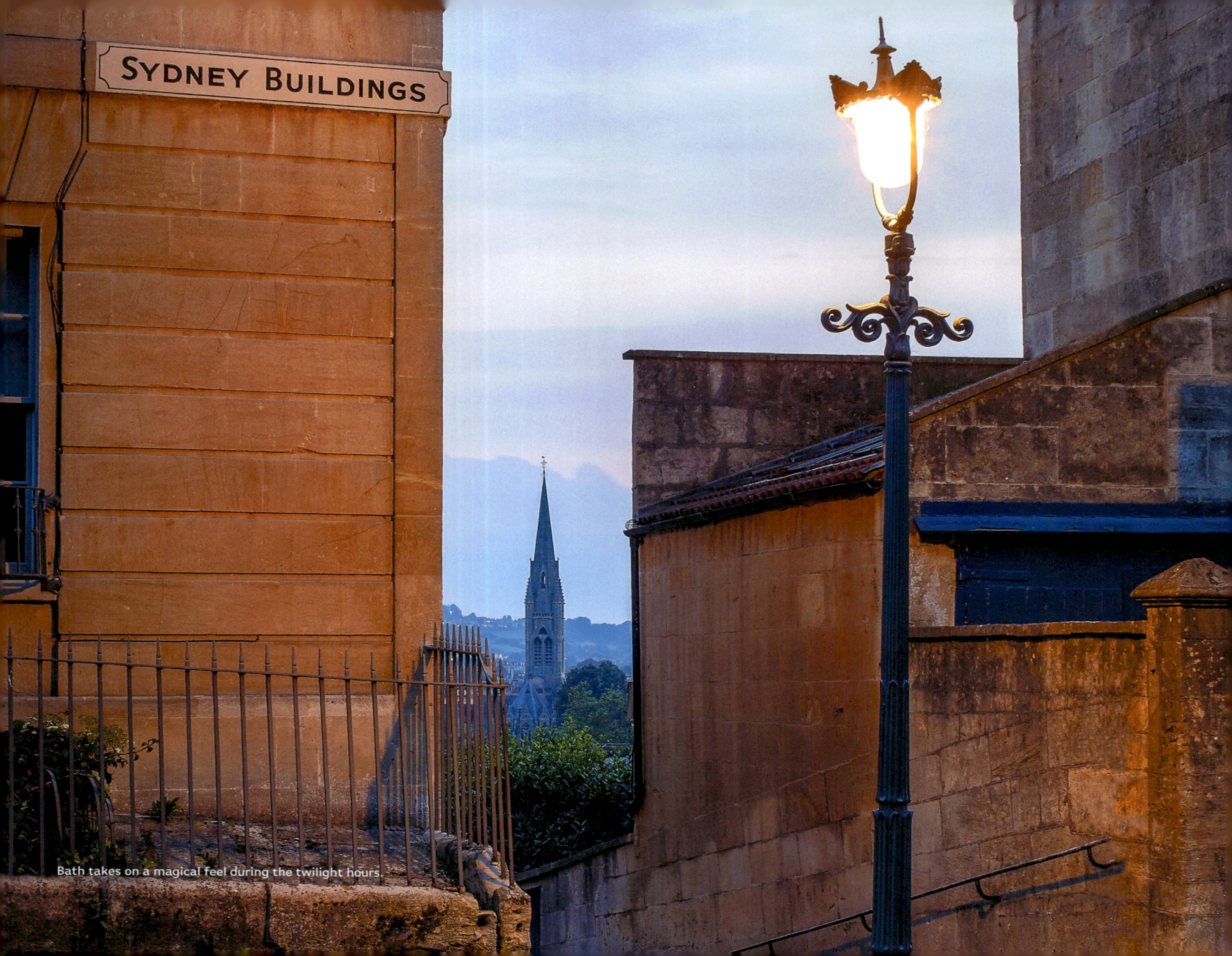

Bath takes on a magical feel during the twilight hours.

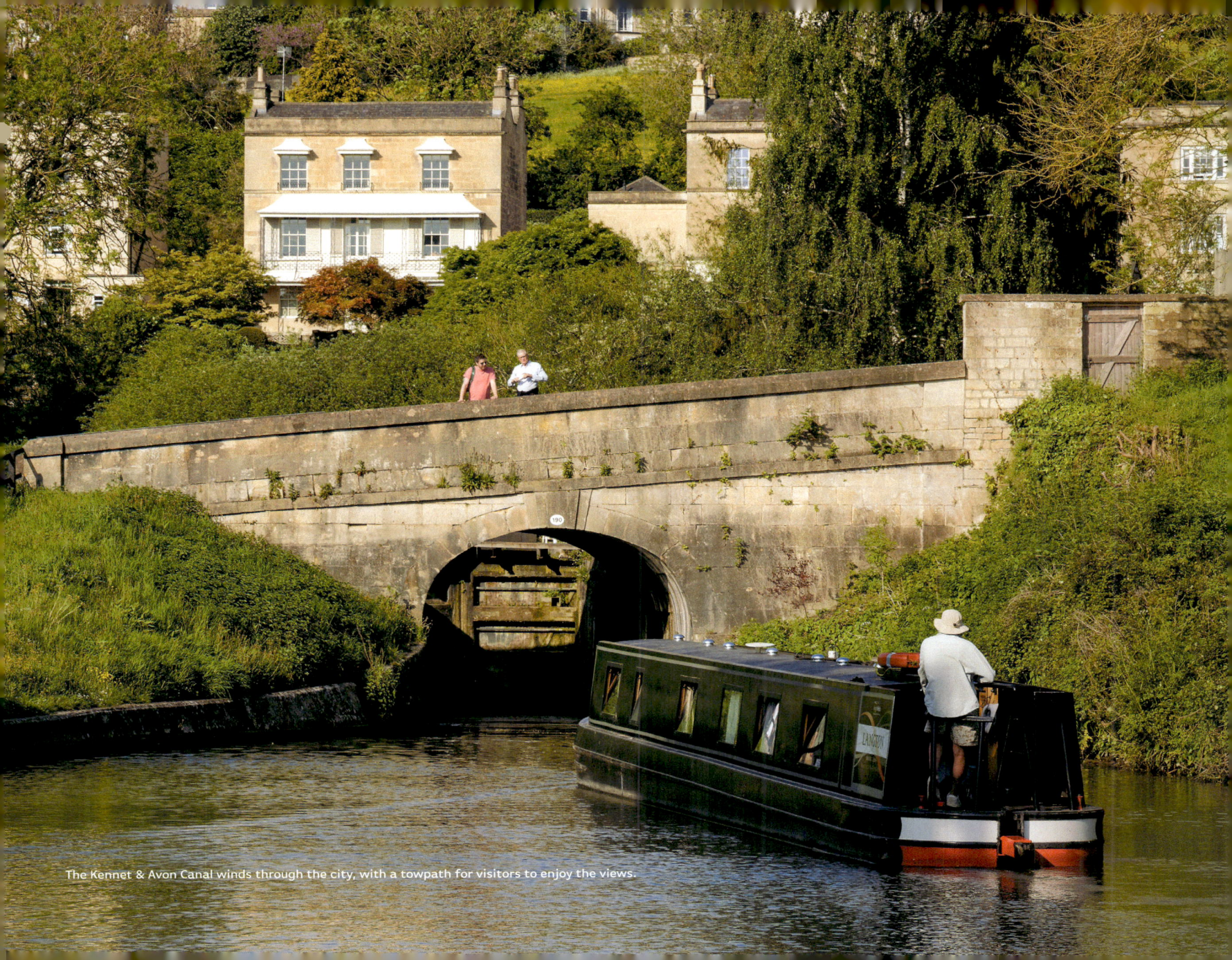
The Kennet & Avon Canal winds through the city, with a towpath for visitors to enjoy the views.

BATH TOP TEN: IN A DAY

Exploring Bath's rich history and stunning architecture is best done on foot, as many of its top attractions are within close proximity. Here's a suggested walking route to experience ten of the city's must-see sights whether you are visiting for a day, or longer. There are many cafes, pubs and restaurants on this route to enjoy.

If you do this walk in sequence it is just short of two miles (3km) and with stops should take between 3 and 4 hours.

 Starting from Charlotte Street Car Park

1 Royal Victoria Park (p.56)
Start your tour with a leisurely walk through this expansive park, opened in 1830 by Princess Victoria. The park features botanical gardens, a children's play area, and offers a serene environment to unwind. Great for stretching your legs after the drive to Bath.

2 The Royal Crescent (p.45)
A brief walk east from Royal Victoria Park leads you to this sweeping crescent of 30 Georgian houses overlooking the park, showcasing the pinnacle of 18th-century design.

3 No. 1 Royal Crescent (p.53)
At the eastern end of the Royal Crescent, this museum offers a glimpse into Georgian life, furnished as it would have been in the late 1700s.

4 The Circus (p.77)
From the Royal Crescent, walk east along Brock Street to this remarkable circular arrangement of Georgian townhouses, exemplifying Bath's architectural grandeur.

5 The Jane Austen Centre (p.32)
Proceed south down Gay Street to learn about the famous author's connection to Bath and the influence the city had on her novels. The Jane Austen Centre is adjacent to Queen's Square which is perfect for a rest on one of the square's benches.

6 The Roman Baths (p.180)
Head south to the heart of the city and ancient history. Explore the well-preserved bathing complex and museum to understand the city's Roman heritage.

7 Bath Abbey (p.149)
Adjacent to the Roman Baths, this magnificent Gothic church offers breathtaking architecture and tower tours with panoramic city views.

8 Thermae Bath Spa (p.192)
Nearby, indulge in Britain's only natural thermal spa, featuring a rooftop pool with stunning city vistas.

9 Sally Lunn's Historic Eating House (p.168)
A short distance away, visit one of Bath's oldest houses, now a restaurant and museum, famed for the original Sally Lunn bun.

10 Pulteney Bridge (p.97)
A short stroll from Sally Lunn's, via the Parade Gardens and along the River Avon, this iconic 18th-century bridge is lined with shops and provides picturesque views of the weir below.

EXTRA
If you have time, especially late afternoon when the sun starts to dip, a visit to Alexandra Park is recommended. From this high viewpoint the whole city will be laid out in front of you.

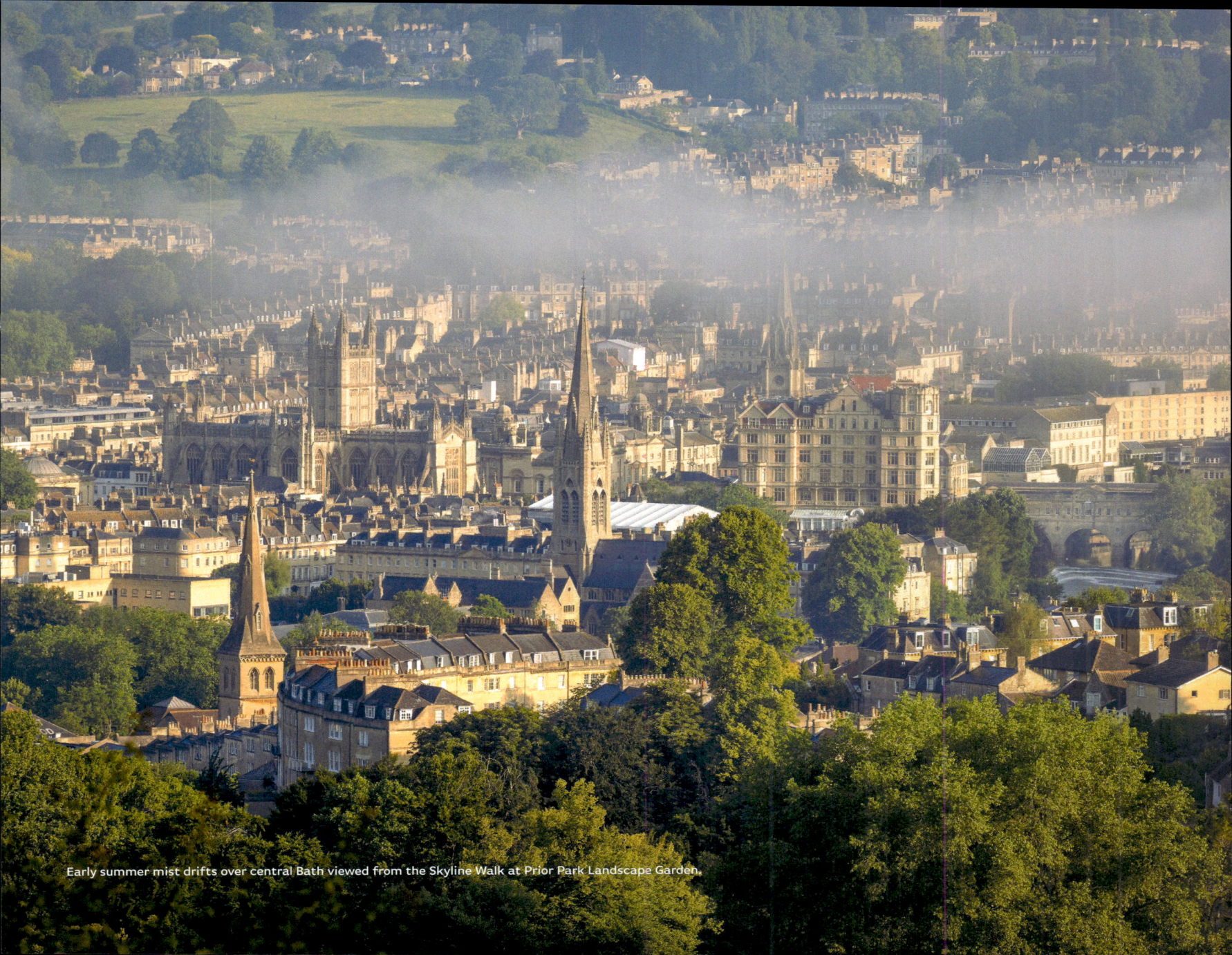
Early summer mist drifts over central Bath viewed from the Skyline Walk at Prior Park Landscape Garden.

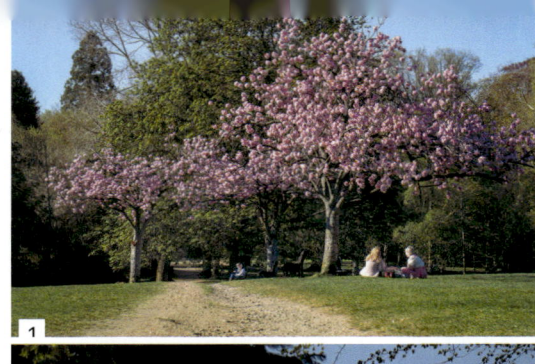
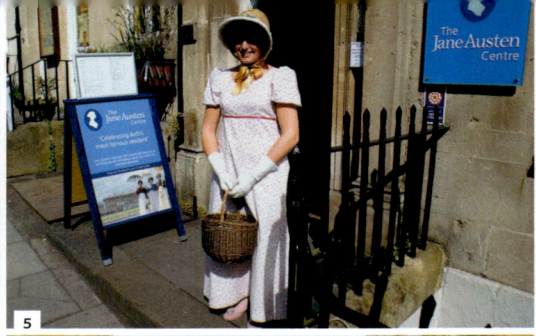
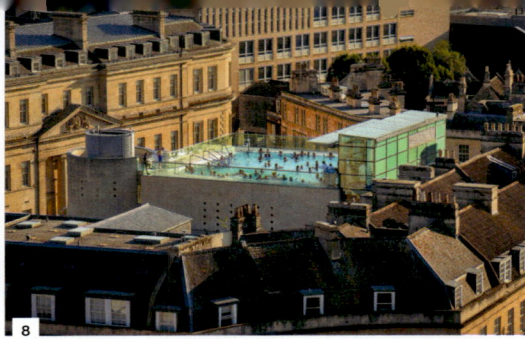
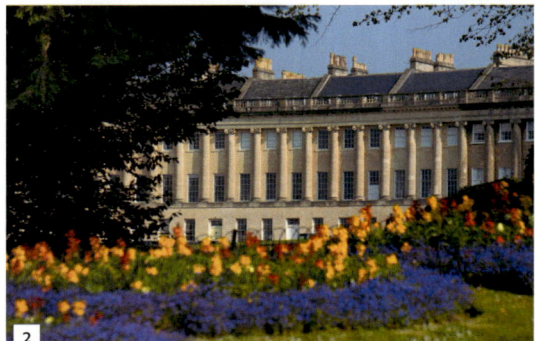
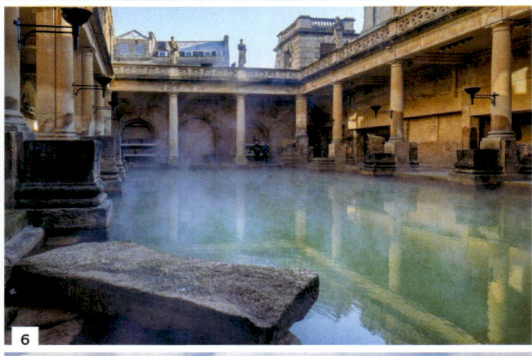
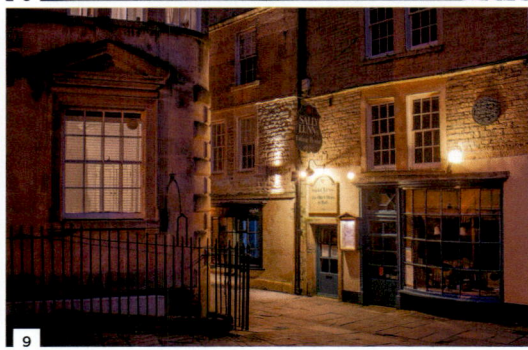
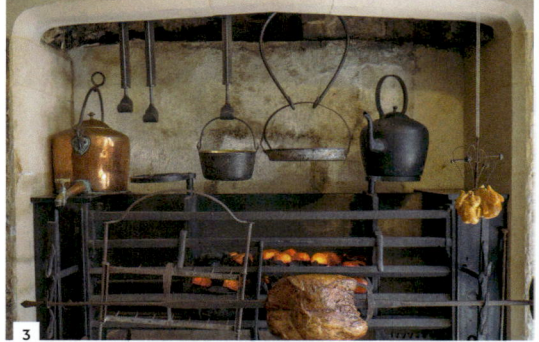
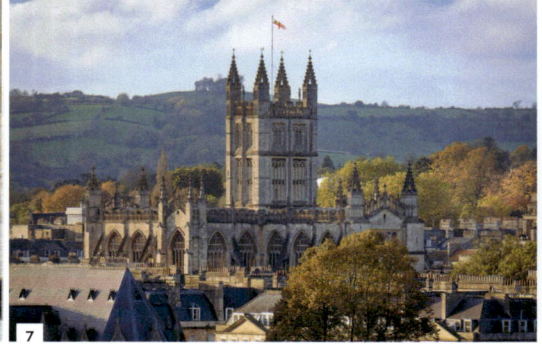
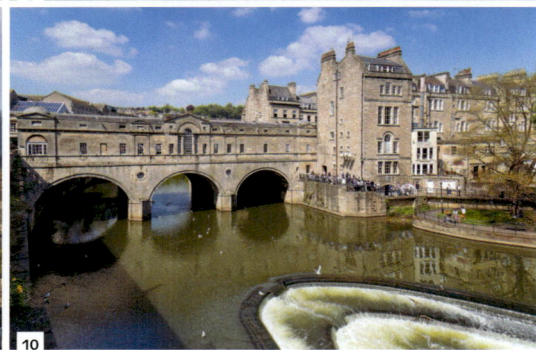
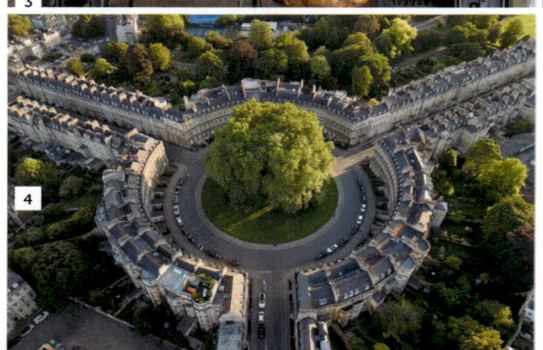

BATH TOP TEN

1 Royal Victoria Park
2 The Royal Crescent
3 No. 1 Royal Crescent
4 The Circus
5 The Jane Austen Centre
6 The Roman Baths
7 Bath Abbey
8 Thermae Bath Spa
9 Sally Lunn's Historic Eating House
10 Pulteney Bridge

OPPOSITE: Alexandra Park viewpoint.

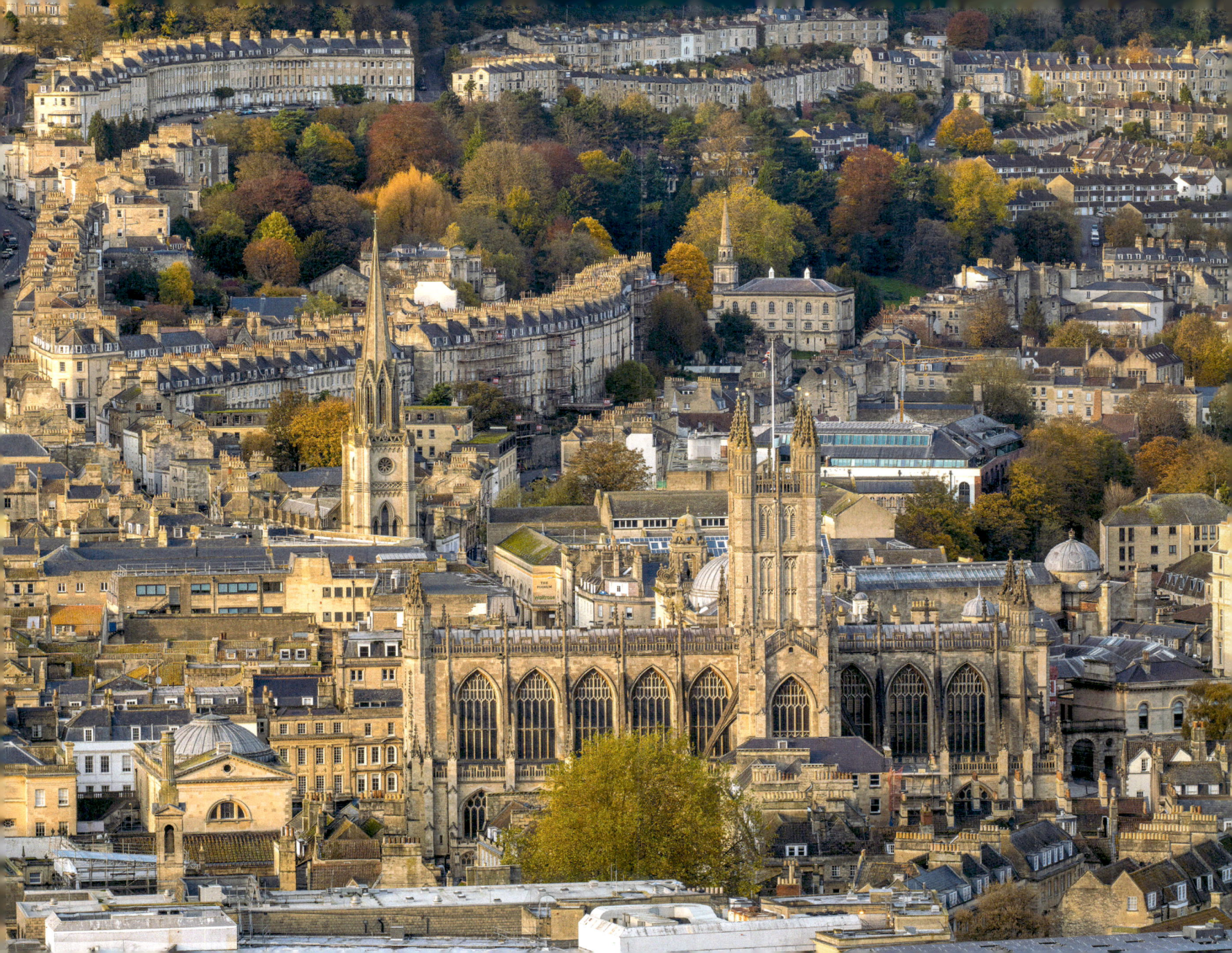

DAY TRIPS FROM BATH

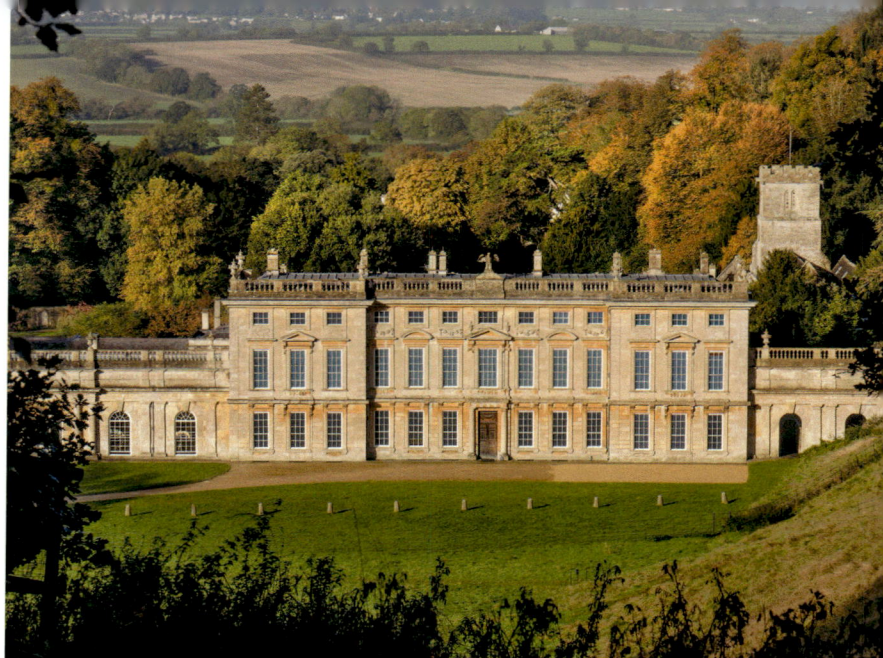

The area surrounding Bath, especially Wiltshire and the Cotswolds, offers a rich tapestry of historical landmarks, picturesque villages, and natural beauty from ancient sites reflecting England's deep-rooted past to charming rural landscapes. Whether you're drawn to cultural heritage, architectural marvels, or serene countryside, there are many options for memorable day trips from Bath.

 Dyrham Park
nationaltrust.org.uk
9 miles from Bath
Dyrham Park is a baroque country house located near the village of Dyrham in South Gloucestershire. Constructed between 1692 and 1704 for William Blathwayt, Secretary at War to William III, the house showcases Dutch decorative arts and is surrounded by 274 acres of parkland, home to a herd of fallow deer. Now managed by the National Trust, Dyrham Park is open to the public, offering visitors a glimpse into 17th-century architecture and landscape design.

 Stourhead Landscape Garden
nationaltrust.org.uk
25 miles from Bath
Stourhead Landscape Garden, located in Wiltshire, is a quintessential example of the 18th-century English landscape garden style. Created by Henry Hoare II, known as "Henry the Magnificent," between 1741 and 1780, the garden features a central lake surrounded by classical temples, including the Pantheon and the Temple of Apollo, inspired by scenes from his Grand Tour of Europe. The design reflects an idealised vision of nature, with carefully planned vistas and architectural elements that evoke the paintings of Claude Lorrain and Poussin.

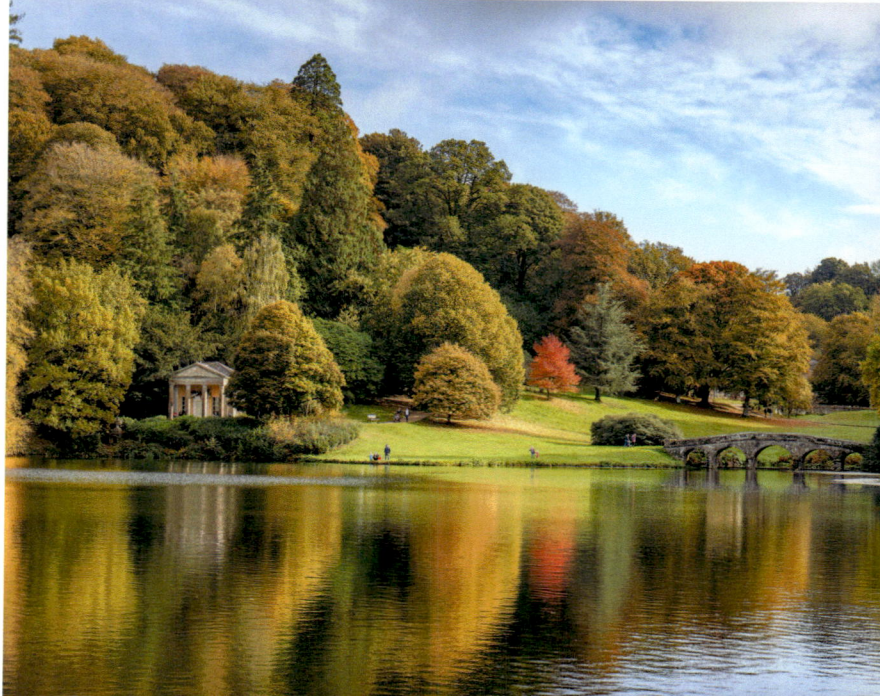

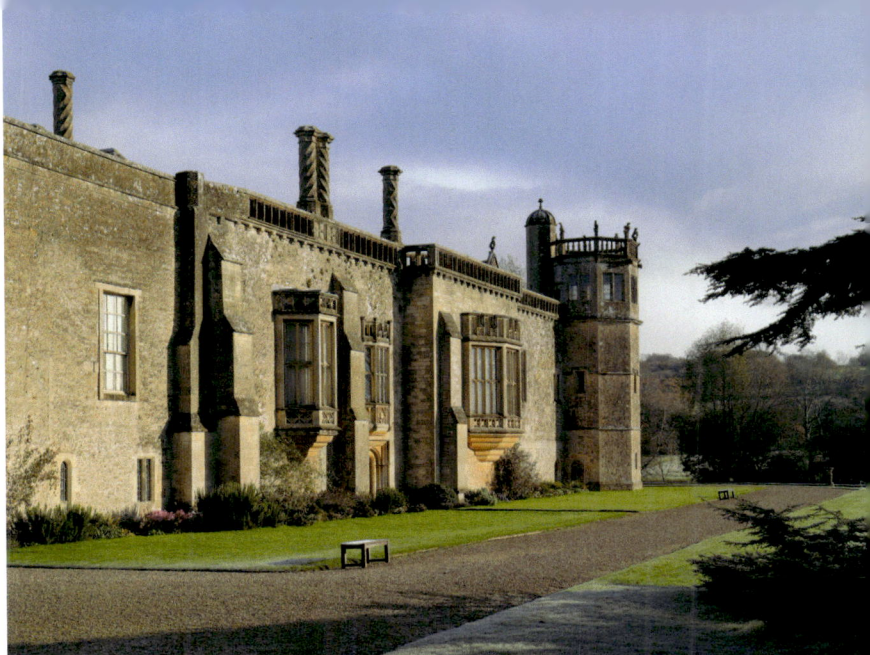

 Lacock Abbey
nationaltrust.org.uk
14 miles from Bath

Lacock is a picturesque village in Wiltshire renowned for its well-preserved historic architecture that dates back to the 13th century. At the heart of the village stands Lacock Abbey, founded in 1232 by Ela, Countess of Salisbury, originally as a nunnery before its conversion into a country house following the Dissolution of the Monasteries. Notably, the abbey served as the residence of William Henry Fox Talbot, a pioneer of photography who in 1835 captured one of the earliest surviving photographic negatives, an image of a window at the abbey. The village and abbey were used to film the Harry Potter series, Fantastic Beasts, Pride and Prejudice, Downton Abbey and Wolf Hall.

 Iford Manor
ifordmanor.co.uk
7 miles from Bath

Iford Manor, located near Bradford-on-Avon in Wiltshire, is a historic estate renowned for its Grade I listed Italianate gardens. These gardens were designed by the esteemed Edwardian architect and landscape designer Harold Peto, who resided at Iford from 1899 to 1933. Peto's design reflects his passion for Italian, Byzantine, ancient Roman, and Oriental styles, incorporating architectural fragments and classical sculptures collected during his travels. Today, the Cartwright-Hignett family, owners since 1965, continue to preserve and share this unique blend of architecture and horticulture with the public. ➔

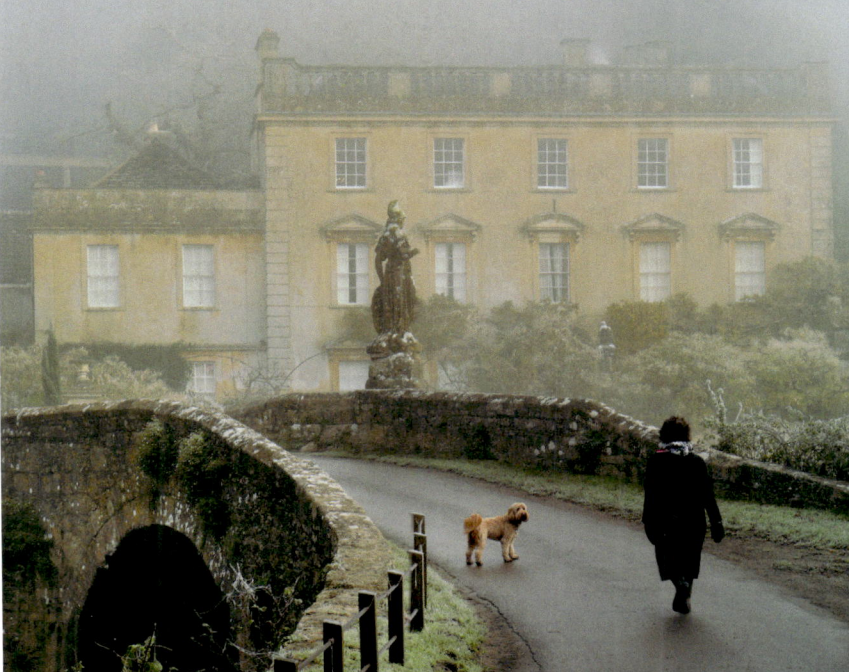

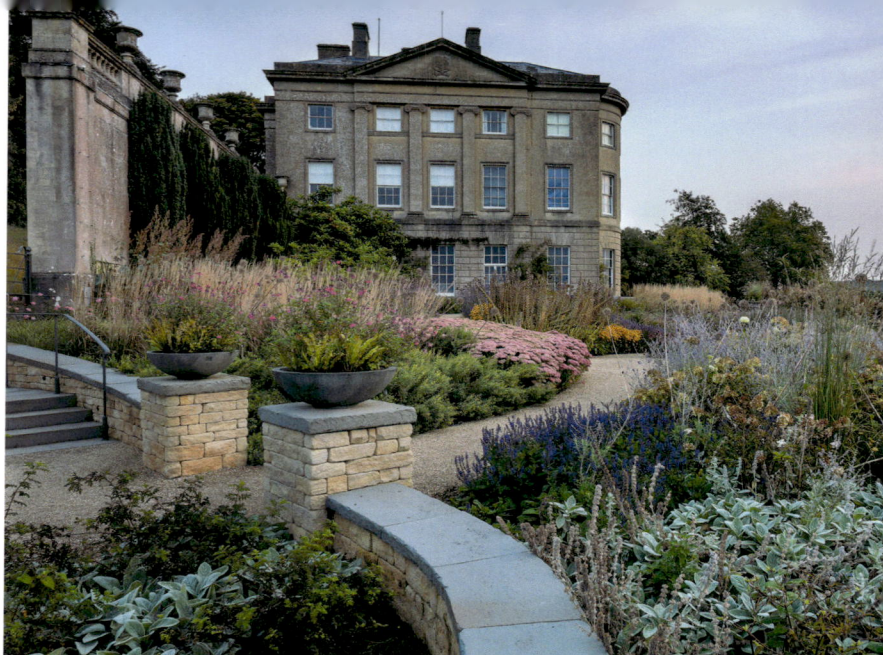

 ### The American Museum (& Gardens)
americanmuseum.org
3 miles from Bath

The American Museum & Gardens, located at Claverton Manor is the only museum outside the United States dedicated to showcasing American decorative arts and cultural history. Founded in 1961 by Dr. Dallas Pratt and John Judkyn, the museum features a diverse collection, including period rooms that illustrate American domestic interiors from the late 17th to the 19th centuries, an extensive quilt collection, and significant folk art pieces. The surrounding 125-acre estate boasts the New American Garden, designed by Oehme, van Sweden, offering visitors a horticultural insight into American flora amidst the picturesque English countryside.

 ### Westonbirt Arboretum
fowa.org.uk
20 miles from Bath

Westonbirt Arboretum, located near Tetbury in Gloucestershire, is a renowned 600-acre arboretum housing approximately 15,000 trees and shrubs from around the world. Established in 1829 by Victorian horticulturist Robert Stayner Holford, the arboretum reflects his passion for collecting rare and exotic plants during the era of Victorian plant hunting. Today, managed by Forestry England, Westonbirt offers visitors 17 miles of marked paths through diverse landscapes, including the carefully designed Old Arboretum and the historic Silk Wood, providing an immersive experience in one of the UK's most significant botanical collections.

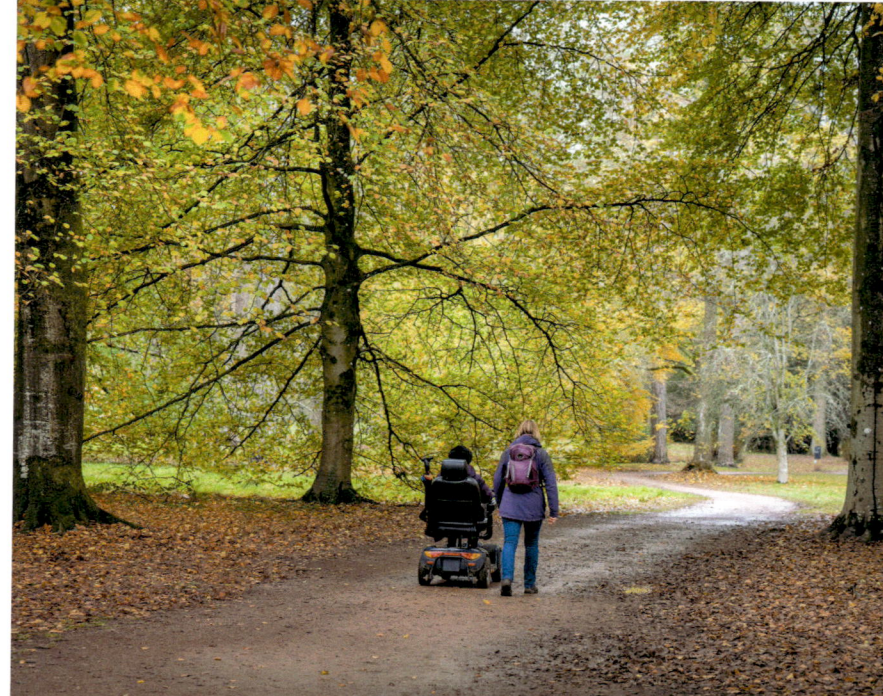

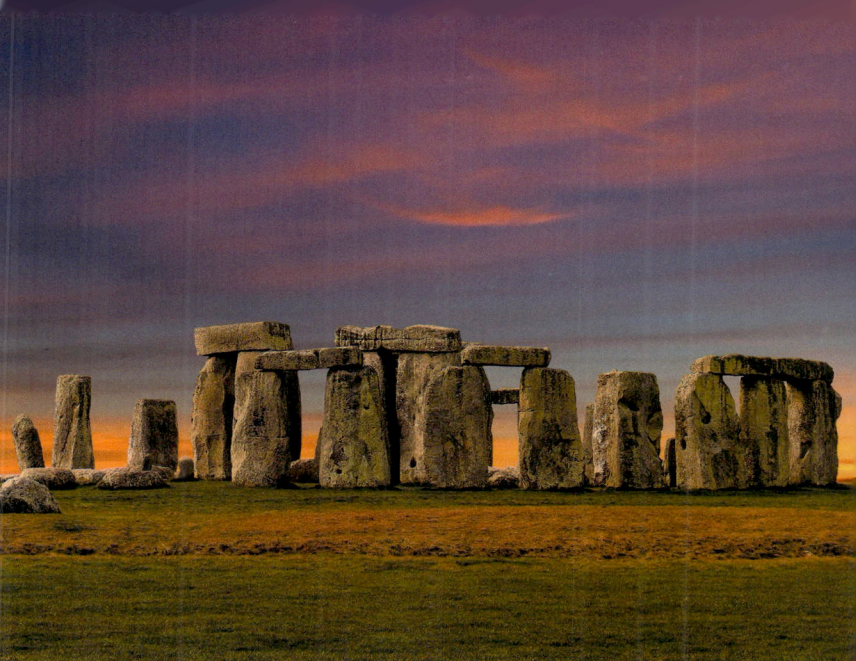

Stonehenge
english-heritage.org.uk
36 miles from Bath

Famous the world over, Stonehenge, located near Salisbury in Wiltshire, is a prehistoric monument consisting of a ring of standing stones, each around 13 feet high and seven feet wide. Constructed in phases between 3000 BC and 2000 BC, its exact purpose remains a subject of debate, with theories suggesting it served as a burial ground, astronomical observatory, or ceremonial site. Notably, the monument aligns with the sunrise of the summer solstice and the sunset of the winter solstice, indicating its builders' advanced understanding of celestial events. Book tickets in advance as the site gets busy, especially at weekends. Early or late in the day midweek are the best times to visit. From the visitor centre, there's approximately a 1.5-mile (2.4 km) walk to the stone circle. While shuttle buses are available, wearing comfortable footwear is advisable if you choose to walk.

Castle Combe
visitwiltshire.co.uk
12.5 miles from Bath

Castle Combe, often hailed as the "prettiest village in England," is a quintessential Cotswold destination characterised by its charming honey-coloured stone cottages and tranquil ambiance. This picturesque village has served as a filming location for notable productions like "War Horse" and "Stardust," offering visitors a sense of stepping into a storybook setting. Its timeless beauty and serene atmosphere make Castle Combe a must-visit for those seeking an authentic English countryside experience. Again better early or late in the day to avoid crowds. ➔

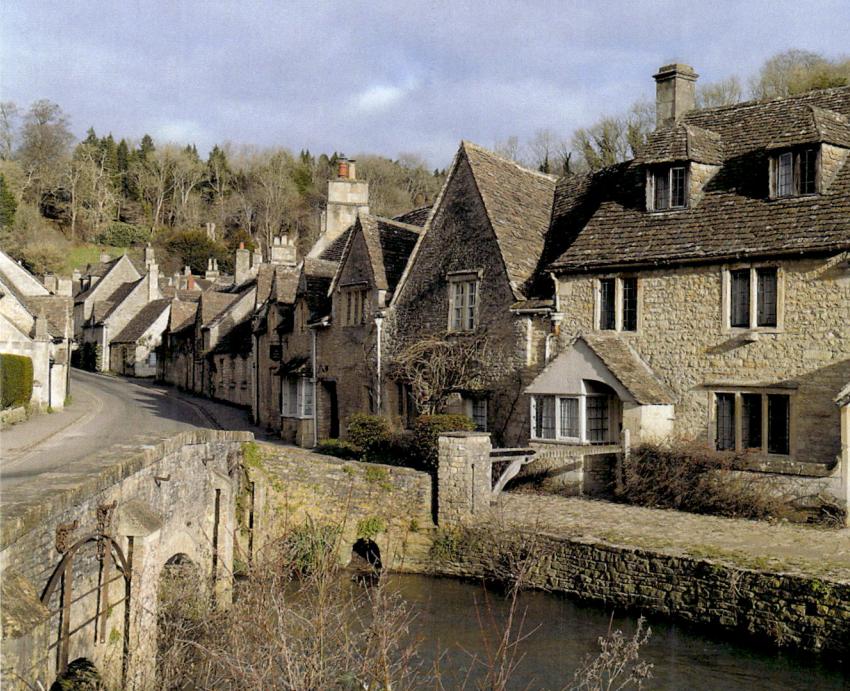

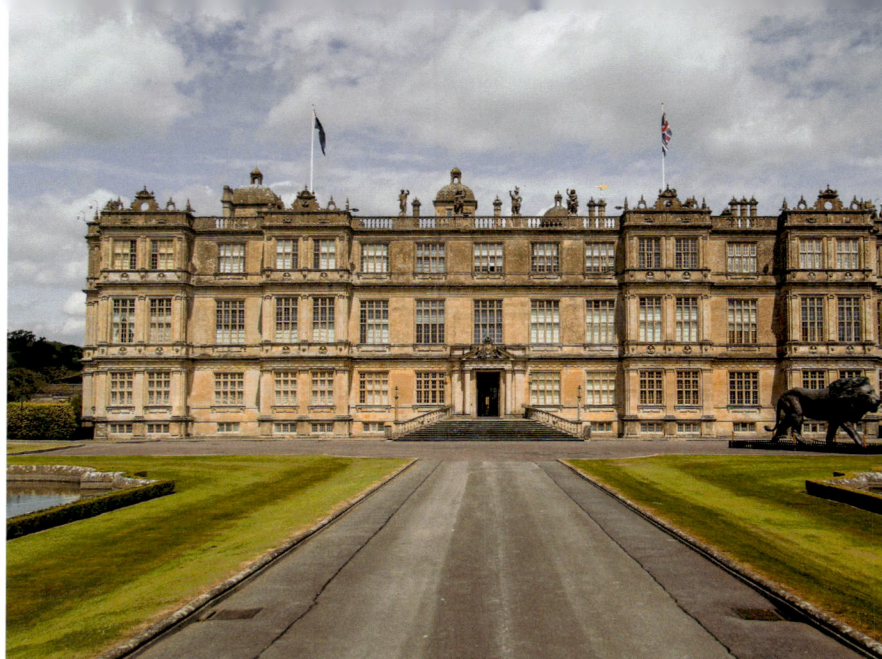

 Longleat Safari Park
longleat.co.uk
20 miles from Bath
Longleat Safari Park in Wiltshire, offers a unique drive-through safari experience where visitors can observe a diverse range of animals, including lions, tigers, and monkeys, roaming in spacious enclosures. Beyond the safari, the park features attractions such as the Jungle Cruise, which provides close-up views of gorillas and sea lions, and the Adventure Castle, a large play area for children. Additionally, the historic Longleat House, an Elizabethan stately home, is open for tours, offering insights into its rich history and architecture.

 Avebury Stone Circle
english-heritage.org.uk
27 miles from Bath
Avebury Stone Circle, located in Wiltshire, is the world's largest prehistoric stone circle, encompassing part of the village of Avebury. Constructed during the Neolithic period, approximately between 2850 BC and 2200 BC, the monument comprises a massive henge with an outer circle originally consisting of about 100 standing stones, enclosing two smaller stone circles. Unlike its counterpart at Stonehenge, visitors to Avebury can freely walk among the stones, offering a unique and immersive experience of this ancient site.

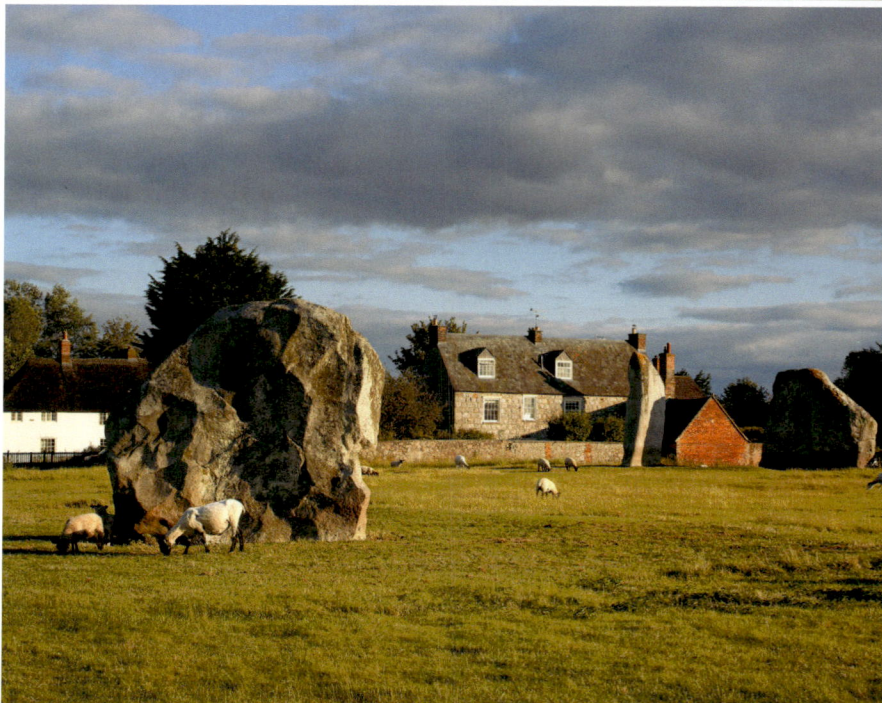

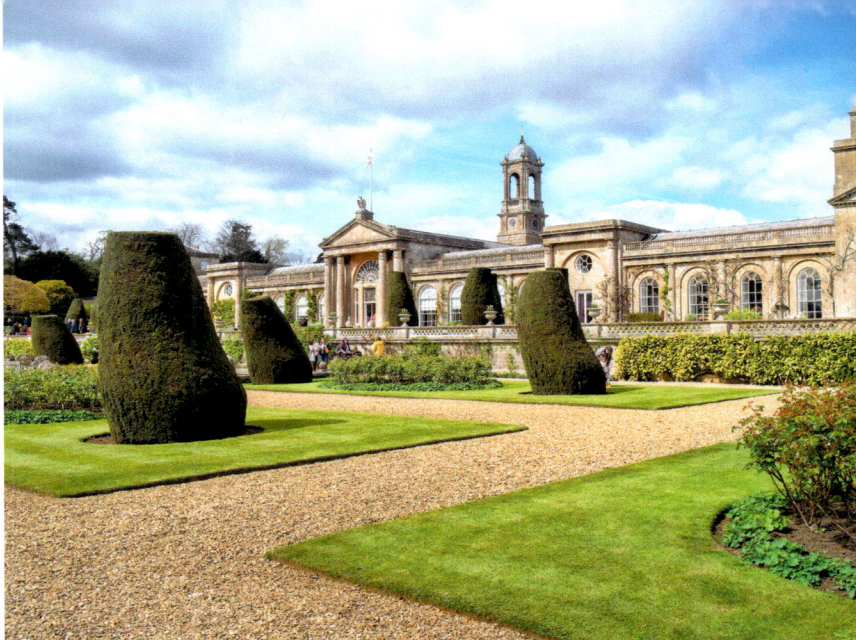

 ### Bowood House & Gardens
bowood.org
19 miles from Bath

Bowood House & Gardens, located near Calne in Wiltshire, is a distinguished Georgian country estate that has been the residence of the Lansdowne family since 1754. The house features interiors designed by renowned architect Robert Adam, while the expansive 2,000-acre parkland was landscaped by the famed Lancelot 'Capability' Brown in the 1760s, showcasing a sinuous mile-long lake and diverse arboretum. Notably, in 1774, scientist Joseph Priestley discovered oxygen in a laboratory within Bowood House, marking a significant contribution to the field of chemistry

 ### The Bishop's Palace, Wells
bishopspalace.org.uk
23 miles from Bath

The Bishop's Palace, located in Wells, Somerset, has been the residence of the Bishops of Bath and Wells for over 800 years. This medieval palace is surrounded by a picturesque moat, famously home to resident swans trained to ring a bell for food – a tradition dating back to the 1800s. Visitors can explore the 14 acres of stunning gardens, which include the well pools that give the city of Wells its name.

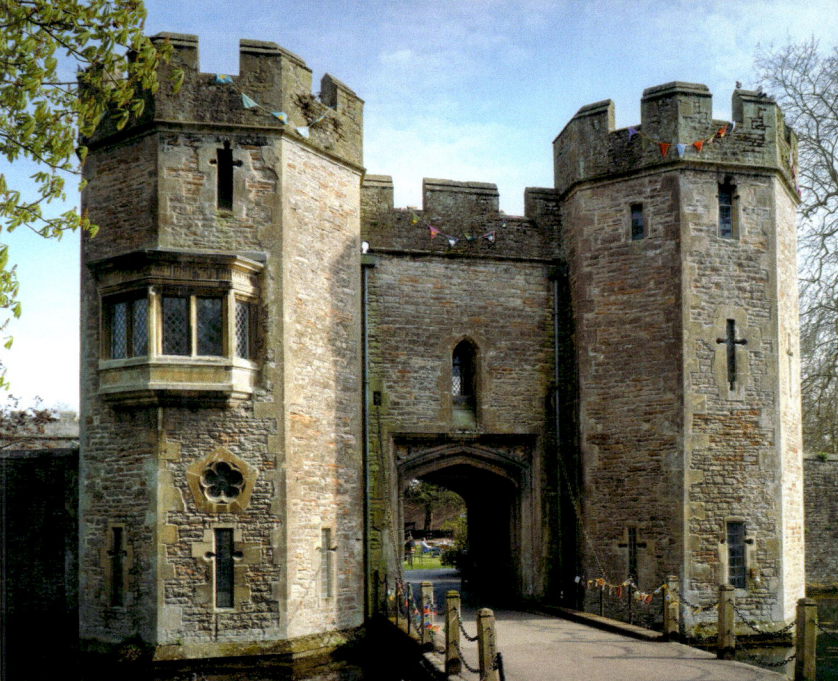

BATH ITINERARY

Here's a three day itinerary to help you experience the city's diverse attractions. Refer to page 232 for some restaurant, cafe and shopping suggestions.

DAY 1
IMMERSION IN BATH'S HERITAGE

Morning:
The Roman Baths: Begin your journey at this iconic site, delving into the ancient bathing complex that dates back to Roman times.
Bath Abbey: Adjacent to the Roman Baths, this magnificent Gothic church boasts stunning architecture and a rich history.

Afternoon:
Pulteney Bridge: Stroll to this unique 18th-century bridge lined with shops, offering picturesque views of the River Avon.
Sally Lunn's Historic Eating House: Enjoy lunch at one of Bath's oldest houses, famous for its original Sally Lunn Bun.

Evening:
Theatre Royal Bath: Experience a performance at this historic venue, renowned for its varied productions.

DAY 2
ARTISTIC EXPLORATION AND SCENIC WALKS

Morning:
The Holburne Museum: Discover a collection of fine and decorative arts in this elegantly designed building.

Sydney Gardens: Adjacent to the museum, these are the only remaining 18th-century pleasure gardens in the UK.

Afternoon:
Jane Austen Centre: Gain insights into the life and works of the famed author who once resided in Bath.
The Circus and Royal Crescent: Marvel at these exemplary pieces of Georgian architecture, showcasing Bath's architectural grandeur.

Evening:
Alexander Park: If you're up for it, walk up to Alexander Park for panoramic views of the city and surrounding countryside.

DAY 3
LEISURE AND UNIQUE EXPERIENCES

Morning:
Thermae Bath Spa: Relax in Britain's only natural thermal spa, featuring a rooftop pool with stunning city vistas.

Afternoon:
Prior Park Landscape Garden: Visit this National Trust site, renowned for its Palladian bridge and landscaped beauty.

Evening:
Local Dining Experience: Conclude your trip with dinner at one of Bath's esteemed restaurants.

BATH PUBS

Traditional British pubs are not merely establishments for drinking; they are often the heart and soul of the community, fostering social bonds and preserving local traditions. Originating from Roman taverns introduced around 43 AD, these 'public houses' have evolved over centuries into gathering places where individuals from all walks of life come together to share stories, celebrate events, and enjoy camaraderie. Bath boasts a rich tapestry of history, and its traditional pubs are no exception. There are around 50 pubs in Bath, here are ten historic pubs in the city, each with its own unique story. For a full listing visit: bathandborders.camra.org.uk/pubguide

The Saracen's Head
42 Broad St, BA1 5LP
Established in 1713, this is one of Bath's oldest pubs. Notably, Charles Dickens is said to have stayed here during his visits to the city.

The Huntsman
1 Terrace Walk, N Parade, BA1 1LJ
Occupying one of Bath's oldest buildings, The Huntsman offers a blend of historic architecture and contemporary comfort, making it a popular spot for both locals and visitors.

The Garrick's Head
7–8, St John's Pl, BA1 1ET
Once the home of Beau Nash, Bath's renowned Master of Ceremonies, this pub became an inn in 1805. It's named after the famous actor David Garrick.

The Raven
7 Queen St, BA1 1HE
Housed in two former Georgian townhouses, The Raven offers a traditional atmosphere across its multiple bars. It's particularly celebrated for its selection of pies and ales.

The George Inn
Mill Lane, Bathampton, BA2 6TR
Located in Bathampton is a Grade II listed, ivy-clad pub situated beside the Kennet and Avon Canal, offering a picturesque setting with a spacious beer garden. Dating back to the mid to late 17th century, the inn retains historical features such as stop-chamfered beams and a winder staircase.

Coeur de Lion
17 Northumberland Place, BA1 5AR
Known as Bath's smallest pub, this establishment dates back to the 18th century. Despite its size, it boasts a rich history and a cozy ambiance.

The Star Inn
23 Vineyards, BA1 5NA
Dating from 1760, The Star Inn retains its traditional multi-room layout with wooden benches and Victorian bar fittings, offering a glimpse into the past.

The Old Green Tree
12 Green St, BA1 2JZ
Built in 1716 on a former bowling green, this pub features three small wood-paneled rooms and an old fireplace, exuding historic charm.

The Bell Inn
103 Walcot St, BA1 5BW
A former 18th-century coaching inn, The Bell is now owned by a cooperative of around 500 people and is known for its bohemian vibe and live music.

The Boater
9 Argyle Street, BA2 4BQ
A historic pub located near the iconic Pulteney Bridge. Established in 1809. The pub boasts Bath's largest beer garden, providing picturesque views of the River Avon and Pulteney Weir.

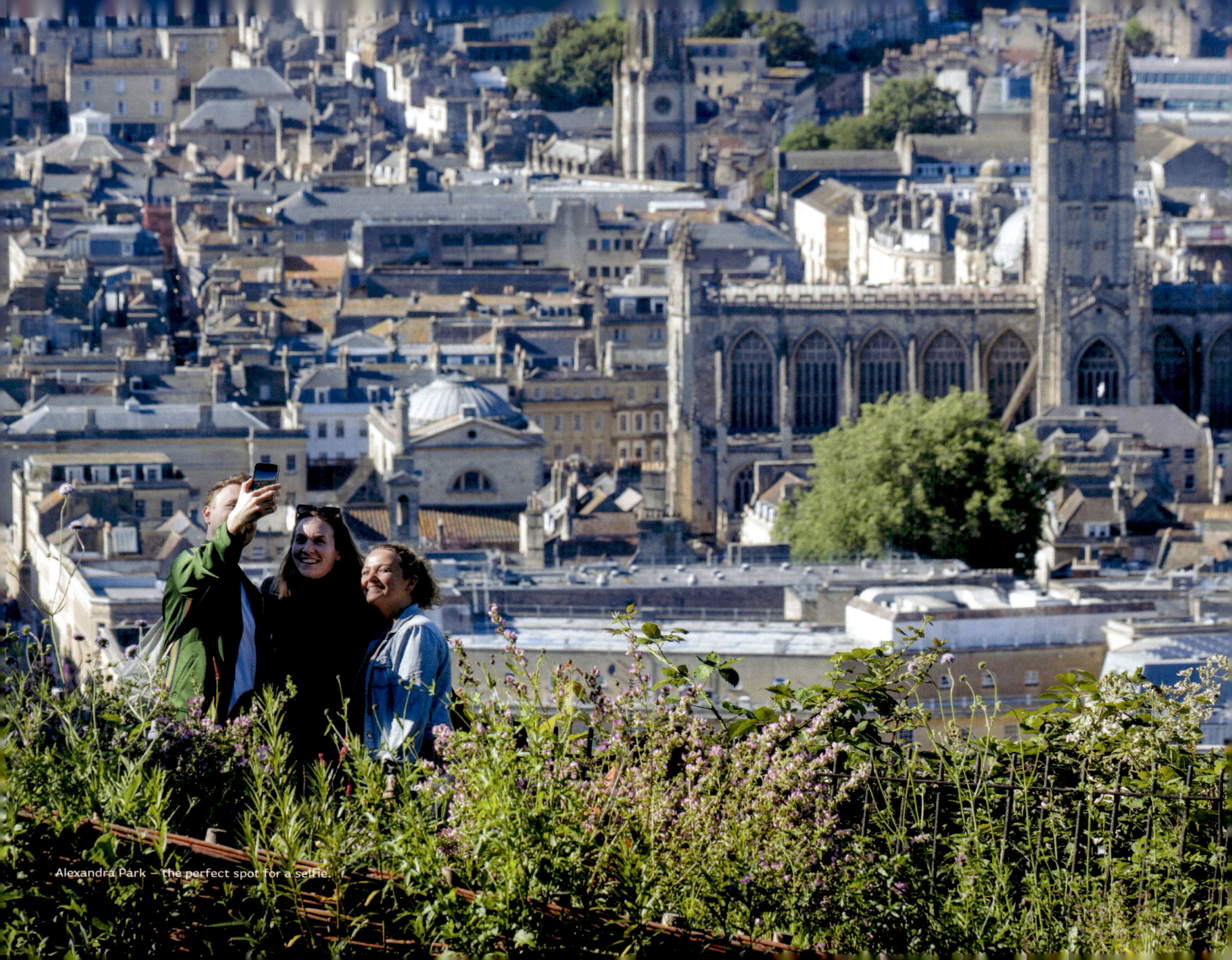
Alexandra Park – the perfect spot for a selfie.

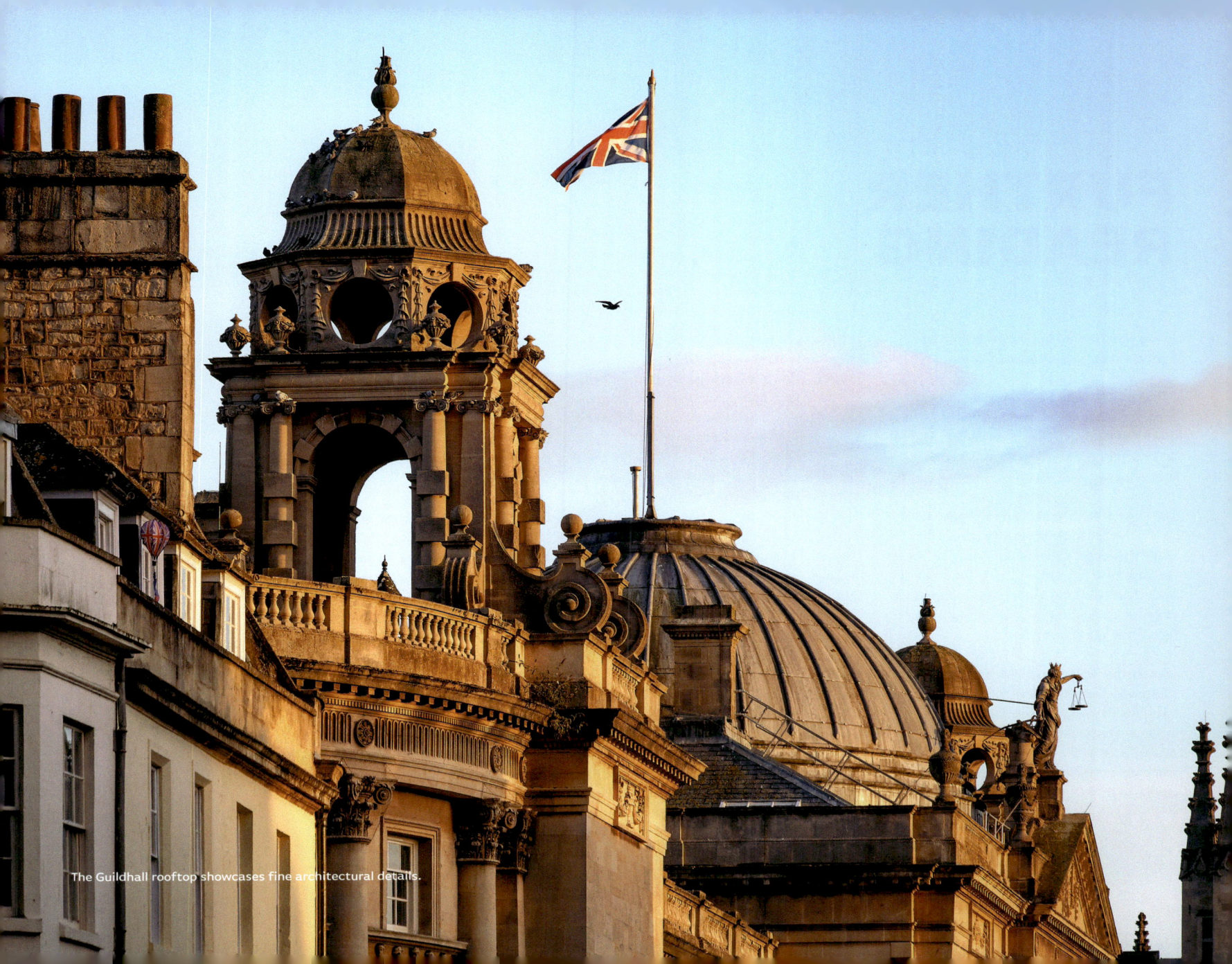
The Guildhall rooftop showcases fine architectural details.

FURTHER READING

If you want to find out more about Bath, here are some recommended books.

"The Little Book of Bath" by Mike Dean (2014)
A compendium of fascinating facts, anecdotes, and lesser-known stories, this book provides an engaging glimpse into the quirky and intriguing aspects of Bath's past.

The Story of Bath by Dr Cathryn Spence (2016)
This richly illustrated history explores the many challenges and triumphs faced by one of Britain's most fascinating cities. The Story of Bath charts the long history of this important city from its beginnings in the Roman period through to the present day.

Jane Austen at Home: 250th Birthday Edition by Lucy Worsley (2024)
Lucy Worsley travels from room to room, house to house, showing us how and why Jane Austen lived as she did, examining the places and spaces that mattered to her. Featuring a guided tour of all the best Jane Austen sites to visit specially written for this birthday edition.

111 Places in Bath That You Shouldn't Miss by Justin Postlethwaite (2017)
Explore Bath's best-kept secrets – stories, locations, and unique personalities from the past and present, who have been neglected by the conventional tourist routes.

Roman Bath: A New History and Archaeology of Aquae Sulis by Peter Davenport (2021)
Peter Davenport, having been involved in most of the archaeological work in Bath since 1980, attempts to tell the story of Roman Bath: the latest interim report on the 'Three Hundred Year Dig'.

An Historical Map of Bath: Medieval, Stuart and Georgian City by History of Bath Research Group (2024)
The Historical Map of Bath shows, on a multi-period map, the many layers of Bath's history, against a background of Bath around 1900. As well as the famous Georgian terraces, it shows how Bath in the 17th century would have looked. A comprehensive gazetteer on the map's reverse, complete with many illustrations and additional maps, explains how Bath developed and introduces its buildings and sites of interest.

Sometimes in Bath, Her Stories and History by Charles Nevin (2019)
The stories and History of 'Britain's most elegant and intriguing city'. Sometimes in Bath is a captivating story-tour through the city's history conducted by Charles Nevin, the award-winning journalist, national newspaper columnist, author and humorist.

Bath Abbey's Monuments: An Illustrated History by Oliver Taylor (2023)
Bath Abbey contains the largest collection of monuments in any UK church or cathedral. But how did the ruined Abbey of 1539 become a Georgian 'gallery of sculpture', where the latest works of art by famous sculptors could be seen? Drawing on a wealth of unpublished material on the Abbey's history, this book tells the story of its monuments for the first time – how they helped the Abbey rise from the aftermath of the Dissolution to give it a new identity, a unique floor, and walls that tell the social history of Bath.

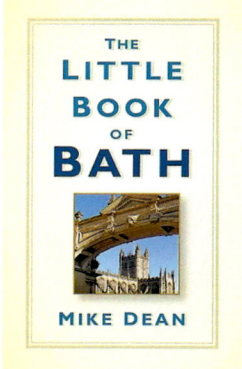

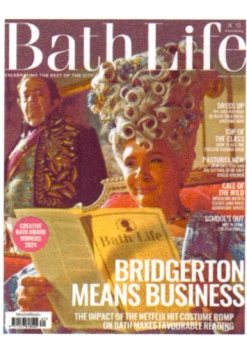

VISITOR INFORMATION WEBSITES

Visit Bath
visitbath.co.uk
The official tourism website for Bath, offering information on attractions, events, accommodation, shopping, and dining.

Welcome to Bath
welcometobath.co.uk
Brought to you by the Bath Business Improvement District (Bath BID), Welcome to Bath will be a hub for events and special offers in the city.

The Bath Magazine
thebathmagazine.co.uk
An independent monthly publication covering local events, culture, and lifestyle in Bath.

Stay In Bath
stayinbath.org
StayinBath.org is owned and run by BIHA, the Bath Independent Hospitality Association.

Bath Festivals
bathfestivals.org.uk
Organises the annual Bath Literature & Music Festivals, featuring a diverse range of events and performances.

Bath UK
bath.co.uk
A general portal for visitors, featuring sections on events, places to visit, and local services in Bath.

Visit Somerset – Bath
visitsomerset.co.uk
Provides a guide to Bath's accommodation, attractions, and things to do, as part of the broader Somerset region

Bath Film Office
bathfilmoffice.co.uk
Managing and promoting Bath and North East Somerset as a filming location

Bath Life Magazine
Bath Life is a luxury lifestyle magazine that celebrates the very best of living in the city of Bath. It's an insider's guide to the city.

Savouring Bath
savouringbath.com
Offers guided food and drink tours, introducing visitors to the city's culinary artisans and local flavours.

Discover Bath
discoverbath.co.uk
A great local website authored by Bath local, Amy. Particularly good for walks and kids activities around Bath, with some great maps.

Bath in Time
bathintime.co.uk
An online image library offering over 40,000 historic images of Bath and its surroundings, allowing users to explore, purchase, and create custom products featuring these images.

Bath World Heritage Site
bathworldheritage.org.uk
Information about Bath's designation as a UNESCO World Heritage Site.

Bath Record Office
batharchives.co.uk
Explore the history of Bath & North East Somerset through archives and collections.

History of Bath Research Group
historyofbath.org
A society dedicated to researching and sharing the history of Bath.

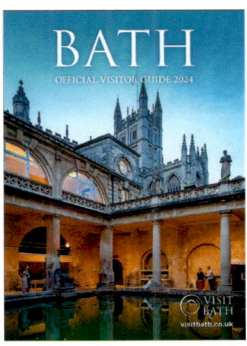

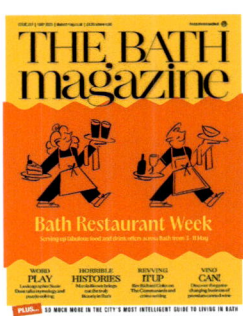

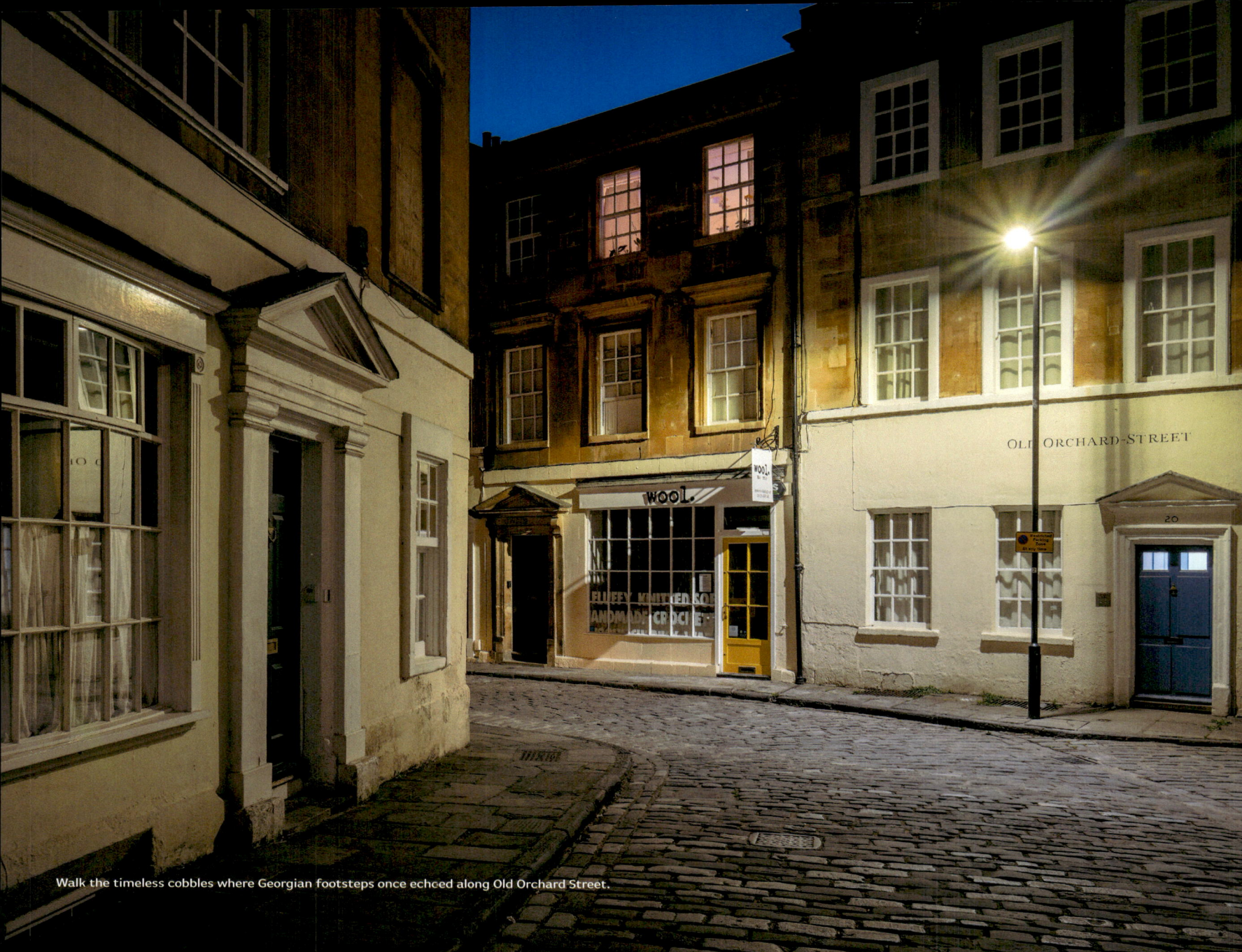
Walk the timeless cobbles where Georgian footsteps once echoed along Old Orchard Street.

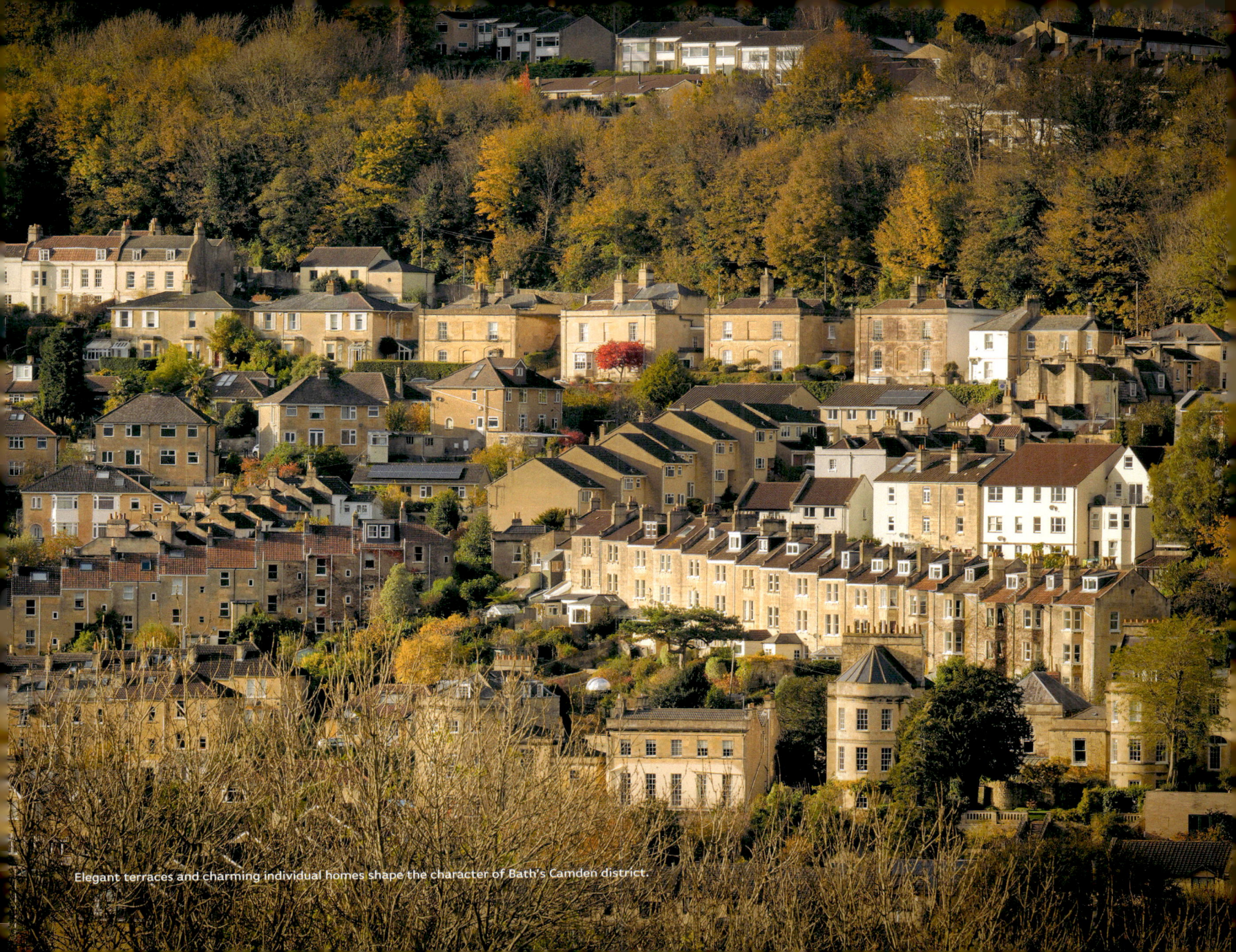
Elegant terraces and charming individual homes shape the character of Bath's Camden district.

ABOUT FOTOVUE

THE BEAUTY OF SERIES

fotoVUE's *Beauty of* series are hybrid books, a visitor guidebook with all the information you need for an enjoyable trip, and also a coffee table-type book with rich array of beautiful images that you can enjoy at home, as a souvenir or memento of your trip, or even as gift for someone to show the beauty of the area.

You hold in your hands second volume of this new series, *The Beauty of Bath*, following on from the first title in this series, *The Beauty of Liverpool*. We plan to roll out more of these titles so please keep an eye on our website – *fotovue.com* – for release dates, and subscribe to our newsletter.

LIKE TAKING PHOTOGRAPHS? THE EXPLORE & DISCOVER SERIES

Our main line of books are called *Explore & Discover* (previously titled 'Photographing') whose main job is to show you the best locations for photography in an area.

See our existing titles on the right covering many areas in the UK, the Dolomites and Iceland, as well as our technical book, *Photographing The Night Sky*.

The *Explore & Discover* series are comprehensive visitor guidebooks with an emphasis on showing you the most beautiful places to visit in an area and when there, how to take the best photographs.

Like your usual visitor guidebook the *Explore & Discover* series have lots of logistical information describing: how to get to the area the book covers, how to get around when there, best time to visit, suggestions on where to stay, and where to eat and drink. Production qualities – paper, reproduction and binding – are high, and the books are full of stunning photographs – they make beautiful coffee table books to browse and plan your trip at home, as well as a guidebook to take with you on your trip.

LOCAL AUTHORS

Typically the author lives in, or near, the area described and each book is the result of approximately 4 years work of photography and writing. In addition there is cultural and historical information to put a photo-location in context, as well as recommendations of places to visit including castles, stately homes, and gardens, as well as natural places.

If you would like to purchase one of our books, please visit: *fotovue.com* When there, use the coupon code **TRAVEL** at the check out for **20% off**, with free UK shipping.

Best regards
Mick Ryan
Publisher at fotoVUE

explore & discover

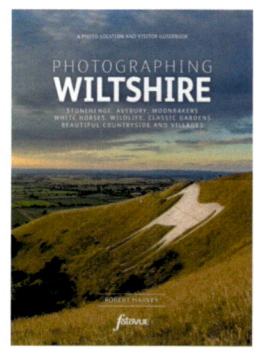

Photographing Wiltshire is the definitive visitor and photo-location guidebook to this fascinating county. Visit and photograph the ancient and mysterious sites of Stonehenge, Avebury and Silbury Hill; the great houses and gardens at Longleat, Bowood, Wilton, Stourhead; villages and churches; Georgian Bradford-on-Avon, Salisbury Plain and Salisbury Cathedral, and the chalk White Horses and the Fovant Badges etched into the hillsides.

Get **25% off** Photographing Wiltshire at *fotovue.com* using the coupon code: **BATH** at the checkout.

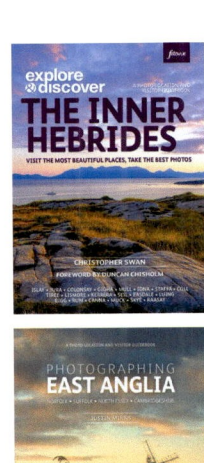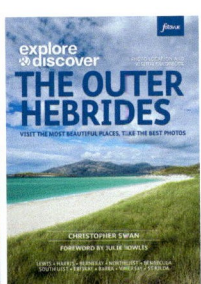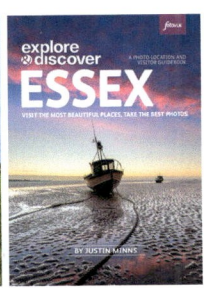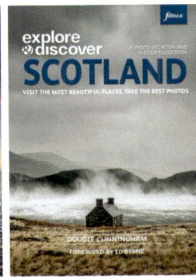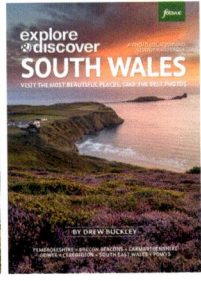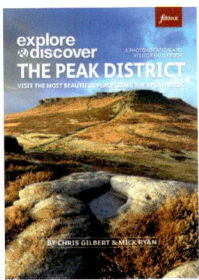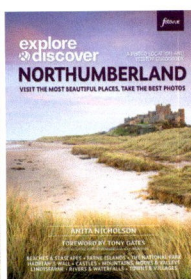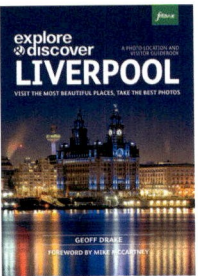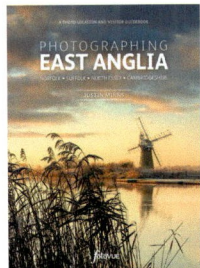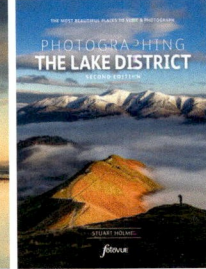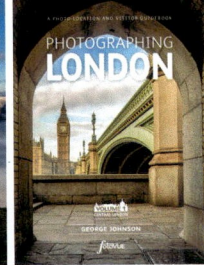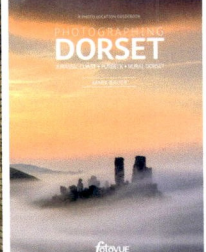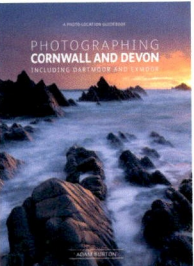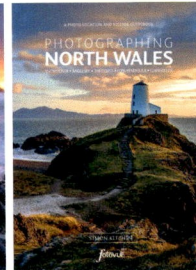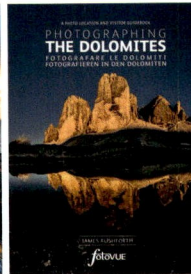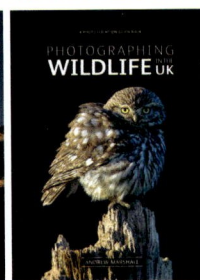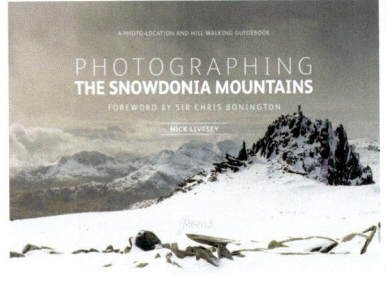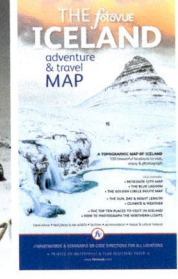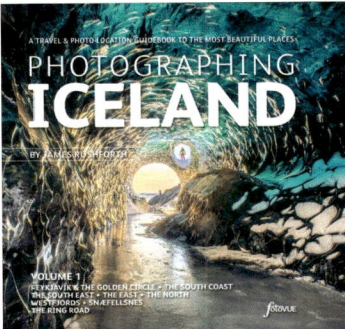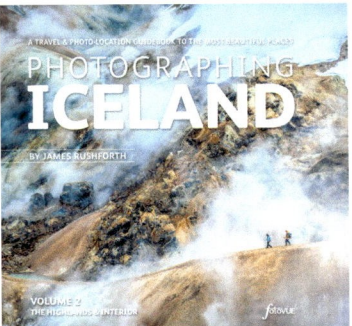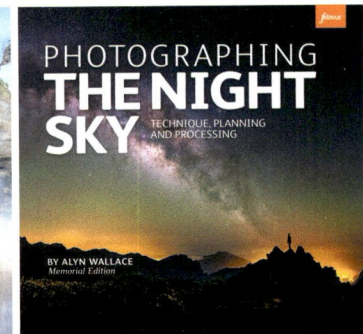

ABOUT FOTOVUE **269**

INDEX

44AD artspace	36
Abbey Green	65
Abbey View Gardens	16
Accommodation	32
Adam Gallery	36
Adam, Robert	29
Afternoon Tea	233
Airports	227
Alexandra Park	202, 250
Alice Park	240
Allen, Ralph	25, 210, 212
Alleyways	163
American Museum (& Gardens), The	236, 240, 256
Anstey, Christopher	25
Aqua Sana at Longleat Forest	242
Aquae Sulis	18, 22
Architecture	28
Art Fair, Bath	234
Art galleries	236
Assembly Rooms, The	30, 79
Austen, Cassandra	33
Austen, Jane	25, 32
Austen, Reverend George	32, 87
Autumn	230
Avebury Stone Circle	258
Babington House	242
Bachfest, Bath	247
Back Streets	163
Baldwin, Thomas	28, 191, 192
Bartlett Street Antiques Centre, The	237
Bath Abbey	149, 250
Bath Chair	25
Bath City Farm	244
Bath Festivals	265
Bath Film Office	265
Bath in Time	265
Bath Magazine, The	265
Bath Map	5, 89
Bath Priory Gardens	240
Bath Record Office	265
Bath Royal Literary and Scientific Institution	236
Bath Skyline	199
Bath Sports & Leisure	244
Bath Stone	28
Bath Street	189
Bath World Heritage Site	265
Bathwick Meadows	206
Beaux Arts Bath	236
Beckford's Tower and Museum	236
Beechen Cliff	202
Bell Inn, The	238
Bicycle Hire	244
Bird of Prey Project	244
Bishop's Palace, Wells	257
Botanical Gardens, The	58
Bowood House & Gardens	257
Bridgerton	38
Bridgerton Tour	38
Brown, Capability	212
Bus	226
Cafes	233
Camden Crescent	72
Car	226
Castle Combe	257
Cavendish Crescent	69
Cavendish Road	69
Chapel Arts Centre	238
Children's Literature Festival, Bath	247
Christmas Market, Bath	247
Cinemas	238
Circus, The	77, 250
City Football Club, Bath	244
City of Bath Guides	246
Climate	228
Comedy Festival, Bath	247
Cork, The	238
Corridor, The	176
Cricket Club, Bath	244
Cross Bath Street	191
Day trips	254
Dining	232
Discover Bath	265
Dobunni	18
Dyrham Park	240, 254
Edge & Andrew Brownsword Gallery, The	237
Egg Theatre	238, 244
Empire, The	102
Events	247
Everyman Cinema	238
Bathonians	23
Farmer's Market, Bath	234
Fashion Museum Bath	236
FilmBath Festival	247
Footprints Tours	246
Forum, The	238
fotoVUE	268
Francis Gallery, The	237
Frankenstein	34
Gainsborough Bath Spa, The	242
Garden Spa by L'OCCITANE at The Bath Priory	242
Gardens	240
Georgian	28
Georgian Garden, The	78, 240
Great Pulteney Street	111
Green Park Brasserie	238
Green Street	173
Guided tours	246
Half Marathon	247
Harington, Sir John	24
Hay Hill	174
Henrietta Park	240
Herschel Museum of Astronomy	236
Herschel, William	24
History of Bath Research Group	265
Holburne Museum, The	121, 236
Homewood Hotel & Spa	242
Hot Bath Street	191
Hot Springs	179
Hotels	232
Iford Manor	240, 253
In & Beyond Bath	246
Independent Market, Bath	234

Inventions	24
Jane Austen Centre	33, 236, 250
Jesters Comedy Club, The	238
Kennet & Avon Canal	135, 137, 138
Komedia Bath	238
Krowd Keepers: Magic Theatre	238
Lacock Abbey	253
Lansdown Crescent	65
Laura Place	117
Literature Festival, Bath	247
Little Theatre Cinema, The	238
Live music	238
Longleat Safari Park	258
Lush Spa Bath	242
Macdonald Bath Spa Hotel	242
Marlborough Buildings	54
Mary Shelley's House of Frankenstein	35
Mayor of Bath's Honorary Guides	246
Milsom Street	234
Minerva	18
Mission Theatre, The	238
Mozartfest, Bath	247
Museum of Bath Architecture	236
Museum of Bath at Work	236
Museum of East Asian Art	236
Museums	236
Music Festival, Bath	247
Narrowboats	244
Nash, Beau	30
New Bond Street Place	177
No.1 Royal Crescent	53, 250
North Parade Alleys	168
Northanger Abbey	18, 33
Northumberland Place	177
ODEON	238
Oktoberfest, Bath	247
Old Orchard Street	172
Old Theatre Royal, The	238
Paddleboard	244
Palmer, John	29
Parade Gardens	106, 240
Paragon, The	83
Park-and-Ride	226
Parking	226
Parks	240
Persuasion	18, 33
Prince Bladud	179
Prior Park Landscape Gardens	212, 240
Pubs	232, 261
Pulteney Bridge	97, 250
Pump Rooms, The	187
Queen Square	91
Rail	226
Restaurants	233
River Avon	143
River Avon Cruises	244
Roman Baths, The	180, 236, 250
Romans	18
Rondo Theatre, The	238
Rostra Gallery	237
Royal Crescent, The	45, 236, 250
Royal Victoria Park	56, 250
Rugby, Bath	244
Sally Lunn Bun	260
Sally Lunn's Cafe	250
Savouring Bath	265
Seasons	228
Sham Castle	210
Shelley, Mary	34
Somerset Place	66
Soul Spa, The	242
SouthGate	234
Spa & Bath House (at The Royal Crescent Hotel)	242
Spa at Lucknam Park, The	242
Spa at No.15 by GuestHouse, The	242
Spas	242
Spring	228
St James's Square	60
St Swithin's Church	87
Star Inn, The	85
Stay In Bath	265
Stonehenge	257
Stourhead Landscape Garden	254
Sulis	18
Sulis Minerva	179, 180
Summer	229
Sydney Gardens	126, 240
Sydney Place	132
The Jane Austen Festival	247
Theatre Royal, The	195, 238
Theatres	238
Thermae Bath Spa	192, 250
Thermal City	179
Timeline	18
Toilet, First Flushing	24
Top Ten, Bath	252
UNESCO	21
Union Street	234
University of Bath	22
University, Bath Spa	22
Ustinov Studio, The	238
Victoria Art Gallery	236
Visit Bath	265
Walcot Chapel Gallery	237
Walcot Market	234
Walcot School, The	85
Walcot Street	234
Walking Tours, Bath	246
Warminster Road	222
Weather	228
Websites, about Bath	265
Welcome to Bath	265
Wellbeing	242
Wera Hobhouse	22
Westonbirt Arboretum, The	256
Wheelchair Accessibility	227
Wilberforce, William	111
Winter	231
Wollaston, William Hyde	24
Wood, John the Elder	28, 212
World's First Postage Stamp	25
Younger, John Wood the	24, 28
Yuup Bath	244

Planning to visit Scotland?
WE'VE GOT YOU COVERED

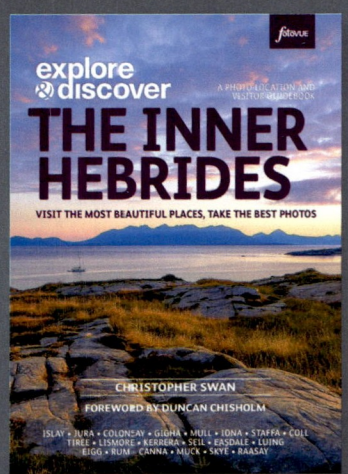 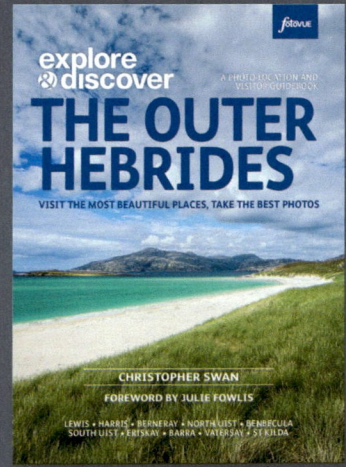 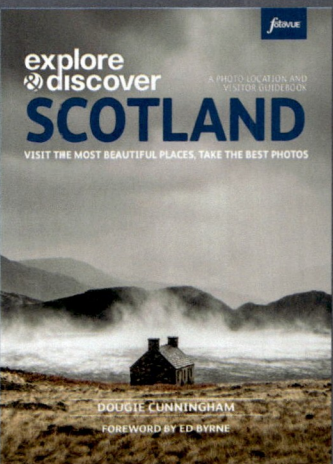

Use coupon code **TRAVEL** at **fotovue.com** for **20% off** all our existing books* – including free UK shipping

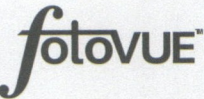

Contact: **mick@fotovue.com**

*Except those on sale